THE ROUGH GUIDE TO

CULT

MOVIES

**ROUGH
GUIDES**

www.roughguides.com

183818
791·4375 SIM

Credits

Contributors:
Paul Simpson, Samantha Cook, Larushka Ivan-Zadeh, David Parkinson
and Jason Wood

Contributors to previous editions:
Jo Berry, Michaela Bushell, Chas Chandler, Andrew Duffy, Mark Ellingham, Caroline Elliott, Angie Errigo, Marianne Gray, Steve Morgan, Ann Oliver, Richard Pendleton, Edwin Pouncey, Helen Rodiss, Victoria Williams, Emma Young

Editing: Kate Berens, Matt Milton, Joe Staines
Layout: Kate Berens
Picture research: Kate Berens, Andrew Lockett
Proofreading: Jason Freeman
Cover design: Tom Cabot
Production: Rebecca Short

Publishing Information

This third edition published August 2010 by
Rough Guides Ltd, 80 Strand, London, WC2R 0RL

375 Hudson Street, New York 10014, USA
Email: mail@roughguides.com

Distributed by the Penguin Group:
Penguin Books Ltd, 80 Strand, London, WC2R 0RL
Penguin Group (USA), 375 Hudson Street, NY 10014, USA
Penguin Group (Australia), 250 Camberwell Road, Camberwell, Victoria 3124, Australia
Penguin Group (Canada), 90 Eglinton Avenue East, Suite 700, Toronto, Ontario, Canada M4P 2Y3
Penguin Group (New Zealand), Cnr Rosedale and Airborne Roads, Albany, Auckland, New Zealand

Typeset in Rockwell and Berthold Akzidenz Grotesk to an original design by Diana Jarvis.

Printed by Toppan Security Printing Pte. Ltd., Singapore.

464pp; includes index

A catalogue record for this book is available from the British Library.

ISBN: 978-1-84836-213-0

1 3 5 7 9 8 6 4 2

Contents

Acknowledgements

Thanks above all to the filmmakers who contributed pieces to this guide: Nick Broomfield, Atom Egoyan, Cari Joji Fukunaga, Keith Fulton, John Hillcoat, Tom Kalin, Asif Kapadia, Stephen Kijak, Gideon Koppel, Andrew Kötting, Joe Lawlor, Christine Molloy, Louis Pepe, James Marsh, Scott McGehee, David Morrissey, Chris Petit, Nicolas Roeg, Ira Sachs, David Siegel, Peter Strickland and Paul Andrew Williams.

The publishers would also like to thank Franz Brown and Marie Reynolds of the Tejeda-Brown Family Limited Partnership for permission to use Reynold Brown's poster design for *Attack Of The 50 Foot Woman*. A book featuring this and dozens of others of Brown's classic designs – *Reynold Brown: A Life in Pictures* by Daniel Zimmer and David J. Nornung – was published in 2009 by the Illustrated Press.

Editorial thanks go to the dedicated writers on this edition, to Sachin Tanwar and Pradeep Thapliyal, to Jason Freeman, Diana Jarvis and Dan May, and to Roger Bardon, Richard Craig and Peter Buckley for additional contributions.

Samantha would like to thank Greg Ward, Jim Cook and Pam Cook, and, at Rough Guides, Andrew Lockett and Kate Berens.

Larushka would like to thank Tom Moggach for all his love and support, her sister Ludmilla for being generally splendid and Kim Newman for lending me *Snakes on a Train*.

Jason would like to thank all the filmmakers listed above, Mia Bays, Walter Donohue and Dave Shear.

Introduction

The movies, where one man's masterpiece is always liable to be someone else's *Air Bud: World Pup*, is a world where no opinion is final and deciding what makes a film "cult" can be as intellectually arbitrary as deciding if a film is "good" or "bad". There is also a big difference between the films we watch over and over again and the films which appear in the critics' lists of greatest-ever movies.

The *Concise Oxford Dictionary* defines "cult" as: 1) a system of religious worship especially as expressed in ritual; 2) a devotion or homage to a person or thing; 3) a popular fashion especially followed by a specific section of society; 4) denoting a person or thing popularized in this way.

The dictionary, in its linguistic wisdom, assigns the last definition to a cult figure or cult movie. In cinematic terms, the word "cult" is often applied to films starring fifty-foot women on a mission of personal revenge, killer tomatoes or an entire Western town populated by midgets. Sometimes this has been extended to include movies that are either "so bad they're good" (the clichéd example of this being any work by the "world's worst director" Ed Wood) or are the objects of quasi-religious worship (*The Big Lebowski*).

The word "cult" also implies knowledge hidden from the masses. So a cult movie may be the preserve of a select few or have depths missed by the casual viewer.

Umberto Eco, author of cult book *The Name of the Rose*, identifies *Casablanca* as a cult movie. This sounds ludicrous, as *Casablanca* is one of the most famous films of all time. But Eco adds: "The work… must provide a completely furnished world so that its fans can quote characters and episodes as if they were aspects of the fan's private sectarian world, a world about which one can make up quizzes and play trivia games so that the adepts of the sect recognize through each other a shared expertise." By this definition, *Casablanca* is certainly a cult movie

For this book, we've reserved the right not to include every title as well known as that, figuring the space would be better given to titles further away from a perennial spotlight. We've also added a few other criteria to Eco's definition. Any movie reviewed here should: 1) prompt people to go around quoting it to each other or inspire an unreasonable amount of devotion long after the masses have forgotten its existence; 2) be good but underappreciated, possibly because, in a market driven by stars and event movies, they were just too different to have a long run at a cinema near you; 3) be an undiscovered gem, perhaps because it's foreign or went straight to video; 4) be so bad it's a hoot; 5) be compelling for some other reason – the script may stink but there's a song, a stunt or scene that makes it all worthwhile; 6) be a mainstream film that has that indefinable something we call "juice"; 7) not be a *Police Academy* sequel.

We've made a conscious effort to include as many different movies as possible. You can thrill to *Battleship Potemkin* and still relish the moment *Springtime for Hitler* breaks into "Don't be foolish, be a smarty, come and join the Nazi party"; you can feel an irrational exhilaration when you hear John Belushi chant "Toga! Toga! Toga!", or be mesmerized by Kurosawa's *Ran*.

For this third edition we've added lots of new categories, from Asian horror to Underground, via Bad girls, Bikers and Mavericks, Psychos and Rock stars – plus many more. Film directors with a nose for the unorthodox and intriguing – from the legendary Nic Roeg to rising stars like Cari Joji Fukunaga – have also told us about their (often rarely seen) favourites. These sections are in special boxes dotted throughout the book. And we have updated all the sections, spending improbably long hours pondering the merits of films to include or to drop. All the while, we've tried to maintain a spirit of fun about the proceedings and the way the book goes about its business, which is to say very seriously in a not so serious kind of way.

Ari tries to find the truth in a tangle of dreams and memories of the 1982 invasion of Lebanon in *Waltz with Bashir*, an animated documentary with a graphic novel look (p.18).

Director Richard Linklater's reverse-engineered Rotoscope animation transforms Robert Downey Jr and Rory Cochrane in *A Scanner Darkly* (p.199).

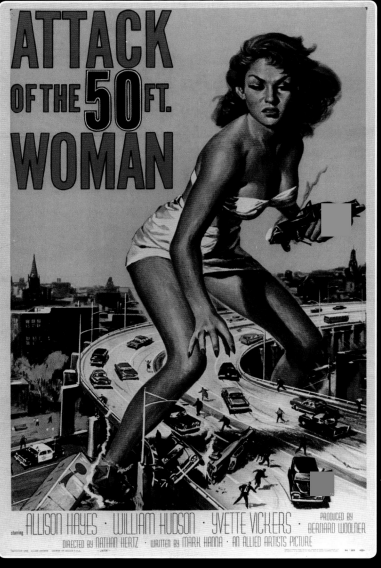

Reynold Brown's vivid poster design has justifiably eclipsed the reputation of the film it promoted. With artwork this good, who needs a credible plot? (p.205).

Don't mess with the one-chick hit squad! Blaxploitation icon Pam Grier as *Coffy* in 1973, a few years before her comeback in Tarantino's *Jackie Brown* (p.49).

A riot of 1970s leisurewear: Will Ferrell creates a splash as sexist Ron Burgundy in *Anchorman* (p.69).

Richard E. Grant as the dishevelled, eponymous failed actor in *Withnail and I*, the classic quotable cult comedy (p.135).

Harsh landscape, harsh characters, vivid filmmaking: Daniel Day-Lewis as oil prospector Plainview in *There Will Be Blood* (p.129).

Vietnam veteran turned chancer, Llewelyn Moss (Josh Brolin) lets off some steam in the Coen

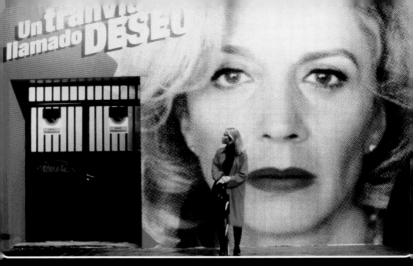

The kindness of strangers: Manuela (Celia Roth) waits for her son under the impassive gaze of Marisa Paredes in *All About My Mother* (p.408).

On the road: the late River Phoenix as rent boy Mike in Gus Van Sant's Shakespearean update, *M*

Blade Runner's dystopian noir vision of the future. William Sanderson and Daryl Hannah go head to head (p.314).

The otherworldly David Bowie as *The Man Who Fell to Earth*, an alien with devastating business

Martial arts mayhem in Thai hit *Ong Bak* (p.221). Tony Jaa stars as orphan Jaa kicking back –

Sharon Stone and Robert De Niro celebrate their gains in *Casino* (p.168), a nostalgic evocation – decor included – of the era when the Mob ruled Vegas.

Art laced with brutality: Lee Marvin keeps his cool in a hot Los Angeles in *Point Blank* (p.95)

Seijun Suzuki's stunning yakuza classic *Tokyo Drifter* combines stylish visuals with highly

Chainsaws are a girl's best friend. Cécile de France has to tackle a murderous stalker in the French slasher *Switchblade Romance* (p.339).

"What is real?" asks Jennifer (Elisha Cuthbert): confinement, horror and pain it appears, at least i

Modern policing: Britcom stalwarts Simon Pegg and Nick Frost are the *Hot Fuzz*, bringing American cop style to postcard-pretty middle England (p.81)

The rock'n'roll lifestyle writ large: actress Anita Pallenberg captures some of the hallucinatory allure and feel of *Performance* (p.301).

Mariah Carey (left) casts aside all airs as dowdy social worker Mrs Weiss in shocking drama *Precious*, aided by an astonishing performance from Gabourey Sidibe in the title role (p.301).

Sci-fi sexploitation. Jane Fonda (covered up, for once) is the eponymous victim of both husband-director Roger Vadim and villain Durand-Durand (Milo O'Shea) in the preposterous 1968 romp *Barbarella* (p.326).

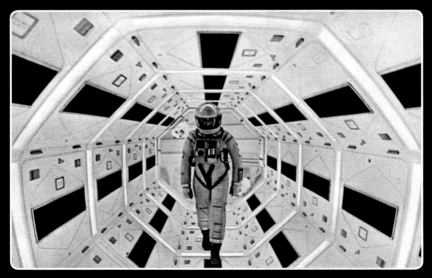

The other side of the sci-fi coin: Gary Lockwood walks into the future in *2001: A Space Odyssey*, where austere set pieces and baffling puzzles abound (p.319).

Favela on film: coming of age in Rio de Janeiro's slums has the compensation of the city's incomparable skyline in *City of Men* (p.77).

This ain't no El Dorado. The wild-eyed conquistador Aguirre (Klaus Kinski, centre) leads his men

Julie Christie as a bordello madam in the mordantly unromantic Western *McCabe and Mrs Miller* (p.414). The fragile-seeming, artfully faded cinematography makes it look like decay being born

ACTION

Formulaic action movies have a plot you can sum up on the back of a business card, a heroic maverick and as many set-piece stunts as the budget can afford. Thankfully, not every action film sticks to the template.

Casino Royale 2006

Director Martin Campbell **Cast** Daniel Craig, Eva Green, Judi Dench 144m

Violent, vulnerable and Fleming-friendly, this **Daniel Craig**-inspired revival of a tired franchise is way more exhilarating and emotionally engaging than a typical 007 romp. Craig put back the acting (and not a little testosterone and grit) into an action movie credited with revisiting the nihilistic tone of the original novel. Amidst all the hooplah over Craig's swimming trunks, it was easy to forget that this hard edge might have owed something to director **Martin Campbell**'s training in British crime drama, with episodes of *The Professionals* and *Minder* amongst his previous credits.

The Castle of Cagliostro 1979

Director Hayao Miyazaki **Cast** Yasuo Yamada, Tao Ishida, Kiyoshi Kobayashi 110m

Hayao Miyazaki's seriously underrated gem is an animated James Bond/Raffles-style adventure in which sympathetic thief **Lupin** must save lovely **Clarisse** from the evil **Count Cagliostro**. The tone is Bondishly light and the violence mostly innocuous although the knife-tastic denouement is startling. Charming, swift, with some wonderful touches, this benefits from a better villain than many 007 movies.

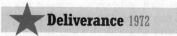

★ Deliverance 1972

Director John Boorman **Cast** Burt Reynolds, Jon Voight, Ned Beatty 109m

Four men go up river for a weekend's sport but are brutalized by the elements, local rednecks and their guilt at surviving the hunt and kill nightmare that ensues. **Boorman**'s hugely influential movie made a star of **Burt Reynolds** who memorably dubbed this "my deliverance from shit". Thank God **James Dickey**, adapting his own novel, ignored studio suggestions that the four men become two couples, drug-crazed hippies or Martians.

★ Die Hard 1988

Director John McTiernan **Cast** Bruce Willis, Bonnie Bedelia, Alan Rickman 132m

McTiernan has some form in the action genre with jungle alien thriller *Predator* (1987), tense submarine drama *The Hunt for Red October* (1990) and anti-action fantasy *Last Action Hero* (1993) in his relatively short CV. Here he gives it to us straight as a youthful **Willis** with white vest and an awful lot of bullets rescues a building full of citizens from the clutches of determined terrorists. Better than all the sequels.

District 9 2009

Director Neill Blomkamp Cast Sharlto Copley, Jason Cope 112m

Aliens have landed on Earth; some 28 years later, the "Prawns" remain confined in squalor outside Johannesburg. Operative Wikus van der Merwe (**Copley**), backed by militia, has the task of evicting them. This is the premise of a surprising and shocking film, which starts off at an arthouse crawl courtesy of *Cloverfield*-like documentary framing before morphing into a body horror turbo-charged action spectacular with a tender side and a satirical subtext.

District 13 2004

Director Pierre Morel Cast David Belle, Cyril Raffaelli, Bibi Naceri, Dany Verissimo 84m

Before *District 9* there was District 13, a walled-off *banlieue* in near-future Paris, abandoned by the authorities to the drug gangs. This unsubtle commentary on the city's present-day social divide provides both backdrop and narrative for a stylish, **Luc Besson**-penned and produced thriller, as B13 homeboy Leïto (**Belle**) and police bulldog Damien (**Raffaelli**) join forces to prevent the district's destruction. The action never lets up: kung fu set pieces, big guns, car chases and explosions galore, alongside astonishing feats of synchronized free running through a graffitied, high-rise cityscape.

⭐ Hard Boiled 1992

Director John Woo Cast Chow Yun-Fat, Tony Leung Chiu-Wai, Philip Chan 126m

American producers made the action movie the monstrous, commercially dominant genre it is today, but in the 1990s Hong Kong directors like **John Woo** gave the action a much harder edge. The plot – dedicated cop **Yun-Fat** is seeking the men who killed his partner – sounds formulaic but with more bullets, more beatings and some classic Wooisms (the Mexican stand-off between adversaries and two-handed gun action), this slick, brilliantly choreographed movie is one of the best in the genre's recent history.

The Hidden Fortress 1958

Director Akira Kurosawa Cast Toshirô Mifune, Minoru Chiaki, Kamatari Fujiwara 123m

Kurosawa's nineteenth directorial effort was one of the main inspirations for *Star Wars*. Two foolish, greedy farmers are dragooned into helping a general escort an exiled princess through war-torn lands. Stealthily evading capture, they observe a nation in turmoil. One of the maestro's strongest medieval sagas, with battles of varying size, impressive stunts and a welcome streak of humour.

El Mariachi 1992

Director Robert Rodriguez **Cast** Carlos Gallardo, Consuelo Gómez, Peter Marquadt 80m

Quentin Tarantino's grindhouse pal **Rodriguez** has never bettered this shaggy-dog tale of a musician mistaken for a drug baron, fighting for his life in a Mexican border town. Clever, fast, and with a hell of a lot of bullets and blood for its $7000 budget. Rodriguez's English-language sequel/remake *Desperado* boasts bigger names (Antonio Banderas, Salma Hayek) but lacks the home-made feel.

The Matrix 1999

Directors Andy and Lana Wachowski **Cast** Keanu Reeves, Hugo Weaving, Laurence Fishburne, Carrie-Anne Moss 136m

Despite an off-putting merchandising frenzy and some vastly inferior sequels *The Matrix* achieved deserved cult status when it first leapt onto the screen. So much now has passed into cliché: the long leather coats, the virtual reality premise, the cloned CGI enemies, but the kinetic action sequences still pack a bigger punch than the tech *noir* trimmings.

Ronin 1998

Director John Frankenheimer **Cast** Robert De Niro, Jean Reno, Jonathan Pryce 121m

The ronin – samurai without a master – in **Frankenheimer**'s world-weary thriller are experts in their field (**De Niro** is ex-CIA, **Reno** an equipment specialist and **Stellan Skarsgård** a technician) enlisted to retrieve an important briefcase, despite the machinations of IRA bad guy **Jonathan Pryce**. An enigmatic, moody tale, worth watching for its violent car chase and De Niro having bullets removed from his chest without anaesthetic.

So Close 2002

Director Corey Yuen **Cast** Qi Shu, Wei Zhao 110m

Move over *Charlie's Angels*; if you want an action movie that delivers kick-ass girl power action try **Yuen**'s uptempo tale of two sibling assassins (**Shu** and **Zhao**) and the rookie cop (**Karen Mok**) assigned to track down Shui (who, in homicidal mode, is sometimes known as the Computer Angel). It's hard to fault any film that kicks off with a version of The Carpenters' "Close to You" that jams security systems.

Terminator 2: Judgement Day 1991

Director James Cameron **Cast** Arnold Schwarzenegger, Linda Hamilton, Robert Patrick 135m

The canal chase is many people's top pick of a host of thrilling action sequences, with **Robert Patrick**'s T-1000 just as eye-catching as **Arnie**'s reformed cyborg this time batting for humanity. The special effects still carry a frisson thanks to some deadpan humour and the bravura with which objects and machines are destroyed onscreen in the cause of entertainment.

ACTORS' LAPSES

If you're watching a bad movie, Jerry Seinfeld noted, it's two hours of your life. If you're in a bad movie, it's two years. Sometimes no one is quite as unhappy with a movie as its actors.

The Appaloosa 1966

Director Sidney J. Furie **Cast** Marlon Brando, Anjanette Corner, John Saxon 98m

Contractual obligation was **Brando**'s main motivation for appearing in this unusual Western. So for much of the film he hides his face in shadow or under a hat as he plays a drifter who owns a prize horse. Brando hated the final film and either **Furie** or the producer penned this doggerel: "Marlon, his heart it bleeds for the masses, but the people he works with, he kicks in the asses."

Batman and Robin 1997

Director Joel Schumacher **Cast** George Clooney, Arnold Schwarzenegger 125m

Clooney was so embarrassed by this sub-standard superhero flick, he called it a "waste of money". Hard as he tries, critics dubbed him the "George Lazenby" of the Batman franchise. The only good to come of

it was that he decided to follow his instinct and make movies like *O Brother, Where Art Thou?* and **Schumacher** handed the franchise to Christopher Nolan.

Highlander II: The Quickening 1991

Director Russell Mulcahy **Cast** Christopher Lambert, Sean Connery, Virginia Madsen 100m

No one liked this movie. **Lambert** was so disgusted by the script rewrite he tried to walk out, returning when lawyers worked out the cost of him ignoring his contractual obligation. Threats of a lawsuit deterred **Mulcahy** from insisting the director's credit be changed to Alan Smithee. As nonsensical sci-fi movies go, this is right down there with *Plan 9 from Outer Space*.

The King and I 1956

Director Walter Lang **Cast** Yul Brynner, Deborah Kerr 133m

Brynner's turn as the king of Siam, humanized by Kerr's governess, won him an Oscar. But Brynner felt the movie didn't have a tenth of the power of the stage show and admitted: "I still get sick when I see it." He felt he lacked the maturity to play the monarch properly. Still, this did give him his most famous line: "Et cetera, et cetera, et cetera and so forth."

The Silver Chalice 1954

Director Victor Saville Cast Virginia Mayo, Jack Palance, Paul Newman 142m

Playing a Greek artisan called Basil in a toga that looked, as the star himself put it, like "a short cocktail dress", could have killed Newman's movie career in an instant. He was so embarrassed by his role as an artist commissioned to improve the cup of Christ that he once put an ad in *Variety* apologizing for it.

Skidoo 1968

Director Otto Preminger Cast Jackie Gleason, Carol Channing, Cesar Romero 97m

Seeing Jackie Gleason trip out on LSD and shout: "I see mathematics! I see mathematics!" is reason enough to watch this unintentionally sidesplitting counter-culture spoof, in which Channing dresses up as Lord Nelson, Groucho Marx is (by his own admission) awful as God and there's a lot of anachronistic body painting. The anti-drugs message hits home when one of the guards hallucinates seeing the Green Bay Packers naked.

Teen Wolf 1985

Director Rod Daniel Cast Michael J. Fox, James Hampton, Susan Ursitti 92m

This cult camp classic, a minor triumph for Fox as the vulpine kid, isn't just celebrated for its humorous portrayal of the difficulties of being a wolf at high school. In the adrenaline-fuelled finale, after Fox has won the championship game, his dad comes down to congratulate him. At this precise point, an extra decides it would be funny to unzip and expose his very own teen wolf.

Trog 1970

Director Freddie Francis Cast Joan Crawford, Michael Gough, Bernard Kay 93m

Crawford is a compassionate scientist trying to protect a troglodytic creature against civilization in a movie so dire that she said afterwards that the mere sight of its name on a cinema marquee might drive her to suicide. The major tension in the film is wondering whether Trog's amateurish make-up will fall off his face.

Valley Girl 1983

Director Martha Coolidge Cast Nicolas Cage, Deborah Foreman 99m

Cage's reputation as one of Hollywood's more thoughtful leading men has mysteriously survived a debut in which, as Foreman's punk love interest, he gets to say lines like: "Well fuck you, for sure, like totally". Even he can't redeem this *Romeo and Juliet* meets *The Graduate* for the MTV generation.

ADVENTURE

Less blood, more finesse and exotic locales. That, in seven words, is the utterly unscientific distinction between action films and adventure movies.

The Adventures of Robinson Crusoe 1954

Director Luis Buñuel **Cast** Dan O'Herlihy, Felipe de Alba, Jaime Fernandez **90m**

This simple telling displays little of **Buñuel**'s flamboyant surrealistic flair. But the additions he made (with blacklisted writer **Hugo Butler**, who had to amend the script by night so as not to arouse the suspicions of **O'Herlihy**) are memorable: Crusoe's furious reaction when Man Friday finds and puts on a dress, and his fevered dream of scrubbing a pig while being lectured by his father. Irish star O'Herlihy was nominated for an Oscar for his stirring, unsentimental portrayal of Crusoe, with strong support from **de Alba**. Would be better known if it wasn't from a relatively unfashionable part of Buñuel's career.

Beau Geste 1939

Director William A. Wellman **Cast** Gary Cooper, Brian Donlevy **120m**

The haunting image of a remote, burning fort, manned by dead legionnaires, is one of the most powerful in the Hollywood action canon and gets this classic version of **P.C. Wren**'s novel off to a cracking start. **Gary Cooper** is charismatic and laconic as the legionnaire hiding from a scandal while **Brian Donlevy** is disturbingly credible as the sadistic sergeant, even though he has to play him as a Russian to avoid offending the French.

Blood Diamond 2006

Director Edward Zwick **Cast** Leonardo DiCaprio, Jennifer Connelly, Djimon Hounsou **143m**

DiCaprio is a former mercenary and **Hounsou** an African fisherman whose lives intersect over a rare pink diamond. **Connelly**, as the journalist trying to expose the trade in blood diamonds, provides the conscience and the sexual tension in a brilliantly made romantic, politically charged yarn that is obviously in debt to *Casablanca*, *Under Fire* and **Ernest Hemingway** but still feels fresh.

Cartouche 1962

Director Philippe de Broca **Cast** Jean-Paul Belmondo, Claudia Cardinale, Jesse Huhn **114m**

Legionnaire's disease

Mickey Mouse, Gary Cooper, Laurel and Hardy and Jean-Claude Van Damme have all served in its ranks with varying degrees of distinction. The strange allure of the French Foreign Legion still attracts filmmakers even though the novel that started it all, *Under Two Flags* by Englishwoman Maria Louise Rame (whose pseudonym was Ouida), was published in 1867.

In Ouida's novel, the Hon Bertie Cecil joins an armed corps called the Chasseurs d'Afrique to forget a homoerotic friendship. Although the novel did not specifically refer to the French Foreign Legion by name, this bestselling potboiler established the idea that if drinking to forget didn't work, you could always join the Legion.

P.C. Wren's 1924 novel *Beau Geste* expanded the myth, making the Legion synonymous with baking deserts, bullying martinets, nifty headgear (the kepi) and heroes seeking redemption. Within two years, Ronald Colman had starred as Beau Geste in the first movie of Wren's novel and by 1931, Laurel and Hardy were spoofing the whole business in *Beau Hunks*. But the legend remained impervious to ridicule: in 1936, Colman starred in *Under Two Flags*, its plot tweaked to resemble Wren's tale, and in 1939 Gary Cooper was a quietly heroic Geste.

Since then the myth has been spoofed – most memorably in *Follow That Camel* (1967), a *Carry On* with Phil Silvers imported to reprise his Sergeant Bilko routine; honoured – by Van Damme in his 1998 turkey *Legionnaire*; and debunked – in *Beau Travail* (1999), Claire Denis's intriguing fusion of *Beau Geste* and *Billy Budd*.

Belmondo is so charming as the noble Robin Hood-style rogue who terrorized Regency France, you even forgive him for two-timing the transcendent **Cardinale** in **de Broca**'s complex swashbuckler full of backstabbings, swordplay and dangerous liaisons.

Dersu Uzala 1975

Director Akira Kurosawa Cast Maximum Munzuk, Yury Solomin 141m

The titular hero (**Munzuk**) is a Siberian native who scouts for a topographic expedition that, as **Kurosawa** beautifully shows us, signals the end of his traditional way of life. Kurosawa's Siberia is full of

visual splendour but it is the relationship between the expedition leader (**Solomin**) and Ursala that forms the heart of this inspiring, sad and resonant film.

Jason and the Argonauts 1963

Director Don Chaffee Cast Todd Armstrong, Nancy Kovack, Honor Blackman 103m

Armstrong is overshadowed as the golden fleece-hunter by **Blackman** as squabbling goddess Hera and by **Ray Harryhausen**'s stop-motion animation. The final battle is Harryhausen's masterpiece. Three minutes onscreen, over four months in the making, the contest between seven skeletons and three men still has a certain grandeur. **Talos**, the monstrous bronze statue, is almost as memorable as King Kong.

Jeremiah Johnson 1972

Director Sydney Pollack **Cast** Robert Redford, Will Geer 108m

In real life, **Redford**'s mountain man was known as "Liver eating Johnson", a reputation he used to scare his enemy, the Crows. Onscreen, no such delicacies are consumed, although **Pollack** and Redford don't pull many other punches in this unflinching account of the brutalities of life in the wilderness. A strange, meandering yet haunting tale, set in stunning scenery, which benefits from the rapport between mountain men Redford and Geer and **Tim McIntire**'s forlorn songs.

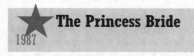

The Princess Bride 1987

Director Rob Reiner **Cast** Cary Elwes, Robin Wright, Mandy Patinkin 98m

In true fairy-tale fashion, a grandfather (**Peter Falk**) reads his grandson a bedtime story of love and adventure. Westley (**Elwes**) and Buttercup (**Wright**, pre-Penn) fall in love, but Westley is lost at sea. Buttercup is seized by a wicked prince (**Chris Sarandon**) and so ensues a fantastical journey with rhyming giants, an embittered miracle man ("You rush a miracle man, you get rotten miracles") and a swordsman extraordinaire. Scripted by **William Goldman** from his

novel, the humour is sharp, and **Reiner** proves he can do more than coax Meg Ryan to orgasm. All together now: "Hello. My name is Inigo Montoya. You killed my father. Prepare to die."

The Prisoner of Zenda 1937

Director John Cromwell **Cast** Ronald Colman, Madeleine Carroll, David Niven 101m

In this lavish, stellar costume adventure, **Colman** has a dual role as King Rudolf and his distant doppelgänger cousin who stands in for the king to save Ruritania from the wicked Duke of Streltsau (**Raymond Massey**). Dashing support is provided by **Niven** and **Douglas Fairbanks Jr**, **Carroll** is as beautiful as ever and the claim – "the most thrilling swordfight ever filmed" – may still hold true.

White Sun of the Desert 1969

Director Vladimir Motyl **Cast** Anatoly Kuznetsov, Spartak Mishulin, Pavel Luspekaev 85m

Motyl's distinctive mash-up of comedy, action, music, drama and Italian Western was such a box office smash in the USSR that some lines – notably "The East is a subtle matter" – were repeated as if they were nuggets of folk wisdom. **Kuznetsov** is the lone hero of the Revolution who, while travelling across the deserts of central Asia, inherits an abandoned harem and tries to instruct them in the ways of liberation with the expected comic consequences.

ALCOHOL

The movies have always had a hypocritical attitude to drunks, condemning them to a tragic fate yet celebrating the mayhem they cause.

Days of Wine and Roses
1962

Director Blake Edwards **Cast** Jack Lemmon, Lee Remick 116m

Young couple **Lemmon** and **Remick** seem to have it all but sink deeper into alcoholism as they set out on the road to hell together. In one powerful scene, Lemmon's cravings are so intense he wrecks his father-in-law's greenhouse in search of hidden booze. Remick copes by effectively denying her addiction's hold on her.

Harvey 1950

Director Henry Koster **Cast** James Stewart, Josephine Hull, Peggy Dow 104m

Mercifully, plans for a cameo by Francis the talking mule were dropped so this enchanting fantasy survived the transition from Broadway to celluloid pretty intact. Elwood P. Dowd (**Stewart**) and his pooka **Harvey** are the unlikely twosome at the heart of this beguiling tale. Harvey is a 6ft 3½in white rabbit who appears only to good-natured alcoholic Dowd. The family's dilemma over how to cope with Elwood and Harvey is finally resolved in a Capra-esque denouement. Devotees insist that **Koster**'s clues – especially the way doors open and shut – prove Harvey is real but any definitive solution would surely dispel the magic.

I'll Cry Tomorrow 1955

Director Daniel Mann **Cast** Susan Hayward, Richard Conte, Jo Van Fleet 117m

As 1930s singing sensation **Lilian Roth**, **Susan Hayward** plays up to her own sexy hellcat image when onstage, but as a merciless stage mum (**Van Fleet**), fame, and the death of an old friend she's fallen for take their toll, the sense of uneasy dread grows as the heroine spirals into alcoholism. The gritty, emotional scene where Hayward leaves her mother is one of Hollywood's greatest exposés of the love/hate dynamic between child and parent.

Ironweed 1997

Director Hector Babenco **Cast** Jack Nicholson, Meryl Streep 143m

Drunken bums don't, alas, put bums on seats. Pity because **Nicholson** and

A bum's rushes

"I hate people don't you?"

"I don't mind them but I seem to feel better when they're not around."

In **Barbet Schroeder**'s *Barfly* (1987), alcoholic Wanda (**Faye Dunaway**) and the **Charles Bukowski**-esque boxing, literary drunk Henry (**Mickey Rourke**) bond over their love of booze and distaste for conventional society.

Such tales of drunken, bohemian low life might sound glamorous when pitched but onscreen they often seem merely dreary. **Marco Ferrari**'s 1981 take on Bukowski (*Tales of Ordinary Madness*) with **Ben Gazzara** as the author's proxy is at least weird enough to fascinate even if the style veers uneasily between voyeurism (notably the scene where the prostitute closes her vagina with a safety pin) and portentous declarations that the desperate, deserted and damned are the "real people of the world".

In 2005, it was **Matt Dillon**'s turn as a surrogate Bukowski in **Bent Hamer**'s wily *Factotum*. Like Ferrari's movie, *Factotum* was at its best, ironically, when the Bukowski character isn't philosophizing and trying to sound like a poet on Skid Row.

Bukowski has written an entertaining book called, a trifle unimaginatively, *Hollywood*, about his experiences in Tinseltown, and it's just possible that he's got more out of the movies than the movies have got out of him.

Streep are wonderful as two alcoholic drifters who meet in their hometown after years on the road. The movie is full of desperation and despair – especially when Nicholson, who works in a cemetery, visits the grave of his infant son – and features one of Jack's best, least mannered performances. Surpasses the **William Kennedy** novel it is based on.

suicidal ambition by **Shue**, a gorgeous, abused prostitute, but as their romance deepens and fractures, the end is inevitable. Based on the novel by **John O'Brien**, an alcoholic who committed suicide, **Figgis'** unflinching portrayal of dependency rings utterly, agonizingly true. Cage had a friend film him on a fortnight's binge-drinking spree in Dublin to prepare for this.

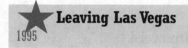

Leaving Las Vegas
1995

Director Mike Figgis **Cast** Nicolas Cage, Elisabeth Shue 112m

Cage has come to Vegas to drink himself to death. He is briefly diverted from his

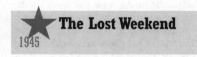

The Lost Weekend
1945

Director Billy Wilder **Cast** Ray Milland, Jane Wyman 99m

So frank in its depiction of the perils of alcoholism that the drinks industry offered to buy the negative and take it

> **"** Most men lead lives of quiet
> desperation. I can't take quiet
> desperation! **"**
> **Don Firnam, The Lost Weekend**

out of circulation, **Wilder**'s melodrama inspired a series of social problem movies in the 1940s and early 1950s. Writer **Milland** relies on the booze to fuel his creativity. Although an optimistic ending has been tacked on, the most forceful sequences – Milland lugging his typewriter around to find an open pawn shop or raiding his various hiding places for booze – are truly heart-rending.

My Name Is Joe 1998

Director Ken Loach **Cast** Peter Mullan, Louise Goodall 105m

The plot could have been lifted straight from Hollywood – a recovering alcoholic endangers his relationship with a nurse when he gets involved with a drugs deal to help a friend in trouble – but since this is directed by **Loach** in characteristically angry and brutally honest style, the result could not be more different. **Mullan** deservedly won best actor at Cannes for his performance as a man walking a very fine line between right and wrong. Painful and grim, but the atmosphere Loach creates makes it absorbing viewing.

Nil by Mouth 1997

Director Gary Oldman **Cast** Ray Winstone, Kathy Burke 124m

Gary Oldman's directorial debut, which he also wrote, is uncompromising in its portrayal of a family living under the pressures of poverty, drugs and alcohol. The film's most harrowing scene is probably where a drunken **Winstone** phones round friends and family trying to find **Burke** after he has given her a savage beating. The movie is presented as a story to watch, not as a lesson to be learned or a set of people to judge. Take from it what you will.

16 Years of Alcohol 2003

Director Richard Jobson **Cast** Ewen Bremner, Kevin McKidd, Laura Fraser 102m

Jobson's intense, imaginatively made debut feature captures the anguish of a young man in Edinburgh (**McKidd**) trying to turn his back on the drink and violence that have characterized his life. Jobson could have trimmed the melancholic voiceover, but this is still a powerful portrait of McKidd's turbulent life and, we are led to assume, early violent death.

The Sound of One Hand Clapping 1998

Director Richard Flanagan **Cast** Kerry Fox, Kristof Kaczmarek 93m

Directing from his novel, **Richard Flanagan** delivers a sombre, contemplative movie about people surviving in a wilderness. **Kerry Fox** is the daughter returning home to Hobart after twenty years. She fled when her father beat her in a drunken rage and he is now a lonely alcoholic.

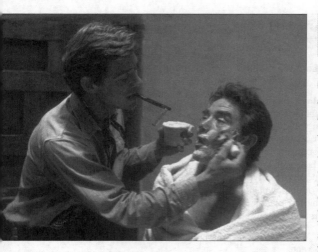

Albert Finney, as the alcoholic ex-consul, is tended to by his half-brother (Anthony Andrews) in moving drama *Under the Volcano*.

Under the Volcano 1984

Director John Huston **Cast** Albert Finney, Jacqueline Bisset, Anthony Andrews 111m

An in-depth study of a drunk. What action there is takes place over the course of a day, as **Finney**'s ex-consul (stripped of his official duties) struggles to remain coherent and able to communicate with his wife (**Bisset**) and half-brother (**Andrews**). Unusually for a screen alcoholic, the consul's family is supportive but there's nothing they can do to help him. The fact that Finney knows he is doomed, his sad intelligence clear in every scene, makes this even more moving.

Some scenes – the child with snow in her socks looking for her father who's in the pub – have a rare poetic power.

Trees Lounge 1996

Director Steve Buscemi **Cast** Steve Buscemi, Chloë Sevigny 95m

Tommy Basilio has lost his job and his girlfriend. In fact, the only thing he hasn't lost is his bar stool. A job in an ice-cream van ends in a relationship with his ex's seventeen-year-old niece and her father is not happy about it. The various drunks and misfits hanging out in the bar (**Samuel L. Jackson** has a cameo) provide this slow, compelling character study with many of its lighter moments, and **Buscemi** handles the actor/director role with a lot of style.

Whisky Galore! 1949

Director Alexander McKendrick **Cast** Basil Radford, Gordon Jackson 82m

Arguably the best comedy inspired by a politician: the *S.S. Politician* that is. The ship, which ran aground off a Hebridean island, was carrying fifty thousand bottles of scotch. This accident is the perfect platform for one of the funniest Ealing comedies, which, among other things, reveals a remarkable variety of ways to conceal copious amounts of whisky. In the US it was retitled, bizarrely, *Tight Little Island*.

ANIMALS

Ever since Rin Tin Tin got more fan mail – thirty thousand letters a week – than many actors, the movies have always had a place for a shaggy dog story that might strike box-office gold.

Amores Perros 2000

Director Alejandro González Iñárritu Cast Emilio Echevarría, Gael García Bernal 154m

A startling, Tarantino-esque tale of betrayals, weaving stories from a cross-section of society – a model and her lover, a youth in love with his brother's wife, a strange down-and-out, all with a particular connection to their dog – to a climax in which their lives fatefully intersect. Intriguing, brutal and controversial for its depiction of animal abuse, it alerted an international audience to the vibrancy of Mexican cinema.

Attack of the Crab Monsters 1957

Director Roger Corman Cast Richard Garland, Pamela Duncan 62m

Giant crabs try to kill scientists stranded on a shrinking atoll. Typical **Corman** fare with more ideas than budget. Look very closely and you'll notice the crabs have wheels and legs. They can talk too: "So you have wounded me! I must grow a new claw – well and good, for I can do it in a day. But will you grow new lives when I have taken yours from you?" Maybe the crabs would have been better off boring their victims to death.

Bambi 1942

Director David D. Hand 70m

Greeted on release as an "insult to American sportsmen", *Bambi*'s most notorious scene – the murder of Bambi's mother – can still horrify today. Despite the cheery presence of **Thumper** and the incredible artistry of the animation, this powerful portrayal of the cycle of a deer's life bombed on release. The ecological subtext – man is presented as the villainous intruder to the forest's Edenic idyll – was pretty heavy for the 1940s. But watching this classic – and weeping – has become a rite of passage for children across the world.

Best in Show 2000

Director Christopher Guest Cast Christopher Guest, Parker Posey, Eugene Levy 90m

Alas, no one has yet launched a magazine called *American Bitch* (focusing on the issues faced by lesbian owners of purebred dogs), possibly because they're still laughing at the memory of **Guest**'s wicked skewering of the dog show scene and the eccentric characters it attracts. Actually, the lesbian owners aren't quite as entertaining as the gay couple who own a ribbon-festooned Shih Tzu or **Fred Willard**, the commentator who once dressed up as a bloodhound in a Sherlock Holmes outfit to get the crowd pumped.

The Birds 1963

Director Alfred Hitchcock Cast Tippi Hedren, Rod Taylor, Jessica Tandy 119m

Alfred Hitchcock's movie never explains why the birds turn vicious, but critics have suggested it's a disguised Western (with the birds as Indians) or an allegory for sexual repression (the first attack stops a couple getting together). **Hedren**, who spent days with birds attached to her dress by nylon threads to film the famous attack scene, had to be taken to hospital after one of them cut her face. But it's hard not to marvel at the results, which took three years and 1360 shots (including 370 trick shots) to make.

Donnie Darko 2001

Director Richard Kelly Cast Jake Gyllenhaal, Mary McDonnell, Katherine Ross 113m

When a jet engine ploughs into his bedroom, disturbed teenager Donnie escapes death thanks to a six-foot rabbit called Frank, who tells him the world will end soon. The rabbit continues to visit Donnie, leading him to commit acts of vandalism and filling his mind with the complexities of worm holes. Written and directed by first-timer **Kelly**, this is the blackest of comedies with a splash of apocalyptic horror, social satire and teenage angst. It's original and well acted, but perhaps the best part is that you're allowed to make your own judgements about its meaning. (If you want to know, see the director's cut.)

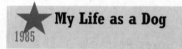

My Life as a Dog 1985

Director Lasse Hallström Cast Anton Glanzelius, Tomas von Brömmsen 101m

A cheeky eleven-year-old trying to fathom adults and the trials of life, Ingemar (**Glanzelius**) is sent to live with his uncle and meets a string of eccentrics, including an uncle with a passion for the song "I've Got a Lovely Bunch of Coconuts" and a green-haired school chum. The dog of the title is Laika, the doomed Russian space dog with whom he identifies. Funny and touching, this is *Stand By Me* without the emotive soundtrack.

Never Cry Wolf 1983

Director Carroll Ballard Cast Charles Martin Smith, Brian Dennehy 105m

In **Carroll Ballard**'s resonant masterpiece, green biologist Tyler (**Martin Smith**) is sent to the Canadian wilds to prove wolves are to blame for shrinking caribou herds, but ends up learning the rules of coexistence from an Eskimo and a wolf. Ballard's imaginative, intense use of landscape is especially exhilarating when Tyler runs with a wolf pack.

ANIMATED

If you've seen a peanut stand or heard a rubber band,
watched a needle that winked its eye or – especially – seen an
elephant fly, you'll know the magic of the animated movie.

⭐ Alice 1988

Director Jan Svankmajer **Cast** Kristina
Kohoutová **85m**

In the hands of the Czech master of the
surreal, the story of *Alice in Wonderland*
becomes a terrifying nightmare. Combining stop-frame animation, puppetry and
live action, *Alice* creates a world of intense
malevolence. The white rabbit is constantly
splitting open and sewing himself back
together, large lumps of raw meat crawl
around, and skulls of dead birds come to
life and peck their way out of eggs.

Belleville rendez-vous 2003

Director Sylvain Chomet **Cast** Béatrice
Bonifassi, Lina Boudreault **81m**

Comic-book artist **Sylvain Chomet**'s
second movie is surreal, ingenious and
visually stunning. An orphan, raised by his
club-footed grandmother-cum-obsessive
cycling coach, is kidnapped on the eve of
the Tour de France. Granny and their overweight dog set off to rescue him, aided by
the **Belleville Triplettes**, a faded close-
harmony act now living in penury. Only
the odd word is spoken and the animation

is best described as a homage to Max
Fleischer, but at eighty minutes the pace
is snappy, the songs are pretty catchy and
the comedy at times almost macabre.

The Brave Little Toaster 1987

Director Jerry Rees **Cast** Jon Lovitz, Timothy
Stack, Deanna Oliver **90m**

Inspired by the CGI wizardry of *Tron*,
Disney drone **John Lasseter** set out to
produce the first 3-D computer-animated
feature. He chose this dark little tale of a
discarded set of household appliances:
a cowardly lamp, a brave toaster, a radio,
an electric blanket and a vacuum cleaner,
who set out on a perilous journey to find
their lost masters. Sadly Lasseter was
ahead of his time. He got sacked by Disney
(who reassigned the movie to *Tron* effects
man **Jerry Rees**) and instead set up Pixar
studio and made *Toy Story* – and millions
of dollars.

Fantasia 1940

Directors James Algar, Samuel Armstrong,
Ford Beebe, Norm Ferguson, Jim Handley,

T. Hee, Wilfred Jackson, Hamilton Luske Cast
Bill Roberts, Paul Satterfield 120m

Over sixty years on, *Fantasia* still looks
grand, bold and imaginative. The animation was so effective that generations have
grown up believing hippos are loveable
creatures instead of vicious killers, while
musician **Leonard Bernstein** had to
instruct students to forget Disney's dancing centaurs when listening to Beethoven's
Pastoral Symphony. **Walt Disney** said the
failure of *Fantasia* loomed like a shadow
over his whole life. Some failure.

Heavy Metal 1981

Director Gerald Potterton **Cast** John Candy,
Harold Ramis 90m

Good and evil, swords and sorcerors, sex
and toasters, plus lots of very, very loud
music: *Heavy Metal* may have limited
appeal, but it broke new ground in bringing Japanese anime to the West. Six stories
are tied loosely together, with music by
bands like Black Sabbath, Grand Funk
Railroad, Blue Öyster Cult and Nazareth.

Hugo the Hippo 1976

Director William Feigenbaum **Cast** Burl Ives,
Paul Lynde, Robert Morley 90m

This Hungarian-American musical animation, about a hippo who saves the
clove trade in Madagascar, has a tiny
band of devotees. Not every animated
movie can combine sharks wearing biker
jewellery with the vocal talents of Jimmy
Osmond singing a lyric that spells out the
word hippopotamus. The psychedelic

animation makes *Yellow Submarine* seem
about as far out as Doris Day.

The Jungle Book 1967

Director Wolfgang Reitherman **Cast** Phil
Harris, George Sanders, Louis Prima 78m

True, **Disney** emasculated **Kipling**'s
story of an Indian boy brought up by
wolves. But it has the best characters, most
memorable songs and the best jokes of
any Disney film. Its real star is Baloo the
bear, **Phil Harris** doing a near-approximation of John Wayne, while for King Louie
(the swinging ape), **Louis Prima** (an Italian) makes a good stab at sounding like
Satchmo. Myth to be dispelled: The Beatles
didn't do the voices for the vultures – they
were booked, but Walt thought they were
only a flash in the pan.

The Nightmare Before Christmas 1993

Director Henry Selick **Cast** Danny Elfman,
Chris Sarandon 76m

While offering a macabre twist on the
festive movies that fill the Christmas TV
schedules, **Tim Burton**'s movie also
pays homage to them. Halloweentown
king Jack Skellington (a loveable misfit like
Beetlejuice) decides to bring his peculiar
genius to bear on Christmas, but somehow
kids don't appreciate his gifts of shrunken
heads and toy snakes. With its stop-motion
three-dimensional animation and a fine,
subtle score by **Danny Elfman**, this may
be Burton's most accomplished movie,
but it couldn't have been realized without

For adults only

Ralph Bakshi's *Fritz the Cat* (1972) was the first (officially) X-rated cartoon. Based on Robert Crumb's underground comics, it sees a cat go through college trying to score as much drugs and graphic sex as possible. Filled with unlikely and unholy couplings of cats and birds, aardvarks and zebras, the movie tackles racism, sexism, unemployment and American youth's sense of alienation. Notable for its limited portrayal of black people as jive-talking crows, further accusations of racism also dogged Bakshi's 1975 animation, *Coonskin*, causing Paramount to drop it. The bad boy Brooklyn-born animator subsequently switched his focus from street life to fantasy. His biggest commercial success, *Lord of the Rings* (1978), may have put most people off fantasy till Peter Jackson, but its rotoscoping technique influenced Richard Linklater's dystopian Philip K. Dick animated adaptation, *A Scanner Darkly* (2006) – one irrefutable instance of Keanu Reeves giving an animated performance. Bakshi's finest critical hour was *Heavy Traffic* (1973), a part-live-action head trip through New York's underbelly that led the *Hollywood Reporter* to recklessly dub Bakshi "the most creative American animator since Disney". His career declined thereafter. Brad Pitt, star of Bakshi's final feature *Cool World* (1992), describes it as "Roger Rabbit on acid", which makes it sound way more fun than it is.

director **Selick**. Although there were a hundred crew members, they could only produce some sixty seconds of film a week, so the project took three years. Repeated viewing is rewarded – you always spot something new tucked away in a corner.

South Park: Bigger, Longer & Uncut 1999

Director Trey Parker Cast Trey Parker, Matt Stone, Mary Kay Bergman 81m

Uncle Walt must've been spinning in his cryogenic chamber on release of this full-length animated feature that parodies classic Disney movies – you certainly never got songs like "Uncle Fucka" in *Beauty and the Beast*. Satirizing the controversy whipped up by the cartoon

TV series, the movie sees the children of South Park watch "Asses of Fire", an R-rated Canadian movie that "warps their fragile little minds" causing them to run riot, spouting obscenities, and their parents to pressure the US government to wage war on Canada, whilst Saddam Hussein repeatedly takes Satan from behind.

Toy Story 1995

Director John Lasseter Cast Tom Hanks, Tim Allen 80m

Heroically, **Disney** and **Pixar** didn't rely on technological wizardry for this first computer-generated movie, about a toy cowboy whose world is rocked when a new astronaut toy, **Buzz Lightyear**, enters the playroom. Instead a great plot, witty

"I've got a hole in my pocket!" Surreal, clever and stylishly animated, the forgotten 1960s classic *Yellow Submarine* so impressed the Beatles themselves that they contributed a performance.

script and inspired casting (such as **John Ratzenberger** from *Cheers*, as **Hamm** the piggy bank) make it a genuine classic.

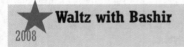

Waltz with Bashir 2008

Director Ari Folman **Cast** Ari Folman, Ori Sivan, Ron Ben-Yishai **90m**

Enter a new sub-genre: the animated documentary. Fluidly animated in vivid colours, this is a remarkable memoir of Folman's time as a young conscript during the 1982 invasion of Lebanon, when Israeli troops stood by as Christian Phalangists massacred eight hundred Palestinians. With its bold lines and equally strong subject matter it's closer in feel to a graphic novel. A hypnotic evocation of the surreal horrors of war.

Yellow Submarine 1968

Director George Dunning **Cast** Dick Emery, Lance Percival, The Beatles **87m**

Deadpan understatement, inventive animation, great songs, an intelligent script: *Yellow Submarine* is the most successful blend of animation and music since 1940's *Fantasia*. The Beatles had little input into this contract-filler, but liked the first cut so much they agreed to appear singing "All Together Now". The movie was unjustly neglected, and watching it today is like discovering a lost masterpiece – not just for the songs, but the offbeat humour.

ANIME

There's more to animation than Walt Disney, Pixar and Matt Groening. The Japanese anime tradition has inspired some amazing, too little-known work.

 Akira 1988

Director Katsuhiro Otomo **Cast** Mitsuo Iwata, Nozomu Sasaki 124m

Tokyo was destroyed by a psychic blast from Akira (the most advanced form of human being), which started World War III. By 2019, when the film is set, Neo Tokyo has risen from its ashes, various parties are struggling for control of Akira, and one child, Tetsuo, develops his ESP and nearly destroys everything. A classic slice of Japanese anime, it's bloody, violent and visually astonishing. Most of the movie takes place at night, so the animators had to create a new range of dark colours, rather than relying on standard blue tones. *Akira* is an abbreviated version of the director's 37-volume manga. Fans say it starts to make sense after the seventh viewing.

Alakazam the Great 1960

Directors Lee Kresel, Daisaku Shirakawa, Osamu Tezuka, Taiji Yabushita **Cast** Frankie Avalon 88m

Once listed as one of the fifty worst movies of all time, but don't let that put you off.

> It's no place for women. Besides, magicians don't like girls. They saw them in half.
> **Alakazam, Alakazam the Great**

In the English-language version of this Japanese animation based on *Journey to the West*, 1950s teen idol **Frankie Avalon** is the singing voice of the mischievous monkey Alakazam. For its time, this was a sympathetic repackaging with a decent vocal cast, also featuring **Dodie Stevens** and improv comedian **Jonathan Winters**. There's a neat moral, too, in the way Alakazam is forced to learn humility.

Ghost in the Shell 1995

Director Mamoru Oshii **Cast** Atsuko Tanaka, Akio Ōtsuka 83m

Co-produced with British funding, this was designed to be a breakthrough for Japanese anime, with hopes it would take the genre mainstream. Unfortunately the convoluted story and conceptual dialogue left it languishing. The curvaceous Major Motoko Kusanagi (**Tanaka**) is the cyborg head of a special intelligence operation.

The magic of Miyazaki

To call **Hayao Miyazaki** the Japanese Walt Disney is cheap, reductive and partly true. Between them, they have done more than anyone to shape movie animation. They are both associated with certain studios – Miyazaki usually works with **Studio Ghibli**. And they are both masters of their craft.

But the similarities are not endless. Miyazaki's work has always ranged more freely. As an animator/writer/director he has touched on environmental destruction (in *Castle in the Sky* and many others), war (*Princess Mononoke*), drawn on folk tales/myths (the forest sprites in *Totoro*), and shown that there's a surprising number of ways you can use pigs as a theme if you're a truly gifted moviemaker.

Totoro is an utterly charming introduction to his work – note the way he avoids what, in the West, would be an obligatory happy ending. But all his films have something to offer – from the darkness of *Princess Mononoke* to the mind-reeling, fantasy/adventure story of love and friendship that is *Spirited Away*.

Investigations lead her and her crack team to the Puppet Master, the "most dreaded cyber-criminal of all time". The animation is superb and the cyborgs are entertaining, but the story is far more complicated than it really needs to be.

Grave of the Fireflies 1988

Director Isao Takahata Cast Tsutomu Tatsumi, Ayano Shiraishi 93m

Not a movie to watch if you're feeling blue, this was based on writer **Akiyuki Nosaka**'s experiences of his younger sister dying of malnutrition during the war. Nosaka said writing this book helped him to come to terms with her death. He may have been uplifted, but few audiences were, the movie subsequently released alongside *My Neighbour Totoro* to liven the experience up. A welcome change from sci-fi anime all the same, it's filled with a rare emotional intensity.

★ My Neighbour Totoro 1988

Director Hayao Miyazaki Cast Hitoshi Takagi, Noriko Hidaka 86m

Often voted one of the best family movies of all time. Totoro is a benevolent, mute, slightly fierce-looking forest sprite, who acts as a kind of chaperone for two sisters – Mei and Satsuki – who have moved out to the country with their personable dad, while they wait for mum to recover from an unspecified illness. **Miyazaki** avoids the generational conflict cliché, a staple of so many Western family films (dad is entirely open to the possibility that Totoro and the Cat Bus exist). The handcrafted animation is simply astonishing. The movie is as inconclusive, occasionally sad, sometimes a bit frightening, and often as funny, as, well, life itself – only much more entertaining.

Perfect Blue 1998

Director Satoshi Kon Cast Junko Iwao, Rica Matsumoto, Shinpachi Tsuji 80m

Mimi, a tiny-skirted, teen pop sensation, quits music to become an actress. Her fans are distraught, particularly a stalker called Me-Mania. Soon Mimi finds every detail of her life on the Internet and, after landing a part in a sexually charged murder mystery, starts to spiral into a vortex of paranoid delusion. Drawing comparisons with Alfred Hitchcock, Philip K. Dick and David Lynch, this suspenseful and disturbing psychological thriller was actually intended to be a live-action series, before the 1995 Kobe earthquake damaged the production studio, reducing the budget.

Porco Rosso 1992

Director Hayao Miyazaki Cast Shûichirô Moriyama, Tokiko Kato, Sanshi Katsura 94m

Japan Airlines hired **Miyazaki** (fresh from *Kiki's Delivery Service*) to direct a half-hour in-flight movie. Fortunately, he decided his story of a World War II flying ace cursed with the head of a pig was too good to be seen only by those struggling with an on-board meal. Pigs are a key element in many Miyazaki movies and here our hero, **Porco Rosso**, who patrols the skies saving the distressed from sky pirates, desperately searches for a way to reverse the curse, win his love and beat his rival. Kids may struggle with some gags, but the story is original and the animation rich in detail.

APOCALYPSE

This is the way the world ends, according to filmmakers: with flu, infertility and computers that are too clever by half.

Amerika 1987

Director Donald Wrye **Cast** Kris Kristofferson, Sam Neill, Mariel Hemingway 870m

An Emmy nomination for outstanding achievement in hairstyling is not the highest commendation, but this mini-series is genuinely compelling crap. Made in response to the 1983 TV movie *The Day After* (about the effects of nuclear war on a US town), which conservatives saw as left-wing propaganda, this sees the US taken over by the USSR. More than fourteen hours long, it's spectacularly clichéd.

Armageddon 1998

Director Michael Bay **Cast** Bruce Willis, Ben Affleck, Liv Tyler 150m

As subtle as the asteroid that is hurtling towards Earth, **Bay**'s scientifically illiterate epic has **Willis** as the John Wayne-style hero determined to save the planet from a very nasty bump. If you suspend disbelief, the scenes in which our heroes drill into an asteroid while trying not to be shot into the fatal void of space are genuinely tense. Standout line: "The fate of the planet is in the hands of a bunch of retards I wouldn't trust with a potato gun."

★ Children of Men 2006

Director Alfonso Cuarón **Cast** Clive Owen, Julianne Moore, Michael Caine 109m

It's 2027, the human race can no longer procreate and a fascist Britain is, it seems, the last nightmarish hope for civilization. The nuclear mishaps, environmental disasters and wars all seem disgustingly, appallingly familiar in **Cuarón**'s urgent, heartbreaking adaptation of the **P.D. James** novel. The redemption of Theo (**Owen**), a former rebel apparently content to watch the world turn hellish, offers some hope in a cogent warning of an all too plausible, dystopian future.

The Forbin Project 1969

Director Joseph Sargent **Cast** Eric Braeden, Susan Clark 100m

Also known as *Colossus*, the name of the computer that gets a bit too clever for man. **Colossus** controls the US defence systems, but once the machine detects that it has a Russian counterpart (**Guardian**), the two machines merge to become one supercomputer. This works best in the uncompromising, non-Hollywood ending (which studio executives disliked so much they shelved the movie – until they saw the box-office success of *2001* in 1968).

On the Beach 1959

Director Stanley Kramer Cast Gregory Peck, Ava Gardner, Fred Astaire 134m

Stanley Kramer was almost as fond of messages as Western Union. So **Nevil Shute**'s horrifically humdrum take on the end of the world was perfect for him, especially with the Cold War then at its very hottest. **Peck** is the commander of a sub that's escaped the nuclear holocaust, who spends his last days finding love at second sight with alcoholic Moira (**Gardner**); meanwhile English scientist Julian (**Astaire**) prefers car racing when he should be trying to correct a dodgy English accent.

Red Dawn 1984

Director John Milius Cast Patrick Swayze, C. Thomas Howell, Lea Thompson 114m

Reaganite Soviet evil empire nonsense that entered the *Guinness Book of Records* as the movie containing the most acts of violence. Worth watching if only to see **Patrick Swayze** as the leader of a group of high school kids battling with Cuban and Soviet invaders. The cast spent eight weeks in military training to achieve the authentic guerrilla look and, presumably, learning to keep straight faces while uttering the corny dialogue. Probably the best Brat Pack teen apocalyptic action movie of 1984.

The Stand 1994

Director Mick Garris Cast Ed Harris, Rob Lowe, Gary Sinise 366m

At six hours, **Garris**'s TV mini-series from Stephen King's prophetic, apocalyptic opus is too long and too anguished to be viewed in one sitting. Opening to the chilling strains of Blue Öyster Cult's "Don't Fear the Reaper", this imagines a world where ninety percent of humanity has been wiped out by a government-spawned superflu and the other ten percent don't have much humanity left in them. The first half is the strongest – the scenes of mass death in the Lincoln tunnel and the streets covered with bodies are horribly memorable – but enough of **King**'s terrifying vision endures throughout to make this genuinely unsettling.

War of the Worlds 1953

Director Bryan Haskin Cast Gene Barry, Ann Robinson, Lee Tremayne 85m

Interplanetary invaders disturb the Eisenhowerian idyll of Barry and Robinson by sending a mechanized eye through their farmhouse and destroying it with a hovercraft. **Haskin** alludes to Bosch, Munch and Picasso as hysteria mounts in a visually inspired, scary Cold War interpretation of **H.G. Wells**' classic. This is weirder than the Spielberg/Cruise remake but neither has the force of **Orson Welles**' radio adaptation.

ART

Most movies about artists, starving or otherwise, have one fatal flaw: they grind to a halt when they have to show us the artist at the easel.

Andrei Rublyov 1966

Director Andrei Tarkovsky **Cast** Anatoly Solonitsyn, Ivan Lapikov, Nikola Grinko 183m

Andrei Tarkovsky's episodic epic about the fifteenth-century icon painter isn't for the faint of heart or the short of attention span. Long on symbolism, short on snappy dialogue (our hero has taken a vow of silence), this is a stunning, draining experience – but the final mysterious sequence where the painter is redeemed by a young nobleman casting a bell will stay with you forever.

Caravaggio 1986

Director Derek Jarman **Cast** Sean Bean, Nigel Terry, Dexter Fletcher, Tilda Swinton 93m

One of **Jarman**'s more accessible pieces, exploring the tumultuous life of the sixteenth-century painter (**Fletcher/Terry**). The crux is his relationship with his muse and lover Ranuccio (**Bean**) and Ranuccio's mistress (**Swinton**). Visually it works like a piece of art, each frame a masterpiece of cinematography, but as an insight into the man himself, it remains a puzzle.

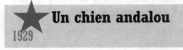 ## Un chien andalou 1929

Director Luis Buñuel **Cast** Simone Mareuil, Pierre Batcheff 16m

Buñuel insisted this collaboration with the Surrealist painter **Salvador Dalí** meant nothing at all. But critics have since pronounced at length on the psycho-sexual significance of images like **Mareuil**'s eyeball being sliced with a cutthroat razor, ants scurrying from a hole in **Batcheff**'s hand and a dragged piano encumbered by a dead donkey and two perplexed clerics. Dalí was dismayed that Buñuel prioritized politics over poetry in their second collaboration *L'âge d'or* (1930), but the Parisian premiere audience responded to his "desperate, passionate call to murder" by rioting.

Edvard Munch 1974

Director Peter Watkins **Cast** Geir Westby, Gro Fraas, Kerstii Allum 210m

You get the gist of this experimental biopic from Munch's harrowing assertion: "Illness, insanity and death were the

Orson Welles in the groundbreaking *F for Fake* (*Vérités et mensonges*): the artist himself faces the camera in this witty film about art hoaxes that's also very much a self-portrait.

black angels that watched over my cradle and accompanied me all my life." The painter of *The Scream* was never likely to have had a blissfully happy existence, but **Peter Watkins** densely combines flashbacks, interviews, diary extracts and an encyclopedic commentary to submerge the audience in the domestic tribulations, psychological strains and everyday realities that shaped Munch's art and set him at odds with his times. Deeply personal, stylistically audacious, brilliantly realized.

Having hoaxed the US into a state of panic with his 1938 broadcast of *The War of the Worlds*, amateur magician Orson Welles furthered his fascination with fakery in this acute post-modern dissection of creativity, celebrity and criticism. The focus falls on modern art forger **Elmyr de Hory**, whose biographer Clifford Irving falsely claimed to have collaborated with Howard Hughes on his memoirs. But this is also a mischievous self-portrait by cinema's most profligate genius.

F for Fake 1973

Director Orson Welles **Cast** Orson Welles, Oja Kodar, Joseph Cotten 85m

Love is the Devil 1998

Director John Maybury **Cast** Derek Jacobi, Daniel Craig, Tilda Swinton 91m

Francis Bacon (**Jacobi**) knows how to disarm a burglar, telling George (**Craig**): "Take your clothes off and come to bed. Then you can have whatever you want." Later, in a neat counterpoint, George threatens to kill himself and is told by Bacon there's a beam in the studio "screaming to have a rope thrown around it". **Maybury**, not allowed to show Bacon's work, makes the movie look like a Bacon painting, with appropriate distortions, reflections and anguish.

Moulin Rouge 1952

Director John Huston Cast José Ferrer, Zsa Zsa Gabor 123m

Biopics of bohemian painters were a minor craze in repressed, conformist, 1950s Hollywood. **John Huston** brings **Toulouse-Lautrec** and his milieu to vivid life here, with **Ferrer**, as the painter, and **Gabor**, as one of the women in his life, on top form. A year before, Huston had paid homage to another artist, Matthew Brady, whose Civil War daguerreotypes set the visual tone for Huston's underrated adaptation of the Stephen Crane anti-war novel, *The Red Badge of Courage*.

★ The Quince Tree of the Sun 1992

Director Victor Erice Cast Antonio López García, Marina Moreno, Enrique Gran 137m

Spain's greatest modern painter **Antonio López García** is trying to capture the light of the sun at midday on the quince tree in his garden. **Victor Erice** takes this simple premise and, in this intriguing documentary, creates something moving, compelling and lightly profound.

Rembrandt 1936

Director Alexander Korda Cast Charles Laughton, Gertrude Lawrence 85m

Charles Laughton is touching as the artist struggling to handle the loss of his adored wife and his public's growing indifference. Like the artist's work, this is too dark and slow for many, but it's held together by Laughton's moving performance and aided by some fine camerawork by **Georges Périnal**.

Van Gogh 1991

Director Maurice Pialat Cast Jacques Dutronc, Alexandra London, Bernard Le Coq 159m

Van Gogh biopics abound. But what distinguishes **Maurice Pialat**'s portrait from Vincente Minnelli's *Lust for Life* (1956), Paul Cox's *Vincent* (1987) and Robert Altman's *Vincent & Theo* (1990) is an uncompromising rigour that makes the painter's last 69 days feel like life being lived. Whether in Auvers-sur-Oise or Montmartre, the improvised action eschews period melodramatics and psychological speculation. Instead, it shows **Jacques Dutronc**'s Vincent being enslaved by the bipolarity that spawned eighty canvases in a frantic burst of creativity before sending him spiralling towards his suicide.

ASIAN EXTREME

Schoolgirl serial killers, squid-eating psychos, witchy-haired women crawling out of your TV... to find the furthest reaches of far-out horror, look East.

⭐ Audition 1999

Director Miike Takashi **Cast** Ryo Ishibashi, Miyuki Matsuda, Renji Ishibashi 115m

With seventy productions to his name and counting, Japanese director **Takashi** is the daddy of Asian Extreme. As well as perversely sexualized violence (check out *Gozu*, where a woman gives birth to a fully grown yakuza gangster), he's also a rug-pulling master of tone. Witness this deranged mix of *Sleepless in Seattle* and *Reservoir Dogs*. Seven years after his wife's death, a widower decides to find new love by pretending to audition actresses for his new movie; only his perfect-seeming choice turns out to be a hypodermic needle-wielding sadistrix with a thing for eyelids. Takashi has insisted: "Audition is not horror. It's just a story about a girl who has just slightly strange emotions." Right.

Battle Royale 2000

Director Kinji Fukasaku **Cast** Tatsuya Fujiwara, Aki Maeda, Taro Yamamoto 113m

Think Japan's answer to *A Clockwork Orange*. It's the dawn of the new millennium. With national unemployment and juvenile crime spiralling out of control, Japan's government introduces the Battle Royale Act, where a random school class is taken to an island and forced to fight to the death until only one survivor remains, as a warning to other youths. Even Japan was shocked by this explosive scenario, that today seems one scarily small step away from the extremes of reality TV. It's yet to receive US distribution.

Ichi the Killer 2001

Director Miike Takashi **Cast** Tadanobu Asano, Nao Omori, Shinya Tsukamoto 129m

Sick bags were passed out at the Toronto premiere of this violent manga adaptation. You'll see why. When a yakuza mobster goes missing with 300 million yen, his sadistic henchman sets out to find him. Instead he crosses paths with Ichi, a mysterious, sexually repressed, mentally deficient martial artist with blades in his shoes. The (real) semen used in the close-up intro sequence was provided by **Shinya Tsukamoto**, director of *Tetsuo*.

Oldboy 2003

Director Park Chan-wook **Cast** Choi Min-shik, Yu Ji-tae, Kang Hye-jeong 120m

Outrage at a yucky scene where the hero eats a real-life wriggling squid was eclipsed after the man behind the 2007 Virginia Tech massacre posted copycat video re-enactments of other, more violent scenes to US news stations. Yet the second instalment of **Park**'s "Vengeance" cycle is no mere video nasty. A South Korean businessman is mysteriously held captive in a hotel room for fifteen years. On escape he finds himself framed for his family's murder, tools up with a claw hammer and sets out for revenge. A morally sophisticated symphony of violence, it won the Grand Prix at Cannes 2004 – but then, Tarantino did head the jury that year.

In the second part of Park Chan-wook's Vengeance trilogy, *Oldboy*, businessman Oh Dae-su (Choi Min-shik) goes on the rampage armed with a hammer. Fifteen years in one room and you'd have a ravaged, driven-beyond-sanity look too.

Ringu 1998

Director Hideo Nakata Cast Nanako Matsushima, Miki Nakatani 95m

An unmarked video tape brings death, one week later, to anyone who watches it. More restrained, quieter, and way more creepy than its US remakes, this franchise spawned a genre of "curse" scary movies (*The Grudge* et al), not to mention four spin-offs wherein witchy-haired women variously crawl out of bathroom taps, mobile phones, mirrors, cameras and what have you, in between burping incomprehensibly down the phone at you. An allegory about Japan's phobia of out-of-date technology, *The Ring* is truly the one J-horror to rule them all.

Tetsuo: The Iron Man 1989

Director Shinya Tsukamoto Cast Tomoroh Taguchi, Kei Fujiwara, Shinya Tsukamoto 67m

The horrific opening shot sees a man ("the metal fetishist") cut open his leg and insert a rusty pipe inside it. When maggots subsequently infest the gash, he runs screaming into the street and gets knocked down. The guilty driver finds his own flesh then gradually mutating into scrap metal. Surreal cyberpunk body horror shot in atmospheric black and white, unlike its similar, but bigger budget 1992 colour sequel. It's like a retooled Asian version of Davids Lynch and Cronenberg.

B-MOVIES

Your mouth feels like the Sahara desert, there are thumb marks at the base of your neck and in the back of your mind a faint suspicion that something awful happened last night... don't panic, you're just trapped in a B-movie. Normal service will be resumed in 85 minutes.

The Blob 1958

Director Irvin S. Yeaworth Jr **Cast** Steve McQueen, Aneta Corsaut, Earl Rowe 86m

Paramount bought producer **Jack H. Harris**'s movie – originally called *The Glob* – to play alongside *I Married a Monster from Outer Space. The Blob* turned out to be the more successful and helped create a star in **McQueen**. He plays a high-school kid (despite his 27 years) who finds a mysterious snot-like being that consumes the local townspeople, gradually becoming bigger and redder in the process. The adults blame the irresponsible youths, yet only these youths have the sense to be very, very afraid. McQueen was initially signed to a three-movie deal, but he proved such a nightmare to work with they released him to go on to bigger and better things.

Blonde Ice 1949

Director Jack Bernhard **Cast** Leslie Brooks, Robert Paige, Russ Vincent 73m

Leslie Brooks is chillingly believable as the columnist who discovers how much fun it can be to murder people and read all about it in your own paper. Good as this B-*noir* is, it didn't help the leads' careers: it was Brooks' last film and not long after **Paige** was doing beer commercials.

Cat People 1942

Director Jacques Tourneur **Cast** Simone Simon, Kent Smith 73m

One of several classy, psychologically complex horror pictures overseen by **Val Lewton**'s unit at RKO Studios, *Cat People* relies on suspense and mood rather than cheapo special effects. The film concerns a young fashion designer (**Simon**) whose chance encounter with a stranger leads her to believe that she is a member of an ancient Serbian tribe who will metamorphose into a panther on experiencing sexual desire. Having fallen for a handsome stranger (**Smith**), it's not too long before the claws come out. A metaphor for both female sexuality and xenophobia, the

Q, The Winged Serpent (1982, 93m)

" Torn between *O Sangue*, a sublime, super-slow black-and-white Portuguese art movie and *Ice Station Zebra*, simply because it was Howard Hughes's favourite film... but the nod goes to... an old B-movie seen 25 years ago. *Q, The Winged Serpent* is pre-9/11 menace out of a clear blue sky whose threat comes not from commandeered planes but a prehistoric bird that squats on top of the Chrysler Building and preys on the citizenry. Godfather to Larry Cohen's cheapie is that master of economy Roger Corman, while an Italian-American sub-plot rips off *Mean Streets*, with a Walken-ish Michael Moriarty as an inept criminal who does good vocal jazz and gets his fifteen minutes of fame. Better for being played straight, especially by the late David Carradine, wearily professional as the cop and with the stoic air of an actor who knows his roles aren't going to improve, this is fast, daft and deft. "

Chris Petit

Chris Petit's Radio On *(1979; executive produced by Wim Wenders) redefined the road movie, setting a template for subsequent films and novels examining melancholia and popular culture in urban environments. Petit returned to the road movie with* Content *in 2009.*

---

film, shot on sets used in *The Magnificent Ambersons*, heralded a run of fine work from director **Tourneur**.

Detour 1945

Director Edgar G. Ulmer **Cast** Tom Neal, Ann Savage, Claudia Drake **68m**

Justly famous for its last line where **Neal**, as he climbs into the police car, says: "At any time, fate or some mysterious force can put the finger on you for no good reason at all." Probably the closest Hollywood came to existentialism in the 1940s, the Camus-influenced line would prove heavily ironic when Neal killed his wife in a jealous rage. This tale of an innocent hitchhiker who gets embroiled in crime, like all of **Ulmer**'s B-movies, was shot in just six days.

Five Came Back 1939

Director John Farrow **Cast** Chester Morris, Lucille Ball, Wendy Barrie **75m**

The all-star disaster movie begins here – the stars in this case all B-movie favourites (like **Morris** and **John Carradine**) or on their way to better things (**Ball**), while the budget wouldn't stretch to Charlton Heston's limo. As for the disaster, a plane crashes in the Amazonian jungle and the dozen survivors know there's only enough fuel to carry five people. Meanwhile, a nearby tribe is making plans to shrink heads... Ignore **Farrow**'s own 1956 remake (*Back from Eternity*) in favour of the superior original, which feels far more real than it ought to, given the jungle's obviously artificial nature.

Forty Guns 1957

Director Samuel Fuller **Cast** Barbara Stanwyck, Barry Sullivan 80m

Samuel Fuller had to tone down the climax of this strange, dark movie. The studio wouldn't accept that when **Stanwyck**'s crazed brother uses her as a shield, the cop (**Sullivan**) would just shoot through her. Pity, because that would have been entirely in keeping with what had gone before. Stanwyck is more hard-boiled than ever as the Amazonian baroness of Tombstone Territory with her own ranch and ranch hands (who are also, it is heavily implied, her sex slaves).

Gonks Go Beat 1965

Director Robert Hartford-Davis **Cast** Kenneth Connor, Lulu 90m

Robert Hartford-Davis made one truly notable movie (*The Sandwich Man*) and one archeological curiosity: this genre-straddling sci-fi/comedy/musical variation on *Romeo and Juliet*. An alien visits Earth to settle a dispute between two great factions: one loves rock, the other loves ballads. Solomon wasn't around to solve this bitter debate so *Carry On* star **Connor** must do his best. **Lulu** sings and **Ginger Baker** plays the drums in a prison cell. Don't ask.

Jail Bait 1954

Director Edward D. Wood Jr **Cast** Lyle Talbot, Dolores Fuller 72m

A rare foray into crime movies, *Jail Bait* is prized for its startling dialogue, a neat plot twist and for **Wood**'s thrifty genius in borrowing the score from *Mesa of Lost Women*, one of the worst horror films of all time (though he hadn't made it). The best exchange may be where the cop turns to the plastic surgeon's daughter and says: "Carrying a gun can be a dangerous business", to which she replies: "So can building a skyscraper." The surgeon's son and a crook rob a theatre, shooting a night watchman fatally and injuring a woman by mistake. The crook kills his accomplice, goes to the surgeon and tells him to give him a new face or he'll never see his son alive again. But his plan of hiding the son's corpse in the closet backfires and, realizing his boy is dead, the surgeon turns the villain into the spitting image of his son.

Machine Gun Kelly 1958

Director Roger Corman **Cast** Charles Bronson, Susan Cabot 80m

Bronson got this leading gangster role by default after a squabble over two other actors (one of whom was the screenwriter's brother), but he grabs his chance. The silent opening robbery sequence is well done, thanks partly to *High Noon* cameraman **Floyd Crosby**. **Cabot** deserves a lifetime achievement Oscar for consistent overacting as Bronson's moll.

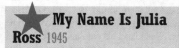

★ My Name Is Julia Ross 1945

Director Joseph H. Lewis **Cast** Nina Foch, Dame May Whitty, George Macready 65m

Elements of *film noir* and horror are never far away from the look of the B-movie. Here Nina Foch encounters a shadowy hand in Joseph H. Lewis's thriller *My Name Is Julia Ross*.

What do you do when you go to your new company as a secretary in London and wake up with a headache in a stately pile in Cornwall, apparently married to a man who is rather too fond of icepicks and knives? That is the problem facing **Foch** in this efficient and pacy British B chiller by one of the genre's most talented directors. It was later remade by Arthur Penn as *Dead of Winter*.

The Narrow Margin 1952

Director Richard Fleischer Cast Charles McGraw, Marie Windsor 71m

Charles McGraw's cynical cop tells his charge (a witness in a Mob trial, beautifully played by **Windsor**): "You make me sick to my stomach", to which

she replies, "Well, use your own sink." With a tight budget and just thirteen days to get the film in the can, more directors should do as **Fleischer** does: focus on one specific locale (the train taking the witness and cop to the trial) and the dialogue.

When Strangers Marry 1944

Director William Castle Cast Robert Mitchum, Kim Hunter 67m

Robert Mitchum's screen debut is one of the best B-movies ever. **Castle**, not famed for his subtlety, builds the suspense slowly, in a tale of a small-town girl who discovers her hubby may be a murderer. Sadly it didn't do well enough to inspire a sequel.

Just William

The title of **William Castle**'s memoirs says it all: *Step Right Up, I'm Gonna Scare the Pants off America!* Born William Schloss in New York in 1914, he spent most of his professional life in the backlots of studios like Columbia and Monogram, producing mostly rather average low-budget thrillers. *When Strangers Marry* is a classic; others, especially *The House on Haunted Hill*, have become cult favourites.

While his movies were seldom out of the ordinary, he had a fertile imagination for stunts to promote them. For *Macabre* he took out insurance in case any member of the audience died during it. For *The House on Haunted Hill* he wired up plastic skeletons to fly over audiences' heads. And for *The Tingler* he gave cinemagoers electric shocks from their seats.

Castle's last film as a director, *Shanks* (1974), was a strange movie, with minimal dialogue, starring Marcel Marceau as a persecuted deaf mute who brings his mentor back to life. Having scared America's pants off with his memoirs in 1976, he died a year later from a heart attack.

X 1963

Director Roger Corman **Cast** Ray Milland, Diana Van der Vlis, Harold Stone **80m**

This may just be **Corman**'s best movie (also known as *X: The Man with the X-Ray Eyes*). As great B sci-fi movies go, its only serious rival is *The Incredible Shrinking Man*. **Milland** gives a searing portrayal of a decent man who acquires a gift (X-ray vision) which, ultimately, he can't cope with. Corman chucks in the idea that Milland can now see God, and the images of his eyes staring out of the screen are incredibly haunting.

BAD GIRLS

With a penchant for tormenting gormless gents (and troubled girls), movie bad girls must be punished, humiliated, maybe even killed – but not before having wreaked havoc, ruined the fabric of respectable society and had enormous amounts of fun, quite often while wearing a catsuit.

Faster, Pussycat! Kill! Kill! 1965

Director Russ Meyer **Cast** Tura Satana, Lori Williams, Haji 83m

You've got to love Varla (**Satana**), the catsuited stripper from hell who, with her two terrifyingly proportioned pals – each one a friend of liquid eyeliner, fist fights and wild gogo dancing – rampage through the desert in an orgy of sex, violence and crime. One of **Meyer**'s more watchable movies, less overtly pornographic than some; the fact you root for these big, badass mamas is testimony to their jawdropping charisma.

Girl Boss Guerilla 1972

Director Norifumi Suzuki **Cast** Miki Sugimoto, Reiko Ike 84m

A biker gang offshoot of the schlocky Japanese *sukeban* (bad girl) genre, with a lipsmacking dash of twisted S&M, brutal punch-ups, nasty revenge scenarios and corny slapstick pratfalls. The term kick-ass doesn't do justice to these girls ("don't mess with us just cos we're chicks!"), zooming around on giant bikes, peeling back their leathers to reveal matching tattoos and much, much more.

Girl Gang 1954

Director Robert C. Dertano **Cast** Joanne Arnold, Mary Lou O'Connor 63m

Ahh, the 1950s. The decade that brought us exploitation movies and more bad girls than you could shake a reefer at – *So Young, So Bad* (1956), *So Evil, So Young* (1957), and so on, ad infinitum. These particular bad girls are very bad indeed, in what is really an insanely bad film. Watch the delinquent dollies stealing, shooting smack, beating up their boyfriends – with the obligatory catfight and frenzied dance number for good measure. For something less chaotic, dig out **Roger Corman**'s *Teenage Doll* (1957), in which the exploitation maestro transforms the girl gang movie into something approaching art.

CULT MOVIES: BAD GIRLS

Leave Her to Heaven 1945

Director John M. Stahl **Cast** Gene Tierney, Cornel Wilde 110m

Though this is *film noir* territory – never was a femme as fatale as Ellen, whose obsessive love for her tiresome husband makes bunny boiling seem compassionate – the feverishly intense (and Oscar-winning) Technicolor presages the overwrought 1950s melodramas of Douglas Sirk, in which neurosis and hysteria lurk under every glossy suburban surface. **Stahl**, himself an accomplished melodrama director, gives us a tragedy of Shakespearean proportions, with an anti-heroine the Bard could only have dreamed of.

Of Human Bondage 1934

Director John Cromwell **Cast** Bette Davis, Leslie Howard 83m

The movie that made a star of **Davis**, never more deliciously bad than as the fiery cocktail waitress **Mildred** (a Cockney of all things, with an accent only marginally better than Audrey Hepburn's as Eliza Doolittle). A single mother, she torments poor old **Leslie Howard**, typically drippy as the besotted, clubfooted masochist who loves her. Aged just 25, Davis is already a scene-stealer, her doll-like vulnerability only underlining her decidedly unladylike behaviour.

★ The Wicked Lady 1945

Director Leslie Arliss **Cast** Margaret Lockwood, James Mason 104m

So bawdy that some scenes were reshot for the US to show less of **Lockwood**'s cleavage, this rollicking Gainsborough romp draws on the legend of highwaywoman Lady Katherine Ferrers. But **Arliss**'s drama is less concerned with history than with the sparks that fly between Lockwood, as the bored noblewoman who turns bad, and **Mason**, as the highwayman who partners her in crime, loves her and two-times her. Lockwood was one of British cinema's most entertaining villainesses.

BANNED

There's nothing like the thrill of the forbidden, except of course when the forbidden is a movie about DIY dentistry or other people's pain thresholds. Often a ban is just grist to the PR machine's mill or makes a movie annoyingly hard to find. Then there are some films, devoid of any artistic merit, that can only be defended on the grounds of free speech.

Blood Sucking Freaks 1978

Director Joel M. Reed **Cast** Seamus O'Brien, Viju Krem **91m**

Are you into "home-style brain surgery!" or "dental hijinks!" (with or without the exclamation marks)? Then this is the movie for you. The synopsis almost says it all: "**Sardu** is into the theatre of the macabre. Sardu is into S&M. Sardu likes to kill people in public and make them think it's fake." All this may explain why Women Against Pornography campaigned, successfully, to ban this in the US. **Reed**'s other movies? *Blood Bath* and *GI Executioner*. Nuff said.

A Clockwork Orange

1972

Director Stanley Kubrick **Cast** Malcolm McDowell, Patrick Magee, Michael Bates **136m**

The funniest thing about this much-analysed movie is that so many of its actors ended up in British TV shows like *Last of the Summer Wine*, *May to December* and *Coronation Street*. **Kubrick** withdrew the film after stories that real criminals had felt inspired to copy crimes committed by **McDowell** and his gang – doubly ironic when one of the messages of this savage satire is that you can't escape the law of karma. Kubrick was accused of creating "intellectual pornography". The furore is a tribute to the movie's disturbing power.

Ilsa, She Wolf of the SS 1974

Director Don Edmonds **Cast** Dyanne Thorne, Gregory Knoph, Maria Marx **96m**

As an example of the 1970s' sleaziest contribution to cinematic history, the Nazi sexploitation film, *Ilsa* is as good (ie bad) a specimen as any. **Ilsa** wants to prove that women can stand more pain than men so she decides to do some experiments. From the people who brought you *Bummer!* and *Larceny*, both of which apply to this movie. This spawned two sequels (*Harem Keeper of*

Verboten!

You just never know how movies are going to affect a country's film censors...

Abbott and Costello Meet Frankenstein Banned in Finland – as was *Abbott and Costello Meet Dr Jekyll and Mr Hyde*.

The Adventures of Barry McKenzie This Barry Humphries comedy upset the New Zealand censor. He said he'd approve it with one cut "from beginning to end".

Catch-22 Banned by Portuguese censors, worried about the damage the glimpse of a naked Yossarian in a tree might do to the national psyche.

Life of Brian Banned in Norway and Runnymede and marketed in Sweden as: "The film that is so funny it was banned in Norway."

Mickey Mouse Banned in Romania in 1935 because the authorities feared he would scare children. How prescient they were.

Monkey Business The Marx Brothers' comedy was banned in Ireland because censors feared it would encourage anarchic tendencies.

Pink Flamingo John Waters' exercise in poor taste was deemed in too poor taste to be screened in Australia, the land which gave us Rolf Harris and Barry McKenzie.

Schindler's List Banned in Malaysia for being pro-Jewish.

---

the *Oil Sheikhs* and *The Tigress of Siberia*). The Norwegians banned *Ilsa* on the not unreasonable grounds that having been invaded by the Nazis, they'd already suffered enough without being forced to watch this nonsense.

resembling dialogue, characters or an intellectual rationale. It was banned in the UK and many other places. **Keaton**, who married into the Garland/Luft showbiz dynasty, appeared as "Girl in the toilet" in her next film.

I Spit on Your Grave 1978

Director Meir Zarchi **Cast** Camille Keaton, Eron Tabor, Richard Pace 100m

Produced at the height of the media pandemic about snuff movies, this was also known as *Day of the Woman* in a bid to give it some feminist credentials. The plot, about a woman who is horribly raped and wreaks murderous revenge, could be described as an updated Jacobean revenge tragedy if only it had anything

Maîtresse 1976

Director Barbet Schroeder **Cast** Bulle Ogier, Gérard Depardieu 112m

Featuring **Depardieu** in an early role, this tale of a small-time crook who becomes involved, both romantically and otherwise, with a professional dominatrix sparked huge controversy in the UK and US. A work in which submissive and dominant roles are examined, the film's graphic depictions of sadomasochistic acts, including the nailing of a penis to a plank of wood, led to the film being denied a release by the BBFC, who deemed it "miles in excess of anything we have released in this field". Not until 2003 was it passed in the UK without cuts.

The Millionairess 1960

Director Anthony Asquith **Cast** Peter Sellers, Sophia Loren, Alastair Sim **90m**

Hard to believe anyone could object to this comedy (except, perhaps, on the grounds that it isn't as funny as it thinks it is), but King Bavendra, the Eton-educated monarch of Nepal, decided that **Sellers**'s Indian doctor was too close to him in both manner and appearance and the only appropriate response to this slight on his royal honour was to ban all Peter Sellers films.

Natural Born Killers 1994

Director Oliver Stone **Cast** Woody Harrelson, Juliette Lewis, Robert Downey Jr **119m**

Although based on a **Tarantino** story, subsequent changes made by **Stone** have led Tarantino to all but disown the film. This is Stone's satire on the media frenzy engulfing the USA, with **Harrelson** and

Lewis as Mickey and Mallory, young, ruthless killers whose main priority on their killing spree is that they take all the credit. Initially banned, the movie holds the record for the largest number of cuts and reshots needed on a film to secure an R-rating (150).

★ Peeping Tom 1960

Director Michael Powell **Cast** Carl Boehm, Anna Massey, Moira Shearer **101m**

"The only really satisfactory way to dispose of *Peeping Tom* would be to shovel it up and flush it swiftly down the nearest sewer. Even then the stench would remain." That was a not untypical reaction when **Powell**'s movie about a serial killer who films his victims as he kills them was first released. The question today is: how good is the film? Answer: very good

Carl Boehm's creepy killer about to film his blonde victim (Pamela Green) in *Peeping Tom*: all very Hitchcock and just as good.

It's only words

Clark Gable wasn't the first man to say "damn" onscreen. Here's our list of linguistic premieres.

Bastard A breakthrough for the British film-making industry: first heard on celluloid in *The Blue Lamp* (1950).
Bloody First heard in *Pygmalion* (1938).
Damned First uttered (in the phrase "Well, I'll be damned") by Emma Dunn in *Blessed Event* (1932).
Fuck First used by Marianne Faithfull in Michael Winner's *I'll Never Forget What's His Name* (1967). Also used by critics at the movie's preview. Later heard 206 times in *Scarface* and 254 times in *Reservoir Dogs*.
Shit Made its big screen debut in Truman Capote's film *In Cold Blood* (1967).

indeed. Powell makes the audience confront their own voyeurism: we are invited to sympathize with the mad, abused hero even as we despise him.

Quiet Days in Clichy 1970

Director Jens Jørgen Thorsen **Cast** Paul Valjean, Wayne Rodda, Ulla Koppel 96m

Thorsen caused a storm in 1970 by adapting this **Henry Miller** book – which had been banned in the US – for the screen. The movie was subsequently banned in the US and UK for being too explicit, though the sex scenes aren't hardcore, just continuous and, as in Miller's books, sometimes monotonous as Joey and Carl screw their way round Paris. Thorsen uses a series of devices to jar his audience, including speech bubbles, voiceovers and subtitles. Fascinating as an example of early sexual liberation onscreen, but **Rodda**'s poor acting is a distraction.

Straw Dogs 1971

Director Sam Peckinpah **Cast** Dustin Hoffman, Susan George, Peter Vaughan 118m

Banned in the UK from home viewing under the 1984 Video Recordings Act and not shown on TV until 2003, it's a moot point whether **Peckinpah**'s West Country western, in which geeky mathematician David Sumner (**Hoffman**) takes on the village thugs who raped wife Amy (**George**), would cause such controversy today. Whether that says more about censorship in 1971 or the decline in moral standards since is another matter. Still, if Peckinpah's intention was to get up people's noses, he did a fine job.

BEACHES

Love, lust and surfing, you can do it all at the beach – in the movies as well as on holiday. Once beach movies get arty, though, you may feel it's safer to get back in the water.

Beach Party 1963

Director William Asher **Cast** Frankie Avalon, Annette Funicello 101m

Picking up where the *Gidget* franchise left off, this amusing anthropological artefact spawned numerous sequels and imitations – most with the word "bikini" in the title. Erstwhile teen idol **Avalon** and busty ex-Mouseketeer **Funicello** were teamed to phenomenally popular effect in innocent antics that epitomized America's riposte to the British Invasion: scantily clad, deeply tanned California kids surfing, smooching and gyrating in the sand to pop pap. It was followed by *Muscle Beach Party*, which, unsurprisingly, wasn't as good, then *Beach Blanket Bingo*, best remembered for having a character called Eric Von Zipper. Frankie, sensing that the tide was out on the beach movie phenomenon, only appeared for six minutes in the follow-up *How to Stuff a Wild Bikini*, in which **Buster Keaton** had a minor role.

> Bring me my pendulum, kiddies, I feel like swinging.
> **Big Daddy, Beach Party**

Big Wednesday 1978

Director John Milius **Cast** Jan-Michael Vincent, William Katt, Gary Busey 119m

This great, cool, cult surfing movie spans the early 1960s and mid-1970s episodically, in snapshots of three friends' lives. Dramatically all over the place, it takes in carefree, youthful adventure involving wine, women and surf, incorporates the Vietnam draft, and culminates poetically in the older, calmer trio's wistful reunion to catch the legendary, perfect big wave. An oddly affecting paean to youth, it's justly famous for its spectacular surfing sequences.

Follow That Dream 1962

Director Gordon Douglas **Cast** Elvis Presley, Anne Helm, Arthur O'Connell 109m

Elvis Presley made some dodgy beach movies (notably *Girl Happy*, in which he tries to launch a dance craze called the clam and escapes from jail in drag) but this is underrated and funny, if slow to start. Elvis is the innocent scion of a hapless family who run out of gas on a beach which is outside state laws and, as a result, attracts gamblers and crooks. A nicely observed study of innocence triumphing over evil, with a handful of so-so songs, this is a minor gem.

The Piano 1993

Director Jane Campion **Cast** Holly Hunter, Harvey Keitel, Sam Neill 121m

Sunhats and spades are never much in evidence on arthouse beaches, which must, by law, be cold, gusty and grey (think *The Seventh Seal*; *Becket*; *Eternal Sunshine of the Spotless Mind*). True to form the cloud cover never breaks for mute Ada (**Hunter**), her spirited daughter Flora (Oscar-winning **Anna Paquin**), and her beloved piano, all dramatically trans-

The arthouse beach is no summer holiday: Holly Hunter, Anna Paquin and the eponymous instrument newly arrived in New Zealand.

planted from Scotland and set down on a wild New Zealand beach to herald Ada's new life in an arranged marriage to a stuffy man she does not love. Those crashing waves, that wind, the rousing, passionate music; all linger like sand in your beach bag in **Campion**'s exquisite examination of erotic love.

★ Point Break 1991

Director Kathryn Bigelow **Cast** Patrick Swayze, Keanu Reeves 122m

Nonstop extreme stunt action from surfer/ bank robber Bodhi (**Swayze**) and the undercover FBI agent (**Reeves**) sent to find him. Plenty of sex, sun and surf ensures that, as long as you don't ask too many questions, the testosterone-fuelled action never drags – despite all the false endings. Swayze, an experienced sky-diver, did some of his own stunts, and Reeves, who learnt to surf for the movie, is still an avid surfer today.

Psycho Beach Party 2000

Director Robert Lee King **Cast** Lauren Ambrose, Thomas Gibson, Nicholas Brendon 95m

Led by future *Six Feet Under* star **Lauren Ambrose**, this is a cross between a spoof of Frankie Avalon's *Beach Party* movies and a slasher horror. Ambrose is schizophrenic, one side the innocent Chicklet, Malibu's first female surfer, the other a foul-mouthed, libidinous potential murderess. Writer **Charles Busch**, better known for his love of cross-dressing, adapted his own play for the screen,

Sonatine (1993, 94m)

"Written, directed, edited and starring Takeshi Kitano, *Sonatine* is not your typical yakuza film. A world-weary gangster, Murakawa is ordered to take his clan to settle a dispute between two factions, but it is a set-up and many of his men die. He takes his gang to hide out in a house on a remote beach. This is where the majority of the film takes place, far away from the city and their troubles. What do bored yakuza do when they have time to kill? They play like kids, but every activity seems to have an undercurrent of violence. They set off fireworks, play 'paper, rock, scissors', sumo wrestle on the beach and play Russian roulette, leading to the memorable image of Kitano blowing out his brains in slow motion...

The heart of the film at the beach is what makes *Sonatine* so unique: there are no scenes of wisecracking dialogue, few shoot-outs and what violence there is, is mainly offscreen, like in the climactic shoot-out where the camera remains passively outside the building so we only see the flashes of gunshots inside.

What makes *Sonatine* so interesting compared to most Hong Kong or Japanese yakuza films of the time is that it is so stylized, slow, poetic, minimalistic – like Kitano's acting, the film shows that less is more."

Asif Kapadia

British Asian director Kapadia's debut, The Warrior, *set in the deserts of feudal Rajasthan, won the best British film BAFTA and was lauded for its use of location and cinematography. The director's subsequent films have been murder thriller* The Return – *featuring Sarah Michelle Gellar – and the visually arresting* Far North.

and is seen here as Captain Monica Stark. If you didn't know Ambrose from her TV success, you might think the bad acting on display here wasn't intentional, but viewed as a pastiche of those often cringingly bad beach movies and *Psycho*, it's a potential camp cult favourite.

Woman of the Dunes 1964

Director Hiroshi Teshigahara **Cast** Eiji Okada, Kyoko Kisida 123m

While not literally set on a beach, this existential classic – edgy, anxious and riven with sandflies – is defined, dominated and consumed by sand, and will touch the buttons of anyone who gets distressed by those gritty little bits that get stuck in seaside sarnies. Cruel, surreal and relentlessly dark – much like an English seaside town out of season – the endless dunes, which a man and woman must "shovel to survive", provide a deranged, ever-shifting stage for one of those savage erotic battles in which Japanese cinema excels. You may never dig a sandcastle again.

BIKERS

Hell's Angels, hoodlums and hot-riding hotheads – movie bikers represent everything that's wrong with society. The open road gives disaffected teens the freedom and space to grapple with existential angst, and with so much leather and darkly revving engines, dirty sex is never far from the surface.

Easy Rider 1969

Director Dennis Hopper **Cast** Peter Fonda, Dennis Hopper, Jack Nicholson 95m

Fonda and **Hopper** were in a pretty bad state while filming this countercultural road movie, in which the bikes – huge, gleaming Harleys – just about avoid playing second fiddle to the drugs. Fonda, as Captain America, is ineffably cool, and constantly stoned, roaring through the Southwestern deserts, but it's **Nicholson** who steals the show as the alcoholic lost soul in this landmark New Hollywood classic. Melancholy and full of longing, it's a genuinely haunting piece of cinema, with something real to say about American disillusionment and despair.

Girl on a Motorcycle 1968

Director Jack Cardiff **Cast** Marianne Faithfull, Alain Delon, Roger Mutton 91m

Faithfull has always wanted to be taken seriously – this piece of Swinging Sixties psychedelic schlock, in which a free-spirited married woman mounts her Harley to zoom off to meet her lover, didn't really help her case. All most people remember about it is that the angelic Sister Morphine (just around the time that a certain Mars Bar story rocked the headlines) is completely starkers beneath her zip-up leather catsuit.

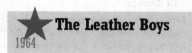 ## The Leather Boys 1964

Director Sidney J. Furie **Cast** Colin Campbell, Dudley Sutton, Rita Tushingham 108m

Splendid British New Wave classic in which a penchant for leather and huge phallic symbols alludes to a love that dare not speak its name. Stylish black-and-white cinematography and great performances convey a real sense of the Brit biker scene of the 1960s – much of it set in and around the iconic Ace Café, the biker hangout that still stands on London's North Circular road.

The Loveless 1982

Directors Kathryn Bigelow, Monty Montgomery **Cast** Willem Dafoe, Robert Gordon 85m

Bigelow brings her trademark style and edgy vigour to her directorial debut, a homage to B-movies, road movies, Westerns and *film noir*, in which a cycle gang clash with a small Southern town in the 1950s. **Dafoe** gives a suitably hip performance as skinny greaser Vance, while **Gordon**, a real-life rocker, snarls right back at him. All switchblades, rumba music, rippling tattoos and sexy rockabilly broads, with the essential dash of homo-erotic brooding – and the vintage bikes aren't bad, either.

Orphée 1950

Director Jean Cocteau **Cast** Jean Marais, François Perier, Maria Casarés **95m**

Cocteau brings us a characteristically magical retelling of the Orpheus legend that's part fairy tale, part gloomy beatnik poem (featuring dark-eyed boho beauty **Juliette Gréco**). The Hell's Angels here are literally that, a sinister brace of bikers kitted out in black gear and shades who accompany Death (the glorious **Casarés**) as she glides through the Underworld in a black Roller.

The Wild Angels 1966

Director Roger Corman **Cast** Peter Fonda, Nancy Sinatra, Bruce Dern **93m**

They may be angels from hell, "with a God called hate", they may rape and pillage and punch preachers in the face, they may smoke weed and wig out to bongo beats, but these Angels have simple needs, according to **Fonda**, as gangleader Heavenly Blues: "We wanna be free! We wanna be free to… er… Do what we wanna do! We wanna be free to ride our machines without being hassled by the Man!" Three years before *Easy Rider*, **Corman**'s B-movie classic has all the nihilism of the later movie, double the pace and triple the violence – one group of real Hell's Angels, in high umbrage, tried to sue for defamation.

★ The Wild One 1953

Director László Benedek **Cast** Marlon Brando, Lee Marvin, Mary Murphy **79m**

Beautiful **Brando** in white cap and leathers, sulkily straddling a 1950 Triumph Thunderbird 6T, is the archetypal biker bad boy, spawning imitators from James Dean (T-shirts, moody squirming) to Elvis (sideburns, pouting). The story was supposedly inspired by a real biker get-together in Hollister, California, in 1947 – though that event didn't end in violence – but the real drama is in Johnny's angst-ridden psyche. It could barely get any hipper – the gangs' jive talking has to be heard to be believed – but whether **Marvin**'s rival gang, The Beetles, inspired the lovable moptops to name their pop combo is a matter of some debate. The movie was banned in Britain until 1968, when it was greeted with wild enthusiasm by greasers facing slow annihilation through flower power.

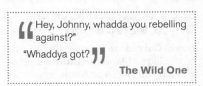

> **"** Hey, Johnny, whadda you rebelling against?"
>
> "Whaddya got? **"**
>
> **The Wild One**

BIOPICS

From musicians to military leaders, artistic prodigies to medical geniuses, the lives of the famous (at least on film) usually chart a course from miserable beginnings to glittering success – followed by inevitable fall. Sometimes, though, it's the historical backdrop that provides the real interest.

An Angel at My Table 1990

Director Jane Campion **Cast** Kerry Fox, Alexia Keogh, Karen Fergusson 158m

Unflinching without being morbid, this is a deeply moving film. **Kerry Fox** piled on the pounds for **Jane Campion** and **Laura Jones**'s epic adaptation of New Zealand writer **Janet Frame**'s autobiographical trilogy, which was originally conceived as a TV mini-series. But Fox's junior co-stars also excel, as the domestic travails of a hardscrabble Depression childhood lead to crippling shyness, a misdiagnosis of schizophrenia and over two hundred electroshock treatments – "each one equal in fear to an execution".

Bound for Glory 1976

Director Hal Ashby **Cast** David Carradine, Ronny Cox, Melinda Dillon 148m

David Carradine inherited this account of folk legend **Woody Guthrie**'s politicization on the Depression road from Oklahoma to California after singer **Tim Buckley** died during preproduction. Acknowledging that Guthrie had flaws as well as genius, Carradine's "Dust Bowl Troubadour" shares the wounded dignity that Henry Fonda brought to *The Grapes of Wrath* (1940) and the film shows a dedication to authentic period mood and detail. All the same, Hal Ashby and Oscar-winning cinematographer **Haskell Wexler** managed to incorporate the first Steadicam shots in a Hollywood feature.

The Chronicle of Anna Magdalena Bach 1968

Directors Jean-Marie Straub, Danièle Huillet **Cast** Gustav Leonhardt, Christiane Lang, Paolo Carlini 93m

Straub and **Huillet** succeed in presenting life being lived and emotions being experienced in this rigorously anti-biopic. Musician **Gustav Leonhardt** and singer **Christiane Lang** exist rather than act amidst narrated extracts from a faux journal and tableau renditions of

Johann Sebastian Bach's sublime music. The result is an immersive film that's as spiritually thrilling as it is cinematically audacious.

Control 2007

Director Anton Corbijn **Cast** Sam Riley, Samantha Morton, Alexandra Maria Lara 122m

Plucked from folding T-shirts in a Leeds warehouse, **Sam Riley** was cast as Joy Division frontman **Ian Curtis** on his birthday. Jude Law and Cillian Murphy had been linked with the role, but **Anton Corbijn** (who had remortgaged his house to fund the picture) was right to trust his instincts, as not only is Riley's impersonation of Curtis's onstage submersion uncanny, but he also nails the bipolar recklessness that made his relationships with bandmates and lovers alike so combustibly unpredictable.

The Glenn Miller Story
1954

Director Anthony Mann **Cast** James Stewart, June Allyson, Harry Morgan 116m

Facts are at a premium in this classic piece of Tinseltown myth-making. **Glenn Miller**'s lengthy search for a distinctive swing sound didn't end, for example, when a trumpeter split his lip and a clarinettist took over "Moonlight Serenade". But sincerity trumps accuracy here, with **James Stewart** exuding a charisma that Miller himself failed to exhibit in *Orchestra Wives* (1941) and *Sun Valley Serenade* (1942). Joe Yukl dubs

Stewart's trombone playing, but the real musical highlights are Louis Armstrong and Gene Krupa's jam on "Basin Street Blues" and the anachronistic radio broadcast of "Little Brown Jug", as **June Allyson** learns that her husband's plane is missing.

The Music Lovers 1970

Director Ken Russell **Cast** Richard Chamberlain, Glenda Jackson, Max Adrian 123m

From his earliest TV films, composers have loomed large in **Ken Russell**'s work. Scripted by **Melvyn Bragg**, this is a gleefully fanciful portrait of **Peter Ilych Tchaikovsky**, which posits that his music was an emotional safety valve for the psycho-sexual traumas that blighted him from childhood. Alan Bates rejected the lead and **Richard Chamberlain** never quite matches the courage of **Glenda Jackson** as his nymphomaniacal wife. But Russell atones with an audiovisual overload that is simultaneously disconcerting, infuriating and intoxicating.

Napoléon 1927

Director Abel Gance **Cast** Albert Dieudonné, Edmond Van Daële, Alexandre Koubitzky 333m

Abel Gance initially envisaged a six-part biography, complete with full-colour and 3-D sequences. Even concentrating just on Bonaparte's youth and first Italian triumph, this epic still took twenty months to shoot and seven more to edit. The resulting six-hour masterpiece was seen by scandalously few viewers, as only a handful of venues could accommodate the majestic Polyvision triptychs. Moreover, its novelty value was undercut by the advent of talkies and Gance was forced to issue a sound edition in 1934. Supposedly nineteen versions of the film exist, with the closest to the original being the 330-minute restoration **Kevin Brownlow** produced in 2000.

The Scarlet Empress 1934

Director Josef von Sternberg **Cast** Marlene Dietrich, John Lodge, Sam Jaffe 109m

The nearest this gets to historical accuracy is the fact that both Catherine the Great and **Marlene Dietrich** were German. Nevertheless, **Von Sternberg**'s "relentless excursion into style" was a slyly perceptive study of the role of women in a patriarchal society. Dietrich is essentially part of the décor here, but she remains eminently magisterial as she dallies with her lovers and plots the overthrow of imbecilic husband **Sam Jaffe**.

Séraphine 2008

Director Martin Provost **Cast** Yolande Moreau, Ulrich Tukur, Anne Bennent 125m

Dismissed for much of her life as a mentally unstable skivvy in her home town of Senlis, **Séraphine Louis** was discovered as a primitive artist of rare talent by Wilhelm Uhde, the gay German champion of Picasso. Both are depicted as outsiders misunderstood by socio-cultural convention either side of the Great War in this multi-César-winning gem. But the galumphing **Yolande Moreau** consistently upstages **Ulrich Tukur**, whether she's communing with nature, furtively gathering the soil, candle wax and animal blood necessary for her paint, or succumbing to the temptations of unexpected celebrity. Rarely has a treatise on preconception and prejudice been so exquisitely photographed or unsentimentally poignant.

★ The Story of Louis Pasteur 1935

Director William Dieterle **Cast** Paul Muni, Josephine Hutchinson, Anita Louise 87m

William Dieterle was Hollywood's biopic king in the 1930s, with lives of Emile Zola, Benito Juárez, Paul Erlich and Paul Julius Reuter to his credit. But his finest achievement was this tribute to French microbiologist Louis Pasteur, which earned **Paul Muni** an Oscar. Obviously the science is grossly simplified, as Pasteur develops effective vaccines against anthrax and rabies. But even though Dieterle's faith in science is a touch naïve, he refuses to patronize his audience, as is the case with too many modern biopics.

> ❛❛ I won't tolerate such practices. We're not living in the Middle Ages. This is France… Paris… the nineteenth century. ❜❜
> **Napoleon III, The Story of Louis Pasteur**

BLAXPLOIT-ATION

Shaft's success kick-started this afrolicious genre and soon every studio wanted a piece of the action. But the craze inspired a few cracking movies, not all of them following the gangster-ghetto template...

Black Caesar 1973

Director Larry Cohen **Cast** Fred Williamson, Gloria Hendry, Art Lund, D'Urville Martin **89m**

A Harlem version of the 1930s gangster movie, charting the murderous misadventures of Tommy Gibbs (**Williamson**) in his rise from shoeshine boy to mafioso boss. You suspect the bloodbaths are there merely to titillate, but then this is essentially a blaxploitation movie with a Mob twist.

Blacula 1972

Director William Crain **Cast** William Marshall, Vonetta McGee **93m**

A horror/blaxploitation hybrid starring **Marshall** as an eighteenth-century African prince, Mamuwalde, who is transformed into a vampire whilst visiting Transylvania. Two centuries later he rises from his coffin in the Watts district of LA in search of young, female blood. Followed by a sequel, *Scream, Blacula, Scream*, American International Studios' production overcomes its meagre budget to deliver a smidgeon of social commentary and some genuinely bone-chilling moments.

Coffy 1973

Director Jack Hill **Cast** Pam Grier, Robert DoQui **91m**

"Coffy" Coffin (**Grier**) is a nurse who decides to take the law into her own hands when her sister becomes a drug addict. Spurned by the police and seemingly corrupt politicians in her quest for help, Coffy poses as a prostitute in order to infiltrate the seedy underworld. Making a star of **Pam Grier**, alluringly dominant in her signature role, *Coffy*'s potent cocktail of sex and violence made it a sensation when released. Pre-dating Michael Winner's *Death Wish*, the film peddles a similar vigilante wish-fulfilment fantasy.

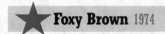

Foxy Brown 1974

Director Jack Hill **Cast** Pam Grier, Antonio Fargas 91m

The film that took **Grier**'s star to international levels and solidified her position as female icon of the blaxploitation movement. **Hill** exceeds even *Coffy*'s high quotient of sex and violence. To avenge the death of her lover at the hands of vicious mobsters on the trail of her ne'er-do-well brother (**Fargas**), Foxy Brown poses as a hooker (sound familiar?) in order to find out exactly who was responsible and have her revenge. Balancing the more outrageous moments (a fight in a lesbian bar) with a more political bent (a community watch group inspired by the Black Panthers fight to stop black areas turning into ghettos), the film became an immediate hit on the grindhouse circuit.

> **“** Dawes: Sister, I think what you're looking for is revenge.
>
> Foxy Brown: You just handle the justice, and I'll handle the revenge myself. **”**
>
> **Foxy Brown**

Jackie Brown 1997

Director Quentin Tarantino **Cast** Pam Grier, Samuel L. Jackson, Robert Forster 154m

For Tarantino's third movie he chose to adapt **Elmore Leonard**'s novel *Rum*

Punch, which has a plot so convoluted he could well have written it himself. (This is, Leonard says, his favourite screen adaptation.) **Grier** plays Jackie Brown (a homage to her 1970s character Foxy Brown) supplementing her air stewardess wage by handling laundered money for her boss, Ordell (**Jackson**). Rumbled, she has to play the situation to stay alive and out of jail. Reading the novel, Tarantino failed to realize the main character was white and wrote the script with Grier in mind (she auditioned for a role in *Pulp Fiction* and Tarantino had promised her a role in his next movie). All the characters are smart, from Ordell to bail bondsman Max (**Forster**, in his best role) and **Michael Keaton**'s FBI agent Ray Nicolette (the same character he played in another Leonard adaptation, *Out of Sight*).

Super Fly 1972

Director Gordon Parks Jr **Cast** Ron O'Neal, Carl Lee, Sheila Frazier 98m

Super Fly was **Gordon Parks Jr**'s antithesis to his previous year's *Shaft*, the hero a drug-pusher with a natty pimp-style wardrobe and a super-cool motor. Summed up in the tagline "Never a dude like this one! He's got a plan to stick it to the man!", Priest was the "super fly" guy making one last score that was to set him up for life. **O'Neal** is perfect as Priest, his swagger and, as one reviewer described, "facial expression that says 'you mess with me and I'll stomp on your balls'" carrying the movie. It boasts one of the best blaxploitation soundtracks thanks to Curtis Mayfield's funky tunes; so good, in fact, that the album outgrossed the movie.

The original Shaft

Former model **Richard Roundtree** experienced the blunt end of the movie business. His 1971 debut, *Shaft* (see p.343), propelled him to superstar status, but his failure to find equally iconic roles brought him back down to earth with a bang.

Though not strictly the first blaxploitation feature, *Shaft* launched the genre, saved MGM from bankruptcy and made Roundtree an idol, but meaty roles for black actors just weren't out there and Roundtree made more blaxploitation sequels like the terminally average *Shaft in Africa*. Despite his good looks and laid-back, droll manner, the succeeding decades weren't kind to him, and he was relegated to bit parts and dire TV movies. After Pam Grier's revival, maybe Roundtree is next in line.

Sweet Sweetback's Baadasssss Song 1971

Director Melvin Van Peebles **Cast** Simon Chuckster, Melvin Van Peebles 97m

Dedicated to "Brothers and sisters who have had enough of the Man" and considered the first blaxploitation movie, preceding *Shaft* by a matter of months, *Sweet Sweetback* was a labour of love for **Van Peebles**. No studio would back his tale of a black man taking matters into his own hands when a black kid is beaten up by two white cops. So Peebles wrote, directed, starred, produced, edited and composed the music, financing the project thanks, in part, to a $50,000 loan from Bill Cosby. Luckily it was a resounding success in the US, grossing $10 million.

TNT Jackson 1974

Director Ciro H. Santiago **Cast** Jeanne Bell, Chiquito, Stan Shaw 72m

Filipino-born **Ciro H. Santiago**'s work successfully exploits the combination of sex, violence and sassy leading ladies pioneered by Jack Hill. Casting former Playboy Playmate **Jeanne Bell** as the titular TNT Jackson ("She'll put you in traction"), Santiago scored one of his biggest hits as he tracks Jackson from Harlem to Hong Kong in search of a missing brother who has, you've guessed it, fallen foul of the Mob. Featuring topless karate, the film was twice reincarnated – as *Firecracker* and then *Angelfist*.

Thomasine & Bushrod 1974

Director Gordon Parks Jr **Cast** Max Julien, Vonetta McGee, George Murdock 95m

A blaxploitation Western, this *Bonnie and Clyde* rip-off is worth viewing for novelty value alone. Thomasine (**McGee**) and Bushrod (**Julien**) are a pair of thieves in the American South in the 1910s, stealing from rich, white capitalists to give to the poor. It proved to be Julien's last film for over twenty years, although rumour has it Tarantino wanted to cast him as Marsellus Wallace in *Pulp Fiction*.

BOLLYWOOD

Like Hollywood, Bollywood is a place, a movie factory and a way of looking at the world. And there's more to the best Bollywood movies than a guy, a girl, parental disapproval and a few cracking musical numbers.

Bandit Queen 1994

Director Shekhar Kapur **Cast** Seema Biswas, Aditya Srivastava, Agesh Markham 121m

Banned by the Indian censors and sued by the real **Phoolan Devi**, who wanted to prevent the movie's release, this Channel 4 production had a tough time reaching audiences but the struggle was worth it. In India, Devi is immortalized as a Robin Hood figure, but elsewhere few will know her name, never mind her story. Sold in marriage by her parents for a cow and a bicycle, Devi bucks society's expectations when kidnapped by bandits by leading her own gang and killing thirty men – in a truly horrifying scene – in revenge for her gang rape and her lover's murder. The unusual amount of graphic sex and violence guaranteed headlines and helped obscure some of the more serious points **Kapur** was making. Grim, but gripping.

Black 2005

Director Sanjay Leela Bhansali **Cast** Amitabh Bachchan, Rani Mukherjee, Ayesha Kapoor 122m

The biggest (by titles released) film industry in the world isn't sufficiently appreciated overseas for its quality arthouse films. Yet this story of an ageing teacher trying to connect with a blind and deaf pupil (who later returns the favour) is full of subtlety and sensitivity and wonderfully framed images. Tearjerker? Yes, but with such aplomb are the movie's emotions communicated it is not surprising the film won many awards in India or that it retains a solid claim to be one of the best ever films concerned with disability.

 ## Monsoon Wedding 2001

Director Mira Nair **Cast** Naseeruddin Shah, Lillete Dubey, Shefali Shetty 113m

This starts almost like a Robert Altman movie – we're plunged into the middle of an event, a family wedding, and invited to figure out who everyone is. It's the kind of movie, critic Roger Ebert noted, ''where you meet characters you have never been within 10,000 miles of, and feel like you know them at once.'' **Nair** has a gift for swift, deft comedy and for weaving musical numbers into her storyline more unobtrusively than many directors of Hollywood musicals. To cap it all, there's a touching gesture of adoration involving some marigolds. A work of genius that overcame cultural boundaries.

Mughal-E-Azam 1960

Director K. Asif **Cast** Prithviraj Kapoor, Madhubala, Dilip Kumar 191m

K. Asif spent at least ten years working on this Bollywood high drama. (Although called the Samuel Goldwyn of India, he only completed one other movie, *Phool* in 1944.) The premise – prince falls out with father, the emperor, over love for servant-dancer – may not be original, but Asif fills the screen for three hours with everything

Madhubala and Dilip Kumar engage in one of *Mughal-E-Azam*'s quieter romantic moments, amidst the thrilling fights and musical numbers.

from swashbuckling swordplay to raucous musical numbers via tender romantic liaisons. **Madhubala**, the Venus of the Indian screen, seemed destined for great things, but died in 1969 aged just 36.

Satya 1998

Director Ram Gopal Varma **Cast** J.D. Chakravarthy, Urmila Matondkar 171m

The uncomfortable proximity between the Mumbai underworld and Bollywood can be glimpsed in this high octane thriller. Reluctant gangster Satya meets Vidya, an aspiring singer, but gets caught up in a tragic high stakes confrontation between rival mobsters and the authorities. With 171 minutes of violence, documentary-style realism and stirring musical numbers, *Satya*'s uncompromising intensity broke new ground in India.

★ Sholay 1975

Director Ramesh Sippy **Cast** Dharmendra, Amitabh Bachchan 188m

Consistently topping polls as one of the best Bollywood offerings ever, *Sholay* is a music- and action-packed epic (the longest in Indian cinema history) about two small-time criminals hired by an ex-policeman to get rid of a dangerous bandit who killed the policeman's family. If you've never watched a Bollywood movie, start here – there's a lot more going on than singing and dancing, while the plot echoes many a Western. Hollywood stunt men and technicians helped **Sippy** give proceedings a certain slickness.

BUDDY

The world is full of great twosomes. Some sing, some dance and some just hit the road together after one of them's shot a man. The quirky relationship of two mismatched characters (usually of the same sex) has changed as the buddy act became commonplace, with increasingly desperate twists.

A Better Tomorrow 1986

Director John Woo **Cast** Chow Yun-Fat, Ti Lung, Leslie Cheung **95m**

The most famous scene in this movie is the dinner-table assassination by **Yun-Fat** wearing, a little implausibly given the Hong Kong setting, a trenchcoat. Yet it struck such a chord with the youth of Hong Kong that all the hippest kids were wearing them in 1986. The action sequences are just trappings; at the heart of the movie is the relationship between two brothers: one a gangster (**Ti Lung**) and the other a cop (**Cheung**).

Butch Cassidy and the Sundance Kid 1969

Director George Roy Hill **Cast** Paul Newman, Robert Redford **110m**

Paul Newman liked to say of this movie: "It's a love affair between two men – the girl is really incidental." **Katharine Ross**'s incidental status is confirmed in a famously unchivalrous scene where Sundance (**Redford**), told that Butch (Newman) is flirting with his girl, waves a tired hand and says: "Take her." The tale of outlaws who wisecrack all the way across the West and then down to Bolivia isn't really popular with Western aficionados, probably because the backdrop is almost incidental too. This is just an excuse for writer **William Goldman**'s witticisms and for the male leads to spark off each other, which they do beautifully.

Kikujiro 1999

Director Takeshi Kitano **Cast** Takeshi Kitano, Yusuke Sekiguchi **121m**

A refreshing excursion from the violent crime films with which **Kitano** had established his reputation, *Kikujiro* merges buddy and road movie elements to pleasing effect. Kitano portrays the gruff title character whose wife instructs him that he must help neighbourhood waif Masao (**Sekiguchi**) find his estranged mother. Before even leaving town, Kikujiro drinks and gambles away their travelling money, and so they are forced to undertake the quest on foot.

The Man Who Would Be King 1975

Director John Huston **Cast** Sean Connery, Michael Caine, Christopher Plummer 129m

John Huston believed the most important part of his job was casting, and **Connery** and **Caine** are perfect as British soldiers in India, conning the local people into believing Connery is a god. Originally, Huston had envisaged Gable and Bogart or Redford and Newman as our heroes, but neither pairing would have been able to provide the story with the Englishness it needs. Fine support is provided by **Saeed Jaffrey**, and a 103-year-old **Karroom Ben Bouih** in his first and only screen appearance, as the high priest Kafu-Selim.

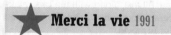 **Merci la vie** 1991

Director Bertrand Blier **Cast** Charlotte Gainsbourg, Anouk Grinberg 118m

It is hard to forget any movie that begins with a scene of a beaten woman in a wedding dress in a supermarket trolley with a seagull on her head, being pushed down an empty road by a girl she has just met. Released the same year as *Thelma and Louise*, this is a road movie on the road to nowhere. **Gérard Depardieu** appears as the appropriately named Dr Worms who, for reasons we will never know, is using **Gainsbourg** in a medical experiment which involves her sleeping with as many men as possible, to see how many of them get sexually transmitted diseases. Anyone heard of the Hippocratic Oath? Depardieu is horribly convincing; an odd role in an odd movie.

Midnight Run 1988

Director Martin Brest **Cast** Robert De Niro, Charles Grodin 126m

One of the best buddy movies of the 1980s and perhaps **De Niro**'s finest – and most foul-mouthed – comedy, *Midnight Run* looks at what happens when a belligerent bounty hunter escorts an accountant wanted by both the FBI and the Mafia bosses he swindled across country to his appointment with justice. Trading on De Niro's taciturn, tough guy persona, the film's brilliance lies in its casting of **Grodin** as his philosophical foil. The quick-fire exchanges between the pair come thick and fast and are deftly delivered.

> ❝ Mardukas: No, I don't have to do better than that, because it's the truth, I can't fly: I suffer from aviaphobia.
> Walsh: What does that mean?
> Mardukas: It means I can't fly. I also suffer from acrophobia and claustrophobia.
> Walsh: I'll tell you what: if you don't cooperate, you're gonna suffer from 'fistophobia'. ❞
>
> **Midnight Run**

★ The Odd Couple 1968

Director Gene Saks **Cast** Walter Matthau, Jack Lemmon 105m

In the popular imagination, **Lemmon** and **Matthau** seemed to spend their closing years eternally appearing in movies together. They co-starred in ten films but this, about two friends who become flatmates, is the most enduring. Neither actor could waste lines like: "You leave little notes on my pillow, 'We're all out of cornflakes, F. U.' It took me three hours to figure out F. U. was Felix Unger." Lemmon improved on **Neil Simon**'s play (based on the writer's brother's divorce) by giving his character something Simon often failed to create, a sense of genuine human emotion and melancholy. The 1998 sequel may star the irrepressible twosome, but it's best left alone if you want to preserve the memory of this classic.

Scarecrow 1973

Director Jerry Schatzberg **Cast** Gene Hackman, Al Pacino, Dorothy Tristan 115m

Riding high from *The French Connection* and *The Godfather*, **Hackman** and **Pacino** opted for this low-key buddy picture which barely managed to create a blip on the Hollywood radar. Hackman is an ex-con eager to go straight as a car-wash proprietor, Pacino a former sailor heading back to the child he abandoned. What they do and where they've been is of little consequence, *Scarecrow* being a character study of two very different people, one a wound-up recluse, the other an amiable optimist, who find companionship and a purpose to life in one another. Directed by former *Vogue* photographer **Schatzberg**, the movie won the Cannes Palme d'Or but remains a little-seen gem.

Thelma and Louise 1991

Director Ridley Scott **Cast** Geena Davis, Susan Sarandon, Michael Madsen 129m

Ground-breaking feminist buddy movie, or exploitative piece of cinematic styling? Whatever your take on **Scott**'s lavish production about two women on the run in the Southwest US after one of them kills an attempted rapist on a weekend away, there's no denying it's a stunning movie, beautifully acted, with an Oscar-winning script from **Callie Khouri**. Delicious scenes include Thelma's boorish husband Darryl (**Christopher McDonald**) trying to be nice to her on the phone, and **Harvey Keitel** verbally beating up **Brad Pitt** for seriously escalating the women's problems after his night of passion with Thelma. All this, along with the breathtaking cinematography, makes for a truly wonderful movie.

BUSINESS

It may not seem the sexiest of subjects, but the boardroom is as fine a setting as the bedroom for a good old morality tale. While the French make thrillers about the banking system, Hollywood business movies either worship the individual or wring hands over the evil of corporations.

Änglar, Finns Dom? 1961

Director Lars-Magnus Lindgren **Cast** Jarl Kulle, Christina Schollin 108m

Sweden's contribution to comedy is usually held to be on a par with Switzerland's contribution to naval warfare, so this little gem comes as a surprise. Jan Froman (**Kulle**) decides to become the boss of his local bank but having few qualifications and less clout, he's obliged to start as a janitor. He falls in love with a married woman and, in 1961, the movie achieved notoriety for its seaside love scenes, a fuss that rather obscured the quality of the rest of the film.

L'argent des autres 1978

Director Christian de Chalonge **Cast** Jean-Louis Trintignant, Catherine Deneuve 105m

Bank worker Henri Rainier (**Trintignant**) is blamed when his bank's loan to a big investor goes awry. The bank tries to cover it up but news soon leaks and Rainier is sacked. **Chalonge** directs an intriguing political-financial thriller known in English as *Other People's Money*, not to be confused with the less convincing Danny DeVito film of the same name.

★ The Crime of Monsieur Lange 1936

Director Jean Renoir **Cast** René Lefevre, Florelle, Jules Berry 80m

The "crime" of the title is the murder by an aspiring young writer of his unscrupulous boss; the story of the events leading up to that murder, however, freewheels over, around and through so much more that the crime itself becomes relatively unimportant. Placing people, dreams and love above business, the idealism of this bighearted, strange movie – assuredly a product of the fiercely left-wing Popular Front – in which the workers' co-operative, rather than any one individual, becomes the hero, is no longer fashionable. It is all the more charming, striking and affecting for that.

The Devil and Miss Jones
1941

Director Sam Wood Cast Jean Arthur, Charles Coburn 92m

Department-store owner (**Coburn**) goes undercover to track down union agitators (led by **Arthur** as Miss Jones) but is soon won over to their demands. Sounds a bit trite, but this comedy is one of the last products of the liberal optimism that pervaded Hollywood after the New Deal. **Wood**'s direction lives up to his surname. He later formed the Motion Picture Association for the Preservation of American Ideals (with a name like that you just know those ideals didn't include free speech).

The Fountainhead 1949

Director King Vidor Cast Gary Cooper, Patricia Neal 114m

Gary Cooper is the first movie superman, but in the Nietzschean sense rather than in the underpants-flaunting sense. Here he stars as a visionary architect who defends "the individual against the collective", sees his new building designs vindicated and meets an heiress whose chat-up lines include: "I'll cook, I'll wash, I'll scrub the floor." Good as Cooper and **Neal** are (their torrid affair began on set), there's more than a hint of those Nazi "mountain" movies, where the lone blonde hero triumphs over the Alpine heights.

Glengarry Glen Ross 1992

Director James Foley Cast Al Pacino, Jack Lemmon, Alec Baldwin, Ed Harris, Alan Arkin, Kevin Spacey 100m

David Mamet's screenplay never stops looking like a play but it's hard to complain about a movie where the real-estate salesmen who come third in the monthly contest are told their reward is to be fired. **Lemmon** once said this was the best cast he'd ever worked with, and the overall level of thespianry is so high that even **Baldwin** rises to the occasion in the role of a nauseating motivator.

The Man in the Gray Flannel Suit 1956

Director Nunnally Johnson Cast Gregory Peck, Jennifer Jones 153m

Gregory Peck has always seemed like a decent, slightly idealized version of how America would like to see itself. The same heightened normality that made his Captain Ahab so hard to accept works for him here, as a Madison Avenue ad-man who has to choose career or family. At least he thinks he does, and picks family, but with typical Hollywood fudge he suddenly inherits a huge chunk of land. Watch out for **DeForest Kelley** (*Star Trek*'s Dr McCoy) as the army doc who gets to say: "This man's dead, Captain." Spooky, eh?

The Marriage of Maria Braun 1978

Director Rainer Werner Fassbinder Cast Hanna Schygulla, Klaus Löwitsch 120m

The main character Braun (played wonderfully by **Schygulla**) inadvertently (plot spoiler alert) kills herself at the end, having committed emotional suicide long ago. (**Fassbinder** took a fatal overdose three years after this movie was made.) This isn't a film about business as such, but it shows how an entire country, in its urge to forget an unforgettable past, became a corporate enterprise. The "economic miracle" is a personal disaster for Braun's lover (her boss), and finally for Braun, a Thatcherite heroine before Thatcherism was invented.

Modern Times 1936

Director Charles Chaplin Cast Charles Chaplin, Paulette Goddard 85m

One of the more enduring movie clichés is that **Chaplin** should have stuck to being a clown and not tried to make message pictures. *Modern Times*, a film that sends up capitalism and automation something rotten and gets the message across while still making you laugh, exposes that for the utter balderdash it is. The movie is silent – Chaplin sings in gibberish and the only other spoken voices are from the machines that enslave the workers. The film was banned as Communist propaganda in Germany and Italy.

Thank You for Smoking 2006

Director Jason Reitman Cast Aaron Eckhart, William H. Macy, Katie Holmes 92m

It's not really the tobacco industry, but human nature and perhaps capitalism itself that this comedy puts under a satirical spotlight. The ever-excellent **Aaron Eckhart**, spokesman for the so-called Academy of Tobacco Studies, is unable to spin his way out of career meltdown after being betrayed by a beautiful reporter; can a barnstorming performance at a senate hearing save him? Though sharp and snappy, with some superb performances, not least from **Rob Lowe** as the slimy movie agent, and **William H. Macy** as an anti-smoking senator, the movie's message – that all life is about risk – eventually feels more like fence-sitting than a daring challenge to political correctness.

 **Tin Men** 1987

Director Barry Levinson Cast Richard Dreyfuss, Danny DeVito, Barbara Hershey 112m

Two aluminium salesmen feud after one prangs the other's car in this comedy set in 1950s Baltimore. Their feud, in a classic example of what shrinks call transference, is an outlet for frustrations about things they can't change: a commission investigating high-pressure sales techniques, the IRS and the mysterious success of *Bonanza*, a show with a 50-year-old dad and three 47-year-old sons. The movie peters out but the journey is so enjoyable the lack of any apparent destination doesn't matter.

CARS

In the movies, cars can eat small towns in Australia, inspire existential musings – and always seem find to a parking space for their drivers.

★ The Blues Brothers
1980

Director John Landis **Cast** Dan Aykroyd, John Belushi 133m

This is especially worth watching if you're the kind of person who goes "Hang on, is that…?" because the odds are the answer is yes, given the cameos from **James Brown**, **Aretha Franklin** and **Twiggy** here. Two blues-lovin' brothers are on a mission in their 1974 Dodge Monaco (aka the Bluesmobile) to raise money for a kids' home. The movie holds the auspicious record for the largest number of cars destroyed in one film with twelve Bluesmobiles and thirty or sixty (depending on which statistician you believe) police cars demolished. Thirteen Bluesmobiles were made in total, the only surviving vehicle now owned by **Ackroyd**'s brother-in-law.

Bullitt 1968

Director Peter Yates **Cast** Steve McQueen, Robert Vaughn, Jacqueline Bisset 114m

Even being hijacked for a smug car advert can't dim the lustre of **Peter Yates**'s slick, visually enthralling car chase epic. The sparse dialogue and **Lalo Schiffrin**'s jazzy soundtrack perfectly complement **McQueen**'s ice-cold portrayal of the rebellious police officer who is utterly dedicated to his duty. The plot is decent but it's the car chase over the bumpy San Francisco streets that stands out. Each car hit over 110mph and one ten-minute scene took over three weeks to shoot.

The Cars That Ate Paris
1974

Director Peter Weir **Cast** John Meillon, Terry Camilleri 91m

The movie's plot, such as it is, follows nice-but-dim Arthur (**Camilleri**), who wakes up in an Aussie outback hospital after a car crash. It takes 91 minutes of wandering through a town full of blood-crazed youths driving spiked jalopies for him to twig the mental patients upstairs are lobotomized "accident" victims and the contents of their car wrecks are the local currency. Hysterical.

Christine 1983

Director John Carpenter **Cast** Keith Gordon, Alexandra Paul, Harry Dean Stanton 110m

The screen rights to **Stephen King**'s *Christine* were snapped up before the book was published. **Carpenter**'s tale of a possessed 1958 Plymouth Fury (25 were used during filming) requires a definite suspension of disbelief. Nerdy kid Arnie (**Gordon**) buys a battered car and falls in love with it. When his friends try to destroy his beloved, both the car and Arnie hit back with terrifying results. A pulp classic, with some nice continuity errors to watch out for and a fine tagline to boot: "Hell had no fury… like Christine."

Crash 1996

Director David Cronenberg **Cast** James Spader, Holly Hunter, Deborah Unger 100m

When **J.G. Ballard** completed his novel *Crash* it was rejected by one publishing house with the words: "This author is beyond psychiatric help. Do Not Publish!" **Cronenberg**'s movie received a rather similar reception. **Spader** and **Unger** are in search of ways to spice up their sex life. After a collision with **Hunter**, they're introduced to a circle of car crash fetishists. Dig deep and you'll discover meaning, but this is far from a pleasant experience.

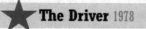 **The Driver** 1978

Director Walter Hill **Cast** Ryan O'Neal, Bruce Dern, Isabelle Adjani 91m

Hill's badass *noir* stars **Ryan O'Neal** at his toughest as the best getaway driver in the business, pursued by obnoxious, maniacal cop **Dern** and aided by the mysterious, beautiful **Adjani**. Though car chases abound, the standout scene in this compelling, weird amalgam of *Bullitt* and *Vanishing Point* is O'Neal's demonstration of how to destroy a Mercedes bit by bit in an empty garage.

Mad Max 1979

Director George Miller **Cast** Mel Gibson, Joanne Samuel 88m

George Miller was searching for someone rough-looking for the title role when **Gibson** turned up with his face cut from a bar fight. Set in the post-apocalyptic near-future, Gibson plays one of the few cops left to maintain law and order. Made for $400,000, it grossed $100m, its budget aided by Gibson being paid by the word in a film where atmosphere is almost everything. The film's vehicular star, the "Pursuit Special", returned in modified form for *Mad Max 2*.

Tucker: The Man and His Dream 1988

Director Francis Ford Coppola **Cast** Jeff Bridges, Joan Allen, Martin Landau 111m

Coppola's exhilarating, extravagant take on the life of maverick car designer Preston Thomas Tucker (**Bridges**) is sunny, heartfelt and resonant. It's hard not to see Tucker's story as a parallel to Coppola's struggles in Hollywood. *The Washington*

Jeff Bridges as maverick car designer Preston Thomas Tucker alongside one of his co-stars in Coppola's *Tucker: The Man and His Dream*.

Post described Bridges as "Jimmy Stewart with plastic seat covers".

Two-Lane Blacktop 1971

Director Monte Hellman **Cast** James Taylor, Dennis Wilson, Warren Oates 102m

Less sensational, but more enduring than *Easy Rider*, **Hellman**'s road movie casts singer/songwriter **Taylor** and Beach Boy **Wilson** as two taciturn drag racers challenged by **Warren Oates**' loquacious Pontiac GTO driver. Oates, a leading player in Hellman's stock company, invests his role with much pathos in a film that starts out like any other road movie but ends up as a study of disconnection and the emptiness at the heart of the 1970s USA.

Vanishing Point 1971

Director Richard Sarafian **Cast** Barry Newman, Cleavon Little 107m

Cross an ex-cop with a racing car driver and you get a man who, behind the wheel of a 1970 Dodge Challenger R/T, has to drive as fast as he can, even though there's a fleet of cops on his tail. The driver, Kowalski (**Newman**), does have meaningful reasons for such bizarre behaviour in this surreal interpretation of the ultimate car chase with blind DJ Super Soul (**Little**) acting as a mysterious guiding light. The superbly shot chases are interspersed with esoteric scenes of gay hitchhikers and naked motorcyclists. The remake, with **Jason Priestly** as the DJ, has none of the original's existential urgency.

CHICK FLICKS

These movies can make you weep, laugh, roar, sometimes all in the same storyline – but only if you're in touch with your feminine side.

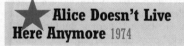

Alice Doesn't Live Here Anymore 1974

Director Martin Scorsese **Cast** Ellyn Burstyn, Kris Kristofferson, Diane Ladd 112m

When Alice Hyatt's (**Burstyn**) husband dies in an accident, she decides to sell the house and, with her twelve-year-old son in tow, realize a lifetime dream of becoming a singer. Along the way she meets some creeps, some new friends and a gentle, available farmer who just might be Mr Right – "he even makes his own ice cream!" **Ladd** plays Flo, a waitress with an astounding repertoire of curses and, if you look closely, you'll see a young **Laura Dern** (Ladd's daughter) eating an ice cream at the diner.

All About Eve 1950

Director Joseph Mankiewicz **Cast** Bette Davis, Anne Baxter 138m

Backstabbing bitchery and catty one-liners make this a must-see. **Davis** plays a Broadway legend whose star is on the wane, and **Baxter** is an ingénue (Eve) who manipulates her position as Davis's assistant to steal her lover and her limelight. Davis's immortal line, "Fasten your seatbelts, it's going to be a bumpy night" is delivered deadpan, only hinting at the turmoil going on inside. (Years later, Davis was to star in the TV series *Hotel* but became ill and was replaced by Baxter.) The effect is summed up by **Thelma Ritter** as the wardrobe woman: "What a story! Everything but the bloodhounds snappin' at her rear end."

Antonia's Line 1995

Director Marleen Gorris **Cast** Willeke van Ammelrooy, Els Dottermans 102m

This wandering tale of three generations in a poor, matriarchal Dutch family won a deserved Oscar for best foreign language film. When Antonia returns home as an unmarried mother after World War

63

II, it takes time for her to be accepted again, but her family finds its place over the years. The movie is a celebration of domestic stories and women's concerns of love and family, and **Van Ammelrooy** is a delight as the sturdy yet appealing Antonia.

Bagdad Café 1987

Director Percy Adlon **Cast** Marianne Sägebrecht, C.C.H. Pounder 91m

Jasmine (**Sägebrecht**), a large German housewife, is left in the desert by her husband after an argument. She ends up living and working at a lonely truck stop and strikes up an unlikely friendship with Brenda, the free-thinking, black café owner (**Pounder**). As Jasmine teaches Brenda about running the café with efficiency and cleanliness, Brenda reciprocates by helping her to become unbuttoned both physically and emotionally. Background characters (including **Jack Palance** as a former Hollywood set painter) help create an offbeat, charming movie that has real emotional depth without being cutesy. Released in the US as *Out of Rosenheim*.

Casa de los Babys 2003

Director John Sayles **Cast** Maggie Gyllenhaal, Marcia Gay Harden 96m

Six women, all hoping to adopt a child, are living in a Mexican guesthouse, waiting for the authorities to allow them to take their babies home. But this is not some schmaltzy feel-good tale – there's a refreshing amount of real-life bitchery and malice as the women's

stories unfold. It's a complex and honest account of the positive and negative issues surrounding international adoption and doesn't ignore the women who are giving up their babies. The scene in which **Susan Lynch** and **Vanessa Martinez**, not understanding each other's language, speak of their hopes for their children, is particularly poignant.

Dance, Girl, Dance 1940

Director Dorothy Arzner **Cast** Maureen O'Hara, Lucille Ball, Louis Hayward 90m

Judy and Bubbles are dancers with very different ambitions. Judy (**O'Hara**) wants only to be a ballerina, Bubbles (**Ball**) seeks only financial success. Bubbles leaves for a burlesque career and when Judy's ballet troupe folds, gives her a demeaning job as her stooge. Then they fall for the same man, Jimmy (**Hayward**)… **Arzner** was the first female director to join the Directors Guild of America, and this is one of her best, with Ball on top form.

Gone With the Wind 1939

Director Victor Fleming **Cast** Vivien Leigh, Clark Gable 238m

Visually stunning, wildly ambitious, overblown to the point of hysteria, **David O. Selznick**'s adaptation of **Margaret Mitchell**'s Civil War novel is among the highest box-office earners of all time. A lush melodrama and a passionate love story, *GWTW* features one of the feistiest heroines ever to grace a screen. **Leigh** is astonishing as the foot-stamping firebrand who manages to be both irritating and inspirational – and **Gable** was born to play Rhett, a romantic hero the like of which they don't make any more.

I Know Where I'm Going! 1945

Directors Michael Powell and Emeric Pressburger **Cast** Wendy Hiller, Roger Livesey 92m

Much has been written about **Powell** and **Pressburger**'s use of saturated colour to convey emotion – just think of *Black Narcissus*, *A Matter of Life and Death*, *The Red Shoes*. This enchanting romance, however, is a study of passion in black and white. **Wendy Hiller** is superb as the strong-willed modern woman whose journey to a remote Scottish island to marry a rich industrialist is thwarted by eccentric locals, wild storms and the irresistible siren song of good old-fashioned romance.

The Mother 2003

Director Roger Michell **Cast** Anne Reid, Daniel Craig, Peter Vaughan 112m

When her husband dies suddenly, May (**Reid**) decides to stay on down south with her self-absorbed, grown-up children and their families. Feeling lost and alone, she starts an affair with Darren (**Craig**), a builder working for her son and having an affair with her daughter. A compassionate tale of a later-life

Anne Reid engaging in a May–December affair with Darren, the irresistible builder (a pre-Bond Daniel Craig) who is also involved with her daughter, in *The Mother*.

reawakening, scripted by Hanif Kureishi, it captures perfectly the frantic disharmony of modern family life.

Muriel's Wedding 1994

Director P.J. Hogan **Cast** Toni Collette, Rachel Griffiths 106m

Overweight and rejected by her trendy friends, Muriel (**Collette**) spends her days being ridiculed by her father, listening to Abba and dreaming of the day someone will want to marry her. It's an old premise – sad case trying to get a life – but it's handled with such hilarity, pathos and flair that you can't help but root for Muriel. The farcical sex scene at the flat she shares with her trashy, fabulous friend Rhonda (**Griffiths**) is brilliant and the wedding is a glorious piece of over-the-top wish fulfilment.

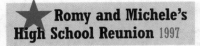

Romy and Michele's High School Reunion 1997

Director David Mirkin **Cast** Mira Sorvino, Lisa Kudrow, Alan Cumming 91m

Quirkiest and funniest of the not-so-dumb-blonde genre that fizzled through Hollywood in the 1990s and early 2000s (*Clueless*, *Legally Blonde* et al), this is a slyly clever cult hit disguised as a frothy guilty pleasure. The premise – two best friends (brilliantly skewed performances from Kudrow and Sorvino) attempt to exorcize their low-self-esteem demons by turning up at their high school's ten-year reunion, claiming they've made a million inventing Post-it notes – sets the tone. With its surreal dialogue, smart 1980s soundtrack, and career-best performances all round (including from **Janeane Garofalo**, who relishes her dark and grumpy teen rebel role) this is the archetypal thinking chick's girly flick.

Waitress 2007

Director Adrienne Shelly **Cast** Keri Russell, Cheryl Hines, Nathan Fillion 108m

Shelly, perhaps best known for starring in **Hal Hartley**'s indie movies, moved on to become an accomplished director, making sweet, smart, offbeat women's films. This disarmingly candy-coloured treat is nowhere near as sugary as it looks – Jenna (**Russell**), the waitress in question, works through her more murderous emotions by cooking pies called things like "I Hate My Husband" and "Pregnant Miserable Self Pitying Loser" – and the film is given an extra layer of dark disquiet by the fact of Shelly's murder shortly before it was released.

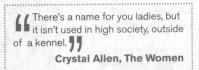

> There's a name for you ladies, but it isn't used in high society, outside of a kennel. **"**
> **Crystal Allen, The Women**

The Women 1939

Director George Cukor **Cast** Norma Shearer, Joan Crawford 132m

There are over 130 roles in this movie, each one played by a woman. The dogs and horses were female, and even the art on the set was devoid of male imagery. This is not, however, a story of female solidarity in a man-free utopia. Far from it. You'd be hard-pushed to find a more vicious and catty bunch as **Shearer** plays the good wife who loses her husband to trashy homewrecker **Crawford**. **Rosalind Russell** and **Joan Fontaine** also feature, with **Anita Loos**'s sparkling script shining in every scene.

CIRCUS

Roll up! Roll up! To watch a movie where triple somersaults abound – we're talking about the plot – and trapezes and clowns aren't what they seem...

The Circus 1928

Director Charlie Chaplin **Cast** Charlie Chaplin, Merna Kennedy, Allan Garcia **71m**

Circus comedies that make you laugh are rare. This may not be on a par with *City Lights* or *Modern Times*, but **Chaplin** does have a few decent jokes as he falls in love with a bareback rider and joins her circus. The funny finale is something of a feat of professionalism: two-thirds of the way through filming, the star/producer/ writer/director/composer had a nervous breakdown.

Circus of Horrors 1960

Director Sidney Hayes **Cast** Anton Diffring, Erika Remberg, Donald Pleasence **91m**

"Spectacular towering terror! One man's lust made men into beasts, stripped women of their souls!" Cecil B. DeMille, eat your heart out. A mad plastic surgeon (**Diffring**) and his accomplices flee Britain and murder their way into controlling a French circus. Diffring plays the kind of doc who makes you wish you ate an apple a day.

The Clowns 1970

Director Federico Fellini **Cast** Federico Fellini, Anita Ekberg, Scotti the Clown **92m**

This documentary deserves to be cherished if only for the scene in which **Fellini** sits down for one of those profound discussions of his art with a journalist and a bucket of water falls on his head, followed by another on his questioner's head. Clowns and circuses had intrigued the director since he ran away from boarding school to join a circus. This apparently jovial but also sinister world was the setting for one of his finest early works, *La strada*, starring Anthony Quinn as a malevolent strongman.

★ Freaks 1932

Director Tod Browning **Cast** Wallace Ford, Olga Baclanova, Leila Hyams **64m**

A true one-off, this darkly surreal horror, a wistful story of true-life carny folk starring real-life "freaks", was pulled soon after its release. MGM were happier to lose $164,000 on a movie they commissioned to be "more horrifying than *Dracula*" than face the guardians of public morality.

Louis B. Mayer insisted MGM's logo wouldn't be on it, which set conspiracy theorists wondering: did Mayer decide the circus master's relation to its "freak" performers was an allegory of the studio and its stars? Or that the cigar-smoking dwarf who deluded himself beautiful women would love him for himself (not his wealth) was a representation of the short, cigar-smoking producer?

Killer Klowns from Outer Space 1988

Director Stephen Chiodo **Cast** Grant Cramer, Suzanne Snyder, John Allen Nelson 88m

This cult favourite closed **Chiodo**'s career as a director – nine years later he was making the creatures for a *Power Rangers* movie. It was a sad fate for someone who directed and co-wrote (with his brothers **Charles** and **Edward**) this bizarre movie about aliens invading a small Californian town and, disguised as clowns, wreaking havoc. Seminal lines include: "It was a spaceship. And there was these things, these killer clowns, and they shot popcorn at us!"

Lola Montès 1955

Director Max Ophüls **Cast** Martine Carol, Peter Ustinov, Anton Walbrook 111m

There's very little funny business here, in this staggeringly beautiful, mannered movie – **Ophüls**' last, and his only film in colour (Technicolor, at that). **Ustinov**, as the ringmaster, invites us to gawp at the nineteenth-century cabaret-dancer-cum-courtesan, displaying her in a gold cage in a New Orleans circus. Whether French bombshell **Carol**'s sullen, dead-eyed performance hints at hidden depths or a simple lack of skills, it's effective in this context, where the spectacle is the thing, and the woman is relegated to sideshow attraction. Hacked before its release to lessen the complexity of its flash-back structure, the film has since been restored to something closer to Ophüls' intention: a swooping, sweeping Cinema-Scope carnival that hits you with, as he put it, "a punch in the stomach".

Something Wicked This Way Comes 1983

Director Jack Clayton **Cast** Jonathan Pryce, Jason Robards, Diane Ladd 95m

The darkest movie Disney has ever made, the circus comes to town but the ringmaster (**Pryce** as Mr Dark) is a demon soon engaged in mortal combat with the town librarian (**Robards**). Based on a **Ray Bradbury** novel, this is for adults, older children and those who don't know the meaning of squeamish. The scene with the skeleton and the merry-go-round is terrifically terrifying and the final confrontation between Robards and Pryce is an unsettling treat.

COMEDIES

How do you like your comedy? Black? Dry? Slapstick? Sexy? Screwball? Sadly, you can't bottle humour, but you can preserve it on celluloid. So go on, have a laugh. Alright, don't then, have it your way.

★ The Anchorman: The Legend of Ron Burgundy 2004

Director Adam McKay **Cast** Will Ferrell, Christina Applegate, Paul Rudd 94m

You can forgive **Will Ferrell** almost anything – except *Talledega Nights: The Legend of Ricky Bobby* – for giving us this genius piece of inspired silliness. He's Ron Burgundy, a 1970s sexist local TV newsman who calls his biceps "guns" and finds himself both threatened by and attracted to the station's first anchorwoman. "I'm very important", he tells her. "I have many leather-bound books and my apartment smells of rich mahogany." Watch out for cameos by **Ben Stiller** and **Tim Robbins** and a yet-to-be famous **Seth Rogan** as the cameraman at a panda birth.

> ❝ You're so wise. You're like a miniature Buddha, covered in hair. ❞
> **Ron Burgundy to his dog in Anchorman**

Annie Hall 1977

Director Woody Allen **Cast** Woody Allen, Diane Keaton, Carol Kane 93m

Semi-autobiographical (**Allen** and **Keaton** were lovers who split up and Keaton's real name is Diane Annie Hall), this is Allen's finest, if not cinema's all-time best, romantic comedy. Realistic rather than sickly sweet, we watch people meet, fall in love and then fall out of it. Full of snappy one-liners and Allen's usual peppering of insights into love, sex, death, New York and the meaning of life, the movie offers early sightings of **Sigourney Weaver**, **Beverly D'Angelo** and **Jeff Goldblum**. It's Allen's first film where the characters have adult emotions.

The Apartment 1960

Director Billy Wilder **Cast** Jack Lemmon, Shirley MacLaine 125m

Deeply satisfying comedy drama about an ambitious executive who curries favour with his seniors by lending them his apartment for their extra-marital trysts. His collusion becomes a problem when he falls for his manager's latest mistress. **Lemmon** is at the peak of his everyman persona – amoral and cringing to begin with, but growing a backbone with every scene – while **MacLaine** is perfect as the elevator girl with zero self-esteem. Stuffed full of great dialogue and delightful detail (Lemmon straining his spaghetti through a tennis racket is as good a representation of bachelordom as you'll find), it was the last black-and-white movie to win a best picture Oscar until *Schindler's List* in 1993.

La cage aux folles 1978

Director Edouard Molinaro **Cast** Michel Serrault, Ugo Tognazzi 110m

Ageing gay couple Renato (**Tognazzi**) and Albin (**Serrault**) are forced to conceal their lifestyle when Renato's son announces he's marrying the daughter of a right-wing politician. The movie went Hollywood in 1996 (*The Birdcage*) with Mike Nichols directing and Robin Williams and Nathan Lane in the leading roles. The original may have done nothing to dispel gay stereotypes but it remains one of the funniest French comedies ever.

Carry On Up the Khyber 1968

Director Gerald Thomas **Cast** Sid James, Kenneth Williams, Charles Hawtrey 88m

A historically insignificant movie (although probably no more inaccurate than Mel Gibson's *The Patriot*), this is a genuinely funny send-up of the British Empire, the nation's psychotic need to maintain a stiff upper lip and what Scots may or may not wear under their kilts. Like *Carry On Cleo* (1964), this is a good spoof of the kind of history young Britons used to learn by rote in school. **Bernard Bresslaw** had to reshoot the scene where he shouts "Fakir off", putting a longer pause between the words in order to please the censors. Production never quite made it to the real Khyber Pass, Welsh Snowdonia serving as the perfect double.

The Castle 1997

Director Rob Sitch **Cast** Michael Caton, Anne Tenney, Eric Bana 82m

It's rumoured that so tight was the budget on this ripping comedy, shooting was cut from twenty to eleven days because the producers couldn't afford to feed cast and crew. The fact that it was picked up by Miramax boss **Harvey Weinstein** for $6m is testament to director **Sitch**'s talent. Mind you, the movie's success owes a lot to the cast's hilarious portrayal of bluecollar-ites refusing to give in to corporate ball-busters as the Kerrigan family fight to stop the family home being swallowed up by an airport. So charming are the characters and sharp the script, that you can forgive the slightly dodgy production values.

Chopper 2000

Director Andrew Dominik **Cast** Eric Bana, Simon Lyndon 94m

Extraordinarily accomplished blacker-than-black comedy by first-time writer/director **Dominik**, featuring a captivating performance by top Aussie comedian **Bana** – in his first major movie role – as notorious criminal Mark "Chopper" Read. Read himself suggested Bana after seeing him in the Aussie sketch show *Full Frontal*. The story, told in flashback, follows Read from fit, fast and furious fighter in prison to enraged, overweight paranoid on the outside – and then back to prison as a media celebrity. Bana's portrayal of this eloquent, complex crook who asks "are you alright?" of someone he's just shot in the head is utterly enthralling but never glorifies his atrocities. Gruesomely shocking, funny and tragic.

Clerks 1994

Director Kevin Smith Cast Brian O'Halloran, Jeff Anderson, Marilyn Ghigliotti 92m

Smith sold his comic book collection to raise the cash for this $26,800 debut described by one reviewer as "an era-defining portrait of Generation X". Filmed at night in the store where Smith worked by day, it records a day in the life of store clerk **Dante** and is loosely based on the *Divine Comedy*. Working on his day off, Dante deals with wacky customers, the death of an ex-girlfriend, the marriage of another and his current girlfriend's dubious sexual past. Smith's brilliant dialogue was sadly lacking from the long-awaited 2006 sequel *Clerks II*, mainly memorable for its gags about donkey sex.

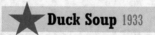

Duck Soup 1933

Director Leo McCarey Cast Groucho, Harpo, Chico and Zeppo Marx 68m

The funniest **Marx Brothers** movie, this war spoof marked the irrepressible foursome's last outing, the least charismatic of the group, **Zeppo**, preferring to work behind the scenes. Astonishingly, on its release, it was a flop. When asked about the movie's political significance, **Groucho** remarked "What significance? We were just four Jews trying to get a laugh." Not everyone was so flippant: Benito Mussolini banned it in Italy as he felt it was a direct attack on him. What plot there is sees Groucho as Rufus T. Firefly, leader of Freedonia, going to war because he's paid a month's advance rent on the battlefield. A showcase of the most inventive comedy: whether you're a fan of physical comedy, puns, slapstick or satire, *Duck Soup* has it all.

Hairspray 1988

Director John Waters Cast Sonny Bono, Divine, Debbie Harry 92m

John Waters placed the social message of racial segregation at the heart of this, his most easily digestible movie, but ultimately *Hairspray* is a comedy about teenage life. A pre-TV talk show **Ricki Lake** is Tracy Turnblad, a teenage dancing whiz who wins a place on her favourite TV dance showcase, the Corny Collins Show, where she becomes a plus-sized poster girl for racial integration. Waters' transvestite muse, **Divine**, is Tracy's mother, a role embodied by an in-drag John Travolta for the 2007 musical movie – a remake Waters to which gave his blessing with a cameo appearance as a flasher.

In Bruges 2008

Director Martin McDonagh Cast Colin Farrell, Brendan Gleeson, Ralph Fiennes 107m

Dwarves, guns, cocaine-fuelled sex, swans and "fairy-tale fucking bridges" all play a part in this brutally black tragi-comedy where two Irish hit men bodge a job and are sent to hide out in Bruges. Try to imagine *Father Ted* meets *Don't Look Now* where splutter-inducing one-liners target everything un-PC from midgets to child abuse. Beautifully acted and scripted (by playwright **McDonagh**), *In Bruges* is essentially an allegory for purgatory, which, as **Farrell** puts it, is "where you go if you weren't really great, but you weren't really shit either – you know, like Tottenham".

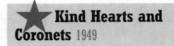

Kind Hearts and Coronets 1949

Director Robert Hamer Cast Dennis Price, Alec Guinness, Joan Greenwood 106m

One of the first truly black comedies, with a wonderful, heartless wit at its core and a neat twist at the end. **Price** plays Louis Mazzini, a young man whose mother was rejected by her aristocratic family when she ran off with an opera singer. On discovering that he is ninth in line to a dukedom, Louis sets about murdering the members of the D'Ascoyne family one by one. **Guinness** plays all eight of them, including Lady Agatha, and it's his performances, along with **Greenwood**'s seductive minx Sybilla, that raise this to classic status.

Admiring the scenery: Bruges's canals and steepled roofs provide context for the darkly funny tale of two gangsters (Brendan Gleeson and Colin Farrell) hiding out after a hit goes disastrously wrong.

Monty Python and the Holy Grail 1975

Directors Terry Gilliam, Terry Jones Cast John Cleese, Eric Idle, Graham Chapman 90m

Now lucratively reincarnated as the Tony Award-winning musical *Spamalot*, the first real Python feature failed to impress its original investors (including **Led Zeppelin**, **Pink Floyd**, **Tim Rice** and **Andrew Lloyd Webber**). However, the mix of English slapstick wit, phoney sets, chivalric spoofs and speculation about the coconut carrying abilities of African swallows saved the day. If you find the ending weak, bear in mind it's not the original scripted version – which was to wrap up with King Arthur and his knights in Harrods.

The Music Box 1932

Director James Parrott Cast Stan Laurel, Oliver Hardy 29m

Stan Laurel's favourite of his 99 collaborations with **Hardy**, *The Music Box* not only demonstrates the pair's impeccable timing, but the darkness behind their comedy. They live in a world where nursemaids, professors, horses and electric sockets are united in a vast comic conspiracy against them. Cynics have criticized the movie for endless repetition of one gag, as Stan and Ollie are relentless in their efforts to get a piano up 131 steps, but this is sublime comedy, with some surrealist touches, an astonishing dance and a nod to another movie with famous steps in it, *The Battleship Potemkin*.

Ninotchka 1939

Director Ernst Lubitsch Cast Greta Garbo, Melvyn Douglas 110m

In **Garbo**'s penultimate movie you do see her laugh – but not for the first time, as MGM insisted in the posters. She shines as the humourless Russian envoy sent in pursuit of three comrades to find out what is delaying their mission. In a role which is almost a send-up of her own onscreen persona, she meets and falls in love with a dashing count, **Douglas**, who does indeed make her laugh. Great performances all round, aided by a witty script (which **Billy Wilder** had a hand in). At the test screening, a member of the audience wrote on his preview card: "I laughed so hard I peed in my girlfriend's hand." Censors in Bulgaria, Estonia, France, Italy and Lithuania weren't as amused: it was banned for making fun of Communism.

Passport to Pimlico 1949

Director Henry Cornelius Cast Stanley Holloway, Margaret Rutherford 85m

Wonderfully funny and good-natured movie in which the Pimlico locals find themselves living on foreign territory and, as such, are free of post-war rationing restrictions. **Holloway** and **Rutherford** turn in typically terrific performances. The movie was inspired by the story that Princess Juliana of the Netherlands, exiled in Canada during the war, was about to give birth, and to be sure her baby would be heir to the Dutch throne, the Canadian government declared the room to be a territory of the Netherlands.

The Producers 1968

Director Mel Brooks **Cast** Zero Mostel, Gene Wilder, Kenneth Mars **88m**

The "Springtime for Hitler" number led to this being banned in Germany. It was first shown in the Führer's homeland at a festival of work by Jewish filmmakers – the kind of irony in which **Brooks** surely would have revelled. This movie about producers who try to create a musical flop on Broadway needs no introduction, especially since its re-invention as a Broadway musical, which in turn spawned a decent, if inevitably inferior, remake. An outraged lady once told Brooks that his movie was vulgar. "Lady", he replied, "it rose below vulgarity."

The Royal Tenenbaums 2001

Director Wes Anderson **Cast** Gene Hackman, Gywneth Paltrow, Ben Stiller **110m**

Wes Anderson and co-writer and star **Owen Wilson** deliver a deliciously odd family portrait of former child prodigies in this superb comedy drama. Led by **Hackman**'s patriarch Royal Tenenbaum, who is attempting a reconciliation with his kids, the brood features **Paltrow**'s precocious adopted Margot, paranoid widower Chas (**Stiller**) and **Luke Wilson**'s failed tennis player Richie, while **Bill Murray**, inevitably, almost steals the show as Margot's downtrodden husband, Raleigh St Clair. Well-played, quirkily scripted, hilarious at times, this ultimately feels a bit ephemeral.

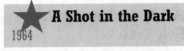 **A Shot in the Dark** 1964

Director Blake Edwards **Cast** Peter Sellers, George Sanders, Elke Sommer **101m**

Released just three months after its predecessor *The Pink Panther*, this was originally written for a detective team which had **Sellers** opposite **Walter Matthau**. When Sellers threatened to quit, *Panther* director **Edwards** came in and rewrote the script into an Inspector Clouseau vehicle. **Sanders**'s chauffeur is murdered with the beautiful **Sommer** as the prime suspect. The bumbling Clouseau falls for her and refuses to believe she is capable of such acts, despite the escalating body count and the evidence pointing to her. Supporting characters **Herbert Lom**, as the inspector's despairing boss ("Give me ten men like Clouseau and I could destroy the world"), **Graham Stark** as his long-suffering assistant Hercule, and **Bert Kwouk** as Kato, all hold their own against what was, for a while, one of cinema's most hilarious creations.

Sleeper 1973

Director Woody Allen **Cast** Woody Allen, Diane Keaton, John Beck **88m**

One of **Allen**'s funniest early movies, this sci-fi spoof was filmed in fifty days for $2m, with futuristic costumes designed by **Joel Schumacher**. Allen plays a twentieth-century man, frozen for two hundred years. He wakes in a world where there is no sex (hence the need for the orgasmatron) and the USA is ruled by a dictator's nose. He discovers a field of giant fruit and the world

Classic comedy scenes

Sometimes just one scene is all it takes to recompense for any other shortcomings in a movie.

Hair gel in There's Something About Mary
Before the Farrelly brothers sank to new depths of un-PC low with *Stuck On You*, they managed to persuade Hollywood leading lady Cameron Diaz to ruin her street cred with some particularly unsavoury hair gel.

Urn of ashes in Meet the Parents
Meeting future in-laws is a disconcerting experience most go through at one time or another. No wonder audiences empathized with Gaylord Focker's plight when the cork from the cheap bottle of fizz he'd bought to impress his future father-in-law Jack smashed the urn holding Jack's beloved mother's ashes.

Man waxing in The 40-Year-Old Virgin
A moment all the more painfully hilarious for (a) being real, (b) knowing the actress playing the waxer lied about having previous waxing experience on her CV, (c) the waxee, Steve Carrell, being Hollywood's second hairiest funnyman, after Robin Williams.

Lou Gehrig disease in Fathers Day
One hilarious moment in the Robin Williams/Billy Crystal paternal comedy. Discussing tragic heroes, Billy says: "Everybody knows Lou Gehrig. He's the baseball player who died of Lou Gehrig's disease." To which Robin replies: "Wow, what are the odds on that?"

of film is treated to the best banana skin sight gag ever. Completely and utterly daft, it remains the best film in its genre.

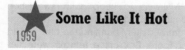

Some Like It Hot

1959

Director Billy Wilder **Cast** Marilyn Monroe, Jack Lemmon, Tony Curtis 121m

Although **Monroe**'s contract stipulated that all her movies be shot in colour, director **Wilder** eventually persuaded her they needed to shoot in black and white as the make-up worn by **Lemmon** and **Curtis**

made them look green. This was the end of his easy ride with the siren (she went so far as comparing Wilder to Hitler; it did take her 47 or 59 takes to say one simple line). But she still carries the movie as Sugar Kane, the alluring member of the all-girl band which Lemmon and Curtis join in drag to hide from the Mob. Lemmon, in a role offered to Frank Sinatra, keeps the zany momentum going, relishing his drag character, while Curtis's concern about being seen as effeminate makes him perfect in the straight man role. Famously basing the voice of his oil industry heir on Cary Grant, he reportedly modelled Josephine's body language on Grace Kelly.

Son of Paleface 1952

Director Frank Tashlin **Cast** Bob Hope, Jane Russell, Roy Rogers, Trigger **95m**

Bob Hope reprises a favourite role as a cowardly dude, here playing the son of the original Paleface, in search of his father's missing gold. **Russell** is the sassy leader of a gang of bandits on the run from marshal **Rogers** and his ever-faithful **Trigger**. Rogers' send-up of his screen persona, along with all the usual Western clichés, makes the movie superior to its predecessor, but it is Trigger who steals the film when he shares a bed with Hope.

That Sinking Feeling 1979

Director Bill Forsyth **Cast** Robert Buchanan, Billy Greenlees **92m**

Bill Forsyth, who *was* the Scottish movie industry in the early 1980s, made his feature debut with this surreal comedy about Glasgow teenagers who decide there's money in stainless-steel sinks. A bizarre plan to dress up as women and raid a sink warehouse is hatched, and the movie just gets weirder and more wonderful from there. The characters are a delight, a well-observed group trying to be angsty and nihilist but failing miserably, and the comatose van driver and canalside chase sequence are particular joys. There are moments when even a Brit might struggle to catch all the dialogue, but if you liked the wandering penguin in *Gregory's Girl*, you'll love this.

Top Secret! 1984

Directors Jerry Zucker, Jim Abrahams, David Zucker **Cast** Val Kilmer, Lucy Gutteridge **90m**

"I'm not the first guy who fell in love with a woman that he met at a restaurant who turned out to be the daughter of a kidnapped scientist only to lose her to her childhood lover whom she last saw on a deserted island who then turned out fifteen years later to be the leader of the French." So sums up **Kilmer**, in his first big screen lead, as an American pop star invited to Nazi Germany as a propaganda stunt. Fantastically stupid fun that becomes even funnier if you know German (the officer replies to his orders "I love you, my treasure").

Zoolander 2001

Director Ben Stiller **Cast** Ben Stiller, Owen Wilson, Christine Taylor **89m**

Derek Zoolander (**Stiller**) is a fading male model with a size-zero intellect, effortlessly brainwashed by **Will Ferrell**'s evil poodle-haired fashion mogul into assassinating the prime minister of Malaysia to keep child sweatshop labour costs down. Malaysia retaliated by immediately banning the film, as did Singapore. Box office returns were further hit by a release date just two weeks after 9/11. However it's since attracted a widespread following, with devoted fans not quoting lines but imitating Zoolander's trademark poses: Magnum, Blue Steel and Le Tigre – indistinguishable to the uninitiated.

COMING OF AGE

In a classic coming-of-age movie lessons about life are learned by angst-ridden teens, often in the 1950s, though any period of cultural upheaval is ripe for a growing-up drama.

City of Men 2007

Director Paolo Morelli **Cast** Douglas Silva, Darlan Cunha, Jonathan Haagensen 106m

Spun off from a hit TV series, this poignant story centres on eighteen-year-olds **Darlan Cunha** and **Douglas Silva**, as the first searches for his long-lost father and the latter struggles to be a good parent to his infant son. Criticized for not being as visceral as **Fernando Meirelles'** City of God (Cidade de Deus, 2002), this much less self-consciously arty insight into life in the Rio favelas does a better job of illustrating the transience of youth, as impoverished kids are peer-pressured into the temptations of sex, drugs and crime.

The Devil's Playground 1976

Director Fred Schepisi **Cast** Arthur Dignam, Nick Tate, Simon Burke 107m

Set in an Australian seminary in 1953 and reclaiming the clichés of the Catholic school movie, **Fred Schepisi's** debut feature has a ring of autobiographical authenticity. But while he clearly identifies with thirteen-year-old Tom (**Burke**), as lusty thoughts cause him to question his nascent vocation, Schepisi also relates to the berobed teachers played by **Dignam** and **Tate**, undergoing their own struggles with sins of the flesh. Sensitively observed, and evocatively photographed by **Ian Baker**, this won six Australian Film Institute Awards.

I Was Born, But 1932

Director Yasujiro Ozu **Cast** Tomio Aoki, Hideo Sugawara 91m

Before **Ozu** became known for his minimalist work, he made this light-hearted silent movie about Japanese society. Two young brothers become local gang leaders before shamefully discovering, through their father's subservient relationship with his boss, the differences between their childhood world and the adult society they will soon move into. Twenty-seven years later Ozu would rework this classic as *Good Morning* (*Ohayu*). But his chronicling and questioning of Japan's rigid social structure – sugared with plenty of visual comedy – is more poignant here. Especially considering, ten years after it was made, many of the boys on the cast list inherited this society before it stole their young lives in World War II.

Last Summer 1969

Director Frank Perry **Cast** Barbara Hershey, Richard Thomas, Bruce Davison 95m

Pipping Robert Mulligan's *Summer of 42* (1971) for its nostalgic depiction of a holiday crush, this underrated adaptation of **Evan Hunter**'s novel shatters its carefully established idyll with a shocking climax. There's a touching mix of camaraderie and curiosity about **Hershey**'s Fire Island friendship with **Thomas** and **Davison**. But it's plumply idealistic outsider **Cathy Burns** who has the most lasting impact. Sadly, Burns all but disappeared after being Oscar-nominated for her debut role, while Hershey briefly changed her surname to Seagull in atonement for her character's moment of petulant cruelty.

Il posto 1961

Director Ermanno Olmi **Cast** Sandro Panseri, Loredana Detto 90m

Shy Domenico leaves his Italian village for Milan, in the hope of securing a desk job in a faceless big-city corporation. After a bizarre but successful interview, where he answers maths puzzles, completes bending and stretching exercises and undergoes psychological testing ("Does the future seem hopeless to you?"), he starts his job as an errand boy, before being promoted to a revered desk job after a clerk dies. He meets Antonietta at his interview, who seems his only release from the monotonous future mapped before him in this touching, funny movie.

★ Rushmore 1998

Director Wes Anderson **Cast** Jason Schwartzman, Bill Murray, Olivia Williams 93m

The story goes that **Murray** loved the script for this odd comedy drama so much, he actually offered to appear in the movie for free. Written by actor **Owen Wilson** and director **Anderson**, it's the story of fifteen-year-old Max Fischer (**Schwartzman**), who runs just about every extracurricular activity at Rushmore Academy yet is failing his classes. His relationship with businessman Herman Blume (Murray) and widowed teacher Rosemary (**Williams**) form the heart of this quirky, melancholy and very funny tale.

★ Stand By Me 1986

Director Rob Reiner **Cast** River Phoenix, Corey Feldman, Will Wheaton 89m

Based on **Stephen King**'s novella *The Body*, four pre-teen boys from a sleepy 1950s town set out in search of the body

> ❝ I never had any friends later on like the ones I had when I was twelve. Jesus, does anyone? ❞
>
> **Gordie, Stand By Me**

of a local missing teenager. There's a clever one (**Wheaton**), a tough-but-sensitive one (**Phoenix**), an oddball with a death wish (**Feldman**) and a fat one (**Jerry O'Connell**). But this isn't a movie that repeats the clichés – it created them. Racing the boys to find the gruesome prize is a gang of older bullies, led by **Kiefer Sutherland**. The dialogue successfully negotiates the wafer-thin line between poignant and sappy, and the performances are stunning (helped, no doubt, by Sutherland's picking on the four younger boys during filming breaks to "keep in character").

Thirteen 2003

Director Catherine Hardwicke Cast Holly Hunter, Evan Rachel Wood, Nikki Reed 100m

Loosely autobiographical story written – in just six days – by thirteen-year-old **Reed** and director **Hardwicke**. Reed is Evie, a popular bad girl who leads a more-than-willing straight-A student, Tracy (the excellent **Wood**), astray. The action opens with the girls sniffing aerosols and testing how hard they can punch each other in the face, and gets more disturbing from there.

Melanie (**Hunter**), single mum to Tracy and recovering alcoholic, struggles to cope as her newly teen-aged daughter discovers sex, drugs and heavy eye make-up before your popcorn's had a chance to cool. **Elliot Davis**'s hand-held camera work draws you in to the bleakness. Reed's real-life experience shows onscreen – she looks far too old to play a thirteen-year-old, even though she was only fourteen during filming.

Tracy (Evan Rachel Wood) being led astray by Evie (Nikki Reed) in the semi-autobiographical *Thirteen* – navel piercings and thick black eyeliner were just the start .

COPS

In the movies, being a cop is all donuts, coffee and corruption.
And occasionally, the right to make your father beg in the streets.

Across 110th Street 1972

Director Barry Shear **Cast** Anthony Quinn, Yaphet Kotto, Tony Franciosa 102m

Elvis Presley knew the script for this tough police drama word for word. **Kotto**, a by-the-book black lieutenant, is partnered with crude, racist Italian cop **Quinn** to find three murdering robbers. Shot on location in Harlem – 110th Street was the ghetto's informal boundary – with a cracking theme song by **Bobby Womack**, this smart script features plenty of brutal, matter of fact violence. But Elvis had a point: it's the dialogue and the characters that have helped it endure.

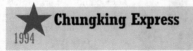

Chungking Express 1994

Director Kar Wai Wong **Cast** Brigitte Lin, Takeshi Kaneshiro, Tony Leung 97m

This movie – about two Hong Kong cops who cope with the loneliness of losing their girlfriends in different ways and take up with new women with problems of their own – made **Quentin Tarantino** cry because he was "just so happy to love a movie this much". The plot is decidedly quirky (one cop buys a tin of pineapple a day for a month, equating its sell-by date with the end of his hopes of being reunited with his ex), but this is also a visual *tour de force*, combining handheld shots, video and slow-motion images with a kaleidoscope of colours portraying the hustle of a pop-culture-soaked Hong Kong.

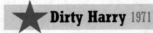

Dirty Harry 1971

Director Don Siegel **Cast** Clint Eastwood, Harry Guardino, Andrew Robinson 101m

Eastwood's maverick, Magnum 44-wielding cop makes fighting crime at any cost, with the end justifying the means, look so cool that the Italians launched a microgenre of films called *poliziotteschi*. Director and star revel in Harry's dirtiness as the frustrated hero duels with a brilliantly deranged killer (**Robinson**). In some ways, this is a riveting, testosterone-powered, technically adept reworking of the earlier Siegel/Eastwood collaboration *Coogan's Bluff*. Derided by some as a "Fascist fantasy", a print was used to train police in the Philippines.

Hana-Bi 1997

Director Takeshi Kitano **Cast** Takeshi Kitano, Kayoko Kishimoto 103m

Actor, writer and director **Kitano**'s thoughtful cop movie is full of agony (the cop's wife is dying and his partner is wheelchair-bound), ecstasy (his childlike joy at playing with a kite with his wife), startling violence and frantic action. Kitano's underplaying may not be entirely deliberate – he was recovering from a motorcycle crash at the time – but it brilliantly conveys the angst of a cop who turns to crime to fund a last trip with his wife.

High Crime 1973

Director Enzo G. Castellani **Cast** Franco Nero, James Whitmore, Delia Boccardo 100m

Paying obvious, but unobtrusive, homage to *Dirty Harry*, **Castellani**'s thriller (*La polizia incrimina la legge assolve*) is brisk, brutal entertainment. Whenever the plot threatens to slow things down, Castellani can usually be relied upon to cut to a skull bouncing off a windscreen. **Nero** is smouldering yet weary as the cop trying to crack a drug ring, **Fernando Rey** is entertaining as the gangster, but the movie is stolen by **Whitmore**'s police commissioner who, for once, is not a blustering bureaucrat but a credible character.

Hot Fuzz 2007

Director Edgar Wright **Cast** Simon Pegg, Nick Frost 115m

Arresting Britcom that spoofs cop action movie clichés and British society. For once, the criminal masterminds are not reclusive billionaires or berserk tycoons but the members of the Neighbourhood Watch Alliance, who murder to keep their village picture-postcard pure. The transposition of *Lethal Weapon* to Somerset works well although, by the end, you wonder if buddy cops **Pegg** and **Frost** would rather just be Gibson and Glover.

Insomnia 1997

Director Erik Skjoldbjaerg **Cast** Stellan Skarsgård, Sverre Anker Ousdal 96m

The 2002 Christopher Nolan remake was unbalanced by Al Pacino's unwittingly self-parodying turn as the cop who, on the trail of a killer, accidentally shoots his partner. The original, **Sjkoldbjaerg**'s debut, is stronger and more original, more of a character study with **Skarsgård** simply immense as the anguished cop for whom the real killer becomes a shadow of his own torment.

Lantana 2001

Director Ray Lawrence **Cast** Anthony LaPaglia, Geoffrey Rush 121m

An adulterous cop experiencing a midlife crisis investigates a woman's murder. So far, so clichéd, but **Lawrence**'s intelligent, ingenious *noir* is as interested in exploring the mystery of human relationships – and such issues as trust and forgiveness – as in solving the murder. **LaPaglia** gives the performance of his career in this superior psychological thriller.

The Man on the Roof 1976

Director Bo Wideberg Cast Carl Gustaf Lindstedt 113m

Wideberg has the guts and the good sense to honour the intent of **Per Wahloo** and **Maj Sjowall**, whose novel *The Abominable Man* mixes social comment and sleuthing to great effect. This investigation into the murder of a violent and brutal policeman is a fine police procedural thriller that becomes more vivid as the murderer loses control and the cops realize they are all in the firing line.

Narc 2002

Director Joe Carnahan Cast Chi McBride, Jason Patric, Ray Liotta 105m

Narcotics cop **Patric**, sidelined after accidentally shooting a pregnant woman, is reinstated to help terrifying cop **Liotta** find his partner's killers in a clever thriller that compensates for its predictable outcome with panache, cynicism and violent verve. Liotta is as watchable as in *Goodfellas* but bearded, heavier, hinting at interesting depths even while he's going OTT.

The Pledge 2001

Director Sean Penn Cast Jack Nicholson, Benicio Del Toro 124m

Poignant drama in which **Nicholson**'s retiring small-town cop is left adrift as fate conspires to prevent him fulfilling his pledge to find a girl's murderer. Based on **Friedrich Durrenmatt**'s story *It Happened in Broad Daylight* (filmed previously as *The Cold Light of Day* with Richard E. Grant), **Penn**'s understated, atmospheric detective thriller is enriched by Nicholson's restrained portrayal of a man whose obsession runs deeper than we first think.

Police 1985

Director Maurice Pialat Cast Gérard Depardieu, Sophie Marceau 113m

Depardieu's brutish, charismatic cop Mangin, is corrupt, but no baddie, and briskly gets on with the serious business of staying alive, protecting his lover (**Marceau**) from Tunisian gangsters who want their two million francs back and sorting out a few criminals on the side. Mangin knows he's being used but when the user looks as lovely as Marceau he's not going to complain.

★ Serpico 1973

Director Sidney Lumet Cast Al Pacino, John Randolph, Jack Kehoe 129m

Al Pacino is outstanding in this fictionalized account of a real-life cop who has nothing to fear except his colleagues. A black sheep (and possibly a righteous pain in the ass) due to his "hippie" appearance and his refusal to take bribes throughout his NYPD career, Serpico finally informed on the entire corrupt squad. Fair enough: this was the kind of police station where a superior complained: "Who can trust a cop who don't take money?"

Britcops

One of the ironies of *Hot Fuzz*, as Simon Pegg pointed out, is that the British have almost stopped making cop movies. Perhaps the genre never recovered from the demise of the old-style certainties of the 1950s – as showcased in such classics as *An Inspector Calls* – but in the 1970s, the boys in blue staged a bit of a comeback.

The Sweeney (1977) and **Sweeney 2** (1978) were lively spin-offs that lived up to the sawn-off shotgun shtick of the seminal TV series but worked as movies even if you'd never seen John Thaw and Dennis Waterman play Carter and Regan.

Neither was quite as sleazy as Michael Apted's **The Squeeze** (1977) in which Stacy Keach's alcoholic ex-cop agrees to fake his own death in the hope that he can save his kidnapped wife and daughter. Apted's squalid, depressing film was damned for stamping on everything that Britain had been proud of in the 1960s and is now remembered largely for the incongruous, but inspired, casting of hamster-eating comic Freddie Starr as Keach's accomplice.

The most original British police movie of the 1970s may have been made by an American. Sidney Lumet directed **The Offence** (1972), with Sean Connery – cast as a favour for returning as 007 in *Diamonds Are Forever* – as a sergeant who snaps and beats a suspect into a coma. Lumet's film avoids the obvious – corrupt cover-ups and legal redress for the sergeant's crime – to ask what had driven the officer to break down. In an unconventional – and largely unknown – cop movie, Lumet focuses on the utterly believable torment endured by Connery's sergeant.

Stray Dog 1949

Director Akira Kurosawa **Cast** Toshirô Mifune, Takashi Shirumi 122m

A twist on American *noir*, **Kurosawa**'s first genuine masterpiece sees **Mifune** play a rookie detective who has his gun stolen. The director takes us on an anti-travelogue of a ruined Tokyo as Mifune's quest to find the culprit – who is using the gun to commit a series of awful crimes – turns manic and the parallels between cop and criminal become ever more telling.

Torrente, el brazo tonto de la ley 1998

Director Santiago Segura **Cast** Santiago Segura, Javier Cámara 97m

Right-wing, drunken, sexist Madrid cop Torrente (**Segura**) inspired one of the most successful Spanish comedy movie franchises ever. But then it's not every cop who has the chutzpah to force his own dad to beg on the streets in a wheelchair. While pursuing a local nympho, Torrente becomes convinced drugs are being trafficked through a Chinese restaurant and takes on the villains with the nympho's nerdy cousin. Enough said?

COSTUME

As the original motivation for almost any actor is the urge to dress up in some fancy outfits, the continued appeal of the costume drama isn't so mysterious.

Barry Lyndon 1975

Director Stanley Kubrick **Cast** Ryan O'Neal, Marisa Berenson 187m

An Oscar-winner for cinematography, art direction, costumes and score, **Kubrick**'s fastidious, downbeat, deliberately paced period piece – adapted from **William Makepeace Thackeray**'s novel about the rise and fall in society of a roguish eighteenth-century Irish adventurer – is revered by cineastes and filmmakers for its candlelit compositions and striking set pieces. To many, however, it's a magnificently handsome but cold, detached movie in which the characters' follies and protracted poses of inner suffering could usefully be alleviated by some of Tom Jones's cheery lustiness.

Beau Brummell 1954

Director Curtis Bernhardt **Cast** Stewart Granger, Elizabeth Taylor, Peter Ustinov 111m

Beau Brummell (**Granger**) was the original Regency dandy – a man who charmed and seduced his way to power, and had an intimate friendship with the Prince of Wales, future king of England (the movie's classic line has Granger refer to Wales with "Who's your fat friend?"). His rags-to-riches tale is perfect stuff for this rich period drama, a colourful remake of the 1924 silent movie. Full of lavish costumes, lots of dialogue and stunning sets (many of the interiors were shot in the well-preserved fifteenth-century Ockwell Manor, near Windsor Castle in England).

Camille 1936

Director George Cukor **Cast** Greta Garbo, Robert Taylor 108m

By 1936 there had already been six silent versions of this tale of love and loss in Paris in 1847. But this re-telling, with dialogue full of the wit director **Cukor** was famous for, had **Garbo** as the tragic heroine Marguerite and resplendent costumes designed by **Adrian**, Hollywood's greatest costume designer. Unashamedly glamorous and romantic, this timeless classic, adapted from the novel by **Alexandre Dumas** (Marguerite is based on a woman he had an affair with), inspired a contemporary song called *I'll Love Like Robert Taylor, Be My Great Garbo*. Winston Churchill was so besotted by Garbo's allure in these films that, meeting her on a yacht in the 1950s, he was found trying to rip her top off to see her breasts, shouting "I must know if they're real."

Carry On Don't Lose Your Head 1966

Director Gerald Thomas **Cast** Sid James, Kenneth Williams, Jim Dale 90m

Despite a switch of studio prompting this French Revolutionary romp to be originally released without its Carry On tag, the thirteenth film in the franchise ranks among the best. **Talbot Rothwell**'s script riffs shamelessly on Baroness Orczy's *The Scarlet Pimpernel*, while **Gerald Thomas** revels in the atypical opulence of three National Trust properties: Clandon Park, Cliveden and Waddesdon Manor. But it's the pantomimic performances that make this so enjoyable, with **Williams**'s police chief Citizen Camembert meeting his match in **James**'s effete aristo, Sir Rodney Efing, who rescues **Charles Hawtrey**'s decadent Duc de Pommfrit while masquerading as The Black Fingernail.

Heart of Glass 1976

Director Werner Herzog **Cast** Josef Bierbichler, Stefan Güttler, Clemens Scheitz 94m

Werner Herzog is known as the visionary of New German Cinema and his decision to hypnotize the bulk of his non-professional cast for this variation on

Herbert Achtenbusch's novel *The Hour of Death* was certainly innovative. Herzog generates a chilling sense of a civilization on the cusp of ruinous transformation in this story of an Alpine village whose fortunes decline when the secret of its famous ruby glass is lost forever. With **Jörg Schmidt-Reitwein**'s cinematography being inspired by the art of Pieter Bruegel and the German Romantics, this is a mesmerizing parable.

The Hours 2002

Director Stephen Daldry **Cast** Nicole Kidman, Julianne Moore, Meryl Streep 115m

A story of three different women's relationship with the Virginia Woolf novel *Mrs Dalloway* (*The Hours* was its working title), the book's underlying theme of suicide might not seem like an uplifting way to spend two hours. But **Daldry** extracts such intense performances from the three leads (for her Oscar, **Kidman** spent hours in make-up each day and learnt to write with her right hand) and supporting cast. Even the most painful moments are shot through with honesty and clarity and stop it from being a depressing dirge. Worth a look, if only to see if you can spot the join on Kidman's nose.

Jassy 1947

Director Bernard Knowles **Cast** Margaret Lockwood, Patricia Roc, Dennis Price 102m

Jassy is the final movie of the Gainsborough Studios costume cycle, which was intended to compete with the big Hollywood epics. The elegant costumes are complemented by the set – which profited from having the company's biggest ever budget. Filmed in Technicolor, this nineteenth-century melodrama about a Gypsy girl whose second sight leads to her isolation in the local village, gave its audiences a glimpse of the luxury their own wartime lives lacked.

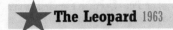

The Leopard 1963

Director Luchino Visconti **Cast** Burt Lancaster, Alain Delon, Claudia Cardinale 205m

Burt Lancaster delivers the performance of his life as nineteenth-century Italian nobleman Prince Saldina, powerfully presiding over **Visconti**'s sumptuous epic of social revolution. Thick with authentic history, socio-political themes and ideological symbolism, this is rated as one of the finest literary adaptations ever undertaken. But even if all this goes over your head, the emotional power and visual magnificence are spellbinding, particularly in the ballroom sequence that constitutes a third of the movie and revolves around the marriage the prince has arranged for his nephew with a daughter of the empowered bourgeoisie: **Delon** and **Cardinale** at their peaks of gorgeousness.

The Little Princess 1939

Director Walter Lang **Cast** Shirley Temple, Richard Greene 93m

After her father is believed to have been killed in the Boer War, the young Sara Crewe (**Temple**) quickly finds herself shifting from privileged student at a Victorian boarding school to becoming a servant there. This is Temple's first Technicolor production – albeit one of her last real classics – so fans can see her at her all-singing, all-dancing best. A full-on corn-fest by today's standards, but don't you just love it? The **Alfonso Cuarón** 1995 remake is also worth a look.

Little Women 1994

Director Gillian Armstrong **Cast** Winona Ryder, Susan Sarandon, Claire Danes 118m

In this fifth movie adaptation of **Louisa M. Alcott**'s classic, director **Armstrong** wanted the costume design to be faithful to the real clothing of the time. So she insisted all the dresses were made from authentic fabrics that would have been available during the civil war. The set followed the same philosophy – the design was based on the layout of Orchard House, Alcott's family home in Massachusetts, where she lived while writing her book and where she imagined the events of the novel taking place. The story of four sisters growing up in the American Civil War benefits from this attention to detail and impressive performances from **Sarandon** as the mother and her young supporting cast.

Picnic at Hanging Rock 1975

Director Peter Weir **Cast** Rachel Roberts, Vivean Gray, Helen Morse 115m

Echoes of *A Passage to India* and *L'avventura* reverberate around the outback in this eerie adaptation of Joan Lindsay's novel about the disappearance of three Australian schoolgirls and a teacher on St Valentine's Day, 1900. A master of pitching folk into alien environments, **Peter Weir** captures the sense of Victorian propriety with the same rhythmic insouciance with which **Russell Boyd**'s camera roves the landscape. The effect is hallucinatory, obfuscatory and deeply disconcerting.

La Reine Margot 1994

Director Patrice Chéreau **Cast** Isabelle Adjani, Daniel Auteuil 162m

A big-budget adaptation of **Alexandre Dumas**'s novel about the Massacre of St Bartholomew in 1572. The action opens with the marriage of the Catholic queen Margot (**Adjani**) to her Protestant husband, Henri de Navarre (**Auteuil**), in a bid to calm the raging religious war, and goes on to graphically depict the stabbings, rapes and violent bloodshed that follow. This was nominated for an Oscar for best costume design – and they are impeccable – but if you're expecting a pretty period fashion parade, be warned.

Isabelle Adjani's amazing get-up shows why *La Reine Margot* was Oscar-nominated for its costumes. However, it remains best remembered for its unrelenting bloodiness.

 **The Secret Garden**
1993

Director Agnieszka Holland **Cast** Kate Maberly, Maggie Smith, John Lynch 100m

Holland's interpretation of the **Frances Hodgson Burnett** novel is so good you forget that it was originally made with kids in mind. No detail was spared: seventeen thousand pots of annuals and grasses, twelve hundred perennials and four thousand wild geraniums were used to create the secret garden. In the guise of a story about an orphaned girl (**Maberly**) who exposes the secrets of a gloomy, forbidding manor, the movie – and the book – make some pertinent points about the nature of life. **Caroline Thompson**'s script helps retain the book's gothic ambience.

COURTROOM

The law may be an ass but it's provided some of the movies' favourite stereotypes: idealistic young lawyers, blinkered or corrupt old judges, cynical (often drunken) has-been lawyers dragged into one last combat, psychopaths who escape justice on a technicality…

The Accused 1988

Director Jonathan Kaplan **Cast** Kelly McGillis, Jodie Foster 111m

One reason this movie seems so realistic is that it echoes the horrific case of a woman who was raped on a pool table in a Massachusetts bar. **Kaplan** has a clear, unwavering eye for the realities of the legal system as it deals with rape – particularly the speed with which the victim becomes the suspect. **Foster** won an Oscar as Sarah, the victim with a past that does not bear more than cursory examination. Debate still swirls about the gang-rape scene, which some see as confronting the audience with the reality of the crime (and the responsibility of those who stood by and watched) but others see as sheer sexploitation.

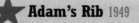 Adam's Rib 1949

Director George Cukor **Cast** Spencer Tracy, Katharine Hepburn, Judy Holliday 101m

The best of the nine movies **Hepburn** and **Tracy** made together, this takes the battle of the sexes and multiplies it with a courtroom battle in which the co-stars (and offscreen lovers) are lawyers on opposing sides of an attempted murder case. But the real star is **Holliday** as a woman on trial for shooting her adulterous husband. There is a theory that her role was part of a conspiracy between **Cukor**, Hepburn and **Garson Kanin** (who co-wrote the script) to get Columbia to give Holliday the lead part in *Born Yesterday*. She got it, but wasn't as effective as she is here, which, considering the quality of her co-stars, is praise indeed.

Anatomy of a Murder 1959

Director Otto Preminger **Cast** James Stewart, Lee Remick 160m

If the judge in this movie strikes you as a bit too goofy to be a real judge, you'd be wrong. He is **Joseph Welch**, who famously represented the army against Joe McCarthy in the hearings that brought down the 1950s Red-baiting senator. Welch's dialogue isn't up to his line which destroyed McCarthy – "Have you no sense of decency, sir, at long last?'' – but the rest of the script crackles, especially when **Stewart**, as the country lawyer defending a man accused of murdering his wife's rapist, exchanges barbs with **George C. Scott**.

Close-Up 1990

Director Abbas Kiarostami **Cast** Hossain Sabzian, Mohsen Makhmalbaf 97m

An Iranian printer's assistant, **Hossain Sabzian** impersonated his favourite movie director to feel important, but was arrested when the hoax was exposed, and tried for fraud. (As the fake director, he obtained money from a family who thought he would shoot a movie in their house.) The trial, which **Kiarostami** got permission to film, is included, although the scenes showing the hoax are re-enactments. The result erases the line between real life and movies for both the audience and for the participants who play themselves. This is a film so full of ideas and themes that it's not easily digested on a single viewing.

My Cousin Vinny 1992

Director Jonathan Lynn **Cast** Joe Pesci, Marisa Tomei, Fred Gwynne 120m

Debunking the po-faced courtroom drama at every turn, **Pesci** plays hilariously to type as a good-hearted, if greasy, rookie personal injury lawyer with no trial experience, while **Tomei** is in her element as his sexy, gum-snapping, car-mechanic fiancée. Much of the humour comes from the clash and the chemistry between these Italian-American Brook-lynites – all leather jackets, gold chains and abrasive backchat – and the Deep South they encounter when trying to save his young cousin from an unjust prison sentence. All that, plus Herman Munster (**Gwynne**) as the worldweary judge: there are more laughs per reel here than in all the other movies in this chapter put together.

A Short Film About Killing 1988

Director Krzysztof Kieslowski **Cast** Miroslawa Baka, Krzysztof Globisz 85m

The clumsy (and protracted) murder of a taxi driver by a young punk is followed by the brutal and protracted execution of the aforementioned punk. **Kieslowski** doesn't try to explore the murderer's motivations, but that only adds to its power. You've read those reviews about movies being the emotional equivalent of going through a meat grinder? In this case, it's true.

To Kill a Mockingbird 1962

Director Robert Mulligan **Cast** Gregory Peck, Mary Badham, Robert Duvall 129m

Robert Duvall spent six weeks in the sun bleaching his hair blond for this often-heard, seldom-seen portrayal of the elusive, possibly mad neighbour Boo Radley. It was the beginning of his long, slow climb into the big league. **Peck** is principled lawyer Atticus Finch, called on to defend a black man accused of rape in 1930s small-town Alabama. Underrated because of its very decency, the movie has more breadth than it's given credit for: the scene where the children are attacked on the way home from a pageant is genuinely scary.

The Trial 1962

Director Orson Welles **Cast** Anthony Perkins, Jeanne Moreau, Romy Schneider 120m

Orson Welles once said this movie (based on Kafka's book) "was much closer to my own feelings about everything than any other picture I've ever made." Certainly he suffered recurring nightmares of guilt and imprisonment, and this movie is very like a nightmare, with Josef K (**Perkins**) trapped in it. Welles played on a suspicion of Perkins' homosexuality, showing three women (**Moreau**, **Schneider** and **Elsa Martinelli**) failing to seduce him, and suggesting another reason why he might live in a state of fear. Critic Roger Ebert suggests this film is an allegory of Welles's own career. After *Citizen Kane* he too was pursued by beautiful women but doomed to wander in search of benefactors, never sure of the crime for which he had been condemned.

12 Angry Men 1957

Director Sidney Lumet **Cast** Henry Fonda, Martin Balsam, Lee J. Cobb, Jack Warden 95m

Sidney Lumet's cinematic debut was a low-budget affair, with two weeks for rehearsals and just seventeen days to shoot. **Fonda** was canvassed to star, typecast as a liberal do-gooder, but with **Reginald Rose**'s measured yet absorbing script and surrounded by New York's finest theatrical talents (including **Jack "Quincy" Klugman** and **Ed Begley**), Juror No. 8 is one of his best performances. The only one of twelve jury members not convinced a young man is guilty of murdering his father, he has to persuade his fellow jury members to look more closely at the evidence. Cinematographer **Boris Kaufman** helped by taking a very stylized approach, gradually closing in to heighten the claustrophobic effect. Fonda, never a fan of his own work, watched most of the film before proclaiming: "Sidney, it's magnificent."

★ Witness for the Prosecution 1957

Director Billy Wilder **Cast** Tyrone Power, Marlene Dietrich, Charles Laughton 116m

Posters warned "You'll talk about it, but please don't tell the ending!", though the final twist(s) in this **Agatha Christie** adaptation are actually pretty lame. It's still a cracker, though, camp as Christmas – if only for the moment when **Dietrich**'s trousers are ripped off, revealing one of those infamous gams in all its glory. And then there's that Cockney woman (but we've been sworn not to talk about her); **Laughton** in fine fettle as the monocle-sporting attorney; and to top it all **Elsa Lanchester**, Bride of Frankenstein herself (and Laughton's real-life wife), playing Laughton's marvellous fusspot of a nurse, Miss Plimsoll.

CRIME

A catch-all term that encompasses dozens of genres and microgenres, crime definitely does pay – but usually only for filmmakers and actors.

Big Bad Mama 1974

Director Steve Carver **Cast** Angie Dickinson, William Shatner, Tom Skerritt 85m

In **Roger Corman**'s take on the Bonnie and Clyde heists, **Dickinson** and her equally sparsely clad teenage daughters travel through rural America bootlegging, robbing and picking up men: if the likes of Dillinger and Capone can have it all, why shouldn't they? **Shatner** and **Skerritt** play the lovers, the only real fault in this comic caper being too many shots of Shatner's hairy legs. Avoid the 1987 sequel.

The Big Lebowski 1998

Directors Joel and Ethan Coen **Cast** Jeff Bridges, John Goodman 117m

Bridges (the Dude) revisits Philip Marlowe territory as an unlikely ageing slacker sleuth. Then there is bowling buddy **Goodman** as Walter Sobchak (a star turn), an angry Vietnam vet, a ridiculous plot (best not go there) and numerous unbelievable characters. It sounds like a mess but this surreal noirish pastiche begat a cult, an annual festival and the religion of Dudeism. It would be criminal not to like it.

Black God, White Devil 1964

Director Glauber Rocha **Cast** Othon Bastos, Geraldo Del Rey, Mauricio do Valle 110m

Rocha's first major movie is an intriguing fictionalized account of the last days of Brazilian banditry. Manuel (**Del Rey**) descends into crime, joining Coriso (**Bastos**), sworn enemy of hired gun Antonio (**Valle**), the eponymous "hero" of the 1969 sequel. Even if you don't know the real story that inspired these events, this works as a crime drama that sheds light on Brazilian society.

Bloody Mama 1970

Director Roger Corman **Cast** Shelley Winters, Bruce Dern, Robert De Niro 90m

Normally the words "based on a true story" make your heart sink. With **Corman** in charge what you have here is not the dogged, small-minded, pursuit of literal truth but a gorgeously OTT confection, symbolized by **Winters**' own melodramatics as the evil Ma Barker, sex-crazed mother and leader of her sons' violent, robbing and murdering criminal gang. **Dern** and **De Niro** give able support in a trashy classic.

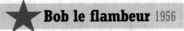

Bob le flambeur 1956

Director Jean-Pierre Melville **Cast** Roger Duchesne, Isabelle Corey 98m

Former bank robber Bob (elegantly played by **Duchesne**) is such a compulsive gambler (*flambeur*) he even has a fruit machine in his apartment. A losing streak turns his thoughts to a big score at the Deauville casino. Montmartre has seldom looked so glamorously sordid as in

Melville's impressive gangster movie, a thoroughly French masterpiece that harks back to *noir*, anticipates the French New Wave and inspired Leone and Woo. Neil Jordan's remake, *The Good Thief* (2002), with Nick Nolte as Bob, is also worth a look.

Charley Varrick 1973

Director Don Siegel **Cast** Walter Matthau, Andrew Robinson, Joe Don Baker 111m

---

The Honeymoon Killers

❝ One of the movies that provoked me to make *Swoon*, **The Honeymoon Killers** (1970) blazes an indelible true crime trail: the low-rent, sordid cousin of *Bonnie and Clyde*. Though the director credit belongs to Leonard Kastle, both Donald Volkman and Martin Scorsese shared duties (Scorsese apparently fired for working too slowly). Remarkably, this was the first feature for stage actors Shirley Stoler and Tony Lo Bianco and cinematographer Oliver Wood (who later shot the *Miami Vice* TV series and the *Bourne* movies, among many others). Stoler and Lo Bianco capture the feral sweat and the darkly funny grime of the notorious 'Lonely Hearts Killers' perfectly. Stoler's performance as Martha Beck – sullen, voluptuous, heartbreaking – remains electrifying.

The other cult movies that make up my top five are:

Night Nurse (1931, William Wellman)

Gun Crazy (1950, Joseph Lewis)

White Dog (1982, Samuel Fuller)

Querelle (1982, Rainer Werner Fassbinder)

or

The Night of the Hunter (1955, Charles Laughton). **❞**

Tom Kalin
Producer, writer and director Tom Kalin's dark debut feature, Swoon, *about two gay lovers who murdered a child, was awarded best cinematography at Sundance, drawing critical comparisons with Alfred Hitchcock. His most recent film,* Savage Grace *starring Julianne Moore, dramatizes the famous Barbara Daly Baekeland murder case.*

Siegel's pacy, violent thriller features **Matthau**'s best dramatic performance as the titular anti-hero, a crop-duster with a sideline in bank heists who outfoxes the Mafia all the way to the thrilling denouement at an airfield. Matthau is ably supported by **Baker** as a hit man with a great line in putdowns and **Robinson** as his impetuous sidekick. An obvious influence on *Pulp Fiction*, especially when the idea of a hoodlum torturing some poor sap with "a pair of pliers and blowtorch" is floated.

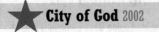

City of God 2002

Directors Kátia Lund, Fernando Meirelles
Cast Alexandre Rodrigues 130m

Based on actual events outlined in the novel by **Paulo Lins**, this sweeping gangster saga achieves all the hyperkinetic brutality of a movie like *Goodfellas* using a largely untrained cast of teenagers, making it all the more powerful and disturbing. On the mean streets of the titular favela on the edge of Rio de Janeiro, life is cheap and frequently short. The struggles of various youngsters are seen through the eyes of narrator Buscapé (**Rodrigues**), who wants to be a photographer. The villain is sociopathic Li'l Ze (**Firmino da Hora**), who runs much of the city's drug trade, but even he earns some sympathy in this utterly involving experience.

Dog Day Afternoon 1975

Director Sidney Lumet **Cast** Al Pacino, John Cazale, Chris Sarandon 130m

The real bank robber whose unfortunate caper inspired **Lumet**'s classic was described as "a thin, dark-faced fellow with the broken good looks of Al Pacino". And it was to **Pacino** that Lumet turned to play Sonny, a complex, unhappy man who tries to rob a bank to fund his lover's sex change operation. **John Cazale**, as Pacino's partner in crime, is almost as brilliant as the headlining star. Cazale made only five movies before his untimely death in 1978 but what a CV: *Dog Day*, *The Godfather I* and *II*, *The Conversation* and *The Deer Hunter*.

Falling Down 1993

Director Joel Schumacher **Cast** Michael Douglas, Robert Duvall, Barbara Hershey 115m

In one of his best performances, **Douglas** plays a defence worker who has just been laid off and experiences meltdown that same hot LA afternoon. Abandoning his car in a traffic jam, he's soon running around with a sports bag full of heavy armaments making a few forceful points about society's flawed social and economic mechanisms. **Duvall**'s performance as the pursuing cop is good enough to help us forget that his character – public servant on the cusp of retirement who takes on one last case – is such a cliché.

Fargo 1996

Director Joel Coen **Cast** Frances McDormand, William H. Macy, Steve Buscemi 98m

The North Dakota town of Fargo is only onscreen for a few seconds but the

Coens, rightly, thought it made a more intriguing title than Brainerd, the Minnesota city that hosts most of the action in this sublime dark comedy. **Frances McDormand** excels as the pregnant police chief with a singsong voice investigating the kidnapping of **William H. Macy**'s wife. It's hard not to empathize with Macy's conniving, kidnapping, car dealer who turns to small-time crooks **Steve Buscemi** and **Peter Stormare**.

The Fourth Man 1983

Director Paul Verhoeven Cast Jeroen Krabbé, Renée Soutendijk, Thom Hoffman 102m

Verhoeven's final movie before Hollywood recognized his talent for persuading actresses to strip is an intriguing work. **Krabbé** plays a bisexual writer who meets hairdresser **Soutendijk** at one of his lectures. They strike up a rapport, but Krabbé is more interested in her lover, **Hoffman**. Krabbé then begins to have visions, possibly warning him about his relationship with a woman who has had three husbands, all of whom died mysteriously. Is he or Hoffman the "fourth man" of the title, the next target of this *femme fatale*? Or is she *fatale* at all? A gothic crime thriller with plenty of Verhoeven's usual eroticism.

Gun Crazy 1949

Director Joseph H. Lewis Cast Peggy Cummins, John Dall 87m

A precursor to *Badlands*, *The Getaway* and *Bonnie and Clyde*, this hard-boiled movie stars **Dall** and **Cummins** as bank robbers whose aversion to work is so extreme, they kill people to earn a living. In part, a Gandhian parable about the perils of violence, **Lewis**'s urban *noir* features many of his favourite motifs: duels, spirals, odd sexual undercurrents and men in uniform. Welsh actress Cummins shines as the *femme fatale* in a masterful movie made in 49 days for $300,000.

The Hitch-hiker 1953

Director Ida Lupino Cast Edmond O'Brien, Frank Lovejoy, William Tallman 71m

The premise is simple: two fishermen (**O'Brien** and **Lovejoy**) give a lift to a hitchhiker (**Tallman**) who proves to be a psycho and promises to kill them both before the ride is over. Tallman makes a fine, unpredictable, intelligent, droopy-eyed psycho and **Lupino** has the sense and craft to avoid almost all the usual clichés in this gem.

Milano calibro 9 1972

Director Fernando Di Leo Cast Gastone Moschin, Barbara Bouchet, Mario Adorf 97m

There's nothing too original about the premise – small-time gangster **Moschin** tries to go straight even though everyone thinks he knows where a large bundle of missing loot is – but Moschin and his girlfriend (**Bouchet**) are fun to watch and **Di Leo** builds nicely to a fantastic double twist at the finale.

Mr Reliable 1996

Director Nadia Tass Cast Colin Friels, Jacqueline McKenzie 113m

In 1968, as the rest of the world was rocked by war, riots and assassinations, the only dramatic event in Australia was an eight-day hostage drama in New South Wales. **Friels** is hilarious as the hapless Mellish, who pulls a gun on cops questioning him about stolen car hood ornaments. Glimpsing Mellish's girlfriend (**McKenzie**) and baby, the police assume they're his hostages. It takes Mellish a while to realize a SWAT team is lurking outside, but he quickly turns the situation to his advantage. In the US this would be an oddball drama where the lovable rogue is blasted to smithereens. But this is Australia in the 1960s and Tass uses a certain artistic licence and dry humour to emphasize the relative innocence of the times.

Out of Sight 1998

Director Steven Soderbergh Cast George Clooney, Jennifer Lopez, Ving Rhames 123m

"Is this your first time being robbed? You're doing great." This is how the suave **Clooney** as Jack Foley robs banks. Based on another **Elmore Leonard** novel, this has a plot as complex as *Jackie Brown*, with the action flitting between past, further past and present. But it's Leonard's colourful characters that propel the movie, notably the buddy relationship between Jack and, er, Buddy (**Rhames**), and Jack and FBI agent **Lopez**. There's also a cameo by **Samuel L. Jackson** and five hundred convicts from Glades penitentiary.

★ Paradise Lost: The Child Murders at Robin Hood Hills 1996

Directors Joe Berlinger, Bruce Sinofsky 150m

In this documentary three teenagers are accused of killing three young children, supposedly through their involvement in Satanism. But there is no real evidence apart from a statement by one of them who has learning difficulties and later says the confession was forced. As the movie progresses, interviews with the victims' parents, police and locals show that the teenagers have been singled out because they are the town's black sheep. They're interested in the occult, listen to heavy metal and wear black, which was enough to get them convicted in the US Bible Belt. The fact that one of the accused is called Damien adds a ludicrous, chilling twist to this compelling, terrifying movie.

Point Blank 1967

Director John Boorman Cast Lee Marvin, Angie Dickinson 92m

Existential torpor, romanticized fatalism, dishonour among thieves, **Boorman**'s great late *noir* has all these – and it is decked out with New Wave trimmings. Left for dead after being double-crossed by his partner in crime and abandoned by his wife, **Marvin** seeks brutal revenge, despite the distraction of sexy sister-in-law **Dickinson**. It is rare to see an American movie of the 1960s that celebrates such pure, unadulterated violence. The action, and Marvin's quiet brutishness, perfectly balance Boorman's artier conceits.

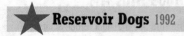

Reservoir Dogs 1992

Director Quentin Tarantino **Cast** Harvey Keitel, Tim Roth, Michael Madsen, Steve Buscemi 99m

Only **Tarantino** would have **Madsen** slicing off a cop's ear to the tune of "Stuck in the Middle With You". The scene is so effective that horror director Wes Craven walked out of the cinema the first time he saw it. Tarantino's seminal retelling of the events before and after a heist is stylish, violent, funny and gruesome, with swathes of quotable dialogue. But there is some merit in Roger Ebert's observation that, as entertaining as Tarantino's debut is, it doesn't seem that curious about the characters.

Roxie Hart 1942

Director William Wellman **Cast** Ginger Rogers, Adolphe Menjou, George Chandler 75m

Ginger Rogers (in a role originally intended for Alice Faye until she fell pregnant) escaped from her dancing partner long enough to dazzle as the dancer who claims to be a murderess to grab some headlines, in this story based on the play *Chicago* that would, years later, be turned into a hit musical and Oscar-winning movie. Director **Wellman** doesn't do this kind of material quite as well as Howard Hawks might have but it still zings and Rogers plays with real zest.

Séance on a Wet Afternoon 1964

Director Bryan Forbes **Cast** Kim Stanley, Richard Attenborough, Nanette Newman 116m

Forbes' best movie will have the hair standing on the back of your neck and a lump forming in your throat. In this compassionate, atmospheric thriller, **Stanley** (hitherto most famous as the uncredited narrator in *To Kill a Mockingbird*) excels as a medium who persuades her asthmatic hubbie (**Attenborough**) to kidnap the daughter of a wealthy couple so she can prove her prowess to the police. The story is so odd that, as the medium's mind unravels, you feel you are watching a real story.

Straight Time 1978

Director Ulu Grosbard **Cast** Dustin Hoffman, M. Emmet Walsh, Harry Dean Stanton 114m

Grosbard's brave, gritty movie starts by presenting **Hoffman** as a wounded soul ground down by the wheels of injustice, but as the exploration of the career criminal's psyche drills deeper, we realize this is not the case. Hoffman gives one of his finest, and seldom seen, performances as the doomed parolee. **Walsh**, as the parole officer who hassles Hoffman onto the wrong side of the law, and **Stanton**, an ex-con in suburbia dreaming of one last score, offer superb support.

Dustin Hoffman in action as Max Dembo in the all but forgotten *Straight Time*, rejecting parole and returning to a life of crime.

The Thin Blue Line 1988

Director Errol Morris 101m

In 1976 Dallas policeman Robert Wood was shot dead on duty. Drifter Randall Adams was convicted and served eleven years until **Morris** made this documentary. After two years of investigation, he discovered the main testimony against Adams was flawed and following the film's release, the case was reopened. Far more than a documentary, the movie features a slightly surreal restaging of Wood's death, and Morris is clearly a man who is interested in more than just what people say, as his camera highlights quirks and reactions to great effect. With **Philip Glass**'s hypnotic soundtrack it becomes a masterpiece of true-life storytelling.

The Watchmaker of St Paul 1974

Director Bertrand Tavernier
Cast Philippe Noiret, Jean Rochefort, Jacques Denis 105m

Tavernier's directorial debut is such a gem, it's no great surprise that he went on to become one of the greatest moviemakers of the late twentieth century. **Noiret**, Tavernier's alter ego, is the thoughtful, middle-aged clockmaker trying to work out why his son has committed a murder. Tavernier stays true to the spirit of the **Georges Simenon** novel by telling us a story that starts with a crime and ends by showing us a personality. By exploring the characters – father, son and police chief – and making judicious use of the Lyon locations he knows so well, Tavernier delivers something completely unexpected, transcending the genre.

Wild Target 1993

Director Pierre Salvadori Cast Jean Rochefort, Marie Trintignant 88m

Rochefort's hesitant hit man never really had a chance. Trained as an assassin by his mother, he finds himself unable to kill an attractive young female thief (**Trintignant**) in a beautifully dark comedy that sets off down one route, then backtracks into a chase before finally deciding to explore the mystery of Rochefort's killer.

CROSS-DRESSING

Some guys simply love the sensation of silk stockings against their skin; for others, a slick of lipstick is enough to send them off on a murdering rampage. As for girls, dressing as boys – from Dietrich in *Morocco* to Hilary Swank in *Boys Don't Cry* – is guaranteed to win fashion kudos and gay icon status.

Boys Don't Cry 1999

Director Kimberley Peirce **Cast** Hilary Swank, Chloë Sevigny 118m

Based on the real life of Teena Brandon, this is the story of a teenage girl who preferred to live as a boy (Brandon Teena) in a tiny Nebraskan town. Brandon meets and falls in love with Lana (**Sevigny**), who right up until the end has no idea that Brandon is not a man. But this is not a movie about lesbianism; it's about the bigotry and homophobia of the other characters. Peirce fought for a long time to get this movie made, and the critical approval it received, including a best actress Oscar for **Swank**, is testament to her tenacity.

Dressed to Kill 1980

Director Brian de Palma **Cast** Michael Caine, Angie Dickinson, Nancy Allen 105m

You'd expect this kind of slick, razor-sharp slasher horror from **de Palma**, that cold-blooded maestro – but from nice **Michael Caine**? Loveable Cockney and national treasure? Wonders never cease. De Palma, often accused of amoral filmmaking – and violent misogyny – pulls off another breathtaking *coup de cinéma*. Creepy, sexy and chilly, and with more than a nod to his hero, Hitchcock, *Dressed to Kill* brought transvestite and transgender protesters out in droves.

★ Glen or Glenda 1953

Director Edward Wood **Cast** Daniel Davis, Bela Lugosi, Dolores Fuller 65m

Whether **Wood** really yearned to bring the plight of innocent transvestites to the world, or just wanted, as was his wont, to dress up in angora sweaters and blonde wigs (using **Davis**, in a nice bit of identity-swapping, as a pseudonym), is hard to say. Either way, this is a nutty gem – points for anyone who can explain the rampaging buffalo scene – and more poignantly engaging than Woods' *Plan 9 from Outer Space* (commonly agreed to be the worst film ever). The producer tacked on an earnest PS about sex change operations, and added a bit of S&M porn to spice things up; **Lugosi**, meanwhile, as a sinister and superfluous scientist, was just waiting for his next fix.

I Was a Male War Bride
1949

Director Howard Hawks Cast Cary Grant, Ann Sheridan 105m

Though best remembered for cutting a dash in debonair suits, **Cary Grant** was no stranger to dragging up on screen – from his infamous "I just went GAY all of a sudden!" while wearing a negligee in *Bringing up Baby* to the denouement of this screwball in which the dapper one is reduced to disguising himself as a nurse in order to consummate his marriage. Based on a true story called *I Was an Alien Spouse of Female Military Personnel Enroute to the United States Under Public Law 271 of the Congress* (why did they change the name?), the movie also features a feisty turn from **Sheridan** as the WAC lieutenant who falls for Grant's French soldier.

Let Me Die a Woman 1974

Director Doris Wishman 79m

Part-shockumentary, part trashy sexploitation flick, in which transsexuals talk about their sex lives in (some would say far too gory) detail; a surgeon opines; and a real-life sex-change operation unfolds. **Wishman** – a prolific grindhouse moviemaker who was never afraid to exploit the horrific potential of male genitalia – spares us nothing during the crucial castration moments.

★ Sylvia Scarlett 1936

Director George Cukor Cast Katharine Hepburn, Cary Grant 95m

"Woman's director" **Cukor** was always intrigued by artifice – how appearances can mask the way we really are – and this picaresque tale, in which **Hepburn**, a scrap of a girl, goes on the lam disguised as a boy, is no exception. A dismal flop on its release, it has since won rafts of gay and feminist fans; Hepburn, all gamine beauty and ambiguous sexuality, is just superb, and the movie is notable too for **Grant**'s performance as a Cockney chancer who catches her eye.

CULT STUDIOS

Top of the list is Hammer, of course, but let's not forget the other studios responsible for a uniquely recognizable catalogue of pictures – not all of them low-budget horror.

The House That Dripped Blood 1970

Director Peter Duffell **Cast** Ingrid Pitt, Peter Cushing 102m

One of the finest films from the **Amicus** stable, this sharp anthology of horror tales is framed by the device of a police search for a missing film star. Featuring Hammer Studios veterans **Peter Cushing** and **Christopher Lee**, the film also made a screen icon of **Pitt**, whose formidable vampire teeth (and bust) featured heavily in the marketing campaign.

The Man in the White Suit 1951

Director Alexander Mackendrick **Cast** Alec Guinness, Joan Greenwood 85m

One of the lesser known of the **Ealing** comedies and a film dwarfed by the success of *The Lavender Hill Mob*, this offers a sharp satire of British industry. The ubiquitous **Guinness** stars as a would-be chemist in a textile mill who invents a miraculous new fabric. Much trouble ensues until, at the film's conclusion, the gleaming white yarn is finally revealed to have a fatal flaw. Ambitious in theme, its stature has grown in recent years.

The Masque of the Red Death 1964

Director Roger Corman **Cast** Vincent Price, Hazel Court 89m

Produced by **American International Pictures**, a company dedicated to releasing low-budget films aimed at teens, *The Masque of the Red Death* has justifiable iconic status. One of **Roger Corman**'s finest films as director, it's a riveting adaptation of **Edgar Allan Poe**'s macabre tale of an evil prince (**Price**) who sells his soul to the devil in exchange for a life of debauchery. Beautifully shot by a young cinematographer, **Nicolas Roeg**.

Amicus: the other studio that dripped blood

Badly financed, and in reality not really a studio at all, Amicus nonetheless is exceeded only by Hammer in its contribution to British horror films of the 1960s and 70s.

The brainchild of scriptwriter **Milton Subotsky** and fast-talking hustler **Max J. Rosenberg**, Amicus made movies cheap and fast, and yet did so with A-grade talent (frequently hired on day-by-day release from other studios). Defined from the outset by their brooding, claustrophobic style and pretensions towards psychology, Amicus helped originate the portmanteau horror, finding success with anthology pictures such as *Dr Terror's House of Horrors*, *Torture Garden* and *Asylum*.

The Quatermass Xperiment 1955

Director Val Guest **Cast** Brian Donlevy, Jack Warner 82m

One of the finest and most critically acclaimed films to have emerged from **Hammer Studios**, this disturbing tale of an astronaut who, as the result of Professor Quatermass's (**Donlevy**) scientific experiment, begins to mutate into something not of this world, still packs a powerful punch. Making fine use of London locations, the *Xperiment* of the title was a characteristically cheesy marketing ploy to highlight the film's adult-only certificate.

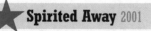 ## Spirited Away 2001

Director Hayao Miyazaki **Cast** Daveigh Chase, Jason Marsden 125m

The story of a headstrong ten-year-old whose capricious ways are brought sharply into focus when she unwittingly finds herself in a new universe inhabited by ancient gods and magical beings, this Oscar-winning animation is one of the jewels in the crown of Japan's **Studio Ghibli**. Loved by adults and children alike, the film is steeped in Japanese culture with an ecological concern that's typical of **Miyazaki**'s work.

The Toxic Avenger 1984

Director Lloyd Kaufman, Michael Herz **Cast** Andree Maranda, Mitch Cohen, Pat Ryan 87m

A wimpy health club cleaner (**Cohen**) is transformed into a disfigured muscle-bound superhuman mutant vigilante when bullies cause him to plummet into a vat of toxic waste. The most successful film ever made by **Troma Productions**, a shoestring-budget studio set up in the mid-1970s to make campy exploitation flicks, and also its first horror release, *Toxic Avenger* has since generated three movie sequels, a stage musical and a kids' TV cartoon. The infamous head-crushing scene, where a child's head is apparently splattered by a car, was achieved by injecting a melon with corn syrup and red food dye and sticking a wig on it.

CULTURE CLASH

The conflict and eventual coming together of two different cultures, whether religious, extraterrestrial or simply one of class, is a subject that never gets old.

Coneheads 1993

Director Steve Barron **Cast** Dan Aykroyd, Jane Curtin, Michael McKean **88m**

More akin to *The Addams Family* than *E.T.*, this *Saturday Night Live* spin-off extols the virtues of America's melting pot ethos, while lampooning the insularity and ignorance of the average citizen. The neighbours readily accept crash-landed Remulakians **Dan Aykroyd** and **Jane Curtin** as French, but INS agents **Michael McKean** and **David Spade** are less convinced. The big laughs come from the speed of conespeak and the contrasts between alien and suburban aspiration. But this possesses a more subversive intelligence than satirized sitcoms like *Mork and Mindy*.

East is East 1999

Director Damian O'Donnell **Cast** Om Puri, Linda Bassett, Jordan Routledge **96m**

A surprise international success, this adaptation of **Ayub Khan Din**'s semi-autobiographical play seeks to disprove Rudyard Kipling's contention that "East is East, West is West, and never the twain shall meet". Indeed, it's hard to imagine a better adjusted family than the one raised in 1970s Salford by Pakistani chippy owner **Om Puri** and his English wife, **Linda Bassett**. But when the hypocritical Puri discovers the extent to which his seven offspring have become Westernized, he attempts to impose his lapsed Muslim values upon them. Exposing the problems of integration and the perniciousness of racism, this has become increasingly pertinent since 9/11.

 Games of Love and Chance 2003

Director Abdellatif Kechiche **Cast** Osman Elkharraz, Sara Forestier, Sabrina Ouazani **117m**

There's something Rohmeresque about this César-winning drama, which charts the romance between the self-assured Lydia (**Forestier**) and emotionally stunted Krimo (**Elkharraz**) as they rehearse a school production of Marivaux's *A Game of Love and Chance*. Although several scenes involve inarticulate adolescents shrieking street argot, this perspicacious teenpic crackles with authenticity. The performances are fresh and confrontational, the cinematography energetic. But the real strength lies in **Kechiche**'s understanding of language and his insights into the similarities between the play characters trapped by destiny and the *banlieue* youths condemned to inevitable struggle by the prejudices of wider society and their own reluctance to break from self-perpetuating stereotype.

The Mission 1986

Director Roland Joffé Cast Robert De Niro, Jeremy Irons, Ray McAnally 125m

Scripted by **Robert Bolt** and the recipient of the Palme d'Or at Cannes, this imposing study of clashing cultures and conflicting interests might have been even more momentous had it been directed by David Lean. The allegorical allusions to Washington's interference in Latin America are a little strident, but there is powerful drama in the stand-off between the eighteenth-century Spanish and Portuguese imperialists that engulfs Jesuit missionary (**Irons**), penitent slave trader (**De Niro**) and cardinal (**McAnally**), who must quell the dispute while keeping both powers loyal to Rome. Civilization has rarely seemed so barbaric.

Shanghai Noon 2000

Director Tom Ley Cast Jackie Chan, Owen Wilson, Lucy Liu 110m

This is essentially a transposition to the Wild West of **Jackie Chan**'s English-language debut, *Rush Hour* (1998), with **Wilson** supplanting Chris Tucker as the wisecracking sidekick. Consequently, the mood is altogether more genial and the humour less abrasive, as Chan's Forbidden City guard forges an unlikely alliance with Wilson's wannabe outlaw to rescue **Liu**'s runaway princess from the dastardly tutor played by **Jason Connery**. Gleeful anachronisms abound between Chan's trademark bouts of knockabout chopsocky, but there are plenty of witty cultural observations too, many of them relating to **Russell Badger**'s highly cultivated tribe of Native Americans.

Zorba the Greek 1964

Director Michael Cacoyannis Cast Anthony Quinn, Alan Bates, Irene Papas 146m

Bates is nominally the hero of this adaptation of **Nikos Kazantzakis**'s novel, as the British writer returning to his Cretan roots to reconnect with his muse. However, **Quinn** dominates as the Greek peasant teaching him how to enjoy life by indulging his desires and dancing on the beach (ironically, Quinn's iconic shuffling step to **Mikis Theodorakis**'s theme was occasioned by a broken foot). Yet the picture's biggest beneficiary was **Lila Kedrova**, who followed her Oscar win with a Tony for the 1968 Broadway version.

CUT

Movies can be cut to placate high-minded censors, as part of a deal between directors and anxious studios, or simply so they can be re-released as "the director's cut".

The Draughtsman's Contract 1982

Director Peter Greenaway **Cast** Anthony Higgins, Janet Suzman 103m

Alan Parker once described this as "a load of posturing poo-poo", so who knows what he'd have made of **Greenaway**'s original four-hour cut, which he aimed to release (with added outtakes) as *The Hedgecutters*. The version released thankfully omitted a scene where one of the characters in this seventeenth-century comedy/drama apparently uses a cellphone. The contract of the title, between a draughtsman (who is hired to draw an estate) and the mistress of that estate, is less straightforward and much darker than it appears. In this instance, the director's cut is, alas, likely to be awaited with bated breath only by Greenaway and his pals.

Greed 1925

Director Erich von Stroheim **Cast** Gibson Gowland, Zasu Pitts 140m

You might find this lengthy classic hard going. But not as hard as **von Stroheim**

did. In his quest for realism in this tale of an innocent dentist driven to double murder, he filmed the final Death Valley scene in Death Valley itself. The crew mutinied, von Stroheim slept with a pistol under his pillow and during one scene, where the actors weren't fighting with enough venom, he shouted: "Fight! Try to hate each other as much as you hate me!" Was the movie worth it? Yes, if for no other reason than the last scene, where the hero frees his pet canary in the desert: it then flutters a little and dies.

The Idiot 1951

Director Akira Kurosawa **Cast** Minoru Chiaki, Chieko Higashiyama, Toshirô Mifune 165m

Akira Kurosawa transplants **Dostoevky**'s *The Idiot* to Japan, in what was supposed to be a two-part movie running a grand 265 minutes, but was cut for release. The story (about a prince and his friend in love with the same woman) isn't that easy to follow but then nobody reads the Russian novelist for his plots either. The movie's rather stately progress is interrupted by sudden flashes of brilliance and is preferable to the faithful 1960 Russian version.

Lost Horizon 1937

Director Frank Capra **Cast** Ronald Colman, Jane Wyatt, Edward Everett Horton 132m

Despite advertising Columbia's $2.5 million adaptation of **James Hilton**'s *Shangri-la* novel as "The Mightiest of All Motion Pictures", famously philistinic studio chief **Harry Cohn** insisted that **Frank Capra**'s three-and-a-half-hour version was slashed after a disastrous preview in Santa Barbara. He also forced Capra to shoot two alternative endings. Despite winning two Oscars from seven nominations, the film flopped, as a world teetering on the brink of war was in no mood for an allegorical pacifist tract. Over time, the original negative deteriorated and the American Film Institute's 1970s restoration was cobbled together using blown-up 16mm inserts and production stills.

Whisked away from a rebellion in China, British escapees find a peaceful refuge in Tibetan Shangri-la in Capra's slashed *Lost Horizon*.

 The Magnificent Ambersons 1942

Director Orson Welles **Cast** Joseph Cotton, Dolores Costello 88m

This was the movie of which **Orson Welles** said: "The studio are cutting my movie with a lawnmower." Not satisfied with slashing fifty minutes, RKO also tacked on a happy ending. This saga is cited as the definitive triumph of Hollywood's crass commercialism over artistic integrity and genius, but the truth isn't that simple. Welles's biographer, David Thomson, suggests he chose to chase carnival girls in Rio rather than come back and fight for his film. That said, the 88-minute studio version is enough to show that this could have been Welles's best movie after *Citizen Kane*, with an even greater emotional depth, possibly because the story of a child who destroys his family struck a guilty chord. For Welles, it was the start of death by a thousand cuts.

DANCE

Break out the legwarmers and leap into a crazy world where everyone's gonna live forever and nobody puts Baby in a corner (or in this selection).

Breakin'2: Electric Boogaloo 1984

Director Sam Firstenberg **Cast** Lucinda Dickey, Adolfo Quinones, Michael Chambers 94m

Reuniting the cast of 1984 hit *Breakin'*, including a young, skinny **Ice-T**, this sees our plucky group of young breakdancers attempt to stop a mean ol' developer from bulldozing their community centre. A cult flick less for its dance than for the fact that the phrase "Electric Boogaloo" has, in the words of Wikipedia, become synonymous with "a sequel that is ridiculous, disappointing, unwanted, unnecessary, formulaic, or simply obscure".

A Chorus Line 1985

Director Richard Attenborough **Cast** Michael Douglas, Terrence Mann, Alyson Reed 113m

The backstage musical came of age with this bitter picture of the humiliations and stresses of desperate-to-please dancers. **Douglas** is the voice in the dark, hectoring dancers auditioning for his Broadway show and prompting confessional monologues about their hopes and fears. Its

departures from the long-running stage hit didn't find favour and many find it stodgy, but it has intelligence, some wicked one-liners and virtuoso dancing.

Fame 1980

Director Alan Parker **Cast** Maureen Teefy, Irene Cara, Barry Miller 134m

Still fresh, raw and edgily dark, this is your classic blood, sweat and tears story of a mixed bunch of young wannabes chasing their dreams of fame through four years at a New York stage school. (This was an era when you needed talent to be a celebrity.) It's fulfilled its Oscar-winning "I'm gonna live forever!" anthem by spawning a long-running TV series, a hit stage show, a reality TV contest and an utterly pointless 2009 remake.

Flashdance 1983

Director Adrian Lyne **Cast** Jennifer Beals, Michael Nouri, Lilia Skala 95m

"It's corny, but it's kind of true, you know?" is how Brit director **Lyne** describes this shamelessly sensational movie that flaunts almost as much sentiment as nubile flesh.

Jennifer Beals stars as Alex, vulnerable eighteen-year-old welder by day, and stripper by night, who dreams of being a "proper" dancer. The script's surprisingly sweet but it's the electrifying, notoriously body-doubled dance numbers we remember. Look closely at the "What a Feeling!" finale: one Jennifer even has a moustache.

> ❝ When you give up your dream you die. ❞
>
> **Nick, Flashdance**

Ginger and Fred 1986

Director Federico Fellini **Cast** Giulietta Masina, Marcello Mastroianni 125m

Two aged entertainers who'd made a modest career imitating Fred Astaire and Ginger Rogers are anxiously reunited after decades of estrangement for a vulgar variety show. The crassness of Italian TV is a gift for **Fellini**'s satirical gaze, but the presence and delightful footwork of Italian cinema legends **Masina** (Fellini's wife) and **Mastroianni** bring a magical if offbeat romantic element.

Mad Hot Ballroom 2005

Director Marilyn Agrelo 105m

Spellbound meets *Strictly Come Dancing* in this heartwarming documentary about a ballroom dance programme introduced in New York's inner city schools. The kids are aged around eleven and the camera beautifully captures their unselfconscious commentary on life lived within a cultural melting pot. This being a dance flick it all culminates in a big contest, but for once the outcome is far from guaranteed. A real breath of fresh air.

★ The Red Shoes 1948

Directors Michael Powell, Emeric Pressburger **Cast** Moira Shearer, Anton Walbrook 133m

Victoria Page (**Shearer**) is a talented young dancer torn between her brilliant but controlling dance master (**Walbrook**) and her penniless composer lover (**Marius Goring**) in this loose adaptation of a Hans Christian Andersen tale. With fabulous dancing from a huge corps de ballet, Oscar-winning art direction (**Hein Heckroth** made over six hundred sketches for the central ballet sequence alone) and gorgeous Technicolor photography from **Jack Cardiff**, it's a British film classic.

Singin' in the Rain 1952

Directors Stanley Donen, Gene Kelly **Cast** Gene Kelly, Debbie Reynolds 103m

Where to begin? Well how about posing the question, what is it that puts *Singin' in the Rain* repeatedly in people's top ten movie lists? **Kelly**'s funny and innovative story about the fates of two silent screen stars during the transition to talkies seems to strike a chord with almost everyone who sees it. It helps that the supporting cast is so strong: **Donald O'Connor**'s "Make 'Em Laugh" is one of the greatest numbers in musical history, and the inspired **Jean Hagan** as Lina Lamont, the actress whose voice is like salt in a wound, gained a cult following. Whatever it is – the

Gene Kelly's wannabe hoofer is lured off the path to stardom by temptress Cyd Charisse in *Singin' in the Rain*'s dream ballet sequence.

music, the dancing, the romance – that makes *Singin' in the Rain* such a joy, we should just be thankful.

Staying Alive 1983

Director Sylvester Stallone Cast John Travolta, Cynthia Rhodes 93m

Set six years on from *Saturday Night Fever*, this sees self-taught, white trash dancer Tony Manero (**Travolta**) transplanted from Brooklyn to Broadway, where he's trying to make it into a show. Writer, producer, director and Travolta's personal trainer, **Stallone** unsurprisingly fixates on the more athletic aspects of dance, particularly the bouffant-haired star's sweaty muscles, to the point that this starts to resemble *Rambo* in tights.

Strictly Ballroom 1992

Director Baz Luhrmann Cast Paul Mercurio, Tara Morice, Bill Hunter 94m

Baz Luhrmann's debut movie and first in his "Red Curtain Trilogy" is a gloriously camp Aussie rom-com that sees a maverick young dancer attempt to introduce "new steps" to the ossified world of ballroom dancing. But will they be too radical to win him the Australian Pan Pacific Championships? A lovingly tongue-in-cheek take on the dance flick that nonetheless respects all the "just follow the rhythm of your heart" clichés.

DECADENCE

In an industry famed across the world for excess, a few filmmakers have felt the need to redefine decadence.

Affairs of Anatol 1921

Director Cecil B. De Mille **Cast** Wallace Reid, Gloria Swanson 117m

Even by the standards of the licentious 1920s, **De Mille**'s star-studded drama, adapted from Arthur Schnitzler's play, was a tad risqué. Anatol (**Reid**) is a stuffy, self-righteous soul who, despite being married to the gorgeous **Swanson**, can't stop trying to save troubled women. His affairs are the least interesting feature of a movie in which De Mille shows women smoking, drinking, showing off their bodies and chasing men.

The Damned 1969

Director Luchino Visconti **Cast** Dirk Bogarde, Ingrid Thulin, Helmut Griem 164m

Visconti's twisted masterpiece kicks off his trilogy on German decadence, completed by *Death in Venice* (1971) and *Ludwig* (1972). Ostensibly exploring the relationship between German big business and the Nazis, Visconti gives us something more baroque and berserk in which **Helmut Berger**, as the wealthy heir in Marlene Dietrich drag, cavorts with the boys in the Bund. Compelling,

absurd and self-indulgent, it should be called *Mein Camp*.

Eyes Wide Shut 1999

Director Stanley Kubrick **Cast** Tom Cruise, Nicole Kidman, Sydney Pollack 159m

Ex-couple **Kidman** and **Cruise** are centre stage in a tale of a New York doctor who is tormented by jealous fantasies before fetching up at a mysterious high-society sex orgy. Yet there's something distinctly old world about **Kubrick**'s swansong and it's not just the script idea loosely adapted from a novella by Austrian playwright **Arthur Schnitzler**, but rather the typically cool styling and the meticulous framing of every image that refuses to cater to the audience hunger for brisk thrills that it incites. *La ronde*, Schnitzler's infamous sexual merry-go-round play, got the Max Ophüls treatment in 1950 and is a more direct evocation of that decadent Viennese spirit.

Night Games 1966

Director Mai Zetterling **Cast** Ingrid Thulin, Keve Hjelm, Jorgen Lindstrom 105m

In **Zetterling**'s Felliniesque maze, a man returns to the ancestral seat to confront – and defeat – the hang-ups crippling his life. We soon realize how formidable those hang-ups might be, as he confronts memories of a mother who indulged in orgies and incest and an insane grandmother who effectively raised him. His liberation is only achieved after almost every sexual taboo has been paraded onscreen.

Salò 1975

Director Pier Paolo Pasolini **Cast** Paolo Bonicelli, Giorgio Cataldi, Umberto Paolo 117m

In the dying days of Mussolini's Fascist regime (aka the republic of Salò), four libertines kidnap, torture and execute eighteen boys in a progress through Pasolini's own version of Dante's infernal circles. (The director's circles being the rather unpoetic obsessions of shit and blood.) The debate over this controversial movie was deflected by Pasolini's brutal murder by a young male prostitute soon after its release.

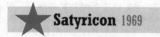 **Satyricon** 1969

Director Federico Fellini **Cast** Martin Potter, Hiram Keller, Max Born, Salvo Randone 129m

Drawing on degenerate versions of Greek and Roman myth, **Fellini** celebrates and mocks the decadence of the 1960s in a reckless gallery of amorality, cruelty and debauchery, which the director, with characteristic wit, hailed as "science fiction of the past". *Satyricon* features almost as many human gro-

tesques as the rest of his films combined, but they seem utterly at home in a film where a young woman must kindle fires from her genitalia to warm a village.

Young Törless 1966

Director Volker Schlöndorff **Cast** Mathieu Carrière, Marian Seidowsky, Bernd Tischer 87m

Schlöndorff stays true to the puzzle at the heart of **Robert Musil**'s novel: the detachment with which young Törless (**Carrière**) regards the sadistic tortures that punctuate life at an Austrian military academy at the turn of the twentieth century. Lynchings, prostitutes and blackmail intrigue him less than the mathematical idea of imaginary numbers. His laugh, as his mother drives him away from the academy for good, is especially chilling, a laugh that, for some, prefigures the horrors to be inspired by the imagination of an Austrian corporal.

THE DEVIL

Whether you call him Beelzebub, Lucifer or Satan, there's no baddie quite as bad – or as charming – as the devil. And if the Prince of Darkness doesn't appear himself, there are always curses, possessions and occult gatherings.

Angel Heart 1987

Director Alan Parker **Cast** Mickey Rourke, Robert De Niro, Lisa Bonet 113m

Some movies come pre-packaged as cult and this is one of them. First, there are the character names (**Rourke** is private eye Harry Angel, hired to find a man called Johnny Favourite, and **De Niro** is devilish Louis Cyphre), then there's the gore and generous helpings of occultism. And it works, partly because Rourke has seldom looked so rancid and Cosby Show kid **Bonet** seldom more beautiful. **Charlotte Rampling** is intriguing as a voodoo debutante and De Niro overacts as Satan. Doesn't everybody?

Bedazzled 1967

Director Stanley Donen **Cast** Peter Cook, Dudley Moore, Eleanor Bron 103m

While Liz Hurley was curvaceously tempting in the 2000 remake, there is something delightfully un-Hollywood about **Peter Cook**'s portrayal of the devil as a seedy nightclub owner called George Spiggott. A patchy, Swinging Sixties retelling of the Faust myth, this co-stars Cook's long-suffering comedy partner **Dudley Moore** as a Wimpy Bar cook who fails to commit suicide, then sells his soul to the devil for seven wishes and a raspberry ice lolly.

The Devil and Daniel Webster 1941

Director William Dieterle **Cast** Edward Arnold, Walter Huston, James Craig 112m

Based on a short story by **Stephen Vincent Benet** about famed statesman and orator Daniel Webster, this movie adaptation was lucky to reach the screen. Thomas Mitchell was originally cast as Webster but fractured his skull during filming, forcing delays and reshoots using **Arnold**. There was also a title issue: not everyone was happy with referring to the devil, and the name was changed to *All That Money Can Buy* in some US states. **Craig** plays a troubled farmer who agrees to sell his soul to the devil for seven years of prosperity. Only towards the end of the seven years, when he is all alone through his greed, does he realize his mistake and persuade Webster to take on the devil to win his soul back.

The Devil Rides Out 1968

Director Terence Fisher **Cast** Christopher Lee, Charles Gray, Nike Arrighi **95m**

Christopher Lee finally got to play the good guy in this top-drawer Hammer Horror adaptation of his old chum, **Dennis Wheatley**'s occultist thriller. He's a toff hero, the Duc de Richeleau, determined to save his friend Simon from falling in with a gang of socialite Satan worshippers. First floated in 1963, it was only greenlit four years later once censorship worries over Satanism had died down. Dated demonic effects range from silly to surprisingly sinister, or both, in the case of the notorious climactic scene where the devil himself appears in the form of a randy goat.

The Devil's Advocate 1997

Director Taylor Hackford **Cast** Keanu Reeves, Al Pacino, Charlize Theron **144m**

Eye-popping, teeth-flashing, sinister-laughing Al Pacino is a lawyer called John Milton who, you guessed it, proves to be the devil. Reeves's monochrome acting is handily thus the ideal balance, playing the greedy young attorney ready to sell his soul for career advancement. Bit like *The Firm* with more special effects.

The Nun and the Devil 1975

Director Peter Sasdy **Cast** Joan Collins, Eileen Atkins, Donald Pleasence **95m**

Also known as *The Monster*, *I Don't Want to Be Born*, *Sharon's Baby* and *The Devil Within Her*, any way you label it,

this hootsome horror is hellishly bad. **Joan Collins** gives birth to a huge evil baby. Her sister-in-law, a bewilderingly accented Italian nun, is convinced he's possessed by the devil. Her doctor thinks it's all just post-natal blues. Whilst Joanie suspects a curse cast by a cackling hunchbacked dwarf (1975 was not a PC era) she used to do a striptease act with. The one genuinely terrifying element is Joan's orange flared culottes.

The Omen 1976

Director Richard Donner **Cast** Gregory Peck, Lee Remick, David Warner, Billie Whitelaw **111m**

American ambassador **Peck** has a lovely wife (**Remick**) and a baby son Damien who just happens to be the Anti-Christ – it's tough, but them's the breaks. Various people have to be dispatched in various grisly ways before Peck realizes his son isn't a cutie, including a nanny who goes flying off a roof, proclaiming her love for the devil in diapers, and **David Warner**'s photographer, who is memorably decapitated by a plate of glass falling off a truck. Packed with truly creepy moments – including the family visit to Windsor Safari Park, when the car is attacked by baboons.

The Private Lives of Adam and Eve 1960

Directors Mickey Rooney, Albert Zugsmith **Cast** Mickey Rooney, Mamie Van Doren **86m**

How can you resist a movie in which **Mickey Rooney** plays a devil in a snakeskin suit and gives the kind of performance which defines that much underrated genre of acting known as "scenery chewing"? A bunch of travellers en route to Reno take refuge in a church, where two of them dream they are Adam and Eve. Tiresomely overloaded with "nudge wink" humour, it boasts the occasional comic gem.

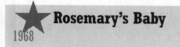

Rosemary's Baby

1968

Director Roman Polanski **Cast** Mia Farrow, John Cassavetes, Ruth Gordon **136m**

Newly wed, newly pregnant Rosemary (**Farrow**) falls under the stifling atten-

tions of a neighbourhood coven. In the movie, Rosemary says "Pain, begone." In real life, it wasn't that simple. In 1969 **Polanski**'s pregnant wife, Sharon Tate, would be murdered by Charles Manson. Farrow was handed divorce papers on-set from husband Frank Sinatra. Polanski's pal **Krysztof Komeda**, who wrote the music, slipped into a coma months before the movie's release. Producer **William Castle** received bags of hate letters. One said simply "Die! Die! Die!". Days later, Castle had surgery for acute uremic poisoning. Coming round from the anaesthetic he shouted: "Rosemary, for God's sake, drop the knife."

Cursed films

Hollywood Babylon's Kenneth Anger thought that movies released demons which affect cast and crew. Sounds stupid...

The Crow (1994)
Brandon (son of Bruce) Lee had a premonition he would die on the set of a movie. He was shot with a gun supposedly loaded with blanks, but the tip of a dummy bullet came loose and killed him.

Gone With the Wind (1939)
One of the highest box-office earners of all time – but at what cost? Three of the cast (Belle Watling, Paul Hurst and George Reeves) killed themselves, while the husband of Evelyn Keyes (Scarlett's sister) shot himself soon after the movie was released and the author Margaret Mitchell died in a car crash in 1949.

Rebel Without a Cause (1955)
James Dean died in a car crash a month before this was released (soon after appearing in a road safety ad urging the public: "Drive safely, because the next life you take may be mine"). Of his co-stars, Sal Mineo was stabbed to death by a stranger in 1976 and Natalie Wood drowned in 1981 whilst sailing with her husband Robert Wagner and Christopher Walken.

DISASTER

Volcanoes, earthquakes, floods, plane crashes, biblical plagues, nuclear wipeouts, meteor landings, towering infernos... and something worse can happen in the sequel. No, wait, that something worse *is* the sequel.

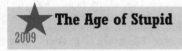 The Age of Stupid

2009

Director Franny Armstrong **Cast** Pete Postlethwaite 92m

A fascinating melange of fiction, documentary and animation, structured around the concept of an archivist in the year 2055 looking back at news footage and reportage that shows how the human race failed to heed the signs of impending disaster through global warming and ended up destroying itself. Recent years have seen no shortage of films dealing with environmental meltdown, but this is one of the most successful, largely down to its ability to engage and provoke, as well as educate.

Airport '77 1977

Director Jerry Jameson **Cast** Jack Lemmon, Lee Grant, Joseph Cotten 114m

The best of the series of four *Airport* films that kicked off the disaster genre in 1970, this one offers a triple whammy – a hijacking, a smash with an oil rig and a crash landing in the Bermuda Triangle. Also stars the ubiquitous **George Kennedy**, who appears in all the *Airport* films, as well as *Earthquake* and *Sonic Boom*, a little-known disaster spoof short in which he co-stars with Ricky Nelson and Keith Moon.

Alive 1993

Director Frank Marshall **Cast** Ethan Hawke, Vincent Spano 127m

The true story of a Uruguayan rugby team who, after a plane crash in the Andes, resort to cannibalism to survive. They endure three months of the most appalling conditions amidst beautifully photographed scenery, with only their faith and their teammates' corpses to sustain them. The story is narrated by an uncredited **John Malkovich**. Much earlier, in 1976, the same subject was covered by the Mexican film *Survive*.

Earthquake 1974

Director Mark Robson **Cast** Charlton Heston, Ava Gardner 123m

Like all good disaster movies, *Earthquake* begins with a rundown of the characters so you can predict who'll go first. There are the usual wives, widows and mistresses, a hot-tempered cop and a psychotic shop owner. This won the Oscar for best sound as the first Universal film presented in Sensurround, four special, low-frequency bass speakers powerful enough to crack plaster at some cinemas. Look out for **Walter Matthau** as a drunk, and some model cows that stay upright when their truck is upturned.

Nippon Chinbotsu 1973

Directors Andrew Meyer, Shirô Moritani **Cast** Hiroshi Fujioka, Lorne Greene 143m

It's all hands to the rescue of a Japan undergoing destruction by natural forces. Volcanoes, hurricanes and earthquakes send the citizens running for shelter before the ultimate tsunami threatens to sink the country. The movie was released in two versions: this uncut and subtitled original, and the cut and dubbed American version, featuring less of the action and more of Lorne Greene, variously titled *Submersion of Japan*, *Japan Sinks* or *Tidal Wave*.

The Poseidon Adventure
1972

Director Ronald Neame **Cast** Gene Hackman, Ernest Borgnine, Red Buttons 117m

In this titanic disaster movie, a vast tidal wave throws New Year's Eve partygoers

Shelley Winters, Red Buttons and Ernest Borgnine among an array of disaster film archetypes, mostly destined for a watery grave in *The Poseidon Adventure*.

aboard a luxury liner into chaos. As the ship capsizes and sinks, cop **Borgnine** and priest **Hackman** compete for leadership of the survivors and for overacting honours. Hackman has by far the juiciest part: he gets to tell **Stella Stevens** to take her top off and **Pamela Sue Martin** to get rid of her skirt. The ship's décor was left over from the set of *Cleopatra*, nine years earlier. You can happily skip the sequel, *Beyond the Poseidon Adventure.*

The Quiet Earth 1985

Director Geoff Murphy Cast Bruno Lawrence, Alison Routledge 91m

"Zac Hobson, July 5th. One – there has been a malfunction in Project Flashlight. Two – it seems I am the last man left on Earth…" Scientist Zac (**Lawrence**) believes he's the sole survivor of the apocalypse in this end-of-the-world saga. This New Zealand production tackles the question every kid has: once we've ransacked the toy shop and stuffed ourselves silly with ice cream, what would we really do if we were alone in the world? More thoughtful than a straight disaster flick, you'll either love or hate the ending.

The Road 2009

Director John Hillcoat Cast Viggo Mortensen, Kodi Smit-McPhee 111m

Hillcoat's adaptation of **Cormac McCarthy**'s Pulitzer Prize-winning novel offers a terrifying glimpse into a possible future. An unnamed man (**Mortensen**) and his son (**Smit-McPhee**) travel through a post-apocalyptic landscape,

ravaged by an unspecified catastrophe. The road is littered with corpses and patrolled by marauding gangs who feast on the flesh of the living to survive. Eschewing CGI in favour of locations that have suffered real environmental and economic disaster, the film retains the realism and sobering relevance of its source material, if not perhaps its intimacy.

San Francisco 1936

Director W.S. Van Dyke Cast Clark Gable, Jeanette MacDonald, Spencer Tracy 115m

This love story is set just before the big San Francisco earthquake, which comes as divine retribution. **Gable** is gambling drinker Blackie, who hires **MacDonald** as a singer in his Paradise Club. Rumour has it Gable wasn't keen on playing second fiddle to MacDonald and only agreed to star after rewrites gave him more scenes. He turned up for love scenes stinking of garlic, so MacDonald's swooning after their first kiss isn't an act.

When Time Ran Out 1980

Director James Goldstone Cast Paul Newman, Jacqueline Bisset, William Holden 121m

There are disaster movies and there are disastrous movies, and this is the latter. A desperate bid to cash in on a formula past its sell-by date, by a director who would later helm a TV movie about Charles and Diana. **Newman** and **Holden** had the excuse that they were contractually obliged to appear in one more Irwin Allen-produced movie. The talented cast look lost, ashamed and fearful for their careers.

DOCTORS

On celluloid, doctors can be the knight in the shining surgical smock (Ronald Colman in the 1931 movie *Arrowsmith*), powerless but decent (*Awakenings*) or the butt of countless "ooh matron!" comedies. When doctors go bad, they go very bad.

Awakenings 1990

Director Penny Marshall **Cast** Robert De Niro, Robin Williams 121m

This is a rare cinematic beast: an underrated **De Niro** movie. Based on the experiences of **Dr Oliver Sacks**, author of *The Man Who Mistook His Wife for a Hat*, it's a poignant drama about a doctor (**Williams**) who brings patients out of their comas but has (spoiler alert) to watch as they slip back into a living death. Williams underplays brilliantly and De Niro is superb, his time spent watching Sacks's patients put to moving effect.

Britannia Hospital 1982

Director Lindsay Anderson **Cast** Leonard Rossiter, Graham Crowden, Joan Plowright 116m

A royal visit to open a hospital wing coincides with a reporter arriving to shoot a documentary, a protest against the hospital's decision to treat an African dictator, and industrial unrest. Anderson's hospital-as-society metaphor isn't subtle, and although the fine cast includes almost every British actor of note (and **Mark Hamill**), they can't prevent the dialogue sounding like rhetoric at times.

Dirty Pretty Things 2002

Director Stephen Frears **Cast** Audrey Tautou, Chiwetel Ejiofor, Sergi López 97m

An absorbing, romantic *noir* penned by **Steven Knight**, creator of *Who Wants to Be a Millionaire?* Okwe (**Ejiofor**), a Nigerian doctor working in England as a hotel porter and minicab driver discovers a human heart in a blocked toilet. He and fellow immigrant Senay (**Tautou**), who left Turkey to escape an arranged marriage, uncover sinister criminal activities within the hotel. The movie is both a thriller and a touching examination of the good in people despite their circumstances. Few directors are as good as **Frears** at empathizing with their characters, but Ejiofor makes his job easy, creating a subtle, dignified hero.

⭐ The Kingdom 1994

Director Lars Von Trier **Cast** Udo Kier, Ernst-Hugo Järegård, Kirsten Rolffes 280m

Few realize that just before he made *Breaking the Waves*, maverick Danish arthouse director **Lars Von Trier** created this hilarious, eerily supernatural eight-episode TV hospital series, edited into a lengthy movie for UK/US distribution. Voodoo hexes, ghost children and eugenic experimentation are just a few of the extremely peculiar goings-on in this hospital, run by a Masonic board of surgeons who dress as stags. **Stephen King** adapted it for US television, but sterilized out its uniquely surreal appeal. Think a Danish *Twin Peaks* with surgical gowns and subtitles.

M*A*S*H 1970

Director Robert Altman **Cast** Donald Sutherland, Elliott Gould, Sally Kellerman 116m

The third biggest box-office success of 1970 (after *Love Story* and *Airport*), *M*A*S*H* is often seen as an anti-war comedy, but it's really anti-authority. Although the antics of rebel surgeons Hawkeye (**Alan Alda**) and Trapper John (**Wayne Rogers**) are set in Korea, audiences often see this as an attack on what was going on in Vietnam. You didn't have to hate the war to enjoy this movie, you just had to sympathize with the guys in their struggle to have fun, often at the expense of Major Frank Burns (**Robert Duvall**) and Hotlips (**Kellerman**). The film wouldn't have been nearly as effective without Altman's dialogue. Not that the actors recognized this at the time: Sutherland and Gould both rebelled on set, telling the studio that Altman, the eighteenth choice to direct the movie, would ruin their careers. Gould later apologized.

The Men 1950

Director Fred Zinnemann **Cast** Marlon Brando, Teresa Wright, Everett Sloane 85m

Marlon Brando's promising debut also marks the first time **DeForest Kelley** (Dr McCoy in *Star Trek*) played a doctor. To Brando's disappointment, the movie, about paralysed war veterans, was given a more hopeful ending than planned. Released the year the Korean war started, and as the McCarthy witch-hunt (which would force writer **Carl Foreman** into exile after he worked with **Zinnemann** on *High Noon*) gathered momentum, this movie still goes beyond the usual cardboard celluloid heroics.

Seducing Doctor Lewis 2003

Director Jean-François Pouliot **Cast** Raymond Bouchard, David Boutin, Benoît Briére 109m

This movie took Québec, where it was made, by storm, grossing more in 2003 than *The Lord of the Rings*. Set in the village of St Marie-le-Mauderne, where all 150 of the population live on welfare since the fishing industry collapsed. When a plastics company decides to move in, they must find a doctor willing to live in the village. Enter Dr Lewis (Boutin). The locals then do all they can to make St Marie his perfect place.

DOCUMEN-TARIES

Documentaries can tell stories that are so outrageous an audience would never accept them as fiction: characters so grotesque even Fellini would spurn them, endings so sweet Meg Ryan would sneer, and conspiracies so tortuous that Oliver Stone would believe them instantly.

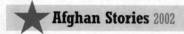 Afghan Stories 2002

Director Taran Davies 60m

Following 9/11, **Davies** and Afghan American **Walied Osman** travelled around Afghanistan interviewing everyone from a local warlord to a foreign aid worker, not to judge, but to find answers. They paint a brilliant portrait of the diverse people who make up this complex, war-torn country and avoid bias or sentimentality. A revelation for those who would dismiss Afghanistan as little more than a cradle for terrorists.

Biggie and Tupac 2002

Director Nick Broomfield 108m

One of **Broomfield**'s wandering epics (having already tackled Kurt Cobain and Courtney Love in *Kurt & Courtney*) following a lead about the possible involvement of the LAPD in the murders of **Biggie Smalls** and **Tupac Shakur**. Their deaths have been officially blamed on the East Coast/West Coast hip-hop rivalry of the late 1990s, and much aggressive posturing (particularly at a 1995 awards show, where threats and challenges are caught on film) seems to back that up. However, an ex-LA policeman has a different take on the case. Broomfield provides excellent interviews, especially with **Suge Knight**, the imprisoned head of Death Row Records, and old footage of Biggie and Tupac in better times is very touching.

Bowling for Columbine 2002

Director Michael Moore 120m

The Columbine High School massacre was a catalyst for this examination of America's relationship with violence. **Moore**'s previous work, *Roger and Me*, looked at the de facto destruction of Flint, Michigan, when Ford closed the car factory there, and this uses similar tactics, doorstepping NRA president **Charlton Heston** and picketing bullet-selling K-Mart. Although some of Moore's own prejudices come through, this is a brilliant documentary, full of black humour.

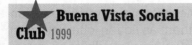

★ Buena Vista Social Club 1999

Director Wim Wenders 101m

Cuba was once the playground of the rich and famous, and had clubs full of musicians playing the best Latin jazz. With Castro in power, the music was still there, but very few outside Cuba had heard it. **Wenders**' movie follows **Ry Cooder** to Cuba as he meets the cream of Cuba's music scene. Every interviewee has an amazing story. The musicians – old men who make stunning music – simply capture your heart.

Crumb 1994

Director Terry Zwigoff 120m

Think your family is dysfunctional? Well, you have nothing on the Crumbs. **Robert Crumb**, creator of *Fritz the Cat,* is a legend among fans of underground comics. **Zwigoff** gets some astoundingly intimate interviews with Crumb, his mother, wife and brothers. Like Crumb's work, the documentary is politically incorrect, hilarious and disturbing; as he says: "Perhaps they should just take away my pencils and lock me away."

Don't Look Back 1967

Director D. A. Pennebaker 96m

A landmark documentary that evolved from the first generation of *cinéma vérité* directors. Filmed using a hand-held camera and distinguished by an absence of voiceover and the replacement of montage with extended takes to offer an approximation of real time, **Pennebaker**'s film accompanies a young **Bob Dylan** on his 1965 tour of Britain. Beginning with Dylan performing "Subterranean Homesick Blues" with the aid of outsized cue cards and culminating in a tumultuous concert at London's Royal Albert Hall, this captures the musician and his entourage as he undergoes the uneasy transition from folk singer to rock star.

Gallivant 1996

Director Andrew Kötting 100m

In **Kötting**'s best-known work, the artist-filmmaker embarks on a coastal trip around Britain with his octogenarian grandmother and his young daughter **Eden**, who suffers from Joubert's Syndrome. This freeform journey, which involves various encounters with the flotsam and jetsam of the British public, is at once larky and epic, and a quirky homage to national eccentricity and identity. It's also an emotional voyage around the ties that bind Kötting's family. *Gallivant* also serves as an entertaining document of Britain's changing coastline.

Garlic Is as Good as Ten Mothers 1980

Directors Les Blank, Maureen Gosling 54m

This is a gentle celebration of the many uses for garlic, including ice cream, but also a fun study of the people of Berkeley, California, in the late 1970s. **Werner Herzog** makes an appearance in the film: he bet **Blank** he would never finish the movie. After Blank made his feature, they made a short showing Herzog losing the bet, called *Werner Herzog Eats His Shoe.*

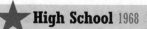 ## High School 1968

Director Frederick Wiseman 75m

A major influence on filmmakers such as Nick Broomfield, **Frederick Wiseman** is one of cinema's great observers. In *High School*, Wiseman freely roams through Philadelphia's Northeast High School, documenting a continual clash of teens with administrators who confuse learning with discipline. A potent chronicler of institutions and their failings, Wiseman returned to observe more progressive teaching methods at a high school in New York's Spanish Harlem in 1994's *High School II.*

Primate (1974, 105m)

❝ Frederick Wiseman's *Primate* is one of the great unacknowledged masterpieces of non-fiction filmmaking. It is also one of the strangest and most unsettling experiences I've had watching a movie. The film is an observational study of the Yerkes Primate Research Center in Atlanta, Georgia: Wiseman's detached, unforgiving camera scrutinizes all the primates within the institution, but it is the species in control whose behaviour seems the most alien and inexplicable.

Quite what is being achieved by the experiments conducted by the humans on the apes is never exactly clear – and that is no reflection on the abrasive clarity of Wiseman's images and editing. It is rather that the cruelties inflicted on these highly intelligent animals in the name of science are no more or less than that – the whims of the scientists with no other discernible point or instructive outcome.

The film contains images of the most visceral horror and sadness, not least a sequence involving the removal of a brain from a live monkey. Wiseman's film is an incomparable example of pure cinema and its surreal, pitiful images are amongst the most memorable I've ever seen, not least for the questions they raise. ❞

James Marsh
First garnering attention with his unnerving Wisconsin Death Trip, *documentary filmmaker James Marsh cemented his reputation as a highly original director with Oedipal drama* The King *(2005). His subsequent film,* Man on Wire *(2008), a heist-movie/documentary hybrid about French wire-walker Philippe Petit, won a BAFTA and an Academy Award.*

The Life and Times of Rosie the Riveter 1980

Director Connie Field 65m

The title is taken from the World War II propaganda character who urged women to do their best for the war effort. Interviews with five women across the USA, all of whom heeded Rosie's call and became metal workers, are intercut with war footage and hilarious propaganda films. There are some fascinating revelations from the women who were encouraged to become docile housewives again when the men returned to claim their jobs.

Nanook of the North 1922

Director Robert J. Flaherty 70m

Flaherty follows traditional Inuit **Nanook** hunting and trading... except it turns out many events were staged for the movie. Instead of being a simple soul, untouched by the outside world, as **Flaherty** depicted him, it later emerged Nanook even owned a snowmobile. Many of the techniques used (including faking the evidence) are still part of documentary filmmaking today.

Night Mail 1936

Directors Harry Watt, Basil Wright 25m

Short film of a **W.H. Auden** poem, set to footage of the night mail train between London and Edinburgh. The music is by Benjamin Britten, and the rhythm of the poem fits perfectly with the shots of the speeding train and post sorters on the night shift. A terrific evocation of how things used to be.

Olympia 1 1938

Director Leni Riefenstahl 121m

Leni Riefenstahl, a personal friend of **Hitler**, was commissioned by him to film the 1936 Berlin Olympics. It is an extraordinary (and long) piece of filmmaking, Riefenstahl's camera lingering over the bodies of the athletes, creating cinematic gods out of ordinary men. Not that this excuses some of the content, or the lack of footage of Jesse Owens, who won four gold medals that year.

Portrait of Jason 1967

Director Shirley Clarke 100m

Portrait of Jason is the engrossing final part in a 1960s triptych of films in which former experimental filmmaker **Clarke** challenged the ideologies and documentary practices of the American *cinéma vérité* movement. This 100-minute film evolved from a continuous, twelve-hour, single-take interview with **Jason Holiday** (real name Aaron Paine), a black, 33-year-old homosexual prostitute and would-be raconteur. Filmed on a single camera in real time, Jason's initially highly entertaining and colourful monologue is prompted by an offscreen Clarke who becomes increasingly antagonistic, finally reducing her subject to tears. Uncomfortable viewing.

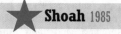

Shoah 1985

Director Claude Lanzmann 566m

"Shoah" is the Hebrew word for chaos or annihilation. This nine-hour epic chronicles the chaos and annihilation caused by the Holocaust, through interviews with perpetrators and witnesses, and the accounts of a few survivors, all trying to understand how such a thing could happen. There is no stock footage, no newsreels of the camps and none of the war itself. There are shots of the camps today, the Polish countryside and rolling meadows, under which thousands are buried. An incredibly moving and, at times, shattering experience.

Sisters in Law 2005

Directors Kim Longinotto and Florence Avisi 104m

An uplifting and enlightening documentary looking at justice in the village of Kumba Town, Cameroon, where prosecutor **Vera Ngassa** and court president **Beatrice Ntuba** together help women to speak out and fight back against assumptions of patriarchal privilege in modern-day Africa. A warm, witty and involving portrait of two remarkable characters and an example of grassroots action at its most effective, this is that rarest of things, a film that makes you believe things might actually get better rather than worse.

What would have been the end of the journey to the concentration camps in Poland, filmed in the 1980s for *Shoah*, an unflinching nine-hour chronicle of the Holocaust that uses no stock footage.

Sleep Furiously 2008

Director Gideon Koppel 97m

Returning to the adopted Welsh home of his refugee parents, **Koppel** films a people and place undergoing rapid change as the generation engaged in traditional, small-scale farming dies out. Resisting any traditional documentary structure, Koppel's camera very quietly observes as the population grows older, the local primary school faces closure, and the mobile library resists a move into the twenty-first century. A lyrical, arresting film enhanced by a soundtrack by Aphex Twin.

Spellbound 2002

Director Jeffrey Blitz 97m

You wouldn't think that a movie following **Neil**, whose father drills him in the spelling of six to seven thousand words a day, could be that gripping. Somehow, though, Neil and the various other National Spelling Bee finalists are fantastic documentary subjects. There are high achievers backed up by ludicrously competitive parenting, and there are high achievers who have no academic family background whatsoever, but together these children provide a lot of funny, touching and downright nailbiting moments.

To Be and to Have 2001

Director Nicolas Philibert 104m

In isolated communities throughout France, there still exist so-called "single class schools", bringing together children of all ages in one class around one teacher. Philibert's remarkably humane and affecting documentary features one such school, and the mutually dependent bond between teacher and pupils. Though seemingly stern and traditionalist, Monsieur Lopez cannot conceal his affection for the kids in his care. The film is filled with extraordinarily unselfconscious characters; sadly, its success spurred a number of lawsuits from its subjects.

The Moon and the Sledgehammer (1974, 105m)

"Seminal aphorisms and insightful anecdotes, a glue for their nonsensical living. A portrait of a fantastical family at odds with the world and then themselves. Scrap metalists, steam driven lumberjacking glorious self-sufficientists. If you go down to the woods today you'll hardly believe your eyes."

Andrew Kötting

Andrew Kötting's features encompass the ground-breaking road movie Gallivant, This Filthy Earth *and* Ivul. *Working across a diversity of media, Kötting's projects are characterized by his collaboration with other artists and by his exploration of family life.*

DRAMA

The ancient Greeks didn't rate a drama until incest had been committed, cast members had died and the tragic hero had ripped his own eyes out. The movies aren't quite that harrowing – unless you're watching a true-life TV movie – but high emotion and a nail-biting finish are the least you can expect.

Alfie 1966

Director Lewis Gilbert **Cast** Michael Caine, Shelley Winters, Julia Foster, Jane Asher 114m

Womanizing Alfie, who thinks getting tied down would be worse than death, realizes his happy-go-lucky life is not as rosy as it seems. **Millicent Martin**, **Alfie Bass** and the rest of the 1960s cast round out a story filled with humour and pathos. A shocking scene for the time features **Denholm Elliott** as a seedy abortionist. The movie was a radio play, stage play and novel before it reached the screen, and these roots are apparent in **Caine**'s direct addresses to the audience, explaining his actions and complaining about his lot.

> **"** I don't want no bird's respect – I wouldn't know what to do with it. **"**
>
> **Alfie in Alfie**

Australia 2008

Director Baz Luhrmann **Cast** Nicole Kidman, Hugh Jackman, Brandon Walters 165m

Critics insisted, drearily, that Australia's history "didn't really happen like that", but audiences loved it. **Luhrmann** and his team apply their usual big-hearted braggadocio to this love letter to not only his native land but also to classical Hollywood – Gone With the Wind and The Wizard of Oz are influences – in which the feisty Lady Sarah (**Kidman**, as always when teamed with Luhrmann, shines), who travels from England to northern Australia to sell her husband's ranch. **Jackman** is delightfully brusque as the hunky Drover, while **Walters** is a revelation as the Aboriginal boy who joins them on their narrative journey. Camp without being crass, romantic without being saccharine, smart without an agenda; critics sniffed that it was too ambitious, but Luhrmann, as ever, storms ahead fearlessly, creating something indefinable, resonant and brave.

★ Bicycle Thieves 1948

Director Vittorio De Sica **Cast** Lamberto Maggiorani, Enzo Staiola **96m**

David O. Selznick was such an admirer of **De Sica**'s work, he offered to fund this movie. All De Sica had to do was cast Cary Grant as the father whose bicycle is stolen and who spends the rest of the film, accompanied by his son, in search of this bike, without which he can't do his flyposting job. De Sica turned Selznick down. Just as well, because a few volts of star power would have destroyed the balance of a piece cast entirely with amateurs. **Maggiorani** and **Staiola** give performances of guileless simplicity as father and son. Their only cheer is when they feast on wine and bread. This is now slightly out of fashion, but watch it and be astounded by its freshness.

The Chant of Jimmie Blacksmith 1978

Director Fred Schepisi **Cast** Tommy Lewis, Freddy Reynolds **122m**

Fred Schepisi's brilliant transposition of **Thomas Keneally**'s novel follows the plight of mixed-race Aborigine Jimmie (**Lewis**), who, though educated, honest and hardworking, is constantly mistreated by his white bosses. Marrying a white girl in the mistaken belief that it will endear him to the white folk, Jimmie finds himself ostracized by both white and Aboriginal, and wages war on his oppressors. The extreme violence may seem overzealous, but it merely mirrors the horrific fate of Jimmie's ancestors. A serious indictment of racism, as relevant today as it was in 1978.

The Conformist 1970

Director Bernardo Bertolucci **Cast** Jean-Louis Trintignant, Stefania Sandrelli **108m**

Bertolucci's first American hit follows the lifelong quest of a member of the Italian Fascist party to lead a normal life. Upper-class Marcello (**Trintignant**) feels closed off from the rest of the world, reviling his dope-addict mother and insane father, and feeling his molestation by the family chauffeur has cut him apart from society. He agrees to become the faceless assassin of his old professor to gain full acceptance by the Fascists. An intriguing examination of one man's desperate need to belong.

★ Farewell My Concubine 1993

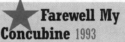

Director Kaige Chen **Cast** Leslie Cheung, Fengyi Zhang, Li Gong **156m**

Winner of the 1993 Palme d'Or at Cannes, this is an epic tale told on two levels. At its base is the friendship of two Peking Opera members who grow up together into stage stars. Dieyi (**Cheung**) is gay and in love with Xiaolou (**Zhang**), who loves and marries the prostitute Juxian (**Gong**). The story's backdrop is China's tumultuous twentieth-century history: World War II, the Communist takeover of China and the Cultural Revolution. Beautifully filmed and performed, this works as both an intimate examination of friendship and as an historical epic.

Fight Club 1999

Director David Fincher **Cast** Edward Norton, Brad Pitt, Helena Bonham Carter 139m

One of those movies where you think you know what's going on until the last reel, when you realize you were completely off the mark. Adapted from **Chuck Palahniuk**'s novel, the film has a different ending, which Palahniuk preferred to his own. **Norton** is a bored, repressed, white-collar salesman whose meeting with **Pitt** and **Carter** – and the blowing-up of his apartment – changes his life. From here on we're in fight-club territory: repressed males getting kicks from beating one another up. Stylishly directed, it's a mesmerizing ride through contemporary culture, fuelled by fantastic performances including a turn by Meat Loaf.

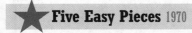 **Five Easy Pieces** 1970

Director Bob Rafelson **Cast** Jack Nicholson, Karen Black 98m

The second of six collaborations between maverick director **Rafelson** and the equally off-the-wall **Nicholson**. Playing a man on the run from himself, Nicholson is a labourer living with a Tammy Wynette-obsessed waitress (**Black**), an existence that's so mundane you know there has to be a secret. It's not until he jumps into the back of a truck during a traffic jam and starts playing the piano that we realize he's from a wealthy family of musicians, a background he's chosen to escape. When his dad has a stroke he revisits the family, the collision of two very different worlds. This was a landmark movie of

the 1970s, but it is the performances that make it a must-see.

Intolerance 1916

Director D.W. Griffith **Cast** Mae Marsh, Robert Harron, Lillian Gish 163m

Fresh off the back of *The Birth of a Nation*, which was scandalous in its sympathetic portrayal of the Ku Klux Klan, **Griffith** came back bigger and better with this monumental melodrama. The statistics, and the hubris, involved boggle the mind, but more to the point is its sheer emotional power – less so from its four interwoven stories of intolerance (in Babylon; towards Jesus Christ; in France in the 1500s; and in early twentieth-century America) than for its astonishing formal brilliance. The movie may have bankrupted Griffith – but its legacy to the art of filmmaking? Priceless.

Irreversible 2002

Director Gaspar Noé **Cast** Monica Bellucci, Vincent Cassel, Albert Dupontel 97m

Irreversible's notoriety as the most shocking movie of 2002 is far from exaggerated. Critic Roger Ebert branded it "so violent and cruel that most people will find it unwatchable." Many will turn off, but this is an intelligent movie, particularly in **Noé**'s decision to tell the story backwards. **Bellucci** and **Cassel** were married at the time and were perfectly at ease with one another, making what happens to them all the more disturbing. Bellucci is the movie's centrepiece, the actress enduring six takes of the rape scene; the only constraint Noé placed on the actors was that it didn't run over twenty minutes. Worth a look even if through half-closed eyes.

The Milagro Beanfield War 1988

Director Robert Redford **Cast** Ruben Blades, Sonia Braga, Chick Vennera 118m

Whimsical tale pitting the Hispanic farmers of Milagro, New Mexico, against each other, evil golf-playing land developers and their henchman (**Christopher Walken**). **Redford** lapses into soft-focus liberal fantasy, but there are some fine moments, including a stand-off between a truckload of octogenarians and a cop whose brains are all in his holster.

 **Petulia** 1968

Director Richard Lester **Cast** Julie Christie, George C. Scott 105m

John Haase's novel *Me and the Arch Kook Petulia* is the source for this modern American tragedy, virtually ignored when it was released but now seen as **Lester**'s finest work. Set in San Francisco in the mid-1960s, this tale of a recently divorced doctor's relationship with an unhappily married nut, Petulia (**Christie**), becomes an indictment of an entire society. On a television set in the background, the Vietnam war is continually blaring, a reminder of what American violence is doing to the world. The relationships between the characters are unusually be-

lievable, Christie giving a more effective performance than she ever did for her future beau, Warren Beatty.

The Servant 1963

Director Joseph Losey **Cast** Dirk Bogarde, James Fox, Sarah Miles 115m

In this **Harold Pinter** screenplay, **Fox** is a rich young gentleman who acquires a townhouse and a manservant, **Bogarde**. Fox's girlfriend warns him about Bogarde's character, but it's the experienced valet who assumes control, bringing in his own fiancée (pretending to be his sister) to seduce Fox to get rid of the girlfriend. A series of mind games and a battle of wills ensues, with Fox becoming enslaved to his own servant. Bogarde is suitably menacing, while Fox, in only his second movie, is perfect as the prissy upper-class toff.

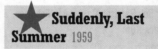 **Suddenly, Last Summer** 1959

Director Joseph L. Mankiewicz **Cast** Elizabeth Taylor, Katharine Hepburn, Montgomery Clift 114m

This is scary in a way many horror movies aren't because the sense of evil springs from the characters. A homosexual youth (**Clift**) uses his sister's beauty (**Taylor**) to lure boys to a beach but ends up devoured by them. **Hepburn**, a New Orleans *grande dame*, is chilling as the mother who wants Taylor to have a lobotomy to hide her son's shame. **Tennessee Williams**, who wrote the play, had objected to Taylor's casting but changed his mind after seeing her give the speech where her character's mind clears. After five takes, Taylor was sobbing in the dressing room and the director told the crew they would make a fresh start tomorrow. "Fresh start my ass", said Taylor, and proceeded to give the whole agonizing speech in one take.

The Sum of Us 1994

Directors Kevin Dowling, Geoff Burton **Cast** Russell Crowe, Jack Thompson 100m

While Hollywood was congratulating itself on the mainstream success of the gay-sympathetic *Philadelphia*, first-time directors **Dowling** and **Burton** had already gone several steps further in this realistic, non-sensationalist movie. Their big-screen adaptation of **David Stevens'** off-Broadway smash is a gay-themed father-and-son story that has the distinction of being accessible to both gay and straight audiences. **Crowe** is superb as the macho gay son looking for love, and **Thompson** is at his career best as ultra-liberal widowed dad Harry, whose open-minded attitude destroys both their budding romances and leads to tragedy.

The Tarnished Angels 1958

Director Douglas Sirk **Cast** Rock Hudson, Robert Stack, Dorothy Malone 91m

If you want to see a grown man cry, sit him down in front of *The Tarnished Angels*. Based on **William Faulkner's** relentlessly downbeat Depression novel *Pylon*

(1935), this male melodrama teams the director and cast from *Written on the Wind*, three years earlier, carrying with it the same hopeless intensity. **Sirk** brings his trademark psychological sophistication to what was widely criticized as a B-movie subject, about a bunch of lost souls working the airshow circuits.

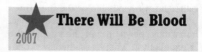

There Will Be Blood
2007

Director Paul Thomas Anderson **Cast** Daniel Day-Lewis, Paul Dano, Dillon Freasier 158m

The adjectives just got bigger and bigger in the reviews of this movie – it's as though the sheer hugeness of the film demanded it. **Day-Lewis's** performance as the monstrous oil prospector Plainview was unanimously agreed to be "barnstorming" – and watching him, it's hard to argue. The story, based loosely on **Upton Sinclair's** novel *Oil!*, may unravel until the gaps are big enough to walk through, but it matters not. As well as Day-Lewis, **Dano** is transfixing as the unsettling religious zealot, but it's also the hypnotic, frightening soundtrack that lingers like blood in the ears, and the harsh, visceral images that sear themselves into your brain like a branding iron.

Three Colours: Blue 1993

Director Krzysztof Kieslowski **Cast** Juliette Binoche, Benoît Régent 98m

In the first instalment of **Kieslowski's** contemporary trilogy based on the colours of the French flag (blue symbolizing liberty, white for equality and red for fraternity), **Binoche** plays a young woman whose husband and daughter die in a car crash at the start of the movie. The theme manifests itself in how Binoche chooses to rebuild her life: cutting ties with her previous existence, moving to the heart of Paris and living as an anonymous entity. Yet she cannot escape either her previous life or the memories of her composer husband, whose music constantly plays in her head. Binoche is excellent in what is essentially a one-woman vehicle – quiet yet emotionally charged. Together with the Red and White films (starring Julie Delpy and Irène Jacob), this is Kieslowski's finest work.

The Treasure of the Sierra Madre 1948

Director John Huston **Cast** Humphrey Bogart, Walter Huston, Tim Holt 126m

This was a box-office flop when first released – the public wanted to see the reluctant hero **Bogart** of *Casablanca*, not the repugnant, mumbling gold-prospector Fred C. Dobbs. Today, though, it's regarded as one of Bogie's finest performances, with sterling support from **Huston** as the old prospector who knows the damage that a lust for gold can do to a man, and **Holt** as the straightforward, if naïve, young thing. The mismatched group find gold and lose it, with Dobbs losing both his mind and his life in the process. The only letdown is the obviously studio-based location shots.

Walkabout 1971

Director Nicolas Roeg **Cast** Jenny Agutter, Lucien John, David Gumpilil 100m

Nicolas Roeg's masterpiece is still as jaw-dropping as it was in the 1970s. Part travelogue, part coming-of-age fable, it's also an examination of what happens when modern society collides with nature – played out through the tale of two schoolkids stranded in the Outback who meet an Aboriginal man-child on "walkabout". As brother and sister roam through the bush, their enigmatic guide leads them not only to "civilization" but also to self-realization, although **Agutter**'s plummy fourteen-year-old won't admit this. To help create an eerie, otherworldly feel, Roeg preferred clever cinematic techniques over dialogue, intercutting freeze-frames and zoom shots of beady-eyed lizards and slithering scorpions. The result is often terrifying as well as visually stunning.

A Woman Under the Influence 1974

Director John Cassavetes **Cast** Peter Falk, Gena Rowlands 155m

Between his stints as the popular detective Columbo, **Falk** made several notable movies with his friend **John Cassavetes** and this is their finest collaboration. Falk is a construction worker trying to cope with his mentally unstable wife (**Rowlands**) and three children, while ignoring his own bizarre behaviour. He comes to believe he must have Rowlands committed but the family, despite her previous unruly behaviour, are left bereft by her exit. It's moving stuff, even if Rowlands' performance is OTT at times. The US Library of Congress lists this as a national treasure: they're right.

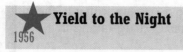

Yield to the Night

1956

Director J. Lee Thompson **Cast** Diana Dors, Yvonne Mitchell, Michael Craig **99m**

The movie that saw blonde bombshell **Dors**, a Rank starlet usually associated with bubblegum bawdiness, pared down, barefaced, and deadly serious. She's terrific, bringing a shadowy intensity to the role of prickly Mary Hilton, thought to be (though the production team denied it) based on Ruth Ellis, the last woman to be hanged in Britain. One of the best British ''social problem films'' from the era that excelled in them.

It Always Rains on Sunday (1974, 92m)

" I saw this film on TV when I was a kid and it stuck in my mind for years afterwards. This was long before DVDs and downloads so I had no way of finding it again, or discovering anything more about it. But a few years ago I ordered it online and was able to enjoy it all over again. It's a classic British *noir* movie, directed by Robert Hamer, which tells the story of a barmaid, Rosie Sandigate (Googie Withers), who is the second wife of an older man and is bringing up his two grown-up girls as well as their own young son. But into her life comes ex-boyfriend Tommy Swann (John McCallum), an escaped prisoner who she hides from the police and tries to help get away to another country. The tension of hiding him in the small house while the husband and the children go about their regular Sunday activities is heart-stopping. The final chase scene in the railway yard (even with some low-budget special effects) is up there with any Dashiell Hammett or Raymond Chandler climax.

It's also a wonderful portrait of London in the 1940s. Not only do we get the exciting central story but we see the post-war East End, teeming with brilliant characters including two Jewish brothers, one a philandering musician trying to carry on an affair with the eldest of Rosie's stepdaughters. The other brother is a shady "businessman", doling out favours and money to the desperate people around him. Shot brilliantly by Douglas Slocombe, it all takes place over one day, the rainy Sunday of the title. Brilliant. **"**

David Morrissey

With film credits including Drowning by Numbers, Hilary and Jackie, Is Anybody There? *and* Nowhere Boy, *David Morrissey is one of Britain's most acclaimed contemporary actors. Screened at the 2009 Times BFI London Film Festival, Morrissey's* Don't Worry About Me, *a tale of juvenile love in his native Liverpool, was his directorial debut feature.*

DRUGS

There's one sure way to make a movie go straight into the cult bag, and that's to put liberal amounts of drug-taking in it.

Drugstore Cowboy 1989

Director Gus Van Sant **Cast** Matt Dillon, Kelly Lynch, James LeGros, Heather Graham 101m

In the best performance of his career, **Dillon** plays a pharmacy-robbing dope fiend. **Van Sant** shows the junkie lifestyle the way it is – depressing and bleak with a few good times thrown in – and leaves the audience to make their own moral judgement. Based on the autobiographical novel by **James Fogle** who, at the time of the movie's release, had spent 35 of his 53 years in prison on drugs-related charges. **William Burroughs** has a role as a junkie former priest.

Fear and Loathing in Las Vegas 1997

Director Terry Gilliam **Cast** Johnny Depp, Benicio Del Toro 118m

Too weird to win over the masses, too rare to sink without trace, **Gilliam**'s *Fear and Loathing* is a healthily bizarre curio. Devotees of writer **Hunter S. Thompson's** account of his drug-fuelled voyage around Vegas with his Samoan attorney will love this, even though it can't quite capture the laugh-out-loud quality of the book. But if you don't like Thompson and prefer movies to have a plot, this won't impress you much.

Go 1999

Director Doug Liman **Cast** Sarah Polley, Katie Holmes, Scott Wolf, Jay Mohr 101m

A drugs deal told from three different points of view is the basis for this hectic, convoluted and (in parts) screamingly funny saga. A girl (**Polley**) reckons selling drugs might just solve her rent problems and with that is launched a chain of extraordinary events. The sequence of two gay soap stars helping the police after they have been caught with drugs is a blast, as is the scene where a very stoned and paranoid customer is convinced the drug dealer's cat is talking to him.

High Art 1998

Director Lisa Cholodenko **Cast** Ally Sheedy, Radha Mitchell 101m

Contrasting the New York art scene crowd – all cliques and cut-throat ambition – with the equally self-obsessed bohemian (read heroin-addicted) loft-living types, *High Art* drew rave notices for its inspired casting of 1980s teen legend **Ally Sheedy**. The film follows a magazine assistant editor (**Mitchell**), who unwittingly uncovers the whereabouts of Sheedy's reclusive photographer. As the pair tentatively sketch out an assignment together, a passionate lesbian affair unfolds. As well as presenting a cogent argument against heroin addiction, **Cholodenko** offers a peek at love, life and the artistic process.

 ## The Man With the Golden Arm 1955

Director Otto Preminger **Cast** Frank Sinatra, Eleanor Parker, Kim Novak 119m

Shockingly for its time, this movie tells the story of Frankie Machine, a heroin addict returning from prison to find himself stuck in a loveless marriage with a crippled wife, unable to leave her for his understanding lover (**Novak**). Parts of the film have dated now, but **Preminger**'s noirish photography and **Sinatra**'s performance (a revelation if you've only ever seen him in musicals) make it well worth seeing.

Marihuana 1935

Director Dwain Esper **Cast** Harley Wood, Gloria Browne 57m

Also known as *Marihuana, the Weed with Roots in Hell*, this sees a bunch of teenagers become helplessly addicted to marijuana after just a single toke. As a direct result, an innocent summer is soon blighted by drowning, alcoholism, heroin addiction, kidnapping, pregnancy and

death. But of course! Gloriously inept performances and terrible direction make this a classic among B-movies, although the tag line: ''Weird orgies! Wild parties! Unleashed passions!'' hints that Esper may have been more interested in exploitation than social responsibility.

Naked Lunch 1991

Director David Cronenberg **Cast** Peter Weller, Judy Davis, Ian Holm 115m

Cronenberg's fantasy masterpiece interweaves parts of **William Burroughs**' bizarre novel with episodes from his real life. Bill Lee (**Weller**) accidentally shoots his own wife and is embroiled in dodgy dealing in a shadowy port called Interzone. Then his typewriter morphs into a giant cockroach. More a movie about drug-induced creativity and destruction rather than a coherent story of a man's life. Be warned – while watching this, you may start to suspect that someone has slipped something in your popcorn.

The Panic in Needle Park 1971

Director Jerry Schatzberg **Cast** Al Pacino, Kitty Winn, Alan Vint, Raul Julia 110m

Al Pacino, in only his second role, plays a junkie, Bobby. When he meets Helen, (**Winn**) she is drug-free, living with wayward artist Marco (**Julia**), who she leaves for Bobby. She soon becomes addicted too, funding her habit with prostitution. Unlike many drug-related movies, there is no concluding redemption. Former photographer **Schatzberg** creates a bleak New York in distressed, gritty hues, and the lack of any music helps to emphasize the desperation.

Requiem for a Dream 2000

Director Darren Aronofsky **Cast** Ellen Burstyn, Jared Leto, Jennifer Connelly 101m

Darren Aronofsky's follow-up to his critically acclaimed *Pi* is a portrayal of addiction, disturbing both in the achingly emotive performances and in its suggestion we could all go down that road. **Burstyn** is Sara, whose addiction to sugar and TV becomes an addiction to diet pills as she tries to lose weight to go on a TV show. Her son, Harry (**Leto**), is addicted to drugs, as is his girlfriend Marion (**Connelly**). Adapted from the **Hubert Selby Jr** novel, this is no addicts-come-clean story, but a brutal look at what addictions can lead to.

Traffic 2000

Director Steven Soderbergh **Cast** Michael Douglas, Catherine Zeta-Jones 147m

A politician with a heroin-addict daughter spearheads an anti-drugs campaign; a wife tries to help her dealer husband's business; DEA agents protect a witness against the dealer; and a corrupt Mexican cop fights with his conscience. Originally a Channel 4 TV series, these interconnected stories get a stylish twist from **Soderbergh**, with clever direction and a distinctive colour-soaked look. **Douglas** (in a part written for Harrison Ford) and **Zeta-Jones** are surprisingly good, but

Benicio Del Toro steals every scene and won the Oscar.

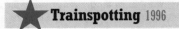 ## Trainspotting 1996

Director Danny Boyle **Cast** Ewan McGregor, Johnny Lee Miller, Robert Carlyle 93m

Fresh from their success with *Shallow Grave* (1994), **Boyle**'s team turned to **Irvine Welsh**'s novel about addicts in Edinburgh. **John Hodge**'s script is shocking, funny and heartbreaking, creating the junkie's junkie movie, where even the minor characters light up the screen. **Ewan Bremner** as the hopelessly stupid Spud gets the funniest moments, while **Carlyle**'s psychopath Begbie is simply terrifying. For a movie with such explicit scenes of drug-taking and withdrawal, it has a surprisingly upbeat ending – although you won't leave thinking heroin should be your next lifestyle choice.

Up in Smoke 1978

Director Lou Adler **Cast** Cheech Marin, Tommy Chong 86m

The first and best of **Cheech and Chong**'s good-natured movies about their eternal quest for the best grass. Here they head to Mexico, where they agree to drive a highly suspect van back to the US. That's about it really: just a long, hilarious road movie about meeting weirdos and getting high, with cameos from **Stacy Keach** and **Tom Skerritt** and inspired silliness that will get you laughing as if you'd shared one of the boys' monster joints.

The casually psychotic Begbie (Robert Carlyle) takes Renton (Ewan McGregor) to task in the Danny Boyle's *Trainspotting*. Edinburgh never looked quite so squalid.

Withnail and I 1987

Director Bruce Robinson Cast Richard E. Grant, Paul McGann, Richard Griffiths 107m

You could call this a story about two unemployed actors in the 1960s who share a holiday in the country, but that doesn't convey the achingly brilliant acting, script and direction, nor the compelling weirdness on offer. Not a huge success when first released, this is now hailed as one of the funniest British movies of all time. The inspired supporting role of Uncle Monty is played with treacherous pathos by **Griffiths**. Various substances come in for abuse (alcohol and lighter fluid among them), but the scene with Danny the drug-dealer (**Ralph Brown**) rolling his multi-Rizla Camberwell Carrot lingers longest in the mind

DYSTOPIAS

Welcome to a world not unlike this one, but with some serious omissions: food, free speech, um, men? Usually set in the future, occasionally in the past, these dystopic visions inspire fear, horror and despair – and make us grateful for what we've got.

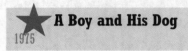

★ A Boy and His Dog

1975

Director L.Q. Jones **Cast** Don Johnson, Susanne Benton, Jason Robards **89m**

This might have been an even bigger cult success had the producers followed through on casting James Cagney as the voice of Blood, the dog who communicates telepathically with **Don Johnson** as they travel through a perilous post-apocalyptic landscape. Instead, **Tim McIntire** voices the mutt who sniffs out food and females for his master, but can't prevent his being lured into the underground bourgeois hell of Topeka, where **Jason Robards** hopes Johnson can replenish the dying civilization's sperm bank. Kinky perhaps, but also bleak and darkly comic.

Fahrenheit 451 1966

Director François Truffaut **Cast** Oskar Werner, Julie Christie, Cyril Cusack **112m**

Truffaut's first colour film and his sole English-language directorial venture proved something of a trial. Having failed to recruit a number of big-name actors to play the fireman who is persuaded by wife **Julie Christie**'s rebellious lookalike to question the wisdom of burning books to suppress free thought, he reunited with *Jules et Jim*'s temperamental **Oskar Werner** and promptly fell out with him. The scripting is awkward, but Truffaut memorably recreates the disconcerting vision of censorship and conformity delineated in **Ray Bradbury**'s futuristic novel.

Hell Comes to Frogtown

1988

Directors Donald G. Jackson & R.J. Kizer **Cast** Julius LeFlore, RCB, Roddy Piper **86m**

With his precious genitals protected by an electronic chastity belt, wrestler **Roddy Piper** debuts here as a rare potent male in a gynaecocratic colony. However, he's surpassed by **Sandahl Bergman**'s glacial nurse, as they rescue some fertile females from the chainsaw-wielding amphibian mutants of Frogtown. Nobody is going to pretend this is a lost classic, but it makes the most of its bargain budget and has its tongue firmly in its cheek as it parodies such post-armageddon landmarks as *Planet of the Apes* and *Mad Max 2*.

No Blade of Grass 1970

Director Cornel Wilde Cast Nigel Davenport, Jean Wallace, John Hamill 96m

A protypical eco movie that contemplates how quickly humanity will return to a primal state once survival becomes the sole reason for existence. Aside from some tedious flashforwards and occasional bouts of sermonizing, this is a tense and provocative film. Architect John Custance (**Davenport**) is compelled to make some drastic moral choices as his family competes for dwindling food supplies with a rabid biker gang and an angry mob after a virus depletes the planet's crops.

Pleasantville 1998

Director Gary Ross Cast Tobey Maguire, Reese Witherspoon, Joan Allen 124m

Nostalgia ain't what it used to be in this parable that pitches modern-day bickering siblings **Maguire** and **Witherspoon** into a 1950s sitcom, whose cosy idyll turns out to be a conformist nightmare. Impeccably designed by **Jeannine Oppewall**, the monochrome TV world is subtly transformed by the ensemble's liberated emotions. But the interlopers also learn valuable lessons about their own dysfunctional times, even as their presence unleashes a backlash of intolerance, paranoia and mob hysteria. Slyly ambiguous and deftly tempering caricature with poignancy, this ranks among Hollywood's sharpest critiques of the American Dream.

Turkey Shoot 1982

Director Brian Trenchard-Smith Cast Steve Railsback, Olivia Hussey, Michael Craig 93m

Reworking *The Most Dangerous Game* (1932) as a totalitarian nightmare set in 1995, this typifies the kind of Ozploitation churned out by maverick producer **Antony I. Ginnane**. The untamed setting evocatively reinforces the dangers faced by **Steve Railsback** and **Olivia Hussey** as they attempt to survive the deadly blood sport devised for his VIP guests by Behaviour Modification Camp commandant Thatcher (Michael Craig). Unsophisticated political commentary it may be, but there's a chilling viscerality to the fascistic excesses.

EPICS

Size has always been the cinema's big advantage over television. And in the 1950s, the mantra in the movie industry almost became "If a story's big enough, it's good enough".

Ben-Hur 1950

Director William Wyler **Cast** Charlton Heston, Stephen Boyd, Jack Hawkins 212m

A great spectacle, but not a great movie. **Wyler** shot 263 feet of film for every foot of the famous chariot race that made it into the movie. **Gore Vidal**, who had a hand in the script, suggested that **Boyd**'s Messala's resentment of **Heston**'s Jewish prince was motivated by a homosexual crush. Wyler thought this a fine idea but told Boyd not to mention it to Heston unless he wanted a punch in the nose. *Ben-Hur* does sag but it contains some of the most stirring scenes in the epic genre.

Fanny and Alexander 1982

Director Ingmar Bergman **Cast** Bertil Guve, Pernilla Alwen, Ewa Fröling, Allan Edwall 189m

A semi-autobiographical labour of love, **Bergman**'s sumptuous masterpiece dwells on spirits, madness, magic, deformity, infidelity, terror, joy and cruelty in the strange history of the Ekdahl family. The opening, a Christmas party that lasts almost as long as a real Christmas party, is a triumph and surprisingly warm. But the story darkens as Alexander's father (who bears an odd resemblance to Hitler) dies, his mother remarries a psychotic bishop and an eccentric Jewish merchant has to come to the family's rescue.

Fitzcarraldo 1982

Director Werner Herzog **Cast** Klaus Kinski, José Lewgoy, Miguel Ángel Fuentes 158m

This movie pushed Herzog to the limit. He had dropped his original idea of **Kinski** as Fitzcarraldo, but when both **Mick Jagger** and **Jason Robards** pulled out weeks into production, the temperamental star was Herzog's only hope as the man who decides to build an opera theatre in the jungle and bring Verdi to its natives. But first he must drag a steamship over the Amazonian mountains… Herzog's account of the filming is equally enthralling and features the only footage of Robards and Jagger in the lead role.

Hercules 1958

Director Pietro Francisi **Cast** Steve Reeves, Sylvia Kocsina 93m

After losing an arm wrestling contest, **Reeves** took up body-building and was the perfect beefcake when the Italians began churning out sword and sandal epics in the late 1950s and early 60s. In this epic, Reeves as Hercules effectively replaces Jason in the Argonauts story and grunts almost as often as he talks. **Kocsina**, as Hercules' bride, almost steals the movie, a surprise box office hit in the US.

Kagemusha 1980

Director Akira Kurosawa **Cast** Tatsuya Nakadai, Tsutomo Yamazaki, Kenichi Hagiwara 181m

Akira Kurosawa had to rely on sponsorship by **George Lucas** and **Francis Ford Coppola** for this, since the $6m budget, puny by Hollywood standards, was a bit steep for Japanese studios. If not quite up to the standard of *Ran*, this is fine work. Kurosawa conveys both the sweep of events in the clan wars of sixteenth-century Japan and shows how the conflict affects individual lives. The battle scenes are glorious, and the warlords' intrigues are of almost Shakespearian subtlety.

Kings of the Sun 1963

Director J. Lee Thompson **Cast** Yul Brynner, George Chakiris, Shirley Anne Field 107m

Long before Mel Gibson's *Apocalypto*, Mayan monarch **Chakiris** led his people out of Mexico to the Mississippi Delta where they fought/learned to live in peace with **Brynner**'s Indian tribe. A love triangle is shoehorned into an unusually intense Hollywood epic, which is both spectacular and thoughtful.

Land of the Pharaohs 1955

Director Howard Hawks **Cast** Jack Hawkins, Joan Collins 103m

If you find **Hawkins**' pharaoh a) dull and b) unconvincing, **Hawks**' comment on the making of this movie may help explain why. "William Faulkner said: 'I don't know how a pharaoh talks – is it all right if I write him like a Kentucky colonel?' And [Harry] Kurnitz [dialogue writer] said: 'I can't do it like a Kentucky colonel, but I could do it as though it were *King Lear*.'" So what you see onscreen is Kentucky colonel crossed with *King Lear*, rewritten by Hawks and plonked down in Egypt in 3000 BC. But you do get a good look at Joan Collins' midriff.

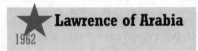 ## ★ Lawrence of Arabia 1962

Director David Lean **Cast** Peter O'Toole, Omar Sharif, Alec Guinness 222m

Luckily Katharine Hepburn persuaded **Lean** that Albert Finney wasn't the man to play the enigmatic T.E. Lawrence but the virtually unknown **O'Toole** was. The camels grew to love O'Toole so much that when he was downed in a fight between extras, they formed a protective circle around him. O'Toole is perfect as Lawrence, making him vivid, fascinating and just as hard to decipher as in real life. The desert has seldom looked more seductive.

Royal Hunt of the Sun 1969

Director Irving Lerner **Cast** Christopher Plummer, Robert Shaw, Nigel Davenport 121m

Too wordy for many, but once you refuse to be distracted by **Plummer**'s bizarre German-Mexican accent as the Inca emperor **Atahualpa**, this version of **Peter Shaffer**'s play offers thoughtful parallels to conflicts in Iraq and Vietnam. **Shaw** is superb as Pizarro, a conquistador who has lost his belief in the mission, while Plummer, vocal tics and all, is fascinating to watch as a living god.

Sign of the Cross 1932

Director Cecil B. DeMille **Cast** Fredric March, Elissa Landi, Claudette Colbert **124m**

This Christian-Roman saga suggests how kinky **DeMille**'s movies might have been without the Hays Code. It stars **Charles Laughton** as an OTT (but clearly homosexual) Nero and has **Colbert** reveal her nipples (you have to look very closely) and invite one of her servants into her bath. Re-released in 1944 without the steamier scenes, it's now available again in its original, compelling form; DeMille was evidently deaf to bad dialogue.

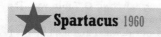 ## Spartacus 1960

Director Stanley Kubrick **Cast** Kirk Douglas, Laurence Olivier, Jean Simmons **196m**

Now chiefly famous for the much parodied "I am Spartacus!" scene, *Spartacus* is one of the few Hollywood epics to acquire a sizeable cult following. Partly, it's thanks to its political cred in backing the slaves, but there are also strange undercurrents (which become explicit when **Laurence Olivier's** patrician seduces **Tony Curtis**'s slave) and unusually intimate performances by **Douglas** as Spartacus, Olivier, Curtis, **Jean Simmons** as Spartacus's wife and **Peter Ustinov** who, as the slave dealer, became the only actor to win an Oscar in a Kubrick movie.

The Ten Commandments
1956

Director Cecil B. DeMille **Cast** Charlton Heston, Yul Brynner, Anne Baxter **220m**

"Oh Moses, you stubborn, splendid, adorable fool". **DeMille** never met a treatment he didn't think he could improve – even if that story had come from God – and he pulls out all the stops in this Biblical blockbuster, an event movie before the term even existed. It's fantastic to look at, stiffly acted, with some kitsch dialogue and a cast of thousands. Look out for trumpeter **Herb Alpert** as a Hebrew drummer.

War and Peace 1968

Director Sergei Bondarchuk **Cast** Ludmila Savelyeva, Vyacheslav Tikhonov **484m**

The most expensive film ever made – £440m in today's money – fearlessly slims down the plot of **Leo Tolstoy**'s novel. Enough complexity remains for **Bondarchuk** to rely, too often, on a voiceover. But he orchestrates the action superbly, the landscapes are epic and the show-stopper burning of Moscow is worth the price of admission alone.

EROTICA

Erotic movies cross genre boundaries and can be intensely challenging, unlike porn (see p.271). Whether explicit or not, they usually have something to say about sex as a theme.

★ Ai No Corrida 1976

Director Nagisa Ôshima **Cast** Tatsuya Fuji, Eiko Matsuda, Aoi Nakajima 109m

This study of an intense and ultimately destructive liaison between maid (**Matsuda**) and married lover (**Fuji**) was inspired by actual events in 1930s Japan. **Nagisa Ôshima** sought to question the extent to which male totalitarianism continued to thrive, but his bold political stance was ignored in the furore caused by the graphic depiction of penetrative sex. Despite obscuring any pubic hair (to meet the strict censorship regulations), Ôshima was charged with obscenity and spent four years arguing his case before the courts.

The Beast 1975

Director Walerian Borowczyk **Cast** Sirpa Lane, Lisbeth Hummel, Elizabeth Kaza 93m

Horror? Fairy-tale fantasy? Porn? This erotic take on the Beauty and the Beast legend defies categorization. Originally an eighteen-minute short about a woman getting raped by a hairy "beast" (a man in a ratty gorilla suit), then realizing she rather enjoys it – footage which visionary Polish surrealist **Borowczyk** then incorporated into this spurious story about a fragrant young heiress coming to visit her suitor in his remote French country mansion, prowled round by… you guessed it. The opening close-up of a horse's vagina (followed by an eight-minute stallion penetration sequence) merely hints at the eye-opening ride ahead.

Dracula: Pages from a Virgin's Diary 2002

Director Guy Maddin **Cast** Zhang Wei-Qiang, Tara Birtwhistle 72m

An unusual interpretation of **Bram Stoker**'s classic, this is a modern silent movie starring the Royal Winnipeg Ballet. The film begins with stage director **Mark Godden**'s production of Dracula before **Maddin** arrives to transform the piece into an erotic, poetic horror, with only the sounds of ballet shoes dancing across the floor to **Mahler**'s first and second symphonies. With its misty, monochrome imagery, it recreates a bygone era, though Bela Lugosi and Christopher Lee were never this sexy.

Friday Night 2002

Director Claire Denis **Cast** Vincent London, Valerie Lemercier 88m

Few directors evoke an erotic atmosphere with the style and panache of **Denis**. Following a woman (**Lemercier**) as she engages in a one-night stand with a handsome stranger (**London**), Denis offers an entirely non-judgemental and swoonsome meditation on sexual desire. The spur for the woman's affair is a rain-sodden traffic jam, a move that is typical of the director's ability to mix the mundane and the magical.

Lady Chatterley 2006

Director Pascale Ferran **Cast** Marina Hands, Jean-Louis Coullo'ch, Hippolyte Girardot 168m

Lady meets gamekeeper and sexual awakening follows. The boiled-down plot of a version of English novelist **D.H. Lawrence**'s famously explicit novel (banned until the 1960s) sounds similar to many a porno flick (okay, not the class bit), but its French female director has made by far the best of the six versions of the tale with a remarkably earthy, lush, fresh and yes, erotic film. It takes its time, though, so not for arthouse phobics.

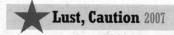 **Lust, Caution** 2007

Director Ang Lee **Cast** Tony Leung, Tang Wei 157m

Set in an occupied Shanghai in the 1940s, *Lust, Caution* weaves together a dark tale of obsessive love and a political spy thriller. The two leads sizzle, caught up in a passionate relationship that's doomed from the start: **Wei** plays Wang Jiazhi, a Chinese resistance fighter charged with seducing the powerful Mr Yee (**Leung**). **Ang Lee**'s fascination with the emotional connection between socially and culturally opposed lovers continues from *Brokeback Mountain*, but with a lot more explicit sex.

Rendez-vous 1985

Director André Téchiné **Cast** Lambert Wilson, Juliette Binoche, Wadeck Stanczak 93m

A stylish drama that gave **Binoche** her first major role, as Nina, a free-spirited actress freshly arrived in Paris. Enjoying a string of sexual encounters, Nina meets a shy estate agent whose attentions she spurns in favour of his sexually liberated actor flatmate. This erotic exploration of love and art amongst a damaged group of people won **Téchiné** the award for best director at Cannes.

EURO HORROR

The gore-splattered, "arty" lesbian-laden nudity that defined Euro horror in the 1960s to 1980s has magically metamorphosed into exquisite modern gothic fairy tales that scare the very goosebumps off you.

Black Sunday 1960

Director Mario Bava **Cast** Barbara Steele, John Richardson **87m**

Bava's feature-length directorial debut was originally released as *La maschera del Demonio* or *Mask of Satan*, which sums up the movie's plot far better. A witch, Princess Vajda, and her servant return from the dead with plans to capture the body of Vajda's descendant Katia, only Katia's brother and doctor standing in her way. Having honed his skills as cinematographer to **Roberto Rossellini**, Bava created a new horror style, adding erotic elements, realistic violence and shooting in black and white, to give this an eerie, gothic dimension. His relationship with his actors was also novel. Bava insisted **Steele** only saw the script on a day-to-day basis, the actress forced to learn her lines on the spot. Nominated by **Tim Burton** as his favourite horror movie.

The Devil's Backbone 2001

Director Guillermo del Toro **Cast** Marisa Paredes, Eduardo Noriega, Federico Luppi **106m**

The title suggests lurid horror in *The Mark of the Devil* mould, but this elegant political allegory from *Hellboy/Hobbit* director **del Toro** is undoubtedly a world apart. Produced by the modern maestro of Spanish cinema, **Pedro Almodóvar**, it's a powerful and affecting coming-of-age tale set in a haunted orphanage during the Spanish Civil War. Infused with his trademark gothic imagination, del Toro describes this as his "spiritual" prequel to *Pan's Labyrinth*.

Eyes Without a Face 1960

Director Georges Franju **Cast** Pierre Brasseur, Alida Valli, Edith Scob **88m**

Wracked with guilt after disfiguring his daughter in a car crash, an eminent plastic surgeon experiments with unorthodox

The Italian Hitchcock

Dario Argento is the maestro of **gialli**: hard-boiled, blood-soaked melodramas named after pulp fiction books with yellow (*gialli*) covers. Yet Hans Christian Andersen, The Brothers Grimm and an aunt who told him terrifying bedtime stories were all crucial influences on a director preoccupied by childhood trauma.

Born in Rome to a movie producer father and Brazilian model mother, Argento started as a writer, collaborating with **Bernardo Bertolucci** on the screenplay of *Once Upon a Time in the West* before completing his own directorial debut, **The Bird with the Crystal Plumage** (1970), a smash-hit suspense thriller with a violent, sado-masochistic bent (see p.374). More highly charged, supernatural thrillers followed, culminating in his scarlet masterpieces **Suspiria** (see p.145), **Tenebrae** (1982) and the seminal **Profondo Rosso** (1975). Widely considered the best *giallo* ever made, *Profondo Rosso* marked Argento's first collaboration with **Daria Nicolodi**, his lover/co-writer/mother of their actress-poet-model-director daughter **Asia**, a chip off the old block who recalls how she was "lonely and depressed" as a child because her parents read her their scripts as bedtime stories.

Now nearly seventy, Argento has ceased to make Hitchcock-type cameos in his own movies – though he only ever cast himself as the killer's gloved hands.

face transplant techniques for her: luring unwitting "donors" into his shadowy basement. An inspiration for *Face/Off* and *Halloween* (note the daughter's chilling white mask), French director **Franju** went easy on the gore to get censorship approval, relying on **Maurice Jarre**'s eerie score to get nerves jangling. Even so seven audience members fainted during a screening at the 1960 Edinburgh Film Festival, prompting Franju to scoff "Now I know why Scotsmen wear skirts".

Häxan 1922

Director Benjamin Christensen **Cast** Maren Pedersen, Oscar Stribolt 87m

Over eighty years on, **Christensen**'s disturbing documentary, subtitled *Witchcraft Through the Ages*, has lost none of its ability to shock. His silent scenes of demonically possessed nuns and friars – and the tortures to which they were submitted in order to extract confessions of sorcery – are made more upsetting by the fear-filled expressions of the actors. Elsewhere, his hideous re-enactment of a witches' sabbat gives you the uneasy feeling that the Danish director might have been present at such events in real life.

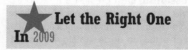 ## Let the Right One In 2009

Director Tomas Alfredson **Cast** Kåre Hedebrant, Lina Leandersson, Per Ragna 115m

Tender, creepy and poetic, this Swedish vampire movie is as much sensitively observed coming-of-age romance as horror flick. Based on **John Ajvide**

Lindqvist's bestseller, it's set in 1981 on a snowy housing estate. Here bullied, blond twelve-year-old loner Oskar (**Hedebrant**) falls for brown-eyed Eli (**Leandersson**), the hungry vampire girl next door. Much is left to linger, unexplained, in this haunting child's-eye look at loneliness, violence and the redemptive power of love. Highlights being the beautifully nuanced child performances, a vein of dark absurdist humour and an exquisite opener where all you hear is the delicate patter of snowflakes.

★ Suspiria 1977

Director Dario Argento **Cast** Jessica Harper, Stefana Casin, Flavio Bucci **98m**

A naïve American newcomer at a posh European ballet school gradually realizes the staff are a coven of witches. Remarkable for what *Entertainment Weekly* called "the most vicious murder scene ever filmed" and an iconic soundtrack by Italian prog rock band Goblin (since sampled by Ghostface Killah), the title for this nightmarish scenario came from Thomas De Quincey's *Suspiria de Profundis*. However, **Argento**, who co-wrote this with his then girlfriend, actress Daria Nicolodi (herself a white witch), declared himself more heavily influenced by *Snow White and the Seven Dwarves*, notably in the use of imbibition Technicolor, a process also used for *The Wizard of Oz* and *Gone With the Wind*.

More than just the pale, creepy girl next door, Eli's (Lina Leandersson) nature is revealed in all its gory inevitability to Oskar in *Let the Right One In*.

EYE CANDY

How is it that some of the world's worst movies feature some of the world's best bods? All of these, cool or kitschy, clunky or classy, have a definite sizzle factor.

★ American Gigolo 1980

Director Paul Schrader **Cast** Richard Gere, Lauren Hutton 117m

There's always been something of the night about **Schrader**'s movies, and this pre-AIDS morality tale is no exception. The sexually ambivalent **Gere** is a knock-out as the glossy gigolo in question, a role he was born to play – hard to say whether he looks better in those Armani suits or out of them. Either way, his beauty steals the show – an unsettling combination of drop-dead gorgeousness, raw sex and icy narcissism that seduces even while it repels.

The Crimson Pirate 1952

Director Robert Siodmak **Cast** Burt Lancaster, Ava Bartok 105m

If an oiled-up **Burt Lancaster** swashbuckling, swinging on ropes and somersaulting on the poop deck can't crush ye barnacles, then nothing can. This tongue-in-cheek bit of buccaneering derring-do set the standard for all pirate movies to come, and Lancaster was never more dizzyingly, heart-thumpingly athletic.

★ The Girl Can't Help It 1956

Director Frank Tashlin **Cast** Jayne Mansfield, Tom Ewell 99m

Plump-lipped, pneumatic and platinum blonde, **Jayne Mansfield** defined the blonde bombshell and **Tashlin**, who spent years as a Looney Tunes animator, knew how best to display her cartoonish, candy-sweet charms. The rock'n'roll sub-plot delivers some fab musical moments, too – along with numbers from **Eddie Cochran** and **Little Richard** there's a stunning "Cry Me a River" cameo from **Julie London**, no slacker in the looks department herself.

Modesty Blaise 1966

Director Joseph Losey **Cast** Monica Vitti, Terence Stamp, Dirk Bogarde 119m

This kitsch op-art comedy thriller, inspired by a 1960s *London Evening Standard* comic strip, was too quirky even for swinging London cineastes. A flop on release, today its off-kilter pacing and dated affectations are sheer delight, while sultry arthouse darling **Vitti** – more usually seen in the throes of existential angst in Michelangelo Antonioni movies – soars above the nuttiness as the super-cool spy with frocks to die for.

One Million Years BC 1966

Director Don Chaffey **Cast** Raquel Welch, John Richardson, Percy Herbert **91m**

"This is the way it was!" said the tagline, though there is little scientific evidence to suggest that Neanderthal woman was as beautiful – and as hair-free – as the lovely **Raquel**, whose image, coiffed and gleaming in her animal-hide bikini, still adorns the bedroom walls of teenage boys around the world. The film's marauding dinosaurs pale in comparison.

Perfect 1985

Director James Bridges **Cast** Jamie Lee Curtis, John Travolta **115m**

Perfect may have halted its stars' careers in their tracks – **Travolta** earned a Razzie nomination for worst actor – but there's no denying that the gorgeous **Curtis** looks "buff". Jiggling and grinding in slinky Lycra, she's the aerobics teacher of every schoolboy's dampest dreams, straddling the moral high ground while spurning Travolta's *Rolling Stone* reporter. Travolta himself indulges in more than a little legwarmer action and pelvic thrusting.

Taza, Son of Cochise 1954

Director Douglas Sirk **Cast** Rock Hudson, Barbara Rush **79m**

After years of starring in B-movies like this, **Hudson** moved into the big league, delivering great performances in classy melodramas and sophisticated comedies. In this rare foray into the Western he plays the peace-loving son of an Apache chief. Adorned with wig, body paint and feathered headdress, Rock's buckskin get-ups display his spectacular pecs to great advantage. Oh, and it's in 3-D, and there's some sort of plot concerning sibling rivalry.

Viva Las Vegas 1964

Director George Sidney **Cast** Elvis Presley, Ann-Margret **85m**

Once seen, never forgotten: **Ann-Margret** in scarlet sweater and black tights shimmying in the school gym, fingers clicking and red hair tossing, while **Elvis** cuts a dash with his sharp suit and sexy hip shakes. Of all his co-stars Ann-Margret was the only one who could match Elvis for sheer animal sexuality – the two were having an affair during the shoot and the "chemistry" practically drips from the screen.

What a Carve Up! 1961

Director Pat Jackson **Cast** Shirley Eaton, Kenneth Connor, Sid James **87m**

Contrary to rumours, British bombshell **Shirley Eaton** did not die after being sprayed gold from head to toe in *Goldfinger*. The blonde comedienne, who spent more than a decade in classic Brit comedies, simply retired. This goofy horror spoof sees her at her funny, alluring best, dressed in her undies and given ample support from a stalwart cast.

FAMILIES

Love 'em or hate 'em, you can't choose 'em. In movies, even the happiest of families hides a dark secret. Most, though, are just plain dysfunctional from the start.

Buffalo 66 1998

Director Vincent Gallo **Cast** Vincent Gallo, Christina Ricci, Ben Gazzarra 110m

Thrumming with visual and comedic ideas (not all of them good), **Vincent Gallo**'s directorial debut can be excused on account of its excoriating denunciation of suburban dysfunction. The sequence in which Gallo's newly released jailbird kidnaps dance student **Christina Ricci** and persuades her to pose as his adoring wife to impress disinterested parents **Ben Gazzara** and **Anjelica Huston** is grimly compelling. Ricci astounds throughout (her tap routine at the bowling alley is mesmerizing) and roots Gallo's preternatural surrealism in a quirkily quaint reality.

Burnt by the Sun 1994

Director Nikita Mikhalkov **Cast** Nikita Mikhalkov, Oleg Menshikov 134m

The image of **Mikhalkov** slinging daughter Nadia over his shoulder after receiving his Oscar for best foreign language film will be indelibly linked to this masterly evocation of the transient joys and persistent perils of life in Soviet Russia during the Stalinist purges of the 1930s. Mikhalkov's revolutionary hero basks in the approbation of his family at their country dacha; but the mood darkens, as apparatchik Oleg Menshikov's morbid mission and his past relationship with Mikhalkov's wife (**Ingeborga Dapkunaite**) become apparent. Stuffed with wry symbolism, this is period lyricism at its most mordant.

Hannah and Her Sisters 1986

Director Woody Allen **Cast** Mia Farrow, Michael Caine, Barbara Hershey 107m

Despite its obvious debts to Ingmar Bergman, **Woody Allen** claimed a line from *Anna Karenina* as the inspiration for this witty saga: "All happy families resemble one another, but each unhappy family is unhappy in its own way". Dividing the action into sixteen chapters, Allen clearly intended a bookish feel. But while he's occasionally guilty of allowing theatricality to intrude on proceedings, this amalgam of showbiz, autobiography and domestic melodrama proves supremely cinematic, as **Farrow**, **Hershey** and

Dianne Wiest make sense of both their lives and the kith and kin that complicate them.

The Happiness of the Katakuris 2001

Director Takashi Miike Cast Kenji Sawada, Keiko Matsuzaka, Shinji Takeda 113m

Kim Ji-woon's delirious black comedy *The Quiet Family* was the chief inspiration for **Takashi Miike**'s uproarious zombie musical. Jettisoning his trademark grotesque schlock style, he adopted a kitsch candy-coloured aesthetic and studded the story of a rural retreat whose guests keep getting slaughtered with mischievous references to *Psycho* and *The Sound of Music*. With claymation reveries evoking Jan Svankmajer, this is much camper and cultier than *The Rocky Horror Picture Show* and markedly less smug.

Heimat 1984

Director Edgar Reitz Cast Marita Breuer, Michael Lesch, Dieter Schaad 3282m

Taking all four of **Edgar Reitz**'s masterworks together, this peerless epic sprawls over 3282 minutes, as it chronicles the fate of the Simon family from 1918 to the new millennium. Juggling numerous plotlines without ever resorting to melodrama or caricature, Reitz explores the key social, political and cultural issues that impacted upon the entire continent. But this always remains an intimate study of everyday people, particularly in this first production, which focuses on Hunsrück hausfrau Marita Breuer, as her sons cope with their father's desertion and the rise of Nazism.

The Holly and the Ivy 1952

Director George More O'Ferrell Cast Ralph Richardson, Celia Johnson, Margaret Leighton 83m

The rural England depicted in this adaptation of **Wynyard Browne**'s stage hit would seem foreign to anyone reared on the social realism that transformed British cinema over the subsequent six years. But this tale of a clergyman accepting that his daughter would drown her sorrows following the death of the illegitimate son she bore to a GI killed in the war would have seemed daring to contemporary audiences. Sadly, its themes of faith, fidelity and family now also seem like relics of a distant past.

Junebug 2005

Director Phil Morrison Cast Amy Adams, Embeth Davidtz, Ben McKenzie 106m

As garrulous mother-to-be Ashley, **Amy Adams** lights up **Phil Morrison**'s understated study of clashing cultures and backwater ennui. Her enthusiasm for her visiting art dealer sister-in-law Madeleine (**Davidtz**) is tinged with a gauche inelegance that contrasts with

Davidtz's determined grace in tolerating the sulky introspection of her husband George (**Alessandro Nivola**, anything but pleased to be back in North Carolina) and the waspish asides of his disapproving mother (**Celia Weston**). Elliptical and enigmatic, but accessible and affectionate, this feels like a throwback to folksy screwballs of the 1940s.

Late Marriage 2001

Director Dover Koshashvili **Cast** Lili Koshashvili, Lior Ashkenazi, Ronit Elkabetz 100m

Lili Koshashvili, the debuting director's mother, excels in this astringent satire on cultural conformity and emotional blackmail, set within Tel Aviv's Georgian community. While Koshashvili attempts to matchmake her perpetual student son (**Ashkenazi**) with a variety of teenage virgins, Zaza instead falls for an older Moroccan divorcée (**Elkabetz**), whose toddler daughter makes the ensuing rows with his highly traditional parents all the more ferocious. The dark humour cuts to the quick, while the disintegration of a family riven by much more than a generation gap is excruciating to behold, especially during the denouement.

Love Finds Andy Hardy 1938

Director George B. Seitz **Cast** Mickey Rooney, Lewis Stone, Judy Garland 91m

The fourth of the sixteen *Andy Hardy* features made between 1937 and 1958 is the series standout. Needing quick cash to buy a car, **Mickey Rooney** agrees to chaperone his best buddy's girlfriend over the Christmas holidays. But **Lana Turner** doesn't want to confine her kissing to the mistletoe and, with Rooney also having to deal with a besotted neighbour (**Garland**), he urgently needs one of those regular man-to-man chats with his judge father (**Stone**) before his own steady, **Ann Rutherford**, returns to town. Oozing rascally charisma, Rooney proved somewhat irresistible in real life, too – he married eight times.

Spanking the Monkey 1994

Director David O. Russell **Cast** Jeremy Davies, Elizabeth Newett, Benjamin Hendrickson 100m

The Graduate gets a very 1990s twist in **David O. Russell**'s vaguely autobiographical and queasily erotic debut study of parental power, pesky pooches, masturbation and incest. With his salesman father on his travels, sardonic undergrad Ray (**Davies**) is forced to pass up a prestigious Washington internship to nurse his mother (**Alberta Watson**) through the broken leg she sustained in a failed suicide bid. However, everyday ablutions engender an unwonted intimacy and the son's arousal eventually overcomes his aversion. Watson makes a suitably voluptuous Mrs Robinson, while Russell remarkably ensures that the shocking contrivances seem pseudo-tastefully plausible.

FANTASY

No fantasy is more seductive to Hollywood than a second chance at life. This is the root of *Field of Dreams* and *The Fisher King*. Yet some fantasies are just excuses to scare us – not that there's anything wrong with that.

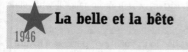

La belle et la bête

1946

Director Jean Cocteau **Cast** Jean Marais, Josette Day 92m

Writer, director, poet, playwright, artist and set designer, **Cocteau** used all his skills on this classic fairy tale. Starring his lover **Marais** as the beast, this adaptation was Cocteau's second movie, following a fifteen-year break since his debut with the short *The Blood of a Poet*. While filming, Cocteau was in hospital with the skin condition impetigo and wrote in his diary: "I look at myself in the mirror… it's awful. The pain is now a torture so horrible I am ashamed of ever showing myself." Like director, like beast.

Chinese Ghost Story 1987

Director Ching Siu-Tung **Cast** Leslie Cheung, Michelle Li, Wu Ma 95m

This first tale in a trilogy sees a tax collector arriving in a small town. Unappreciated, he seeks refuge in a haunted temple and there meets the ghost of a woman whose curse is to lure men to their

death. The fun doesn't stop there: a hideous tree spirit goes around sucking the yang from people and a Taoist swordsman appears. The action sequences and the soul-sucking demon make this one of the better recent ghost stories – terrain revisited in two sequels (1990 and 1991), the last with *Do Do Do* added to its title.

The City of Lost Children
1995

Directors Marc Caro, Jean-Pierre Jeunet **Cast** Ron Perlman, Daniel Emilfork 112m

There's a brain in a tank on an island. It's uncle to five identical guys who are giving it a birthday party, which is broken up by another guy who has no sense of humour, can't cry, and has to kidnap children and connect them to thought-stealing equipment because he needs innocent dreams to prolong his life. But the children are scared, so they only have nightmares. Then a circus strongman arrives with an orphan to find the kids. After that things start to get weird. An orgy of sick jokes, startling images and twisted ideas, this makes *Twelve Monkeys* look like Enid Blyton.

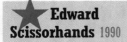

Edward Scissorhands 1990

Director Tim Burton **Cast** Johnny Depp, Winona Ryder, Dianne Wiest 105m

Tim Burton's left-field follow-up to his *Batman*. Edward (**Depp**) is an incomplete man-made boy (and possible Christ figure) whose inventor father (**Vincent Price**) died before he could replace his scissor hands with human ones. Finding him living alone, the local Avon lady (**Wiest**) takes him under her wing, introducing him into society through his topiary and hairdressing skills. Burton's idea, an updated *Frankenstein*, came to him as a kid. Depp makes this – he's one of the few actors who is physically as expressive as silent stars.

Field of Dreams 1989

Director Phil Alden Robinson **Cast** Kevin Costner, Amy Madigan, Ray Liotta 106m

Farmer Ray (**Costner** in his favoured role as everyman) hears voices in his field telling him: "If you build it, he will come." "He" is Shoeless Joe Jackson, a White Sox baseball player who became known as one of the ten "Black Sox" for throwing the World Series in 1919. Spurred on by his love for baseball and his own lost dreams, Ray turns his field into a baseball pitch and Jackson and the other players do indeed come. In **W.P. Kinsella**'s novel (on which this faithfully draws), Ray enlisted reclusive author J.D. Salinger to help him understand the meaning of what is going on. Salinger was so incensed by the novel that a fictitious writer, Terence Mann (**James Earl Jones**), was created so the movie could avoid legal action.

The Fisher King 1991

Director Terry Gilliam **Cast** Robin Williams, Jeff Bridges, Mercedes Ruehl 137m

It's easy to spot the key **Gilliam** moments (the ghost horseman for example), but this is fantasy cemented in the real world. Jack (**Bridges**) was a radio talk DJ who, after a listener goes on a killing spree, fell into alcohol-fuelled despair, supported only by his long-suffering partner (**Ruehl**). **Williams**, a homeless man, rescues him from muggers and Bridges decides to help Williams' quest for the Holy Grail, believing it could cleanse his own soul. Encompassing many elements (the Grail quest, real and imaginary demons, despair and love), this is a touching, exhilarating and frightening tale, aided by fantastic performances from Bridges, Ruehl and **Amanda Plummer** in particular, with Williams' manic character allowed to shine without taking over the movie.

If... 1968

Director Lindsay Anderson **Cast** Malcolm McDowell, David Wood, Richard Warwick 111m

A scathing view of a year in a bizarre English public school, where the boys rebel against the establishment. A movie of its time, with jarring cutting and swaps from colour to sepia (dictated by lack of funds but curiously effective), *If...* still has a frantic appeal, and the sociopathic performance by the then-unknown **McDowell** is mesmerizing. The title is

Elves – the uncool years

Once upon a time, before Peter Jackson and Harry Potter, sword'n'sorcery films were seriously embarrassing. Some guilty pleasures:

Conan the Barbarian (1982)
Breakthrough role for bodybuilder-turned-movie star-turned-ruler of California Arnold Schwarzenegger, which wisely demanded minimal dialogue and maximum body oil.

Krull (1983)
Star Wars meets *Dungeons and Dragons* in a (very un-)special effects cheese fest. The supposedly high speed, gravity-defying Fire Mares were portrayed by shire horses.

Legend (1985)
Ridley Scott's soft-focus, unicorn-filled folly. Memorable as one of the last onscreen sightings of Tom Cruise's original, imperfect teeth.

Willow (1988)
Originally titled *Munchkins*, George Lucas's gorgeous turkey boasts a plot even tinier than its suspiciously hobbity cast.

an ironic nod to the Kipling poem of that name, which celebrates an Englishman's fortitude and restraint. With its beatings, homoeroticism and machine gun battles, this educational establishment couldn't be further from Kipling's vision.

The Last Unicorn 1982

Directors Jules Bass, Arthur Rankin Jr **Cast** Alan Arkin, Jeff Bridges, Christopher Lee **93m**

Tolkien scholar **Peter Beagle**'s novel made "unicornucopia" trendy in 1968; co-directors **Bass** and **Rankin Jr** marketed his book as "hip Tolkien" to raise the money to make this animated fantasy. The final unicorn (voiced by **Mia Farrow**) is turned into a human and must

decide whether to become a unicorn again to save her species or stay as she is so she can love Prince Lir (**Bridges**). There are some fine lines ("No cat anywhere ever gave anyone a straight answer"), sub-Tolkien dialogue, uneven animation and songs. But the strength of Beagle's original fantasy carries it.

The Lord of the Rings
2001–2003

Director Peter Jackson **Cast** Elijah Wood, Sean Astin, Ian McKellen, Viggo Mortensen **558m**

Playing devil's advocate, isn't Gollum just the thinking man's Jar-Jar Binks? Couldn't the walking-talking trees have made their minds up a little quicker in *The Two Towers*? And if **Jackson** really wanted to differentiate the female characters, why didn't he make each gorgeous long-haired, mystical lass distinct? Such minor caveats aside, Jackson's achievement across this trilogy is simply magnificent. **Tolkien**'s fantasy saga was always going to be a tall order to recreate, but its making was almost as epic as the story itself. **Mortensen** lost a tooth, **Orlando Bloom** broke a rib and **John Rhys-Davies** had an allergic reaction to his make-up. The shoot lasted more than a year, during which 1600 pairs of latex ears and feet were used.

Pan's Labyrinth 2006

Director Guillermo del Toro **Cast** Ivana Baquero, Sergi Lopez, Maribel Verdu 119m

Its main character may be an eleven-year-old girl, but **Guillermo del Toro**'s film is far too sophisticated and downright disturbing for children. A spellbinding fable set in post-Civil War Spain, it sees Ofelia escape the brutal realities of Franco's militarist regime by entering her own fairy-tale world. It's hardly a cosy place, however, populated by a fabulous bestiary including the Pale Man – a hairless, eyeless cannibal who makes *Chitty Chitty Bang Bang*'s Child Catcher look like Mary Poppins. Ravishing, unsettling and poetic.

Paperhouse 1988

Director Bernard Rose **Cast** Charlotte Burke, Jane Bertish, Ben Cross 92m

A terrifying adaptation of **Cathe-rine Storr**'s children's book, *Marianne Dreams*, by the director of *Candyman*. An ill little girl from a troubled family discovers that when she dreams she can escape into the house she's drawn herself – only for the house to become a prison. Horror? Fantasy? Thriller? Psychological drama? Not easy to categorize, this British take on *A Nightmare on Elm Street* unjustly fell through the box office net on release, but definitely rewards a look, if you can bear to peek through your fingers…

Repo Man 1984

Director Alex Cox **Cast** Harry Dean Stanton, Emilio Estevez, Tracey Walter 92m

Alex Cox's most original movie is a fantastic conflation of every budget sci-fi theme: a dystopian future, a government conspiracy, aliens and atomic power. Otto (**Estevez**, in his first and best role) is a disaffected youth who meets a car repossession man (**Stanton**, in his funniest role) and is persuaded to join the agency. In mortal danger, he's caught up in the hysteria surrounding a mysterious 1964 Chevy and its glowing cargo. Cox adds to this strange brew the details that define a cult movie: each character except Otto is named after a kind of beer and all the cars have Christmas tree air fresheners. Plus there's the all-time cult movie catchphrase: "Intense? Repo man always intense!"

The Seven Faces of Dr Lao 1964

Director George Pal **Cast** Tony Randall, Barbara Eden 100m

In this film based on **Charles Finney**'s 1935 cult novel, *The Circus of Dr Lao*, the mysterious Dr Lao (**Randall**) arrives at a turn-of-the-century western town and, with his magical circus, mesmerizes the townsfolk and confronts them with their own prejudices and foibles. Randall, who had presumably been let out on parole from Doris Day and Rock Hudson movies, plays each of the circus characters, but is hardly recognizable beneath **William Tuttle**'s Oscar-winning make-up.

The Seventh Seal 1957

Director Ingmar Bergman **Cast** Gunnar Björnstrand, Bengt Ekerot, Nils Poppe 95m

In a script originally rejected by the studio as too dour, a knight (**Max von Sydow**) and his squire return home from the Crusades only to meet Death (**Ekerot**). Even if you've never seen a Bergman movie, you may recognize the chess-playing scene from the *Bill and Ted* spoof. The final scene when Death and his followers dance away was acted out by a group of technicians and tourists, as the actors had all left the set. In a spooky coincidence, Ekerot died shortly afterwards.

Synecdoche New York 2008

Director Charlie Kaufman **Cast** Philip Seymour Hoffman, Catherine Keener 124m

Having sucked us inside John Malkovich's brain and chased us through Jim Carrey's, you'd expect the directorial debut of *Eternal Sunshine of the Spotless Mind* writer **Charlie Kaufman** to be something

mental. This time we're inside the head of hypochondriac theatre director Caden Cotard (**Hoffman**), who is awarded a grant to produce an artistic work of "great truth" that becomes an ever-expanding study on himself. Loop-the-looping complex themes such as mortality, infidelity, impotence, the relationship of artist to work and art to life, this is a fantastically funny, intellectual roller-coaster ride where you never know what's real and what's not.

The Thief of Bagdad 1940

Directors Michael Powell, Ludwig Berger, Tim Whelan **Cast** Sabu, Conrad Veidt 106m

British wartime audiences needed a bit of magic in their lives, and this sumptuous Arabian Nights fantasy provided it in spades. It's lost none of its power to whisk us away to a magical world, the luscious cinematography, audacious special effects and exquisite Technicolor presaging much of **Powell**'s later work. Loosely based on the *Tales of the 1001 Nights*, this has it all: flying carpets and evil wizards; giant spiderwebs and genies in bottles; jewels, souks and evil viziers. Enchanting.

Les visiteurs 1993

Director Jean-Marie Poiré **Cast** Christian Clavier, Jean Reno, Valérie Lemercier 107m

France's biggest domestic hit at the time stars **Reno** as medieval knight Godefroy, who is transported – along with his faithful squire (**Clavier**, who co-wrote the script) – into the future. The bumbling pair were heading back in time to change his-

Marion (Solveig Dommartin), trapeze artist and target of an angel's love in Wim Wenders' fantastical *Wings of Desire*.

tory, but ended up in the twentieth not the twelfth century. The action resembles an extended *Benny Hill* sketch as they battle with cars, steal food and learn to cope with modern life.

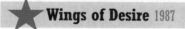

Wings of Desire 1987

Director Wim Wenders **Cast** Bruno Ganz, Solveig Dommartin, Peter Falk **128m**

Wenders' masterpiece was remade eleven years later as *City of Angels*, with Nicolas Cage and Meg Ryan. The original, with **Ganz**'s angel Damiel wandering around Berlin comforting unhappy souls until he sees a trapeze artist and falls in love, is an incredibly moving exploration of what it means to be human. Ganz's gentle melancholy makes the movie, and the remake just couldn't compete

with **Henri Alekan**'s sumptuous photography.

Xanadu 1980

Director Robert Greenwald **Cast** Olivia Newton-John, Gene Kelly, Michael Beck **96m**

This can only have been made because some Hollywood executive had a fantasy about **Newton-John** on roller skates. She plays Greek muse Kira, whose role in life is to inspire men to achieve. With the help of **Kelly** (who only took the role because he wouldn't have far to travel to work), she persuades musician Sonny (**Beck**) to build a roller rink. It's a rare privilege to see a star light the touch paper and watch their career explode on camera. *Grease* had made her a movie star. After this, she couldn't get a leading role in Greece.

FIGHT CLUB

Boxing and wrestling have provided the excuse for many a director to thoughtfully explore male machismo, corrupt societies and self-expression – while making sure to weave in a few crowd-pleasing fight scenes.

Cockfighter 1974

Director Monte Hellman **Cast** Warren Oates, Harry Dean Stanton, Ed Begley Jr 83m

Given the choice of cockfighting or his fiancée, **Oates**'s character feels he has no choice and with obsessive single-mindedness sets out to win the Cockfighter of the Year award. **Hellman**'s offbeat drama, a brilliant adaptation of the **Charles Willeford** novel, has a wonderful grasp of the milieu, showing us the pathetic ruse – nicking his bird's beak – Oates uses to try and boost his winnings.

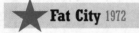 ## Fat City 1972

Director John Huston **Cast** Stacy Keach, Jeff Bridges, Susan Tyrell 96m

The antithesis to *Rocky*. **Huston**'s late great movie, drawing on a novel and script by **Leonard Gardner**, is a powerful, understated character study of the empty lives of two marginalized boxers. **Keach** is the alcoholic with emptiness ahead, **Bridges** the optimist on the way up. An amateur lightweight champion in his youth, Huston gives this a sad, realistic

resonance, aided immeasurably by **Conrad Hall**'s noirish cinematography.

Girlfight 2000

Director Karyn Kusamo **Cast** Michelle Rodriguez, Jaime Tirelli, Paul Calderon 110m

A troubled teen in Brooklyn learns to express herself in the boxing ring in this fascinating, low-budget movie. Despite an unnecessary romantic sub-plot, **Kusamo**'s debut feature works brilliantly, thanks in part to **Rodriguez** who is every bit as dedicated, easily wounded and quick to defend herself as her character.

Hard Times 1975

Director Walter Hill **Cast** Charles Bronson, James Coburn, Jill Ireland, Strother Martin 97m

Bronson's best film. His weathered contours were made for the role of Charlie, the taciturn New Orleans street fighter, and contrast brilliantly with **Coburn**'s grinning, flashy turn as his backer and partner. **Hill**'s classic exploration of machismo is bitter, tough and steeped in the ambience of 1930s America.

Kid Galahad 1937

Director Michael Curtiz **Cast** Edward G. Robinson, Bette Davis, Humphrey Bogart 102m

Romance, betrayal, men beating each other into a bloody pulp, **Curtiz's** melodrama has all these and more. But it's the star power on display that really gives this its kick. **Robinson** is the promoter enraged by rival **Bogart's** corrupt ways, while **Davis**, as Robinson's girlfriend, just wants him to leave well alone. Ultimately, the rivalry destroys them all and, for once, the innocent boxer and his girl are the winners.

Raging Bull 1980

Director Martin Scorsese **Cast** Robert De Niro, Joe Pesci 129m

This is about boxing in the same way *Battleship Potemkin* is about a boat. Like all the best sports movies, the sport itself is a vehicle for exploring more complex themes, not least the relationship between masculinity and violence. This shows its subject, Jake LaMotta, as a figure whose capacity for violence in the ring is indivisible from his capacity for violence outside it. **De Niro**, in arguably his finest performance, went into full-on Method mode and gained several stones to provide the film's most arresting image: the young winner who becomes a fat loser. The juxtaposition of soaring strings above scenes of brutality would be done again, but seldom have beauty and savagery been allied to such devastating effect.

Santo vs las mujeres vampiro 1962

Director Alfonso Corona Blake **Cast** Santo, Lorena Velázquez, María Duval 89m

Masked Mexican wrestling legend **El Santo** is hired to use his strong-arm tactics to protect a girl doomed to be taken away by vampires. Can Santo defeat the curse? You betcha – even if it means wrestling with a werewolf (who, the footage suggests, only grow hair on their faces). This cheesy adventure is delightfully bizarre. The more accomplished entries in Santo's canon – notably *Santo contra el Doctor Muerte* (1973) – don't exert the same strange fascination.

The Wrestler 2008

Director Darren Aronofsky **Cast** Mickey Rourke, Marisa Tomei, Evan Rachel Wood 109m

There is so much autobiographical resonance for **Rourke** in this character study of a once famous wrestler reduced to loading boxes at a supermarket that it's easy to see why his iconic performance struck such an award-winning chord. It's as if, one review noted, *Rocky* had been remade by Scorsese in his *Mean Streets* prime. Though Rourke dominates, **Tomei** deserves credit for making her stripper more than a cypher.

FILM NOIR

For about ten years from the mid-1940s the screen was filled with doomed heroes, their lives wrapped around the little finger of a *femme fatale* who looked like an angel but schemed like the devil. *Film noir* is the oddest of mainstream movie genres, with a look, feel and tone far removed from most other Hollywood pictures of the era.

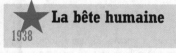

La bête humaine
1938

Director Jean Renoir **Cast** Jean Gabin, Simone Simon 104m

Film noir owes much to French films like this, part of a movement critics have dubbed poetic realism. Fritz Lang remade this story as *Human Desire* in 1954, with Glenn Ford in the Gabin role as an engineer who has fits of uncontrollable violence against women who helps plot his lover's husband's death. **Renoir** wrote the script from the **Emile Zola** novel and you'll enjoy this more if you read the book first.

The Big Combo 1955

Director Joseph H. Lewis **Cast** Cornel Wilde, Richard Conte, Jean Wallace 84m

Wilde plays a cop obsessed with bringing down a mobster (**Conte**), while in love with the gangster's moll (**Wallace**). This movie is full of strange moments that don't fit the formula, such as the homo-erotic banter between two hoodlums (one played by **Lee Van Cleef**). And the scene where Conte kisses Wallace on the face and neck and disappears out of shot, the implication being his kisses have travelled south. Even an unusually happy ending can't disguise the oddness.

Blast of Silence 1961

Director Allen Baron **Cast** Allen Baron, Molly McCarthy 77m

Swift, brutal and black-hearted, **Baron**'s New York *noir* is a lost gem that was dumped on release by its distributor but has recently had a revival of fortune. Made for peanuts and with borrowed equipment and largely non-professional actors, it's a portrait of a hit man on assignment in Manhattan during Christmas. Showing a flair for the oddball idiosyncrasies of urban living, the film has a pronounced melancholy enhanced by the seasonal setting. The tough as nails voiceover narration is performed by *noir* regular **Lionel Stander**.

Whose noir?

Film noir is probably cinema's finest international co-production. The term was first applied by French critics to the hard-boiled school of American crime fiction written by **James M. Cain** and **Dashiell Hammett**. But its distinctive visual techniques, especially the high contrast black-and-white look, were borrowed from German expressionist movies such as Fritz Lang's *M*, and their themes were often based on the French "poetic realist" films of the 1930s, such as *Rue sans nom* (1934). **John Alton**, the cameraman who created the chiaroscuro look of **Anthony Mann**'s great *noir* movies was born in Hungary. Most *noir* directors were from central or eastern Europe: **Fritz Lang**, **Otto Preminger**, **Edgar Ulmer** and **Billy Wilder** were all from the old Austro-Hungarian Empire and **Robert Siodmak** was from Germany. Given what was happening to their old homeland, it's not hard to understand *noir*'s peculiar combination of cynicism, fatalism and pessimism.

Blood Simple 1984

Director Joel Coen **Cast** Frances McDormand, John Getz, Dan Hedaya **95m**

An early example of the flurry of American indie films labelled "neo-*noir*", **Joel** and **Ethan Coen**'s debut owes much to the hard-boiled novels of **James M. Cain**. Set in a blisteringly hot Texas, the plot has sleazy bar-owner Marty (**Hedaya**) hiring private eye **M. Emmet Walsh** to deal with his adulterous wife (**McDormand**) and the man she's having an affair with (**Getz**). So far so *noir*. But things rapidly get out of whack, in an unpredictable, sometimes gory black comedy that marked the Coen brothers as filmmakers to watch.

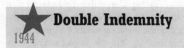 **Double Indemnity**

1944

Director Billy Wilder **Cast** Fred MacMurray, Barbara Stanwyck **106m**

Even in a movie industry increasingly content to pillage its past for future profit, *Double Indemnity* has been largely left alone, sacrosanct apart from *Body Heat* and a Mr Magoo spoof (*Trouble Indemnity* in 1950). **Wilder** deserves most of the credit for this classic yarn of a woman who persuades her lover/insurance salesman to murder her husband. But spare some praise for **Stanwyck** – she had to wear a wig (which the studio boss said made her look like George Washington) and look as sleazy as possible to, as she put it, "go into an out-and-out cold-blooded killer." Wilder asked her if she was an actress or a mouse. The answer's right there onscreen.

Force of Evil 1948

Director Abraham Polonsky **Cast** John Garfield, Thomas Gomez **78m**

The only movie **Polonsky** helmed before he was blacklisted, like his "comeback" Western *Tell Them Willie Boy Is Here*, takes itself a tad too seriously. That said, **Garfield** shines as a lawyer for the Mob who has a cash register where his heart should be. Polonsky gave cinematographer **George Barnes** a book of Edward Hopper paintings to show how he wanted this to look and Barnes did his best.

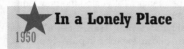

In a Lonely Place
1950

Director Nicholas Ray **Cast** Humphrey Bogart, Gloria Grahame **93m**

Nicholas Ray takes the ambiguity inherent in many *noir* films and runs with it in this movie, using **Bogart** as a frustrated screenwriter who may or may not have murdered a waitress. **Grahame** gives Bogart an alibi because she likes his face, although when Bogie tries to kiss her she objects: "I said I liked it; I didn't say

I wanted to kiss it." This may be as close as we get to the real Bogie onscreen. Grahame came in when Warners refused to lend Bacall and had to sign a contract which forbade her influencing her husband director in a "feminine fashion".

The Killing 1956

Director Stanley Kubrick **Cast** Sterling Hayden, Marie Windsor, Vince Edwards, Coleen Gray **84m**

This study of a racetrack heist made **Kubrick**'s name. For once, it's not the robbery that goes wrong but the aftermath, when the suitcase to carry the money becomes critical. Blacklisted **Jim Thompson** wrote the dialogue, and the use of multiple flashbacks anticipates *Reservoir Dogs*. **Hayden** leads well as the mastermind and **Windsor** is definitive as the treacherous temptress.

The power of Gloria

This lady really was a tramp – onscreen at least – although when **Gloria Grahame** married her stepson **Tony Ray**, son of director **Nicholas Ray**, some decided she hadn't played temptresses by accident. Descended from King Edward III (but raised in Los Angeles), she was offered a contract by **Louis B. Mayer** in 1944 after he saw her on Broadway. She appeared in various movies (including *It's a Wonderful Life*) but never fitted the Hollywood star system and MGM sold her contract to RKO. There she achieved absolute greatness in *In a Lonely Place* (1950), directed by her then husband Ray. She excels as the pretty neighbour who falls for likeable loser Humphrey Bogart, only to discover just how dark the nights of his soul really are.

Grahame won an Oscar for her hilarious turn as a writer's wife in *The Bad and the Beautiful*, but the decline of *film noir*, marital problems and a reputation for being difficult on set meant that, from 1959, she faced twenty years of supporting roles and minor films. Her smirk would later inspire Annette Bening in the noirish 1990 classic *The Grifters*.

The Lady from Shanghai
1948

Director Orson Welles **Cast** Orson Welles, Rita Hayworth 127m

Based on **Sherman King**'s novel *If I Die Before I Wake*, in the hands of **Orson Welles** this simmering if somewhat hackneyed tale of lust and deceit is transformed into something truly remarkable. As with many *noirs*, the plot is pretty impenetrable (Welles plays a loveable Irish rogue who falls in with a wealthy couple with a mutual hatred of each other) but the execution is thrilling and audacious. Climaxing with a gunfight in a hall of mirrors, the film was intended as a vehicle for **Hayworth** (then Welles' wife) and like so many Welles masterpieces was savagely recut by studio bosses.

Laura 1944

Director Otto Preminger **Cast** Gene Tierney, Dana Andrews, Clifton Webb 88m

This emerged from a degree of chaos: studio boss Darryl F. Zanuck banned **Preminger** (replacement for the first sacked director) from the Fox lot, refused to cast **Webb** until a screen test was made, and tried to change the ending. Set against such intrigue and subterfuge, the movie is simplicity itself. **Andrews** is the detective falling for the girl whose murder he is investigating (but who hasn't been murdered). Webb shines as a villainous columnist but had a breakdown afterwards.

The Locket 1946

Director John Brahm **Cast** Laraine Day, Brian Aherne, Robert Mitchum 86m

Day's *femme fatale* is set to marry until her ex-husband (**Aherne**) turns up and tells her fiancé she is a habitual liar and kleptomaniac. Told using the now famed flashback within a flashback within a flashback device, **Brahm** never lets this lapse into an exercise in pure style, keeping a close eye on the plot and the finale.

The Naked Kiss 1964

Director Samuel Fuller **Cast** Constance Towers, Anthony Eisley 93m

Samuel Fuller can sometimes be as subtle as a nuclear strike but he has an undeniable knack for telling images. The scene that opens this movie, where the hooker beats her pimp to a pulp with the heel of her shoe and is revealed to be bald, is one of his most notorious. But this bleak tale of a woman who was sexually abused as a child (a daring theme in 1964) and gives up prostitution to seek redemption in a small town has many more such moments, including the scene where she stuffs money into the mouth of the local brothel-keeper. **Towers** is simply remarkable in the demanding lead role.

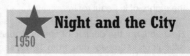

Night and the City
1950

Director Jules Dassin **Cast** Richard Widmark, Herbert Lom 100m

Adapted from the lowlife novel by **Gerald Kersh**, *Night and the City* drips corruption, paranoia and doom. **Widmark** delivers an indelible performance as Harry Fabian, a nightclub tout and desperate dreamer who tries to worm his way into the wrestling rackets of post-war London. In his path lie a number of formidable obstacles, including his own tendency towards failure. Much of the filming was done in actual after-midnight hours, shooting night scenes in a London still shattered and skeletal from wartime bombings. Locations included Soho, Piccadilly and the Festival of Britain construction site on the South Bank.

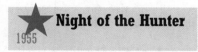

Night of the Hunter

1955

Director Charles Laughton **Cast** Robert Mitchum, Lillian Gish 92m

As **Laughton** himself liked to say, he had a face like an elephant's backside, so it's surprising that he didn't go behind the camera more often. He may, though, have been depressed by the commercial and critical failure of this movie, with its storyline about a psychotic preacher who pesters two kids to find out where their dad has hidden the loot from a robbery. **Gish**'s casting is just one of many nods by Laughton to D.W. Griffith. Nobody has

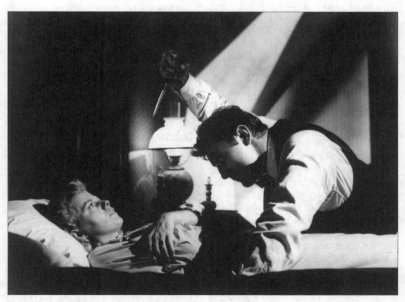

The charismatic Robert Mitchum seen here in full-on psychopath mode in *Night of the Hunter*.

ever played a psychopath with the nonchalant charisma of **Mitchum**.

Out of the Past 1947

Director Jacques Tourneur **Cast** Robert Mitchum, Jane Greer, Kirk Douglas **97m**

Tourneur's complex *noir*, in which **Mitchum** is a private eye sent by gambler **Douglas** to find his runaway dame and inevitably falls for her, plays beautifully on the ambiguity that marked all of Mitchum's best movies. Douglas is excellent as the chief villain, while **Greer** is slipperiness personified as she switches between good and evil, often from line to line. The voiceover narration does, at times, lapse into Chandler parody, but otherwise this is a true classic.

Pickup on South Street 1953

Director Samuel Fuller **Cast** Richard Widmark, Jean Peters, Thelma Ritter **80m**

The experience of watching this for the first time was described by one reviewer as "like finding gold in the back yard while mowing the lawn." One of the best *noir* thrillers of the 1940s and 50s, its brilliance was overshadowed by politics. Some were offended by the Communist agent portrayed as the baddie; and others didn't understand why the hero wouldn't play ball with the Feds. But **Fuller** is more concerned with people and what drives them than political issues. Shot in twenty days, this is the director at his best, creating a grimy criminal underworld and draw-

ing superb performances from his cast, particularly **Ritter** as stool pigeon Moe.

Shadow of a Doubt 1943

Director Alfred Hitchcock **Cast** Teresa Wright, Joseph Cotten **108m**

Noir's ambiguous blend of good and evil so suited **Hitchcock** that many of his movies could have been listed here. **Wright** plays a bored young girl called Charlie who invites her uncle Charlie (**Cotten**) to visit but soon discovers that he is a murderer. The movie is full of pairs, both obvious and subtle: the two Charlies, two detectives, two suspects, even two conversations about murder techniques and the double brandy Charlie orders in the Till Two bar. This is said to be Hitchcock's favourite movie, possibly because he worked some of the details of his early life into the script, including a glimpse of a screen mum called Emma.

The Stranger 1946

Director Orson Welles **Cast** Edward G. Robinson, Loretta Young, Billy House **95m**

One of the odder ironies of *film noir* was that it turned **Robinson** from a gangster into a good guy. Here he is the dogged detective who tracks **Welles**' war criminal in disguise to a small town in Connecticut. This is the director being a good boy, delivering a movie under budget and conventional enough to be a commercial success. His biographer David Thomson suggests that it might have been better if Robinson had taken Welles' role and, as the director originally wanted, Agnes Moorehead played the detective. Welles himself reckoned it was his worst film.

Touchez pas au grisbi 1954

Director Jacques Becker **Cast** Jean Gabin, René Dary, Jeanne Moreau **94m**

Max (**Gabin**) and Riton (**Dary**) are two ageing gangsters who manage to pull off their final heist, a spectacular gold bullion robbery at Orly airport. All is well until Max's former girlfriend Josy (**Moreau**) tips off a rival gangster. The latter kidnaps Riton and threatens to kill him unless Max hands over the spoils from his robbery… Helping to birth the French *policier, Touchez pas au grisbi* influenced subsequent directors such as Jean-Pierre Melville, not least in its spectacularly staged robbery and conniving female protagonist.

★ Touch of Evil 1958

Director Orson Welles **Cast** Orson Welles, Charlton Heston, Janet Leigh **108m**

Orson Welles is Hank Quinlan, a corrupt cop who asks **Marlene Dietrich** to read his future. "You're all used up, you haven't got any" she tells him, but you don't need to be Mystic Meg to see that. By then he is almost friendless, pursued by his old sidekick and by do-gooding Mexican lawyer **Heston**. But the plot is almost incidental in this study of corruption and menace in a small border town: it's scenes like the one where **Leigh** retreats up her hotel bed while a gang prepare to pump her with heroin that stick in the memory. The focus on Quinlan unbalances the

movie and underlines that Welles the actor is not on top form. Quinlan is too much of a monster, while Heston's troubled lawyer is more convincing.

You Only Live Once 1937

Director Fritz Lang **Cast** Sylvia Sidney, Henry Fonda, Barton MacLane **86m**

Fonda impresses as the ex-con who tries to go straight but fails. Even more impressive is **Lang**'s grasp of the Hollywood idiom only three years after arriving from Nazi Germany without speaking a word of English. He fled after Josef Goebbels had offered him a senior role in the German film industry. Lang had declined, saying he had Jewish grandparents, to which Goebbels replied: "We'll decide who's Jewish." This is one of a pair of American movies he made in the late 1930s about society's outcasts, the other being *You and Me* (1938), again with Sidney and MacLane.

FOOD

Cordon bleu noodles, homicidal tomatoes, prime cuts of beef which aren't quite what they seem – they're all allegorical grist to the moviemaker's mill.

Attack of the Killer Tomatoes 1978

Director John De Bello **Cast** David Miller, George Wilson, Sharon Taylor, Jack Riley **87m**

Director **De Bello** set out to create a bad spoof of the sci-fi B-movies of the 1950s, and there's no doubt that he succeeded. Giant tomatoes (red beach balls in real life) attack people, and a crack team – a parachute-clad lieutenant, a diver never without his scuba gear and a master of disguise dressed as Adolf Hitler – is sent to destroy them. Disturbingly compulsive viewing.

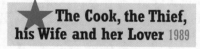

The Cook, the Thief, his Wife and her Lover 1989

Director Peter Greenaway **Cast** Richard Bohringer, Michael Gambon, Helen Mirren **124m**

The food featured in **Peter Greenaway**'s tale of love, greed and revenge is often overshadowed by the sumptuous sets, Gaultier costumes and **Gambon**'s portrayal of evil, but the image of brut-ish gangster Spica (Gambon) about to tuck into the naked, cooked man laid out before him, is simply unforgettable. The action is surrounded by the creations of the chef (**Bohringer**). This was originally rated X, but Miramax released it with no rating. In case you were wondering, the dog poo was chocolate mousse. There's supposed to be an allegory about Thatcherism here, somewhere.

Dumplings 2004

Director Fruit Chan **Cast** Miriam Yeung Chin-Wah, Tony Leung **131m**

Mrs Lee, a former TV star and now wife of a prominent businessman, is driven by a desperate need to appear youthful. She learns of a mysterious chef whose delicious dumplings are said to make women appear younger. But what is the secret ingredient in the dumplings and at what cost has it been devised? A darkly satirical look at the obsession with looks and beauty, this sinister work, beautifully shot by **Christopher Doyle**, also plays on the old adage that we are what we eat.

Eat Drink Man Woman 1994

Director Ang Lee **Cast** Sihung Lung, Yu-Wen Wang, Chien-Lien Wu, Kuei-Mei Yang 124m

Like **Lee**'s previous work, *The Wedding Banquet*, this is a tale of love, relationships and traditions played out with the metaphor of food. A Taipei master chef, Chu (**Sihung Lung**) tries to communicate his feelings for his three daughters through his ritual Sunday banquets. Rating this movie by the food alone, *Eat Drink* ranks alongside the delectable chocolates in Lasse Hallström's pleasant time-passer *Chocolat*.

Our Daily Bread 2005

Director Nikolaus Geyrhalter 130m

A sobering look at the world of industrial food production, *Our Daily Bread* is one of the most provocative documentaries of recent times. To the visual and aural rhythm of conveyor belts and immense machines, **Geyrhalter** offers a look at the surreal and monumental European factories where the majority of our food supply is produced. In these sterile environments, people, animals, crops and machines play a supporting role in the logistics of a system that provides our society's standard of living. Austere in style (there's neither voiceover nor music), the film contains images that range from the terrifying to the strangely contemplative.

Parents 1989

Director Bob Balaban **Cast** Randy Quaid, Mary Beth Hurt, Sandy Dennis 82m

The blackest of black comedies, *Parents* is a tale of suburban cannibalism. There are moments of horror, but **Balaban**'s big-screen debut is best enjoyed for its humour and wackiness. **Quaid** and **Hurt** play seemingly perfect, perky 1950s parents, feeding their son Michael (**Bryan Madorsky**) nutritious meat every night. He isn't convinced these are prime beef cuts and becomes increasingly wary. Quaid puts in a particularly freaky performance, with Hurt perfect as his seemingly cutesy wife. If your appetite for urban cannibalism is still unsatisfied, check out Jean Caro and Jean-Pierre Jeunet's *Delicatessen*.

★ Tampopo 1986

Director Juzo Itami **Cast** Tsutomu Yamazaki, Nobuko Miyamoto, Koji Yakusho 114m

Tampopo (**Miyamoto**) is a widowed noodle chef whose knight in shining armour (**Yamazaki**) teaches her to become the very best noodle chef possible. Food isn't a metaphor in this movie, it is the movie. It envelopes the lives of every protagonist, from the gangster who misses sex and food to the finicky old lady driving a shopkeeper insane. An early foray into directing by **Itami**, and one of his less offensive pieces.

GAMBLING

The great thing about gambling movies, if you're making one, is that your losses are tax-deductible. Not that this has influenced directors at all…

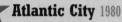 Atlantic City 1980

Director Louis Malle **Cast** Burt Lancaster, Susan Sarandon, Michel Piccoli 105m

If Robert Mitchum hadn't been so vain he would have won the role of small-time gangster Lou. **Malle** was keen to cast the rough-and-ready actor, but his recent facelift forced a rethink and the casting of **Lancaster**. Set in the poor man's Vegas, Lou dreams he was once a gangland big shot and meets Sally (**Sarandon**), an aspiring croupier hoping to make it to Monte Carlo. They become embroiled in a drug deal and a love story against the backdrop of dismal Atlantic City.

Bay of Angels 1963

Director Jacques Demy **Cast** Jeanne Moreau, Claude Mann, Paul Guers 79m

A lesser-known *nouvelle vague* work from **Demy**, in which the mild-mannered Jean (**Mann**) becomes addicted to gambling and even more so to **Moreau**'s dangerous blonde divorcée, herself a slave to the roulette wheel. The roller-coaster ups and downs of the gambling life – its repetitive compulsion and its wild impulsiveness – are echoed in the breathlessly swooping camerawork and on the swirling piano soundtrack, leading you to believe totally in the crazy ending. Moreau and Mann epitomize 1960s French chic, and Nice never looked more seedily glamorous.

Casino 1995

Director Martin Scorsese **Cast** Robert De Niro, Sharon Stone, Joe Pesci 178m

In the first hour of *Casino*, the detail about how the Mafia ran casinos in Vegas is so intense it's like watching a documentary. **De Niro** is the casino owner who marries a hooker (**Stone**) who then has a fling with hubby's hit man (**Pesci**). This triggers the Mafia's undignified exit from Vegas. In a strong cast, Stone carries the movie, without uncrossing her legs. An intriguing exercise in one of **Scorsese**'s favourite sports, historical revisionism: while the rest of the world cheers the sanitizing of Vegas, Scorsese sounds a note of quiet regret that an outlaw's paradise has become another Disneyland.

The Cincinnati Kid 1965

Director Norman Jewison **Cast** Steve McQueen, Edward G. Robinson 113m

When professional poker players gather in New Orleans for a high-stakes game, **McQueen**'s ambitious hotshot gets a chance to challenge **Robinson**'s master. Despite the seductive distractions of **Ann-Margret** and **Tuesday Weld**, most riveting is the game of wills between the old and new icons. Not the cardsharp variation on *The Hustler* it aspired to be, this has plenty of cool and a great cult ensemble including Joan Blondell, terrific as wisecracking dealer Lady Fingers.

The Croupier 1998

Director Mike Hodges **Cast** Clive Owen, Gina McKee, Alex Kingston 94m

Mike Hodges' best movie since *Get Carter* in 1971 is an original, philosophical morality play/crime drama with a tough, brooding script by **Paul Mayersberg**. An edgy, glinting **Owen** is a struggling writer using his job in a London casino for explosive material in his novel. Despite his coolly watchful, cynical gaze, he is lured into a heist with a sting in its tale (sic). **Kingston**, on hiatus from *ER*, showed another facet of her talent as a duplicitous South African seductress.

5 Card Stud 1968

Director Henry Hathaway **Cast** Dean Martin, Robert Mitchum, Inger Stevens 103m

Critics pooh-pooh this Western collision with Agatha Christie-like murder mystery, in which the lynching of a card cheat is avenged by a strangler picking off the saloon's poker-playing regulars. The rest of us can't quite resist natty gambler **Martin** turning sleuth, **Mitchum**'s suspicious, hellacious preacher, **Stevens**' suspicious, razor-brandishing lady barber, some nicely dry wit and, especially, Dino crooning the swinging title song, wooing the gals, shooting down the bad guys and wearing the same coat as in all his Westerns.

The Lady Gambles 1949

Director Michael Gordon **Cast** Barbara Stanwyck, Robert Preston 99m

Las Vegas hadn't long stopped being a chicken run when this movie – about a woman who accompanies her husband there and becomes addicted to gambling – was made. **Gordon** would later direct Doris Day comedies, but here he shines a pretty remorseless light on the ugly seam running through Vegas life. The scene where **Stanwyck** gets beaten up by thugs in an alley is remarkable for what is, for all its *noir* trappings, a star vehicle. Look out for Tony Curtis as a bellboy and for the film crew reflected in the window of the bus Stanwyck is on.

GANGSTERS

Organized crime, disorganized crime – there's something therapeutic about cheering on the bad guys. Since gangster films came into their own in the 1920s, the criminal underworld – from Moscow to Hollywood, Hong Kong to Brighton – has exerted a fascination for filmmakers. See also the Mafia (p.213) and Yakuza (p.423) sections.

Bonnie and Clyde 1967

Director Arthur Penn **Cast** Warren Beatty, Faye Dunaway, Gene Hackman 111m

Despite Warner Bros giving the movie only a limited release, it was an unprecedented success and appeared to usher in a new Hollywood. The old Hollywood wasn't impressed: Jack Warner, after a private screening, scolded **Beatty** about its length: "This is a three-piss picture." The tale of a 1920s gang of bank robbers led by Clyde Barrow and Bonnie Parker is essentially a movie about reacting against the establishment.

Borsalino 1970

Director Jacques Deray **Cast** Jean-Paul Belmondo, Alain Delon, Michel Bouquet 126m

François (**Belmondo**) and Roch (**Delon**) are two small-time crooks making their way in the Marseilles crime world in the 1930s. What begins as simple race-fixing and running errands for the local Mob bosses rapidly turns more serious as the two decide to go into business for themselves. **Claude Bolling**'s delightful score, the nods to masters like Howard Hawks and the sparkling performances of the stars make this a very entertaining, if sometimes bloody, pastiche. Followed in 1974 by the slightly less engaging *Borsalino & Co*.

Brighton Rock 1947

Director John Boulting **Cast** Richard Attenborough, Carol Marsh 92m

Richard Attenborough gives his finest performance as babyfaced gang-leader Pinkie who, after murdering a rival racketeer, spirals out of control. Although author **Graham Greene** applauded Attenborough's chilling portrayal, the movie, one of Britain's best *films noirs*, is marred by Greene's decision to give his screenplay an overly optimistic ending, with which **Boulting** went OTT. This aside, the movie, known rather reductively in the US as *Young Scarface*, remains a bleak, perfectly crafted slice of gang life.

Brother 1997

Director Aleksei Balabanov **Cast** Sergei Bodrov Jr, Viktor Sukhorukov 96m

This caused a stir in Russia, accused by the authorities of glamorizing the Russian mafia. There is much to like here. Danila (**Bodrov**) finds an elusive father figure in his older brother (**Sukhorukov**), who leads him into being a Mob killer. Danila comes to realize this isn't the life for him, the movie closing with a refreshingly honest, if downbeat scene of him heading out into the world to try his luck again.

Eastern Promises 2007

Director David Cronenberg **Cast** Viggo Mortensen, Naomi Watts 100m

Reuniting **Cronenberg** with his *History of Violence* leading man, this violent thriller follows a harrowing chain of murder, deceit and retribution amidst London's Russian organized crime families. Sharply scripted by **Steven Knight**, the film's centrepiece is an astonishingly choreographed bathhouse scene in which a lithe and game Mortensen battles in the buff with two fearsome assassins. Meticulously designed, the authentic evocation of the Russian mafia clans is augmented by **Howard Shore**'s wonderful score.

 **Get Carter** 1971

Director Mike Hodges **Cast** Michael Caine, Ian Hendry, Britt Ekland 112m

Cool, unrelenting and vicious, Jack Carter (**Caine**) returns to Newcastle to find those responsible for killing his brother and falls into a world of corruption, pornography and murder. Forty years on, the coolness with which Jack dishes out violence remains disturbing, and anticipates the measured violence of *The Godfather*. Playwright **John Osborne** is surprisingly effective as the crime boss. **Caine** didn't get to know him well: "He seemed to be someone who didn't like many other people, so I kept out of his way in case I was one of them." Sly Stallone's remake is to be avoided.

Gloria 1980

Director John Cassavetes **Cast** Gena Rowlands, Julie Carmen, John Adames 121m

The idea of teaming tough-talking gangsters with smart-mouthed kids isn't new, but the casting of **Rowlands** as Gloria is what carries the movie. A family is wiped out by the Mob for giving information to the FBI, only the seven-year-old son surviving. Gloria (Rowlands) is the former gangster's moll who begrudgingly looks after him. From here a cat-and-mouse chase ensues, with Gloria's street smarts saving the kid and herself. **Cassavetes** gives the movie a suitably smoky feel but it's devoid of some of his usual touches. Avoid the 1999 Sharon Stone remake.

★ Infernal Affairs 2002

Directors Wai-Keung Lau, Alan Mak **Cast** Andy Lau, Tony Leung 102m

Later remade by **Scorsese** as *The Departed*, *Infernal Affairs* looks at the world of the contemporary Hong Kong triads through the parallel lives of a cop who secretly reports to a ruthless crime boss and a rookie undercover officer posing as a member of the same boss's gang. Concluding in an inevitable confrontation, the film avoids stylized violence in favour of a slower accruement of emotional and psychological tension. Featuring Asian superstars **Andy Lau** and **Tony Leung**, the film was a huge domestic success and deservedly gained international critical acclaim.

Miller's Crossing 1990

Director Joel Coen **Cast** Gabriel Byrne, Marcia Gay Harden 115m

The **Coen brothers**' terrific tribute to *film noir* features a scheming young political advisor caught in shifting loyalties between two crime bosses when a war erupts over a bookie who has been cheating one of them. **Byrne** plays the utterly callous manipulator running rings around the other characters, even though he doesn't really gain anything from it himself. There are flashes of the blackest humour, like the scene where a gang is being ripped to shreds by machine-gun fire to the strains of "Danny Boy".

New Jack City 1991

Director Mario Van Peebles **Cast** Wesley Snipes, Ice-T, Judd Nelson, Bill Nunn 100m

Gangster Nino (**Snipes**) is modelled on Al Pacino's *Scarface*, but the gangland world over which he presides is a reversal of the traditional Mob. Here the Mob is trigger-happy with no code of honour, making it susceptible to infiltration, in this case by ex-cops Appleton (**Ice-T**) and Peretti (**Nelson**, back from the dead). This is an interesting take on the ambitious boss turns megalomaniac, but the plot often spirals out of control with too many characters to get to grips with. Still, there's a grim and suitably menacing feel to the movie, its music helping maintain the pace.

Pete Kelly's Blues 1955

Director Jack Webb **Cast** Jack Webb, Janet Leigh, Edmond O'Brien 95m

Pete Kelly (**Webb**) and his band of jazz musicians come under threat from the Kansas City mob. When the drummer is killed, Pete allows the wise guys to take over the band. Although it can be hard to separate Pete from Jack's alter ego Joe Dragnet Friday, the music and the cast are impressive, with appearances from **Peggy Lee**, **Ella Fitzgerald** and **Jayne Mansfield** in her first screen role.

The Sicilian Clan 1969

Director Henri Verneuil **Cast** Jean Gabin, Alain Delon, Lino Ventura 120m

This isn't about the Sicilian Mafia but a group of gangsters in France planning to make a jewel heist aboard an aircraft. Based on an Auguste le Breton novel, **Gabin** plays the old Don in charge, with **Delon** as a Corsican who dares to fool around with the boss's daughter-in-law. The performances aren't as good as you'd expect from these leads, but the heist itself is a work of genius.

Paul Andrew Williams, *director of* London to Brighton, *writes about* The King of New York *in the Mafia section on p.217. Here he describes three more of his favourite gangster films.*

The Road to Perdition (2002, 117m)

❝ Not only is this my favourite gangster film but it is also my all-time, most perfect film in the world. This film has everything right – and in harmony. From the performances, to the Thomas Newman score, the pace of the movie; but it is also one of the most beautifully shot films ever made. So much more poignant than the graphic novel, it's an absolute master class in filmmaking. ❞

State of Grace (1990, 134m)

❝ Another brilliant film, with a standout performance from Gary Oldman. It's also the first film that introduced me to the talents of Ed Harris and John C. Reilly, playing it straight in a story about Irish mobsters. A work all about family, friendship and a sense of belonging, the film also has a sweet little cameo from Burgess Meredith. Look out for the actor James Russo, who plays the stooge that the undercover Sean Penn hooks up with in the beginning. Russo is a brilliant and underused actor who links me to my next choice. ❞

Donnie Brasco (1997, 126m)

❝ Al Pacino's finest hour. It's the only film of his in recent times where he has played a sympathetic character. His loyalty to Johnny Depp makes the final double cross heartbreaking. Michael Madsen, Bruno Kirby and James Russo make up a perfect team, underplaying to the max. Add Ann Heche who is crazy, sexy and a desperate wife, and you've got an awesome cast. Watch out also for Paul Giamatti in a tiny role. ❞

White Heat 1949

Director Raoul Walsh **Cast** James Cagney, Virginia Mayo, Edmond O'Brien 114m

James Cagney may never have said "You dirty rat!" on celluloid but he does say "Made it, Ma! Top of the world!" in this. In the convoluted way of Hollywood, the movie started life as a police thriller, mutating when Cagney, who needed cash for his production company, signed on.

Under veteran director **Walsh**, Cagney makes ruthless gang-leader Cody one of his most brutal and mesmerizing villains. The scenes emphasizing Cody's unnatural affection for his ma are compelling if OTT, but then Cagney plays him as a universal monster. It was his last great gangster part. Maybe that's why he's so reluctant to die in the end; poor old **O'Brien** (the film's official hero) has to keep pumping bullets in him, asking: "What's keeping him up?"

GAY

In 1927 Hollywood's first self-regulating code banned "any inference of sexual perversity." Ruthlessly applied, this could have ended the careers of Marlene Dietrich, Anthony Perkins and Cecil B. DeMille. Times may have changed, but many in the movie business still live in fear of gossip.

Anders als die Andern 1919

Director Richard Oswald **Cast** Conrad Veidt, Leo Connard **50m**

A rich man falls prey to blackmail when he makes advances to a stranger at a men-only dance. Ahead of its time and a product of German expressionist cinema, this silent movie deals frankly and sympathetically with gay relationships. Almost every copy was destroyed when the Nazis came to power, but a fragmented print was discovered and restored in the 1970s. It was years before Hollywood would show the same maturity towards the subject, with *Victim* in 1961.

The Boys in the Band 1970

Director William Friedkin **Cast** Kenneth Nelson, Frederick Combs **118m**

Mart Crowley's play about a homosexual birthday party made it to the screen as one of the first movies where it was taken as a basic fact that the characters were gay and they were allowed to discuss their lives openly. Not that these men are exactly happy with their lot – the evening progresses to a drunken slanging match about how much they hate themselves – but it's a landmark in gay cinema in that no one dies or commits suicide, and in that the implication is, despite the bitching, that these men will always be there for each other.

The Celluloid Closet 1995

Directors Robert Epstein, Jeffrey Friedman **Cast** Lily Tomlin, Tom Hanks **101m**

Fascinating and sometimes hilarious documentary (narrated by **Tomlin**) tracing the development of gay characters and themes in Hollywood's history. Terrific interviews with performers, filmmakers and camp icons like **Harvey Fierstein** and **Quentin Crisp** are intercut with footage of all sorts of movie characters you might not think were gay at first glance. The film was to feature biopics that made clear the sexual leanings of the likes of Alexander the Great, Hans Christian Andersen and Michelangelo, but the filmmakers refused to release the clips, proving that homophobia still flourishes in parts of Hollywood.

Eating Out 2004

Director Q. Allan Brocka **Cast** Scott Lunsford, Jim Verraros, Emily Stiles 90m

A screwball comedy in every sense of the term, this fag hag farce has straight stud **Lunsford** pretending to fancy hunk **Ryan Carnes** because his flatmate, **Stiles**, only falls for gay men. However, Lunsford's roomie (**Verraros**), has the hots for Carnes. Despite the script dripping with acidic one-liners (many of them being zinged by **Jillian Nusbaum** as Stiles' irksome younger sister),

this may not always be the most original rom-com. But the phone sex sequence is very sensual indeed.

Happy Together 1997

Director Kar Wai Wong **Cast** Leslie Cheung, Tony Leung, Chui Wai 97m

Refreshingly, being gay is not an issue here – being and staying together is. Ho Po-Wing (**Cheung**) and Yui-Fai (**Leung**) are on holiday, but their relationship is unravelling. Jealousy and betrayal sour their feelings and they part, only to remain linked despite moving in very different directions. It's visually frantic, with **Wong**'s trademark flashy style, but if you can handle the roving camera and

L'homme blessé (1983, 109m)

Like a fevered dream, *L'homme blessé* is a film you can't get out of your head. The story of a repressed young man's longing and lust for a beautiful street hustler he meets in the bathroom of the local train station, Patrice Chéreau's film should join the ranks of those other dark-night-of-the-soul classics like Jules Dassin's *Night and the City*, and Scorsese's *Taxi Driver*. In each, compulsion itself drives the narrative, as well as the filmmaking itself. Fuelled by an extraordinary performance by Jean-Hugues Anglade, who plays the central role like a caged dog in heat, the film is also an eloquent metaphor for gay sexuality in a broader sense. I have never seen a movie that better depicts the ways in which desire can take hold of one's every thought and action, and refuse to let go. It almost makes you wish for the days when as gay men, we could only have sex in the bushes, or the movie theaters.

Ira Sachs
The films of Ira Sachs (born in Memphis, Tennessee) have dealt with themes of infidelity, longing and betrayal in gay and straight relationships. They include Married Life, The Delta, *and* Forty Shades of Blue, *the story of an irascible Memphis music producer (played by Rip Torn) that won the Grand Jury prize at Sundance.*

the black-and-white film intercut with garish colour, you'll find a revealing and genuine movie about love and growing into relationships.

Hustler White 1996

Directors Rick Castro & Bruce La Bruce **Cast** Tony Ward, Bruce La Bruce, Alex Austin 80m

Canadian maverick **Bruce La Bruce** established himself as Queer Cinema's shock king with titles like *No Skin Off My Ass* (1991), *Super 8½* (1995) and *The Raspberry Reich* (2004). But while La Bruce's German writer encounters an amputee fetishist, a razor masochist and a kinky mortician in pursuing hustler **Tony Ward**, this owes as much to Billy Wilder's *Sunset Boulevard* as Andy Warhol's *Flesh*. Stuffed with graphic sex scenes.

 **My Own Private Idaho** 1991

Director Gus Van Sant **Cast** River Phoenix, Keanu Reeves 104m

Mike (**Phoenix**) and Scott (**Reeves**) are rent boys in Portland, Oregon. Mike is a narcoleptic, and Scott the bisexual son of the mayor, slumming it with deadbeats. An offbeat reworking of Shakespeare's *Henry IV*, the relationship of the two men is the heart of the movie. Mike is looking for someone to love him and thinks he has found him in Scott, but Scott isn't sure. The scenes shot on the road and by the campfire are stunning, visually and emotionally, and **Van Sant** gets one of the best performances from **Phoenix**.

Nighthawks 1978

Director Ron Peck **Cast** Ken Robertson, Tony Westrope, Rachel Nicholas James 113m

The first British feature to deal unapologetically with homosexuality stresses the importance of coming out, while providing a frank discussion of the potentially alienating effects of doing so. With extras drawn from the London gay scene, this courageous picture uses long 16mm takes to reinforce the hesitancy and mundanity of Jim's life (**Robertson**), whether he's cruising or teaching questioning and often cruel comprehensive kids. Moreover, by focusing on the endless round of empty sexual encounters, **Peck** succeeds in politicizing public conceptions of same-sex relationships, while capturing the grim awfulness of marginalization.

Querelle 1982

Director Rainer Werner Fassbinder **Cast** Brad Davis, Jeanne Moreau, Franco Nero 108m

Jean Genet's Querelle is a sailor who finds himself in a brothel with a difference. Here you can play dice with the madam's husband. If you win you get to sleep with her. But if you lose, you have to sleep with her husband instead. The movie is violent and explicit, and although **Davis**, **Moreau** and **Nero** work well together, some performances seem leaden and the overall look of the film is odd. That said, this is director **Fassbinder** at his most decadent, and fans of *Midnight Express* will enjoy the chance to see Davis in one of his final roles.

 **Torch Song Trilogy**

1988

Director Paul Bogart **Cast** Harvey Fierstein, Anne Bancroft, Matthew Broderick 119m

Harvey Fierstein's adaptation of his successful play for the big screen is a touching, funny, sad and uplifting study of a camp gay man who simply wants life's blessings – love, success and a caring family. Female impersonator Arnold (Fierstein) is a hopeless romantic, and the movie tells of his love life alongside terrific scenes with **Bancroft** that delve into the murky mother–son relationship. Fierstein is a delight throughout, with his gentle manner and gravelly voice, and this is a humane, engaging movie that has stood the test of time and fashion.

A moment in the close, complex relationship between Harvey Fierstein as Arnold and his ma, Anne Bancroft, in *Torch Song Trilogy*, a movie that's stood the test of changing dressing gown fashions.

GROSS OUT

From exploding zits to urinating santas, "juvenile toilet humour" is considered high praise by these unashamedly crude comedies.

American Pie 1999

Directors Chris and Paul Weitz **Cast** Jason Biggs, Chris Klein, Alyson Hannigan 95m

A new gross-out generation was born with this teen sex comedy – think the Brat Pack with sperm jokes. The plot is hardly mould-breaking: a group of (male) friends vow to lose their virginity by graduation night. Yet this is stuffed with original gags and memorable characters such as **Hannigan**'s sexually rapacious band camp nerd, the fruity dad (**Eugene Levy**) trying to have a frank sex talk with his embarrassed eighteen-year-old son and the first use of the term MILF (Mom I'd Like to Fuck) in mainstream cinema. Not to mention the titular incident where our hero (**Biggs**) masturbates with his mom's apple pie after being told that's what "third base" feels like.

The Aristocrats 2005

Director Paul Provenza 89m

Steve Wright once called "The Aristocrats" a "secret handshake" amongst comedians. It's an exceptionally filthy joke that's been retold, always differently, by generations of stand-ups since the vaudeville era. This masterclass documentary sees the likes of **Billy Connolly**, **Robin Williams**, **Chris Rock** and **Eddie Izzard** line up to perform said joke, which always starts with the same setup: a family goes to a talent agent and describes their act. The revolting details, always improvised by the teller, typically involve taboos like bestiality and coprophilia, but always end with the same punchline, where the shocked agent asks "what the heck do you call this act?!" Answer: "The Aristocrats!"

Bachelor Party 1984

Director Neal Israel **Cast** Tom Hanks, Tawny Kitaen, Adrian Zmed 105m

Forrest Gump does gross out? Surely not! Yes, in his young, foolish, pre-Oscar-winning days, **Hanks** slummed it in this crude but fondly remembered comedy, wherein his fiancé tries to catch him cheating on her during his stag night. It's otherwise mediocre, though the notorious scene involving a quaalude-dropping, cocaine-snorting donkey who dies of a drug overdose remains eye-popping stuff.

Bad Santa 2003

Director Terry Zwigoff **Cast** Billy Bob
Thornton, Tony Cox, Brett Kelly 91m

Darker and smarter than average, this
"alternative" gross out was produced by
the Coen brothers. **Thornton**'s gift of a
role sees him play a bitter alcoholic, borderline suicidal shopping mall Santa who
unofficially views his grotto as urinal/shag-
pad. The more sentimental Hollywood
twinkles that occur as he forms ye olde
unlikely friendship with a fat bullied child
were later excised by **Zwigoff**, meaning
his "director's cut" actually ran three minutes shorter.

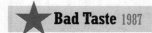

Bad Taste 1987

Director Peter Jackson **Cast** Terry Potter,
Peter Jackson, Pete O'Herne 91m

In the mists of time before *The Lord of the
Rings*, **Peter Jackson** created this aptly
named low-budget debut: a delirious sci-
fi comedy-action splatterfest about aliens
who invade Earth in order to turn humans
into intergalactic fast food. A four-year
labour of love, shot mainly on weekends
and starring the director and his mates,
it demonstrates Jackson's early interest in
special effects. He concocted alien vomit
by mixing green food dye with muesli and
hand-baked the masks in his mum's oven.

Borat: Cultural Learnings of America for Make Benefit Glorious Nation of Kazakhstan 2006

Director Larry Charles **Cast** Sacha Baron
Cohen, Ken Davitian 84m

Like *Ali G Indahouse* and *Brüno*, this brilliantly outrageous mockumentary is based
on a character from **Baron Cohen**'s TV
series. Borat (Baron Cohen) is a cultural
attaché from Kazakhstan who arrives "in
America's airport with clothings, US dollars, and a jar of gypsy tears to protect me
from AIDS" and proceeds to guilelessly
insult his way across the States, coaxing
real Americans to expose their own prejudices along the way (several of whom later
sued). Often accused of the homophobia,
sexism, racism and anti-Semitism it supposedly satirizes, *Borat* is still banned in
almost all Arab countries and was never
distributed in Kazakhstan, though it's a
favourite of the Kazakhstan football team.

National Lampoon's Animal House 1978

Director John Landis **Cast** Tim Matheson,
Peter Riegert, John Belushi 109m

Considered the first gross-out movie, this
was the blueprint for all the lucrative frat
boy comedies to come. Rejected by other
college fraternities, "a wimp and a blimp"
join the misfits at Delta House – whose
anarchic, toga-partying antics are under
threat from the dean. Set in the more
innocent era of 1962, it's tame by modern
standards, with the burden of gross out
shouldered by **Belushi** (then 29), who
envisaged his character, Bluto, as a cross
between Harpo Marx and the Cookie
Monster. Costing $2.7 million, it's since
grossed over $140 million, making it one
of the most profitable movies of all time.

GUILTY PLEASURES

Movies we cannot defend but cannot, alas, resist...

 **Clueless** 1995

Director Amy Heckerling **Cast** Alicia Silverstone, Brittany Murphy, Paul Rudd **98m**

The thinking woman's guilty pleasure, if the huge critical acclaim this audacious chick flick/teen movie garnered is anything to go by. Sassy and knowing, brimming with sly wordplay and visual humour, it's as hip a high-school comedy as you'd expect from the director of *Fast Times at Ridgemont High*, with a charming performance from the seventeen-year-old **Silverstone**, who allows us to like Cher – the matchmaking valley girl based on Jane Austen's Emma – as much as we mock her.

The Court Jester 1956

Directors Melvin Frank, Norman Panama **Cast** Danny Kaye, Angela Lansbury **101m**

Of all his roles, zany court jester Hubert Hawkins was **Kaye**'s best loved, and fans frequently recited his famous tongue-twister "The pellet with the poison's in the vessel with the pestle; the chalice from the palace has the brew that is true!" to him. In this Robin Hood skit, Kaye stars as a "merryman" to **Edward Ashley**'s Black Fox, charged with looking after the heir to the English throne when plans to usurp his position are revealed. Kaye was forced to wear false attachments to his legs, so unimpressed were the producers by his appearance in tights.

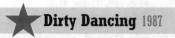 **Dirty Dancing** 1987

Director Emile Ardolino **Cast** Jennifer Grey, Patrick Swayze, Jerry Orbach **100m**

This joyously sexy coming-of-age story, a massive sleeper hit that became the highest-banking indie movie ever, has long been something of a joke – "No one puts Baby in the corner!" – but it's a fond joke, and following a high-profile twenty-year-anniversary re-release, the huge success of the stage show, and then **Swayze**'s untimely death, its cult status has been eternally guaranteed. And you can forget the cheesy "I've Had the Time of My Life" – the real *Dirty Dancing* soundtrack is studded with classy soul from the likes of **Otis Redding** and **Solomon Burke**.

Dream Girls 2006

Director Bill Condon **Cast** Jamie Foxx, Beyoncé Knowles, Jennifer Hudson 130m

So let's get this straight: the story here, of the trials and tribulations of a sequin-clad Detroit R&B girl group called The Dreams, is definitively *not* based on that sequin-clad Detroit R&B girl group called the Supremes... Despite that, this slick adaptation of a popular 1980s stage show has the weepie biopic formula down to a tee, and if you can get over the fact that the characters sing more than they talk, you'll love it. Watch for Oscar-winning **Hudson**'s staggering "And I Am Telling You I'm Not Going" number alone – barnstorming just isn't the word for it.

Ferris Bueller's Day Off 1986

Director John Hughes **Cast** Matthew Broderick, Alan Ruck, Mia Sara 103m

To be blunt, Ferris is a pain in the butt. We're talking about a guy whose biggest gripe is that he got a computer instead of a car from his parents, but **Hughes** makes this trickster loveable all the same. Ferris convinces his parents, yet again, that he is sick and skives school, dragging his girlfriend Sloane (**Sara**) and best mate Cameron (the superbly dry, not to say neurotic, **Ruck**) around Chicago. Despite his dubious, 1980s sweater-vests, you can't help liking this smug little bastard as he succeeds in outwitting **Jeffrey Jones**' cartoon-villain school principal.

Havana 1990

Director Sydney Pollack **Cast** Robert Redford, Lena Olin, Alan Arkin 145m

Even though an hour too long, this doesn't detract from the desire to watch *Havana* again and again. **Redford**'s gambler, Jack, is the fascinating crux of the movie. For most of it he is very seedy indeed. When he propositions **Olin** she rebukes him. He shrugs and says "Hey, I can be suave but I figure you know lots of suave guys. I got no edge that way. But how many crude guys do you know?" This is a rarely glimpsed Redford and thus a must-see movie experience.

Mamma Mia! 2008

Director Phyllida Lloyd **Cast** Meryl Streep, Pierce Brosnan, Julie Walters 108m

How can a movie whose first sickly sweet minutes sap you of the will to live win you over so quickly and so totally? Is it the post-menopausal **Meryl Streep** leaping about in dungarees? **Brosnan**'s endearingly cracked singing voice? The dancing Greek mammas? The holiday brochure setting? Or the pop-perfect Abba songs? Don't waste a moment wondering: the sheer glory of *Mamma Mia!* defiantly defies definition.

Paris Blues 1961

Director Martin Ritt **Cast** Paul Newman, Joanne Woodward, Sidney Poitier, Diahann Carroll 98m

There are clear incongruities in the notion of hipster jazz musician buddies **Newman** and **Poitier** digging a free-wheeling life on Paree's Left Bank while romancing **Woodward**'s and **Carroll**'s sweet tourists. But the naturalism, pungent atmosphere, presence of **Louis Armstrong** and terrific **Duke Ellington** compositions make this a must-see for jazz fans.

See Spot Run 2001

Director John Whitesell **Cast** David Arquette, Paul Sorvino, Michael Clarke Duncan **97m**

This movie about a dog (Spot) taken into a witness protection programme was universally loathed for its obsession with jokes about faecal matter. But there's nothing quite as pompous as a critic pontificating about what kids ought to watch, especially when the film is held as yet more evidence things ain't what they used to be. A future cult classic.

Serial Mom 1994

Director John Waters **Cast** Kathleen Turner, Sam Waterston, Ricki Lake, Matthew Lillard **93m**

Taking a pop at those movies that put mass murderers at the centre of a media frenzy, this is the tale of a whiter-than-white, suburban middle-class family whose mom happens to be a serial killer. **Turner** is astounding as the beaming wife of a perfect husband and mother to the two best-behaved teenagers imaginable, who also strikes down those she feels are unjust towards her family – such as boyfriends who stand up her daughter

or little old ladies who fail to rewind their video cassettes. A nasty yet hilarious piece of kitsch.

Smokey and the Bandit 1977

Director Hal Needham **Cast** Burt Reynolds, Sally Field, Jackie Gleason **97m**

Burt Reynolds perfected every nuance of his loveable rogue persona. Here he stars as truck driver Bandit, who bets he can drive a load of illegal beer from Georgia to Texas and back in 28 hours, breaking the odd speed limit along the way. **Field** is his romantic interest, their offscreen relationship adding to their onscreen chemistry. A former stuntman, **Needham** created some ground-breaking car chases, the cast ad-libbing some funny lines. Don't bother with the sequels.

Tales of Ordinary Madness 1981

Director Marco Ferrari **Cast** Ben Gazzara, Ornella Muti, Susan Tyrell **108m**

You won't know whether to laugh, cover your eyes, or just gape at this movie based on one of cult writer **Charles Bukowski**'s semi-autobiographical novels, with **Gazzara** as the writer. The erotic scenes may disappoint those who tune in to see erections and ejaculations but there's plenty of other stuff to savour, with hard to forget moments of unadulterated, authentic weirdness.

HEIST

Stealing may break the eighth commandment but it has inspired some intriguing movies, especially in the decadent, licentious 1970s.

The Anderson Tapes 1971

Director Sidney Lumet **Cast** Sean Connery, Dyan Cannon, Martin Balsam 99m

Instead of chalking off the days on the cell wall, Anderson (**Connery**) puts his prison time to good use, devising the complicated robbery of an entire apartment block. On release, with his girlfriend (**Cannon**) living in the aforementioned block, all seems to be proceeding to plan. But Connery is already under surveillance. **Lawrence Sanders**' novel is based on the transcripts of real wiretappers and this intriguing thriller perfectly captures an era in American history when tapes would bring down a president.

The Asphalt Jungle 1950

Director John Huston **Cast** Sterling Hayden, Jean Hagen, Sam Jaffe, Louis Calhern 112m

Seminal Hollywood heist movie which memorably suggested that "crime is only a left-handed form of human endeavour". **Huston**'s noirish, nocturnal caper has no heroes or villains, just a cast of tragic losers, headed by **Jaffe** as criminal mastermind Doc who is ultimately undone by his admiration for feminine beauty. **Hayden** is impressive as the doomed thug in the gang that Doc puts together for a jewel heist and **Marilyn Monroe**, in a minor role, lights up the picture as a *femme fatale*. A classic example of the "one last big job" heist movie.

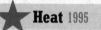 ## Heat 1995

Director Michael Mann **Cast** Al Pacino, Robert De Niro, Val Kilmer, Jon Voight 171m

"A guy once told me: 'Do not have any attachments, do not have anything in your life you are not willing to walk out on in thirty seconds flat if you spot the heat around the corner.'" Spoken by master thief McCauley (**De Niro**), these words sum up his and cop Hanna's (**Pacino**) lives. Hanna, the 1990s Dirty Harry, puts his heart and soul into his work at the expense of his family, while McCauley continually pulls off that final job. One of the best cops-and-robbers movies, with impressive acting from both leads and their crews, an intelligent script based on **Mann**'s own TV movie *LA Takedown*, and his fast and furious direction.

Heist 2001

Director David Mamet **Cast** Gene Hackman, Danny DeVito 109m

Entertaining, not too mannered **Mamet** movie, in which fence **DeVito** blackmails jewel thief **Hackman** into one last job. Double crosses and different perspectives abound but this works well, partly because Mamet is yet to fall in love with his own dialogue, though he does have the gall to give us an answer to the eternal "why did the chicken cross the road" question.

The Hot Rock 1972

Director Peter Yates **Cast** Robert Redford, George Segal, Zero Mostel, Ron Leibman 105m

Redford and **Segal** lead a talented ensemble cast as the schemers trying to steal the precious Sahara Stone for a

Caper movies

Caper movies usually focus on an audacious criminal act – swindle, burglary, sometimes a kidnapping, often in an unusual location – and, as a rule, invite us to sympathize with the crooks. Cops may have some screen time but the caper movie belongs to the criminal masterminds, small town crooks with big ambitions.

If anyone invented the caper movie it's probably **Jules Dassin**, the American director who fled to Europe in the 1950s after being blacklisted in Hollywood. His two great movies – *Topkapi* (1954) and *Rififi* (see opposite) – laid the foundations for the genre, being full of wanted jewels, criminal ambitions and plot complications. Capers are rarely easy. Sometimes it's the crime itself that tests the gang's resources but often it's the aftermath that's the challenge, the crime changing their lives in ways they never imagined.

The genre became especially popular in the 1960s with the Rat Pack's *Ocean's Eleven* (1960), *The Thomas Crown Affair* and *The Italian Job* (both covered in the following pages). Sometimes, the crimes were a bit more original: in Jack Smight's charming *Kaleidoscope* (1966), Warren Beatty breaks into a card factory so he can win in all the casinos in Europe. By the late 1970s, the caper movie had more or less petered out, until **Bruce Willis** (with *Hudson Hawk*) and **Robert Redford** (with *Sneakers*) rode to its rescue in the early 1990s.

The world was once again awash with caper movies as diverse as *Lock, Stock and Two Smoking Barrels* and Steven Soderbergh's plush, all-star remake of *Ocean's Eleven*, which did well enough to lead to a series of increasingly dodgy sequels. Paul McGuigan's *Lucky Number Slevin* (2006) is at least ingenious, original and entertaining with **Josh Hartnett** as the victim of mistaken identity who has to plot to survive in a crime war. But the modern caper movie, certainly the Hollywood version, seems to be all about style, stars and plot rather than character or ambience.

shyster lawyer (**Mostel**). **Yates** and his cast – **Leibman** is splendid as the gang's wild, wacky driver – extract a great deal of comic mileage from their repeated failures. Occasionally, Yates changes register adroitly – most notably when the gang "drop" Mostel's son down a shaft – in what must be one of the most entertaining heist movies of the 1970s.

Idiot Box 1996

Director David Caesar **Cast** Ben Mendelsohn, Jeremy Sims 85m

Corrosive Australian crime caper about two unemployed suburban bums who spend their days setting off car alarms, swigging beer and watching the "idiot box" from which they get the idea of a heist. But a much more adept crook who robs banks to fund his girlfriend's drug habit is casing the same joint. Debut director **Caesar's** careering plotline is carried by clever camera work punctuated by growling grunge music and cheerfully insistent four-letter dialogue. But it's **Mendelsohn** and **Sims** as the adrenaline-fuelled meathead and his slightly less addled mate who top the whole thing off. Fast, furious and, above all, funny.

The Italian Job 1969

Director Peter Collinson **Cast** Michael Caine, Noel Coward, Benny Hill 100m

Some parts of this movie – the cliffhanger ending, "You're only supposed to blow the bleedin' doors off" and the self-preservation society – are so well known that it's hard to think this flopped at the box office. A very British heist flick, celebrating a gang with gold bullion on their mind. **Michael Caine** and **Noel Coward** are in fine form as mobster and criminal mastermind. The car chases are great and it's nice to have a gang run by an effete dandy called Camp Freddie.

★ Rififi 1955

Director Jules Dassin **Cast** Jean Servais, Carl Möhner, Robert Manuel, Jules Dassin 117m

The nearly silent heist scene was such an effective masterclass in breaking and entering that the film was banned in Mexico after a spate of copycat burglaries. **Servais**, **Möhner**, **Manuel** and **Dassin** are the surprisingly decent criminals whose lives become complicated when they rob a Parisian jeweller. Dassin's darkly comic, visually atmospheric and beautifully detailed classic is probably the best heist movie ever made. The title, by the way, is slang for "trouble".

> ❝ You got very nice eyes, DeeDee. Never noticed them before. They real? ❞
>
> **Don Logan, Sexy Beast**

★ Sexy Beast 2001

Director Jonathan Glazer **Cast** Ray Winstone, Ben Kingsley, Ian McShane 88m

Gal (**Winstone**) is a former gangland bank robber, happy with his wife (**Amanda Redman**), life and swimming

Future Bond villain Yaphet Kotto as Carl, loading the loot in the stylish heist flick *The Thomas Crown Affair*.

pool on the Costa. Enter Don (**Kingsley**), who won't take no for an answer when he wants Gal to do one last job. The plan is to break into the bank through a Turkish bathhouse next door – but no one thinks to drain the pool first. Originating from the same script as *Gangster No.1*, this is the only recent British gangster flick to rival *Get Carter*. Each character is richly portrayed with exceptional turns from Winstone and Kingsley, while **McShane** plays a criminal version of Bryan Ferry.

The Thomas Crown Affair
1968

Director Norman Jewison **Cast** Steve McQueen, Faye Dunaway, Yaphet Kotto, Jack Weston 102m

Even though **Weston** called this a "victory of style over substance", it was **McQueen**'s favourite of his own movies. On **Jewison**'s advice, he plays his criminal art dealer as Cary Grant. His chemistry with **Dunaway** – and **Noel Harrison**'s haunting, indecipherable version of "The Windmills of Your Mind" – take this away from pure slickness. The Pierce Brosnan–Rene Russo remake isn't as compelling.

HISTORICAL

Sam Goldwyn once asked a writer for a script about the kidnapping of Charles Lindbergh's baby. But the family couldn't be called Lindbergh, there would be no baby and, er, no kidnapping. Welcome to Hollywood history.

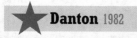

Danton 1982

Director Andrzej Wajda **Cast** Gérard Depardieu, Wojciech Pszoniak 136m

Difficult to go wrong with a movie which a) stars **Depardieu** as one of his nation's greatest historical figures and b) is about a man who, just before he was guillotined, told his executioner: "Show them my head. It will be worth it." Good as it is, it does plod in places. For a romantic view of 1789 and all that, it's hard to top Ronald Colman in *A Tale of Two Cities*.

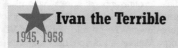

Ivan the Terrible 1945, 1958

Director Sergei M. Eisenstein **Cast** Nikolai Cherkassov, Ludmila Tselikovskaya 100m, 88m

Never one to be swayed by conventional wisdom, Stalin had decided by the end of the 1930s that Tsar Ivan the Terrible was due for rehabilitation. **Eisenstein** researched his subject for two years, sketching every scene. Part one premiered in 1945 and got a good review from you-know-who. Relieved,

the director collapsed and, as he lay in hospital, Stalin got a sneak preview of part two, which he didn't like. Eisenstein died in 1948 and his *Terrible* sequel wasn't shown to the public until 1958. The parallels between Ivan and Stalin are bitterly obvious in part two. But both movies are alternately slow-moving and startling, unlike almost anything else you'll see.

Jeanne la Pucelle 1994

Director Jacques Rivette **Cast** Sandrine Bonnaire, André Marcon 238m

Meticulously researched and comprising two parts – *The Battles* and *The Prisons* – this is a companion piece to *The Passion of Joan of Arc* (1927) and *The Trial of Joan of Arc* (1962). But it feels more like medieval reportage than costumed re-creation, capturing a world that's much bleaker and more brutal than its façade suggests. The Maid of Orleans has proved an elusive character since she was first portrayed on-screen in 1899, but **Bonnaire** conveys the innocence of an illiterate peasant girl at the mercy of treacherous and vengeful men, whose hypocritical chauvinism contrasts with her patriotic zeal and spiritual purity.

The Lion in Winter 1968

Director Anthony Harvey Cast Katharine Hepburn, Peter O'Toole, Anthony Hopkins 134m

King Henry II summons his sons to join him for Christmas, when he plans to decide on his successor. What follows is the ultimate dysfunctional family Yuletide – dad's young mistress is there, and his wife's been let out of the tower for the holiday. A darkly comic historical drama, with witty and infinitely quotable dialogue (it was first a stage play). **Hopkins** and **Timothy Dalton** make their screen debuts here, while **Hepburn**'s portrayal of Eleanor of Aquitaine won her an Oscar – the fact she is descended from both the French and English sides of Eleanor's family might have helped.

Ludwig, Requiem for a Virgin King 1973

Director Hans-Jürgen Syberberg Cast Harry Beer, Ingrid Caven 139m

The faint-hearted may prefer Visconti's *Ludwig* (with Helmut Berger as the mad Bavarian monarch) but **Syberberg**'s take is odder, telling Ludwig's story through episodic tableaux and visual metaphors and finding time to attack the English ideology of industrialism.

Queen Christina 1933

Director Rouben Mamoulian Cast Greta Garbo, John Gilbert, Ian Keith 100m

When **Greta Garbo** realized she had no chemistry with personally selected co-star Laurence Olivier, she hired one-time lover and silent idol **John Gilbert**. He's dashingly charismatic as the Spanish ambassador persuading the seventeenth-century Swedish queen to resist a dynastic marriage. But the film's highlight is the climactic close-up of the abdicated Christina sailing into exile, which **Mamoulian** wanted to be beguilingly enigmatic. So, he advised Garbo "to think of nothing… absolutely nothing".

The Rise to Power of Louis XIV 1966

Director Roberto Rossellini Cast Jean-Marie Patte, Raymond Jourdan, Silvagni 102m

Rossellini was determined to arrest the media's "cretinization of adults" when he inherited this biopic of the Sun King from Jacques Rivette. As he told Pope Paul VI during a Vatican audience, he wanted to break down the detachment and moral decay of modern life and make people think by showing them reflections of themselves in the past. By using long takes and zoom lenses, he created *histoire vérité* and exploited office clerk **Jean-Marie Patte**'s inability to learn lines by having him read from cue cards to enhance his air of supercilious superiority.

Village of the damned? The children in *The White Ribbon* are not quite as innocuous as they seem.

The Story of Mankind 1957

Director Irwin Allen **Cast** Ronald Colman, Vincent Price, Hedy Lamarr, Peter Lorre 100m

You might think any movie which purports to tell the story of mankind might be monstrously long, but **Allen** zips through it. Mankind is on trial (for discovering the super-H-bomb sixty years early), with **Price** as the devil prosecutor and **Colman** defending mankind. Any movie which casts **Dennis Hopper** as Napoleon and **Harpo Marx** as Sir Isaac Newton can't be all bad, although the enterprise suffers from a certain predictability.

The White Ribbon 2009

Director Michael Haneke **Cast** Burghart Klaussner, Christian Friedel, Susanne Lothar 144m

Haneke's dark vision here focuses on a north German village on the eve of World War I, where a series of hideous and apparently motiveless crimes opens up a web of deceit within a seemingly respectable community. The pillars of society are not what they seem, however, and neither is the prim group of children who wander the village expressing concern after each incident. Filmed in starkly beautiful black and white, and with an excellent cast of professionals and non-professionals, the film is both mesmerizing and disturbing, not least in the way it leaves so many questions unresolved.

HOLLYWOOD

Hooray for Hollywood! If the world's biggest dream factory didn't exist, what, you wonder, would moviemakers do for subject matter?

Auto Focus 2002

Director Paul Schrader **Cast** Greg Kinnear, Willem Dafoe, Rita Wilson 105m

The moral majority has always insisted that Tinseltown is a den of depravity; **Paul Schrader** forensically exposes the peccadilloes of *Hogan's Heroes* star Bob Crane in this sordid biopic. It's sex, lies and videotape a-go-go once Crane (**Kinnear**) is introduced to new-fangled home movie equipment by Sony rep John Carpenter (**Dafoe**). But Crane's delusional sense of entitlement costs him his career and two marriages. The 1960s aesthetic is as kitschily authentic as Kinnear's glib charm. Rarely has transgression seemed so joyless and celebrity so tawdry.

The Bad and the Beautiful 1952

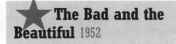

Director Vincente Minnelli **Cast** Lana Turner, Kirk Douglas, Walter Pidgeon 116m

"Don't worry. Some of the best movies are made by people who hate each other's guts", says **Douglas**'s movie mogul, Jonathan Shields. But no one was at each other's throats in this tale of a manipulative tycoon whose rise and fall are told from the point of view of a director, a writer and an actress. The movie began life as a story in the *Ladies Home Journal* about a "bad" Broadway producer. "Beautiful" was added when **Turner** was cast.

The Big Knife 1955

Director Robert Aldrich **Cast** Jack Palance, Ida Lupino, Shelley Winters 111m

Writer **Clifford Odets** was never renowned for his subtlety, but he had enough inside knowledge to make this tale of a Hollywood hunk (**Palance**) with a secret uncompromising, compelling and dead on. Shot in a documentary style, making the message – that it's lethal at the top – even harder to ignore.

Day of the Locust 1975

Director John Schlesinger **Cast** Donald Sutherland, Karen Black, Burgess Meredith 143m

A walk on the seamy side of Tinseltown. **Black** glitters as the cheap, conniving, but sexy wannabe actress while **Sutherland** excels as the accountant who loves Black but is mocked by her, and **William Atherton** is suitably glib as the art director who tries to help her. Like the **Nathanael West** novel, this is dark stuff – too dark to make an impact at the box office in the 1970s.

Ed Wood 1994

Director Tim Burton **Cast** Johnny Depp, Martin Landau, Sarah Jessica Parker **127m**

Two cheers for **Burton** for creating an affectionately amusing piece about the man who was posthumously dubbed the worst film director in the world. It would have been easy to camp it up: Wood (**Depp**) was a director who claimed to have gone to war wearing panties and bra underneath his uniform; a director whose cast, as his girlfriend (**Parker**) says, consists of "the usual gang of misfits and dope addicts". Burton gets one more cheer for giving the movie emotional depth, with its depiction of Wood's relationship with Bela Lugosi (**Landau**), who is his co-star, friend and patient.

The Front 1976

Director Martin Ritt **Cast** Woody Allen, Zero Mostel, Michael Murphy **95m**

Woody Allen is just perfect in this cautionary serio-comedy of the Communist witch-hunt in the 1950s – written, directed, acted and crewed by survivors of the blacklisting, including the brilliant **Mostel**. When a successful TV writer finds himself unemployable he enlists Allen's twerp to put his name on scripts. Soon he is fronting for a pool of blacklisted writers and letting the success of his work go to his head, with attendant hilarious complications.

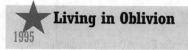 **Living in Oblivion** 1995

Director Tom DiCillo **Cast** Steve Buscemi, James LeGros, Catherine Keener **90m**

Too little-known satire that rips into moviemaking with savagery, outshining Steve Martin's *Bowfinger* by at least 60 watts. **LeGros** excels as narcissistic Hollywood star Chad, who works for independent director **Buscemi** on the cheap, even though, as Chad says, he's so hot he's got two movies scheduled. He is supposed to be a lampoon of Brad Pitt, the blond bombshell due to play this role before schedules clashed; LeGros insists he drew his mannerisms from an actor he'd worked with. **Keener** is quietly effective as the movie-within-the-movie's heroine.

Matinee 1993

Director Joe Dante **Cast** John Goodman, Cathy Moriarty, Simon Fenton **99m**

William Castle's finest movie. Pity he didn't make it. He is the thinly disguised model for **Goodman**'s flamboyant director Lawrence Woolsey, who comes to Key West – just as the Cuban missile crisis breaks – to promote the movie *Mant*, about a man who mutates into an ant. Goodman is superb here, helped by **Moriarty**'s portrayal of his big, blonde girlfriend who dons a nurse's uniform and makes the kids sign "medical consent" forms promising not to sue if they suffer medical trauma from the shock of seeing the mutated ant.

A Star Is Born 1954

Director George Cukor **Cast** Judy Garland, James Mason, Jack Carson 175m

Groucho Marx described Grace Kelly's best actress victory over **Judy Garland** at the 1955 Oscars as "the biggest robbery since Brinks". But this scathing demythologization of Hollywood trod on too many toes to be loved. Cary Grant, Humphrey Bogart, Gary Cooper, Frank Sinatra, Ray Milland and Laurence Olivier had all rejected the role of the monstrous, drunken has-been eventually taken by **James Mason**. But what cut the deepest was the unflinching snapshot of the studio system imploding in the face of stress, addiction, unprofessionalism and television.

Sullivan's Travels 1941

Director Preston Sturges **Cast** Joel McCrea, Veronica Lake, William Demarest 91m

Things go from bad to worse for director Sullivan (**McCrea**), his plans to make a "picture of dignity, a true canvas of the suffering of humanity" foundering. He ends up losing his freedom and identity and discovering the uplifting power of Disney. Strong stuff for 1941, it's a celluloid miracle it was ever made. **Sturges** was interpreted as suggesting directors should stick to entertainment, which wasn't what he meant; ironically his own career would soon begin a Sullivan-like slide.

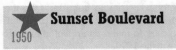 **Sunset Boulevard**

1950

Director Billy Wilder **Cast** William Holden, Gloria Swanson, Erich von Stroheim 111m

Film writer Richard Corliss calls this "the definitive Hollywood horror movie" but it can be watched as a satire and/or *film noir*. It originally opened with **Holden** as one of a number of talking corpses, narrating the story from the morgue. Yet the movie is dark enough already, with Holden vacillating charismatically between the right and the wrong woman, the wrong woman a silent-movie actress (**Swanson**). The pairing of Holden and Swanson was fortuitous: it could have been Montgomery Clift and Mary Pickford, but Pickford turned it down, viewing it as vulgar. She was right, but it is also one of the most compelling Hollywood movies ever made

Tropic Thunder 2008

Director Ben Stiller **Cast** Ben Stiller, Robert Downey, Jr, Tom Cruise 107m

Few will miss the ironies coursing through this smug satire on the lengths that movie stars will go to for their art. Despite its dubious gags about white actors in blackface, testy Jewish studio executives and wannabe thespians award-fishing by playing mentally disadvantaged characters, this vulgar farce about the making of a combat actioner acquired a cult following. **Stiller** and **Jack Black** chew scenery, while **Robert Downey, Jr** parodies his own Method obsessions. But the nadir is **Tom Cruise**'s egotistical cameo.

HORROR

From stomach-fluttering dread to screamworthy shocks, horror movies offer perhaps the most vital of viewing experiences. What's more, they've provided some of the most memorable moments (and characters) in movie history. What's your favourite scary movie?

El Barón del Terror 1962

Director Chano Urueta **Cast** Abel Salazar, Ariadna Welter, Rubén Rojo 77m

Probably the weirdest and most disturbing horror movie ever created. Made in Mexico on a shoestring budget, it tells the grisly tale of a seventeenth-century evil baron (**Salazar**) who is reincarnated and returns from outer space as a brain-eating monster with an enormous forked tongue. He uses this gruesome appendage on his unsuspecting dinner guests, killing them with a campy kiss before scooping out their grey matter and gulping it down (hence the sometime US title *The Brainiac*). The hallucinatory feeling that one experiences while watching this movie is hard to shake off.

A Bucket of Blood 1959

Director Roger Corman **Cast** Dick Miller, Barboura Morris, Antony Carbone 64m

It's not scary nor a roller coaster of tension but horror comedy has few finer moments than this knowing, queasy quickie from legendary hack helmsman **Roger Corman**. Reputedly made in five days – and for Corman that could mean a long shoot – it has **Dick Miller** offer the perfect performance as a sculptor who uses corpses and is hailed as an artistic sensation. Set around a superbly skewered Greenwich Village beat café milieu, satire not slashing is the dish of the day served here.

The Blair Witch Project 1999

Directors Daniel Myrick, Eduardo Sànchez **Cast** Heather Donahue, Michael C. Williams, Joshua Leonard 81m

Who knows if this project would have garnered as much acclaim if it had been released by a major studio and not launched through a clever guerrilla marketing campaign over the Internet. Initial praise for its budget *cinéma vérité* style soon lapsed into backlash. Still, it puts a chilling spin on the "if you go down to the woods today…" line and the ending is thoroughly disturbing.

The Corpse Grinders 1972

Director Ted V. Mikels **Cast** Sean Kenney, Monika Kelly 72m

Outrageous horror comedy from legendary exploitation movie mogul **Mikels**. The plot rotates around the owners of a failing cat-food company who, to spice up their product, employ a couple of grave-robbing maniacs to supply them with dead bodies. Soon the felines develop a craving for human flesh and start attacking their owners. This leads to a factory visit by veterinarian Dr Howard Glass (**Kenney**) and his nurse assistant Angie Robinson (**Kelly**), whose covert investigation uncovers the entire ghastly scheme. The star of the movie is the prop of the title: a painted cardboard box which, every time a body is pushed through it, has hamburger meat dropping out of the other end into a bucket.

The Devil-Doll 1936

Director Tod Browning **Cast** Lionel Barrymore, Maureen O'Sullivan 79m

Best known for *Freaks* and 1931's *Dracula*, former circus clown **Browning**'s twenty-year career also included this little oddity. His last-but-one movie before retirement, it was originally called *The Witch of Timbuctoo*, but the title was changed because of censorship concerns. Co-written by actor/director **Erich von Stroheim**, the story follows a Devil's Island escapee and former banker Paul (**Barrymore**) who, with a fellow escapee, hits upon the idea of shrinking humans to doll size for his

Things that go splat in the night

What's the difference between "slasher" and "splatter"? Not much, one might think, given both consist of young women running away from psychopaths with axes. Basically meaning a movie with loads of blood and guts (and little else) the term "splatter cinema" was first coined by **George A. Romero** to describe his 1978 film *Dawn of the Dead*. However, 1963's **Blood Feast** is generally considered the first splatter movie. "Filmed in BLOOD VISION!", it's a ludicrous tale of sacrificial slaughter and cannibalism wreaked by psychotic Egyptian caterer/high priest Fuad Ramses in suburban Miami. Hired to supply an exotic banquet, Ramses takes to hacking out the vital organs of girls as an offering to his goddess (a shop-window mannequin) before serving them up to unsuspecting diners. Ramses gets his just desserts, by falling into a garbage-truck compactor – a fair, if self-critical, comment on his own performance. Director **Herschell Gordon Lewis** was dubbed "the Godfather of Gore" for creating this celluloid equivalent of the French theatrical form *Grand Guignol*. Costing under $25,000 *Blood Feast* was a huge drive-in hit, launching a thousand cheap imitators, including Lewis's own 1972 *Gore Gore Girls* (aka *Blood Orgy*), and some genuine genre classics like *Bad Taste* (see p.179) and *The Evil Dead* trilogy. Lewis is now a direct marketing consultant. Go figure.

own evil ends. Undeniably silly, this bizarre movie mixes horror, sci-fi, melodrama and revenge thriller, and contains a plethora of ideas and images (Barrymore in drag being one of them) that were deemed shocking in 1936 and still unsettle today.

The Evil Dead 1982

Director Sam Raimi **Cast** Bruce Campbell, Ellen Sandweiss **86m**

With a budget of less than $100,000 this was essentially director **Raimi**, his brother **Ted** and a group of mates (including assistant film editor **Joel Coen**) making a jokey horror movie set in a woodland cabin. Despite the lack of cash, they produced some great effects, as **Campbell** and pals accidentally unleash some demons. (Many of the crew returned five years later to do it all again in *Evil Dead II* – budget $3m – with even more gore and humour. *Evil Dead III: Army of Darkness* cost $30m.) Some have complained about the graphic gore (especially the raped-by-a-tree scene) but all three are among the funniest, most cleverly made horror movies around.

The Exorcist 1973

Director William Friedkin **Cast** Ellen Burstyn, Max von Sydow, Linda Blair **122m**

Regularly voted the scariest movie of all time, thanks to **Friedkin**'s taut direction, wonderful performances (especially from **Jason Miller** as Father Karras and **Burstyn**) and the gripping source material by **William Peter Blatty** (who has a cameo as the producer of the movie

Burstyn is acting in). Many scenes have become the stuff of legend: possessed child Regan (**Blair**) vomiting pea soup or getting a bit graphic on the bed with a crucifix – but the creeping horror of the movie remains embedded in your mind well after the credits have rolled.

Poltergeist 1982

Director Tobe Hooper **Cast** JoBeth Williams, Craig T. Nelson, Heather O'Rourke **114m**

The role of Carol Anne Freeling, the little girl kidnapped by poltergeists, is one Drew Barrymore is probably pleased she didn't win. **Dominique Dunne**, who played elder Freeling sibling, Dana, was strangled to death by her ex-boyfriend shortly after the movie was released. **O'Rourke**, who won the role of Carol Anne (Spielberg himself spotting her in an LA restaurant), died suddenly during filming of *Poltergeist III* in 1988 from intestinal stenosis. And **Julian Beck**, who played evil Reverend Kane, died of stomach cancer during the making of *Poltergeist II*. That's why this series became known in the industry as "the film that kills".

★ The Shining 1980

Director Stanley Kubrick **Cast** Jack Nicholson, Shelley Duvall **146m**

The best movie adaptation of a **Stephen King** novel it may not be, but *The Shining* is certainly the most memorable. Devoted fans were upset the ending was changed, but **Kubrick** makes other contributions – that jaw-dropping tracking shot of the boy on the tricycle – to this psychological horror, essentially a haunted-house movie of the first degree. **Nicholson** chews up the scenery as Jack Torrance, who becomes caretaker of the remote Overlook Hotel during the winter months when it's cut off from the rest of civilization by snow drifts; **Duvall** is the wife who goes through hell when he begins to lose his marbles. Most impressive of all is six-year-old **Danny Lloyd** as their son who has the gift of "shining" (clairvoyance). Legend has it that Kubrick kept a careful eye on Lloyd so he didn't know he was involved in the making of a horror movie until a few years later.

Shivers 1975

Director David Cronenberg **Cast** Paul Hampton, Joe Silver 87m

Canadian director **Cronenberg**'s early low-budget movies remain his most effective, *Rabid* and *Scanners* delivering more yuckiness than, say, *The Fly* and *Naked Lunch*. The plot here centres on parasitic creatures that turn everyone in an apartment block into sex maniacs. But it's really an excuse for Cronenberg to pile on the grossness as the little buggers burrow into people's bodies or are transferred from body to body during snogging (watch out for the flying parasites that attach themselves to a victim's face – the one time in the movie you'll laugh instead of shiver).

Whatever Happened to Baby Jane? 1962

Director Robert Aldrich **Cast** Bette Davis, Joan Crawford 133m

The tale of two ageing sisters and showbiz has-beens plays off the real-life **Crawford–Davis** feud so wonderfully it carries the film. Crawford got through the movie on Pepsi spiked with vodka, while Davis survived the shooting on ego, watching in horror as (she claimed) her co-star strapped ever larger fake boobs to her chest as shooting progressed. Crawford got her revenge on her co-star for cutting her scalp by strapping weights to herself for a scene where Davis had to carry her. All of which was how you imagine their characters behaving – sometimes it really is all in the casting.

★ The Wicker Man 1973

Director Robin Hardy **Cast** Edward Woodward, Britt Ekland 105m

A horror fantasy classic that plays on the unease engendered by remote, isolated communities. **Woodward** is the Christian policeman sent to investigate the disappearance of a girl on the Scottish island of Summerisle. He arrives to find the islanders have strange rituals – and different stories about what happened to the girl. Beautifully written by **Anthony Shaffer** ("You'll simply never understand the true nature of sacrifice") and tautly directed by **Hardy**, this has stood the test of time thanks to a terrific twist and fine performances from Woodward and **Christopher Lee** as the island's lord. Atmospheric and unforgettable, although usually only available in the cut 85-minute version.

INDEPENDENT

Distinguishing independent from Hollywood isn't easy these days as the boundaries become ever more blurred. But none of the movies that follow were made by major studios, or even minor studios about to become major ones.

★ Born in Flames 1983

Director Lizzie Borden **Cast** Honey, Adele Bertei 80m

A self-financed project that took seven years to complete, *Born in Flames* is a seminal chapter in both independent and feminist filmmaking. It's been ten years since a peaceful revolution ushered in equality for all, but the streets of New York City are murmuring with the discontent of the seemingly forgotten female populace. A call for liberation and sexual equality, this partly improvisational work (which features **Kathryn Bigelow** in a small role) is a skilful blend of art, activism and anger.

Clean, Shaven 1993

Director Lodge Kerrigan **Cast** Peter Greene, Molly Castelloe 80m

Filmed over a two-year period, **Kerrigan**'s debut feature is representative of the more radical end of the independent spectrum. Rejecting convention, the film offers an impressionistic, fractured and ambiguous portrait of Peter Winter (**Greene**), a schizophrenic and self-mutilator who undertakes a cross-country search for his daughter. Largely rejecting dialogue for a soundtrack that's a cacophony of discordant screeching, the film's representation of mental illness is likewise far removed from traditional Hollywood productions.

Go Fish 1994

Director Rose Troche **Cast** Guinevere Turner, V.S. Brodie, Anastasia Sharp 83m

Black-and-white movie about a group of women conspiring to matchmake **Turner**, a young and pretty lesbian, with the older, plainer **Brodie**. Meanwhile, promiscuous Daria (**Sharp**), is berated for sleeping with a male friend. The Chicago-set movie suffers from the usual budget problems of using friends as actors, static cameras and never having enough film to do more than two takes, but it's so sweet and good-hearted that such things can be forgiven.

Gummo 1997

Director Harmony Korine **Cast** Jacob Reynolds, Nick Sutton, Linda Manz, Chloë Sevigny 89m

Minnie and Moskowitz (1971, 114m)

" The cult of **Cassavetes** is firmly established on the foundation of some of his more emotionally harrowing masterpieces like *A Woman Under the Influence* and *Opening Night*, films that push both performer and audience to uncomfortable limits. Love, family, fidelity, madness, motherhood, ageing, identity – all usually chased with a healthy dose of drink – are the themes that engage his brilliant family of actors, chief among them his wife and leading lady Gena Rowlands.

Minnie and Moskowitz is Cassevetes' twist on the screwball romantic comedy, an often overlooked gem that approaches almost surreal levels of zany. It's a tale of star-crossed lovers: Minnie (**Gena Rowlands**) works at a museum and is just about to end an affair with an abusive married man (Cassavetes). Seymour Moskowitz (another regular, **Seymour Cassell**) is a hippyish drifter who moves to LA and gets a job as a parking-lot attendant. They meet as Minnie is escaping the worst blind date ever committed to celluloid – a lunch with Zelmo Swift (a deliriously tragic **Val Avery**) that boasts countless hilarious one-liners.

Seymour's slapstick courtship of Minnie escalates towards one of the most beautiful moments in the Cassavetes oeuvre, when Cupid's arrow finally strikes Minnie's heart just as Seymour seems ready to stab himself with a pair of scissors during a desperate spasm of lovelorn hysteria. Instead of a fatal blow, he accidentally chops off half of his handlebar mustache. It's one of those rare moments when actor and character experience a seemingly spontaneous transformation right before our eyes. A moment the director and actors must have rehearsed for days – or maybe not at all… and that's what's so wonderful about this film. It's like true love itself, the grand theme of all Cassavetes' work, which is best accepted as something completely irrational and completely perfect. "

Stephen Kijak

Director Kijak followed up his bohemian family drama Never Met Picasso *with the highly acclaimed* Cinemania, *a documentary about the culture of cinephilia in New York City. Kijak's subsequent* Scott Walker: 30 Century Man *provided a rare glimpse into the working methods of pop enigma Scott Walker.*

There's no plot to speak of in this portrait of social decay set in tornado-ravaged Xenia, Ohio. A funny and disturbing ensemble piece, it centres on a couple of glue-sniffing youngsters who shoot cats and sell the carcasses to a local butcher. Lit with fluorescent lights to achieve a haunted look, it's a movie about people nobody wants to know doing things few of us want to think about. Critics denounced it as exploitative garbage. It might make your teeth itch, but you can't argue with its logic: "Life is beautiful… Without it, you'd be dead."

Happiness 1998

Director Todd Solondz **Cast** Jane Adams, Jon Lovitz, Philip Seymour Hoffman 139m

Focusing on three middle-class New Jersey sisters and their families, this movie is full of eccentric grotesques, from the paedophile who is disturbingly honest with his son to a telephone stalker whose target rings him back for more. A film about such topics as murder, child molestation and pornography shouldn't really manage to stir a titter, but it does.

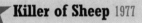 ## Killer of Sheep 1977

Director Charles Burnett **Cast** Henry Gayle Sanders, Kaycee Moore 84m

One of the most perceptive films ever made about family and community, this is the tale of a black slaughterhouse worker suffering from profound disillusionment. A work that consciously opposes the 1970s blaxploitation style, **Burnett** instead favours low-key characters and situations employing a striking neo-realist cinematography to capture the nitty-gritty of urban, working-class lives. One of the first films selected for the Library of Congress's prestigious National Film Registry for its cultural and artistic significance.

The Last Seduction 1994

Director John Dahl **Cast** Linda Fiorentino, Peter Berg, Bill Pullman 110m

Bridget (**Fiorentino**) is a rare cinematic creation: a *femme fatale* for the 1990s who isn't a camp send-up of Barbara Stanwyck, but so evil even Freddie Krueger would steer clear. She and her doctor hubbie start working for professional drug dealers, until Bridget runs off with the loot. On the run she persuades **Pullman**, a hapless suitor, to get rid of her husband. **Dahl** set out to make a movie where you didn't fall in love with the central character. He almost succeeded – but a Last Seduction Club was founded by women who'd been screwed over by men.

Mutual Appreciation 2005

Director Andrew Bujalski **Cast** Justin Rice, Seung-Min Lee 108m

This charming lo-fi look at the relationship struggles of a group of twentysomething New Yorkers is one of the key works of the recent mumblecore movement. And likewise it's characterized by a reliance on dialogue (talk is cheap to film) over action and a fixation on fey, vaguely directionless archetypes, but no less engaging for that.

A Scanner Darkly 2006

Director Richard Linklater **Cast** Keanu Reeves, Robert Downey Jr, Winona Ryder 100m

Linklater has developed cult status amongst the strokey-beard brigade with films such as *Slacker* and gentle romance *Before Sunrise*. Hard-core fans of **Philip K. Dick** hailed him as the first director to successfully commit one of the writer's dystopian tales to the big screen. An intelligent countercultural ethos infuses proceedings in which a detective addicted to the mysterious "Substance

D'' has to spy on himself to help the government uncover the secrets of the drug. The graphic novel styling – it's a unique blend of animation and film – is just one element of a cocktail calculated to blow smoke rings in your mind.

sex, lies, and videotape 1989

Director Steven Soderbergh **Cast** James Spader, Andie Macdowell, Laura San Giacomo 100m

Arguably the most influential American independent picture in recent memory, though the majority of the film's $1.2 million budget was financed by the video division of Columbia, *sex, lies, and videotape* also ranks among the most important feature debuts. Risqué title aside, it's a beautifully written account of relationships breaking down between two sisters, a husband (**Peter Gallagher**) and his catalyst friend. A harbinger of **Soderbergh**'s formal daring, it scooped the 1989 Palme d'Or and became a huge critical and commercial success.

Stranger than Paradise 1984

Director Jim Jarmusch **Cast** John Lurie, Richard Edson 89m

Announced as a "new kind of American movie", *Stranger than Paradise* is another US indie watershed moment. Esoteric and accessible, the film – a look at cultural difference and communication issues between a Hungarian and an American

on a road trip – established **Jarmusch** as a guru of cool. Characterized by its long, stationary shots and resolutely minimalist style (not to mention its hip soundtrack), *Stranger than Paradise* altered the way American independent movies were shot, produced, distributed and exhibited.

Tongues Untied 1989

Director Marlon T. Riggs **Cast** Kerrigan Black, Blackberri 55m

One of the first black independent productions to openly address the issue of black homosexuality and of the experience of being hidden from both contemporary society and history on the dual grounds of race and sexuality. Intelligently and passionately exploring the intersections of racism and homophobia, the film gives a defiant voice to the previously silenced black gay male community. Largely autobiographical, it was produced, edited and shot by the director, **Riggs**.

Totally F***ed Up 1993

Director Gregg Araki **Cast** James Duval, Roko Belic, Jenne Gil 80m

A nihilist angst-fest about a group of gay and lesbian LA teenagers who have been disowned by their parents and drift aimlessly from café to mall and from one sexual relationship to another. Hailed as a breakthrough youth movie, it's not that far from standard Hollywood coming-of-age stuff. **Duval** is excellent though, and went on to star in Araki's *The Doom Generation* and *Nowhere*.

KIDS

Welcome to a magical world where dogs talk, dads build you flying cars and the best friend a child can have is a chocolate tycoon. Great kids' films entertain while imparting some greater truth; the same cannot be said of *Santa Claus Conquers the Martians.*

Bolt 2008

Directors Byron Howard, Chris Williams **Cast** John Travolta, Miley Cyrus **96m**

Disney's first 3-D animation was also their first produced under new Chief Creative Officer **John Lasseter**, the director of *Toy Story*. He's also head of Pixar, the guys who brought you *Ratatouille*, who tend to pitch their computerized cartoons equally at grown-ups. *Bolt* is definitely one for kiddies, but has Lasseter's paw prints all over it. A fuzzy-hearted, smartly scripted tale of Bolt the Super Dog, a canine TV star who deludedly believes his superpowers are real, it's essentially Buzz Lightyear with fur.

Bridge Over Terebithia 2007

Director Gábor Csupó **Cast** Josh Hutcherson, AnnaSophia Robb, Zooey Deschanel **96m**

It's hard to wow the kids visually, now that big bucks CGI digital effects are the norm. What's so effective about Hungarian animator **Csupó**'s US fantasy is that it largely doesn't try. Instead, when bullied twelve-year-old Jesse meets artistic, free-spirited neighbour Leslie and introduces him to the imaginary land of Terebithia, it pretty much stays imaginary, and is all the more magical for it. Based on **Katherine Paterson**'s 1977 novel, it's a profound celebration of the transcendent power of art, of human difference and the value of life – prepare to blub like a babe.

★ The Goonies 1985

Director Richard Donner **Cast** Sean Astin, Josh Brolin, Corey Feldman **114m**

He directed *Superman* and *Lethal Weapon*, but Spielberg's kiddie treasure quest is the film **Donner** called "the best experience I've ever had in my life". Why? His eclectic young cast, many of whom found fame later. Okay, *Lost Boys* star **Corey Feldman** (Mouth) hit the career skids but **Sean Astin** (Mikey) became Sam Gamgee in *The Lord of the Rings*; **Josh Brolin** (Brand) became George Bush in *W*, whilst **Jeff Cohen**

(Chunk) became one of Hollywood's top entertainment lawyers, presumably so he could sue anyone who ever asked him to do the "truffle shuffle" again.

Holes 1996

Director Andrew Davis **Cast** Shia LaBeouf, Sigourney Weaver, Patricia Arquette 117m

A lot of kids rate **Louis Sachar**'s book as one of their absolute favourites so this Disney movie stayed faithful to it, give or take a cameo from Whoopi Goldberg and a soundtrack that rocks. Stanley Yelnats (**LaBeouf**), a poor New York kid, is wrongly accused of stealing a pair of sneakers and sent to a juvenile prison camp in Texas. There, along with an engaging cast of delinquent detainees, he is forced to dig endless holes in the desert, under the eye of a cruel warden (**Weaver**). She hopes the kids will unearth a secret treasure, buried by a Wild West-era female outlaw whose tale is told in flashback. Just sit back and enjoy.

★ The Iron Giant 1999

Director Brad Bird **Cast** Jennifer Aniston, Harry Connick Jr, Vin Diesel 87m

Based on poet **Ted Hughes**' story and executively produced by Pete Townshend, this animated feature is about a boy trying to hide an alien from his mum. It's also a Cold War parable and a fantasy about a paranoid government. It's full of tributes to the greats of animation: the newspaper headline, "Disaster Seen As Catastrophe Looms" is the same as one in *Lady and the Tramp*, and the two trainmen, Frank and Ollie, are caricatures of Disney animators Frank Thomas and Ollie Johnston.

Kiki's Delivery Service 1989

Director Hayao Miyazaki **Cast** Kirsten Dunst, Debbie Reynolds 103m

This tale of a nice young witch who has to learn her trade in a strange new city is so sweet-natured it's impossible not to be won over. **Miyazaki**'s cast of characters is more human than many other animators', with frequent roles for sympathetic, intelligent, older people who aren't annoyingly cute. Kiki's broom-flying delivery service gives the director ample excuse to indulge in his obsession for flight. And the story, in which Kiki loses and rediscovers her magic powers, stresses the importance of friendship and independence.

Labyrinth 1986

Director Jim Henson **Cast** David Bowie, Jennifer Connelly 101m

A flop on release, Muppets creator **Henson**'s last feature achieved belated popularity: **David Bowie** action figures were launched in 2007 and Tim Burton's considering a remake. Certainly there's a Burtonesque flavour to this dark fantasy wherein fairy-tale-obsessed fifteen-year-old Sarah wishes away her baby half-brother to the goblins then has to save him by completing a muppet-populated labyrinth. Bowie beat off competition from Sting and Michael Jackson to play the Goblin King, which he does magnificently, despite looking like an extra from *Cats*.

Hang in there for the incredible staircase-whirling finale, inspired by M.C. Escher.

Matilda 1996

Director Danny De Vito **Cast** Mara Wilson, Danny De Vito, Pam Ferris, Embeth Davidtz 98m

Danny De Vito had to convince Roald Dahl's widow he was a fan of the original book before she would sell him the movie rights for this magical fantasy. De Vito plays Matilda's hideous dad and his other half **Rhea Perlman** is the selfish mum. The heroine with the power to move things by concentrating on them triumphs, finally, over her parents and the horrendous child-throwing headmistress (British TV star **Ferris**). **Wilson** as Matilda centres the movie: any more – or less – innocent and the whole concept would collapse.

The Mighty 1998

Director Peter Chelsom **Cast** Sharon Stone, Harry Dean Stanton, Gena Rowlands 100m

Lumbering outcast Max (a sensational performance from **Elden Henson**) teams up with another misfit (**Kieran Culkin**), a hunchback who's been dubbed Freak by his classmates. For succour against a cruel world, the misfits try to live by the chivalrous code they have learned from reading tales of King Arthur and his knights. The movie is shot through with humour and has some touching scenes. **Stone** is a revelation as Kevin's mother.

Fantasy 1980s-style for David Bowie and Jennifer Connelly in *Labyrinth*.

Panda and the Magic Serpent 1958

Directors Kazuhiko Okabe, Robert Tafur **Cast** Mariko Miyagi, Hisaya Morishige 76m

This classic was the first colour, feature-length Japanese anime and the first to reach the US. It's an enthralling tale based on a Chinese legend about a boy, Xu-Xian, forced to give up his pet snake. The snake, however, is a goddess who, on reaching adulthood, searches for her love, Xu-Xian. When a wizard tries to separate them, Xu-Xian's panda and cat come to love's rescue. Every shot is breathtaking in its use of stunning, almost psychedelic imagery.

The Phantom Tollbooth 1969

Directors Chuck Jones, Abe Levitow **Cast** Butch Patrick, Mel Blanc 89m

A real curio this. **Chuck Jones**, best known for creating *Roadrunner* and embellishing *Bugs Bunny*, leaves Looney Tunes behind to take on a children's classic about a bored boy who drives through a magical tollbooth to enter a pun-infested world where characters have names like Officer Short Shrift. Some found Jones' part-animated fantasy too preachy, others found the songs icky, but a few loved it.

Santa Claus Conquers the Martians 1964

Director Nicholas Webster **Cast** John Call, Leonard Hicks 82m

The Martians haven't got a Santa so they kidnap ours. That's the plot of this cult classic often described as the worst Christmas movie of all time. Some insist it is an allegory about the dangers of technology, with the Martians as hard-boiled scientists who have to be softened by Santa/Christ's good cheer. Others may see some sinister significance in the fact Santa's reindeer is called Nixon.

The Secret of Roan Inish 1993

Director John Sayles **Cast** Jeni Courtney, Pat Slowey, Dave Duffy, Declan Hannigan 103m

Fiona (**Courtney**) believes she and her family are half-descended from the selkies (seals). She knows this is possible because she's seen a child carried out to sea in a cradle by seals on Roan Inish. With this conceit – and this being Ireland – **Sayles** could have easily gone for blar-

ney and whimsy but he keeps this tale grounded, taking the girl's story at face value. Good to look at, thanks to some fine cinematography from **Haskell Wexler**.

Snow White and the Seven Dwarfs 1937

Director David Hand 83m

Dubbed "Disney's Folly" by Hollywood execs who saw the costs of his first full-length feature balloon from $250,000 to $1,480,000, this became Walt's cash cow. Yet its tale of a jealous queen and her beautiful stepdaughter might not have been as successful if the creators had stuck with these original suggestions for the names of the dwarves: Awful, Biggy, Blabby, Dirty, Gabby, Gaspy, Gloomy, Hoppy, Hotsy, Jaunty, Jumpy, Nifty, and Shifty.

Willy Wonka & The Chocolate Factory 1971

Director Mel Stuart **Cast** Gene Wilder, Jack Albertson, Peter Ostrum 100m

Tim Burton's 2005 take on **Roald Dahl**'s deliciously nasty tale of five children who win tickets to visit a magic chocolate factory – and mostly meet sticky ends – is the better movie. But there's a zany charm to this 1970s musical incarnation, mainly thanks to **Wilder**'s superbly unsettling Wonka: at times firm but fair; at others downright perverse. Keep an eye out for the scene where the Paraguayan newsreader holds up the photo of the man whose chocolate bar held a lucky ticket: the photo is of Nazi exile Martin Bormann.

KITSCH

Kitsch is defined by the dictionary as "garish, tasteless or sentimental art". On that basis it must be the fastest-growing genre in the movies. You can normally find at least two of those qualities in any John Waters film, and in Michael Sarne's *Myra Breckinridge* you can find all three.

★ Attack of the 50 Foot Woman 1958

Director Nathan Juran **Cast** Allison Hayes, William Hudson, Yvette Vickers **66m**

What a paranoid decade the 1950s were. Dominated by worries about Commies and bodysnatchers (or were they the same thing?), the end of the decade saw a plethora of B-movies where the forces doing the attacking were giant leeches, killer tomatoes and, of course, a 50ft woman. **Hayes**, enlarged after a meeting with aliens, takes revenge on her husband and her tormentors, playing the loosest woman the filmmakers could get past the censors. Remade in 1993 (by Christopher Guest and starring Daryl Hannah) with more money but less conviction.

Bedtime for Bonzo 1951

Director Frederick de Cordova **Cast** Ronald Reagan, Diana Lynn **83m**

Until Bonzo's co-star became president of the United States, this was just another Hollywood comedy, albeit one about a professor who treats a chimp (Bonzo) as if it's a child. It isn't even **Reagan**'s worst performance as an actor. After his 1980 election victory, the vicious rumour was spread that he was out-acted by the chimp. But Bonzo just wasn't that great an actor.

Bela Lugosi Meets a Brooklyn Gorilla 1952

Director William Beaudine **Cast** Bela Lugosi, Sammy Petrillo, Duke Mitchell **74m**

In the course of this curious movie, **Lugosi** (a mad scientist on – hey! – a jungle-covered Pacific island) injects a de-evolution serum into "entertainer" **Mitchell**, turning him into a singing gorilla. After watching this film, the only rational conclusion is that a similar serum must have been used on **Beaudine** and scriptwriter **Tim Ryan**. This movie's only purpose is to emphasize how far Lugosi had sunk since he personified Dracula for Universal in 1931. By 1955, he had succumbed to drug addiction and died a year later.

Dr Goldfoot and the Bikini Machine 1965

Director Norman Taurog **Cast** Vincent Price, Frankie Avalon, Dwayne Hickman 88m

Vincent Price sends up his own image as the evil genius of the title, whose mad plan it is to make lady robots marry wealthy men and persuade them to sign away their assets. **Avalon**, having tired of an endless beach party, tries to foil him. This was successful enough to spawn an Italian-American sequel *Dr Goldfoot and the Girl Bombs*. It's the same plot only this time the girls, as the slogan for the movie says, have thermonuclear navels.

Jesse James Meets Frankenstein's Daughter 1966

Director William Beaudine **Cast** John Lupton, Narda Onyx 88m

If Ed Wood hadn't existed, the world could have lived happily in the knowledge that in **William Beaudine** we had the next best/worst thing. "One Shot" Beaudine had developed a new micro-genre of B-movie (some would call it a rut) where two major genres collided onscreen. This was Beaudine's 199th movie and, even though he never reshot a scene, you can sense that exhaustion is finally setting in. The fantastic comic/horror/Western possibilities of a charismatic outlaw coming into conflict with a girl whose birthright was a bolt through the back of her neck were never really explored. Bizarrely, Beaudine decides to play this one straight.

Matango: Attack of the Mushroom People 1963

Director Ishirô Honda **Cast** Akira Kubo, Yoshio Tsuchiya, Kumi Mizuno, Hiroshi Koizumi 89m

Ishirô Honda wasn't a director who ever became a household name in the West, though he worked as assistant director on Akira Kurosawa's late masterpiece *Ran* and the great man gave the eulogy at his funeral. This movie sums up just why Honda gave up directing his own films. Having made *Godzilla* in 1956, he found himself increasingly confined to sci-fi and monster movies like this one, a strange tale of a group of shipwreck survivors who get turned into mushrooms. It's all right to watch on a Saturday afternoon but not the kind of film you'd want to spend your life making.

Myra Breckinridge 1970

Director Michael Sarne **Cast** Mae West, John Huston, Raquel Welch, Rex Reed 94m

This movie was promoted with the slogan: "Everything you've heard about *Myra Breckinridge* is true." Unfortunately, most of what people heard was the critics saying it was rubbish. Any movie whose plot involves **Rex Reed** becoming **Raquel Welch** is up against it, and the decision to cast the 78-year-old **Mae West**, still using her come-up-and-see-me-sometime routine (she wrote her own dialogue), didn't help. The rest of the actors don't seem to have been cast but rounded up from a nearby party and kept against their will. Welch (as the man-hating Myra who enrols in acting school to get into Hollywood to

Hazardous Waters

Hairspray, the smash Broadway musical based on his film, may've kidnapped him into family-friendly territory, but **John Waters** is still the shock-merchant who made his 300lb transvestite star, Divine, eat real dog poo in their first famous movie *Pink Flamingos* (1972).

The title of his 1969 debut, *Mondo Trasho*, sums up Waters' artistic oeuvre. His early work is a pornucopia of hooliganism, sex, drugs and gleeful depravity. That anarchic energy diminished after the original *Hairspray* movie (1988) drew the pimp-moustached auteur closer to the mainstream. Some found his Hollywood satire *Cecil B. Demented* unwatchable, others hailed it as sly, strange and funny. *Cry Baby* (1990), his companion to *Hairspray*, starring Johnny Depp as a juvenile delinquent, was more entertaining. But for aficionados, his masterpiece is *Female Trouble*, a grotesque precursor to *Serial Mom* equally inspired by Jean Genet's theory "crime equals beauty" and Waters' prison visits to one of the Manson family.

Obsessed by pop culture, Baltimore and true crime (he attends murder trials for a hobby), over the years Waters has created an eccentric stable of stars including heiress Patti Hearst and the *Jackass* star Johnny Knoxville.

He once declared "If someone threw up at one of my screenings, it would be like a standing ovation."

destroy the American male) struggles valiantly to stop this from sinking, but fails.

Sgt Pepper's Lonely Hearts Club Band 1978

Director Michael Schultz **Cast** The Bee Gees, Peter Frampton, Frankie Howerd 111m

While the plot is terminally average – local band (the Gibbs plus Frampton) battle it out with music industry and bad band (Aerosmith) – and the decision to only have spoken dialogue from the narrator (**George Burns**) is a brave one, what really lifts this into a class of its own is the use of Beatles songs – and the director's insistence that this film should allude to the Fab Four as little as possible. The sight of **Donald Pleasence** disco dancing,

however unnerving, fails to prepare you for the horror of seeing **Howerd** singing "When I'm 64" to a young woman called Strawberry Fields he's hoping to seduce.

Snakes on a Train 2006

Directors The Mallachi Brothers **Cast** A.J. Castro, Julia Ruiz 91m

You read that right. And this isn't a sequel to Samuel L. Jackson's *Snakes on a Plane*, but a cheeky "mockbuster" from The Asylum, the straight-to-DVD studio behind suspiciously familiar-sounding titles as *The Da Vinci Treasure* and *Transmorphers: Fall of Man*. Likewise, this one preys on inattentive video store browsers who'll discover too late that "100 Trapped Passengers. 2000 Venomous Vipers!" is a wildly misleading tagline given the cast of under ten cheapo actors being terrorized by three very small, confused-looking grass snakes.

The Terror of Tiny Town
1938

Director Sam Newfield **Cast** Billy Curtis, Yvonne Moray, "Little Billy" Rhodes **62m**

The first and probably only midget Western, this movie has to be seen to be believed. Starring a cast of midgets, the standard story sees an evil cowboy terrorizing innocent townspeople. This is really a novelty movie, yet the mostly amateur cast take themselves very seriously, making the experience all the stranger. The producers hoped to make a follow-up using the same cast telling the story of Paul Bunyan, but thankfully the idea was shelved.

The Tingler 1959

Director William Castle **Cast** Vincent Price, Darryl Hickman, Patricia Cutts **82m**

More showman than director, **Castle** was an extremely average filmmaker with an extraordinary flair for stunts. For *Macabre* (1958) he took out insurance in case the audience died of fright whilst watching it. For *House on Haunted Hill* (1959) he hooked up plastic skeletons to fly over the audience's heads. But he surpassed himself with *The Tingler*, starring **Price** as a pathologist who discovers that spine-tingling fear is caused by a wriggling parasite that can only be destroyed by screaming. Castle literally shocked his audience by wiring up their seats and sporadically zapping them with electric shocks.

Vincent Price as the pathologist who makes a startling discovery in screamworthy kitsch horror *The Tingler*.

Trouble Man 1972

Director Ivan Dixon **Cast** Robert Hooks, Paul Wonfield, Ralph Waite **99m**

"So man if you don't dig this super cool black… stay away from the box office you motherf–." That, at least, was how one critic greeted the arrival of the original Mr T – not the *A-Team* star, but the hero of this blaxploitation movie. Another reviewer obviously felt threatened by **Hooks'** bulletproof private eye (who can close pool halls with a stern glance), complaining that the character looked "so cool as to make one suspect it isn't Coke he is constantly drinking but antifreeze". The soundtrack is by Marvin Gaye and it's a pity he didn't write the script. It's a pity somebody didn't write the script.

LESBIAN

While women who love women can be a surefire recipe for box office success, forming the basis of a slew of super-trashy exploitation flicks, for a more sensitive study of lesbian love, you might need to turn to European art cinema.

The Bitter Tears of Petra von Kant 1972

Director Rainer Werner Fassbinder **Cast** Margit Carstensen, Hanna Schygulla 124m

Talky, moody and static, this is a classic **Fassbinder** study of female relationships. Petra (**Carstensen**) is a successful fashion designer, arrogant, tough and rude. As she begins an affair with a model (**Schygulla**), her life starts to unravel. Fassbinder uses an ornate bedroom to convey the prison of Petra's mind, and shots using mirrors, gauzy fabric and the bars of the bed hem her in further. Meticulous camera work is the perfect foil for the story of erotic power and sexual cruelty.

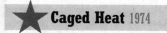 Caged Heat 1974

Director Jonathan Demme **Cast** Barbara Steele, Erica Gavin, Juanita Brown 83m

Steele – the Northern lass and lesbian icon who made it big in 1960s Italian horror movies – camps it up to the max as the sadistic, bespectacled, wheelchair-bound warden in this chicks-in-chains exploitation classic. **Demme**, Roger

Corman's protégé, brings humour and style to his lively directorial debut, and there are enough bad-girl shenanigans, tongue-in-cheek titillation and feisty female solidarity to have won the movie everlasting lesbian cult status.

The Children's Hour 1961

Director William Wyler **Cast** Audrey Hepburn, Shirley MacLaine 107m

In 1936 **Wyler** made *These Three*, a discreet version of **Lillian Hellman**'s play, with the references to lesbians removed because of the Hays Code. In 1961 he returned to the material, making this overt, if uneasy, story of two teachers wrongly accused of a lesbian affair. Ground-breaking and undeniably powerful melodrama, the film ultimately falters: in not actually using the word "lesbian", the whole "issue" is treated with coy distaste, the kind of thing that nice people don't discuss.

Desert Hearts 1985

Director Donna Deitch **Cast** Helen Shaver, Patricia Charbonneau 96m

In 1950s, divorce-happy Nevada, Vivian (**Shaver**), a literature professor, comes to a ranch to end her marriage and is drawn to the ranch-owner's daughter, a liberated lesbian, Cay (**Charbonneau**). A refreshingly simple love story that refuses to get bogged down in endless should-they-shoudn't-they teasing. The desert settings, representing the freedom of Cay's life versus Vivian's, are sumptuous, and the ethereal soundtrack featuring Elvis, Patsy Cline and Kitty Wells suits perfectly.

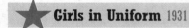

Girls in Uniform 1931

Director Leontine Sagan **Cast** Hertha Thiele, Dorothea Wieck **88m**

Lesbian love was rather fashionable in pre-war Germany, and this romantic school story – based on the autobiographical novel by **Christa Winsloe** and with an all-female cast and a lesbian director – became a cult classic from the word go. Banned by the Nazis as decadent, and heavily censored until the 1970s, it is a touching and visually lovely film, in which a motherless girl at a cruel Prussian boarding school falls for her teacher. The famed kissing scene is short, sweet and genuinely startling.

The Incredibly True Adventure of Two Girls in Love 1995

Director Maria Maggenti **Cast** Laurel Holloman, Nicole Ari Parker, Maggie Moore **94m**

Low-budget indie movie that gives the well-worn kids-from-the-opposite-sides-of-the-tracks formula a lesbian twist. Blue-collar tomboy Randy (**Holloman**, who went on to star as Tina in top US lesbian TV soap *The L Word*) and rich kid Evie start a tentative affair against all the odds. Sweet, edgy and quirky, and notable for a sex scene that manages to be neither coy nor exploitative.

101 Reykjavík 2001

Director Baltasar Kormákur **Cast** Hilmir Snær Gudnason, Hannah María Karlsdottir **88m**

There aren't many movies about Icelandic lesbians, but this off-the-wall comedy makes up for that. If you're over thirty and still living with your mother, you might want to see how Hlynur (**Gudnason**), perennial loafer and Internet porn addict, handles life when he finds out his mother is having an affair with Lola, her flamenco teacher. Bizarre, a little twisted and very funny.

Show Me Love 1998

Director Lukas Moodysson **Cast** Rebecka Liljeberg, Alexandra Dahlström **89m**

Declared a masterpiece by Ingmar Bergman and more successful at the Swedish box office than *Titanic*, poet **Lukas Moodysson**'s debut feature is part teen movie, part lesbian romance. Known in its rather less buttoned-up home country as *Fucking Amal*, it's a pared-down love story about two adolescent girls struggling to come to terms with their sexuality in the small Swedish town of Amal. Sensitive, intelligent and affecting, with superb performances from the two young leads, and a grainy, stylishly naturalistic patina.

MADE FOR MONEY

The movies have always had an eye for talent. Especially for cheap talent of the swimming, skating or singing variety that can be put to use in formulaic, but profitable movies.

Dangerous When Wet 1953

Director Charles Walters **Cast** Esther Williams, Fernando Lamas, Jack Carson 95m

Ironically, the most famous movie to feature swimming star **Esther Williams** is best remembered because of the fantasy scene in which she cavorts underwater with Tom and Jerry. This entertaining musical comedy's thinner-than-water plot has Williams falling for a handsome Frenchman (**Lamas**). The leads fell for real and wed, with Lamas – by Williams' account – making her a virtual prisoner for thirteen years.

Lassie Come Home 1943

Director Fred M. Wilcox **Cast** Pal, Roddy McDowall, Elizabeth Taylor 89m

Lassie was one of Hollywood's first gender benders – she was played by a male dog called Pal, wearing a patch. You know the drill: loyal dog walks length and breadth of land to be reunited with master. Good as Pal is, (s)he is overshadowed by the young **Liz Taylor**, who was once sent back to the dressing room to have her false eyelashes removed, only for the director to be told they were genuine. For some cheap laughs, try Lassie's *Adventures in the Gold Rush* (1951) – easily the worst in the series.

Liane Jungle Goddess 1956

Director Eduard von Brosody **Cast** Marlon Michael, Hardy Kruger 88m

Marlon Michael is beautiful, blonde and topless as the female Tarzan in an ersatz Edgar Rice Burroughs-style adventure where the lion cub out-acts everyone else in the cast. The nudity – though tame by today's standards – gave the movie enough momentum for Michael (who was only sixteen when this was released) to reprise the role in two sequels that lacked the original's bizarre innocence.

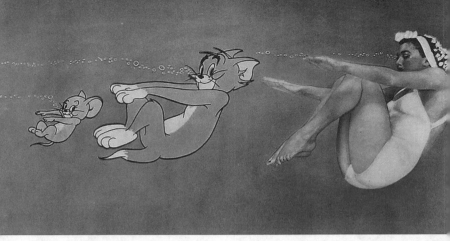

Not so *Dangerous When Wet* at all, really: Tom and Jerry swim in synch with Esther Williams.

Second Fiddle 1939

Director Sydney Lanfield **Cast** Sonja Henie, Tyrone Power, Rudy Vallee 85m

Henie ice skated her way into the movies from Oslo via a gold medal at the 1936 Olympics. By the mid-1940s her movie career had peaked but this escapist fantasy casts Henie as a skating teacher discovered by **Power**'s scheming publicist. The 1920s heartthrob **Rudy Vallee** croons to good effect but **Edna May Oliver**'s sharp aunt steals the movie.

Tarzan's New York Adventure 1942

Director Richard Thorpe **Cast** Johnny Weismuller, Maureen O'Sullivan 71m

Certainly the funniest adventure starring the loincloth hero. **Weismuller** is good enough to make this superior B-movie comedy reasonably convincing – even when he calls for a witch doctor after hearing an opera singer – and **Thorpe** makes sure the movie satisfies hard-core fans by including that essential ingredient: plenty of elephants.

Wake Up and Dream 1934

Director Kurt Neumann **Cast** Russ Columbo, Roger Pryor, June Knight 77m

From Rudy Vallee to Elvis and David Essex, the movie industry has always been quick to exploit the latest singing sensation. **Columbo**, a crooning rival of Vallee and Crosby, would be more famous had he not been shot dead in a freak accident with a French duelling pistol when he was just 26. In this, his best musical comedy (for which he wrote three songs), he is good enough as a member of a vaudeville trio to show why he was hailed as the "crooning Valentino".

MAFIA

The movie industry has always been interested in the Mafia – and the Mafia has always had interests in the movie industry. Here is a selection of cult movies you can't refuse.

The Consequences of Love
2004

Director Paolo Sorrentino **Cast** Toni Servillo, Olivia Magnani 100m

A former stockbroker from southern Italy, Titta di Girolamo (**Servillo**) is a quiet, sober resident in a hotel in a Swiss-Italian town. He once lost Mafia money and has been punished by being forced to deliver the cash to the bank once a week, enjoying no life of his own. Girolamo's detachment is complete, until he begins a liaison with the hotel's beautiful bartender (**Magnani**) and resolves to wrest back control of his own destiny. This elegant look at codes of conduct – mafiosi and otherwise – proved **Sorrentino**'s breakthrough picture.

Il divo 2008

Director Paolo Sorrentino **Cast** Toni Servillo, Anna Bonaiuto 110m

The figure of Giulio Andreaotti looms large over Italy's political landscape. He was prime minister no fewer than seven times and accusations of corruption and Mafia involvement were levelled against him throughout the 1960s, 70s and 80s. This is no mere biopic; **Sorrentino** weaves his source material and characters into an enjoyable political thriller centred on a tremendous performance from **Servillo** as the Nosferatu-like Andreaotti.

The Godfather 1972

Director Francis Ford Coppola **Cast** Marlon Brando, Al Pacino, James Caan

Offers you can't refuse, a horse's head in a bed and **Marlon Brando** chuntering through a mouthful of cotton wool. They're all here in **Coppola**'s powerhouse adaptation of **Mario Puzo**'s bestselling tale of family life – the "family" being the Mafia. Coppola brings the ingredients to a slow pressure boil – and his regular juxtaposition of religious symbolism with claret-spilling lends extra gravitas. Brando is at his cold-eyed best as the ageing boss and **Pacino** announces his arrival as the vengeful heir. It's so good they can even afford to relegate **James Caan** to third lead. If only all soaps were this great.

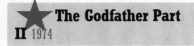

The Godfather Part II 1974

Director Francis Ford Coppola Cast Al Pacino, Robert De Niro 200m

One of those rare instances where a sequel is worthy of, if not better than, the film that spawned it, **Coppola**'s continuing look at cinema's best known Mafia family is audacious and handsomely executed. Tracing Corleone back to his native Italy and depicting his rapid rise to position and power, Coppola drew a striking, career-making turn from **De Niro** as the fearless young Don Vito. De Niro was rewarded with an Oscar and the film also picked up six other Academy Awards.

★ Gomorra 2008

Director Matteo Garrone Cast Maria Nazionale, Salvatore Cantalupo 137m

Power, money and blood: this is the trinity that informs daily life for the residents of the Province of Naples and Caserta. Five stories are woven together in this potent look at the Camorra and their ruling system of fear, threat and retribution. A visceral work, the film is set apart by **Garrone**'s understated style. Based on the bestselling book by **Roberto Saviano**, this is perhaps the most realistic and resolutely unsentimental Mafia picture to emerge from Italy.

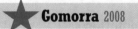

Goodfellas 1989

Director Martin Scorsese Cast Ray Liotta, Robert De Niro, Joe Pesci 145m

The scene of Henry Hill (**Liotta**) swaggering through the Copacabana club with girlfriend Karen (**Lorraine Bracco**), heading for the best seats, with a dedication by Bobby Vinton, sums up why he has always wanted to be a gangster and why a good Jewish girl is willing to believe his "I'm in construction" line. **Scorsese**'s tale of the rise and fall of real-life mobster Hill is a whirlwind adventure with the Mafia at its most seductive: the cars, the houses, the respect and the danger. **De Niro** plays Hill's paranoid mentor, while **Pesci**'s Tommy is mindlessly violent. This is sublime Scorsese, with a rousing soundtrack, frantic sequences (Henry pursued by the helicopter) and a supporting cast that look as if they're straight from San Quentin. The swearing didn't put off Ma and Pa Scorsese, as they both have cameos.

★ Mean Streets 1973

Director Martin Scorsese Cast Harvey Keitel, Robert De Niro, Amy Robinson 110m

"You don't make up for your sins in church. You do it in the streets." Charlie (**Keitel**) and Johnny (**De Niro**) are two hoods establishing themselves in the Mafia. Charlie, thoughtful and guilt-ridden, runs errands for his uncle, while Johnny is the embodiment of gangster glory. Less polished than his later work, many **Scorsese** trademarks are nevertheless in evidence, notably the use of music in the much copied scene of Charlie strutting through a bar to the Stones' "Jumpin' Jack Flash". Not exactly autobiographical, *Mean Streets* stems from a childhood where, in Scorsese's neigh-

It may have been shot in the 1980s, but a keen eye for period detail made sure Robert De Niro and James Woods looked sharp and moody in Sergio Leone's gangster-era *Once Upon a Time in America*.

bourhood, you either entered the Mob or the priesthood. Thankfully he entered neither. Be grateful, too, that Scorsese, who wrote 27 script drafts before anyone bought it, didn't accept Roger Corman's offer to finance it if he made it as a *Shaft* blaxploitation rip-off.

Once Upon a Time in America 1984

Director Sergio Leone **Cast** Robert De Niro, James Woods, Elizabeth McGovern 225m

Sergio Leone's final movie as director (he turned down the chance to direct *The Godfather* to film this, a decision he later regretted) has never yet been released in its entirety. Noodles (**De Niro**, based on mobster Meyer Lansky) and Max (**Woods**) are childhood friends who rise up in the Jewish mafia but whose friendship turns to betrayal. An attempt to edit the movie into chronological sequence proved disastrous. Leone himself edited the 225-minute version, and it is only in this print that you come to realize how the characters relate to one another and the importance that time, seen through the use of flashbacks, has on the narrative. Beautifully photographed, the streets of New York almost resemble the dusty plains of Leone's *A Fistful of Dollars*. Like that movie, this can be brutal, especially the rape scene with Noodles and Deborah (**McGovern**). And you'll need a comfy seat to watch it all through in one sitting.

One Hundred Days in Palermo 1984

Director Giuseppe Ferrara **Cast** Lino Ventura, Giulana de Sio 108m

An enthralling political thriller, *100 Days in Palermo* looks at the last hundred days in the life of Carlo dalla Chiesa (**Ventura**), an Italian general and prefect of Sicily's Palermo who took a stand against the Mafia and their various state- and corporate-related activities. Bringing numerous Mob leaders to justice, Chiesa, his wife Emmanuela (**di Sio**) and his bodyguard met their deaths at the hands of a Mafia hit squad on 3 September 1982. Adopting a sober and realistic approach, the film deserves to be more widely known.

Prizzi's Honour 1985

Director John Huston **Cast** Jack Nicholson, Kathleen Turner 130m

Lovingly transposed to the screen, **Richard Condon**'s novel looks at the powerful Prizzi family, a Mob clan who employ hit man Charley Pantana (**Nicholson**). When Pantana falls in love with Irene Walker (**Turner**), a woman of independent, nefarious means he's been hired to kill, things take a complicated turn. Nicholson and Turner are a perfect match in a film with a very matter-of-fact approach to death.

Salvatore Giuliano 1962

Director Francesco Rosi **Cast** Frank Wolff, Salvo Randone, Federico Zardi 125m

The infamous Sicilian bandit Giuliano remains an enigma, and director **Rosi** preferred to stick to the few facts known rather than create his own dramatic interpretation. With its use of black-and-white photography, the movie has a documentary feel. Although the Christopher Lambert film *Il Siciliano* told the same story, Rosi's is the more stirring, and even prompted Italian authorities to investigate the Mob for a while.

★ Scarface 1932

Directors Howard Hawks, Richard Rosson **Cast** Paul Muni, Ann Dvorak, George Raft 90m

Al Capone liked this disguised story of his life so much it's said he owned a copy. **Paul Muni** is Tony, former bagman to an old-style gang leader, who sets out to rule the (Mob) world. Despite the movie's credits stating, "This picture is an indictment of gang rule in America and of the callous indifference of the government", censors wouldn't endorse it. Re-shoots showing Tony arrested, convicted and hanged failed to persuade them, so **Hawks** stuck to the original. The movie marks **Raft**'s debut as a coin-tossing henchman. He would play a slew of gangsters and his personal association with mobster Bugsy Siegel encouraged rumours he himself was a "made" man.

Scarface 1983

Director Brian De Palma **Cast** Al Pacino, Steven Bauer, Michelle Pfeiffer 170m

King of New York (1990, 103m)

❝ The legendary Christopher Walken, playing it cool the only way he knows how in this epic tale of a modern Robin Hood, trying to put his drug money to good use. With excellent support from Laurence Fishburne, David Caruso, Steve Buscemi and Wesley Snipes, the acting is first class. Fishburne's scene in the fried chicken joint is great: he gives a poor old lady some money and fills up the video game with quarters for the kids, right before screaming at the teller. Young MC provides the tune for a mass shoot-out in the blue-lit club in one of the film's epic gun battles and the film finishes off with a calm and downbeat ending. Nice! ❞

Paul Andrew Williams

After his engaging low budget crime drama London to Brighton *in 2006 Williams was hailed as a rising talent and a director to watch. Horror comedy* The Cottage *was his 2008 follow-up.*

Although the film lacks originality, **Pacino** is suitably menacing as the coke-fuelled, self-made boss Tony Montana – it was actually icing sugar they were bathing their nostrils with. The scene where Montana, surrounded, his arm in a sling, waves his gun at his enemies, death and fate, is one of the most glamorous images of the doomed gangster on celluloid.

La scorta 1993

Director Ricky Tognazzi **Cast** Claudio Amendola, Enrico Lo Verso **92m**

Sicily, 1992: when a high-profile judge and his bodyguard are brutally murdered, four reluctant rookie cops are assigned the unenviable task of guarding his replacement from Mafia assassins. Negotiating the daily threat of car bombs and ambushes, the quartet must also battle personal conflicts and backroom betrayals in an environment rife with high-level corruption and violence. The winner of five Italian Oscars, *La scorta* is based on a real-life incident. Its tense, atmospheric score is by **Ennio Morricone**.

MARTIAL ARTS

The movies with the biggest kick – typically provided by Bruce Lee, Jackie Chan, Jet Li or, ahem, Jean-Claude Van Damme, the "muscles from Brussels".

Above the Law 1988

Director Andrew Davis **Cast** Steven Seagal, Pam Grier 99m

Under Siege may be **Steven Seagal**'s best work (it's a relative term, of course), but it was this cop flick about the Iran-Contra scandal that launched the pony-tailed martial arts teacher on his film career. Seagal is Nico, an ex-akido instructor maverick cop with Mafia connections. Not much of a thespian stretch, given Seagal was discovered whilst teaching akido to Hollywood super-agent Mike Ovitz, a man, apparently rightly, convinced he could make any idiot a star.

Crouching Tiger, Hidden Dragon 2000

Director Ang Lee **Cast** Chow Yun-Fat, Michelle Yeoh 120m

Chow Yun-Fat's first martial arts movie is a breathtaking mix of fighting, choreography and filmmaking. Okay, the story doesn't win any prizes for complexity, but it allows co-star **Zhang Ziyi** to display her impressive acting and fighting. The magical effects of running up trees and jumping over rooftops were created with harnesses and cables, edited out later, rather than by computers.

Drunken Master 1978

Director Yuen Woo-Ping **Cast** Jackie Chan, Siu Tien Yuen 111m

Jackie Chan's finest film: the kung fu is phenomenal, the verbal and physical jokes are laugh-out-loud funny and the action never stops. Chan is sent for a year of training with Beggar Su, aka "Drunken Master", a wine-sloshing kung fu genius with his own unique style. From him Chan learns the secrets of the Eight Drunken Gods movements – including that of Miss Ho, a drunken goddess who flaunts her body (as you'd expect, Chan the clown makes the most of it) – and comes out ready to do battle with a bounty hunter.

The Bruce Lee enigma

When it comes to staging a memorable movie death, the martial arts genre rarely lets you down. Neatly rolled umbrellas, underwear, even twirling moustaches – all have been used as lethal or near-lethal weapons. So when a real-life martial arts hero dies, it shouldn't be that surprising that the fans can't swallow a straightforward explanation. **Bruce Lee** was the first pan-Asian superstar. Turning his back on the supernatural Monkey King style, Lee developed Jeet Kune Do – a street-fighting system inspired by all martial arts.

Lee died in his sleep, aged only 32, on a hot Hong Kong day in 1973. According to the coroner's report, he had suffered a hyper-allergic response to an aspirin. But the Hong Kong press was having none of it. According to which edition of the papers you read, Lee had been murdered by triads, given an untraceable Oriental poison, killed by a psychic, faked his own death to escape gangsters, been the victim of a martial arts "death touch" or been slain by seriously bad feng shui. The fact that Lee had predicted that he would live to only half the age of his father – who died at 64 – only served to fuel the speculation.

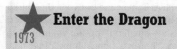

Enter the Dragon 1973

Director Robert Clouse **Cast** Bruce Lee, John Saxon, Kien Shih 98m

The first Hong Kong–US production and the movie **Bruce Lee** hoped would make him a Hollywood star. Here he goes undercover to a martial arts contest on the island of a Hong Kong millionaire. According to **Clouse**, the fight between Lee and **Bob Wall** became real, extras convincing Lee that to save face he'd have to kill his rival. Luckily Clouse persuaded him he didn't. The movie was an instant hit, but Lee died before the final cut.

Hero 2002

Director Zhang Yimou **Cast** Jet Li, Tony Yeung Chiu-Wai, Maggie Cheung 98m

A martial arts epic from China's foremost filmmaker, the comparisons to *Crouching Tiger, Hidden Dragon* are inevitable, especially since they both have scores by **Tan Dun**, but this is the tighter, more visually impressive work. The King of Qin places a reward on the heads of three deadly assassins. A decade later, a warrior called "Nameless" (**Jet Li**) brings their weapons to the palace and is invited to explain how he defeated them. All is revealed in a series of sumptuous flashbacks.

The Karate Kid 1984

Director John G. Avildsen **Cast** Ralph Macchio, Pat Morita 127m

"Wax on, wax off": perhaps the most famous martial arts movie line ever. Daniel is the new kid in town (**Macchio** was actually 23 at the time). Everything goes well until he chats up the school karate star's girlfriend. But wait – the ageing Japanese caretaker turns out to be a crack karate expert. Many crane stances on windswept beaches and much waxing of cars later, our weedy hero is ready to take on the champ. Guess who wins.

Kickboxer 1989

Director Mark DiSalle **Cast** Jean-Claude Van Damme, Tong Po 103m

When **Van Damme**'s mullet-haired brother is paralysed in a kickboxing contest, he swears vengeance against the mighty **Tong Po**. He finds help from the sort of retired forest-living master who tend to frequent martial arts movies. The training sequences – including felling palm trees with bare shins – are spectacular. The dancing is not. For more "classic" Van Damme, try *The Quest*, with **Roger Moore** and a kilt-wearing Scottish fighter.

Kill Bill Vols. 1 & 2 2003, 2004

Director Quentin Tarantino **Cast** Uma Thurman, David Carradine, Michael Madsen, Daryl Hannah, Lucy Liu 111m, 136m

Allegedly based on an idea conceived by **Tarantino** and **Thurman** whilst filming *Pulp Fiction*, the story of a woman seeking revenge on a group of people, crossing them off a list as she kills them, is actually a direct lift from the 1973 Japanese movie *Lady Snowblood* (see p.309). Just one of a whole video-store's worth of martial arts influences battling it out here, including the Japanese softcore movie *Sex and Fury* and the *Female Prisoner Scorpion* series. However *Kill Bill* is samurai Tarantino-

style, with the look as authentic and pre-digital as he could make it. Each fight scene is played out in full, using the traditional Chinese method of condoms filled with fake blood for the injuries.

★ Kung Fu Hustle 2004

Director Stephen Chow **Cast** Stephen Chow, Xiaogang Feng, Wah Yuen 95m

An eye-popping, chop-sockey treat, this Hong Kong belter teams the balletic style of *Crouching Tiger* choreographer **Yuen Wo Ping** with the Tom and Jerry energy of *Shaolin Soccer* director (and star) **Stephen Chow** to laugh-a-minute effect. It's basically one long, crazily inventive fight scene between the quirky tenants of "The Pig Sty" and the dreaded hot-shoe-shuffling, top-hat-wearing Axe Gang. There's a bonus in the older cast members drawn from the golden era of martial arts, including veteran Bruce Lee stuntman **Yuen Wah** as a boozy landlord, and former *The Man With the Golden Gun* Bond girl **Yuen Qiu** as his wife.

Legend of a Fighter 1982

Director Woo-Ping Yuen **Cast** Ka-Yan Leung, Yasuaki Kurata 89m

Set during the Japanese occupation, Chinese hero Yuen Chia (**Ka-Yan Leung**) fights not only the Japanese but also the idea that kung fu should be reserved for a minority. With the plot based on a true story and the acting being top quality, this is a brilliant antidote to the farce and bluster of many poor-quality martial arts hits.

The New One-Armed Swordsman 1971

Director Chang Cheh **Cast** David Chiang, Ti Lung, Cheng Lei 102m

An inauspicious opening, complete with cardboard prop swords, a *Star Trek*-style set and plenty of overdubbed steel-on-steel sounds, leads to an ultimately impressive tale of honour, friendship and sword-fighting. Young knight Lei Li (**David Chiang**) fulfils a pledge to cut off his right arm after losing a fight and is forced to retire. But everything changes with the arrival of a sword-bearing love interest.

Once Upon a Time in China 1991

Director Tsui Hark **Cast** Jet Li, Yuen Biao, Rosamund Kwan 135m

Jet Li plays Wong Fei Hung, a nineteenth-century Chinese kung fu fighter and healer. Li's mastery of the *wu shu* style of fighting makes for thrilling viewing and the final fight sequences are incredible. But then, by the time this movie was released, Li had been in training for years. China's national *wu shu* champion aged eleven, his first US starring role was on the White House lawn for Nixon.

Ong Bak 2003

Director Prachya Pinkaew **Cast** Tony Jaa, Petchtai Wongkamlao 104m

"No wires, no CGI, no stuntmen": this down-and-dirty Thai action thriller sets itself up as a low-budget antidote to the likes of *Crouching Tiger, Hidden Dragon*. The first 45 minutes are a snore, in which baddies steal a Buddha head from a village temple and an orphan (**Tony Jaa**) is sent to Bangkok to recover it from the Big Boss and his many, mysteriously unarmed henchmen. Then the bare-knuckle fighting starts. Astonishing set pieces with inconvenient obstacles – panes of glass, barbed wire etc – all showcase the extraordinary talents of Jaa, poised for international action megastardom, if only his Jackie Chan fight skills were matched by Chan's charisma.

Pantyhose Hero 1990

Director Sammo Hung **Cast** Sammo Hung, Alan Tam, James Tien 99m

A surreal kung fu action "comedy", in which **Hung** and his partner go undercover as a gay couple to investigate a murder. Cue a tightly curled, brilliantined hairdo for Sammo and a mincing walk for **Alan Tam**. The acting is as gruesome as the blood-spurting chainsaw close-ups, but the showdown at a well-equipped but handily deserted construction site is worth the wait.

MAVERICKS

The history of cult movies is littered with the work of maverick directors. However, here's where we celebrate the really special ones – the cult movie director's cult movie directors.

Aguirre: The Wrath of God
1972

Director Werner Herzog **Cast** Klaus Kinski, Alejandro Repules, Cecilia Rivera 95m

Kinski is perfect as the psychotic, idealistic conquistador in search of El Dorado. But then, if he was ever in any doubt about his characterization, he could always watch the man in the director's chair. At one point, **Herzog** threatened to kill himself and Kinski to stop the actor quitting. Spectacularly epic yet meticulously detailed, the movie shows star and moviemaker at their berserk, fascinating best.

Beau travail 1998

Director Claire Denis **Cast** Denis Lavant, Grégoire Colin 90m

Inspired by Herman Melville's *Billy Budd*, *Beau travail* is a stunning combination of literature, music, poetry and dance that explores the near mythical world of the French Foreign Legion. **Denis** creates a dark mounting tension which underlies the exquisite cinematography of **Agnès Godard**, whose stark visual style contrasts vividly with the graceful training rituals of the sculpted young soldiers. Arguably the director's best work, and with a filmography including *Chocolat*

Double trouble

The turbulent relationship between director **Werner Herzog** and the late actor **Klaus Kinski** is the fabric of legend. Both extremists, they understood and inspired each other, and the insults, shrieking and mutual death threats produced a remarkable quartet of movies that significantly extended cinema's sense of compulsive personality.

The Polish-born actor's extraordinary face (part-angel, part-pterodactyl) was his fortune. But, growing up poor, he was attracted by the prospect of cash-in-hand and he appeared in more trashy European movies – frequently playing lunatics, killers and other figures of fear and loathing – than he cared to recall. Few directors before Herzog, young mystic of the New German Cinema of the 1970s, lauded for his studies of people on the fringes of society, noticed the sensitivity behind the chilling stare.

and *Friday Night*, that is really saying something.

Katalin Varga 2009

Director Peter Strickland Cast Hilda Péter, Tibo Pálffy 84m

Disowned by her husband after a brutal incident in her past is revealed, Katalin Varga sets out on a quest through the Carpathians, determined to exact revenge. Owing something to the work of Béla Tarr, the film moves at a slow pace, gradually ratcheting up an unbearable tension. The story of the making of *Katalin Varga* is as remarkable as the film itself, with first time director **Strickland** achieving his ambition to make a feature film after receiving an inheritance from the death of a relative.

My Winnipeg 2007

Director Guy Maddin Cast Darcy Fehr, Ann Savage 80m

Mingling mystical rumination and personal history, city chronicle and deranged post-Freudian proletarian fantasy, **Guy Maddin**'s masterpiece blends local myth with childhood trauma. Part-documentary and part-drop-dead hysterical farce, this extraordinary visual homage to Maddin's home town is all narrated by the Canadian director with both love and hatred.

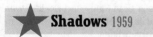

Shadows 1959

Director John Cassavetes Cast Leilia Goldoni, Ben Carruthers 87m

Viewed as the *Citizen Kane* of American independent cinema, *Shadows* opened the door for a new kind of self-sufficient filmmaking. Shot in black and white with a six-person crew, *Shadows* offers a frank observation of the tensions and lives of three siblings in an African-American family. Made for $40,000 with funds accrued by the director's parallel acting career, the film took three years to complete and though not an initial success on release, would come to alter the landscape of American film.

Ten 2002

Director Abbas Kiarostami Cast Mania Akbari 94m

A perceptive and revealing portrait of contemporary Iranian life, *Ten* marked director **Kiarostami**'s conscious break with traditional film form. Opening with a bristling exchange between a woman and her young son in a car, the film goes on to explore the relationships that develop between the driver and her disparate passengers over the course of ten short trips. Undoubtedly the most celebrated director in recent Iranian cinema, Kiarostami has frequently fallen foul of the Iranian authorities but has continued to pioneer digital filmmaking and plough his own furrow.

Violent Cop 1989

Director "Beat" Takeshi Kitano Cast "Beat" Takeshi Kitano, Maiko Kawakami 98m

In his stunning first feature as director, the actor, painter and TV personality

Heart of Glass (1976, 94m)

" What I love about Heart of Glass is that I can't really recommend it. It defies all conventions and standard criteria for what constitutes a "good film". It is the antithesis of films that have been developed and vetted and brought before test audiences. It is a deeply philosophical B-movie. The fact that the cast of the film supposedly performed under hypnosis lends each scene an almost pornographic quality – like it's something you really shouldn't be watching. It's the cast of Night of the Living Dead stumbling onto the set of a Vermeer painting. It is ridiculous and sublime and like most of Herzog's films it explores the ways in which people struggle to make their mark even though they're constantly outdone by the awesome forces of nature that surround them. It is, as the last line of the film tells us, a group of strangers who believe the Earth is flat, and who band together to travel to the edge of the abyss simply because they can. "

Keith Fulton

First making a splash with The Hamster Factor and Other Tales of Twelve Monkeys, *Keith Fulton and Louis Pepe again collaborated with Terry Gilliam for the remarkable* Lost in La Mancha. *Described as the first "un-making of" documentary, the film presented an in-depth look at Gilliam's struggles to bring his adaptation of Don Quixote to the screen. Fulton and Pepe's most recent collaboration is* Brothers of the Head, *a synthesis of fact and fiction that centres on the story of two conjoined punk twins.*

Takeshi Kitano plays Azuma, a brutal but honourable cop whose life unravels when his mentally ill sister is kidnapped by gangsters. Resuscitating the waning yakuza genre, Kitano, who only boarded the project after the veteran Kinji Fukasuku dropped out, gave us an intriguing introduction to what would become a unique directorial vision and filmmaking style.

You, the Living 2008

Director Roy Andersson **Cast** Jessica Lundberg, Elisabet Helander 96m

An assortment of washed-out interiors provide the backdrop for a motley crew of characters: a stout depressive and her long-suffering husband; a young girl with an unrequited crush on a rock musician; an Arab barber taking sweet revenge on a racist customer; a diligent tuba player; and various couples with too much to say – or too little. Swedish director **Roy Andersson** is a filmmaker like no other. Like *Songs from the Second Floor*, *You, the Living* is both funny and riddled with despair in its observations of life's eccentrics and absurdities.

MEDIA

Whether you're a war correspondent, a newsreader or just a guy on the radio, in movies you're only ever a couple of blunders away from death, or – even worse – starring against your will in a 24-hour TV series.

★ Ace in the Hole 1951

Director Billy Wilder **Cast** Kirk Douglas, Jan Sterling 111m

Billy Wilder's most savagely cynical movie was a controversial flop when released but has come to be regarded as a darkly prophetic, increasingly relevant indictment of media sensationalism. (And a much imitated one too, most blatantly in **Costa-Gavras**'s *Mad City*). **Douglas**, never better, is washed-up reporter Charles Tatum. When he finds a man trapped in a cavern he exploits the situation to restore his career and creates a media and merchandising circus. Wilder's wife Audrey suggested the most famous line, where **Tatum** tells the trapped man's tough-nut wife (**Sterling**) to go to church and she retorts: "I don't pray. Kneeling bags my nylons."

All the President's Men
1976

Director Alan J. Pakula **Cast** Robert Redford, Dustin Hoffman 138m

Robert Redford only wanted to produce this movie but no studio would take it unless he starred in it too. Just as well, because he and **Hoffman** make a perfect pair. The account of *The Washington Post*'s investigation into Watergate is full of classic one-liners. The movie takes us back to a time when the very idea that a president would be involved in a third-rate burglary seemed ludicrous. You see Redford and Hoffman piecing it together, not quite believing it. The last word belongs to editor Bradlee, played to perfection by **Jason Robards**: "We are about to accuse Haldeman, who only happens to be the second most powerful man in this country, of conducting a criminal conspiracy from inside the White House. It would be nice if we were right!"

Citizen Kane 1941

Director Orson Welles **Cast** Orson Welles, Joseph Cotten, Agnes Moorehead 119m

One of the many achievements of this all-time great is to redefine the way we see media moguls and powerful men. Not just William Randolph Hearst, whose life partly inspired this, but also Rupert Murdoch or Robert Maxwell. The movie is full of elements of **Welles**' own life that writer **Herman Mankiewicz** and Welles slipped in, and says as much about its star as about its apparent subject (this is especially true of Kane's relationship with his parents). Stick it on again and see if you can remember which scene comes next – one of the film's great gambits is the way it defies time, relying on its emotional chronology to tell the story.

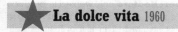

La dolce vita 1960

Director Federico Fellini **Cast** Marcello Mastroianni, Anita Ekberg, Anouk Aimée 176m

A movie inspired by the media (the events that gossip columnist **Mastroianni** cov-

ers come from actual newspaper stories), which influenced the media in ways that **Fellini** could never have foreseen. The character of Paparazzo, the photographer, coined a new word, and the phrase "la dolce vita" became part of a drive for tourism in Italy and Rome. The tale of Mastroianni's descent into decadence was slammed by the Catholic Church, Fellini's old mentor Roberto Rossellini and film critic Pauline Kael, who called it the "come-dressed-as-the-sick-soul-of-Europe party". Perhaps they were missing the point: Fellini didn't approve of the "dolce vita" set, hence his refusal to cast Paul Newman in the Mastroianni role. He didn't want the Hollywood star's charisma to blind the audience to the story and saw the Italian actor as more of an everyman figure. Robert Altman claims the film changed his life.

Life is sweet for both the jet set and the paparazzi in Fellini's satire that was often mistaken for a celebration: *La dolce vita*.

My Favourite Year 1982

Director Richard Benjamin **Cast** Peter O'Toole, Mark Linn-Baker 92m

A young TV writer gets the job of baby-sitting his childhood idol, a famously inebriated ageing movie star called Alan Swann (based on Errol Flynn) when he appears on a live TV show. Meanwhile the star of the show, King Kaiser (based on Sid Caesar), is under fire from a union boss unhappy about Kaiser's on-air impressions of him. Great scenes include **O'Toole** abseiling down a firehose, and the final farcical fight scene.

Network 1976

Director Sidney Lumet **Cast** Peter Finch, Faye Dunaway, William Holden 121m

This gripping satire looked overcooked on release. But all TV producer **Dunaway** really, really wants is her own brand of reality TV – only instead of inmates in a Big Brother house, she wants terrorism telly ("Joseph Stalin and his merry band of Bolsheviks"). Her newscaster, Howard Beale (**Finch**), is doing his bit by threatening to kill himself on air, an event which, as **Holden** says, "will guarantee a 50 share". After the initial thrill of Finch's divine madness the movie loses its way a bit but picks up when Holden tells Dunaway that she and TV destroy everything they touch.

★ Shock Corridor 1963

Director Samuel Fuller **Cast** Peter Breck, Constance Towers 101m

The dialogue in this movie sounds like it's been plucked from a tabloid front page and the plot (about a newspaper reporter (**Breck**), who fakes madness to gain entry to an asylum to win a Pulitzer Prize but really goes mad) is taken to its illogical extreme. The whole film is a "shock corridor": the asylum's inmates are so animated you almost expect them to launch into a high-stepping version of "Anything Goes". You may not like this movie but, as is usually the case with **Fuller**, you won't forget it.

Shoot to Kill 1992

Director Carlos Azpúrua **Cast** Amalia Pérez Diaz, Jean Carlo Simancas, Daniel Alvarado 109m

Carlos Azúrua has made two brave movies about Venezuelan politics. In 1998 he made *Almanecio de Golpe* about the 1992 military coup, and this one, aka *Disparen a matar*, about a woman who persuades a reporter to investigate the death of her son. Like Costa-Gavras's *Missing*, the film uses the techniques of a thriller to tell the story as the reporter comes into conflict with his editor and the state.

Startup.com 2001

Directors Chris Hegedus, Jehane Noujaim

An engrossing, at times traumatic look at the rise and fall of a startup Internet company, *Startup.com* follows the trajectory from boom to bust of GovWorks.com – an Internet site that facilitates interaction between local government, citizens and businesses – led by two entrepreneurs with inflated ideals and dreams of instant wealth. The film, produced by **D.A Pennebaker**, is lent added poignancy by the fact that the two principals involved are lifelong friends. Distilled from over four hundred hours of filmed material, the timing of the documentary perfectly captured the boom to bust nature of the Internet and the shifting sands on which many new media businesses were built.

Talk Radio 1988

Director Oliver Stone **Cast** Eric Bogosian, Alec Baldwin 109m

This is the movie about the talk radio show host who gets murdered. So it's not to be confused with the movie about the DJ whose comments inspire murder (*The Fisher King*), the movie about the pirate radio station that interferes with passing planes (*Big Swinger*) or the movie about the talk radio host who looks like Dolly Parton (*Straight Talk*), all of which were released between 1988 and 1992. This **Bogosian/Stone** effort is easily the best, thanks to Bogosian's intensity and Stone's subtle camera work.

Tout va bien 1972

Director Jean-Luc Godard **Cast** Jane Fonda, Yves Montand 95m

Jane Fonda has spent so long playing news reporters it came as no surprise when she married the media mogul Ted Turner. This is a must-see because it's the kind of film (**Godard**'s first after four years of self-imposed exile) you can debate into the night. Is it a Marxist movie? A parody of a Marxist movie? Or an anti-Marxist movie? The plot is easier to describe: Fonda and **Montand** play a reporter and TV producer whose commitment to each other, and to the revolution, is called into question by the workers occupying a factory.

The Truman Show 1998

Director Peter Weir **Cast** Jim Carrey, Ed Harris, Laura Linney 102m

Whatever else this movie is, it's proof that the only people who are nostalgic for the American small town are those who never lived in one. A better movie than the similarly themed *EDtv*, made around the same time, it has **Carrey** as the unwitting star of a 24-hour TV show whose world is one big special effect. At one point, the show's producer **Harris** even says: "Cue the sun!" Scripted by **Andrew Niccol**, who wrote and directed *Gattaca*, this is an eerie, funny movie with a subdued – for him – performance by Carrey.

MIDNIGHT MOVIES

These films quite simply wouldn't work in the afternoon. These aren't for the matinee. These are films to mess with your head, man.

Equinox 1970

Director Dennis Muren **Cast** Jack Woods, Edward Connell 80m

Equinox, begun in 1967 but not completed and released until three years later, is frequently cited as the inspiration behind The Evil Dead. Four teenagers head into a forest in search of a long-lost scientist. Monitoring their every move is a forest ranger (Woods), who is actually an ancient demi-god in human form. When the teens stumble across a precious book of incantations, the ranger summons up a parade of nightmarish monsters and visions. Featuring a cameo from cult sci-fi writer **Fritz Leiber**, the film is a midnight movie staple.

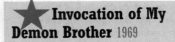

Invocation of My Demon Brother 1969

Director Kenneth Anger **Cast** Kenneth Anger, Bobby Beausoleil 11m

Invocation of My Demon Brother is a later entry to avant-garde filmmaker **Kenneth Anger**'s "Magick" cycle, a series of films that are manifestations of occult practices. Here, powers from the underworld gather at a midnight mass to shadow forth Lord Lucifer. Featuring found footage, it attempts to appeal directly to the subconscious mind, with a hallucinatory Moog synthesizer soundtrack courtesy of **Mick Jagger**.

Liquid Sky 1982

Director Anne Carlisle **Cast** Anne Carlisle, Paula Sheppard 118m

Frequently pitched as a glitzy synthesis of Andy Warhol's *Trash* with *Alien*, this campy, stylish sci-fi is one of the most keenly observed portraits of New York's early 1980s downtown new wave scene. A tale of sex, drugs and alien invaders in which director **Carlisle** also features in a double acting role, *Liquid Sky* offers a powerful mix of surreal imagery, music and potent production design. Very much an underground classic, and quite unlike anything else from its period.

Macunaíma 1969

Director Joaquim Pedro de Andrade **Cast** Rodolfo Arena, Jardel Filho 100m

Choosing an iconic novel of Brazilian modernism by **Mário de Andrade** (no relation), the director noted: "Once I understood that Macunaíma was the story of a Brazilian man devoured by his country, the whole story made sense and everything fell into place." The eponymous protagonist, "a hero with no character", changes from black to white as he travels from the jungle to the big city, along the way meeting con artists, urban guerillas, and an industrialist who likes to eat people. Reflecting a nation caught between a harsh military dictatorship and the anarchic energy of its people, Macunaíma's radical politics and inspired humour made it a regular feature on the midnight movies circuit.

They Live (1988, 93m)

John Carpenter's *They Live* might be the cleverest – and we would also argue most potentially effective – poke in the eye of capitalist culture we've ever seen. While masquerading as a straight-to-video genre movie with nothing but the kicking of alien ass on its mind, the film manages to do for its audience what the special glasses do for our everyman hero, "Rowdy" Roddy Piper, in this film: expose the mind-numbing seduction of consumer media, and unmask the hideously ugly power elite. When the glasses are off, it's the world as we know it. With the glasses on, slick ad campaigns become Barbara Kruger-esque aphorisms like "MARRY AND REPRODUCE". The money in your wallet reminds you: "THIS IS YOUR GOD". And the rich ladies in the gourmet foods aisle look like scary reptiles with Nancy Reagan hair. We first saw *They Live* at a Cineplex in a California stripmall. When we walked out, we found the scary world of the film was waiting right outside the door. And we've been living a bit less easily in that world ever since.

David Siegel and Scott McGehee

Scott McGehee and David Siegel are the writer-producers-directors of highly distinctive genre-bending movies. These include thriller Suture *and the crime mystery* The Deep End. *Both films won the best cinematography prize at Sundance. After* Bee Season *the pair recently completed* Uncertainty, *the story of a young couple whose decision to flip a coin at the film's opening sets in motion two wildly different stories that unfold simultaneously.*

Reefer Madness 1936

Director Louis J. Gasnier **Cast** Kenneth Craig, Dorothy Short **67m**

Originally titled *Tell Your Children* and financed by a small church group as a cautionary tale against the horrors of marijuana, the film became something else entirely in the hands of notorious exploitation producer and director **Dwain Esper**. Structured as a cautionary documentary which follows a lecture to parents during a PTA meeting with a case study of two promising high school students who turn into mindless zombies after imbibing the demon weed, the film became a comedy classic in the hands of 1970s American college students. It ends with an ominous warning: "The dread marijuana may be reaching forth next for your son or daughter... or yours... or *yours*!"

★ The Saragossa Manuscript 1965

Director Wojciech Has **Cast** Zbigniew Cybulski, Kazimierz Opalinski **180m**

Described by David Lynch as "simultaneously horrific, erotic and funny … one mother of a film", *The Saragossa Manuscript* is based on a book by esteemed count Jan Potocki and is set in seventeenth-century Spain. Unfolding in a weird fantasy landscape featuring sexy princesses and other assorted colourful characters who may or may not be dead, the film boasts an astonishing score by **Krzysztof Penderecki**. A counterculture classic, its restoration was at the behest of Jerry Garcia and Martin Scorsese.

Viva la muerte 1971

Director Fernando Arrabal **Cast** Anouk Ferjac, Nuria Espert **90m**

An extremely violent, gory, and surreal meditation on the life of a young Spaniard during the time of the Spanish Civil War as he attempts to find out what happened to his missing father, *Viva la muerte* has an enduring place on the midnight movie circuit largely down to its brilliantly conceived and original grotesque set pieces, many of which feature castration and the devouring of male genitalia. An extremely powerful vision of war, chaos, sex and politics, the film is invariably compared to the work of Alejandro Jodorowsky, and is as ferocious in its taboo-busting sensibilities.

MINIMALISM

Stripped-down cinema is perhaps always fated to end up a cult concern in today's cineplex world, where everything has to be as big as the popcorn helpings.

Ordet 1955

Director Carl Theodor Dreyer **Cast** Henrik Malberg, Emil Hass Christensen 125m

Dreyer made only fourteen full-length feature films in a career spanning almost fifty years, but they are considered amongst the most intensely wrought works in cinema. Based on a play by a Lutheran priest, *Ordet* explores religion versus faith within a rural Danish family. Deceptively simple and shot with extraordinary precision, the closing sequence was borrowed wholesale by Carlos Reygadas for *Silent Light*.

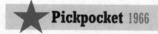 Pickpocket 1966

Director Robert Bresson **Cast** Martin Lasalle, Marika Green 73m

Bresson was known for his attention to detail and uncompromising, austere style. A tale of a petty thief, played by **Martin Lasalle**, for whom crime is a way of life until he finds love with another social misfit, *Pickpocket* is often compared to Samuel Beckett in its interest in only the bare essential components of character and plot. Free of any frills

or flourishes, the cinema of Bresson is cinema at its purest.

Radio On 1979

Director Christopher Petit **Cast** David Beames, Lisa Kreuzer 102m

This film might strike you as utterly pretentious: a black-and-white road movie that drifts through the landscape of late-1970s England in the company of an inscrutable, sharp young man (**Beames**) who sets off in search of his dodgy brother after he receives a parcel of music tapes from him, last seen in the Bristol area. But it isn't. The music (from **Kraftwerk**, **Lene Lovich** and **Robert Fripp**) conspires with the endless motorways, flyovers and country lanes to produce a compelling head-trip where repetition is the whole point.

Rosetta 1999

Directors Luc & Jean-Pierre Dardenne **Cast** Emelie Dequenne, Fabrizio Rongione 91m

Rosetta (**Dequenne**) is obsessed with leading a normal life and with fitting in with society, and she'll go to almost any lengths to remain in work. A documentary-style portrait of a determined and resourceful teenage girl, *Rosetta* is defined by its lack of artifice and artificiality. The winner of the Palme d'Or, the film is perhaps the jewel in the crown of the unique films made by Belgian brothers **Luc and Jean-Pierre Dardenne**.

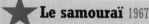

Le samouraï 1967

Director Jean-Pierre Melville **Cast** Alain Delon, Cathy Rosier 105m

A huge influence on Walter Hill's *The Driver*, John Woo's *The Killer* and Jim Jarmusch's *Ghost Dog: The Way of the Samurai*, **Melville**'s minimalist *policier* combines 1960s French pop culture with Japanese lone-warrior mythology. A tale of an impassive lone assassin whose identity is compromised after leaving behind a witness to one of his executions, the film features little dialogue but plenty of cool cars, trench coats and modish interiors.

The Time to Live and the Time to Die 1985

Director Hsiao-Hsien Hou **Cast** You Anshun, Tian Feng 137m

Deliberately spare and simple in style, *The Time to Live and the Time to Die* announced the arrival of a major talent in the shape of Taiwanese director **Hou**. A semi-autobiographical tale of a family that leave the Chinese mainland to settle in a village in Taiwan and decide to remain there, the film spans several years of their lives. A contemplative work that hints at

rather than shows emotions, the static filming style earned comparison to Ozu.

Tokyo Story 1953

Director Yasujiro Ozu **Cast** Chishu Ryu, Setsuko Hara, Chieko Higashiyama 136m

Ozu's films made after World War II are understated domestic dramas, in which his austere style – the camera rarely moves – sharpens the sense of intimacy to an almost painful extent. In *Tokyo Story* an elderly couple from the country decide to visit their grown-up children in the big city, but find themselves largely in the way. Only their widowed daughter-in-law shows them any real tenderness and respect. From such a simple premise Ozu fashions a poignant meditation on generational difference and a rapidly changing world.

The Unbelievable Truth 1989

Director Hal Hartley **Cast** Adrienne Shelly, Robert Burke 86m

The tale of an ex-con (**Robert Burke**) trying to go straight in Long Island but finding life complicated by the romantic attentions of a rebellious teen (**Shelly**), **Hartley**'s first feature established a unique style (pared down and very simple) and revealed an ear for witty wordplay. A self-dubbed tyrant of economy, the director's belief that minimalism could still be pregnant with meaning and emotion was partly dictated by the small budget with which he was forced to work, his only backing for this film being from an ex-employer.

MONSTERS

Be they hairy, scary, scaly or gooey, you don't want to be around when these big boys hit your town.

Cloverfield 2008

Director Matt Reeves **Cast** Lizzy Caplan, Jessica Lucas, T.J. Miller 85m

Producer **J.J. Abrams**, creator of *Lost*, loves an enigma. This no-star blockbuster was as distinctive for its teaser marketing campaign as the fact it reinvented the monster movie for the YouTube generation. The roller-coaster action has a huge, but never fully seen, creature causing mayhem in Manhattan, decapitating the Statue of Liberty, among other things. All supposedly seen from the point of view of one character's lo-fi camcorder, there are no heroes here so much as a blind, uncomprehending panic. If *Godzilla* symbolized the H-bomb, this is essentially the 9/11 attacks in a lizard suit.

Creature from the Black Lagoon 1954

Director Jack Arnold **Cast** Antonio Moreno, Richard Carlson, Julie Adams 79m

In this movie, shot for 3-D, a creature dubbed Gill-Man, the only resident of a black lagoon, falls for Kay (**Adams**), whose habit of swimming in the aforementioned lagoon must count as contributory negligence. Professional swimmer **Ricou Browning** was cast as Gill-Man because he could hold his breath for four minutes underwater. Kitsch, subliminally sexy, and entertaining.

Ghostbusters 1984

Director Ivan Reitman **Cast** Bill Murray, Dan Aykroyd, Sigourney Weaver, Harold Ramis 105m

Aliens, dinosaurs, germs, small fat men who think they're penguins: New York has been attacked by many crazy things in movies, but there's arguably never been a cuter one than the angry 100-foot-tall Stay Puft marshmallow man in this ageless sci-fi comedy. He's more than a match for the bumbling paranormal college geeks turned commercial ghost catchers **Murray**, **Aykroyd** and **Ramis**.

Godzilla vs the Destroyer 1995

Director Takao Okawara **Cast** Takuro Tatsumi, Megumi Odaka 103m

Godzilla 1984 heralded a new era for the film company Toho's creation, inspiring a slew of movies. But for their grand finale, after ten years Toho decided to kill off their biggest star by internal nuclear meltdown. But not before he has met Destroyer (a giant crab-like mantis) and avenged the supposed death of his son Minya with a death ray. Although Godzilla has since arisen (in *Godzilla 2000*), this beautifully photographed, cleverly scripted and ingeniously staged movie is the best of the new batch.

The Host 2006

Director Bong Joon-ho **Cast** Song Kang-ho, Byeon Hie-bong, Park Hae-il 119m

In the year 2000, a US military base empties toxic waste into the Han River. Six years later, a mutant squid leaps forth to attack Seoul. The highest-grossing South Korean film of all time, it brilliantly combines slapstick comedy and creature feature fun with political commentary. Vaguely inspired by a true event – a Korean mortician working for the American military d id indeed flush a large volume of formaldehyde down the drain in 2000 – the blockbuster's anti-US stance led to rare official praise from North Korea.

★ The Hunchback of Notre Dame 1939

Director William Dieterle **Cast** Charles Laughton, Maureen O'Hara 116m

The **Victor Hugo** classic has never been treated better than in this historical pageant, with a gothic atmosphere and a

Hogarthian cross-section of society. Below Quasimodo's bell tower, the city teems with beggars, kings, clergymen and the puritanical chief justice (**Cedric Hardwicke**) lusting for the Gypsy Esmeralda (**O'Hara**), whose kindness to Quasimodo has made her his obsession, too. **Laughton** is colossal in the title role, like a living, crying gargoyle, and his snatching of Esmeralda from execution, holding her high overhead bellowing ''Sanctuary! Sanctuary!'' is one of screen history's enduringly stupendous moments.

Jabberwocky 1977

Director Terry Gilliam **Cast** Michael Palin, Harry H. Corbett, John Le Mesurier 101m

Inspired by Lewis Carroll's poem, **Gilliam**'s first directorial departure from the Flying Circus is still basically Monty Python goes medieval. Not least because fellow Python **Michael Palin** plays the milksop hero coerced into freeing the local town from a ''monster so horrible that people caught the plague to avoid it'', as the tagline put it. At his creative best when faced with tight budget restraints, Gilliam designed the Jabberwocky costume to be worn face-backwards, giving the monster's body an organic, bird-like stance whilst the puppet head was manipulated by a piece of string on a stick.

Jaws 3-D 1983

Director Joe Alves **Cast** Dennis Quaid, Bess Armstrong 99m

Not to be confused with *Jaws*, and not to be confused with a real movie either.

The great white shark heads to Florida to find a more exciting menu. There's the usual mauling of human victims and gnashing of shark's teeth, this time shown (very slowly) in (very basic) red-and-green cardboard 3-D glasses. A period curiosity.

Jurassic Park 1993

Director Steven Spielberg **Cast** Sam Neill, Laura Dern, Jeff Goldblum 127m

Richard Attenborough is the crazed scientist whose theme park goes badly awry, endangering his guests' lives and grossing the movie over $400m at the box office. Screenwriter **David Koepp**, in adapting **Michael Crichton**'s novel, operated on this credo: "Whenever the characters started talking about their personal lives, you couldn't care less. You want them to shut up and go stand on a hill where you can see the dinosaurs."

★ King Kong 1933

Directors Merian C. Cooper, Ernest B. Schoedsack **Cast** Fay Wray, Bruce Cabot, Robert Armstrong 100m

This saved RKO from bankruptcy, helped to create the fantasy monster genre and made a legend out of **Fay Wray**, the Queen of Scream. A re-imagining of the Beauty and the Beast fable, a director heads off with his leading lady (Wray) to a remote island to coerce a giant ape into starring in his film, only for the ape to fall for Wray. **Cooper** and **Schoedsack**, both former wrestlers, acted out the fight scenes between Kong and

the T-Rex to give the animators something to work from. The heart-tugging humanity and wonder that shines from **Willis O'Brien**'s stop-motion models surpasses anything in Peter Jackson's crass multimillion-dollar CGI-heavy remake.

King Kong vs Godzilla 1962

Director Ishiro Honda **Cast** Tadao Takeshima, Yu Fujiki 98m

The ape's creator, **Willis O'Brien**, originally had the idea of pitting his giant gorilla against – somewhat improbably – Frankenstein's monster for this movie. That evolved into a rubber-suited rumble in the jungle in which the mighty US ape clashes with Japan's finest flame-thrower. Entire cities are flattened, Mount Fuji is threatened, a giant octopus is wrestled into submission and, after a furious underwater struggle, a victorious Kong swims off into the sunset. Toho's Kong returned in *King Kong Escapes* (1967) where he meets MechaKong, a robot monkey controlled by, wait for it, Dr Who. We kid you not.

MUSIC

Whether you want movies that put the sin into syncopation, rock the joint or even start making sense of David Byrne, you won't be disappointed by any of these.

The Buddy Holly Story 1978

Director Steve Rash **Cast** Gary Busey, Don Stroud, Charles Martin Smith 114m

The Oscar-nominated **Gary Busey** excels in this top tapping, if factually fanciful biopic, which traces the career of the geek from Lubbock, Texas, who had become an international rock superstar by the time he was 22, the age at which he perished in a plane crash in February 1959. Singing live, Busey captures Holly's unique style and infectious stage presence to such authentic effect that Paul McCartney regularly screens the picture at his annual Buddy Holly birthday bash. The scene in which The Crickets become the first white act to play the Apollo in Harlem is superb.

Can't Stop the Music 1980

Director Nancy Walker **Cast** The Village People, Valerie Perrine, Steve Guttenberg 124m

Never let anyone kid you that 1977's *Saturday Night Fever* is the quintessential disco movie. A real disco movie doesn't worry about plot, character and narrative, it just cares about disco. And that's this one. The movie's "true story" of The Village People is so hilariously disastrous that it ruined **Perrine**'s promising career and saw **Guttenberg** consigned to *Police Academy* hell.

Crossing the Bridge: The Sound of Istanbul 2005

Director Fatih Akin **Cast** Baba Zula, Alexander Hacke, Aynur 103m

A must for world music aficionados, this is a fascinating exploration of Turkey's musical heritage. There's a bit of everything here, with rap, busking and the avant-garde sharing the spotlight with traditional saz (lute) melodies, Kurdish laments and Sufi dance. Established stars like **Orhan Gencebay** and **Sezen Aksu** have the show stolen by prog rockers **Baba Zula**. Featuring travelogue montages juxtaposed with polished performances, this could be retitled *The Bosphorus Vista Social Club*.

Expresso Bongo 1959

Director Val Guest **Cast** Laurence Harvey, Sylvia Syms, Yolande Donlan, Cliff Richard 111m

Wolf Mankowitz's adaptation of his own stage show is the *Pal Joey* of the British pop musical. It coolly captures the atmosphere of the Soho coffee bar scene, while also subverting the naïve optimism of the time (in the form of **Cliff Richard**'s wannabe rocker) with lashings of cynicism (supplied by **Laurence Harvey**'s opportunistic talent agent). A neglected social realist gem, this is a long way from *The Young Ones* or *Summer Holiday*.

A Hard Day's Night 1964

Director Richard Lester **Cast** The Beatles, Wilfrid Brambell, Norman Rossington **85m**

This ragbag assortment of sketches and songs charting a day in the life of the Fab Four escapes the fate of other rock'n'roll capers because its knockabout jocularity seems naturally charming and unforced. **Alun Owen**'s Oscar-nominated script, packed with one-liners, brings out the best in the band, especially the laconic **Harrison**. Good turns too from **Brambell** as Paul's grandfather and **Rossington** as the band's harassed manager, Norm. All that and a stonking title tune as well. Like looking at an old photograph, it's an oddly moving thing and a bona fide slice of social history.

The Harder They Come 1973

Director Perry Henzell **Cast** Jimmy Cliff, Janet Bartley, Carl Bradshaw **110m**

The first independent feature produced in Jamaica, *The Harder They Come* is a hard-edged story of poverty, crime, and outlaw culture that plays like a West Indian corollary to the classic gangster films of the 1930s and 1940s whilst also looking forward to the black urban dramas of the early 1990s. Even though singing sensation **Cliff** had never acted before, he's thoroughly convincing as the tough-as-nails country boy who rises up the charts on the strength of his criminal record. Cliff is also the star of the film's superlative soundtrack.

★ I'm Not There 2007

Director Todd Haynes **Cast** Cate Blanchett, Ben Whishaw, Christian Bale **135m**

Less subversive than his Barbie doll biopic, *Superstar: The Karen Carpenter Story* (1987), but a vast improvement on his glam rock travesty, *Velvet Goldmine* (1998), **Todd Haynes**' homage to the many guises of Bob Dylan is audaciously conceived and even more brilliantly executed. Nods to Dylan's early fascination with Woody Guthrie and Arthur Rimbaud precede reflections on the folk prophet, the difficult husband, the post-bike crash recluse and the religious zealot. But it's **Cate Blanchett**'s Oscar-nominated brittle performance as an electric-era Bob that elevates this to a dazzling treatise on celebrity, artistry and integrity.

Intermezzo 1936

Director Gustaf Molander **Cast** Gosta Ekman, Inga Tidblad, Ingrid Bergman **93m**

In this Swedish movie, **Ingrid Bergman** made her breakthrough as the temptress for whom concert violinist Holger Brandt (**Ekman**) abandons his wife and family. In a life-mirroring-art moment, she was later pilloried for leaving her family for the director **Roberto Rossellini**. The Swedish version has less polish but more water symbolism than the Hollywood remake of 1939, which had a subtitle ("A Love Story") just in case audiences confused "intermezzo" with "mezzanine".

Jailhouse Rock 1958

Director Richard Thorpe **Cast** Elvis Presley, Judy Tyler 97m

Gene Kelly was in the wings applauding as they filmed the title number. This was as close as **Elvis** got to *film noir* in his thirty musicals. He comes good at the end, but for most of the movie he's the perfect heel, sent down for killing a man while defending a woman's honour. His cellmate is played by **Mickey Shaughnessy** – an odd choice considering he'd made a living with a nightclub act ripping Presley to shreds. As Elvis's manager, he gets the star to sign away fifty percent of his earnings – the same as the real Elvis later gave Colonel Parker on some of his income.

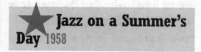

★ Jazz on a Summer's Day 1958

Directors Aram Avakian, Bert Stern **Cast** Louis Armstrong, Big Maybelle, Chuck Berry 86m

Elvis proves he's no lightweight actor in *Jailhouse Rock*, perhaps his grittiest film outing. Though they still got him to take his shirt off...

Woodstock is the most famous festival documentary ever made but the sheer quality of musicianship on offer here – from **Thelonious Monk** to **Mahalia Jackson** – makes this record of the 1958 Newport Jazz Festival a must-see. **Bert Stern** showed the work in progress to jazz critic Martin Williams, among others, and filmed their reactions, which he then mixed into the finished version.

Leningrad Cowboys Go America 1989

Director Aki Kaurismäki **Cast** Matti Pellonpää, Kari Väänänen 78m

In this very funny movie about a Finnish rock band, the Leningrad Cowboys head to the US in search of fame and fortune. Resplendent in huge quiffs, they're possibly the most pathetic rock group ever to tour the US, lurching from one mishap to another, whether it's a failed revolt against their overbearing manager, or having the engine stolen out of their Cadillac (sold to them by **Jim Jarmusch**). An affectionate homage to wannabe rock stars and to an America of run-down gasworks and seedy strip-malls.

Let's Get Lost 1988

Director Bruce Weber **Cast** Chet Baker, Carol Baker, Vera Baker 120m

The finest jazz documentary ever made is simultaneously a fan letter, a *film noir* and an obituary. Inky monochrome images don't hide the price exacted for decades of hard living: trumpeter **Chet Baker** is happy to be profiled as a beatnik portrait of Dorian Gray. He clearly had the devil in him, and played like an angel in some of the last gigs before he fell to his death from an Amsterdam hotel window in 1988.

Lisztomania 1975

Director Ken Russell **Cast** Roger Daltry, Sara Kestelman, Paul Nicholas 104m

Following the success of *Tommy*, we can only presume **Ken Russell** had his business head on when he decided to make *Lisztomania*. Starring his *Tommy* collaborator **Daltry** and a gang of rock-star friends, including **Ringo Starr** and **Rick Wakeman**, Russell tried to cash in on the popularity of the rock opera with this tale of the debauched life of composer Franz Liszt. He created a wild mess of a movie with Starr as the pope and Wakeman performing his highly individual renditions of Liszt and Richard Wagner classics. Has to be seen to be believed.

Nashville 1975

Director Robert Altman **Cast** Ronee Blakley, Shelley Duval, Ned Beatty 161m

One of **Altman**'s trademark ensemble pieces that looks chaotic at first glance but is actually very sharp and utterly engrossing. The stories of various musicians and hangers-on in the music mecca all intertwine, and Altman manages them deftly, never sliding into condescension about country music or letting his extreme characters become unbelievable caricatures. All the actors wrote and performed their own songs live for the movie, which is a treat in some cases, less so in others.

Quadrophenia 1979

Director Franc Roddam **Cast** Phil Daniels, Leslie Ash, Mark Wingett, Sting, Ray Winstone 120m

Franc Roddam expertly weds The Who's boss sounds to his rites-of-passage tale, centred on a 1964 bank holiday skirmish in Brighton between Mods and Rockers.

Brothers of the Head (2005, 93m)

" The insanely ambitious *Brothers of the Head* had us where it wanted us from the first frame of its perfectly pitched phoney Ken Russell-film opening. This is a film with a deft hand and a good sense of humour. But it's no "mockumentary", as it seemed to have been pitched when it had its blink-and-you-missed-it release in the US. A documentary-style narrative fiction about a pair of 1970s punk-rock-star conjoined twins, it ends up being an unexpectedly touching story about both the burden of and the desire for connection. Luke and Harry Treadway, supremely talented non-conjoined twin actors, play the rock stars (and play the rock songs!) in the movie. Why Keith Fulton and Louis Pepe might have thought they would be able to find charismatic twin actor-musicians who could carry a movie is beyond us, but find them they did, and the result is enthralling. This is a beautifully crafted piece of cinema to boot, energetically shot by Anthony Dod Mantle, and directed with aplomb. **"**

Scott McGehee and David Siegel – *for a biography, see p.230.*

More energetic than anyone looking this undernourished has a right to be, **Daniels** has never bettered his role as the artless bodger Jimmy. It's hard to believe that this cast were all unknowns and even harder to work out how **Sting**'s dancing wins him the mantle of "ace face" – you'll have seen better shapes thrown at a wedding to "The Birdie Song".

Sid and Nancy 1986

Director Alex Cox **Cast** Gary Oldman, Chloe Webb, David Hayman, Courtney Love **114m**

Gary Oldman lost so much weight for the role of Sex Pistols bassist Sid Vicious that he ended up in hospital. He gives a *tour de force* performance in this harrowing tale of the tragic relationship of Vicious and groupie Nancy Spungen, which ended in Nancy's death. Cox emphasized this wasn't the story of the Sex Pistols, but the band's self-destruction plays out neatly in the background.

Stop Making Sense 1984

Director Jonathan Demme **Cast** Talking Heads **88m**

One of the many interesting things about this rockumentary is how critics invariably compared Talking Heads' lead singer **David Byrne** to any number of dancers from Hollywood's golden age (Fred Astaire and Donald O'Connor are favourites). **Demme** avoids most of the devices which slow similar efforts (tedious crowd reaction shots and meaningless band interviews), focusing on the music and the geeky quirkiness of Byrne. Compulsory viewing in its time, compelling viewing today.

Topsy-Turvy 1999

Director Mike Leigh **Cast** Jim Broadbent, Allan Corduner, Timothy Spall 160m

The story behind the creation of Gilbert and Sullivan's most popular operetta, *The Mikado*, is given **Mike Leigh**'s trademark low-key treatment, and the result is a brilliant look at backstage life and Victorian society in general. The theatre hasn't changed much in a hundred years: there's plenty of sex, drugs and rivalry going on. Incredible sets and costumes along with perfect casting (**Spall** shines as the ailing Richard Temple playing the Mikado himself) make this an absolute gem – enjoyable, engrossing and funny.

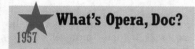

What's Opera, Doc? 1957

Director Chuck Jones **Cast** Mel Blanc, Arthur Q. Bryan 7m

Richard Wagner meets the wacky wabbit in the only Merrie Melody cartoon to have a tragic ending… compensated for by the spectacle of **Bugs Bunny** wearing blonde braids, false eyelashes and a bra, pliéing and pirouetting in pink as Brünnhilde, **Elmer Fudd**'s love object. Brünnhilde's horse's huge rump suggests the exaggerated curves that Bugs didn't have, and "Ride of the Valkyries" provides suitably dramatic backing. One of the best animated movies ever made.

Woodstock 1970

Director Michael Wadleigh **Cast** The Who, Janis Joplin, Jimi Hendrix 184m

The three-day gig that occurred at Max Yasgur's muddy farm in the summer of 1969 was, as this heartfelt record demonstrates, much more than a moment in time – it was the end of an era. **Wadleigh** and his assistants **Thelma Schoonmaker** and **Martin Scorsese** waded through miles of footage and used split screens to capture the numerous iconic moments on stage and in the crowd. **Hendrix**'s "Star-Spangled Banner" is the standout, but almost everything dazzles: the documentary captures idealistic 1960s youth trying to achieve something and occasionally succeeding.

MUSICALS

As long as there have been moving pictures, there have been musicals. Before sound, singers would lip-synch live to onscreen stars. These days, the typical musical star is more likely to be a cartoon lion than Fred Astaire...

Alferd Packer: The Musical 1996

Director Trey Parker **Cast** Juan Schwartz, Dian Bachar, Toddy Walters **95m**

Anyone who enjoyed singing along to *South Park: Bigger, Longer & Uncut* will relish this musical memoir of America's first convicted cannibal. Told largely in flashback from Death Row, the schlocky action is studded with such chokingly funny songs as "Hang the Bastard". It's rough and ready in places, but **Parker** can be forgiven the odd lapse, as he was still a student when he made the picture, which was released three years later by Troma.

All That Jazz 1979

Director Bob Fosse **Cast** Roy Scheider, Jessica Lange **123m**

Bob Fosse more or less tells his own story in this portrait of a Broadway choreographer. A stunning movie, it's packed with standard Broadway dance routines and flight-of-fancy, rock-opera-type numbers. **Scheider** plays Joe Gideon, who has an ex-wife, a current girlfriend, any number of mistresses and a daughter reaching puberty. He drinks heavily, is addicted to speed and has dreamlike dialogues with death (**Lange**), discussing his shortcomings. If you've only seen Scheider in *Jaws*, this will blow you away.

An American in Paris 1951

Director Vincente Minnelli **Cast** Gene Kelly, Leslie Caron **113m**

Possibly the perfect Hollywood musical. A struggling painter is discovered by an heiress interested in more than just his talent; he in turn is in love with a dancer who is engaged to someone else. The screwball plot is played out against some of **George Gershwin**'s loveliest songs, like "I Got Rhythm" and "It's Very Clear", and the final ballet is a masterpiece of Kelly's deceptively easy-going choreography.

The Boy Friend 1971

Director Ken Russell **Cast** Twiggy, Christopher Gable **125m**

Fans of **Russell**'s gothic offerings might be surprised to discover what seems a mundane piece of musical fluff about a finishing school on the French riviera in the 1920s. But this is vintage Russell. He takes **Sandy Wilson**'s lightweight musical and sets it in a run-down regional theatre where the cast outnumbers the audience. While the show itself is being performed onstage, the lives and loves of the company are played out behind the scenes. Entertaining and offbeat, there are wonderfully OTT numbers and great performances from a relatively unknown cast. Look out for the brief uncredited cameo from **Glenda Jackson**.

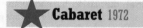

Cabaret 1972

Director Bob Fosse **Cast** Liza Minnelli, Michael York 123m

This deservedly swept the boards at the 1973 Oscars, winning eight, including best supporting actor for **Joel Grey**, the sinister and brilliant MC of the Kit Kat Club. Based on the play *I Am a Camera* adapted from Christopher Isherwood's *Goodbye to Berlin*), *Cabaret* tells the story of a bohemian romance set against the rising tide of Nazism in 1930s Germany. **Fosse**'s outstanding direction and his use of mirrors and odd angles to distort and frame the characters gives the movie a dark edge. Most of the numbers are set in the seedy gloom of the club, but the most chilling of all, '"Tomorrow Belongs to Me'', showing the Germans' unquestioning devotion to Hitler, is set in the dappled sunshine of a country afternoon.

Damn Yankees 1958

Directors George Abbott, Stanley Donen **Cast** Tab Hunter, Gwen Verdon 111m

This all-American musical version of the Faust story has an everyday Joe selling his soul to the Devil, Mr Applegate (**Ray Walston**), in return for becoming the greatest baseball player ever. Featuring choreography by **Bob Fosse**, it's a great version of the Broadway hit. It's a shame that **Verdon** didn't make more movies; she reigned long on Broadway but not much of her work is on film.

East Side Story 1997

Director Dana Ranga 75m

Soviet Russia was an unlikely boom town for musical makers. Fanatically happy workers on the production line and in the fields were routinely bursting into song at the drop of a hammer and sickle. Here, the multitude of songs and stories celebrating the Socialist Republic are explored in a documentary using terrific clips and interviews with elderly Communist tap-dancers and cinemagoers. It's short on real social comment but hugely entertaining (the singing pig farmers are a particular treat).

Eight Women 2002

Director François Ozon **Cast** Danielle Darrieux, Catherine Deneuve, Isabelle Huppert 111m

A *chanson*-stuffed 1950s-style Yuletide whodunnit. Allusions to Minnelli, Hitchcock, Sirk and Truffaut abound in this dazzling ensemble mystery, which makes it irresistible to both film buffs and adherents of Agatha Christie. With the elegantly attired cast revelling in the pop pastiches and catty one-liners, this may be designer kitsch, but a sinister sadness simmers beneath the pristine façade.

The First Nudie Musical
1976

Directors Mark Haggard & Bruce Kimmel **Cast** Stephen Nathan, Cindy Williams **97m**

While the title conveniently ignores Herschell Gordon Lewis's *Goldilocks and the Three Bares* (1963), this cheeky reworking of *42nd Street* is sweet rather than salacious. The skin flick Harry (**Stephen Nathan**) has to make to save his father's studio may be called *Come, Come Now* and the score may include songs entitled "Orgasm" and "Let Them Eat Cake (But Let Me Eat You)", but this is always cornball burlesque rather than pornography. Nevertheless, Paramount tried to suppress it when **Cindy Williams** became a small-screen star in *Laverne & Shirley*.

The 5000 Fingers of Dr T
1953

Director Roy Rowland **Cast** Hans Conried, Tommy Rettig **88m**

Dr Terwilliker is the drudgery of piano practice made flesh. His plan is to capture five hundred boys and force them to play the piano around the clock. But Bart is on hand with a scheme to set them free. Sounds like a children's book? You're not wrong. The screenplay, lyrics and sets were all done by **Dr Seuss**, and the result is a brilliant, colourful fantasy that should be a family classic. **Conried** has been described as an anti-Danny Kaye, and he is outstanding here as the psychotic Dr T.

The Gang's All Here 1943

Director Busby Berkeley **Cast** Alice Faye, Benny Goodman, Carmen Miranda **103m**

Yep, the gang's all here – but more importantly so is **Miranda**'s fruit salad of a hat. The song titles give you a flavour of the kind of treats on offer: "The Lady in the Tutti Frutti Hat" and "The Polka Dot Polka" being two examples. Jazz great **Goodman** provides the swing and you won't believe what improvisational genius **Berkeley** can do with bananas. An exploitation movie that tapped into the craze for swing and the less enduring fascination with the woman with fruit on her head, a typecasting she soon found restrictive.

Harum Scarum 1965

Director Gene Nelson **Cast** Elvis Presley, Mary Ann Mobley **95m**

Too bizarre to be dull, even if the songs vary from average to atrocious, this stars the Pelvis as rock singer Johnny Tyrone, hired by a bunch of Middle Eastern assassins to kill their king with his bare hands while singing "Shake that tambourine, that tambourine…" Things get complicated when he is aided by a money-grabbing midget and falls for the king's daughter, played by **Mobley**. The studio almost added a talking camel – this sub-Valentino yarn certainly had everything else.

Hedwig and the Angry Inch 2001

Director John Cameron Mitchell **Cast** John Cameron Mitchell, Michael Pitt 92m

An East German transsexual glam rocker called Hedwig tells her tragic life story as she travels across America on a B-grade rock tour. Her lover absconds, stealing her songs to further his career, bringing further revelations of another betrayal in her past. The music is packed with vicious lyrics and the performances are full of passion and humanity. A cult interest that deserves a wider audience.

Hum Aapke Hain Kaun 1994

Director Sooraj Barjatiya **Cast** Madhuri Dixit, Salman Khan, Anupam Kher 206m

India's fourth most successful movie is pure Bollywood melodrama. Secret lovers (**Khan** and **Dixit**) look like being prized apart when his brother is widowed by the death of her sister. But fourteen songs later, true love has conquered all. The leads are exquisitely matched, but it was the songs that made this box-office gold. Indeed, **Lata Mangeshkar**'s renditions of ''Chocolate Lime Juice'' and ''Wah Wah Raamji'' revived the masala musical, since become a global phenomenon.

Lili 1953

Director Charles Walters **Cast** Leslie Caron, Mel Ferrer, Jean-Pierre Aumont 81m

A charming, complex story about an orphaned French girl who ends up as part of a travelling circus starring alongside a troupe of puppets and their bitter puppeteer Paul. It's a classic coming-of-age tale but with a darker side. Lili's passion for Marc, the handsome, philandering magician who saves her from a potential rapist, almost undoes her, and her feelings for Paul are clouded by the fact he is only able to express himself through puppets.

Little Shop of Horrors 1986

Director Frank Oz **Cast** Rick Moranis, Ellen Greene, Levi Stubbs 94m

This musical revamp of the 1960 Roger Corman classic tells the story of a nerdy florist's assistant who tends a giant man-eating plant in return for magical intervention in his lacklustre love life. Every song is a jewel, especially those sung by **Levi Stubbs** as the plant's voice, and the film is packed with hilarious cameos like **Steve Martin** and **Bill Murray** playing, respectively, a sadistic dentist and his masochistic patient in a hysterically sickening sequence. The Greek chorus of Motown-style backing singers (called Crystal, Chiffon and Ronette) make this a riotous delight.

Moulin Rouge! 2001

Director Baz Luhrmann **Cast** Ewan McGregor, Nicole Kidman, Jim Broadbent 127m

Hyperbole here we come: **Luhrmann**'s audacious musical is a breathtaking whirl of postmodern theatricality, flinging together operatics with classical

Hollywood, pop music with burlesque, to create a sensational, spectacular and utterly original experience. **Catherine Martin**'s costumes are staggering, and if you don't cry when doomed lovers **Kidman** and **McGregor** sing "Your Song" atop a giant bejewelled elephant, you have a heart made of stone.

El otro lado de la cama
2002

Director Emilio Martínez **Cast** Ernesto Alterio, Guillermo Toledo, Natalia Verbeke 114m

A modern partner-swapping farce of manners and music that invites comparison with Woody Allen and Pedro Almodóvar, but is really a one of a kind. Pedro loves Paula, but Paula is having an affair with Javier, who in turn won't break up with Sonia. You get the drift. Add in some happy bisexuals, a few clunky dance numbers and a dose of Spanish melodrama, and you have this lighthearted treat, in which **Toledo** really stands out as the hang-dog Pedro.

Porgy and Bess 1959

Director Otto Preminger **Cast** Sidney Poitier, Dorothy Dandridge 138m

Bess (**Dandridge**) is a woman with a past and a violent ex-lover, Crown (**Brock Peters**), so the only person who will take her in is crippled Porgy (**Poitier**). But her past, in the shape of Crown and drug dealer Sportin' Life (played masterfully by a cat-like **Sammy Davis Jr**), threatens to overwhelm their relationship. Gershwin's

masterpiece is beautifully adapted for the screen, with wonderful performances. There have been suggestions the movie is racist, but it's been convincingly argued that it's more about human beings in a tragic situation.

Reefer Madness: The Movie Musical 2005

Director Andy Fickman **Cast** Kristen Bell, Christian Campbell, Neve Campbell 109m

Louis J. Gasnier's *Reefer Madness* (1936) was a shockumentary designed to warn parents about the perils of marijuana, but its cult status inspired **Kevin Murphy** and **Dan Studney** to produce an off-Broadway show. The musical sequences riff on everything from Bob Fosse and hip-hop to Vegas cabaret and Bollywood masala, while the increasingly wacky plot incorporates cannibals, zombies, FDR, Uncle Sam and Jesus. But the performances are gleefully camp and the songtrack is sniggeringly satirical.

The Rocky Horror Picture Show 1975

Director Jim Sharman **Cast** Tim Curry, Susan Sarandon 101m

A newly engaged couple break down on a lonely road and find themselves at the mercy of a local weirdo, Dr Frank-N-Furter, in this cultest of cult musicals. **Curry** has never been better as the louche transvestite, and, bearing in mind the kind of dramatic, worthy projects **Sarandon** has chosen since, it's a hoot seeing her running around in her underwear. Great songs, great cameos and a bizarre final number.

Sweet Charity 1969

Director Bob Fosse **Cast** Shirley MacLaine, John McMartin, Ricardo Montalban 149m

Bob Fosse wrings out every last bit of **MacLaine**'s offbeat talent in this psychedelic groove-fest about a downtrodden dancer-for-hire who hopes for better things when she meets a rich young man. Based on Fellini's *Nights of Cabiria*, it's in many ways a warm-up for Fosse's later work, with his trademark choreography, zooming cameras, spaced-out support cast and terrifyingly hip settings. The songs make it worth it, especially **Sammy Davis Jr**'s fabulous "Rhythm of Life".

The Umbrellas of Cherbourg 1964

Director Jacques Demy **Cast** Catherine Deneuve, Nino Castelnuovo 92m

This odd but satisfying French operetta, with every piece of dialogue sung throughout, tells the story of Geneviève (**Deneuve**), whose widowed mother owns an umbrella shop. When her lover goes into the army, a pregnant Geneviève marries a rich older man. The movie's spectacular richness and use of colour will take your breath away, and **Demy** coaxes some truly heartfelt performances out of his cast. All this French chic, coupled with one of the most wonderfully romantic screen endings, gives this huge appeal.

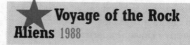 **Voyage of the Rock Aliens** 1988

Director James Fargo **Cast** Pia Zadora, Craig Sheffer, Jermaine Jackson 97m

Pia Zadora has never been in a good movie (well, not in a leading role anyway; she was a beatnik chick in *Hairspray*). But this one wins prizes for its absolutely breathtaking awfulness. Aliens land in Speelburgh (geddit?), searching for the source of rock'n'roll but instead they find the comely Ms Zadora and her beau making the kind of music that only the 1980s could be responsible for. One of the hapless aliens falls for Zadora and all sorts of problems ensue. This is fabulous trash with stupendous outfits and a soundtrack that will torture you for days afterwards.

The Wayward Cloud 2005

Director Tsai Ming-Liang **Cast** Lee Kang-Sheng, Chen Shiang-Chyi, Lu Yi-Ching 114m

Maverick Taiwanese auteur **Tsai Ming-Liang** delights in dropping musical pastiches into his otherwise spartan studies of isolation. The songs are mischievously random in this continuation of *What Time Is It There?* (2001), which sees **Chen** return from Paris to discover that street vendor **Lee** is now a porn actor making his latest opus in her building. The playback sequences are fittingly risqué, with Lee playing a giant penis in one number, while another has chorus girls draping themselves provocatively over a statue of Chiang Kai-Shek.

MUTATIONS

Movies where "You may notice certain changes happening in your body" heralds something a wee bit more drastic than puberty.

★ An American Werewolf in London 1981

Director John Landis **Cast** David Naughton, Jenny Agutter, Griffin Dunne **97m**

It's hard to believe director **Landis** was just nineteen when he wrote this imaginative horror comedy, even if it took another twelve years for it to make it to the screen (after the success of *National Lampoon's Animal House*). David (**Naughton**) and Jack (**Dunne**) are two Yank tourists in Yorkshire who, despite being warned by the regulars of The Slaughtered Lamb, foolishly venture onto the moors and get bitten by a werewolf. David realizes he's half-wolf when he wakes up nude in London Zoo. Gruesomely funny with terrific casting, it also boasted great werewolf effects, which prompted **Michael Jackson** to hire Landis to direct his pop video epic, *Thriller*.

The Bed Sitting Room 1969

Director Richard Lester **Cast** Rita Tushingham, Ralph Richardson, Arthur Lowe **91m**

Only **Spike Milligan** could dream up a black comedy where a respected Shakespearian actor (**Richardson**) gently mutates into a bedsit. His character's not the only one adversely affected by the radiation fallout caused by the "nuclear misunderstanding" that led to World War III. Set in a hauntingly realized, post-apocalyptic London, this surreal social satire follows the wacky travails of a handful of survivors who bravely attempt to "keep calm and carry on" whilst they variously mutate into parrots and wardrobes. Directed by **Richard Lester** (*A Hard Day's Night*), it stars every 1960s comedy icon from **Marty Feldman** to **Peter Cook**, with the cast listed "in order of height".

Black Sheep 2006

Director Jonathan King **Cast** Matthew Chamberlain, Oliver Driver, Tammy Davis **97m**

"Get ready for The Violence of the Lambs!" goes the genius tagline for this hilarious horror yarn. When illegal genetic engineering goes awry on a New Zealand farm it causes the sheep to turn baaaaad. Think *Midsomer Murders* meets *Bad Taste* in a debut Kiwi feature whose effects have a studied rubbishness to them, despite being engineered by WETA (the world-leading FX dudes behind *The Lord of the Rings*). Top moment being whilst our hero, wrestling with one "were-sheep", which looks suspiciously like a hearth rug, reaches for the mint sauce and uses it as mace. Certainly the most bizarre piece of pro-organic propaganda you're ever likely to see.

The Fly 1986

Director David Cronenberg **Cast** Jeff Goldblum, Geena Davis 100m

A mad scientist (**Goldblum**) starts to transform into a revolting house-fly/human hybrid after a matter transference experiment goes hideously wrong. "The king of venereal horror", as he has been dubbed, **David Cronenberg** lives up to that moniker with this stomach-churning, emotionally conflicted remake of the 1958 B-movie. He plays a gynaecologist here – a terrifying thought. Few viewers will forget the scene where Goldblum's ears and penis start sloughing off; he preserves them inside his bathroom cabinet. Cronenberg, who directed an operatic version of *The Fly* in Paris in 2008, firmly believes that "everybody's a mad scientist, and life is their lab" and that his work should be seen "from the point of view of the disease".

The Incredible Shrinking Man 1957

Director Jack Arnold **Cast** Grant Williams, Randy Stuart, April Kent 81m

Scott Carey (**Williams**) gets lost in mist, finds some glitter on his chest and suddenly starts losing height and weight. Not surprisingly, he becomes embittered and runs away, finding brief solace with a sideshow midget called Clarice. He returns to live in a doll's house but has to flee after an attack by a cat and ends up in the basement, while his wife and brother assume he is dead. There aren't too many laughs in this doomy sci-fi movie, made when paranoia about radiation was at its height, but it's compelling and, er, short.

Teeth 2007

Director Mitchell Lichtenstein **Cast** Jess Weixler, John Hensley, Josh Pais 94m

The ultimate Freudian nightmare. Fragrant blonde virgin Dawn (**Weixler**) is her high school's chief cheerleader for chastity. But she has more reasons than modesty for keeping her panties on – as her lustful boyfriend discovers when her be-fanged vagina munches off his penis. "Honey, it's dinner time", calls Mom from downstairs. "No thanks, I just ate!" comes the reply. Tongue-in-cheek lines like that suggest this slippery-toned US indie is more knowing, anti-chastity satire than it is tasteless Z-movie schlock. Or is it? One thing's for certain – it's not a date movie.

NAZIS

Despite competition from Commies and al-Qaeda, the Nazis remain the most enduringly dependable villains in the celluloid universe. Their crimes have inspired serious probing, cheap sensationalism and bizarre psychodramas.

The Boys from Brazil 1978

Director Franklin J. Schaffner Cast Gregory Peck, Laurence Olivier, James Mason, Lilli Palmer 125m

Quite what **Palmer**, who fled Berlin with her family as the Nazis came to power, made of this schlock is anyone's guess. **Schaffner**'s version of Ira Levin's reasonably intelligent thriller is compulsive viewing – often for the wrong reasons. The most original aspect of this film, in which Nazis try to bring back the bad old days by cloning from a piece of Hitler's tissue, is the casting against type. **Peck**'s Mengele is thoroughly hammy, while **Olivier**'s Nazi hunter is entertainingly preposterous.

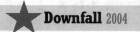 Downfall 2004

Director Oliver Hirschbiegel Cast Bruno Ganz, Alexandra Maria Lars 156m

Attacked in some quarters for humanizing Hitler, **Hirschbiegel**'s harrowing melodrama does the exact opposite. As impressively played by **Ganz**, Hitler seems all the more monstrous because

he coos to his dog, rubs the heads of the Goebbels children, and bemoans the fact that "all the good Germans" are dead. By not portraying Hitler as inhuman, *Downfall* reminds us just how awful humanity can be.

The Great Dictator 1940

Director Charlie Chaplin Cast Charlie Chaplin, Jack Oakie 128m

In **Chaplin**'s first full-length talkie he plays both the part of the dictator Hynkel, who is persecuting the Jews, and the poor Jewish barber who is mistaken for the megalomaniacal leader. If you're thinking that Chaplin would make a great Hitler send-up just on looks alone, you'd be right: a friend of his suggested the similarity, which gave Chaplin the idea. Work on the movie began in 1937, years before the true extent of Hitler's atrocities came to light. Chaplin later said that he would never have made fun of Hitler's "homicidal insanity" if he had known the full facts. The Führer himself banned the film from all occupied countries. He eventually had a copy brought in to Germany through Portugal, which he screened

Charlie Chaplin lampoons Adolf Hitler in *The Great Dictator*.

twice out of curiosity, though no record was ever made of his thoughts on it.

Hitler: A Film from Germany 1977

Director Hans-Jürgen Syberberg **Cast** André Heller, Harry Baer, Heinz Schubert, Peter Kern, Hellmut Lange **442m**

Syberberg's epic experimental movie thoroughly explores the horrors of the Nazis using props, monologues, back-projections, puppets and some startling tableaux to touch on everything from the Holocaust to Wagner, the cult of Hitler's

personality and the regime's odd obsession with the lance that pierced Jesus. Pace yourself – it is over seven hours long.

Hotel Terminus 1988

Director Marcel Ophüls **267m**

A powerful, dogged but also frustrating documentary which follows **Marcel Ophüls'** quest to unearth the truth about the life and crimes of Klaus Barbie, the war criminal whose skills were first used by the Gestapo and then by American intelligence. Ophüls confronts colleagues of his, questions his dupes and interviews his victims.

The Night Porter 1974

Director Liliana Cavani **Cast** Dirk Bogarde, Charlotte Rampling 118m

A concentration-camp survivor (**Rampling**) meets her persecutor (**Bogarde**) in Vienna and they resume their sado-masochistic relationship. Soft porn, cheap exploitation of the Holocaust, or a dark psychological thriller exploring two characters doomed by their pasts? **Cavani**'s most famous movie is a bit of all three. In one notorious scene, Rampling sings in pants, suspenders and an SS cap. Cavani's defenders say the key to the film is Bogarde's remark that he is too ashamed to work in the daylight. Watch it and make up your own mind.

The Shop on Main Street 1965

Director Jan Kadar **Cast** Ida Kaminska, Jozef Kroner 128m

The marvel – given that **Kadar**'s parents and sister died at Auschwitz – is the control and restraint which the director brings to this masterful, disturbing drama, set in Slovakia in World War II, in which a peasant (**Kroner**) is asked to run a sewing shop owned by a nearly deaf Jewish widow (**Kaminska**). The contrast between his torment as he tries to save family, friends and the town with the old woman's refusal to recognize the realities of life under the Nazis builds to a pointed, tragic climax.

Die Wannseekonferenz 1984

Director Heinz Schirk **Cast** Dietrich Matthausch, Gerd Bockman 85m

This TV documentary re-creates the notorious conference at which the Nazis' final solution was finalized. Using archives to reproduce the jokes and pleasantries, facts and figures swapped around the table in 1942, this is the ultimate portrayal of what historian Hannah Arendt called "the banality of evil". Not to be confused with the 2001 dramatization, which is also worth a look.

Went the Day Well? 1942

Director Alberto Cavalcanti **Cast** Leslie Banks, Marie Lohr, Basil Sydney, Elizabeth Allan, Frank Lawton, Mervyn Johns 92m

Chilling, often cruel, adaptation of **Graham Greene**'s short story "The Lieutenant Died Last" in which the Royal Engineers who descend on a quiet English village turn out to be German paratroopers. **Cavalcanti** ensures the villagers' hopes of aid are repeatedly crushed and the post office mistress takes matters into her own hands, killing an unwelcome lodger with pepper and an axe.

NOSTALGIA

Filmmakers as a breed are often nostalgic, taking long, wistful looks at the past – and in particular at the cinema of the past – using music, movies and memories to evoke something forever lost. Perhaps, through the power of film, what is lost is retrievable. For ninety minutes or so, at least.

★ Be Kind Rewind 2008

Director Michel Gondry **Cast** Danny Glover, Jack Black, Mos Def 102m

With his back catalogue of pop music, MTV videos and Levis commercials, **Gondry** is sometimes accused of fussy pretension. But despite its crazy quirks, this hilarious film, about a group of misfits who accidentally wipe all the videos in their store and have to remake them – is at heart a yearning hymn to cinephilia, community and popular memory. Interestingly for a movie that draws so on nostalgia, it pushed the creative possibilities of the web, with a website that allowed viewers to "swede" movies – remake them in one unedited take – themselves.

Cinema Paradiso 1988

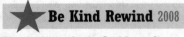

Director Giuseppe Tornatore **Cast** Jacques Perrin, Philippe Noiret, Salvatore Cascio 123m

A successful movie director returns to his Sicilian village for the funeral of his old friend and father figure, the projectionist at the local cinema. Cue flashbacks to his 1950s childhood, when the community gathered to lose themselves in the wonder of the movies. The scene where he watches all the kissing scenes, which had been cut from those old movies by the village priest-cum-censor, is a paean to the glorious power of cinema; shamelessly sentimental and no less powerful for it.

The Cotton Club 1984

Director Francis Ford Coppola **Cast** Richard Gere, Diane Lane, Gregory Hines 128m

This criminally underrated musical suffered on release from poor publicity and the impending collapse of **Coppola**'s Zoetrope studios. Set in the gangster-owned Cotton Club of 1920s Harlem, it melds real-life and fictional figures and incidents to impeccably evoke the Jazz Era. The fantastic musical numbers – check out **Hines'** tap dancing and **Larry Marshall** as a loose-limbed Cab Calloway – form the heart of a movie that combines nostalgia, knowingness and a wistful utopianism.

Distant Voices, Still Lives
1988

Director Terence Davies **Cast** Pete
Postlethwaite, Freda Dowie **85m**

Davies turns his uncompromising and
contemplative gaze upon his own childhood in 1940s Liverpool, where the
brutality of his father, and the harshness
of living conditions, were leavened by
the warmth and connection proffered
by his community, and particularly the
women. It's the songs that give this otherwise chilly movie its heartbreaking
power, whether belted out in smoky
pubs or plaintively warbled over lingering shots of rainy Liverpool streets.
Touching, haunting and unique.

Les enfants du paradis
1945

Director Marcel Carné **Cast** Arletty, Pierre
Brasseur, Jean-Louis Barrault **187m**

Commonly agreed to be the greatest
movie of classical French cinema, *Les
enfants du paradis* was made during the
most taxing years of the Nazi occupation
and returns to the theatrical demi-monde
of a golden, dreamlike mid-nineteenth-
century Paris. An exuberant celebration of
the human spirit, creativity and popular art,
its beautiful re-creation of the Boulevard du
Crime, where carnival sideshows, mime
artistes and classical theatres stood side
by side, is as romantic as the love story that
forms the backbone of the plot.

Denizens of Paris's nineteenth-century Boulevard du Crime enjoy a night out in *Les enfants du paradis*.

The Last Picture Show 1971

Director Peter Bogdanovich **Cast** Jeff Bridges, Timothy Bottoms, Cybill Shepherd 118m

Bogdanovich, aged just 31 and with two B-movies under his belt, made his name with this mature film, using stunning black-and-white cinematography to pay homage to the lost era of the early 1950s and also to the great moviemakers such as Orson Welles and John Ford. Based on the novel by **Larry McMurtry**, and telling a fairly conventional coming-of-age story, it evokes the frustrations of life in a one-horse town with atmospheric intensity, the characters fumbling through their lives as if in an exquisitely sad dream. The scratchy soundtrack – old country music that has largely been forgotten – only makes things more ghostly.

Prairie Home Companion 2006

Director Robert Altman **Cast** Kevin Kline, Meryl Streep, Lily Tomlin 105m

It's fitting that this movie turned out to be **Robert Altman**'s swansong: a musical about the (fictional) final broadcast of a (real-life) downhome radio show from author **Garrison Keillor**. Altman's typically star-studded ensemble cast, and a smart screenplay from Keillor – who, despite playing himself, seems to inhabit a bygone age – create a wry, melancholy and beautiful tribute to lost dreams, lost loves and lost souls.

24 Hour Party People 2002

Director Michael Winterbottom **Cast** Steve Coogan, John Thomson 117m

As a decade, the 1980s has been rather overused by filmmakers looking back; **Winterbottom**, however, eschews cheesy camp to take a drily humorous look at "Madchester", Tony Wilson's Factory Records, and the cool side of Thatcher's Britain in the early 80s. As British as fish and chips – many of the cast have featured in quintessential Manchester soap *Coronation Street* – the movie boasts a virtuoso performance from **Coogan** as the aggravating genius Wilson. The soundtrack – Joy Division, Happy Mondays, and the like – is as impeccable as you'd expect.

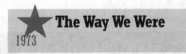 **The Way We Were** 1973

Director Sydney Pollack **Cast** Barbra Streisand, Robert Redford 118m

The kind of big Hollywood movie they don't make any more – a political film made by political people about a political time, which dares to state that even the deepest romantic love is not invincible. **Streisand** is superb as the fiery left-wing intellectual who in the 1930s falls hard for **Redford**'s easy-going blond WASP; the film follows their relationship against a background of huge social and cultural change. Desperately romantic, wistful in the extreme – a whole lifetime of longing is represented by Streisand's gentle brush of the sleeping Redford's hair from his eyes – and with a belting theme song.

NUNS

Whether they're on the run, or trying to solve a problem like Maria, or growing hysterical up a Himalayan mountain, nuns have become habit-forming for filmmakers.

★ Black Narcissus 1947

Directors Michael Powell, Emeric Pressburger
Cast Deborah Kerr, Flora Robson 100m

When Martin Scorsese saw this movie for the first time, he said he'd seen something revolutionary. Outwardly, it's a relatively straightforward story about nuns who try to set up a school and hospital in the Himalayas and who almost go mad in the attempt. But it's more subtle than that: the Archers (as **Powell/Pressburger** called themselves) produced a subtly sensual film, in which the Himalayan scenery sets the mood of the film perfectly. All the more remarkable because it was all created on a sound stage at Pinewood.

Dark Habits 1983

Director Pedro Almodóvar **Cast** Cristina S. Pascual, Julieta Serrano, Marisa Paredes 114m

Pedro Almodóvar's venture into nunsploitation is a satire on secular decadence and religious hypocrisy in which a junkie chanteuse (**Cristina Sánchez Pascual**) discovers that the cloisters of the Convent of Humble Redeemers is

a hotbed of transgression. The Mother Superior (**Julieta Serrano**) succumbs to temptation in order to understand sinners, while Sister Manure (**Marisa Paredes**) experiences lysergic ecstasies, Sister Snake (**Carmen Maura**) tends a pet tiger and Sister Sewer Rat (**Chus Lampreave**) devours racy fiction. Luis Buñuel would have thoroughly approved of such scurrilous Catholic kitsch.

Demonia 1990

Director Lucio Fulci **Cast** Brett Halsey, Meg Register, Lino Salemme 85m

Lucio Fulci insisted that **Luigi Ciccarese**'s amateurish photography ruined this film. But the focusing faux pas only intensified the eerie atmosphere of this grizzly slasher. An archaeologist (**Meg Register**) working in Sicily discovers the skeletons of five heretic nuns crucified five hundred years earlier. The ensuing carnage includes a harpoon attack by a naked, headless nun, a woman having her eyes clawed by her cats, a butcher having his tongue nailed down and a man being torn in two between two trees. Nothing like a bit of old-time religion.

The Devils 1971

Director Ken Russell **Cast** Vanessa Redgrave, Oliver Reed 111m

Oliver Reed described this as his best performance ever. He plays the priest of a small seventeenth-century French town that is needed by Cardinal Richelieu and Louis XIII if they are to exert complete control over the country. The pair plot to destroy him, charging him with a Satanically possessed nunnery and a sexually rampant hunchback nun (**Redgrave**). **Russell**'s flamboyant style sits perfectly with the hallucinatory material, based on **Aldous Huxley**'s novel *The Devils of Loudon*. It was banned in Italy, with Reed and Redgrave threatened with imprisonment if they ever set foot there.

La religieuse 1965

Director Jacques Rivette **Cast** Anna Karina, Liselotte Pulver, Micheline Presle 135m

A combination of Enlightenment trenchancy and *nouvelle vague* subversion makes **Jacques Rivette**'s adaptation of **Denis Diderot**'s 1760 novel so riveting. Like every ingénue in the movies, **Anna Karina**'s disowned waif is subjected to physical and spiritual torment by her envious sisters. But this is as much about freedom of conscience and action than religious hypocrisy, with Rivette using the enclosed spaces to suggest that little had really changed in France between the *ancien régime* and the Swinging Sixties.

Sisters of Satan 1978

Director Juan López Monteczuma **Cast** Claudio Brook, Tina Romero, Susana Kamini 85m

A former assistant to Alejandro Jodorowsky, **Monteczuma** leaves little to the imagination, helped by cinematographer **Xavier Cruz**. There are demonic possessions, blood rituals, throat-ripping, fire storms and a resurrectionist revenge. But this is intelligent exploitation, which explores faith, superstition and the suppression of the self while also generating plenty of horror and hysteria.

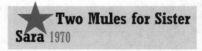

Two Mules for Sister Sara 1970

Director Don Siegel **Cast** Shirley MacLaine, Clint Eastwood 116m

''What the hell is a nun doing out here?'' asks one character, understandably. **MacLaine** plays Sara, a prostitute who is disguised as a nun when she is rescued by Hogan (**Eastwood**) from three cowboys. The two become friends, with Hogan in awe of her chastity, which slips along the way, to great comic effect. MacLaine and Eastwood are a great pairing. Vastly underrated, it's the best **Siegel**/ Eastwood film – their favourite of their five collaborations.

OUTLAWS

There's something cathartic about cheering on glamorous, witty and charismatic law-breakers on the big screen. And the movie industry likes heroes who break the rules... as long as they're not behind the camera.

The Adventures of Robin Hood 1938

Director Michael Curtiz **Cast** Errol Flynn, Olivia de Havilland, Basil Rathbone 111m

Childhood isn't childhood unless you've watched at least one movie where men run around in tights for a good and noble cause and true love triumphs. As men-in-tights movies go, this is probably the finest, with **Errol Flynn** at his energetic best and Roy Rogers' famous steed Trigger turning in one of his more compelling performances as **de Havilland**'s horse. For a variation on this theme try *Ivanhoe* (1952), starring Taylors Robert and Liz.

★ The Assassination of Jesse James by the Coward Robert Ford 2007

Director Andrew Dominik **Cast** Brad Pitt, Casey Affleck, Mary-Louise Parker, Paul Schneider, Sam Rockwell, Sam Shepard 160m

The James family reportedly liked this intriguing reflection on the life of Jesse, which delved into America's obsession with celebrity and the shaping of heroic myths. **Pitt** and **Affleck** play off each other superbly as the heroic outlaw and his "cowardly" assassin. **Dominik** uses the landscape brilliantly, but sometimes you do wish that all concerned would just hurry up a bit.

Cobra Verde 1987

Director Werner Herzog **Cast** Klaus Kinski, King Ampaw, José Lewgoy, Salvatore Basile, Peter Berling, Guillermo Coronel 111m

Shrieks and snarls account for about half of **Klaus Kinski**'s dialogue, playing a nineteenth-century Brazilian bandit sent to Africa on a suicide mission to procure slaves in a tale loosely inspired by Bruce Chatwin's *The Viceroy of Ouidah*. **Herzog** complained the actor became uncontrollable during shooting and he never worked with him again. But Kinski's beastliness suits this unhinged portrayal of a brutal century, in which the rich get their kicks watching slaves get whipped. When Kinski leads an army of topless warrior women in revolt, the spectacular Freudian nightmare is merely the final crowning madness.

Face to Face 1967

Director Sergio Sollima **Cast** Gian Maria
Volonte, Tomás Milián 108m

The political subtext that underpinned
many a spaghetti Western is brought usefully to the surface in **Sollima**'s thoughtful
anti-fascist, anti-capitalist drama. **Volonte**
is the depressed professor taken hostage
by outlaw **Milián**, who decides to kill to
protect his captor. Sounds facile, but in
the hands of Sollima, Volonte and Milián
it's anything but.

Lonely Are the Brave 1962

Director David Miller **Cast** Kirk Douglas, Gena
Rowlands, Walter Matthau 107m

"I'm a loner, clear down deep to my guts.
And you know what a loner is? He's a
cripple". **Douglas**' escaped convict is
painfully aware of his flaws as he tries to
elude **Matthau**'s technologically savvy
lawman in a classic chase Western. A
great horse opera, it can also be read as
an agonized, occasionally strident meditation on persecution – **Dalton Trumbo**,
who penned it, had recently returned
to work after years on the blacklist – or
equally as an insight into what can happen when your brain has been fried by
making too many B-Westerns.

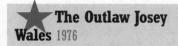 ## The Outlaw Josey
Wales 1976

Director Clint Eastwood **Cast** Clint Eastwood,
Sondra Locke, Chief Dan George 135m

For a movie that starts with rape and
massacre, *The Outlaw Josey Wales* is
an unusually optimistic Western, culminating in a conciliation that, in the
post-Vietnam era, its director clearly
hoped America would achieve. **Eastwood** is unforgettable as the wronged
Confederate guerrilla, a loner who
reluctantly accumulates a band of misfits
as he seeks vengeance and a new life.
Philip Kaufman (who was initially the
film's director) wrote one of the sharpest screenplays in the Western oeuvre,
giving supporting characters such as
John Vernon's Confederate officer and
George's roguish Cherokee their chance
to shine.

The Wild Bunch 1969

Director Sam Peckinpah **Cast** William Holden,
Ernest Borgnine, Robert Ryan, Warren Oates
134m

Few Westerns force the audience to
confront their inner psycho with such
force as *The Wild Bunch*. Pike Bishop
(**Holden**) and his outlaw gang head to
Mexico for one last job, pursued by a
betrayed ex-partner (**Ryan**) where, in
the midst of revolution, they take one
last, mad, suicidal bow. **Peckinpah** had
hoped the cruelty – and Ryan's despairing, demented laughter that closes the
movie – would make audiences think
critically about the carnage in Vietnam.
But many were too busy complaining
about – or thrilling to – the violence of
the movie to notice any contemporary
parallels.

PARANOIA

From darkly brooding melodramas to Cold War political thrillers, moviemakers have got a lot of mileage from that unnerving cliché: just because you're paranoid doesn't mean they're not out to get you.

L'avventura 1960

Director Michelangelo Antonioni **Cast** Gabriele Ferzetti, Monica Vitti, Lea Massari **145m**

Antonioni gives himself a simple narrative to follow – a young couple search for a woman (**Massari**) who vanishes after the first reel – and then takes a massive detour to focus on the burgeoning relationship between the couple (**Ferzetti** and **Vitti**). There is no real resolution, though clues are offered, but part of the point is that the cast of mostly wealthy, spoiled, unfulfilled characters are all, metaphorically, on the brink of disappearance.

Bunny Lake Is Missing 1965

Director Otto Preminger **Cast** Laurence Olivier, Carol Lynley, Keir Dullea **107m**

Many were underwhelmed by this psychological thriller on its release, but as a cult classic it ticks all the boxes. A single mother's desperate search through Swinging London for her missing child involves a hammy **Noel Coward** as a sadomasochist with a chihuahua, a creepy doll's hospital, a headmistress obsessed by children's nightmares, an appearance from darkly cool pop combo **The Zombies**, and super-stylish **Saul Bass** credits. The location shooting is raw and fresh, and the denouement, hinting at incest and regression, is genuinely unsettling.

Les diaboliques 1955

Director Henri-Georges Clouzot **Cast** Simone Signoret, Vera Clouzot **114m**

Spooky things start happening to the wife and mistress of a caddish headmaster after they murder him and the corpse goes missing. The paranoia builds steadily, onscreen and off, with plenty of bumps in the night, a creepy bathroom scene, and some unspeakable business with eyeballs.

Dr Strangelove 1964

Director Stanley Kubrick **Cast** Peter Sellers, Sterling Hayden, George C. Scott **94m**

The more you watch this, the more you get. For example, General Buck Turgidson (**Scott**) is clutching a book entitled *World*

Targets in Megadeaths. General Jack D. Ripper (**Hayden**) may seem purely satirical, but after the Russians began removing their missiles from Cuba, a general did ask JFK: "Why don't we go in anyway?" It's not far from there to Ripper shooting himself rather than reveal the codes that will bring the missiles back. **Sellers** is even more effective as the prissy president than as Nazi Dr Strangelove, who springs to life when he hears the word slaughter.

A Dog's Breakfast 2007

Director David Hewlett **Cast** David Hewlett, Katie Hewlett, Paul McGillon 88m

Believing that Ryan (**McGillon**), his sister's fiancé and a sci-fi soap star, is plotting

The Game charts Michael Douglas's descent from self-satisfied businessman with everything to the wild-eyed gunman with nothing to lose seen here.

to kill her, paranoid Patrick isn't exactly unhappy when Ryan keels over, but has his work cut out trying to hide a corpse that refuses to disappear. **Hewlett**, who stars in cult TV shows *Stargate: Atlantis* and *Stargate SG-1* – along with his sister, McGillon and many other cast members – features enough in-jokes to delight fans, and enough laughs for anyone who enjoys a no-budget indie comedy packed with old-fashioned silliness.

The Game 1997

Director David Fincher **Cast** Michael Douglas, Sean Penn 128m

Fincher has built a career on paranoia and psychological confusion, and this movie, nestled in between *Se7en* and *Fight Club*, fits snugly in the canon. An elaborate riff on conspiracy theories and sibling rivalry, the movie is based on a

real scavenger-hunt-type game much beloved of geeks. Praised by the critics, it was largely ignored by audiences, who were beginning to resent Fincher's habit of toying with them. **Douglas** is superb as the lonely millionaire, channelling some of the intensity and edginess he brought to *Falling Down* four years earlier.

Gaslight 1944

Director George Cukor **Cast** Ingrid Bergman, Charles Boyer, Joseph Cotten 114m

Newlywed Paula (**Bergman**) is plagued by mysterious events when she returns with her husband (**Boyer**) to her childhood home. Driven to distraction by sputtering gaslights and disappearing jewellery – convinced she's nuts and just a stone's throw away from being sectioned – she finds solace in **Cotten**'s dashing detective before revealing she is not averse to playing a few mind games herself. This quality psychological drama was nominated for seven Oscars, and won two – best actress and best art direction.

The Hitcher 1986

Director Robert Harmon **Cast** Rutger Hauer, C. Thomas Howell 97m

The movie that did for hitchhiking what *Single White Female* would do for flatmates six years later. As if we've not got enough to worry about, Hollywood scares the hell out of us with stuff like this and we, suckers that we are, love 'em for it. **Hauer** is strangely credible as the killer without wheels, even if the movie lapses first into self-parody, then beyond.

The finger in the french fries scene has launched a thousand urban myths.

The Manchurian Candidate 1962

Director John Frankenheimer **Cast** Laurence Harvey, Frank Sinatra 130m

This is one of the best political thrillers of the 1960s. A mordant, funny, but tense film that puts **Harvey**'s woodenness to good use as an assassin brainwashed by the North Koreans and sent back to the US to do some unspecified evil. The opening sequences are unforgettable and **Angela Lansbury** is superb as Harvey's smothering mother. Seven members of Harvey's platoon are named after the cast and creator of *The Phil Silvers Show*. Remade in 2004 with Denzel Washington; it's so-so.

Memento 2000

Director Christopher Nolan **Cast** Guy Pearce, Carrie-Anne Moss 113m

Christopher Nolan raised money for this movie by showing its predecessor at a Hong Kong film festival and asking the audience to cough up. Here he asks the audience to concentrate as we follow **Pearce**'s quest to find his wife's killer, a quest complicated by the fact that her death has so traumatized him that he can only remember things for a few minutes. To conquer what, for an amateur sleuth, seems an insuperable obstacle, he stores information on Polaroids and tattoos all over his body. Confused? You will be. The setup of a man without memory trying to solve a crime in which he might be implicated is at least as old as *film noir*, but Nolan has given it a neat new twist.

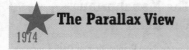

The Parallax View

1974

Director Alan J. Pakula **Cast** Warren Beatty, Paula Prentiss 102m

This movie isn't out to help anybody solve any particular assassination, but it does give you a horribly plausible account of how such things happen. **Beatty** is the reporter whose smug pursuit of the Pulitzer Prize takes him in too deep, as people around him start dying and the shooting of a senator develops connections to a mysterious corporation called Parallax. In a scenario that could have been lifted from the movie, **Pakula** suspected Paramount were refusing to promote the film, becoming so enraged that he broke his umbrella against the wall in a hotel room row with Paramount boss Robert Evans.

Seconds 1966

Director John Frankenheimer **Cast** Rock Hudson, Salome Jens, John Randolph 105m

John Frankenheimer took a risk using **Rock Hudson** in this paranoid sci-fi fantasy and, in box-office terms, the risk didn't pay off. Hudson fans wouldn't pay to see him in this doom-laden scenario, made more alien by the black-and-white format and cameraman **James Wong Howe**'s risky camera work. Noirer than the darkest *noir*, this stars **Randolph** as a banker who gets a chance of a new life from a

mysterious company and re-emerges as a bohemian artist. The final scene is probably one of the most terrifying ever. Suffice to say there's a drill and a head involved.

Spider 2002

Director David Cronenberg **Cast** Ralph Fiennes, Miranda Richardson, Lynn Redgrave 98m

Featuring stellar performances all round, with **Fiennes** as Spider, a schizophrenic released from a mental institution after twenty years, taking lodgings in a halfway house run by a crotchety landlady (**Redgrave**). As the movie unfolds we discover Spider's troubles stem from his childhood memories. Viewing events through Spider's confused eyes, **Richardson** plays the mother and stepmother, allowing the audience to grasp his internal struggle to realize the truth. Fiennes' performance is a welcome return to form, if a little mannered at times. **Cronenberg** does a decent job of transferring **Patrick McGrath**'s novel to the screen, but the story itself is the sticking point, the realization that Spider will never get any better making this a difficult movie to swallow.

Suddenly 1954

Director Lewis Allen **Cast** Frank Sinatra, Sterling Hayden 77m

Sinatra plays John Baron, leading a trio of assassins who arrive in a small town just in time to shoot the president. It's a compelling premise, well performed and well directed, but you probably haven't heard of it for one simple reason: Lee

The Conversation (1974, 113m)

❝ A few years ago, I made the mistake of showing our son – then ten – one of my favourite films. I remembered *The Conversation* as a restrained and evocative character study. Instead, I found myself scrambling to cover his tender eyes as blood began to gush out of a toilet towards the end of the movie. Coppola made four astonishing films in the 1970s, and this is the most exciting for me, though I'm a sucker for any drama that centres on humans and recording machines. Gene Hackman as sound technician Harry Caul delivers an amazingly resourceful performance. What one remembers (instead of the gushing blood), are scenes of Harry blowing softly on a mobile, getting unexpectedly excited about a breakthrough in microphone technology, or destroying his apartment at the end as he looks for a hidden bug. In that final sequence, Coppola uses his camera in an astonishingly muscular way, making it an active participant in Caul's breakdown. ❞

Atom Egoyan

Born to Armenian parents, Canadian stylist Atom Egoyan's work explores the bemusing and distorting interactions of visual media, alienation, paranoia and sexuality. His films include early cult favourite Calendar, *the striptease-structured* Exotica, *the Oscar-nominated adaptation* The Sweet Hereafter *and sexual surveillance thriller* Chloe.

Harvey Oswald was rumoured to have been watching this on the evening of 21 November 1963. Sinatra years later pulled the film out of respect for his friend John F. Kennedy. The colourized version is a rare treat because Ol' Blue Eyes has been given brown eyes, presumably for satirical purposes.

 Vertigo 1958

Director Alfred Hitchcock **Cast** James Stewart, Kim Novak, Tom Helmore **128m**

So keen were novelists **Pierre Boileau** and **Thomas Narcejac** to have **Hitchcock** adapt one of their works for the screen that they wrote *D'entre les morts* especially for him. Initially slated by critics, *Vertigo* is now considered a masterpiece and is one of the few times **Stewart**, as the obsessive detective, managed to throw off his "everyman" persona. Ever the perfectionist, Hitchcock worked closely with costume designer **Edith Head** to create the right look for Madeline (**Novak**). Wanting an eerie appearance, the grey suit was chosen as Hitchcock believed a blonde woman would rarely be seen wearing all grey. Vera Miles was nearly cast as Madeline; fortunately her pregnancy allowed Novak to step in, fresh from *Pal Joey*, and give the best performance of her career.

POLITICS

Politics and movies don't mix. That's the theory. It's just that directors as great as Fuller, Sturges and Puenzo seem determined to prove the contrary.

The Blue Kite 1993

Director Tian Zhuangzhuang **Cast** Lu Liping, Pu Quanxin, Chen Xiaoman, Li Xuejian **138m**

Zhuangzhuang's family saga is so pointed and rich in its portrayal of the tragic human cost of the Communist Party's "progress" from the Hundred Flowers campaign and the Great Leap Forward onto the Cultural Revolution that the Chinese government felt obliged to ban it. The movie's grasp of everyday realities only makes its indictment all the more powerful.

Burn! 1968

Director Gillo Pontecorvo **Cast** Marlon Brando, Evaristo Marquez **132m**

Brando reckoned he did his best acting in this uneven, fascinating, colonial drama – although he also threatened to shoot **Pontecorvo** if he ever met him again. Brando is the *agent provocateur* fomenting revolt in a Portuguese colony so the British Empire can control its sugar cane industry and **Marquez**, a plantation worker in real life who sometimes had to be kicked (below camera level) into

life by the director, is the slave who takes Brando at his word. Brando is playing a British agent but his character, Sir William Walker, has the same name as an American adventurer who, in 1850, led a private invasion of Nicaragua.

The Candidate 1972

Director Michael Ritchie **Cast** Robert Redford, Peter Boyle, Melvyn Douglas **110m**

Jeremy Larner's script uses much of the inside info he gained as a speechwriter for Democratic presidential aspirant Eugene McCarthy. It's all here: the hollowness of the candidates' debate, the vacuous marketing ("The better way with Bill McKay"), the fixer, subtly played by **Boyle**, and the decent liberal who gains office and loses his beliefs. In the back of the limo, **Redford** doles out clichés: "Think of it, the biggest most powerful nation on Earth cannot house its houseless, cannot feed its foodless." The problem is that Redford is too likeable for the satire – you still want him to win. And the satirical speeches Larner writes are more stirring than the hornswoggle we get from politicians today.

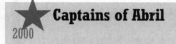

Captains of Abril

2000

Director Maria de Medeiros **Cast** Stefano Accorsi, Maria de Medeiros 123m

The most expensive movie ever made by the Portuguese film industry and one of the best. You probably remember **de Medeiros** as Bruce Willis's girlfriend in *Pulp Fiction*. But here, in her directorial debut, she mixes fiction and fact in this account of the Portuguese revolution of 25 April 1974. The movie is true to the spirit of the revolution – the rebels' tanks really did stop at red traffic lights – although it doesn't dwell on the rumour that the country's entry in the Eurovision Song Contest was a signal to the plotters. Well made, easy to watch and just a few minutes too long.

The Colour of Pomegranates 1968

Director Sergei Parajanov **Cast** Sofia Chiaurelli, Melkon Alekian 73m

This unconventional biopic of the eighteenth-century Armenian poet **Sayat Nova** is really a mesmerizing, but challenging, celebration of that country's culture – eroded by Turkish invasion and the massacres of 1915. The Soviet authorities took this as nationalistic propaganda and in 1973 **Parajanov** was sentenced to five years hard labour in Siberia. Plotless, beautiful, intriguing, this interprets Nova's life poetically through a series of *tableaux vivants*.

The Great McGinty 1940

Director Preston Sturges **Cast** Brian Donlevy, Muriel Angelus 81m

Donlevy enjoys the role of his career as the tramp whose rise to the governor's mansion is facilitated by corruption and a convenient marriage but who ruins it all with one "crazy moment of honesty". The dialogue, often ad-libbed on set, includes the great justification for letting the dead vote: "We knew they were going to vote for us. Why should we be deprived because they were unlucky enough to die?"

Hands Over the City 1963

Director Francesco Rosi **Cast** Rod Steiger, Salvo Randone, Guido Alberti 105m

Steiger is ferocious as the property developer who misuses public funds, manipulates politicians and feels no responsibility for the cataclysmic collapse of one of his slum tenements. Set in Naples, **Rosi**'s blistering depiction of civic corruption is charged with a passion and outrage that has all but vanished from both Italian politics and Italian films.

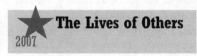

The Lives of Others

2007

Director Florian Henckel von Donnersmarck **Cast** Ulrich Mühe, Martina Gedeck 137m

A poignant, unsettling thriller, coloured with greys and dour greens, which focuses on a Stasi agent (**Mühe**) monitoring an enemy of the state. Mühe's performance is a marvel of muted grandeur, his control of his expressions and gestures matched perfectly by **von Donnersmarck**'s control of telling detail.

The Long Walk Home 1990

Director Richard Pearce **Cast** Sissy Spacek, Whoopi Goldberg 97m

You could view this as a challenging companion to *Driving Miss Daisy*. A white woman (**Spacek**) is brought to an understanding of racial discrimination in the US by her maid (an understated **Goldberg**) in 1950s Alabama, where a black woman, Rosa, has refused to stand at the back of the bus. The movie takes care not to make the leads mere symbols – their understanding is at the heart of the movie. Eventually Spacek is drawn into the civil rights movement, leading to conflict with her racist husband. The acting, the script and the gospel music give this movie, which isn't perfect, real power.

Malcolm X 1992

Director Spike Lee **Cast** Denzel Washington, Angela Bassett, Spike Lee 201m

Lee's epic depiction of the life of civil rights leader Malcolm X (**Washington**) remains his most accomplished movie. Fierce, fascinating and urgent, Lee's biopic is as complex as its subject and Washington has the power and intelligence to create a tension and excitement that isn't always there in the screenplay.

Medium Cool 1969

Director Haskell Wexler **Cast** Robert Forster, Verna Bloom 111m

Forster is a news cameraman who gets caught up in the Democratic Party convention in Chicago, scene of one of the world's most famous riots, while simultaneously trying to keep his private life from disintegrating. An odd, influential movie whose cast includes **Mariana Hill**, an escapee from Elvis's *Paradise Hawaiian Style*. The director, one of the greatest cinematographers of his day, was stunned by the apathy with which this effort was received, and virtually gave up directing.

Moonlighting 1982

Director Jerzy Skolimowski **Cast** Jeremy Irons, Eugene Lipinski 97m

Tradesmen don't make great movie heroes, but this engrossing film is about the tribulations of a group of Polish workers (led by **Irons**) who smuggle themselves into England to renovate an apartment. While working in secret, Irons (who is the only one who speaks English) hears martial law has been declared in Poland. **Skolimowski** wrote the script in a day and the movie used three Polish emigrants living (legally) in his home.

The Official Story 1985

Director Luis Puenzo **Cast** Héctor Alterio, Norma Aleandro, Chunchuna Villafañe 115m

As Argentina's right-wing dictatorship starts to crumble, a mother (**Aleandro**) begins to suspect that her adopted daughter may be the child of a *desaparecido*. In the late 1970s, when thirty thousand Argentines disappeared, there was a small trade in the children of the dictatorship's pregnant victims. **Puenzo**'s accomplished polemical thriller casts a tragic light on a society living in terror of its own history.

In the context of the McCarthy anti-Communist witch-hunt, making a neo-realist movie that rallies behind striking miners and explores racism and sexual politics was an act of professional suicide. Given that Biberman didn't direct another film for fifteen years, it is just as well that *Salt of the Earth* is, despite some wooden acting, an extraordinary movie, a no-holds-barred retelling of a 1951 strike against Empire Zinc.

Salt of the Earth 1954

Director Herbert J. Biberman **Cast** Rosaura Revueltas, Juan Chacon, Will Geer 94m

Salvador 1986

Director Oliver Stone **Cast** James Woods, James Belushi 122m

A martyr to the cause

Doomed tough guy John Garfield didn't actually die for his beliefs. But his commitment to liberal causes did ruin him and hasten his untimely death of a heart attack when he was just 39.

In Thomas Pynchon's 2009 novel *Inherent Vice*, soft-boiled private eye Larry "Doc" Sportello's idolatry of Garfield is so extreme he owns a suit the actor wore in *The Postman Always Rings Twice*. The invocation of Garfield by cultish, left-wing novelist Pynchon is almost official confirmation of his emergence as a countercultural hero.

The man's tough guy cred was genuine: he grew up in the roughest streets of the Bronx. As an actor, he prefigured the Method style of Brando, Clift and Dean. Charming, menacing and vulnerable, Garfield seldom gave a bad performance. His best movies often cast American society in an unflattering light: he was grittily magnificent as a boxer in a corrupt trade in *Body and Soul*, sexy and brooding in *Postman* and utterly convincing as a Mob lawyer in *Force of Evil*.

His last movie was, with terrible irony, called *He Ran All the Way*. And this, in essence, is what he did after his refusal to name Communists to the House Un-American Activities committee effectively ended his career. Realizing that he was caught up in something that was utterly out of control, Garfield tried to placate his persecutors by writing an apologia called *I Was a Sucker for a Left Hook*. But it wasn't enough. He spent his last eighteen months out of work, hounded and stalked by the FBI. So many Americans were moved by his death that his funeral drew a bigger crowd than Valentino's.

Angry, pertinent and taut, **Stone**'s adventure movie is, at heart, a character study of two burnt-out freelancers trying to keep afloat in the midst of a treacherous civil war. But Stone, by encouraging us to identify with **Woods**' sardonic outrage, confronts us with the brutal consequences of US support of right-wing military forces in Central and South America.

Viva Zapata! 1952

Director Elia Kazan **Cast** Marlon Brando, Jean Peters, Joseph Wiseman, Anthony Quinn 113m

John Steinbeck won an Oscar for his screenplay but the real author is **Kazan**, who saw parallels between the rise to (and renunciation of) power by Mexican revolutionary Zapata, and the fate of many of the more idealistic leaders of the Russian Revolution. **Brando** was second choice for Zapata (the studio wanted Tyrone Power) but the key performance is **Joseph Wiseman** as the Stalin figure Fernando, and the film is as much a critique of those who inherited the Russian Revolution as it is a celebration of the Mexican one.

White Dog 1982

Director Sam Fuller **Cast** Kristy McNichol, Paul Winfield, Burl Ives, Jameson Parker 90m

Fuller's unflinching exploration of racism – through the device of a stray dog that has been trained to attack black people – was too controversial to enjoy more than a limited release in the US. A pity because this bombastic, pulpy piece of agitprop is worth seeing and **Winfield**, as the trainer

trying to change the dog's ways, makes an interesting character out of a role that could easily have been a cipher.

Winstanley 1975

Directors Kevin Brownlow, Andrew Mollo **Cast** Miles Halliwell 96m

Scrupulously faithful account of seventeenth-century social reformer Gerrard Winstanley's attempt to found a commune in what is now the Surrey stockbroker belt. Even in Cromwell's Republican England, Winstanley's Diggers were regarded as going a bit far and his socialist experiments ended in disaster as this squalid, austere, beautiful (and rather earnest) movie makes terribly clear.

Z 1969

Director Costa-Gavras **Cast** Yves Montand, Jean-Louis Trintignant 125m

A sensational movie starring **Trintignant** as the judge probing into the death of **Montand**, who begins to uncover proof that the government has blood on its hands. Only his fourth feature, this made **Costa-Gavras**'s reputation, using thriller techniques to expose corruption in a government which is a flimsily disguised version of Greece under the colonels' dictatorial junta of 1967 to 1973.

PORN

The sole purpose of porn is arousal, which usually makes for a fairly simple narrative thrust (as it were). Some films cast a beady eye on the industry, so having their cake and eating it.

★ Boogie Nights 1997

Director Paul Thomas Anderson **Cast** Mark Wahlberg, Burt Reynolds, Julianne Moore 156m

Inspired by the life and flicks of **John Holmes** and expanded from the director's 1988 short, *The Dirk Diggler Story*, this Altmanesque memoir of the California porn scene in the 1970s and 80s gained notoriety through the prosthetic enhancement of onetime rapping underwear model, "Marky Mark" **Wahlberg**. Cast only because Leonardo DiCaprio had signed up for *Titanic*, Wahlberg brought vulnerability, as well as virility, to the role of a misfit who seeks acceptance by baring his soul (and more) for sexploitation auteur **Burt Reynolds**' camera.

The Devil in Miss Jones 1973

Director Gerard Damiano **Cast** Georgina Spelvin, John Clemens, Harry Reems 67m

Hired as the cook, **Michelle Graham** wound up the star of **Damiano**'s follow-up to the epochal skin flick, *Deep Throat* (1972). She didn't want to use her real name, however, and opted for Georgina Spelvin, a feminization of the actor equivalent of Alan Smithee. Along with Linda Lovelace and Marilyn Chambers, Spelvin became an icon of 1970s Porno Chic, here playing the suicidal spinster who becomes a raging nymphomaniac. *Variety* claimed this box-office smash elevated hardcore to the realms of art.

Exposed 1971

Director Gustav Wiklund **Cast** Christina Lindberg, Heinz Hopf, Björn Adelly 99m

Sweden was once the hotbed of porn. The 1969 sex education film *The Language of Love* prompted Cliff Richard to lead a protest march and Travis Bickle to take Betsy to see it in *Taxi Driver*. But the starring vehicles of **Christina Lindberg** were much racier. Despite being a parable on the wages of sin, *Exposed* was banned in 36 countries for its depiction of a teenager's couplings with blackmailer **Hopf**'s swinging clients. **Wiklund** attempts the odd moment of Bergmanesque significance.

Humpday 2009

Director Lynn Shelton **Cast** Mark Duplass, Joshua Leonard, Alycia Delmore 94m

This satire on how differently the genders view intercourse centres on the macho posturing of newlywed Ben (**Duplass**) and his globe-trotting buddy Andrew (**Leonard**) after they come to regret drunkenly agreeing to shoot a gay porno to impress some sexually emancipated Seattle bohemians. The showstopping sequence takes place at the Bonin Hotel, as the two friends test each other's artistic commitment and personal integrity, while desperately seeking to abort the humiliating escapade.

One-Eyed Monster 2008

Director Adam Fields **Cast** Amber Benson, Jason Graham, Charles Napier 84m

A jokey homage to creature features like *Alien* and *The Thing*. Humiliated on the set of his latest humpfest, **Ron "The Hedgehog" Jeremy** is zapped by lightning and his detached manhood goes on a vengeful rampage. **Fields** stages the slayings with an adequate mix of irony and panache, while the supporting cast revels in its caricatures. There's room for poignancy, however, as Jeremy and fellow porn veteran **Veronica Hart** ponder life after their assets no longer command the adulation they've come to crave.

The Pornographer 2001

Director Bertrand Bonello **Cast** Jean-Pierre Léaud, Jérémie Renier, Dominique Blanc 111m

Bonello's pensive portrayal of disillusion sees a penurious porn director (**Léaud**) reluctantly return to an industry that has changed drastically since his 1970s hey-day. It's hard to share Bonello's contention that pornography liberates and empowers. But he does have interesting things to say about the socio-artistic constraints imposed by reputation and the increasing difficulty of making meaningful movies.

Sex and Zen 1991

Director Michael Mak **Cast** Lawrence Ng, Amy Yip, Carrie Ng 99m

Hong Kong cinema in the 1990s was dominated by the softcore equivalent of Japan's "pink" genre, dubbed Category III after its censor rating. It acquired cult status abroad with this adaptation of **Li Yu**'s Ming Dynasty novel *The Carnal Prayer Mat*, which was largely played for laughs, as scholar Mei Yeung-Sheng (**Ng**) comes to regret having a genital transplant of equine proportions. There are plenty of erotic scenes, however, notably a music-room encounter involving two women and a flute.

Torremolinos 73 2003

Director Pablo Berger **Cast** Javier Cámara, Candela Peña, Juan Diego 91m

Loosely based on actual events, timid encyclopedia salesman Alfredo's (**Camara**) adventures in the skin trade are all the more amusing because he fancies himself as the Ingmar Bergman of Super-8 smut. Meanwhile his wife (**Peña**) has only agreed to participate in an audiovisual encyclopedia of reproduction as her best chance of getting pregnant. A gentle but acute satire on how the Spanish circumvented the strictures imposed on them by Franco's regime.

PRESIDENTS

What really goes on behind the closed doors of the corridors of power has long intrigued moviemakers, though the perennial mystery of the Kennedy assassination has proved even more magnetic.

Being There 1979

Director Hal Ashby **Cast** Peter Sellers, Shirley MacLaine, Melvyn Douglas, Jack Warden 130m

Modelling his voice on his idol Stan Laurel, **Sellers** is brilliantly minimal as Chance the gardener, a simple man in every sense whose cryptic aphorisms gain him access to the great and the good, including the US president (**Warden**). A subtle satire on American susceptibility to self-help bullshit, the film also features one of the most excruciating seduction scenes ever, superbly played by **Shirley MacLaine**.

The Best Man 1964

Director Franklin Schaffner **Cast** Henry Fonda, Cliff Robertson 104m

Gore Vidal never quite recovered from the realization that he was not going to be US president and has been amusingly condescending about American politics ever since. Here he scripts a fine tale about presidential hopefuls (**Fonda** and **Robertson**) with dark secrets. The movie zings with savage one-liners, for example when one character says of another: "He has every characteristic of a dog, save loyalty."

Executive Action 1973

Director David Miller **Cast** Burt Lancaster, Robert Ryan, Will Geer 91m

Scripted by former blacklistee **Dalton Trumbo**, this may not be as famous as Stone's *JFK*, but it's a cooler, and ultimately more convincing explanation of the conspiracy that could have led to the murder in Dealey Plaza in Dallas. The sinister machinations, led by a trio of right-wing business types, are interspersed with footage of Kennedy's eloquence which explains why the assassination still troubles millions. Even as a work of fiction, this is more plausible than the Warren Commission's official version.

Gabriel Over the White House 1933

Director Gregory la Cava **Cast** Walter Huston, Karen Morley, Franchot Tone 87m

A strange work of political wish fulfilment by media magnate **William Randolph Hearst**. A do-nothing president (**Huston**), modelled on Herbert Hoover, is nearly killed in an accident and is transformed by archangel Gabriel into a go-getting radical president who cracks down on unemployment, gangsters and foreign debt. Some see this as a soggy liberal fantasy, others as a paean to fascism. The movie's release was stalled by Louis B. Mayer, a staunch Republican, until Hoover lost the 1932 election.

in the 1950s. This movie is full of such incidental delights and some impressive performances, especially by **Woods**, **J.T. Walsh** and **Allen** as the people closest to – and suffering the most from – Nixon. Hopkins captures Nixon's awkward, charmless, incomplete but strangely forceful personality brilliantly.

The Last Mitterand 2005

Director Robert Guédiguian **Cast** Jalil Lespert, Michel Bouquet, Philippe Fretun 116m

Based on the **Georges-Marc Benamou** memoir, but much kinder to its subject, **Guédiguian**'s movie has a young writer (**Lespert**) quietly interrogating the ageing, enigmatic statesman (wonderfully played by **Bouquet**) and trying to solve some of the many mysteries in Mitterand's past. Ultimately, the big question – what did Mitterand do as a junior minister in the Vichy government? – is left hanging but this cerebral, evasive movie is, in its thoroughly understated fashion, pretty riveting.

 ## Nixon 1995

Director Oliver Stone **Cast** Anthony Hopkins, Joan Allen, James Woods, Paul Sorvino 192m

In the middle of a harangue by Kissinger (**Sorvino**), Nixon (**Hopkins**) tries to stroke a dog that yelps and flees. "Aw fuck it," says Nixon, "he doesn't like me." This small scene becomes more telling when you compare it to the shot in the credit montage of *JFK* of a dog eating out of Kennedy's hand. And a dog, Checkers, was invoked as Nixon defused a bribes scandal that nearly wrecked his career

The Price of Power 1969

Director Tonino Valerii **Cast** Giuliano Gamma, Van Johnson, Maria Cuadra 108m

Valerii's biting, politicized Western blurs the 1881 assassination of President James Garfield (**Johnson**) with the 1963 assassination of JFK to suggest they both died for their liberal attitude to race. As Garfield's wife Lucretia, **Cuadra** seems to emulate Jackie Kennedy, and the assassination scene is obviously influenced by the Zapruder footage of the slaying of JFK. Odd, cerebral, yet unforgettable.

Winter Kills 1979

Director William Richert **Cast** Jeff Bridges, John Huston, Anthony Perkins 96m

Based on a novel by **Richard Condon** of *Manchurian Candidate* fame, this neglected dark comedy has a fresh take on the Kennedy assassination, suggesting, metaphorically at least, that the dad did it. **Huston** is unforgettable as the randy old patriarch Pa Kegan, while **Bridges** is quietly effective in the difficult role of Nick Kegan (the Bobby Kennedy figure investigating his brother's death), who unearths enough red herrings to open a fish market.

PRISON

Prison isn't meant to be a holiday camp, but you wouldn't send your worst enemy to a movie clink, where sadomasochistic wardens, ritual beatings and rape seem par for the course.

Birdman of Alcatraz 1962

Director John Frankenheimer **Cast** Burt Lancaster, Karl Malden 148m

Birdman's appeal lies in its powerful conviction that even the most reprehensible life has redemptive value. **Lancaster** gives a sensitive portrayal of Robert Stroud, a murderer who became a world famous authority on birds while in the pen (in Leavenworth; he wasn't allowed birds in Alcatraz). The movie largely ignores the fact that Stroud killed two people in prison, stabbed an orderly and was in solitary for the safety of his fellow inmates, but as Joe E. Brown says in *Some Like It Hot*: "Nobody's perfect."

The Caged Heart 1984

Director Denis Amar **Cast** Richard Berry, Richard Bohringer, Victoria Abril 87m

Directing his own screenplay, **Amar**'s prison drama is hard to swallow, becoming ever bleaker as events progress. Bruno (**Berry**) is an actor destined for trouble. Spotting a female shoplifter (**Abril**) in difficulty, he decides to help, only to be imprisoned for her crime.

There he finds himself in the wrong place again when he is mistakenly blamed for a prison escape and an attack on a guard (**Bohringer**), who takes revenge with sadomasochistic games. A taut psychological drama, Bohringer's frighteningly impressive turn as the psychotic guard makes this a tough movie to watch.

Carandiru 2003

Director Hector Babenco **Cast** Luiz Carlos Vasconcelos, Milton Goncalves 145m

Babenco's doctor, Drauzio Varella, had worked in Carandiru prison in Sao Paulo, Brazil, and this movie is based on his book *Carandiru Station*. Built for four thousand inmates, the prison housed eight thousand, there was no outside authority and the prisoners made up their own rules. Despite their bleak existence, humorous and tender moments are included, such as the marriage of transvestite Lady Di. In 1992 a riot erupted and police killed 111 inmates. That event led to the prison's demolition ten years later, and the scene is used as the movie's last, poignant shot. Brutally shocking at times, Babenco's examination of the inmates' individual tales balances out the violence.

Chained Heat 1983

Director Paul Nicholas **Cast** Linda Blair, John Vernon, Sybil Danning **95m**

Not to be confused with *The Caged Heart*, this is the big mamma of the dodgy "women in prison" sub-genre. Former *Exorcist* child star **Linda Blair** stars as a naïve teen banged up for accidental manslaughter. She's fresh meat for the seething mass of predatory drug-dealing lesbian rapists that unapologetically abound in this deranged, nudity-crammed, exploitation flick. Even the sadistic, sex-taping warden has a Jacuzzi in his office. Positively classy compared to the sequel starring Brigitte Nielsen.

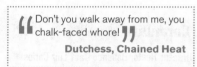

> **❝** Don't you walk away from me, you chalk-faced whore! **❞**
>
> **Dutchess, Chained Heat**

Chicken Run 2000

Directors Peter Lord, Nick Park **Cast** Mel Gibson, Julia Sawalha, Miranda Richardson **84m**

An animation *The Great Escape* – but with chickens. That genius concept goes a long way to endearing you to Aardman's attempt to find their first feature-length wings. If the hens' characterization is at times cringe-makingly clichéd, **Mel Gibson** certainly makes a memorable cock of himself as Rocky the Rooster, determined to save them from a deadly fate of chicken pie. A bumpy-paced test-flight for *Wallace and Gromit: Curse of the Were Rabbit*.

★ Cool Hand Luke 1967

Director Stuart Rosenberg **Cast** Paul Newman, George Kennedy **127m**

Stuart Rosenberg's classic anti-hero prison drama starred **Newman** as the irrepressible, nonconformist Luke only after first choice Telly Savalas refused to fly back from Europe. Released at a time when any sign of rebellion against the establishment was revered, audiences lapped up the opening scene of the destruction of parking meters. The only downer is Rosenberg's use of religious symbolism with Newman as a Christ figure, but his egg-eating feat is the pinnacle of cool. Look out for Dennis Hopper and Harry Dean Stanton.

Escape from New York 1981

Director John Carpenter **Cast** Kurt Russell, Lee Van Cleef, Donald Pleasence **99m**

John Carpenter comes from the "if you want something doing, do it yourself" school of film music, having scored most of his own films, including this one. According to one buff, the melody in this film sounds like one of Casio's digital watches. The movie is set in the future, in 1997(!), when all of New York is a walled-in prison. The president's airplane is crashed into a building inside New York and one of the prisoners is sent on a daring rescue bid.

Female Convict Scorpion: Jailhouse 41 1972

Director Shunya Ito **Cast** Meiko Kaji, Fumio Watanbe, Kayoko Shiraishi 90m

This riveting Japanese exploitation flick teeters between arthouse and B-movie. Second in the *Female Prisoner Scorpion* series, based on the manga, the beautiful Matsu (aka Scorpion) ends a year in solitary by stabbing the warden's face with a sharpened spoon. An orgy of violence is unleashed as the Scorpion escapes in an increasingly surreal jail break. A key inspiration for Tarantino's *Kill Bill* along with **Kaji**'s follow-up *Lady Snowblood*. Bizarre feminist tract or women-in-prison trash? Fight it out yourselves.

I Am a Fugitive from a Chain Gang 1932

Director Mervyn LeRoy **Cast** Paul Muni, Glenda Farrell 90m

In its time this was a shocking exposé of penal practices and the best of the hard-hitting social-protest dramas made by Warner Bros in the 1930s. It vividly depicts an innocent man criminalized by the justice system as a down-on-his-luck war veteran is railroaded into shackles and hard labour. Rock splitting, torture by sadistic guards, escapes (including the seminal pursuit by baying bloodhounds through a swamp), solitary – it's worth seeing just to appreciate how often it has been referenced in other films (most recently in *O Brother, Where Art Thou?*) and for the titanic performance from the great **Muni**.

Kiss of the Spider Woman 1985

Director Hector Babenco **Cast** William Hurt, Raul Julia 121m

Hector Babenco produces a rare, intimate movie from **Manuel Puig**'s novel. **Hurt** is perfectly cast as the homosexual Luis, imprisoned for corrupting a minor. His cellmate is the aggressively straight political revolutionary Valentin (**Julia**). The pair begin as enemies, Valentin opposed to Luis's sexuality and politics, but slowly they begin to respect each other. The Spider Woman of the title refers to an old movie plot, which Luis recounts to Valentin. The film is interspersed with moments of fantasy and classic *film noir* images, Luis using movies to escape from prison life.

 # Midnight Express 1978

Director Alan Parker **Cast** Brad Davis, John Hurt 121m

Following his debut with *Bugsy Malone*, **Parker** produced his best and most gut-wrenching movie. **Davis** keeps your sympathy, just, as Billy Hayes, caught trying to smuggle drugs out of Turkey and sentenced to life in a Turkish prison to "make an example". Enduring physical and psychological abuse (although the rape is only hinted at), Hayes realizes his only chance of survival is escape. Scripted by **Oliver Stone** from **Hayes**' book, the movie would have us believe that it is closer to the truth than it actually is, and Hayes himself doesn't come across as the most pleasant character. The meat-hook scene is, of course, legendary.

Papillon 1973

Director Franklin J. Schaffner Cast Steve McQueen, Dustin Hoffman 150m

Treacherous nuns, gracious lepers and an inventive use for coconuts are among the colourful elements in this penal saga, based on the autobiography of French criminal Henri "The Butterfly" Charrière (named after his tattoo). It's perfectly played by **McQueen**, whose ordeals on Devil's Island (with puny comrade **Hoffman**) are harrowing and exciting by turns, and lead to a growing affection for a man who defies the odds and refuses to be denied his liberty. The last screenplay of blacklist survivor Dalton Trumbo, who appears as prison commandante.

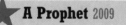 **A Prophet** 2009

Director Jacques Audiard Cast Tahar Rahim, Niels Arestrup 155m

Malik (**Rahim**) is a young Arab banged-up for petty crimes who, on his first day in prison, finds himself ordered by ruthless Corsican gang boss César (**Arestrup**) to murder another inmate or be killed himself. From this opening dilemma **Audiard** creates an almost unbearable tension, which is sustained throughout the film as Malik becomes a skivvy to the Corsicans – to the disgust of his fellow Muslims. But as Malik warily plays the system, the power starts to shift his way. Audiard brilliantly evokes the sweaty machismo and

violence of prison life but also its loneliness and sheer banality.

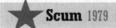 **Scum** 1979

Director Alan Clarke Cast Ray Winstone, Mick Ford, Phil Daniels 97m

Originally made as a BBC play and banned for brutality before it was screened, this was remade as a movie. **Winstone** stars as Carlin, in a stunning debut. Within a budget that wouldn't stretch to shoestrings, **Clarke** uses a documentary style, making the scenes of violence and abuse in a British borstal all the more disturbing. A strong stomach is essential.

The Shawshank Redemption 1994

Director Frank Darabont Cast Tim Robbins, Morgan Freeman 142m

A beautifully crafted, superior adaptation of a **Stephen King** story (Rita Hayworth and the Shawshank Redemption), this is that unlikely thing, a feel-good prison movie. Cultured banker **Robbins** is convicted for murder and, with the friendship of philosophical lifer **Freeman**, endures dehumanization and brutality, but wins the hearts of his fellow inmates and serves up canny comeuppances to tormentors in a great climactic coup. Although it did disappointing business on release, multiple Oscar nominations, video and word of mouth saw it grow into one of the most fiercely loved, uplifting male weepies of modern times.

PRIVATE EYES

An archetype established by the hard-boiled crime fiction of Hammett and Chandler, the world-weary private eye became increasingly more so as the twentieth century wore on. Wisecracking, however, never deserted him.

Alphaville 1965

Director Jean-Luc Godard **Cast** Eddie Constantine, Anna Karina 98m

This futuristic thriller, with **Constantine** as a detective called Lemmy Caution sent to rescue a scientist from a city run by an electronic brain, has some quite extraordinary dialogue. As the electronic brain says: "Sometimes reality is too complex for oral communication. But legend embodies it in a form which enables all over the world." Err... okay. Beautiful, but hard to follow, this is fascinating, irritating viewing. Spot the influences on Philip K. Dick's *Do Androids Dream of Electric Sheep?*, the source for *Blade Runner*.

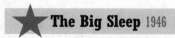 The Big Sleep 1946

Director Howard Hawks **Cast** Humphrey Bogart, Lauren Bacall 114m

After the success of *To Have and Have Not*, Warners didn't really care

what the movie was about as long as it starred **Bacall** and **Bogart**. The plot was changed dramatically because **Raymond Chandler**'s original novel (adapted by William Faulkner and Leigh Brackett) didn't hang together, and because the censors wanted somebody punished: either the decadent Sternwood family or the gangsters. **Hawks** didn't mind: the censors' ending was more violent than his and less complicated than the one Chandler suggested. Chandler's hero, Philip Marlowe, didn't like women much, not a point of view Hawks had much time for, so he made the female characters as available as he could. From these conflicting priorities and commercial considerations a masterpiece emerged.

Charlie Chan at the Opera 1936

Director H. Bruce Humberstone **Cast** Warner Oland, Boris Karloff, Keye Luke 66m

With an opening credit promising "Warner Oland vs Boris Karloff", this is the best entry in the Fox series featuring **Earl Derr Biggers'** Chinese-American detective. As an amnesiac baritone who returns to the wings to reclaim the wife and daughter convinced he'd perished in a theatre fire, **Karloff** essays a cross between Frankenstein's monster and the Phantom of the Opera. But **Oland** is too shrewd to be misled by appearances and the mystery twists several times before the reveal. The Nazis weren't impressed, however: they banned the film for having "too many murders".

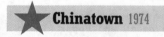

Chinatown 1974

Director Roman Polanski **Cast** Jack Nicholson, Faye Dunaway, John Huston 131m

A well-dressed Jack Nicholson bearing the scars of the memorable nose scene in Polanski's *Chinatown*.

Roman Polanski won the big argument: that a movie called *Chinatown* had to have at least one scene set in a real chinatown. The overruled writer, **Robert Towne**,, insisted it was just a metaphor. The director spent much of the movie rowing with Towne, and telling **Dunaway**, whenever she queried her motivation: "Just say the fucking lines – your salary is the motivation." **Nicholson** charmed enough people to get the movie made without too much violence breaking out, although he may have provided the urine in the cup Dunaway threw in Polanski's face. What ended up onscreen is a real *noir* classic, right down to the downbeat, cynical ending. In memory it is often reduced to a procession of scenes: the nose slitting (performed by Polanski), the joke about the Chinaman having sex, the horror of the closing scene.

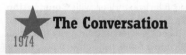

The Conversation 1974

Director Francis Ford Coppola **Cast** Gene Hackman, Robert Duvall 113m

Hackman has seldom bettered his performance as the surveillance expert desperate to prevent a murder he overhears being planned (though he gets excellent support from **Duvall** and, in a small part, a young **Harrison Ford**). With its muffled soundtrack the movie can confuse, but keep an eye on the taped words which run throughout the film. A statement about American society in the 1970s as well as a psychological thriller.

Devil in a Blue Dress 1995

Director Carl Franklin **Cast** Denzel Washington, Tom Sizemore, Jennifer Beals 101m

This is so good you want to write to **Denzel Washington** and **Walter Mosley** to demand that the same team films some of the other novels that star Mosley's black private eye, Easy Rawlins. Here he investigates the murder of his lover Coretta and is paid by a thug to ask questions about **Beals**, a white woman who likes "the company of Negroes". Washington gives Rawlins a character and a conscience in this entertaining tour of the jazz clubs and back streets of 1940s LA.

Farewell My Lovely 1976

Director Dick Richards **Cast** Robert Mitchum, Charlotte Rampling 95m

Former magazine photographer **Richards** directed six films (uncredited on the last, **Burt Reynolds**' *Heat*) of which this is easily the best, a brooding, tense movie based on the Raymond Chandler mystery. **Mitchum** is Marlowe in a way that Dick Powell, and possibly even Bogart, never quite were. The world-weary cynicism he brings to lines like "It's July now and things are worse than they were in spring", sound completely authentic. Marlowe's attempts to trace Velma take him into his usual milieu of lies and double-crosses.

The Kennel Murder Case 1933

Director Michael Curtiz **Cast** William Powell, Mary Astor, Eugene Pallette 73m

Powell is Philo Vance, a dapper detective who takes cases only because they amuse him and certainly for no reason as sordid as paying the rent. The actor toned down some of the hero's foppishness from the books but his ever-present gloves are a sign that this sleuth isn't going to get his hands dirty. This is the archetypal whodunnit, certainly more absorbing on film than any of the subsequent adventures of Hercule Poirot.

Kiss Me Deadly 1955

Director Robert Aldrich **Cast** Ralph Meeker, Albert Dekker 105m

Watch this and feel Mike Hammer's (**Meeker**) pain. He's driven over a cliff, given a needle, knocked out by a blackjack, strapped to a bed, worked over by heavies and finally shot. Not since Rasputin has one man taken so much punishment and lived. Hammer's only mistake was to give a lift to a woman he finds running along the road. And some mistakes you never stop paying for. Probably the biggest single influence on the *nouvelle vague*, this is a thoroughly nasty gem.

Lady in the Lake 1947

Director Robert Montgomery **Cast** Robert Montgomery, Audrey Totter, Lloyd Nolan 103m

Mirroring the first-person narration of protagonist Philip Marlowe, this is the only mainstream film to be shot entirely with a subjective camera – you only get to see the detective when he looks in the mirror. Although interesting at first, it becomes distracting, and it's never fun watching a *femme fatale* pucker up to the screen. Possibly why the technique never caught on.

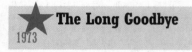

The Long Goodbye 1973

Director Robert Altman **Cast** Elliott Gould, Nina Van Pallandt, Sterling Hayden 111m

Philip Marlowe's most controversial screen incarnation, a laid-back **Elliott Gould**, is also one of his most satisfying. In the final scene he shoots his duplicitous old friend Terry Lennox, something critics insist the old Marlowe would never have done. Cinematographer **Vilmos Zsigmond** adds to the uncertainty – he zooms in and out, arcs around and tracks across. The movie has a nightmarish, haunting quality and Gould strips away the invisible suit of armour that always protected Bogart's Marlowe.

The Maltese Falcon 1941

Director John Huston **Cast** Humphrey Bogart, Mary Astor, Peter Lorre 100m

This was Hollywood's third attempt to capture **Hammett**'s novel on the big screen. The first two bombed, but this one made **Huston** and **Bogart** (who only got the part because George Raft's contract said he didn't have to do remakes). Bog-

art is substantially different to the hero in the book, but this version had the courage to pursue Hammett's original ending. The movie's dark cinematography anticipates *film noir* – and disguised the paucity of the sets at Warners. Spade isn't as moral as Marlowe, but in his refusal to "play the sap" he sums up the private eye's creed.

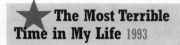

The Most Terrible Time in My Life 1993

Director Kaizo Hayashi **Cast** Masatoshi Nagase, Shiro Sano 92m

The director's love of B-movies can be seen from the fact that Hama (**Nagase**) is possibly the only private eye whose office is also a projection booth. **Hayashi** himself once tried to become a detective (the movie is recommended by the Japan Association of Detective Agencies), and the homage here is deep and affectionate, with Hama (first name Mike) hired to find a waiter's lost brother. Underneath the fun there's a point too about Japan's xenophobia.

Murder, She Said 1961

Director George Pollock **Cast** Margaret Rutherford, Arthur Kennedy, Muriel Pavlow 87m

Despite dedicating *The Mirror Crack'd from Side to Side* to Margaret Rutherford, **Agatha Christie** was never a fan of the screen's first Miss Marple. Perhaps she would have preferred TV incarnation Joan Hickson, who plays a suspect in this brisk take on *4.50 from Paddington*. **Rutherford** clearly had clout on the set, however, as the role of her librarian sidekick was written especially for husband, **Stringer Davis**. The action is quirkier than Christie's, but the satisfying mystery clips along to the jaunty **Ron Goodwin** theme that was later covered by Fun Boy Three.

Night Moves 1975

Director Arthur Penn **Cast** Gene Hackman, Jennifer Warren, Melanie Griffith **99m**

One of the keys to this movie is an apparently innocuous exchange when private eye Harry Moseby (**Hackman**) is watching American football on TV and his wife asks who's winning. "Nobody", he says, "one side's just losing slower than the other." Moseby is no Marlowe, and the deconstruction of the private-eye hero went too far for 1970s audiences; this bombed and remains underrated today.

The Private Life of Sherlock Holmes 1970

Director Billy Wilder **Cast** Robert Stephens, Colin Blakely, Genevieve Page **125m**

Pitching Holmes and Watson into an adventure replete with Russian ballet dancers, missing midgets, malevolent Trappists and the Loch Ness Monster, this will intrigue devotees of the Baker Street sleuth. But it's not the film **Billy Wilder** wanted to make. He originally envisaged a Lerner-Loewe musical, starring Peters O'Toole and Sellers. But the timidity of the suits at United Artists meant that even his 165-minute songless scenario was stripped of an Oxford flashback and cases involving naked honeymooners and an upside-down room. It's accomplished, but it could have been a masterpiece.

The Thin Man 1934

Director W.S. Van Dyke **Cast** William Powell, Myrna Loy **93m**

Nothing in this brilliantly executed work quite matches the dialogue. **Hammett**'s detective Nick Charles (**Powell**) is reviewing his reviews in the papers: "I'm a hero, I got shot twice in *The Tribune*." Nora (**Loy**) responds that it was five times in the tabloids and hubby replies: "It's not true. He didn't come anywhere near my tabloids." The case he's working on is well plotted but incidental, probably not as important as the case of scotch he's working on.

Tony Rome 1967

Director Gordon Douglas **Cast** Frank Sinatra, Jill St John, Richard Conte **110m**

In 1971, Bing Crosby turned down *Columbo* and Frank Sinatra withdrew from *Dirty Harry* with a broken finger. But Ol' Blue Eyes had gotten to crack crime in this dogged attempt to hybridize **Hammett's** *The Thin Man* and **Chandler**'s *The Big Sleep*. The chic 1960s raciness occasionally feels forced. But **Gordon Douglas** makes solid use of the Miami locations and there was enough spark between Sinatra and party girl **Jill St John** to earn him a reprise in *Lady in Cement* (1968).

PROPAGANDA

Despite Hollywood mogul Sam Goldwyn's dictum that messages should be left to Western Union, many governments have exploited the power of film in the ideological battle for hearts and minds.

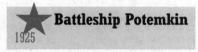

Battleship Potemkin 1925

Director Sergei Eisenstein **Cast** Alexander Antonov, Vladimir Barsky 75m

Eisenstein's most remarkable movie was an assignment from the state Central Committee and shot by a film collective, with the director focusing not on individual characters but class types. The resulting drama of a battleship mutiny, which commemorates the aborted 1905 revolution, is a cornerstone of film studies. Its legendary sequence on the Odessa Steps (mother loses grip on pram, camera follows its inexorable descent and baby's crushing under stampeding feet as crowd escapes Tsarist troops) may be the best known, most imitated scene in the history of motion pictures.

The Green Berets 1968

Directors Ray Kellogg, John Wayne **Cast** John Wayne, David Janssen 141m

John Wayne (who never served in the military) first mooted helping the Vietnam war effort in a letter to president Lyndon Johnson. The result is a gung-ho movie that tries to apply the simplicities of the American West to a new war in the East and gets hopelessly confused. The Pentagon had a hand in the script, so what you see onscreen is a straight good vs evil clash with marauding Indians replaced by massacring Vietcong. It made a mint at the box office but failed to make Americans feel any better about Vietnam.

Kolberg 1945

Director Veit Harlan **Cast** Heinrich George, Kristina Soderbaum 111m

Nazi attempt to create a *Gone With the Wind*-style epic, in which the Prussian city of Kolberg is surrounded by nasty Napoleonic troops but won't give in. It's let down, in the words of one critic, by a "score so sweet it makes *The Sound of Music* sound like punk rock." The fact that **Josef Goebbels** helped write the script didn't help. Even from the Nazi point of view, it seems a strange way to employ 187,000 German troops in the closing months of World War II.

The Silent Village 1943

Director Humphrey Jennings 36m

The solidarity of Welsh miners with the brutalized residents of the Czechoslovakian town of Lidice manifests itself in this poetically powerful tribute. Over 170 men were executed in reprisal for the murder of Deputy Reich Protector Reinhard Heydrich, while countless women and children were dispatched to camps. **Humphrey Jennings** stages the violence offscreen, but he and editor **Stewart McAllister** generate a palpable sense of community that is reinforced by the non-professional Cwmgiedd cast.

Triumph of the Will 1935

Director Leni Riefenstahl **Cast** Adolf Hitler, Josef Goebbels 120m

At Hitler's request, **Riefenstahl** filmed the sixth Nazi Party Congress in 1934, assisted by 30 cameras and 120 technicians. Her brief was to glorify the might of the Nazi state, which she achieved with breathtaking imagery on a spectacularly sinister, epic scale. Its stirring anthems and saluting multitudes provide a fascinating and chilling testament to the ability of film to impose a false, spiritual aesthetic on the overtly political. After the war Riefenstahl was jailed for four years for her propaganda work.

Why We Fight 1942–45

Directors Frank Capra and Anatole Litvak

Roused into recognizing the value of propaganda by Leni Riefenstahl's *Triumph of the Will*, **Frank Capra** produced this seven-film series to provide the US with a moral compass during World War II. The newsreel footage was brilliantly edited by **William Hornbeck**, while **Walter Huston** brought growling authority to commentaries scripted by the **Epstein** twins who would co-write *Casablanca*. **Disney** contributed the animation, but the guiding vision was that of the Sicilian-born Major Capra and *The Prelude to War* deservedly won an Oscar.

John Wayne may not have served in the real-life army, but valiantly attempts to fire up American soldiers in Vietnam in *The Green Berets*.

PSYCHOS

While bad guys (they're usually guys) have always loomed large in the movies, Hitchcock's *Psycho* created the gold standard of sheer demented evil that subsequent movie killers have striven to exceed.

The Big Heat 1953

Director Fritz Lang **Cast** Glenn Ford, Gloria Grahame, Lee Marvin 126m

A blistering *noir* in which **Glenn Ford**'s dogged cop comes up against a brutal gang, **Fritz Lang**'s *The Big Heat* is perhaps most memorable for its creation of the truly unhinged Vince Stone (**Marvin**). A hurricane force of violence and self-loathing, in perhaps the film's most memorable moment Stone scars his girlfriend (**Grahame**) by flinging scalding coffee in her face. The scene redefined onscreen violence.

Cape Fear 1962

Director J. Lee Thompson **Cast** Robert Mitchum, Gregory Peck 102m

After an eight-year prison stretch for rape and assault, Max Cady (**Mitchum**) returns to disrupt the life of the prosecutor (**Peck**) he holds responsible for his conviction. Operating at the height of his physical prowess, a beefed up Mitchum radiates genuine menace and malice in one of his best screen roles. Scorsese later remade the film, with the original stars taking pivotal cameo roles.

Funny Games 1997

Director Michael Haneke **Cast** Susanne Lothar, Ulrich Mühe 108m

The truly disturbing tale of a wealthy Austrian family who shortly after arriving at their lakeside retreat find themselves confronted by two cold-blooded psychopaths who set about their mental and physical torture. The fact that the psychos first appear sporting white gloves and immaculate tennis whites is a clearly ominous sign. A cold, dispassionate work that analyses violence and how it is represented onscreen, the film was later remade in the US by the director.

Hard Candy 2006

Director David Slade **Cast** Ellen Page, Patrick Wilson 100m

A claustrophobic and economically shot psychological thriller, *Hard Candy* excels in pulling the rug from the viewer. Centred on the thorny subject of online grooming, the film plays with expectation, switching audience sympathy from a teenage girl (**Page**) to the lecherous fashion photographer (**Wilson**) who becomes her quarry. Featuring a truly eye-watering finale, the film was the Sundance Film Festival story of its year.

Kontroll 2003

Director Nimrod Antal Cast Sándor Csányi, Zoltán Nagy 111m

Kontroll unfolds amidst Budapest's labyrinthine subway system where the ticket inspectors are universally despised. Amongst the "Kontroll" are a ragtag gang of misfits, led by Bulcsú, a maverick inspector who never leaves the subway. A scourge of the management, Bulcsú also has his own particular nemesis: an uncatchable, fleet-footed fare dodger known as "Bootsie". However, a darker foe has also emerged: a sinister hooded figure who has taken to pushing unwary passengers to their instant deaths. Atmospheric and terrifying, if you've seen this you'll never fare dodge again!

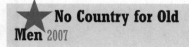

★ No Country for Old Men 2007

Directors Joel and Ethan Coen Cast Josh Brolin, Javier Bardem, Tommy Lee Jones 122m

When a Vietnam vet (**Brolin**) discovers $2 million while wandering through the aftermath of a Texas drug deal gone horribly awry, his fateful decision to abscond with the cash sets a hellhound on his trail in the form of dead-eyed assassin Anton Chigurh (**Bardem**). Determining the fate of his victims on the toss of a coin, Chigurh is compared by one associate to the bubonic plague. The description seems unnecessarily harsh on the plague. Adapted from the novel by **Cormac McCarthy**; brilliantly directed by the **Coen** brothers.

The Proposition 2005

Director John Hillcoat Cast Guy Pearce, Danny Huston, Ray Winstone 100m

In the unforgiving Australian Outback of the 1880s, men live and die by the gun and justice comes at the end of a hangman's rope. Struggling to bring order to the territory, a ruthless English police captain (**Winstone**) hunts down the Burns gang – the brothers wanted for a brutal rape and murder. But while two are taken prisoner, the psychopathic leader (**Huston**) escapes to the hills and plots a horrific revenge. The script's biblical overtones and sense of the macabre come courtesy of **Nick Cave**.

Psycho 1960

Director Alfred Hitchcock Cast Anthony Perkins, Janet Leigh, Martin Balsam 104m

Still deeply disturbing after all these years, not least for the way the audience is made to identify with both the victim and the killer, *Psycho* is a brilliant take on gothic horror, overlaid with the fashionable pop psychology of the day, and a distinctly noirish visual style. **Perkins**, as the mother-fixated Norman Bates, brings a twitchy, awkward charm to the part, but special mention must be made of **Bernard Herrmann**'s unnerving music, which – as Hitchcock acknowledged – ratchets up the tension to an almost unbearable level. Why Gus Van Zant saw fit to re-make Hitchcock's classic frame by frame in 1998 is still a mystery, though it did garner him a Razzie for his efforts.

Something Wild 1986

Director Jonathan Demme **Cast** Jeff Daniels, Melanie Griffith, Ray Liotta 114m

It's hard to say who is the most deranged in **Demme**'s quirky road movie: **Griffith**'s kinky Lulu, or her plainly psychotic ex-husband, Ray (**Liotta**). When Ray discovers that Lulu has taken a dull investment banker (**Daniels**) on a cross-country road trip involving petty thievery and kinky sex, it's fair to say he's none too pleased. Liotta has made a career of playing psychos; this is his first, and best.

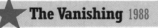 The Vanishing 1988

Director George Sluizer **Cast** Johanna ter Steege, Bernard-Pierre Donnadieu 120m

For many *the* most chilling onscreen psycho, and from this selection possibly the least known. Raymond Lemorne (**Donnadieu**) is a seemingly mild-mannered professor and family man who, it transpires, is actually a cold-hearted technician of terror. Abducting a young woman, Lemorne later promises to reveal her whereabouts to her naturally inquisitive boyfriend. The result is not for the squeamish, nor the claustro-

phobic. Sluizer remade his own film in Hollywood (hence this original version is sometimes known by its Dutch title, *Spoorloos*) but it lacked the Hitchcockian power of the original.

RELIGION

God has always been big in the movies. Back in 1910 a film of the Passion sold out theatres in New Jersey. And in an industry where one studio claimed it had more stars than heaven, heaven's biggest star remains a perennial attraction.

The Bible 1966

Director John Huston **Cast** Michael Parks, Richard Harris, George C. Scott, Ava Gardner 174m

There are 39 books in the Old Testament. Here it takes 174 minutes to tell the first half of the opening one – at that rate, if **Huston** had filmed the rest, the resulting movie would have been over nine days long. God created the world in seven days, but then he didn't have **Dino de Laurentiis** as producer. Huston plays Noah, and his performance shames the rest of the cast, bar **George C. Scott**'s Abraham).

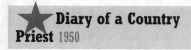

★ Diary of a Country Priest 1950

Director Robert Bresson **Cast** Claude Laydu, Jean Riveyre, Adrien Borel 120m

Frustrated by his failure to finance a biopic of St Ignatius Loyola, **Robert Bresson** turned to Georges Bernanos' novel in his bid to create a new kind of cinema, focusing on a character's inner life. After an extensive search for a suit-able Catholic non-professional actor, he devoted every Sunday for a year to schooling **Claude Laydu**, a 22-year-old Swiss man, who even spent time in a monastery to inhabit the conflicted cleric whose terminal cancer is exacerbated by his inability to reach his new flock. Austere, elliptical and intensely spiritual, this is also a deeply affecting human drama.

The Gospel According to Matthew 1964

Director Pier Paolo Pasolini **Cast** Enrique Irazoqui, Margherita Caruso, Susanna Pasolini 142m

A gay Marxist, drawn to the Gospel message after realizing it was as political as it was compassionate, **Pier Paolo Pasolini** succeeds brilliantly in his ambition to depict both "the life of Christ plus two thousand years of storytelling about the life of Christ". Quoting from scripture and devotional art, yet subverting both with a raw technique inspired by neo-realism and the *nouvelle vague*, the film has an intuitive empathy with its subject matter.

Jesus of Montreal 1989

Director Denys Arcand **Cast** Lothaire Bluteau, Catherine Wilkening 118m

A group of young actors revamp the traditional Passion Play and then start behaving like Jesus and his disciples. Sounds trite, but if you're not allergic to allegory this is worth the effort, especially for **Bluteau**'s intense performance as Danile/Christ. (Bluteau is equally impressive as a Jesuit priest on a spiritual voyage of discovery in 1991's *Black Robe*). As celluloid Jesuits go, Bluteau just shades it over Jeremy Irons in *The Mission*.

The Life of Jesus 1997

Director Bruno Dumont **Cast** David Douche, Majorie Cottreel, Kader Chaatouf 96m

Don't expect Jesus to crop up much in this bleak tale set in rural France. Freddy (**Douche**) and his mates spend their days in Bailleu, or "Nowheresville" as they call it, riding their bikes and taunting Arab immigrants. Their pent-up frustration is released when a young Arabic man, Kader (**Chaatouf**), moves in on Freddy's girlfriend Marie (**Cottreel**), to the group's violent displeasure. Director **Dumont**'s use of novice actors adds a level of realism to events. There's nothing stagey about the performances, right down to Freddy and Marie's sex scenes, which made many ask a perennial movie question: were they really acting?

The Message 1976

Director Moustapha Akkad **Cast** Anthony Quinn, Irene Papas, Michael Ansara 117m

The executive producer of the *Halloween* franchise may seem an unlikely chronicler of the origins of Islam, but **Moustapha Akkad**'s epic (which was filmed simultaneously in English and Arabic) not only received the imprimatur of some senior Muslim scholars, but also funding from Libya's Colonel Gaddafi, who even loaned the production his army for the Badr and Uhud battle scenes. Forbidden from depicting Muhammad, Akkad focused on the exploits of his uncle, Hamza (**Anthony Quinn**), and utilized a combination of subjective perspective and offscreen silence to suggest the Prophet's presence. The result is disorientating, but reverentially effective.

Nazarín 1958

Director Luis Buñuel **Cast** Francisco Rabal, Marga López, Rita Macedo 94m

Religion and death, **Buñuel** famously said, had marked him for life. They certainly left an indelible imprint on his film work. After *Viridiana*, he was attacked for sending up Christ's Last Supper and in *Simon del desierto* he told the bizarre tale of a fourth-century man who climbs up a column to get closer to God, whereupon he is whisked to modern-day New York by the devil. In *Nazarín*, Buñuel's purpose is clearer: to point out how difficult it is for the lapsed priest to live by the laws of Christ. Not as witty as his later masterpieces, this is still a credible work from a director in geographic, political and quasi-professional exile.

The Rapture 1991

Director Michael Tolkin **Cast** Mimi Rogers, Patrick Bauchau, David Duchovny 100m

That rarest of modern American movies: a film that takes the fundamentalist view of the apocalypse seriously. Sharon (**Rogers**) is a bored sex-line operator. One night, in a way that **Tolkin** makes believable, she calls out in the night to God and is born again. It's hard to say more without giving the game away, but the movie ends in an apocalypse and Tolkin has the nerve to press things to the only logical conclusion.

Solomon and Sheba 1959

Director King Vidor **Cast** Yul Brynner, Gina Lollobrigida, George Sanders 139m

Tyrone Power died halfway through the making of this movie, and was replaced by the actor formerly known as the King of Siam. After Power's death, filming only managed to continue because the studio collected $1.1m on the insurance. The result is perhaps one of the rare instances when the world would have been better served if the insurer had refused to pay out. He was a wise king; she was, as they used to say in the markets of old Palestine, no better than she ought to be; so they were destined, according to strict Hollywood rules, to fall in love. You have to wonder how much the free interactive Bible kits that were used to promote the film in schools concentrated on the famous orgy scene that allegedly cost $100,000 to make.

★ Spring, Summer, Fall, Winter... and Spring 2003

Director Kim Ki-duk **Cast** Oh Yeong-su, Kim Ki-duk, Kim Yeong-min 103m

The contrast between the tranquillity of nature and humanity's destructive urges informs this sublime study of the psyche and the soul. **Baek Dong-hyeon**'s camera exquisitely captures the seasonal colours and moods, but **Kim Ki-duk** isn't solely interested in Zen bliss, as the mischievous tot raised by Oh Yeong-su's ageing monk becomes a lustful teenager, and he considers acts of cruelty, carnality and rage, as well as moments of compassion, atonement and love. Visually entrancing, spiritually uplifting and utterly unforgettable.

Wise Blood 1979

Director John Huston **Cast** Brad Dourif, Harry Dean Stanton, John Huston 106m

Hazel Motes (**Dourif**) is a war veteran who returns to the deep south to found the Church Without Christ. Asa Hawks (**Stanton**) is a blind preacher whom Motes meets, and **Huston** plays Dourif's grandfather, a preacher, in flashbacks. Dourif plays the philosopher king, throwing out great lines like: "A man don't need justification if he's got a good car." A grim but compelling slice of southern gothic.

ROAD MOVIES

The ultimate way to strike out for freedom, road movies combine epic scenery with intense in-car dialogue. And although a good plot never goes amiss, in a true road movie you never reach your destination, if you ever had one.

The Adventures of Priscilla, Queen of the Desert 1996

Director Stephan Elliott **Cast** Hugo Weaving, Guy Pearce, Terence Stamp 104m

Two drag queens and a transsexual, hired to perform at a resort in Alice Springs, buy a bus, the eponymous Priscilla, and drive themselves across the country, encountering Aborigines and gay bashers along the way. Unashamedly camp, with more rhinestones and feathers than a Danny La Rue retrospective, the three friends sing, dance and bitch their way through Australia's stunning Outback, astounding the locals wherever they go.

Candy Mountain 1987

Directors Robert Frank and Rudy Wurlitzer **Cast** Kevin J. O'Connor, Tom Waits 92m

A co-production that begins in New York before meandering cross-country and concluding in Canada, *Candy Mountain* is one of the seminal road movies. The film traces the personal odyssey of ambitious but untalented New York musician Julius (**O'Connor**), whose quest for glory leads him to feign an association with Elmore Silk, the J.D. Salinger of guitar making. Charged with luring the legendary crafts-man from hiding and retirement, Julius takes to the road for a series of ultimately spirit-sapping adventures. Boasting an eclectic cast of musicians (**Joe Strummer**, **Dr John** and **Arto Lindsay** all feature), the film looks at the pressure of fame, the journey towards selfhood and the road as a symbol of freedom.

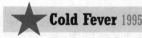 **Cold Fever** 1995

Director Fridrik Thór Fridriksson **Cast** Masatoshi Nagese, Lily Taylor 95m

Staking a claim as Iceland's first road movie, **Fridrik Thór Fridriksson**'s

Cold Fever offers a distinctive and suitably chilly take on familiar genre conventions. Evocative of Aki Kaurismäki and Jim Jarmusch, the film concerns a Tokyo businessman whose vacation plans are interrupted by the need to fulfil Japanese custom and visit the final resting place of his parents: a remote rural river in wintry Iceland. In typical road movie fashion, our hero drives a beautiful car (a Citroën DS), meets some eccentric locals, and finally completes a physical and spiritual journey. Shot during particularly harsh conditions, the film is certainly striking to look at.

The Doom Generation 1995

Director Gregg Araki **Cast** James Duval, Rose McGowan 85m

Gregg Araki explores his favourite theme of troubled teens: Jordan White and Amy Blue pick up a drifter, Xavier Red, and together they embark on an orgiastic crime spree. The humour is of the blackest kind, and at times misses the mark, but no one can deny the movie's impact, with its gore, out-there dialogue and tortured characters. Self-consciously trashy, fast-paced, violent and sexy, this is one for viewers with good concentration spans and strong stomachs.

Duel 1971

Director Steven Spielberg **Cast** Dennis Weaver 90m

Steven Spielberg's made-for-TV movie put him on the map in terms of filmmaking, and deservedly so. This is a road trip gone horribly wrong, with **Weaver**'s businessman harassed by the driver of a tanker after he tries to overtake him. The tension created by one man (we never see the face of the truck driver) and two vehicles will have you on the edge of your seat throughout.

Familia Rodante 2004

Director Pablo Trapero **Cast** Graciana Chironi, Liliana Capurro 104m

At her 84th birthday party, Emilia (**Chironi**) gets a phone call from her sister back home in Misiones asking her to be her niece's matron-of-honour. So Emilia declares that the whole family is going to the wedding. The family motor home is dusted off as the twelve-member family embarks on a mammoth two-day journey. Argentinian writer/director **Pablo Trapero** takes to the road in an amiably sour and bittersweet road movie that adopts a fly-on-the-wall documentary approach to capture four generations of a Latino family. Comprising briefly glimpsed scenes and snatches of conversation, Trapero's observations of this feisty, chattering, emotionally chaotic family are so authentic as to be unnerving.

Get on the Bus 1996

Director Spike Lee **Cast** Richard Belzer, De'aundre Bonds 120m

Spike Lee's movie follows a ragged busload of African-American men travelling from Los Angeles to Washington for the 1996 Million Man March. A mixed bunch, there is the father whose son is shackled to him as a condition of his parole, who hopes this will improve their relationship, the callous salesman, the actor, the policeman and so on. All these men have different hopes for the march, and different stories to tell. Beautifully observed, paced and acted.

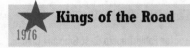

Kings of the Road

1976

Director Wim Wenders **Cast** Rüdiger Vogler, Hanns Zischler 176m

The last, and best, of **Wenders**' road trilogy (the others being *Alice in the Cities* and *Wrong Move*) tells the story of Bruno and Robert, two friends who travel the often deserted roads of the border between East and West Germany, repairing old cinema projectors. The shadow of post-war American cultural imperialism looms large over the whole movie. Deliberately slow and introspective, the characters don't get anywhere, but somehow it's both absorbing and moving.

The Passenger 1975

Director Michelangelo Antonioni **Cast** Jack Nicholson, Maria Schneider 125m

One of **Antonioni**'s very finest achievements, and the best of his English-language films, **Jack Nicholson** gives one of his greatest performances as a disillusioned television journalist covering current affairs in Africa who impulsively decides to exchange identities with an acquaintance he finds dead in a Saharan hotel room. Fashioned from a terse, taut,

imaginative script by **Mark Peploe** and **Peter Wollen**, Antonioni creates a haunting, suspenseful and extremely subtle study of psychological and spiritual disenchantment.

The Return 2003

Director Andrei Zvyagintsev **Cast** Vladimir Garin, Ivan Dobronravov 105m

After an absence of twelve years, the father of two adolescent Russian boys abruptly materializes in the home of their mother. Setting out on what they believe will be a fishing vacation, Andrey and Vanya's excitement soon diminishes under the weight of their dad's awkward and increasingly brutal efforts to make up for a missing decade of parental supervision. Finally arriving at their mysterious island destination, the true nature of the reunion becomes chillingly clear. A combination of road movie, thriller and tragic parable, *The Return* is a remarkable and highly original piece of cinema.

The Straight Story 1999

Director David Lynch **Cast** Richard Farnsworth, Sissy Spacek 112m

Gentle and sweet movie, based on a true story about Alvin Straight (**Farnsworth**), an old man who drove for six weeks on a ride-on lawnmower to visit his sick brother. This is **Lynch** at his lyrical, thoughtful best – concerned with people's underlying quirks and personal stories. Farnsworth, an ex-stuntman, is a joy and deserved his Oscar nomination for the role.

Wild at Heart 1990

Director David Lynch **Cast** Nicolas Cage, Laura Dern, Willem Dafoe 124m

Nicolas Cage was once the darling of independent filmmakers, and *Wild at Heart* marked the peak of his alternative career. He plays Sailor, in love with Lula (**Dern**) but hated by her crazed mother (**Diane Ladd**, Dern's mother). Lula and Sailor take off on a journey along a "Yellow Brick Road" peppered with car wrecks, ex-lovers and the usual bunch of Lynch crazies and dropouts. When Lula says it's all "wild at heart and weird on top", she's not wrong.

Y tu mamá también 2001

Director Alfonso Cuarón **Cast** Gael Garcia Bernal, Diego Luna, Maribel Verdú 105m

Harry Potter director **Cuarón** wrote this script with his brother Carlos. Best friends Julio and Tenoch meet a vivacious older woman at a wedding. Impressing her with plans to drive to a secret beach, she agrees to accompany them, teaching the impressionable youths about life, love and sex. Their road trip is interspersed with realities of life in Mexico: police checkpoints, drug busts and shanty towns. A daring, sometimes shocking movie, it broke Mexican box-office records.

Wanda (1970, 102m)

There's a scene fifty minutes into *Wanda* involving the central characters, Wanda Goronski and Mr Dennis. A bank robber who looks like a university lecturer, Mr Dennis is trying to fix Wanda's hair to make it look "nicer". He eventually gives up and suggests she wear a hat. Wanda tells him she doesn't have a hat: "I never did have anything, never will have anything." Annoyed, Mr Dennis tells her, "You don't want anything, you won't have anything. If you don't have anything you're nothing, you may as well be dead." Wanda, unperturbed, responds, "I guess I'm dead then". Thirty-nine years after it was made, Barbara Loden's incredible film – sadly the only one she ever made – still packs a punch and demands our attention for the purity and clarity of its vision. A low-budget, truly independent 16mm, *Wanda* remains an anomaly. As a filmmaker, Barbara Loden is not unlike her central character Wanda. An ethereal, spectral figure, she's been more or less sidelined at the margins of American film history. But Loden deserves better: she has given us something unique and special.

Joe Lawlor and Christine Molloy

Joe Lawlor and Christine Molloy won an award at the 2004 Edinburgh film festival with the short Who Killed Brown Owl?, *part of a series of community-based shorts entitled* Civic Life *that took the filmmakers to different parts of Britain. The acclaimed, feature-length* Helen *took a police procedural premise deep into art cinema territory.*

ROBOTS

From killer cops to cute li'l 'bots, cinema boasts an infinite variety of robotic performances. Keanu Reeves seems to be particularly good at them.

A.I.: Artificial Intelligence
2001

Director Steven Spielberg **Cast** Hayley Joel Osmet, Frances O'Connor, Jude Law **146m**

Stanley Kubrick spent over twenty years developing this adaptation of Brian Aldiss's short story of a child android called David engineered with the capability to love – mainly because Kubrick thought "David" should be computer-generated and was waiting for big screen technology to catch up. On his death the project passed to **Spielberg**, who lavished Kubrick's chilly arthouse project with his usual family-friendly Hollywood sentiment, right down to a bizarre denouement involving the Blue Fairy from *Pinocchio*. The contrasting visions of these two cinematic legends conflict onscreen to fascinating effect.

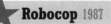 Robocop 1987

Director Paul Verhoeven **Cast** Peter Weller, Nancy Allen **102m**

This unusually smart example of the militant robot genre is set in a dystopian Detroit. When a good cop (**Weller**) gets killed in the line of duty, he returns as a super-powerful cyborg, haunted by his suppressed human memories. Thanks to Dutch director **Verhoeven** (later of *Starship Troopers* and *Showgirls* notoriety), satire and pathos are as much key components here as the unrelenting ultra-violence.

Robot Monster 1953

Director Phil Tucker **Cast** George Nader, George Barrows **66m**

George Barrows is Ro-Man in **Tucker**'s baffling sci-fi schlocker. Instructed by "Great Guidance", an overweight man in a gorilla suit with a toy space helmet on his head, he plots world domination from inside a desert cave. A veritable feast of shaky props and lizards made up to look like dinosaurs, this movie has more going for it than the Golden Turkey Awards judiciary would have you believe. It is surrealist filmmaking at its finest, albeit unintentionally: a warped blend of near-Shakespearian pathos and Ed Wood-like insanity blasts *Robot Monster* into the realm of the remarkable. Incidentally, in John Carpenter's Lovecraftian *In the Mouth of*

Arnold Schwarzenegger as the 1980s-styled, unstoppable cyborg in *The Terminator* – before he turned cuddly in *T2*.

Madness, this is the late-night movie playing on the TV in Sam Neill's motel room.

The Stepford Wives 1975

Director Bryan Forbes **Cast** Katharine Ross, Paula Prentiss, Peter Masterson 115m

Based on the satirical novel by **Ira Levin** (who also wrote *Rosemary's Baby*), the term "Stepford wife" has passed into daily parlance to mean an unnaturally submissive trophy wife. They're the immaculately coiffured helpmeets that young Joanna finds herself surrounded by when she moves to the suburbs to support her husband's career. That you easily guess the secret to these housewives' freakishly robotic perfection doesn't make this dark thriller any less chilling.

The Terminator 1984

Director James Cameron **Cast** Arnold Schwarzenegger, Michael Biehn 108m

"Wow, it's dated" and "Wow, Arnie really can't act" are the main reactions the mother of all robot blockbusters routinely provokes among today's viewers. Governor **Schwarzenegger** is perfectly cast as a monomaniacally steely force housed in a monosyllabic hunk of meat; he's a cyborg hit man sent from the future to kill the mother (**Linda Hamilton**) of future rebel leader John Connor (**Biehn**). This being the pre-CGI era most of the effects are done with smoke and mirrors, or rather dry ice and cheap lasers. You'd have thought Hamilton's backcombed "startled poodle" hairdo would be enough to stop anything dead in its tracks.

The Transformers: The Movie 1986

Director Nelson Shin **Cast** Eric Idle, Judd Nelson, Peter Cullen **84m**

No, not the live-action, Michael Bay blockbuster, but the original animated feature-length 2-D spin-off. Set way off in the year 2005, two warring races of robots, the Autobots (goodies) and Decepticons (baddies) have, for reasons never fully explained, been genetically engineered to transform themselves into things like lorries and cassette tapes. It made an inglorious swansong for **Orson Welles**, who provides the voice of a very fat planet here.

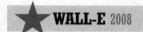

WALL-E 2008

Director Andrew Stanton **Cast** Ben Burtt, Elissa Knight, Jeff Garlin **98m**

"What if mankind had to leave Earth and somebody forgot to turn off the last robot?" That was the starting point for this sophisticated, heart-tugging animation. Left to clean up the mess man left behind, loyal garbage robot WALL-E finds a higher purpose in life when he falls in love with EVE, an iPod-esque ladybot, who's totally out of his league. Together they save the planet. Beaming with Pixar's trademark blend of heart and humour, it's an animation classic. *Time* magazine declared that WALL-E and EVE's on-screen chemistry rivalled that of Spencer Tracy and Katharine Hepburn.

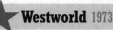

Westworld 1973

Director Michael Crichton **Cast** Yul Brynner, Richard Benjamin **88m**

Michael Crichton, who also wrote *The Andromeda Strain* and *Jurassic Park*, is clearly trying to tell us not to mess with things we don't understand. This time it's the machines that are going to get everyone into trouble. In the future, rich holidaymakers can go to a resort and live out their fantasies with the help of robots – but are stalked by a determined robot assassin (**Brynner**) when the machines begin to malfunction. Avoid the useless sequel, *Futureworld*.

ROCK STARS

The casting of singers and musicians in film roles stretches right back to Louis Jordan and Bessie Smith. There are very few rules when it comes to movies and rock stars, except the one that says that Bob Dylan, Prince and Sting really can't act.

The Book of Life 2000

Director Hal Hartley **Cast** Martin Donovan, P.J. Harvey, Thomas Jay Ryan 63m

Jesus (**Donovan**) materializes in New York on the last day of the century with his assistant, Magdalene (**Harvey**) in tow. Sent to initiate the end of the world, Jesus is having second thoughts. *The Book of Life* features **P.J. Harvey**'s sole acting appearance. Having used one of the West Country singer's songs on the soundtrack to *Amateur*, Hartley primarily cast her in response to the intense Catholic imagery in her songs of tortured love.

Dancer in the Dark 2000

Director Lars von Trier **Cast** Björk, Catherine Deneuve, David Morse 140m

A jarring fusion of classic Hollywood musical, arthouse weepie and overwrought melodrama, the ambitious but ultimately flawed final part of **von Trier**'s "Golden Hearts" trilogy is redeemed by a committed performance from **Björk** as Selma, a Czech immigrant forced into desperate acts by failing health and the wellbeing of her young son. Fans of Björk's yowling vocal style are most likely to enjoy the numbers, but even those unfamiliar with her music will be entranced by the way von Trier weaves the sounds of the machinery she works with, as well as the local railway engines, into the score.

★ Down by Law 1986

Director Jim Jarmusch **Cast** John Lurie, Tom Waits, Roberto Benigni 107m

One of the few musicians to have sustained an acting career, **Tom Waits**' first starring role casts him as Zack, a New Orleans DJ. Framed by the police, he finds himself sharing a cell with a motormouth Italian (**Benigni**) and a pouting pimp (**Lurie**). A characteristically esoteric combination of buddy movie and prison drama, *Down by Law* is driven by the director's interest in American culture colliding with a foreign element and the simmering chemistry between the leads.

Ghosts of the Civil Dead
1988

Director John Hillcoat **Cast** Nick Cave, David Field, Mike Bishop 93m

Having met when **Hillcoat** directed a number of **Nick Cave**'s pop videos, this brutal, nihilistic prison drama marked the Australian duo's first collaboration for the screen. Co-written by Cave, this uncompromising work featured his first character performance as the psychopathic inmate, Maynard. Shorn of his trademark crow-black mane, Cave effec-

tively conveys the sense that Maynard is one of the last people on Earth that you would want to be stuck in a cell with.

The Man Who Fell to Earth 1976

Director Nicolas Roeg **Cast** David Bowie, Rip Torn, Candy Clark 139m

An adventurous examination of alienation, **Roeg**'s film also offers a melancholy critique of capitalist society. **Bowie** claimed he saw the film as a straightforward love story; he also claims never to have read

Cocksucker Blues (1972, 102m)

❝ The first thing to be said about *Cocksucker Blues* (the Robert Frank documentary on the Rolling Stones 1972 Tour) is that it is the ultimate rock'n'roll movie, the second, that it is almost impossible to see, as the Stones have taken out an injunction. Robert Frank and fellow filmmaker Danny Seymour, a drug buddy of the bands, had such ease and intimacy that *Cocksucker Blues* feels more like a home movie of the band at the peak of their greatness, which is what is so unique about it.

There's that amazing scene of the stoned groupie making patterns with the semen on her chest, bodies semi passed out around the room, including the sound recordist, the microphone unattended and propped up by the bed, and then there's the musical brilliance of the band, jamming, rehearsing, creating, topped with the mesmerizing, swirling, crazed performances of Mick Jagger. The 1972 Tour is regarded as the band's best ever. It's a genius film that captures an era, a moment in history, now so long ago that the Stones would risk nothing by finally allowing people to see Robert Frank's masterpiece. ❞

Nick Broomfield

The fearless Broomfield has become Britain's foremost documentary maker, pioneering a new, edgier and entertaining style of non-fiction filmmaking. His profile rose again with his take on cult icons Kurt and Courtney *and* Biggie and Tupac *and serial killer Aileen Wuornos. He has also shot drama, with the immigrant narrative* Ghosts *and, in 2007, the Iraq-set* Battle for Haditha *both shining an unsparing spotlight on awkward social and political issues.*

the script. The former Ziggy Stardust plays Thomas Jerome Newton, an alien from a dying planet who lands on Earth and amasses a vast business empire in order to save his home planet. Harnessing Bowie's otherworldliness, Roeg was vindicated in his instinct that the singer would be perfect as the fallen angel figure undone by earthly temptations.

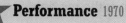

Performance 1970

Directors Donald Cammell and Nicolas Roeg **Cast** James Fox, Mick Jagger 105m

Set in 1960s London, *Performance* begins as a straightforward thriller before deviating into darker terrain. Gangster on the run Chas (**Fox**) takes refuge in the household of a washed-up rock star (**Jagger**) and his two lovers, and soon finds himself exploring the outer limits of sex, drugs and reality. This kaleidoscopic masterpiece left Warner Bros so bewildered that they refused to release it. Deliberately drawing on Jagger's persona, the directors coax a complex performance from him, a fascinating and contradictory blend of arrogance, androgyny and artistry. Jagger would never be so assured onscreen again.

Precious 2009

Director Lee Daniels **Cast** Mo 'Nique, Mariah Carey, Gabourey Sidibe 109m

The Harlem-set story of Claireece "Precious" Jones (**Sidibe**), an illiterate African-American teenager who is pregnant for the second time and abused by a poisonously angry mother. Despite her experiences, Precious has a latent under-standing that other possibilities exist for her, and jumps at the chance to enrol in an alternative school. Banishing the memory of *Glitter*, Mariah Carey gives an entirely credible and naturalistic performance as a care worker alert to Precious's plight. **Lenny Kravitz** also features.

Stardust 1974

Director Michael Apted **Cast** David Essex, Adam Faith, Keith Moon 111m

The follow-up to *That'll Be the Day*, *Stardust* presents the flipside to chart success and fame. Having begun to scale the dizzy heights, homegrown rock'n'roll star Jim Maclaine (**Essex**) soon finds things souring thanks to the actions of his less than honourable manager and one-time friend, Mike (**Faith**). An acutely observed and surprisingly caustic look at the entertainment industry.

★ Videodrome 1983

Director David Cronenberg **Cast** James Woods, Deborah Harry, Sonja Smits 87m

Woods stars as Max Renn, a sleazy TV executive who stumbles across *Videodrome*, an underground show that broadcasts torture and murder. When Renn sets out to find the truth behind the programme, his thrill-seeking girlfriend Nicki (**Harry**) agrees to act as bait. Taking on the role of a dead-eyed attention seeker with masochistic tendencies in a film in which violence, pornography and questions about the nature of reality loom large, Harry made flesh a million unspoken male fantasies.

ROMANCE

The first close-up screen kiss was featured in *The Widow Jones* (1896), a two-minute short recreating the final scene of a popular stage musical. From then on, romance was big box office. If it's a love affair you're after – tragic or cutesy, operatic or kitchen sink – you're going to find it at the movies.

Amélie 2002

Director Jean-Pierre Jeunet **Cast** Audrey Tautou, Mathieu Kassovitz 122m

When a daydreaming Parisian waitress reaches out to her friends, neighbours and customers, she begins an intriguing journey that just might lead her to love, helped by an eccentric cast, a box full of a child's mementos and a garden gnome. The puppy-eyed **Tautou** is perfect as the upbeat innocent Amélie, and the movie is filled with beautiful imagery and memorable characters.

Fear Eats the Soul 1974

Director Rainer Werner Fassbinder **Cast** Brigitte Mira, El Hedi ben Salem 93m

Emmi is a woman past the prime of her life who is determined to marry Ali, a younger Arab man, despite the criticism of her friends and family. The painful irony is once they have been accepted by society, the couple's relationship starts to sour. This is one of Fassbinder's more measured movies, heartbreaking at times but a thoughtful look at the nature of love and what it needs to survive.

Brief Encounter 1945

Director David Lean **Cast** Celia Johnson, Trevor Howard, Stanley Holloway 86m

A happily married housewife meets a handsome stranger, also married, on a station platform. Over the course of a few more weekly meetings, they fall desperately in love, even though they know nothing can happen between them. This romance from another era has lost none of its poignancy and both **Johnson** and **Howard** are so sincere that the slightly dated dialogue hardly registers. It's an expanded version of a **Noel Coward** one-act play (he can be heard making the station announcements in the movie) and is imbued with a certain kind of British clipped restraint, all the while hinting at the repressed passion lurking within the middle-class English soul. You'll never look at a station waiting room in quite the same way again.

Deep End 1970

Director Jerzy Skolimowski Cast John Moulder Brown, Jane Asher, Diana Dors 88m

An initially straightforward romance between a school-leaver working at a public baths and his older woman crush turns dark and disturbing in this ode to love in mod London. **Asher** is a revelation as the provocative Susan – she's a natural screen actress. The movie is full of slightly surreal moments and camera work, which add to its unbalancing effect, such as the bizarre scene where Mike falls from the diving board onto a lifesize cardboard cutout of his crush and then sinks to the bottom of the pool with her.

Eternal Sunshine of the Spotless Mind 2004

Director Michel Gondry Cast Kate Winslet, Jim Carrey, Elijah Wood, Kirsten Dunst 108m

If you could erase part of your romantic past – all those bad memories and lurking resentments – would you? That's the premise of **Charlie Kaufman**'s superficially twisted but sweet love story that **Winslet** and **Carrey** are just perfect for. Clementine has had her memories of ex-boyfriend Joel erased, but when he goes to have the same procedure, he finds he doesn't really want to forget her, and so smuggles her to places in his mind that even the psychiatrists can't find. A complex and thought-provoking movie.

Harold and Maude 1972

Director Hal Ashby Cast Ruth Gordon, Bud Cort 91m

A strange and wonderful black comedy about a young man who is obsessed with death. He falls in love with a 79-year-old woman who is so in love with life that his nihilistic angst seems petty in comparison. Maude lives in a railway carriage, steals cars for fun, and expresses a desire to become a sunflower. She encourages Harold to see his life as more than a boring charade among people he despises. The shocking opening scene is worth seeing the movie for alone.

Heaven Knows, Mr Allison 1957

Director John Huston Cast Deborah Kerr, Robert Mitchum 108m

A decade after her stunning turn in *Black Narcissus*, **Kerr** dons a habit once more for this bittersweet two-hander set during World War II. Sister Anne may be a little less neurotic than Sister Clodagh, but the location is no less exotic – this time Kerr's opinionated, novice nun gets washed up on a Pacific island with a grizzled marine (**Robert Mitchum** was born for the part). Hiding out from the fiendish Japanese,, the odd couple form a tentative, mutually respectful friendship that, it is obvious, should develop into something more. But who will win out in Sister Angela's heart – Jesus or Mitchum? Nuanced, top-notch performances, delicate direction, and an ache-in-the-chest finale – simply delightful.

Lost in Translation 2003

Director Sofia Coppola **Cast** Bill Murray, Scarlett Johansson 102m

A fading movie star and a photographer's wife find themselves adrift in Tokyo and form an intense bond in the face of the city's chaos. This is romance at its most understated, with **Murray** giving one of his best performances as the exhausted Bob, distanced from his wife both physically and emotionally, and unable to find any common ground with his Japanese hosts. **Coppola** gives the movie a stylish sheen with her shots of Tokyo at night and the moody hotel interiors. The big unanswered question is, what does Bob whisper in Charlotte's ear at the end?

Marty 1955

Director Delbert Mann **Cast** Ernest Borgnine, Betsy Blair 90m

Ernest Borgnine rarely plays romantic leads, but his performance here as the butcher who has given up on finding love until he meets Clara (**Blair**) is so tender and genuine it's easy to forget he usually plays heavies. **Paddy Chayefsky**'s beautifully understated script captures how tentative they are at first. Marty's friendship with Angie (**Joe Mantell**), his infantile mate who rubbishes Clara for her lack of sex appeal, is another joy, especially their repeated exchanges of: "What do you wanna do tonight?"

 **A Matter of Life and Death** 1946

Directors Michael Powell, Emeric Pressburger **Cast** David Niven, Kim Hunter 104m

A young British fighter pilot, Peter (**Niven**), exchanges what he assumes are his last words to a female radio operator, June (**Hunter**), as his burning plane plummets towards the English Channel. Miraculously, he is washed up alive, but it turns out his escape is a celestial bureaucratic mistake when "Heavenly Conductor 71", played deliciously by **Marius Goring**, shows up to escort him to heaven. Not only is the story original and entertaining but the technical brilliance of the film is breathtaking. Heaven is shot in black and white, Earth in Technicolor, and whenever Goring appears, all the earthbound characters and movement, bar Peter, freeze – even a mid-air ping pong ball. Such stunning effects don't look ropey, even today. A profound influence on Scorsese, this is simply one of the best films ever.

Il postino 1994

Director Michael Radford **Cast** Massimo Troisi, Maria Grazia Cucinotta, Philippe Noiret 108m

Poet Pablo Neruda is exiled to a small Italian island where the locals have to draft in a new postman just to deliver his fan mail. Gradually, Mario's daily visits give him an understanding of poetry, and the advice of the writer comes in handy when Mario tries to woo a fiery local beauty. A gentle,

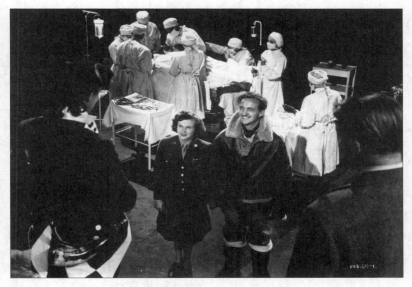

Heaven and Earth colliding: Kim Hunter and a "dead" David Niven plead to be allowed to stay together in *A Matter of Life and Death*.

lyrical movie about finding poetry in every area of life, and finding love even when you think it has passed you by. Tragically, **Massimo Troisi**, who plays Mario with such tentative charm, died of heart failure just twelve hours after filming finished.

Romance & Cigarettes 2005

Director John Turturro **Cast** Susan Sarandon, James Gandolfini, Kate Winslet 105m

On paper it sounds bonkers, certainly, intriguing perhaps – a surreal, blue-collar musical, featuring fabulously over-the-top turns from **Winslet**, **Christopher Walken** and **Steve Buscemi** among others, with quieter performances from the likes of **Sarandon**, **Gandolfini** and **Mary-Louise Parker**, all of whom burst into song when emotion gets the better of them. But **Turturro**'s freewheeling (and scandalously underrated) *tour de force* – touching on the fragile beauty of love, life and everything – is far more than the sum of its quirks, packing an emotional punch that's going to leave you winded.

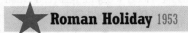 **Roman Holiday** 1953

Director William Wyler **Cast** Audrey Hepburn, Gregory Peck 118m

So ravishing is the doe-eyed **Hepburn** in this gorgeous romance – all stunning Roman locations and Edith Head-designed outfits – that she reduces **Peck**, the cynical news reporter on the trail of her princess-in-disguise, to tears. With all the style but none of the cynicism of other Hepburn hits, such as *Breakfast at Tiffany's* and *Sabrina*, movies simply don't come more lump-in-the-throat lovely than this.

Romuald and Juliette 1989

Director Coline Serreau **Cast** Daniel Auteuil, Firmine Richard 112m

Not another Shakespeare adaptation, but in fact an oddly subversive rom-com about a selfish, wealthy businessman who forms a sweet friendship with a cleaning lady who works in his office building, and her five kids. Quirkily charming not only for its gentle comedy, but also for its patently wishful thinking.

Splendor in the Grass 1961

Director Elia Kazan **Cast** Warren Beatty, Natalie Wood, Pat Hingle 124m

Young love is at its most intense in this powerful study of high-school infatuation, set in the 1920s. **Wood** and **Beatty** play a couple, deeply in love, whose parents think they are far too young to marry. Frustrated by Wood's restraint, Beatty turns to a local floozy for relief and, when she finds out, Wood ends up in an asylum. Melodramatic? Yes, but it is saved from parody by the genuinely moving performance of both leads (who did, of course, become an item during filming), the outstanding supporting cast, including **Hingle**'s authoritarian father, and the bittersweet ending.

 2046 2004

Director Kar Wai Wong **Cast** Tony Leung, Maggie Cheung 123m

The plot is complex and opaque – stories interwoven around a science fiction novel being written by Chow, the lovelorn hero of **Wong**'s *In the Mood for Love*. But plot barely matters in this exquisite piece of filmmaking. If anything, *2046* raises the romance stakes even higher than the earlier movie, revisiting its themes of nostalgia, loss and yearning with a haunting sense of worldweariness. Heartbreakingly beautiful.

White Palace 1990

Director Luis Mandoki **Cast** Susan Sarandon, James Spader 103m

Hollywood has churned out hundreds of love stories where one half of the couple comes from the wrong side of the tracks. This movie is set apart from the rest because **Sarandon**'s Nora, a waitress in a seedy burger joint, is seventeen years older than Max (**Spader**), a widower with a career in advertising. Their relationship is initially one of sexual attraction, but gradually becomes more than that, despite objections from their friends and family. Spader's dissillusioned with the repressed, tidy world he inhabits, even though he can't bring himself to treat Nora as he would a socially acceptable girlfriend. A deeply untypical love story, and a brilliant and moving study about whether or not it's important to find an "appropriate" partner.

Nuptial gigs

Here comes the bride! Filmmakers love a really romantic wedding. Or a truly disastrous one.

Betsy's Wedding (1990)
Alan Alda and Joe Pesci's competitive dads ruin their children's wedding day. If it can go wrong, it does, and more.

Fiddler on the Roof (1971)
When Chava marries Motel and the whole village sings "Sunrise Sunset", you'll be blubbing before they finish the first line.

Goodbye, Columbus (1969)
Proof that money does not buy taste in this over-the-top society wedding that degenerates into a drunken debacle.

The Sound of Music (1965)
Fraulein Maria's wedding scene is often cut on TV. Pity, as she walks down the aisle to one hundred nuns singing a nicely restrained version of "How Do You Solve a Problem Like Maria?" Nice frock, too.

Chicks in White Satin (1993)
A documentary proving even a lesbian wedding cannot escape warring relatives and angst-ridden discussions about commitment and cakes.

The Wedding Singer (1998)
Romance here is for the characters working at the wedding and there's a hard-to-beat 1980s soundtrack.

Rachel Getting Married (2008)
Jonathan Demme's indie masterpiece rips open middle-class bohemian America to reveal its rotten, self-absorbed core. Despite it, you can't help but love the dysfunctional family doing their best to limp through the nuptials.

Wide Sargasso Sea 1992

Director John Duigan **Cast** Karina Lombard, Nathaniel Parker **98m**

Jean Rhys's prequel to *Jane Eyre* is translated wonderfully by this Australian director, who doesn't flinch from the erotic charge which the story (essentially how Mrs Rochester lost her grip on real-ity) has to carry to work. It was given a 17 rating in the US, which pretty much killed its box-office chances. Proof that not all such adaptations have to be as impeccably mannered as the Ivory/Merchant/Jhabvala collaborations.

SAMURAI

There are lots of ways of the samurai, depending on who is directing. Part of the fun is spotting those Western classics that rose first in the East.

Baby Cart at the River Styx 1972

Director Kenji Misumi **Cast** Tomisaburo Wakayama, Kayo Matsuo, Akiji Kobayashi 81m

This is the second film drawn from **Kazuo Koike** and **Goseki Kojima**'s *Lone Wolf and Cub* manga series. Having avenged himself on the shogun responsible for killing his wife, ronin Ogami Itto (**Tomisaburo Wakayama**) and his young son Daigoro (**Akihiro Tomikawa**) resist the female ninjas sent to dispatch them and prevent a dye-maker from betraying his secrets. The action is slick, swift and stylized. But, for all the spurting blood and swordpoint amputations, this never glorifies violence. In the US, it was edited together with its prequel, *Sword of Vengeance*, to form *Shogun Assassin* (1981).

Blind Fury 1989

Director Phillip Noyce **Cast** Rutger Hauer, Terry O'Quinn, Brandon Call 86m

Zatoichi Challenged (1967) was number 17 in the 26-strong series starring Shintarô Katsu as an itinerant blind swordsman and it took producers Tim Matheson and Daniel Gordnik seven years, three studios, two directors and eleven screenplay drafts to rework it into a vehicle for **Rutger Hauer**. As the sightless Vietnam veteran with heightened senses and a blade in his cane, Hauer protects buddy **Terry Quinn**'s son to keep dad from being blackmailed into manufacturing designer drugs. Set pieces like the cornfield pursuit are impeccably choreographed, while the gallows wit gives this cult kudos.

Chushingura 1962

Director Hiroshi Inagaki **Cast** Koshiro Matsumoto, Yuzo Kayama 206m

The tale at the heart of *Chushingura: Hana No Maki Yuki No Maki* (its full title) is a popular one in Japan. In short, when a samurai master is betrayed, his 47 ronin disciples must avenge him. It is said that to understand Japanese culture you need only read *The 47 Ronin*, which schoolchildren were expected to memorize to instil honour and pride. Five versions of the story were made between 1932 and 1962 alone: this one, in which a young lord attempts to challenge official corruption and a choice must be made between following orders and avenging a master, is the most elaborate and visually gorgeous of these, but it never loses the audience.

Ghost Dog: Way of the Samurai 1999

Director Jim Jarmusch **Cast** Forest Whitaker, John Tormey, Cliff Gorman 116m

When a Mob boss (**Tormey**) saves his life, African-American Ghost Dog (**Whitaker**) dedicates his life to him, adhering to the code of the Hagakure: the way of the samurai. He becomes a Mob hit man, but when it's decided he is expendable, he has to decide whether to follow the code or save himself. It may sound straightforward enough, but this is a **Jarmusch** movie. The Mob communicates with its killer via carrier pigeon, and Dog speaks only to a young girl and to a Haitian ice-cream man who speaks no English (Dog speaks no French, so the chat is somewhat limited). Wu Tang Clan member **RZA** provides a hip-hop soundtrack.

Lady Snowblood 1973

Director Toshiya Fujita **Cast** Meiko Kaji, Toshio Kurosawa, Masaaki Daimon 97m

Having launched the *Female Prisoner Scorpion* series, **Meiko Kaji** assumed the role of Yuki Kashima in *Blizzard from the Netherworld* and its sequel, *Love Song of Vengeance*. But while the kimono-clad Yuki is bent on avenging the villains who raped and falsely imprisoned her mother, this is as much a study of honour in a Japan newly opened to Western influence as a gore-gushing chop-sake swordfighting

Here spattered with blood, Yuki (Meiko Kaji) stands for vengeance and honour in *Lady Snowblood*, a huge influence on *Kill Bill*.

epic. Vastly superior to Quentin Tarantino's *Kill Bill* duo, which it inspired.

★ Yojimbo 1961

Director Akira Kurosawa **Cast** Toshirô Mifune, Tatsuya Nakadai, Yôko Tsukasa 110m

Even if you've seen Sergio Leone's 1964 remake *A Fistful of Dollars*, *Yojimbo* is a must-see. Loosely based on Dashiell Hammett's novel *Red Harvest* (although not acknowledged), it's the tale of a nameless samurai who arrives at a small town divided by two gangsters; the warrior decides to play one off against the other until they both fall. The star is Kurosawa regular **Mifune**, who once said: "I am proud of nothing I have done other than with him."

SATIRE

Satire is traditionally seen as the preserve of irate literary types like Jonathan Swift, but from its earliest days the silver screen has loved to poke fun at human frailty. Hollywood happily takes sly swipes at itself, while arthouse directors can use cruel humour to show everyone just how clever they are.

★ The Discreet Charm of the Bourgeoisie 1972

Director Luis Buñuel **Cast** Fernando Rey, Delphine Seyrig, Stéphane Audran 105m

Buñuel's satire is an attack on a certain way of life but also a sendup of our own need for movies that take themselves seriously. Six outwardly respectable members of the upper middle class find their attempts to have dinner together frustrated by an increasingly surreal succession of events, including inconvenient corpses and military manoeuvres. The director was 72 when he made this, probably his most internationally renowned movie, and there's a sense of him doing whatever he feels like. Very funny and, like the best Buñuel, very unsettling to boot.

Eating Raoul 1982

Director Paul Bartel **Cast** Mary Woronov, Paul Bartel, Robert Beltran 83m

Former Roger Corman protégé **Paul Bartel** persuaded his parents to sell their home to help fund his project. Shooting in just 22 days, Bartel stars alongside regular cohort **Mary Woronov** as a conservative couple, the Blands. When Mary Bland is disturbed by a swinging neighbour who mistakes her for his date, her husband comes to the rescue, killing him with a frying pan and hitting upon a beautiful plan. The Blands dream of moving out of LA to open a restaurant, so they take their victim's money and advertise for more rich swingers to kill. A brilliant black comedy guaranteed to please fans of Corman.

The Joke 1968

Director Jaromil Jires **Cast** Josef Somr, Jana Ditetova, Ludek Munzar 80m

For such an audacious soul, **Jires** shows some restraint in his screen adaptation of **Milan Kundera**'s novel. He may, though, have felt that the source was savage enough, with its tale of a student, sentenced to hard labour after a minor political joke backfires, who seeks revenge on his oppressors. No one is spared here: not Communism, Czech society, nor the hero who, after some excruciating experiences, realizes his jokey revenge has gone flat. After the Soviet tanks rolled into Prague that year, this was virtually unseen in Jires's homeland for twenty years.

King of Comedy 1983

Director Martin Scorsese Cast Robert De Niro, Jerry Lewis, Sandra Bernhardt 109m

Reeking of desperation and delusion, **Scorsese**'s satire on celebrity is nastier than *Taxi Driver*, more brutal than *Raging Bull*. De Niro was then at the top of his game – he is positively frightening, and a little sad, as Rupert Pupkin, the deluded would-be stand-up comic who teams up with stalker Sandra Bernhardt (as crazy as you'd expect) to kidnap talk show host Jerry Langford (**Lewis**, affecting and strange in a straight-man role). Cultish cameos include **Tony Randall**, 1950s neurotic extraordinaire, and **The Clash** – as "street scum".

The Player 1992

Director Robert Altman Cast Tim Robbins, Greta Scacchi, Fred Ward, Whoopi Goldberg 124m

A knowing satire of all things Hollywood, **Altman**'s movie stars **Robbins** as a studio executive who is pursued by a writer and finally, almost accidentally, takes the law into his own hands. The satire, funny as it is, is at the expense of some easy targets, but the people you really have to feel sorry for are Tim Curry, Jeff Daniels, Franco Nero and Patrick Swayze. There are an incredible 65 cameos in this movie and they are the four poor souls whose appearances ended up on the cutting-room floor.

To Be or Not to Be 1942

Director Ernst Lubitsch Cast Carole Lombard, Jack Benny, Robert Stack 99m

Though the German-born (and Jewish) **Lubitsch**'s satire on the Nazis was slated on its release as being in poor taste, it was, like Chaplin's *The Great Dictator*, made before the true horror of the Third Reich, and in particular the concentration camps, was fully known; today, its bold comedic swipes appear almost painfully daring. Following the adventures of a Polish theatre company during the Nazi Occupation, who despite their luvvie narcissism get involved with the Resistance, it's a delightful screwball satire. **Benny** has great fun as a hapless ham, while **Lombard** – as ever smart, elegant and very funny – provides a touching swansong: she was killed in a plane crash soon after filming.

To Die For 1995

Director Gus Van Sant Cast Nicole Kidman, Joaquin Phoenix, Matt Dillon 106m

The movie that made the world take notice of **Kidman** as an actor, and brought **Van Sant** mainstream attention, this is a deliciously nasty slice of arch black comedy, mixing up *femme fatale* feminism with a dash of dark misogyny. Quite apart from Kidman, who uses her cool beauty to superb effect as the murderously ambitious newsreader, **Dillon** is typically great as her doomed husband, and there are a number of smart cameos, including David Cronenberg as a Mafia hit man.

SCHOOL

Schools may be more violent these days, with students meeting up to study drugs not maths. But you still find the occasional class dominated by a teacher with the inspirational gifts of Sidney Poitier.

The Belles of St Trinian's
1954

Director Frank Launder **Cast** Alastair Sim, Joyce Grenfell, George Cole **91m**

Any US movie about a school full of wild girls who kidnap a racehorse would have been plotted to dullness with gags emphasized to death. But the writing team of **Launder** and **Gilliat**, well served by **Sim** in drag as the dotty headmistress and **Cole** as her spiv brother Flash Harry (a dry run for Arthur Daley), make this fast, painless and nearly as funny as the Ronald Searle cartoons it's based on. Surprisingly, the girls' antics are more transgressive than in the recent franchise: tiny girls with machine guns and fag-smoking behind the bike sheds being two big no-nos in the twenty-first century.

 **Blackboard Jungle**
1955

Director Richard Brooks **Cast** Glenn Ford, Sidney Poitier, Vic Morrow **101m**

This histrionic social issue movie, ripping the lid off "teenage terror in the schools", trod what is now well-worn territory, pitching an idealistic teacher against a group of sulky delinquents and throwing race issues into the mix in the form of a young **Poitier**. With a dangerous rock'n'roll soundtrack – **Bill Haley and his Comets**' "Rock Around the Clock" inspired Teddy Boys to rampage through cinemas slashing seats with switchblades, apparently – and middle-aged actors jitterbugging in bobby sox and bomber jackets, this one will surely never date.

Blackboards 2000

Director Samira Makhmalbaf **Cast** Saïd Mohamadi, Bahman Ghobadi, Behnaz Jafari **85m**

In Iranian Kurdistan a group of itinerant teachers look for pupils to instruct in exchange for food. As far from a Hollywood school movie as you can get, this isn't for those who worry about plot or like an upbeat message, but it has breathtaking moments and a painfully real sense of hardship.

Carrie 1976

Director Brian de Palma **Cast** Sissy Spacek, Piper Laurie 98m

The high-school-as-nightmare movie to top them all (set, with a not-so-sly nod to Hitchcock's *Psycho*, in a school called Bates High), climaxing with the Prom night from Hell (and we're not talking about the bow ties and polyester ruffles). The first adaptation of a **Stephen King** novel to grace the big screen, it heralded an era of phenomenal movie success for the author; weirdly enough the Broadway musical spin-off won fewer accolades, playing for just five nights before closing.

Election 1999

Director Alexander Payne **Cast** Reese Witherspoon, Matthew Broderick 103m

Witherspoon camps it up as Tracy Flick, the all-American goody two-shoes whose lust for power – in the form of a high-school election – will brook no opposition. A downbeat satire on both high-school movies and electoral politics, it's often remembered for Witherspoon's performance, though she's given a run for her money by **Broderick** – Ferris Bueller all grown up, bitter and gone to seed.

Elephant 2003

Director Gus Van Sant **Cast** Alex Frost, Eric Deulen, John Robinson 85m

Variety's summary – "pointless at best and irresponsible at worst" – is harsh but not entirely unfounded. Little happens at this school until the thrill-less, Columbine-style massacre at the end, but by this time you've got to know the characters, and the documentary style makes it all the more disturbing.

Rock 'n' Roll High School 1979

Director Allan Arkush **Cast** P.J. Soles, Vincent Van Patten, Clint Howard, The Ramones 93m

In this deeply silly, low-budget update of a 1950s teen movie, **Soles** tries to liberate her school, attend a **Ramones** concert and sell her song to them. Adults are chucked out of windows – but only when it's essential to the plot. And there's a nice running gag involving a constantly evolving photo of coach Lombardi. Just thank the gods that **Arkush** persuaded executive producer Roger Corman not to make this a disco movie. A sequel, *Rock'n'Roll High School Forever* is cherished only by those who haven't seen this.

Tom Brown's Schooldays 1951

Director Gordon Parry **Cast** John Howard Davies, Robert Newton, Hermione Baddeley 96m

Nowhere is the young hero vs school bully conflict better described than in the novel on which this is based. This UK film (with a young **Max Bygraves**) is easier on the irony than the 1940 Freddie Bartholomew version. **Davies**, who also played Oliver Twist, graduated from playing urchins to direct *Monty Python's Flying Circus* in 1969.

SCI-FI

Tales of the future – or the future as it was viewed at the time – offer pertinent lessons about the world we live in now (or lived in then). No other genre explores strange new worlds, let alone technology that doesn't yet exist, quite as entertainingly as science fiction.

⭐ Blade Runner 1982

Director Ridley Scott **Cast** Harrison Ford, Rutger Hauer, Sean Young 112m

Regarded as a failure on release, Scott's version of **Philip K. Dick**'s moral tale *Do Androids Dream of Electric Sheep?* became a cult classic, especially once the director's cut was released. Visually stunning, it has **Ford** as a weary LA cop in 2019 hunting down human replicants, and draws on *film noir* (the *femme fatale*, the alienated hero), Lang's *Metropolis* and Westerns like *High Noon* yet remains utterly, compellingly, unique.

The Boy from Mercury 1996

Director Martin Duffy **Cast** James Hickey, Tom Courtenay, Rita Tushingham 87m

Duffy's debut feature, an unjustly neglected gem, is a semi-autobiographical tale in which **Hickey** is thoroughly endearing as the son who compensates for the death of his dad by making Flash Gordon his surrogate father. Duffy pays entertaining homage to kitchen sink drama and comic-book sci-fi. **Courtenay** and **Tushingham** are superb as uncle and mother, enjoying their first shared screen time since *Dr Zhivago*.

Dark Star 1974

Director John Carpenter **Cast** Brian Narelle, Cal Kuniholm 83m

Billed as a "cosmic comedy", *Dark Star* was **Carpenter**'s feature-length debut, co-written by *Alien*'s **Dan O'Bannon**. The daft tale of stoner dude astronauts on a twenty-year mission to destroy unstable planets is surreal stuff (they have to convince a talking bomb not to explode while still attached to their ship), and was originally made for $5000, though the crew were later given $60,000 to finish the film off for cinema release.

The Day the Earth Caught Fire 1961

Director Val Guest **Cast** Edward Judd, Janet Munro, Leo McKern, Michael Goodliffe 99m

Given a cracking premise – journalist (**Judd**) discovers the Earth has been knocked off its axis by recent nuclear explosions and is plummeting towards the sun – and a tight budget, **Guest** creates a minor classic that has aged less than his better-known *The Quatermass Experiment* (1955). Among the many charms of this apocalyptic tale are the jibes at the media ("World Tips Over" reads one scary headline) and the surprisingly sensual scenes between Judd and **Munro**'s telephone operator.

Duck Dodgers in the 24½th Century 1953

Director Chuck Jones **Cast** Mel Blanc 7m

Marvellous *Merrie Melodies* cartoon in which Daffy Duck (as Duck Dodgers) battles Marvin the Martian for the rare element illudium phosdex (aka "the shaving cream atom") in a contest which finally – some see this as an allusion to the futility of the arms race – destroys the planet they fight over.

The Face of Another 1966

Director Hiroshi Teshigahara **Cast** Tatsuya Nakadai, Mikijiro Hira, Machiko Kiyo 122m

Teshigahara's breakthrough movie explores the meaning of identity through the story of a reclusive burn victim (**Nakadai**) who acquires a new face through the work of a pioneering doctor (**Hira**). Nakadai uses the face in secret to see if people will react to him differently, even setting out to seduce his wife (**Kiyo**). This unsettling adaptation

of **Kobo Abe**'s novel is peppered with startling images – horrific masks, flesh being strained through a pasta maker and a woman, pretty in profile, who turns out to have charred cheeks – that allude to the horror of Hiroshima.

The Fifth Element 1997

Director Luc Besson **Cast** Bruce Willis, Milla Jovovich, Gary Oldman 126m

Perhaps the most audacious element of **Besson**'s science fantasy is his suggestion that, in the twenty-third century, a cynical cab driver (**Willis**) will save the world. Mind you, he is distracted by **Milla Jovovich**, who literally falls into his lap and turns out to be the lovely key to saving the planet. Tipping his hat to *Metropolis* and *Blade Runner*, Besson creates a lavish, yet murky world, full of eccentric characters and, through nifty editing and sly humour, ensures time never drags.

Island of Lost Souls 1932

Director Erle C. Kenton **Cast** Charles Laughton, Kathleen Burke, Bela Lugosi, Richard Arlen 72m

Almost eighty years since it was made, this version of H.G. Wells' *The Island of Dr Moreau* can still startle, with its scary animal-faced men and bestial sub-plot. **Laughton**'s Dr Moreau is one of cinema's greatest mad scientists, all the more menacing as his character's madness is revealed through casually inappropriate behaviour. The bestiality stuff upset Wells who thoroughly disliked the film. Shame, because it is one of the best adaptations of his work.

Primer (2004, 77m)

We challenge any first-time viewer to decipher *Primer*'s plot without resorting to the rewind button. But the thrill of this masterfully tuned time-travel ride is well worth the extra brain effort. And an extra bonus: we're pretty sure that watching *Primer* occasionally will actually reduce your chances of early onset Alzheimers. *Primer* – like Gus Van Sant's *Mala Noche*, or Thomas Vinterberg's *Celebration* – is one of those truly rare microbudget indie films that just could not have been any better with more money, more resources or better equipment. It's a hand-made miracle of a film, with an intricate, mind-bending puzzle of a plot, and an atmosphere so incredibly dry and yet so fresh and genuine that you feel like you're spying on your real-life geeky college dorm mates as their lives spin into a dark and bottomless vortex.

Scott McGehee and David Siegel *(co-directors of* Suture, The Deep End, Bee Season, Uncertainty*; for a fuller biography, see p.230).*

Logan's Run 1970

Director Michael Anderson **Cast** Michael York, Richard Jordan, Jenny Agutter **118m**

Soon to be remade, this classic 1970s kitsch sci-fi is set in a world where people are ritually sacrificed when they get to thirty. **York** is paid to hunt down anyone who escapes this fate but is persuaded otherwise by **Agutter**'s beauty and, on the run, they bump into doddery old **Peter Ustinov**. Epic, extravagant, gripping and thoroughly daft.

Metropolis 1926

Director Fritz Lang **Cast** Alfred Abel, Gustav Frohlich **153m**

The basic plot – love across the caste barriers in a futuristic city – makes no real sense but that doesn't stop **Lang**'s futuristic meisterwork casting its spell. Many of the themes we now regard as clichés – the hellish vision of the city of the future, the robot who looks like a human being – were coined by Lang, who took a year and a half to make this, driving his cast – especially the extras – with a frenzied, ruthless determination worthy of the movie's villain, Rotwang. Sci-fi as a movie genre starts here.

Panic in Year Zero 1962

Director Ray Milland **Cast** Ray Milland, Jean Hagen, Frankie Avalon **95m**

LA gets it again, courtesy of a Russian nuclear device, while **Milland**'s family are fishing. They head for a remote cave but find the way blocked by anarchy, highways turned into car parks, and fiends who want to rape Milland's daughter. This was Milland's only film as a director and it's personal. Dystopia seldom seemed so ugly.

The Phantom Empire 1935

Directors Otto Brower, B. Reeves Eason **Cast** Gene Autry, Dorothy Christy 245m

Not to be confused with the 1986 film of the same name – a witless horror about a cave creature who owns a pile of uncut diamonds – this is a twelve-episode serial starring singing cowboy **Gene Autry**, who finds a civilization at the bottom of a mine. Oscillating between his Radio Ranch and Murania, Autry can't stop the Muranians being killed by a death ray, but consoles us by singing "Silver-Haired Daddy of Mine". Why aren't there more sci-fi/Western musical serials?

Pi 1998

Director Darren Aronofsky **Cast** Sean Gullette, Mark Margolis 84m

Aronofsky's complex, dark, psychological movie focuses on a paranoid mathematician (**Gullette**) whose quest for the 216-digit number that will reveal the true name of God leaves him studying chaos theory obsessively and, most of the time, with only a computer for company. An audacious debut that blends sci-fi, Poe and Kafka to create something utterly original.

 Plan 9 from Outer Space 1956

Director Ed Wood **Cast** Gregory Walcott, Bela Lugosi, Mona McKinnon 79m

Widely regarded as the worst movie ever made. The plot is hilarious (aliens whose first eight plans have failed to get mankind's attention try re-animating a few corpses) and the effects are risible (hub caps as UFOs). It's the stories of how **Wood** got it made that make this movie so fascinating. Funding from the local Baptist church led to cast and crew being baptized; Wood mixed footage from a film he had begun with Lugosi (who died before he could appear in this) with scenes played by a much taller man disguising his face with a cape; and cardboard gravestones wobble in the wind.

Planet of the Apes 1967

Director Franklin J. Schaffner **Cast** Charlton Heston, Roddy McDowall 112m

The first of three epic movies in which **Heston** stars as the last voice of reason – he performs the same function in *The Omega Man* and *Soylent Green* – is probably the greatest, an almost perfect sci-fi movie that has spawned four so-so sequels, a TV series, a mediocre remake and a spoof musical on *The Simpsons*. Although Heston's officially the star, **McDowall** never escaped the shadow of his superb, sarcastic simian Cornelius. In breaks in filming, the apes only hung out with members of the same species. Make of that what you will.

Soylent Green 1973

Director Richard Fleischer **Cast** Charlton Heston, Edward G. Robinson 97m

Based on Harry Harrison's novel *Make*

Room! Make Room!, **Fleischer**'s grimly plausible dystopia envisions a world where real food is so scarce people queue for a ration of manufactured nourishment (soylent green), the suicide trade is booming and only a few intellectuals – including **Edward G. Robinson**, a friend of **Heston**'s cop – read books. Heston's horror when he discovers the secret of this pseudo-food leads to one of the most memorable images in sci-fi as he weeps over a lost world.

Stalker 1979

Director Andrey Tarkovsky **Cast** Alexander Kaidanovsky, Anatoli Solonitsyn 161m

The premise is deceptively simple – the stalker leads a writer and a professor across a forbidden territory inside a police state to a room where their innermost desires will be laid bare – but out of this, as is his wont, **Tarkovsky** weaves something unfathomable, unsettling and unforgettable, managing to allude to Joseph Conrad, Jean Cocteau's *Orphée*, Westerns and, seven years before it happened, Chernobyl.

Star Trek 2009

Director J.J. Abrams **Cast** Chris Pine, Zachary Quinto, Leonard Nimoy, Eric Bana 127m

Abrams steers this movie with such finesse he could replace Chekov as navigator of the USS *Enterprise*. Aided by a superb cast, he has squared the circle by satisfying most diehard Trekkers and

Sex and sci-fi

In the future, sci-fi movies would have you believe, two things are a given: we all end up wearing the same clothes (usually a one-piece silver number) and the sex is crap.

Jane Fonda in **Barbarella** (see p.326) is the glorious exception to this rule. But her delight isn't shared by too many other inhabitants of the celluloid future. Robert Duvall's experience in **THX 1138** is more typical. After deciding that making love to his wife is more entertaining than watching androids being beaten, he is dragged away by two chrome cops, found guilty of "malicious sexual perversion" and has a tag stapled into his ear. As inducements to chastity go, this is much more effective than the belt maidens wore in the Middle Ages. In Alfonso Cuarón's **Children of Men** (see p.22), humanity has been infertile for eighteen years without, it would seem, stimulating the characters' sex lives.

But then again, given the standard of pun in **Flesh Gordon** (1974), the erotic spoof of the comic-strip hero, we should probably be profoundly grateful. Calling a character Dr Flexi Jerkoff isn't cheap, it's just rubbish. Even here Gordon's job is to stop humanity being perverted by the sex ray aimed at Earth by Emperor Wang, the evil ruler of the planet Porno. The motto for Gordon and many other sci-fi characters might just be, "No sex please we're in the future."

succeeding as a movie in its own right. This prequel effectively reboots the *Star Trek* saga even if the story doesn't pose the kind of moral challenges Kirk and his crew routinely faced on TV.

The Tenth Victim 1965

Director Elio Petri **Cast** Marcello Mastroianni, Ursula Andress 92m

Italian cinema is not famed for its sci-fi but **Petri**'s frenetic, *Mad*-magazine take on twenty-first-century life – in which war has been replaced by a game called The Big Hunt – makes intriguing use of **Andress** and **Mastroianni** as veteran contestants. Drawn to kill Mastroianni, Andress is attracted to him, but the rules of the game – and the demands of her corporate sponsors – are clear. Petri's stylish, ahead-of-its-time movie touches on all kind of themes with such speed and lightness it is impossible to get bored.

> **❝** Why control births when you can increase death? **❞**
> **Poster in The Tenth Victim**

THX 1138 1971

Director George Lucas **Cast** Robert Duvall, Maggie McOrmie, Donald Pleasence 95m

Lucas's first quixotic tribute to *Buck Rogers* has a simple story – citizen THX 1138 (**Duvall**) takes on the centralized computer system after he has been punished for not taking his drugs and having the nerve to make love – but the visual imagination on display is so unusual it is, at times,

as unsettling as parts of *2001*. In the sterile, featureless white of Lucas's twenty-fifth century, the characters' words are half-audible and half-forgotten and a computer has the final word: "Buy and be happy".

 ## 2001: A Space Odyssey 1968

Director Stanley Kubrick **Cast** Keir Dullea, Gary Lockwood 141m

It's possible that **Kubrick**'s space opera can only be understood if you're on some mind-altering substance. Kubrick would have preferred it if you just puzzled over his most famous movie, which stayed true to the intent of **Arthur C. Clarke**, who said that if you understood his story, he had failed. Such wilful obscurity doesn't prevent this from being the sci-fi movie against which all others are measured, thanks to Kubrick's obsessive attention to detail, audacious juxtapositions (the docking of the spaceship to the tune of *The Blue Danube*) and the sentient computer HAL.

Zardoz 1974

Director John Boorman **Cast** Sean Connery, Charlotte Rampling, Sarah Kestelman 105m

The future, as Roger Ebert noted, seems to be ruled by stoned set decorators in **Boorman**'s self-indulgent, yet interesting apocalyptic epic. **Connery**, a member of the future's warrior class, is overpowered mentally by **Rampling** and **Kestelman** and comes to learn the nature of the Vortex. Barmy, visually enchanting and strangely likeable nonsense.

SCREWBALL

There can be as many pitfalls as pratfalls when it comes to making a zany comedy. Many have tried, and most have failed, to match the sizzling chemistry achieved by Cary Grant and all number of fast-talking dames in the 1930s. When it comes to screwball, it's a simple fact – they just don't make 'em like they used to.

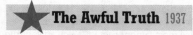
The Awful Truth 1937

Director Leo McCarey **Cast** Irene Dunne, Cary Grant 91m

An Oscar winner for **McCarey**'s smart direction, this warm and playful screwball classic is sublime in its delightful stars, inspired visual gags and brilliant timing. Perfect, urbane couple **Dunne** and **Grant** suspect each other of infidelity. They divorce and embark on new relationships, but their attempts to foil each other's forthcoming nuptials rekindle the fire. Sophisticated, inventive and wildly funny, it established many of the enduring rules of rom-com.

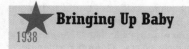
Bringing Up Baby
1938

Director Howard Hawks **Cast** Cary Grant, Katharine Hepburn 102m

This comedic *tour de force* was loosely based on a newspaper story about **Hepburn**'s affair with John Ford during the

making of *Mary of Scotland*. It bombed on release (leading to **Hawks** getting fired from his next production and Hepburn having to buy out her contract) but it has the essentials of the genre: pratfalls, implausible situations, contrary animals, confusion… Hepburn plays a madcap heiress with a pet leopard called Baby, who sets her sights on bumbling paleontologist **Grant**. The two leads are glorious, but Grant hated cats so Hepburn had to do most of the scenes with Baby.

> " When a man is wrestling a leopard in the middle of a pond, he's in no position to run. "
> **David Huxley, Bringing Up Baby**

His Girl Friday 1940

Director Howard Hawks **Cast** Cary Grant, Rosalind Russell, Ralph Bellamy 92m

The story of newspaper editor Walter Burns' attempts to thwart the marriage plans of his star reporter, Hildy Johnson, had already been a hit Broadway play and a movie (*The Front Page*, 1931). But Hawks, nothing if not ambitious, saw no reason why he couldn't create the ultimate retelling. Grant and Russell throw **Charles Lederer**'s sharp lines at one another at a pace of 240 words per minute (normally we talk at 90 per minute). This is one of the greatest comedies of all time, featuring every technique from slapstick to wordplay and was the first movie to feature characters talking over one another, a key facet of the screwball genre.

Intolerable Cruelty 2003

Director Joel Coen Cast George Clooney, Catherine Zeta Jones, Billy Bob Thornton 100m

Not one of the **Coens**' most fashionable movies, but one of their most enjoyable, an honest homage to screwball with their trademark skewed sensibility. Reeling along with schemes, double dealings and battle-of-the-sexes banter, it maintains, nonetheless, that cool Coen detachment – **Clooney**, however, is clearly having a ball pretending to be Cary Grant, and while **Zeta Jones** is no Hepburn, she gives one of her more appealing performances as the slinky, smart-talking gold-digger.

It Happened One Night
1934

Director Frank Capra Cast Claudette Colbert, Clark Gable 105m

This early screwball broke records by winning best picture, director, actor, actress and adapted screenplay Oscars. **Colbert** is likeably feisty as spoiled heiress Ellie, on the run from a father who won't approve her marriage, while **Gable** is all smoulder and wry cocked eyebrows as hardbitten newshound Peter. A chalk-and-cheese road trip through Depression-era America, this crackles with sexual chemistry (the

Clark Gable about to have a profound influence not just on Claudette Colbert but on the entire US male underwear market in *It Happened One Night*.

scene in which Gable strips off his shirt to reveal a bare chest was single-handedly blamed for the demise of vests in the USA) and remains as fresh today as when it was made.

The Lady Eve 1941

Director Preston Sturges **Cast** Barbara Stanwyck, Henry Fonda, Charles Coburn 97m

In this screwball classic, **Sturges**'s third film as director, **Stanwyck** perfects her tough-sexy shtick as the fast-talking con artiste who sets her sights on innocent Charles "Hopsy" Pike (nice-guy **Fonda**, channelling Cary Grant in *Bringing Up Baby*). In cahoots with her dad (the brilliant **Charles Coburn**) she takes him at cards on a luxury liner before the inevitable romantic complications – and a host of mistaken identities – ensue.

My Man Godfrey 1936

Director Gregory La Cava **Cast** William Powell, Carole Lombard 92m

Carole Lombard is better known these days as Mrs Clark Gable but, in her all-too-brief heyday, she was one of Hollywood's funniest comediennes. Here she shines as the dizzy socialite who hires the vagrant **Powell** as a butler for her idle rich family. The dialogue sparkles like champagne, and even the simplest gags work beautifully. When Lombard asks the tramp, would he like to earn five dollars, he replies: "Well, I don't mean to seem inquisitive, but what would I have to do for it?"

What's Up, Doc? 1972

Director Peter Bogdanovich **Cast** Ryan O'Neal, Barbra Streisand, Madeleine Kahn 94m

Bogdanovich's homage to screwball comedy in general – and to *Bringing Up Baby* in particular – is as funny a comedy as Hollywood has produced in the last forty years. This time the absent-minded male is a musicologist (**O'Neal**) desperate for an academic grant. He soon becomes ensnared in the schemes of an eccentric college drop-out (**Streisand**). Streisand, here in her pre-prima donna days, is on top form and displays a genuine gift for comedy. Bogdanovich throws in mistaken luggage, a jewel theft and spies, not to mention a car chase across San Francisco that pokes fun at *Bullitt*.

Women on the Verge of a Nervous Breakdown 1988

Director Pedro Almodóvar **Cast** Carmen Maura, Antonio Banderas 89m

Modern screwball Spanish-style in this crazy comedy about a philandering husband, his wife, his ex-lover and his new lover. **Almodóvar** catches the spirit of sexual unbuttoning in post-Franco Spain, and the frantic humour comes across in buckets, the brightly coloured sets and OTT fashions adding to a sense of unreality. **Antonio Banderas** is almost unrecognizable, but this set him on the road to stardom.

SERIAL KILLERS

Most portrayals of serial killers, even the less sensational ones, end up blaming the mother. Or, in Buñuel's case, a music box.

Coup de torchon 1981

Director Bertrand Tavernier **Cast** Philippe Noiret, Isabelle Huppert 128m

Tavernier's sardonic adaptation of **Jim Thompson**'s novel *Pop* transposes the action from Texas to West Africa but faithfully captures the spirit of its source. **Noiret** is the ineffectual constable who uses his position to murder everyone who has ever mocked him. Noiret's goofiness is the perfect disguise for a heartless killer going off the deep end. Though some found this film too detached, Tavernier makes some good points about the collapse of morality and the restlessness of the colonial life in a film that feels, at times, like an existential parable.

The Criminal Life of Archibaldo de la Cruz 1955

Director Luis Buñuel **Cast** Ernesto Alonso, Miroslava Stern 91m

Everyone labours under some misapprehensions in life but, as a child, Archibaldo (**Alonso**) comes to believe that his music box has killed his governess. Finding the governess's corpse sexually stimulating, he then embarks on a series of sexual adventures which all lead to death until he finds salvation with a woman (**Stern**) who reminds him of Joan of Arc in flames.

★ Deep Crimson 1996

Director Arturo Ripstein **Cast** Regina Orozco, Daniel Giménez Cacho 115m

Arturo Ripstein began his career as an assistant to Luis Buñuel, and is now Mexico's most acclaimed director. Set in that country in the 1940s, this movie retells the story of the infamous Lonely Hearts Killers, a grotesque couple who preyed on lonely, affluent widows. In glossier serial thrillers, you may develop a somewhat uncomfortable attachment to the killer, but neither obese nurse Coral (**Orozco**) nor her lover Nicholas (**Cacho**) display any redeeming qualities – Coral has abandoned her children in pursuit of gigolo/con-man Nicholas. Although often compared to Bonnie and Clyde, these killers are never romanticized.

Hangover Square 1945

Director John Brahm **Cast** Laird Cregar, Linda Darnell, George Sanders 78m

There's much to like here: **Cregar**'s chilling turn as a composer who becomes a homicidal maniac when he blacks out, the way that fire scenes punctuate each murder and a fantastic, atmospheric score by **Bernard Herrmann**. Cregar was so keen to make his psycho romantically neurotic, he took amphetamines on a crash diet, lost a hundred pounds and effectively died from the strain at the age of 28.

Henry: Portrait of a Serial Killer 1986

Director John McNaughton **Cast** Michael Rooker, Tracy Arnold, Tom Towles 83m

Loosely based on the crimes of Henry Lee Lucas, whose 1985 death sentence was later reduced to life imprisonment by the Texas governor, one George W. Bush. Set in a grim, working-class Chicago, this takes us through one graphic killing after another. Although the real Henry was caught, here he remains free, as the movie focuses on a disturbingly realistic examination of killing. The use of unknown actors, coupled with debut director **McNaughton**'s gritty visual approach, leaves the viewer feeling like a voyeur at times. Some scenes proved too much even for the actors, with one actress going into shock after her scene as a victim.

Manhunter 1986

Director Michael Mann **Cast** Brian Cox, William Petersen, Joan Allen, Kim Greist 120m

Although Anthony Hopkins conquered the box office as Thomas Harris's serial killer Hannibal Lecter, many believe that **Cox**'s Lektor (as it is spelt in this movie) is the more convincing psycho. Not as obviously demonic as Hopkins', but more mysterious, ambiguous and credible. **Mann**'s thriller in which a psycho called the Tooth Fairy (**Tom Noonan**) kills families at random is cool, hypnotic and implicates us in its exploitative voyeurism. All it lacks is a strong male lead. With

Inspired by

When **Brian Cox** played serial killer Hannibal he used a fairly obvious source: Scottish serial killer Peter Manuel who, Cox said, had no sense of right or wrong. His successor in the role, **Anthony Hopkins**, modelled his character on magician Tommy Cooper, while drawing vocally on Truman Capote and Katharine Hepburn. **Jack Nicholson** must have been a bit bemused when reviewers suggested he had gone OTT as crazed writer Jack Torrance in *The Shining*: he had based his portrayal partially on Charles Manson.

Brian Cox as Hannibal Lektor (sic), in *Manhunter*, the most convincing version of Thomas Harris's serial killer to appear on film.

Pacino as the FBI agent, this might have made a much bigger smash.

Targets 1968

Director Peter Bogdanovich **Cast** Tim O'Kelly, Boris Karloff 90m

After killing his wife and mother, and unwisely staging a shoot-out atop an oil refinery, **Tim O'Kelly**'s disturbed Vietnam vet flees to a drive-in-movie show where **Boris Karloff** – hardly cast against type as an ageing movie actor making a last promotional appearance – confronts him. In part, it's a clash of different generations of monsters playing by different rules. But it's also **Bogdanovich**'s entertaining homage to his favourite movies from *White Heat* to *The Criminal Code*.

The Young Poisoners Handbook 1995

Director Benjamin Ross **Cast** Hugh O'Conor, Anthony Sher, Ruth Sheen, Roger Lloyd Pack, Charlotte Coleman 105m

Parents are usually relieved when their teenage sons are clear about their goals in life, but Graham (**O'Conor**) would like nothing more than to be the best poisoner in the world. And, in this sick, wicked and brilliant satire – inspired by a real-life case – he pretty much achieves his aim, despite the inconvenience of a prison sentence.

Zodiac 2007

Director David Fincher **Cast** Jake Gyllenhaal, Mark Ruffalo, Robert Downey Jr 157m

Cinemagoers who expected *Eight*, from the director who gave us *Se7en*, were sorely disappointed. But there's much to admire in this intriguing, meandering, exploration of the notorious and unsolved Zodiac killings that occurred in San Francisco in the 1960s and 1970s. Some found the puzzle's lack of resolution unsatisfying, but as **Fincher** draws us into this legendary case, his meticulous character study becomes increasingly suspenseful.

SEXPLOITA-TION

Sexual chemistry sells movies. But its elements can change and each moviemaker has their own set. In 1932 Clark Gable sparked an erotic charge in audiences by telling Jean Harlow to take his boots off. Such innocent times.

★ Barbarella 1968

Director Roger Vadim **Cast** Jane Fonda, John Phillip Law, Anita Pallenberg 98m

According to *Life* magazine, **Vadim** got the idea for this when he saw his wife walking topless around the villa. This, he decided, was something the world should see. Titillation starts with the opening credits and **Fonda**'s famous strip. Somewhere in here is a devastating 1960s satire written by **Terry Southern**. Allegedly. It's a lot of fun even if Vadim couldn't direct to save his life.

Extase 1932

Director Gustav Machaty **Cast** Hedy Lamarr, Aribert Mog 81m

Not the first film to show an actress naked onscreen – Audrey Munson starred in the buff in the 1915 silent *Inspiration* – but arguably the first in which the sex act is depicted. At the crucial moment, **Lamarr**'s passion is inspired by the pin the director had just stuck in her backside.

The Glamorous Life of Sachiko Hanai 2003

Director Mitsuru Meike **Cast** Emi Kuroda, Yukijiro Hotaru, Takeshi Ito 90m

Most of Japan's softcore pink or *eiga* films are best appreciated for their weird titles when rendered in English, with monikers such as *Best Friend's Wife: The Black Panties of a Secret Rendezvous*. Something does get lost in translation. *Sachiko Hanai* started life as *Horny Home Tutor: Teacher's Love Juice* before it was recast and re-released as an off-the-scale zany apocalyptic satire in which an escort gains hyper-intelligence and a cloned copy of George Bush's finger that has the potential to unleash a nuclear holocaust. Then there's a lot of serious sex and serious philosophy too. We may not see its like again.

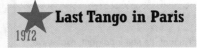

Last Tango in Paris
1972

Director Bernardo Bertolucci **Cast** Marlon Brando, Maria Schneider 129m

As **Brando**'s dresser noted one day: "Something's going on here: he's taking this seriously." He displays intensity and depth, although this may be down to the fact that, so chaotic was this film, he was not reading his lines from cue cards. The sex seems more incidental today, though it might not had **Bertolucci** kept to his plan to show intercourse (Brando persuaded him not to). Whatever else, this is a star vehicle for Brando, playing a man who seeks to obliterate his wife's suicide with an affair with a young Parisienne. The film was perfectly calibrated to trigger outraged horror and exaggerated delight at its taboo-busting potency. It did. Both leads later complained of feeling violated.

9 Songs 2004

Director Michael Winterbottom **Cast** Margot Stilley, Kieran O'Brien 69m

Lisa (**Stilley**), an American student in London for a year, begins an intense sexual relationship with Matt (**O'Brien**) after meeting him at a Black Rebel Motorcycle Club gig. **Winterbottom** shadows the couple, alternating full-on sex scenes with concerts by the likes of Franz Ferdinand and the Dandy Warhols. In a classically deadpan arthouse way, the film worked up a frenzy of interest in its explicit content in the name of art (note the running time), whilst delivering enigma, very little plot and a variable

mood poem that evokes an autumnal London. At least it proved English directors do do sex, though the inspiration was apparently the French novel *Platform* by Michel Houellebecq.

The Outlaw 1943

Director Howard Hughes **Cast** Jane Russell, Thomas Mitchell, Jack Buetel 116m

Jane Russell's breasts are really incidental to this retelling of the Billy the Kid saga – except to billionaire director-producer **Hughes**. He had seen a photo of Russell when she was a chiropodist's assistant and, being an engineer, designed a special cantilever bra for her. But Russell refused to wear it – and to become Hughes's mistress. Still, this did for her cleavage what *The Seven Year Itch* did for Marilyn Monroe's legs.

Pretty Baby 1978

Director Louis Malle **Cast** Keith Carradine, Susan Sarandon, Brooke Shields 110m

The controversy about child model **Shields** playing a twelve-year-old prostitute in a New Orleans brothel circa 1917 is arguably the most interesting thing about **Malle**'s first American movie. Beautifully shot by Bergman favourite **Sven Nykvist**, its calculated eroticism and provocative set piece – the auctioning of young Violet's virginity – serve a story of her acquisition as "wife" by sad sack photographer **Carradine**, a relationship of the innocent and the hopelessly entranced artist that is soooo languid and downbeat.

Satyricon (1969, 128m)

❝ The general verdict on late-period Fellini is that it's self-indulgent, excessive, and just not very good. This was pretty much my response when I first saw *Satyricon*. At the time, I had recently discovered and fallen in love with the man's greatest hits – *La strada*, *The Nights of Cabiria*, *La dolce vita*, *8½* – but *Satyricon* seemed like an entirely different Fellini.

Fifteen years later, I decided to give it a second look. I could still see all the reasons I hadn't liked it, and why it's usually maligned: the lack of any real story per se, the not-so-good performances, an absence of emotional connection to any character. But this time, I was struck by the beauty of its excess: not only is every image an exquisite dream-like fresco, but Fellini's commitment to his self-indulgent choices is so unapologetic that it moved me. Story, character, accessibility? Ha! This was a unique personal vision, a phantasmagoria straight from the man's head! … and much more captivating than anything else I had seen in a long time.

At home, still stirred by the film, I wrote in a journal: 'Even bad Fellini is better than most films.' ❞

Louis Pepe
Co-director with Keith Fulton of Lost in La Mancha *and* Brothers of the Head*; see p.224 for a biography.*

Red Dust 1932

Director Victor Fleming **Cast** Clark Gable, Jean Harlow 83m

The old gag about the "t" in **Harlow** being silent works because she looked like a sex goddess who enjoyed sex. The scandal that almost shut down this movie and could have killed her career (her husband mysteriously committed suicide) added to that aura. This tale of lust and love triangles on a Malaysian plantation broke many rules about the presentation of adultery onscreen.

Shortbus 2006

Director John Cameron Mitchell **Cast** Sook-Yin Lee, Raphael Barker 101m

Director **Mitchell** created a cult sensation with transsexual rock road movie *Hedwig and the Angry Inch* and here blazes another brave trail with a comedy-drama that tells the tales of a handful of dissatisfied New Yorkers gravitating around a hedonistic sex club. Billed as a noughties return to Swinging Sixties-style sexuality, the film's most notorious money shot (of several) was a widely trailed DIY blow job. One of the most explicit works to be released in cinemas, it is also a perceptive look at physical intimacy, though the sex therapist searching for an orgasm story-line gestures more to porn than Pasolini.

SHORTS

Who says a film has to be an hour and a half long? One of the greatest films, *Un chien andalou*, lasts for 16 minutes, whereas *Raise the Titanic* (at 115 minutes) seemed to take longer than it would have done to drain the Atlantic.

The Case of the Mukkinese Battle Horn
1956

Director Joseph Sterling **Cast** Spike Milligan, Dick Emery, Peter Sellers **29m**

This historic curio was finally released as a support feature in the early 1970s. When it was made, **Milligan** and **Sellers** were two-thirds of the Goons and this is a more extravagant version of that brand of humour. As Superintendent Quilt of the Yard, Sellers (as ever) is in a semi-autonomous comic republic of his own. Milligan does his usual shtick, while laying out a comic conspiracy involving an international ring of Mukkinese battle horn smugglers.

The Cat Concerto 1946

Directors Joseph Barbera, William Hanna **8m**

The similarities between this Tom and Jerry classic – the winner of the 1947 Oscar for best short – and Bugs Bunny's *Rhapsody Rabbit* may not be entirely co-incidental. Bugs's studio, Warner Bros, used the same processing firm as MGM and the lab mistakenly sent *Rhapsody Rabbit* back to MGM rather than Warners. MGM took so long to return the film that Warners believed they had plagiarized it in *The Cat Concerto*. MGM then accused Bugs director **Fritz Freeling** of overhearing ideas for *The Cat Concerto* and being guilty of plagiarism himself. Such legal wrangling can't take away the genius of the feuding twosome at their best, with piano-playing Tom never missing a beat during a concert performance, despite Jerry's mischievous efforts.

The Day of the Fight 1951

Director Stanley Kubrick **Cast** Douglas Edwards **16m**

It cost the young **Kubrick** $3900 to make this film, based on his own photoshoot of a boxing match for *Look* magazine. A three-part story focusing on the boxer Walter Cartier, it's rarely seen now. This is a shame because it has a distinctly noirish tone and there are some lovely moments, particularly the scene where the boxer confronts his face in the mirror before the fight. Kubrick made a $100 profit on the movie, selling it to RKO, which incorporated it into a triptych called *This Is America*. A cracking debut.

Bouche-Villeneuve; he chose "Marker" after the Magic Marker pens.

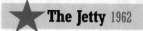 ## The Jetty 1962

Director Chris Marker **Cast** Jean Négroni, Hélène Chatelain, Davos Hanich 28m

It would take you longer to read the synopsis of this 28-minute French short than to watch it. *Twelve Monkeys* buffs will find it awfully familiar: it is the filmmaker's vision of a post-nuclear Earth where the survivors have to travel back in time to find food. The film, **Marker**'s only foray into fiction, is almost completely made up of still frames (one scene contains some movement) but the effect is startling. Marker's real name is Christian

The Play House 1921

Directors Buster Keaton, Eddie Cline **Cast** Buster Keaton, Edward F. Cline 22m

With **Buster Keaton** taking upwards of 25 roles, this homage to Georges Méliès's *L'homme-orchestre* (1900) is also a masterclass in silent technique. Cameraman **Elgin Lessley** used a nine-windowed shutter to shoot the minstrel show sequence, meticulously handcranking and winding back the celluloid to capture Keaton playing each performer with metronomic precision. One to savour.

In the Dark (2004, 40m)

❝ An elderly man fumbles around a room, cramped and a little chaotic. The view from the window tells us we are in a tower block, one of many in a vast zone of housing. As the film unfolds we discover that the man is blind. He is searching for some string and then becomes absorbed in knotting and plaiting it. A radiant white cat appears and seems to mischievously taunt him – prowling round the small space, knocking over a pile of papers, unraveling the ball of string... The old man loves this proud-looking animal, but its antics drive him to tears of anger and frustration.

I am not sure what qualifies a film for the title of "cult", but in the simplicity and quiet of this small room Sergey Dvortsevoy finds the heart and soul of the matter – a universal quality of human experience so poignant and poetic... that for me the experience of watching this film is equivalent to gazing at a Rembrandt self-portrait. **❞**

Gideon Koppel

An astonishing debut by any standards, Gideon Koppel's 2009 meditative documentary Sleep Furiously *unobtrusively observed the changes in the valleys of mid-Wales as the population grows older. Fused with a score by the electronic wizardry of Aphex Twin, it marked Koppel out as a real talent for the future.* **❞**

A Trip to the Moon 1902

Director Georges Méliès **Cast** Georges Méliès, Bleuette Bernon, Henri Delannoy **14m**

The rocket landing in the Man in the Moon's eye ranks among early cinema's most iconic images. However, Thomas Alva Edison distributed pirated prints and ensured that **Georges Méliès** made only peanuts from the US release of this thirty-scene landmark in the evolution of narrative film. Abounding with wit and invention, the Astronomic Club's encounter with the Selenites prompted Chaplin to call Méliès "the alchemist of light". Pioneering director D.W. Griffith conceded, "I owe him everything", but so does anyone who ever made a sci-fi movie.

The unfriendly lunar inhabitants in the ground-breaking, thirty-scene French short, *A Trip to the Moon*: progenitors of every space monster appearing on film, from *Alien* to *Starship Troopers*.

Vincent 1982

Director Tim Burton **Cast** Vincent Price **6m**

Tim Burton based this on a poem he'd written about a boy who wants to grow up to be like **Vincent Price** (who narrates). As Burton's subsequent work shows, he was being completely serious. It was one of the first uses of claymation but the film's charm is provided by Burton's vivid, macabre, imagination.

SHRINKS

Therapists can be peripheral figures, fashion accessories or sounding boards. When they take centre stage, it's either because they're the villain, about to perform a miracle cure, reveal their own inner demons, or, all too frequently, engage in mattress-surfing with their patient.

Le corbeau 1943

Director Henri-Georges Clouzot **Cast** Pierre Fresnay, Ginette Leclerc, Pierre Larquey **91m**

A psychiatrist sends his small town into self-destructive freefall by writing anonymous letters. Though its sly swipes are as much against the Nazi occupiers as at the French bourgeoisie and Vichy France, the movie's nihilism and misanthropy violently upset most people, and **Clouzot** was banned from filmmaking until 1947. While steeped in its own time and place, today it holds up as a darkly disturbing tale with the message that no one can be trusted, and nowhere – not least our own doorstep – is safe.

Face to Face 1976

Director Ingmar Bergman **Cast** Liv Ullmann, Erland Josephson **136m**

This slice of Nordic misery marked **Bergman**'s return to form and the exorcizing of his own personal demons. It tells the story of the breakdown of a psychiatrist (**Ullmann**) overwhelmed

by memories of her past when she returns to her family home. Originally a 200-minute TV series, it had 65 minutes cut for cinemas. It's so harrowing, some might see that as an act of mercy.

Family Life 1971

Director Ken Loach **Cast** Sandy Ratcliff, Bill Dean, Grace Cave **108m**

Grim docudrama that portrays the psychiatric profession as a tool of state oppression. Subtlety has never been one of **Loach**'s strong suits, especially when he has a point to make, and he makes a good case against the state's definition of mental health. The electric shock treatments are especially horrific.

★ Lilith 1964

Director Robert Rossen **Cast** Warren Beatty, Jean Seberg, Peter Fonda **114m**

The premise may be preposterous, and the sexual politics suspect, but this strange and arty movie, **Rossen**'s last, intrigues with its ethereal nihilism.

Carry on screaming

There are three types of shrink in the movies: Dr Wonderful, Dr Evil and Dr Dippy.

Dr Wonderful

Robin Williams as therapist Sean McGuire in *Good Will Hunting*; Barbra Streisand as Susan Lowenstein in *The Prince of Tides*, helping Nick Nolte face the past; Adam Williams as Dr Brown, who leads Jimmy Piersall out of mental illness and back to baseball in *Fear Strikes Out*.

Dr Evil

Hannibal Lecter in *Silence of the Lambs*; Herbert Grimwood as Dr Ulrich Metz, who tries to drive Douglas Fairbanks to suicide in *When the Clouds Roll By*; the anonymous psychiatrists who will "cure" the young woman Karin in Bergman's *Through a Glass Darkly*.

Dr Dippy

Peter Sellers as Dr Fassbender, trying to cure a woman-chasing Peter O'Toole in *What's New Pussycat?*; Dr Dippy in *Dr Dippy's Sanitarium* (1906); Diane Keaton's shrink in *Manhattan*; Ben Kingsley as dope-smoking, Aloha shirt-wearing Dr Squires in *The Wackness*.

Beatty is the troubled Korea vet turned shrink (now, you just know that isn't going to work), who becomes obsessed by the man-eating siren Lilith (**Seberg** without her trademark elfin crop, all back to nature and scrawling on walls); the ensuing relationship descends into a nightmare where schizophrenia's a higher state of being and boundaries are just plain bourgeois. Above all this is Seberg's movie – you simply cannot take your eyes off her.

★ Now, Voyager 1942

Director Irving Rapper **Cast** Bette Davis, Paul Henreid, Claude Rains 117m

Therapists' bank balances were boosted in the 1940s after downtrodden spinster Charlotte (**Davis**) emerges as a beautiful, independent woman after a stint at Dr Jaquith's (**Rains**) sanatorium. She then meets Jerry (**Henreid**) on a cruise, only to find he's married, so she heads back to Dr Jaquith and meets Jerry's troubled daughter. One of Hollywood's greatest weepies, it is carried by Davis, who had to battle Irene Dunne and Ginger Rogers for the part.

One Flew Over the Cuckoo's Nest 1975

Director Milos Forman **Cast** Jack Nicholson, Louise Fletcher 134m

James Caan turned down **Nicholson**'s role because there'd be "too many white walls", a fact for which we and Jack should be eternally grateful. Nicholson and his character Randle McMurphy seem to merge in this harrowing tale of life and rebellion in an asylum. **Ken Kesey**, who wrote the novel, said he'd never watch it. It was his loss. Nicholson returned to similar territory in *As Good As It Gets*, which is one of the few Hollywood films where a patient's medical treatment actually works.

Seventh Heaven 1997

Director Benoît Jacquot **Cast** Sandrine Kiberlain, Vincent Lindon, François Berléand 91m

An ambiguous movie about therapy and marriage where the patient is warned: "If you sleep to the southeast, be prepared to suffer the consequences." Yes, Freud has been superseded by feng shui and hypnotism. **Kiberlain** is a compulsive shoplifter and painter and her therapist's cures are making hubby jealous. Nothing is resolved, but Jacquot leaving things hanging is better than most directors tying up every loose end.

Shock 1946

Director Alfred L. Werker **Cast** Vincent Price, Lynne Bari 70m

The ultimate expression of the psychiatrist as Dr Evil. Woman sees a murder, goes into shock and is handed over to a shrink, who just happens to be the killer. Funnily enough, psychiatrists found this view of their profession less than flattering and Hollywood, eager to make amends, proceeded to make a string of movies where the psychiatrist was the hero.

Spellbound 1945

Director Alfred Hitchcock **Cast** Gregory Peck, Ingrid Bergman 111m

Hitch was never entirely happy with this movie. He had wanted to make the first proper movie about psychoanalysis, and some of that ambition survives onscreen as **Bergman** tries to help **Peck** prove his innocence. There's a great dream sequence put together by **Salvador Dalí**, but other Dalí scenes, such as Bergman being turned into a Greek statue that explodes, didn't make it, sadly.

SILENTS

The universal language of silents died out in the 1930s. But even today the silent era exerts a fascination which can't quite be explained by jerky black-and-white films of actors making the kind of hand gestures for which you can get arrested in some of the world's more repressive regimes.

La antena 2007

Director Esteban Sapir **Cast** Alejandro Urdapilleta, Valeria Bertuccelli 99m

Filmed in eleven weeks and requiring a year-plus's post-production, this media parable is set in the Year XX in the City Without a Voice and is packed with stock heroes and villains fighting over the power of speech. Despite cheating slightly by resorting to CGI effects, **Esteban Sapir** magpies from several silent masters and his use of captions, montage, superimposition, expressionist silhouette and studio-bound decor is impressive.

The Cabinet of Dr Caligari 1920

Director Robert Wiene **Cast** Werner Krauss, Conrad Veidt 71m

Some movies start things – this, the first classic movie of German expressionism, is usually cited as the first true horror film and is sometimes seen as the root from which *film noir* sprang. **Krauss** is Dr Caligari, a sinister fairground showman whose cabinet contains a somnambulist (**Veidt**) who can predict the future. The horror is accentuated by the grotesquely beautiful imagery and claustrophobic camerawork. It's dated but still essential viewing.

The Chess Player 1927

Director Raymond Bernard **Cast** Pierre Blanchar, Charles Dullin, Édith Jéhanne 135m

Banned by the Nazis in 1940 for its incitement to resist Occupation, this masterly adaptation of Henri Dupuis-Mazuel's fact-inspired novel about a Polish rebel concealed inside a chess-playing automaton that's delivered to the court of Catherine the Great was long thought lost. However, ace archivist Kevin Brownlow pieced together this version from prints found in four countries to showcase the lustre of the cinematography and the *mise en scène*, as well as the ingenuity of **W. Percy Day**'s special effects. A classy curio by a neglected master.

Civilisation 1916

Directors Raymond B. West, Reginald Barker and others **Cast** Howard C. Hickman, Enid Markey, Lola May **78m**

Coming between J. Stuart Blackton's *The Battle Cry of Peace* (1915) and D.W. Griffith's *Intolerance* (1916), this reflected the USA's isolationist-interventionist dilemma during the Great War. Diverse hands claim to have directed sequences, but producer **Thomas Ince** was seemingly the guiding light for an allegory that has a count (**Hickman**) return from a submarine mission possessed by the spirit of Christ, who takes the king of Wredpryd (**Herchel Mayal**) on a battlefield tour to convert him to pacifism. Naïve and archaic perhaps, but also sincere and fascinating.

Fantômas 1913–14

Director Louis Feuillade **Cast** René Navarre, Edmund Breon, Georges Melchior **54m**

Five serials are combined in this compendium – *In the Shadow of the Guillotine*; *Juve versus Fantômas*; *The Murderous Corpse*; *Fantômas versus Fantômas* and *The False Magistrate* – which draw freely on the novels penned by Pierre Souvestre and Marcel Allain. Fantômas (**René Navarre**) and Juve (**Edmund Breon**) make admirable adversaries, with the master criminal's devilish ruthlessness being tempered by an irresistibly pulpy blend of fantasy, sensationalism, slapstick and authentic Parisian locations.

It 1927

Director Clarence Badger **Cast** Clara Bow, Antonio Moreno, William Austin **72m**

Louise Brooks is the cineaste's flapper of choice, but **Clara Bow** was a much bigger star during the Jazz Age. Bow's mother tried to slit her throat when she announced she was going into pictures, but she so epitomized youthful spirit that, at the height of her fame, she received forty-five thousand fan letters a month. Rumours abounded about her sexual appetites and this made her the perfect choice to play shopgirl Betty Lou Spence, who entices **Antonio Moreno**'s playboy heir in this racy adaptation of Elinor Glyn's novel. Sadly, her thick Brooklyn accent killed her career and Bow retired from films at 28 after several scandalous court cases.

★ Pandora's Box 1929

Director G.W. Pabst **Cast** Louise Brooks, Fritz Kortner **133m**

"Every actor has a natural animosity toward every other actor, present or absent, living or dead." So said **Brooks** in her amusing account of the making of this psychosexual melodrama. Co-star **Kortner** hated her so much that after every scene he would run to his dressing room and beat the walls with his fists. Some of this oddness infuses the story of Lulu, a woman who doesn't start out as a prostitute but just behaves like one, before having the fatal lack of taste to give Jack the Ripper a freebie. Brooks' Lulu is one of the most enigmatic, erotic presences ever conjured up on celluloid.

Hollywood's first sex goddess

The black bangs, the name, even the essays (*Lulu in Hollywood*) are familiar, even though the films aren't. **Louise Brooks** was the movie business's first – and most enduring – self-made cult, an actress whose one great performance, as vivacious, doomed Lulu in G.W. Pabst's classic *Pandora's Box*, still looks ahead of its time, more than eighty years since its release.

Brooks made many silents – most of them lost – but retired in the late 1930s when she realized Hollywood didn't know what to make of her. She was rediscovered after **Jean Luc-Godard** paid tribute to her in *Vivre sa vie* (1962). In 1986, a year after Brooks' death, her legend was potent enough for **Jonathan Demme** to cast **Melanie Griffiths** as Lulu – an alcoholic sex machine, complete with black bangs – in *Something Wild*.

Her first autobiography, allegedly entitled *Naked on my Goat*, was not, as she claimed, incinerated, but was the figment of an imagination driven by the desire for immortality.

The Thief of Bagdad 1924

Director Raoul Walsh **Cast** Douglas Fairbanks, Julanne Johnston 155m

Raoul Walsh has always been under-rated. His name wasn't mentioned in the glowing reviews of **Fairbanks'** most extravagant fable, not even by the critic who said it had learnt from the errors of D.W. Griffith's *Intolerance*. The marvel is that the Arabian Nights settings seem fresh today, thanks to designer **William Cameron Menzies**, who would later design *Gone With the Wind*.

SLASHERS

"A girl and a gun" is, Godard said, all you needed for a movie. Make that "a babysitter and a kitchen knife" and you've got a slasher.

Black Christmas 1974

Director Bob Clark **Cast** Olivia Hussey, Keir Dullea, Margot Kidder **98m**

John Carpenter certainly saw this Canadian comedy slasher, for there are notable similarities to his 1978 classic *Halloween*. An unseen killer secretes himself in a sorority house at Yuletide. From his attic hideout he phones the girls (incidentally, anyone else out there have a second phone line in their attic?) to run through an impressive array of farmyard noises, in between trotting down the ladder to stab them. The 2006 remake has little original merit, aside from jolly nasty ways with a sharpened candy cane.

Friday the 13th 1980

Director Sean S. Cunningham **Cast** Betsey Palmer, Adrienne King, Harry Crosby **95m**

Jason's hockey mask: a killer piece of iconography that transformed this derivative slasher into one of America's most successful media franchises. It certainly wasn't the script. Jason Voorhees drowns in Camp Crystal Lake as a boy, due to staff negligence (they're having

sex); thereafter any who venture there are butchered. Spawning eleven spin-off features and counting, though *Jason X* (2001), where Jason regenerates aboard a twenty-fifth-century spaceship, was so hootsomely rubbish it almost killed off the series. However a 2009 remake of the original film rebooted it, making this the horror franchise that just won't die.

★ Halloween 1978

Director John Carpenter **Cast** Jamie Lee Curtis, Donald Pleasence, Nancy Kyes **91m**

Its original title, *The Babysitter Murders*, summarizes a classic scary movie which sees nineteen-year-old unknown **Jamie Lee Curtis** stalked by psychotic, boiler-suited serial killer, Michael Myers. Costing just $320,000, and grossing $47 million at the US box office, it's one of the most profitable independent films ever made. Immediately launching lashings of inferior imitators, as well as Curtis's "Scream Queen" career, **Carpenter**'s menacing point-of-view direction was critically praised for championing suspense over gore. Myers' trademark spooky face was created by spray-painting a $1.98 Captain Kirk mask white.

Scream 1996

Director Wes Craven **Cast** Neve Campbell, David Arquette, Courteney Cox 111m

Slashers became an unprofitable joke during the 1990s – witness *Leprechaun* (1993), Jennifer Aniston's best-forgotten debut about a serial-killing leprechaun on a pogo stick. It was up to Freddie Kreuger's daddy, **Wes Craven**, to once again recharge the genre for a new generation with this slick, postmodern, tongue-in-cheek teen flick that then spawned two decent sequels. The whodunnit plot sees bereaved high schooler Sidney Prescott (**Campbell**) persecuted by a giggling, knife-wielding killer in a ghost-face costume. "Do you like scary movies?" purrs the killer. We did again, after this.

Switchblade Romance 2003

Director Alexandre Aja **Cast** Cécile de France, Maïwenn le Besco, Phillippe Nahon 91m

Proving it's not just US teens that get stalked by truck-driving killers with butchers' knives, this twisted French thriller sees two nubile college *femmes* in the same plight. Its French title *Haute tension* more aptly describes Aja's brutishly effective, back to basics, stalk'n'slash flick, only marred by an infuriating plot hole that, as critic Roger Ebert points out "is not only large enough to drive a truck through, but in fact does have a truck driven right through it."

The Texas Chainsaw Massacre 1974

Director Tobe Hooper **Cast** Marilyn Burns, Gunnar Hansen 83m

Real-life killer Ed Gein was the inspiration for Jame Gumb in *The Silence of the Lambs*, Norman Bates in *Psycho*, and (here) Leatherface – member of a strange family who slice and dice a group of travellers who make the mistake of coming near their Texan farm. Not as scary or gruesome now as it seemed at the time, this was nonetheless refused a certificate by the BBFC and only allowed an uncut release in the UK in 2000. Perhaps the censors' main problem with the movie is that there is no explanation for the attacks. A terrific exercise in terror, and one that should be played to all teenagers planning a road trip for their summer holidays.

Gunnar Hansen as quintessential slasher Leatherface in *The Texas Chainsaw Massacre*.

SOUND-TRACKS

Movies have always had music, even silent ones. Sometimes it's forgettable, sometimes intrusive, but there are also films that you simply can't imagine without also hearing the soundtrack in your head.

Close Encounters of the Third Kind 1977

Director Steven Spielberg **Music** John Williams 135m

The famous five-note alien message motif in this sci-fi epic was **Spielberg**'s idea. **Williams** had wanted a longer motif, but they noticed that even adding just one or two notes began to build a tune. So he stuck to five notes and created 350 combinations, all of which were played on the piano with Spielberg to decide which was the most haunting. It later emerged that Williams, who began thinking about the score two years before the deal was finalized, often wrote music for Spielberg to put scenes to.

The Dark Knight 2008

Director Christopher Nolan **Music** Hans Zimmer and James Newton Howard 152m

Eye-popping IMAX visuals and Heath Ledger's legendary, posthumous-Oscar-winning performance as the Joker may've distracted you a tad from the music. But this is an awesome score. Who'd have thought the composers responsible for *My Best Friend's Wedding* and Disney's *The Lion King* would be capable of capturing the menacing psyche of Nolan's Batman? Inspired by The Damned and Kraftwerk, this stands out from most big Hollywood scores by its unusual use of sound. **Zimmer** dragged razor blades over stringed instruments to achieve the Joker's twisted, hackle-raising theme.

The Fabulous Baker Boys 1989

Director Steve Kloves **Music** Dave Grusin 113m

Dave Grusin earned his second Oscar nomination in a row for this score, even though when the music in this movie is mentioned, most people think of Michelle

Pfeiffer making whoopee on a piano. Grusin, who started out accompanying Andy Williams, is an easy-going, jazz-orientated composer – subtle, concise and seldom showy. At its worst, his music for this sounds like a slick, yet distinctly average theme for a hit TV cop series. At its best, it contributes beautifully to the bittersweet mood. Pfeiffer's character memorably observes that the world would not be a vastly poorer place if nobody ever sang Morris Albert's ''Feelings'' in public again. That said, when she says that ''Feelings is like parsley'', you can't help feeling that parsley should be able to sue.

Goldfinger 1964

Director Guy Hamilton **Music** John Barry 112m

This was the score that defined the James Bond sound. Take one fabulously OTT dramatic ballad (preferably sung by Shirley Bassey), work the theme throughout the film and pump in some seriously punchy brass and percussion action. Oh, and make sure there's a dodgy rhyme in there too (William McGonagall would have been proud of goldfinger/cold finger). It's such a perfect mix here that the soundtrack album knocked The Beatles off the number one spot. **Barry** scored nine Bond movies but never really topped this atmospheric gem.

High Fidelity 2000

Director Stephen Frears **Music** Various 113m

How do you pick the top music tracks for a movie that's all about music snobs

judging other music snobs on their top five music tracks? Adapted from Nick Hornby's bestseller, this stars John Cusack as a record shop owner and commitment-phobe whose milder muso decrees include ''Liking both Marvin Gaye and Art Garfunkel is like supporting both the Israelis and the Palestinians.'' Cusack, who also co-wrote the screenplay, listened to over two thousand songs with his writing partners before selecting the contentious fifty-odd featured in the film that span artists from **Apartment 26** to **Stevie Wonder**. What, no Westlife? Shocker.

Juno 2007

Director Jason Reitman **Music** Various 96m

This remarkable, offbeat rom-com about Juno, a wise-cracking teenager who gets up the duff – and decides to have the baby, in order to sell it – required an equally quirky sound. Director Reitman initially envisaged Juno as a glam-rock fan, but actress Ellen Page set him straight. She reckoned Juno would listen to cute anti-folk band **The Moldy Peaches**, downloaded him some tracks and ta-da! 20th Century Fox's first number one soundtrack since *Titanic* was born.

The Moon in the Gutter 1983

Director Jean-Jacques Beineix **Music** Gabriel Yared 137m

Gabriel Yared is best known for his Oscar-winning musical score for Anthony Minghella's *The English Patient* (though some accused him of trying to be a John Barry clone), but thirteen years earlier he had contributed this sumptuous score to Beineix's moody, mesmerizing tale of rape, guilt, class and love set in mysterious, menacing dockland. Indeed there are times when the cinematography by Phillipe Roussellot and Yared's surging, rather grand music completely take over the film and Gérard Depardieu and Nastassja Kinski seem like figures in someone else's dream.

O Brother, Where Art Thou? 2000

Director Joel Coen Music Various 106m

The Coen Brothers' wildly original spin on Homer's *Odyssey* sees George Clooney, John Turturro and Tim Blake Nelson on top form as prison escapees

fleeing across the Deep South in search of treasure. Along the way they record a blues song, "Man of Constant Sorrow", under the band name The Soggy Bottom Boys (dubbed from real-life bluegrass artists). The soundtrack was a surprise hit, topping the US country charts with an eclectic mix drawn from the popular spiritual, Baptist, folk and dirge music of the Depression era, whilst the film itself was merely a modest success.

Pather Panchali 1955

Director Satyajit Ray Music Ravi Shankar 122m

Shot for just $3000, Satyajit Ray's debut of love, redemption and family is a slowburn study of a boy called Apu growing up in 1920s rural Bengal. It was scored by legendary sitar player **Ravi Shankar**, who was yet to become globally super famous

The Soggy Bottom Boys (Tim Blake Nelson, George Clooney and John Turturro with Chris Thomas King, left) recording "Man of Constant Sorrow" at a radio studio in *O Brother, Where Art Thou?*

by becoming George Harrison's guitar teacher. Apparently Shankar composed almost all of his ravishingly plaintive classical Indian soundtrack in just one eleven-hour session because he was in the middle of a demanding tour, so any extra instrumental bits were filled in by Ray's sitar-playing cinematographer.

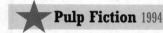 **Pulp Fiction** 1994

Director Quentin Tarantino **Music supervisor** Karyn Rachtman 154m

Purists often complain that the noble art of film music has been corrupted by a pop-rock soundtrack designed to keep MTV viewers tuned in, but Tarantino's selection of songs for *Pulp Fiction* is both eclectic and apt. Tracks vary from **Dick Dale**'s surf guitar to the **Statler Brothers**' apparently innocent but deeply sinister "Flowers on the Wall" to **Urge Overkill**'s true-to-the spirit cover of Neil Diamond's "Girl You'll Be a Woman Soon".

The Sea Hawk 1940

Director Michael Curtiz **Music** Erich Wolfgang Korngold 127m

Some students of film music will tell you **Korngold** was the finest composer of the twentieth century (to which the only response is to smile and head for the nearest exit). He was born in the old Austrian empire and he was a child prodigy, and there the resemblance to Mozart ends. But if anybody can be held to have perfected orchestral film music, it's probably Korngold. *Kings Row* is often held to be his finest movie score, but there's an

adolescent grandeur to his music for this seafaring adventure yarn that is hard to top.

Shaft 1971

Director Gordon Parks **Music** Isaac Hayes 100m

"Who's the black private dick / That's a sex machine to all the chicks? / SHAFT!" pants **Isaac Hayes**' sexed-up title anthem, setting the groove for every inferior blaxploitation flick that followed. Hayes had actually hoped to be cast as badass Harlem detective John Shaft, "the cat that won't cop out". But he had to be content with a small cameo – and the fact his Oscar-winning soundtrack then stole the film from right under lead actor Richard Roundtree's moustache.

 **A Streetcar Named Desire** 1951

Director Elia Kazan **Music** Alex North 122m

When Maurice Jarre's score for *Ghost* was nominated for an Oscar, many felt **North** should have shared it as it was his song, "Unchained Melody" (written for the 1955 movie *Unchained*) that set the musical mood. For *Streetcar*, North did away with the symphony orchestra that had previously underlined every emotion and introduced blues and jazz to the Hollywood movie score. He got his first Academy Award nomination for his gall but, as with the other thirteen nominations, didn't win. Pity, since critics will tell you this is the most important score in the history of American film. They're only exaggerating slightly.

SPACE

Some people think "Houston, we have a problem" was first said by Tom Hanks. NASA may have phased out the shuttle, but the odyssey, as far as filmmakers are concerned, is far from over.

The Astronaut Farmer 2006

Director Michael Polish **Cast** Billy Bob Thornton, Virginia Madsen 104m

Thornton's astronaut never wanted to retire and, having saved the family farm, is determined to build his own rocket even though the government doesn't want him to. Thornton is typically thoughtful in this Capraesque variation on *October Sky* and *Field of Dreams*. There's whimsy aplenty and some sharp dialogue. At one point, Thornton's dreamer rebukes a kid who doesn't know what he wants to do when he leaves town: "You better know what you wanna do before somebody knows it for you."

Capricorn One 1977

Director Peter Hyams **Cast** Elliott Gould, James Brolin, Sam Waterston 124m

The premise of this sci-fi thriller more than makes up for the film's failings. Three astronauts are asked to fake a NASA mission to Mars in a studio when their ship is found to be defective, but discover that part of the plot is that they die in "outer space" so the big secret never gets out. **Hyams** (who also directed the kitschy *Outland*, *2010* and *Timecop*) keeps the pace up, and while some of the dialogue is dreadful (and **O.J. Simpson**'s delivery even worse) this is hugely entertaining. The movie stars both Barbra Streisand's first husband (**Gould**) and her current one, **Brolin**.

Destination Moon 1950

Director Irving Pichel **Cast** John Archer, Warner Anderson, Tom Powers, Dick Wesson 91m

Producer **George Pal**'s prophetic space movie draws together what must be the oddest team of collaborators in Hollywood history: space artist **Chesley Bonestell**, cult novelist **Robert A. Heinlein**, blacklisted director **Pichel** and **Woody Woodpecker**, who drops in to explain the science behind the race to the moon. Flatly directed, with much jingoistic "Let's beat the Russians to the moon" sentiment, *Destination Moon* remains intriguing because of Bonestell's astronomic art and the movie's canny knack of prefiguring what really happened when *Apollo 11* landed in 1969.

The Dish 2000

Director Rob Sitch **Cast** Kevin Harrington, Sam Neill, Tom Long 101m

Wry, sweet comedy about the Australian satellite dish – and its eccentric crew – who became pivotal to the broadcast of the moon landing. **Sitch**'s endearing footnote to the *Apollo 11* mission almost feels, as *The Guardian* noted, a bit like an old-fashioned war movie in which three Australian soldiers and an American officer hold a pass until reinforcements arrive.

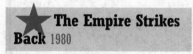

The Empire Strikes Back 1980

Director Irvin Kershner **Cast** Mark Hamill, Harrison Ford, Carrie Fisher 124m

After the genre-defining success of *Star Wars: A New Hope* (1977), many assumed the sequel would be, well, a typical sequel. But *Empire* still shines as the gem in the *Star Wars* crown. The entire movie bristles with excitement and energy – from the awe-inspiring battle of Hoth to the asteroid field pursuit and the brutal encounter between Luke and Vader. At the same time we witness the burgeoning love of Leia and Han, and enjoy some of the saga's most memorable lines, thanks to Leigh Brackett and Lawrence Kasdan's great script – "Laugh it up, fuzzball!"

First on the Moon 2005

Director Aleksei Fedorchenko **Cast** Aleksei Anisimov, Viktor Kotov, Igor Sannikov 75m

Clever mockumentary/alternative history that purports to tell the story of a secret Soviet moon landing in the Stalinist 1930s. **Fedorchenko** and the actors play it straight, presenting us with recently discovered NKVD footage of the training and a plausible rationale for the suppression of this secret mission in a subtle comedy drama that, ultimately, delivers more fun than most of the NASA-faked-the-moon-landings movies.

For All Mankind 1989

Director Al Reinert **Cast** Jim Lovell, Russell Schweickart 90m

Talented as Hollywood is, you can't beat actual footage of man's travels in space for sheer exhilaration. Cameras were on board all 24 *Apollo* space missions between 1968 and 1972. Splicing together excerpts from more than six million feet of film, director **Reinert** captures the beauty of the mission and the **Brian Eno/Daniel Lanois** soundtrack is incredibly haunting.

Moon 2009

Director Duncan Jones **Cast** Sam Rockwell, Kevin Spacey 97m

Rockwell is the starman waiting in the sky – to invoke a line made famous by the director's dad – for his lonely stint on a lunar mining base to end. But after three years of video links to his wife and conversations with a HAL-like computer (**Spacey**), his mind is fragmenting. **Jones** creates in his directorial debut a film in the vein of 1970s classics *Silent Running* and *2001*, and it's similarly packed with ideas,

Bruce Dern as Freeman Lowell, bedraggled but still standing, aided by his robotic friends, as the final bastion against nature's destruction in *Silent Running*.

some of which it doesn't quite know what to do with. Not that this detracts from the intense, solitary atmosphere, only heightened by Clint Mansell's soundtrack.

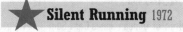 Silent Running 1972

Director Douglas Trumbull **Cast** Bruce Dern, Cliff Potts, Ron Rifkin 89m

Influential ecological sci-fi flick in which astronaut **Dern**, minding the Earth's last nature reserve aboard a spaceship, disobeys orders to ditch the programme, kills his more obedient colleagues and holes up with drones Huey, Louie and Dewey to save nature. Dern instils enough pathos into his character to make such a course plausible.

The Woman in the Moon
1929

Director Fritz Lang **Cast** Fritz Rasp, Gerda Maurus, Willy Fritsch, Klaus Pohl 156m

Lang's last silent movie still managed to stir controversy and make its mark in history. On finding there's gold on the moon, a professor (**Pohl**) joins with an ambitious engineer (**Fritsch**) to get there. Too many cooks spoil the broth, though, and trouble brews between the pair and their crew. Contains the first ever countdown launch, while Lang's vision of a rocket turned out to be a little too close to the mark – the Nazis withdrew the movie to preserve the secrecy of their own rocket.

SPAGHETTI WESTERNS

In the 1960s, Italy stunned Hollywood by making its own Westerns that were cheaper, better and more successful than many traditional horse operas. It wasn't true, as Burt Kennedy told John Ford, that these movies had no stories, just killing. But they did offer a stylized, violent alternative to the increasingly predictable fare coming from the US.

Death Rides a Horse 1968

Director Giulio Petroni **Cast** Lee Van Cleef, John Philip Law 120m

Referenced in *Kill Bill*, **Petroni**'s most famous Western starts like a horror movie – with mass murder on a dark, scary night – but evolves into a weird buddy movie with **Law** as the traumatized young gunslinger looking to avenge the slaughter of his family, palling up with veteran **Van Cleef**, who is after the same bandits for different reasons. Although Law casts a shadow over an entire fake mountain range in one scene, Petroni's Old West in violent turmoil has a certain blunt poetry.

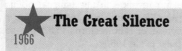 **The Great Silence**
1966

Director Sergio Corbucci **Cast** Jean-Louis Trintignant, Klaus Kinski, Frank Wolff 105m

Corbucci's hauntingly sad, politicized Western was hardly likely to outdo Leone's exhilaratingly violent *Dollars* movies at the box office. **Trintignant** is the mute gunslinger defending local hill folk who, in their fight for survival, have irritated a venal banker. The law – personified by **Wolff**'s inept sheriff – is less of a force than **Kinski**'s terrifyingly amoral bounty hunter who kills for fun. Probably Corbucci's best.

Keoma 1976

Director Enzo Castellari **Cast** Franco Nero, Donald O'Brien, William Berger 105m

By the mid-1970s, industrialized plagiarism and changing tastes had destroyed the spaghetti Western. But there was still time for **Castellari** to make this belated classic, starring **Nero** as a half-breed Indian who returns to find his old town turned into a veritable slave camp by

O'Brien. Castellari seasons this with some Christian symbolism, flashbacks and an excruciating score, and sets the final shoot-out to the strains of a woman screaming as she gives birth.

Kill and Pray 1967

Director Carlo Lizzani **Cast** Lou Castel, Mark Damon, Pier Paolo Pasolini 92m

An entertainingly violent Western, slipping Marxist messages in between the shoot-outs and showdowns as **Castel** tries to save the townsfolk from evil Southern fop **Damon**. Although this movie is best remembered for **Pasolini**'s revolutionary priest, his playing is less remarkable than **Lizzani**'s conceits, especially the duel scene where villain and hero, standing on stools with their heads in nooses, try to shoot the foot off the other's stool.

My Name Is Nobody 1973

Director Tonino Valerii **Cast** Henry Fonda, Terence Hill 117m

Valerii, producer **Sergio Leone** and **Fonda** seem to be suggesting the Western should be left in peace – especially when the camera pans to Sam Peckinpah's name on a gravestone. In Valerii's accomplished comedy Western, **Hill** idolizes Fonda's ageing gunslinger so much he tries to ensure his hero dies in a blaze of glory in a shoot-out against the wild bunch. But ultimately, he stages a fake killing to let Fonda – and by implication the Western? – slip away quietly.

Once Upon a Time in the West 1968

Director Sergio Leone **Cast** Henry Fonda, Claudia Cardinale, Charles Bronson, Jason Robards 165m

Leone's epic, operatic tale of the civilizing of the West by railroad and women (beautifully symbolized by **Cardinale**'s heroine) is packed with thirty significant homages to his favourite Westerns – even the famous eight-minute scene where three men wait for a train is a parodic tribute to *High Noon* – and set to one of **Ennio Morricone**'s most memorable scores. **Fonda** excels as the child-killing gunslinger but he, like his rivals **Bronson** and **Robards**, are all participating in a dance of death in a land where money will increasingly count for more than guns.

The Stranger's Gundown 1969

Director Sergio Garrone **Cast** Anthony Steffen, Rada Rassimov, Paolo Gozlino, Lu Kamante, Teodoro Corra 107m

If you're wondering why **Steffen** walks as if he's recovering from rigor mortis, it's because his mysterious stranger is actually a reincarnated Civil War veteran seeking revenge in this unusual gothic horror Western spun off the *Django* franchise of Eurowesterns that were so popular in the 1960s.

SPOOFS

As relentless as a sequel, there will always be a spoof hard on the heels of any successful movie. Parodies can take on specific films (*High Anxiety*), entire genres (*Blazing Saddles*) or just be an excuse for gags about bodily functions.

Abbott and Costello Meet Frankenstein 1948

Director Charles Barton **Cast** Bud Abbott, Lou Costello, Lon Chaney Jr 83m

On seeing the script, **Lou Costello** reportedly hissed, "No way I'll do that crap. My little girl could write something better than this." Yet it proved a box-office success and launched the chubby comic and **Bud Abbott** on a series of horror lite adventures. **Bela Lugosi** was cast as Dracula only after his agent contacted the producers to quash rumours that he was dead. Boris Karloff refused to play the monster, although he did agree to be photographed queueing to see the picture, which affectionately lampoons Universal's house horror style.

Airplane! 1980

Directors Jerry Zucker, Jim Abrahams, David Zucker **Cast** Leslie Nielsen, Robert Hays 87m

Probably the best-known spoof, *Airplane!* is based on the *Airport* disaster trilogy, though even if you've never seen a 1970s disaster movie this doesn't lose a jot of its humour. Keep your eyes peeled the whole time because there's always a joke on the go, and it's usually other than the one you are currently laughing at. **Robert Hays**, who stars in both *Airplane!* movies, is perfectly cast as dull Ted Striker, who has to overcome his fear of flying and step into the pilot seat when the plane's crew fall victim to severe food poisoning. The sequel is not directed by the same team and suffers as a result.

★ Blazing Saddles 1974

Director Mel Brooks **Cast** Gene Wilder, Cleavon Little 93m

Mel Brooks' first hit movie is a Western spoof, which thirty-odd years on is still hugely popular – it was ranked sixth in the 2003 American Film Institute's funniest US films of all-time. It's offensive, sexist and rude, and one of the few films to have had sound censored: the TV version cut the flatulence of the campfire scene and replaced it with belching. The name of Brooks' character (William J. Petomane) is taken from the stage name of a popular French performer whose speciality was telling stories punctuated with bottom burps.

Cat City 1986

Director Béla Ternovszky **Cast** Rob Roy, Dean Hagopian, Vlasta Vrana 96m

The tyrannized mice of *Cat City* (or *Macskafogó*, to give the movie its not-so easily pronounceable original title) have discovered that a Japanese scientist has designed the ultimate weapon to help them fight their evil cat oppressors. Step up secret agent double-seven-o Gary Gumshoe (**Roy**), brought out of retirement to secure the safe delivery of weapon plans. Hired to stop Gumshoe are the inept Rat Gang in this low-budget Hungarian anime Bond spoof parodying the action and romance of the original spy adventures, with added laughs.

Dead Men Don't Wear Plaid 1982

Director Carl Reiner **Cast** Steve Martin, Rachel Ward, Reni Santoni 88m

Parody of a 1940s thriller with **Martin** playing detective Rigby Reardon, who has to uncover the truth behind the mysterious death of a scientist. Characters and scenes from old *film noir* footage are pasted into the action. Martin's assistant is none other than Humphrey Bogart in his role as Philip Marlowe. The old movie clips also show off the early work of legendary costume designer **Edith Head**. *Dead Men Don't Wear Plaid* was to be the final movie that she worked on.

Galaxy Quest 1999

Director Dean Parisot **Cast** Tim Allen, Sigourney Weaver, Alan Rickman 102m

Washed-up sci-fi actors find themselves transported into space thanks to a race of aliens who have mistaken their TV show for a documentary, built their culture around it and come to ask for help to fight a war. It's obviously *Star Trek* (with a bit of *Alien* thrown in), but you don't have to be a diehard Trekker to get the gags (although

Steve Martin stars alongside old *film noir* greats in *Dead Men Don't Wear Plaid*, here wearing a natty suit that looks as if it could have been made for Humphrey Bogart.

some may pass you by if you're not). In fact, if you are a Trekker, be prepared to come in for a good bit of ribbing. As in all good sci-fi movies, there has to be an evil warlord, and this one is named Sarris, after movie critic Andrew Sarris, who slated producer Mark Johnson's *The Natural*.

High Anxiety 1977

Director Mel Brooks **Cast** Mel Brooks, Madeline Kahn **94m**

Comedy thriller inspired by you-know-who, which includes scenes from *The Birds* (with the tastiest bird droppings ever – spinach and mayonnaise), *Psycho* and *Vertigo*. **Brooks**, a psychiatrist, is promoted to head of the Psychoneurotic Institute for the Very Very Nervous after his predecessor dies mysteriously. Death and mayhem ensue. **Rudy De Luca** (director of spoof horror *Transylvania 6-5000* – see below) appears as a killer and **Albert Whitlock**, Hitchcock's special-effects man, has a cameo.

Schlock 1971

Director John Landis **Cast** John Landis, Saul Kahan **80m**

"Due to the horrifying nature of this film, no one will be admitted to the theatre", is one of the taglines to **Landis**'s first production, closely followed by: "The first musical monster movie in years", which gives you some idea of what you are about to encounter. The premise? A monster falling in love with a blind girl. Listen out for the line "See you next Wednesday", which became a trademark of Landis's movies. It's a line from *2001: A Space Odyssey*, and is the title for a film idea Landis had when he was fifteen. Whenever he finds himself using ideas from this film in his later work, Landis puts in the phrase as a reference to it.

Student Bodies 1981

Director Mickey Rose **Cast** Kristen Riter, Matthew Goldsby, Richard Belzer **86m**

Written and directed by ex-Woody Allen collaborator **Mickey Rose**, this amusingly amateurish account of the murderous misdeeds of The Breather beat *Scream* to the high-school horror parody punch by fifteen years. Producer Michael Ritchie wasn't impressed, however, and insisted on an Alan Smithee credit, while the actor playing Malvert the oddball janitor is billed only as The Stick. Despite an opening caption setting the action on Jamie Lee Curtis's birthday, more gags miss than hit. But there are so many throwaway one-liners and bits of schlock schtick that resistance is futile.

★ Team America: World Police 2004

Director Trey Parker **Cast** Trey Parker, Matt Stone, Kristen Miller **98m**

How can anyone resist a film whose R rating certificate reads: "For graphic crude and sexual behaviour, violent images and strong language – all involving puppets"? Shot in Supercrappymation and combining *South Park* attitude with *Thunderbirds* aesthetics, this is as much a satire on Dubya's foreign policy posturing as a lampoon of Jerry Bruckheimer movies. The mockery of Kim Jong-Il and Hollywood's leading liberals is mercilessly hilarious, as are the songs. But nigh-on every frame contains a blink'n'miss it sight gag.

Theatre of Blood 1973

Director Douglas Hickox **Cast** Vincent Price, Diana Rigg 102m

Vincent Price does such a good job playing a not-very-good classical actor, you almost wonder… no, stop that. Here, aided by his daughter (**Rigg**), he takes revenge on his critics by killing them in ways selected from the works of the Bard. Yes, one is taken from *Titus Andronicus*. While you can sense some spoof movies winding down as they run out of gags, that never happens here. You can see Price's eyes gleaming with merriment as he tells a victim: "I'll kill you when I'm ready – next week, next month, next year."

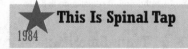

This Is Spinal Tap 1984

Director Rob Reiner **Cast** Michael McKean, Christopher Guest, Harry Shearer 82m

A monumental mockumentary which suggests that Rob inherited comic genes from old man Carl and, ironically, influenced more serious rock biopics like Oliver Stone's *The Doors*. The lead actors and director were given $10,000 to write a script and make a twenty-minute film to convince investors. Lucky they got the go-ahead, because this is one of the most dead-on satires ever. Rock, especially this kind of pompous heavy rock, still hasn't recovered from this skewering. The name of the album (*Smell the Glove*), their hit (*Lick My Love Pump*), even the cold sores, are so right it's scary. The people behind *A Mighty Wind* will be quite happy if they do for folk what this did for metal.

Transylvania 6-5000 1985

Director Rudy De Luca **Cast** Jeff Goldblum, Joseph Bologna 93m

Great title. Frankenstein has reappeared and two reporters go to Transylvania to investigate. You'll either love **Goldblum** in his deadpan role, or hate the cheap lines. You might prefer Mel Brooks' *Young Frankenstein* for a parody of the monster horror genre, which was shot in the same castle (with the same props) as *Frankenstein* (1931).

Zelig 1983

Director Woody Allen **Cast** Woody Allen, Mia Farrow, Patrick Horgan 79m

Filmed with period cameras and recording equipment, yet making exemplary use of modern matting techniques, this monochrome profile of the human chameleon who became a Jazz Age celebrity makes exceptional use of archive footage to show Zelig rubbing shoulders with America's glitterati, as well as Hitler and the pope. It's slick, clever fun. But the satirical insights into the melting pot ethos, anti-Semitism and psychotherapy have a keen edge.

SPORT

Only in a sports film could an actor utter the words "win just one more for the Gipper". The genre has always been about suspension of disbelief, and if two tons of disbelief hang from the ceiling by the final credits, all the better.

L'arbitro 1974

Director Luigi Filippo D'Amico **Cast** Joan Collins, Lando Buzzanca 108m

An Italian comedy of manners about a referee who can't concentrate on what's happening on the pitch because he's too busy thinking about what's happening in his bedroom. But then one of the things happening in his bedroom is **Joan Collins**. This was one of several forays into sport by the director: he also made the bizarre *La vida sigue igual*, starring former goalkeeper Julio Iglesias as a football-playing troubadour.

Bang the Drum Slowly 1973

Director John Hancock **Cast** Robert De Niro, Michael Moriarty, Vincent Gardenia 96m

After over half a decade learning his trade in movies like Roger Corman's *Bloody Mama* and Ivan Passer's *Born to Win*, **De Niro** made his mark in 1973 with two very different performances. His volatile Johnny Boy stole Scorsese's *Mean Streets* and his dying baseball

player here had critics raving – once they'd dried their eyes. De Niro brings a youthful innocence to the role of Bruce Pearson, a borderline simpleton doomed to an early trip to the great locker room in the sky by Hodgkin's disease in what is essentially a chick flick for blokes.

Body and Soul 1947

Director Robert Rossen **Cast** John Garfield, Lilli Palmer 104m

Body and Soul is both a *film noir* and a classic sports movie. There is a flawed protagonist faced with a terrible moral dilemma, in this case young boxer Charlie Davis, who has to decide between throwing a fight for Mob money or winning it for himself. Shot with newsreel realism, *Body and Soul* won a place in the canon of sports movies in its own right, but it will also be remembered as the film that helped launch a genre.

Breaking Away 1979

Director Peter Yates **Cast** Dennis Christopher, Dennis Quaid, Daniel Stern 101m

Earning **Steve Tesich** an Oscar for his autobiographical screenplay, this rite of passage pitches somewhere between *American Graffiti* (1973) and *Say Anything...* (1989). But **Peter Yates** captures the last summer anxieties of wannabe Italian cyclist **Dennis Quaid**'s teenage pals as precisely as the rivalry between Bloomington, Indiana's townie cutters and its campus jocks. Consequently, the Little 500 bike race becomes as much a tribal showdown as an athletic contest, which is what all good sport should be.

The Club 1980

Director Bruce Beresford **Cast** Jack Thompson, Graham Kennedy **99m**

Nailing the ocker mentality that still prevails in much sport down under, **David Williamson**'s adaptation of his own play relocates the characters and themes of *This Sporting Life* to an Aussie Rules setting. Civil war breaks out in the dressing and board rooms when Collingwood president (**Kennedy**) pays a record fee for callow newcomer John Howard, yet the club still climbs the table towards the grand final. **Jack Thompson** excels as the coach, but the stinging (and often uproariously crude) one-liners are distributed equally among the ensemble.

Cool Runnings 1993

Director John Turteltaub **Cast** John Candy, Leon, Doug E. Doug, Rawle D. Lewis **98m**

Mining the same formula as movies like 1976's *Rocky* and *The Bad News Bears* – rank outsiders become worthy competitors through heart, determination, elbow grease and the encouragement of a has-been coach – this juvenile Disney comedy fictionalized the true story of the Jamaican bobsledding team at the Olympics. The colossally unathletic **Candy** is the disgraced ex-champ who takes them to Calgary in a long, clichéd round of feel-good daftness.

The Creator's Game 1999

Director Bruce Troxell **Cast** Dakota House, Al Harrington **102m**

It's more than just field hockey with bags on sticks – *The Creator's Game* is easily the best movie about lacrosse (for obvious reasons). The plot concerns Daniel Cloud (**House**), an Iroquois who aspires to coach American football at university. As luck has it, the only coaching vacancy left open is for the lacrosse side, a game Daniel plays rather well. Lacrosse was invented by native Americans, and with a big game coming up, it's up to Daniel to draw on his Iroquois heritage for inspiration.

Escape to Victory 1981

Director John Huston **Cast** Sylvester Stallone, Michael Caine, Pelé, Bobby Moore **117m**

It's hard to work out what is more surprising. The fact that this movie stars an eclectic combination of first division footballers and character actors, or that it was directed by **Huston**. Either way, it's fantastic. A team comprising POWs raises a football team to play the Germans. Given the chance to escape at half time, they stick around, put a few past them and escape anyway. Honour is satisfied, and even the German manager (**Max von Sydow**, who else?) goes all dewy-eyed at the end. It's only mildly less laughable than an overweight **Michael Caine** pretending to be an ex-international so obviously modelled on his pal Bobby Moore that the England skipper should have got royalties. Legend has it that **Pelé**'s overhead kick was filmed in one take. Moore sent over a perfectly weighted cross and Pelé hit it first time. Pure brilliance.

Hoop Dreams 1994

Director Steve James **Cast** William Gates, Arthur Agee **171m**

Filmed between 1986 and 1991, this is a compelling insight into the intolerable pressures placed upon **William Gates** and **Arthur Agee**, as well as the sacrifices made by their families, as the teenagers strive to escape their tough Chicago neighbourhoods and fulfil their basketball potential. Even more sobering is the exposé of the cynical way in which African-American aspiration is exploited by the US sporting system and society at large. Coach Gene Pingatore and St Joseph's school sued the filmmakers for misrepresentation, but settled for a charitable donation. A catch-up sequel is long overdue.

 **The Hustler** 1961

Director Robert Rossen **Cast** Paul Newman, Jackie Gleason, Piper Laurie **135m**

It's hard to think of a more equivocal hero than **Newman**'s Fast Eddie Felson.

Determined to beat pool legend Minnesota Fats (**Gleason**), Fast Eddie loses the game and his self-belief, only to find redemption in the love of alcoholic misfit Sarah Packard (a towering performance by **Laurie**). Just as the couple seem to have found salvation, Fast Eddie risks it all by selling out to **George C. Scott**'s pool hustler Bert Gordon for another shot at Minnesota Fats. *The Hustler* has generated its own mythology, and Fast Eddie's alliance with Gordon is said to parallel **Rossen**'s own decision to name names in the McCarthy era.

Lagaan 2001

Director Ashotosh Gowariker **Cast** Aamir Khan, Rachel Shelley, Paul Blackthorne **224m**

It's 1893 and the Indian village of Champaner is beset by drought and dastardly Brits threatening to triple the land taxes (the "lagaan") unless the villagers can defeat them at cricket – despite having never played before. Alternatively titled *Once Upon a Time in India*, this is the first Bollywood production to include British actors and, unlike many Indian movies, the musical sections advance the story instead of just providing gratuitous interludes. Needless to say, steer clear if you don't like cricket. The match itself swallows eighty minutes of screen time.

The Mean Machine/The Longest Yard 1974

Director Robert Aldrich **Cast** Burt Reynolds, Eddie Albert **122m**

As fallen American football idol Paul Crue, **Burt Reynolds** plays a washed-up hero, fallen from grace for throwing a game and imprisoned for stealing his ex-girlfriend's car and punching out a police officer. Told to build a prison team to challenge the guards at a game, Burt creates the Mean Machine; when the governor offers Crue the chance for an early release he can redeem his honour, or sell out his buddies one more time. There's a distinct post-Watergate disaffection to **Albert**'s corrupt prison governor and Reynolds' equivocal hero, making this movie more complicated than the trot through prison movie clichés it might seem.

The Natural 1984

Director Barry Levinson **Cast** Robert Redford, Robert Duvall, Kim Basinger 137m

Unless you've never seen a movie before, you know what's going to happen in The Natural before **Redford** has spoken. He's a washed-up baseball player who joins a team of no-hopers. Guess what happens next. Yet of all the zero-to-hero characters, Redford's Roy Hobbs is one of the most likeable. **Levinson** uses baseball to retell the Arthurian legend of the search for the Holy Grail. Baseball fans voted this as having three of the top ten great diamond moments in the movies, the most inspiring being when Redford knocks the cover off the ball.

Personal Best 1982

Director Robert Towne **Cast** Mariel Hemingway, Scott Glenn, Patrice Donnelly 127m

Eyebrows were raised when raging bull **Robert Towne** made his directorial debut with the story of two athletes who become lesbian lovers while competing for a spot on the US Olympic team. But there's nothing voyeuristic about this celebration of the power and beauty of the human body. Indeed, passion comes a poor fourth behind ambition, discipline and dedication. With both **Patrice Donnelly** and **Kenny Moore** being genuine Olympians, this is as authentic as it's sensual.

Searching for Bobby Fischer 1993

Director Steven Zaillian **Cast** Joe Mantegna, Max Pomeranc, Joan Allen, Ben Kingsley 110m

Quietly powerful melodrama that actually makes chess interesting. It's the true story of a seven-year-old chess genius, adapted from the book by his father. Josh Waitzkin is torn between playing in the park for fun (and minor financial gain) and studying with his coach to win prestigious tournaments and become the next Bobby Fischer, the uncompromising and mysterious grand master who became a fugitive from US justice.

Slap Shot 1977

Director George Roy Hill **Cast** Paul Newman, Michael Ontkean, Lindsay Crouse 124m

Slap Shot is, by turns, funny, profane and violent. Despite the humour, the darkness prevails. **Newman** takes over a struggling ice-hockey team based in an industrial town suffering a similar reversal of fortune and recruits three violent players to bludgeon opponents into submission. The movie raises questions about the morality of a win-at-all-costs mentality, and deplores the ensuing violence. It never answers convincingly, but the action and the anarchic humour of the dressing room make up for its faults, and the scene where the leading scorer circles the ice naked lives long in the memory.

This Sporting Life 1963

Director Lindsay Anderson **Cast** Richard Harris, Rachel Roberts, Alan Badel 134m

Adapted from a **David Storey** novel, the tale of a Yorkshire miner who briefly samples celebrity while playing rugby league for his home-town team is kitchen sink cinema's most complex and least commercial picture. Northern audiences didn't appreciate the allusions to Michelangelo Antonioni and Ingmar Bergman, while softy cineastes spurned the sporting savagery. **Richard Harris** isn't always sure whether he's playing Marlon Brando, Richard Burton or an emotionally and intellectually stunted everyman. But his gauche romance with fellow Oscar nominee **Rachel Roberts** is as savage as the mud-spattered action.

When We Were Kings 1996

Director Leon Gast **Cast** Muhammad Ali, George Foreman 87m

By 1974 **Ali**'s star seemed to be descending. His refusal to be drafted cost him his title and the ensuing ban cost him the best years of his career. His decision to challenge champion **George Foreman** for the heavyweight title at the age of 32 seemed suicidal. Foreman was rumoured to be the hardest hitter in boxing history. But in the soaring temperatures and the clamour of Kinshasa… heck, you can guess the rest. The Greatest in the greatest sports documentary.

> **❝** I'm gonna let everybody know that thing on your head is a phony and it comes from the tail of a pony. **❞**
>
> **Muhammad Ali, When We Were Kings**

Yesterday's Hero 1979

Director Neil Leifer **Cast** Ian McShane, Adam Faith 95m

Pre-*Lovejoy* and *Deadwood*, McShane plays a boozer, a maverick whose sublime footballing skills are undermined by a defiant spirit that refuses to bow down. It's not hard to guess which real-life football hero McShane's character is based on. Naturally, he makes a glorious cup-final comeback from the bar – sorry, bench – as the whole thing unfolds like an accident in slow motion. **Jackie Collins** wrote the script and **John Motson** provides the commentary, while **Faith** and **Paul Nicholas** co-star. Whatever did McShane's dad, who used to be a Manchester United scout, make of this?

SPY MOVIES

When you're a spy you never know how the villains will take over the world. They might nuke Florida or take control of the weather. And all you have to fight the nefarious forces of evil is your raised eyebrow and some fancy gizmos.

Army of Shadows 1969

Director Jean-Pierre Melville **Cast** Lino Ventura, Paul Meurisse 145m

Jean-Pierre Melville had already commemorated the extraordinary sacrifices made by ordinary men and women in the Vichy dramas *Le silence de la mer* (1949) and *Léon Morin, prêtre* (1961). But this determinedly anti-heroic mix of **Joseph Kessel**'s novel and Melville's own experiences extols the quiet courage and calculating ingenuity required to treat wartime treachery, tragedy and triumph with the same steely dispassion. **Ventura** is outstanding, but all the performances are as taut as the spartan direction, making this as authentic as it's tense.

Danger: Diabolik 1968

Director Mario Bava **Cast** John Phillip Law, Marissa Mell 105m

Yet another James Bond spoof that's funnier than *Austin Powers*. This Italian-French production stars **Law** in the title role as a super-thief who has a fine old time stealing gold and murdering inno-cent people. Catherine Deneuve should have had a lead role but the director, as an Italian schlock artist, found her acting wanting. Cheesy, badly acted fun.

★ The End of an Agent by Means of Mr Foutka's Dog 1967

Director Vàclac Vorlícek **Cast** Jan Kacer, Kveta Fialova 87m

The name's… Cyril Juan, Agent W4. Not as catchy as 007, but funnier than some of the later Bond capers, this is a marvellous spy spoof, complete with freeze frames, fist fights, groovy gadgets and an agent who deals with the baddies without ever getting his white trousers dirty.

The Falcon and the Snowman 1985

Director John Schlesinger **Cast** Timothy Hutton, Sean Penn, Pat Hingle 131m

Either side of filming Alan Bennett's Cambridge spies duo (*An Englishman*

Abroad and *A Question of Attribution*) for the BBC, **John Schlesinger** sought to show how naïveté and greed rather than misplaced idealism led disillusioned seminarian Christopher Boyce (**Hutton**) and drug dealer Andrew Daulton Lee (**Penn**) to sell secrets to the Soviets through their Mexican embassy. Essentially revisiting *Midnight Cowboy*, Schlesinger seems more fascinated by the code of espionage conduct than the morality of treason. However, the CIA hardly emerges unsullied, while Penn hired Daulton Lee as his assistant on his release from prison.

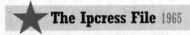

The Ipcress File 1965

Director Sidney J. Furie **Cast** Michael Caine, Nigel Green **109m**

Producer **Harry Saltzman**, **Furie** and **Caine** needed a name for the spy in **Len Deighton**'s novel. They wanted a boring name and Caine suggested Harry. Saltzman's acolytes waited to see if the boss would take umbrage. But he laughed and just said: "Harry it is. My real name's Herschel." Saltzman added that the most boring man he'd ever met was called Palmer, and so Harry Palmer was born. They did have one difference of opinion: Saltzman was worried a scene where Palmer pushed his own supermarket trolley would be taken to mean the spy was gay. They solved it by using the trolley as a weapon. This and *The Spy Who Came In from the Cold* vie for the best spy flick of the 1960s.

Ivan's Childhood 1962

Director Andrei Tarkovsky **Cast** Nikolai Burlyayev, Yevgeni Zharikov **95m**

This, **Tarkovsky**'s first feature, was made in the Khruschev era. (He would not be so lucky with his second – *Andrei Rublev* – of which the Brezhnev drones disapproved and only allowed to be screened at 4am on the last day of the Cannes festival.) Here the spy is a twelve-year-old boy (a fantastic performance by Burlyayev), prematurely aged by the Great Patriotic War. His inner life – his dreams are beautifully shot – is more important than what he does, although we see him growing into his spy role to the point where he starts ordering the men around. A wonderful, difficult film, which is also known as *My Name Is Ivan*.

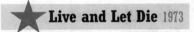

Live and Let Die 1973

Director Guy Hamilton **Cast** Roger Moore, Jane Seymour **121m**

New Bond, new bloke writing the theme tune (some chap the tabloids call Macca) and a new Bond girl (the future Dr Quinn, medicine woman). It was too much change for some Bond die-hards, who also missed Q and his gadgets, but this remains an entertaining caper. Bond has to escape a few hungry crocodiles, deal with a different kind of villain (**Yaphet Kotto** as a drug baron) and there are some neat touches too (Tee-Hee and his mechanical arm). *Goldfinger* may be the best Connery Bond, but Moore was always closer to Ian Fleming's ideal.

Mata Hari 1931

Director George Fitzmaurice **Cast** Greta Garbo, Ramon Novarro 88m

Greta Garbo vamps it up and camps it up in this cracking slice of historical nonsense. Chronicling the life and crimes of the world's most famous woman spy, Mata Hari, was really just an excuse for Garbo to play the fallen woman, again, and suffer moral retribution (although she is "purified" by being escorted to her execution by a squad of nuns). Bizarrely, this got into censorship trouble over a scene which showed **Novarro** peering at the Virgin Mary and then turning to Garbo. Cue cries of blasphemy! But Garbo pays for her sins. As her colleague tells her: "The only way to resign from our profession is to die."

Notorious 1946

Director Alfred Hitchcock **Cast** Cary Grant, Ingrid Bergman, Claude Rains 102m

How to choose just one of the master's spy movies? This script was turned down by Warner Bros because they didn't believe the plot, which mentioned uranium. The FBI liked the uranium angle so much they spied on **Hitchcock** for months. The director always said the uranium was incidental. **Grant** was also the object of FBI interest. Two years earlier his *None But the Lonely Heart* was cited as Communist propaganda by the FBI for the line: "You're not going to get me to work 'ere and squeeze pennies out of little people poorer than I am." You wonder how that experience affected his ambiguous portrayal of an FBI agent in the movie.

The Million Eyes of Su-Muru 1967

Director Lindsay Shonteff **Cast** Shirley Eaton, Frankie Avalon 95m

If you haven't already met Su-Muru (**Eaton**), it's high time you were introduced. She's a diabolical, man-hating, sadistic Amazonian goddess. The movie, which also stars **Avalon**, isn't as good as *Grease* but it's not as bad as *How to Stuff a Wild Bikini* either. Take the worst dialogue from all the Bond movies put together, the stupidest stunts from the era's kung-fu movies and the daftest plot this side of a Matt Helm spoof and you're thinking along the right lines.

Operation Kid Brother 1967

Director Alberto De Martino **Cast** Neil Connery, Lois Maxwell 104m

That's **Neil Connery** (as in Sean's brother) playing the "brother of a British secret agent". **Bernard Lee** plays a man who does a job rather like M in a certain spy movie series and **Maxwell** plays a secretary. But is the film any good? Well, the ads proclaimed "Operation Kid Brother too much for one mother!" and Neil plays a hypnotist, plastic surgeon and lip reader. So that'll be a no then.

OSS 117: Cairo, Nest of Spies 2006

Director Michel Hazanavicius **Cast** Jean Dujardin, Bérénice Bejo, Aure Atika 99m

Created by **Jean Bruce** in 1949 (four years before James Bond), Hubert Bonisseur de la Bath has featured in 265 novels and nine movies. Borrowing from Hulot and Clouseau, **Jean Dujardin** bestows vacuous suavity and imperialist condescension upon OSS 117 in this gleefully politically incorrect romp. But while there's a sly causticity to the political satire, the biggest laughs come from the ridiculous running gags and the pantomimic parodying of such classic espionage tropes as the racially stereotyped villain and the imperilled love interest.

The President's Analyst 1967

Director Theodore J. Flicker **Cast** James Coburn, Severn Darden 103m

James Coburn starred in a couple of spy semi-spoofs as Derek Flint, but they were the kind of movies that assumed they were wittier than they were. But in *The President's Analyst*, Coburn casts off the smugness in a very funny satire, as a shrink who is soon pursued by every spy on Earth. Most original character? An armed and dangerous Canadian agent who hates Americans. Maybe that's why Americans have all those guns: you never know when Canada might invade.

Spione 1928

Director Fritz Lang **Cast** Willy Fritsch, Rudolf Klein-Rogge, Gerda Maurus 178m

Spy number 326 (**Fritsch**) can't close down a spy ring because he's in love with Sonja (**Maurus**), much to the chagrin of the ring-master (**Klein-Rogge**). This is the German grandaddy of Bond (known as *Spies* in the US) and probably the most distinguished silent spy movie. It was a genre to which Lang would return (most notably with *Man Hunt*), and to watch this is to see many of the genre's clichés for the first time, even the daft bits.

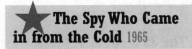 ## The Spy Who Came in from the Cold 1965

Director Martin Ritt **Cast** Richard Burton, Claire Bloom, Sam Wanamaker 112m

John Le Carré didn't want **Burton** to play his spy, Alec Leamas. He preferred Trevor Howard, whom he thought had a more lived-in look. There was a further complication: Burton's co-star **Bloom** had been the other woman in Burton's marriage before Liz Taylor came along. And Burton didn't like the director's ideas about his character: Ritt wanted to flatten him out, denying Burton his trademark magnetic flamboyance. Yet the movie works brilliantly. Burton was drunk and miserable during filming, and when Le Carré first saw the film he realized he'd been wrong: Burton was perfect.

The Tailor of Panama 2001

Director John Boorman **Cast** Pierce Brosnan, Geoffrey Rush, Jamie Lee Curtis 109m

Still in Her Majesty's Service as James Bond at the time, **Brosnan** relishes the role of a very British MI6 agent, sent to the backwater of Panama in disgrace. There he falls in with an expat tailor (**Rush**), who has an ear to the ground and a wife (**Curtis**) with access to valuable information. **Boorman**'s vision is of a glitteringly unreal, post-colonial expatriate bubble, while the twisty plot is scripted from the **John Le Carré** novel by Boorman, **Andrew Davies** and Le Carré himself. Look out for a pre-Hogwarts Harry Potter.

The 39 Steps 1935

Director Alfred Hitchcock **Cast** Robert Donat, Madeleine Carroll, Lucie Mannheim 93m

Risking the censor's ire to warn British audiences about the growing fascist threat, this chase thriller secured Alfred Hitchcock's international reputation. It's full of trademark flourishes and there's plenty of saucy banter between **Robert Donat**'s fugitive (who has been wrongly accused of murder) and **Madeleine Carroll**, as the cool blonde he meets on a train and who overcomes her initial misgivings to help him expose Godfrey Tearle's spy ring. This is less faithful to John Buchan's novel than the 1959 and 1978 versions, but Hitch liked the story so much, he remade it as *Saboteur*, *North by Northwest* and *Torn Curtain*.

Three Days of the Condor 1975

Director Sydney Pollack **Cast** Robert Redford, Faye Dunaway, Cliff Robertson, Max von Sydow 118m

After Nixon quit, almost every movie made in America was described as showing "post-Watergate disillusionment". Well, this one really does. **Redford** plays Joseph Turner, a CIA researcher who returns from lunch to find all his co-workers dead. For a movie star of his magnitude, Redford was refreshingly willing to play characters who were slightly out of their depth, and Turner's only unqualified victory is to be still alive when the film finishes. The anti-climactic ending, where Turner doesn't even have the satisfaction of knowing he's blown the whistle, is a bonus. An under-rated gem.

What's Up Tiger Lily? 1966

Directors Woody Allen, Senkichi Taniguchi **Cast** Tatsuya Mihashi, Woody Allen (narrator) 79m

As early as 1964 the James Bond formula had inspired a Japanese spoof entitled *Kokusai Himitsu Keisatsu: Kagi No Kagi*. Allen bought the rights to it and dubbed a completely new narration, so that the plot now centred on the fight to control a top secret recipe for egg salad. Funnily enough, two actresses in the original movie became Bond girls.

STEAMPUNK

Go back to a fantastical future where steam power and clockwork still rule and Jules Verne might be popping round for tea by zeppelin.

Brazil 1985

Director Terry Gilliam **Cast** Jonathan Pryce, Robert De Niro, Kim Greist 132m

Bleak yet humorous tale where Sam (**Pryce**) feels oppressed by technology and bureaucracy, and fantasizes about flying off with his dream girl Jill (**Greist**), whom he's never met. **Gilliam**'s experience directing was almost as nightmarish as the story. He fought with Universal Studios' chairman Sid Sheinberg (as documented in the book *The Battle of Brazil*), with Sheinberg insisting on an upbeat ending (shown in a US TV version). Gilliam was also unhappy with Greist's performance so he cut several of her scenes – which Sheinberg put back into his studio version, referred to as *Love Conquers All*.

The Golden Compass 2007

Director Chris Weitz **Cast** Daniel Craig, Nicole Kidman, Dakota Blue Richards 113m

Set in a parallel steampunk universe powered by anarbic energy and populated by talking polar bears, author **Phillip Pullman**'s bestselling *His Dark Materials* trilogy bewitched the world. Sadly this multimillion-dollar movie adaptation was less magical: production walkouts landing it, last minute, with the director of *American Pie*. Lyra, a girl with a magic clockwork space/time compass and a shape-shifting "daemon" familiar, realizes her destiny as the One who will overthrow the despotic Church. A conflict which went down like a lead zeppelin in the US Bible Belt, crucifying any ideas of a sequel.

Hellboy II: The Golden Army 2008

Director Guillermo del Toro **Cast** Ron Perlman, Selma Blair, Doug Jones 120m

Variety praised **del Toro**'s "clockmaker's preoccupation with detail" and the Spanish director allows his marvellous mechanical imagination to run riot here. Gorgeous sequel to the 2004 fantasy, based on **Mike Mignola**'s comic books, our anti-hero is a foul-mouthed, cigar-chewing devil's spawn with a stone club hand created by mad boffin Nazi occultists. The overdrawn plot takes second place to del Toro's fabulous bestiary, which includes vicious tooth fairies, the titular mechanical army created by goblin blacksmiths and an underground library lair straight out of Captain Nemo.

The Prestige 2006

Director Christopher Nolan **Cast** Hugh Jackman, Christian Bale, Michael Caine 130m

Nolan shot this curiosity in between *Batmans*. Here **Bale** sheds the mask to play a magician whose inexplicable illusions are the talk of turn-of-the-century London. Dead set on uncovering his secrets, his rival (**Jackman**) travels to quiz Tesla (**David Bowie**), a real-life engineering wizard with a living room full of arty-looking lightbulbs, who claims to have invented a teleporter. **Christopher Priest**, author of the original novel, was already a fan of Nolan's and insisted he directed: no wonder this feels like *Memento* in tweeds.

How many Victorians does it take to change a lightbulb? Hugh Jackman and Andy Serkis experiment in *The Prestige*.

Steamboy 2004

Director Katsuhiro Otomo **Cast** Anna Paquin, Patrick Stewart, Alfred Molina (English dubbed version) 126m

Ten years in the making, **Otomo**'s second major anime since *Akira* was the most expensive full-length Japanese animated movie to date. It didn't make its yen back due to its baffling eccentricity for both Japanese and Western audiences. Set in an alternate reality version of Victorian Manchester, it's about a steam-obsessed thirteen-year-old boy inventor who gets drawn into a caper that involves Robert Louis Stevenson, a flying evil fortress, the Rovers Return pub and an infuriating girl called Scarlett O'Hara. Nice zeppelin/steam train chase though.

Wild Wild West 1999

Director Barry Sonnenfeld **Cast** Will Smith, Kevin Kline, Kenneth Branagh 106m

A fan of the original TV series, **Will Smith** turned down the lead role in *The Matrix* to star in this adaptation. He later admitted it was the worst decision of his career. Warner Bros' most expensive production ever, you could file this sci-fi/comedy genre collision equally under "Steampunk" or "Weird West" or just plain "Turkey".

SUPER-HEROES

What makes a superhero? Is it superpowers? Or just super gadgets? Whatever their source of superiority, with their great power comes great responsibility...

The Adventures of Buckaroo Banzai Across the 8th Dimension 1984

Director W.D. Richter **Cast** Peter Weller, John Lithgow, Ellen Barkin, Jeff Goldblum 102m

In his first crack at saving the world (**Weller** went on to play Robocop), Buckaroo Banzai is a superhero/rock star/brain surgeon/samurai warrior who must fight evil creatures from the eighth dimension. Able to travel through solid matter, he can call on a band of Hong Kong cavaliers, including a cowboy brain surgeon and a six-foot ET rasta. All the baddies are called John, with **John Lithgow** as evil boss Lord John Whorfin stealing scenes.

American Splendor 2003

Directors Shari Springer Berman, Robert Pulcini **Cast** Paul Giamatti, Harvey Pekar 101m

Blurring the lines between documentary and drama, **Giamatti** plays the charac-ter Harvey Pekar and the real-life Pekar plays himself, the real Harvey Pekar. Pekar has a wife, a daughter and a menial nine-to-five job. He draws on his love of music as he becomes a superhero to fight his anally retentive boss and his testicular cancer. Pekar's very ordinariness led graphic artist Robert Crumb to build a comic around him after Pekar, in one of his rants, moaned that comics were never about people like him.

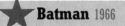 Batman 1966

Director Leslie H. Martinson **Cast** Adam West, Burt Ward, Burgess Meredith 105m

This may lack a catchy tagline – "For the first time on the motion picture screen in color! Adam West as Batman and Burt Ward as Robin together with all their fantastic derring-do and their dastardly villains too!" – but this spin-off has all the virtues, and vices, of the TV series. The Dynamic Duo fend off four villains: The Joker (**Cesar Romero**), The Rid-dler (**Frank Gorshin**), Catwoman (**Lee**

Meriwether rather than Julie Newmar) and The Penguin (**Meredith**), and, at one point, the not-so Dynamic Duo are saved by a porpoise.

Flash Gordon 1980

Director Mike Hodges **Cast** Sam J. Jones, Melody Anderson, Max von Sydow 111m

"Flash / Ah-ahhh / He'll save every one of us!" Queen's title track makes you feel like you've already watched this psychedelically camp 1930s comic strip adaptation, even if you never had. Former *Playgirl* centrefold **Jones** plays the titular American football player who finds himself skyjacked on a rocket to planet Mongo where he has only 24 hours to save the Earth from Ming the Merciless. Federico Fellini was the first director to wisely pass on a project whose production nightmares led eventual eighth choice **Mike Hodges** (*Get Carter*) to call this "the only improvised $27-million movie ever made."

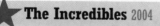 **The Incredibles** 2004

Director Brad Bird **Cast** Craig T. Nelson, Holly Hunter, Samuel L. Jackson 115m

Smart, mid-life-crisis humour and a groovy retro feel characterize this Oscar-winner about the incredible adventures of a family, whose 2.4 kids suburban life masks their Fantastic Four-style powers. Brought to you by Pixar, it's their first movie to ever get a PG certificate: clear sign it's too good to be wasted on children. Think *The Simpsons* in tights.

Iron Man 2008

Director Jon Favreau **Cast** Robert Downey Jr, Gwyneth Paltrow, Terrence Howard, Jeff Bridges 126m

Nicolas Cage and Tom Cruise were both interested in playing previously little known Marvel Comics creation Iron Man aka Tony Stark the billionaire playboy industrialist/engineering genius who builds his own body armour. Thankfully, the part went to notorious substance-abuser/acting genius **Robert Downey Jr**, officially rehabilitating his star status with studio bosses still haunted by the 2000 incident where the actor got busted in a Palm Springs hotel room with cocaine and a Wonder Woman costume.

Mystery Men 1999

Director Kinka Usher **Cast** Hank Azaria, Janeane Garofalo, William H. Macy, Ben Stiller, Greg Kinnear, Eddie Izzard, Geoffrey Rush 120m

As the movie's tagline enthuses, these are not your classic heroes, these are the other guys. To be specific, they're The Shoveler ("I shovel well"), The Blue Raja (hurls forks and spoons), The Spleen (uses flatulence to bring down evil), The Bowler (complete with golden bowling ball encasing her dead dad's head), Mr Furious (a time bomb of fury) and a host of new recruits. This amiable spoof basically has one joke – these guys are crap.

Superheroes just don't fly like this any more: Christopher Reeve as the definitive version of the red-caped crusader, *Superman*.

My Super Ex-Girlfriend
2006

Director Ivan Reitman **Cast** Uma Thurman, Luke Wilson, Anna Faris 95m

Fresh, funny with surreal moments that touch the cloak hem of genius, this rom-com was unjustly overshadowed on release by *Superman Returns*. **Uma Thurman** stars as G-Girl, a neurotic superheroine who falls for a normal guy, who dumps her. Super-big mistake. Bunny-boiling has nothing on G-Girl's increasingly loopy revenge acts that lead her ex to defend his breakup behaviour with the immortal line: "Well, you DID throw a shark at me". It's the only superhero film to address the delicate issue of "super-sex". As one hilariously painful coital scene confirms, all G-Girl's muscles are steel-like.

Superman 1978

Director Richard Donner **Cast** Christopher Reeve, Marlon Brando, Gene Hackman 143m

Forget the lacklustre 2006 remake starring Brandon Routh – oh, you had. **Christopher Reeve** remains the big screen's definitive man in red knickers. Yet having amazingly battled off big hitters like Robert Redford, Clint Eastwood, Warren Beatty, Burt Reynolds and even Neil Diamond (it was the 1970s, man) for the role, Reeve found his super-luck turn to bad when finally trying to escape it. A horse-riding accident left him paralysed for the rest of his life, whilst a car crash left his Lois Lane co-star, **Margot Kidder**, unable to work for two years, resulting in bankruptcy and alcoholic depression.

Brandon Routh should count himself lucky all *Superman Returns* did was send him back to career oblivion, faster than a speeding bullet.

Unbreakable 2000

Director M. Night Shyamalan **Cast** Bruce Willis, Samuel L. Jackson, Robin Wright Penn **107m**

A lifelong comic-book fan, **Shyamalan**'s companion to the sleeper hit *The Sixth Sense* is rife with superhero references. **Willis**, in a fine performance, is David Dunn (note the superhero-style alliterative name), sole survivor of a train wreck. Reading David's astonishing story, Elijah (**Jackson**) is convinced David is the answer to understanding his purpose in life. If David is superhuman, Elijah is the opposite, nicknamed Mr Glass because he suffers from a rare but real condition, osteogenesis imperfecta, which means his bones are easily broken.

The Watchmen 2009

Director Zack Snyder **Cast** Malin Akerman, Billy Crudup, Matthew Goode **162m**

Clocking up six studios, five directors and over two decades in development hell, many thought **Alan Moore** was right when he declared his ground-breaking 1985 graphic novel "unfilmable." Yet **Zack Snyder** makes a surprisingly fair fist of it. Adapting what Terry Gilliam once called "the *War and Peace* of comic books" to a popcorn audience ain't easy. But this dark realization of Moore's sophisticated tale of ageing, emotion-ally damaged caped crusaders battling beneath the shadow of the Cold War is anything but cartoonish.

Who Wants to Kill Jessie?
1966

Director Václac Vorlícek **Cast** Dana Medrická, Jiri Sovák **80m**

A scientist (**Medrická**) invents a formula which removes elements from dreams, but which also unexpectedly transports them to the real world, something she only realizes when her husband's dreams of Jessie, a voluptuous blonde comic-book heroine, become real. It's light and bright, with some nice touches.

SUPER-NATURAL

There are things that just can't be explained. Things that go bump in the night. Levitating tables and flickering lights. More than any other art form, the movies demand we believe.

 Bell, Book and Candle 1958

Director Richard Quine **Cast** James Stewart, Kim Novak, Jack Lemmon 103m

This Broadway comedy is a charming romantic fantasy on film, with **Novak** as the Greenwich Village witch who can make men fall in love with her when she isn't keeping an eye on her mischievous warlock brother (**Lemmon**) and doddering aunt (**Elsa Lanchester**). **Stewart** is Novak's blissfully unaware upstairs neighbour, on whom she casts a spell so that he ditches his fiancée and falls for her in this inspiration (along with *I Married a Witch*) for the TV series *Bewitched*.

Blithe Spirit 1945

Director David Lean **Cast** Rex Harrison, Kay Hammond, Constance Cummings 96m

Based on a play by **Noel Coward**, this comedy zips along with witty repartee from a raft of British actors (including the ever-wonderful **Margaret Rutherford** as the madcap medium) at the peak of their powers. The blithe spirit in question is Elvira, the ex-wife of **Harrison**'s urbane novelist, returned to make his life with his new wife a misery – robed in fluorescent green, with scarlet lips and nails, she's a siren from the Other Side. A cult classic today, the film failed to make an impression at the box office, despite the wild success of the play – famously, Coward demanded of **Lean**: "How the hell did you fuck up the best thing I ever did?"

Ghost 1990

Director Jerry Zucker **Cast** Demi Moore, Patrick Swayze, Whoopi Goldberg 128m

You may try to dismiss it, but you won't be able to resist it: **Swayze**, oddly touching as the beleaguered spook, and **Goldberg** as the charlatan psychic who eventually comes good, will have you believing – or longing to believe – that there's more out there than we know. Everyone remembers the iconic potters' wheel sequence, but this movie has as much edge as it does schmaltz: those shadow demons (their wails made by slowed-down tape of crying babies) are pretty scary, and how come no one ever mentions the scene where Whoopi and **Demi** smooch?

I Married a Witch 1942

Director René Clair **Cast** Frederic March, Veronica Lake 76m

Veronica Lake is seductively coy as the seventeenth-century witch burned at the stake who returns three centuries later as part of a curse on the Puritan family who condemned her. Her task is to spoil descendant **March**'s upcoming marriage by making him fall in love with her, but a mix-up with the love potion has her ingesting it instead. A promised remake, directed by Danny DeVito and possibly starring Tom Cruise, has yet to materialize.

★ The Orphanage 2007

Director Juan Antonio Bayona **Cast** Belén Rueda, Fernando Cayo, Roger Príncep 105m

Produced by Guillermo del Toro, director of *Pan's Labyrinth*, this poignant ghost story gets under the skin with all the tried-and-trusted ingredients – a gothic mansion, strange old ladies, bumps in the night and small children standing stock-still in long corridors (this one has the USP of his head being hidden by a small, misshapen sack) – and more than the usual share of grief and loss. The haunting here is one of sadness; Spanish Catholic melancholy at its best.

The Witches 1990

Director Nicolas Roeg **Cast** Angelica Huston, Mai Zetterling, Jasen Fisher 91m

Roald Dahl's twisted children's book became a scary movie in **Roeg**'s hands. **Fisher** is Luke, the small child taken by his grandmother (**Zetterling**) to a grand hotel in England, where he discovers a secret coven of witches, led by the Grand High Witch (**Huston**, who steals the film, but then she did spend eight hours in make-up each day), who are preparing to change all children into mice. Jim Henson's Creature Workshop (this was the last movie to be overseen by the man himself) provided the rodent effects (using real mice and animatronic ones), while **Rowan Atkinson**, **Jane Horrocks** and **Brenda Blethyn** offer support.

Witchfinder General 1968

Director Michael Reeves **Cast** Vincent Price, Ian Ogilvy 87m

Known in the US as *The Conqueror Worm*, this horror classic features one of **Price**'s best performances, in a role originally offered to Donald Pleasence, until the distributor AIP demanded Price be offered the part. Seen as excessively bloody and gruesome when it was first released, Price is the witchfinder Matthew Hopkins (who, in just one year, 1645, was reported to have killed almost two hundred witches), scouring Civil War England for worshippers of the devil to torture in the most sadistic ways possible. *Witchfinder* was the final movie of 25-year-old director **Reeves**, who overdosed the year after it was released.

TEEN

Rebel Without a Cause (see p.113) didn't quite invent the genre, but the 1950s was the decade in which the teen movie came of age (as it were). Youths have been mumbling inarticulately, looking angst-ridden and sneering at grown-ups ever since.

American Graffiti 1973

Director George Lucas **Cast** Richard Dreyfuss, Ron Howard, Charles Martin Smith 110m

A group of friends in 1962 spend their last night together before going their separate ways into adult life, in this funny, nostalgic piece of cinema which filmmakers have been paying homage to ever since. One of the first mainstream movies to use music as such a fundamental part of the action, the rock'n'roll slots perfectly with the sex, booze, music and cars. This launched a thousand careers, but **Lucas** hardly spoke to the actors (he hired a drama coach instead).

Badlands 1973

Director Terrence Malick **Cast** Martin Sheen, Sissy Spacek 94m

One of the most stunning directorial debuts, this movie, based loosely on the Starkweather-Fugate killings of the 1950s, was from **Malick**'s own script. **Sheen** is a James Dean lookalike and garbage collector Kit, who goes on the run with his girlfriend (**Spacek**) after she kills her father. The pair leave a trail of seemingly random yet brutal killings in their wake. Spacek's flat monotone narration helps avoid any sensationalism.

The Breakfast Club 1985

Director John Hughes **Cast** Emilio Estevez, Anthony Michael Hall, Molly Ringwald 97m

If the 1980s were your years, *The Breakfast Club* was your signature movie, capturing the highs and lows, not to mention the fashion for fingerless gloves. **Hughes**' best foray into teen cinema, the film showcases a wealth of young talent – though few went on to great careers. Despite the clichés, notably the premise of putting a stereotype jock, princess, criminal, basket case and brain in the same room and watching them react, the film plays well on teenagers' instinctive belief that the world is against them.

Com licença, eu vou à luta 1986

Director Lui Farias **Cast** Fernanda Torres, Marieta Severo 85m

Teen angst in Brazil as seen through the eyes of a fifteen-year-old girl and her suburban family. One of the more realistic tales of its type, it shows Elaine (**Torres**) trying to cope with the usual trials and tribulations and the unnatural animosity shown by her mum (**Severo**). Torres went on to win best actress at Cannes for her role in *Eu sei que vou te amar*. The soundtrack boasts a rather fine selection of Brazilian pop.

Cosh Boy 1953

Director Lewis Gilbert **Cast** James Kenney, Joan Collins 73m

Britain's first X-rated movie tells the salutory story of "a post-war tragedy: the juvenile delinquent". With all the trademarks of the "social problem" genre, this plays like a public information movie – one that comes right out and blames the parents – with a stilted script delivered in cringeingly bad Cockney accents. It's a fascinating slice of history nonetheless (bleak, bombed out London locations; post-war anxiety), with a highly watchable performance from a very young **Collins** as the good girl gone (very) bad.

Dazed and Confused 1993

Director Richard Linklater **Cast** Jason London, Wiley Wiggins 102m

Two years after director **Linklater** captured 24 hours in the life of twenty-something misfits in *Slacker*, he was back in Texas with the disaffected youth, this time celebrating the last day – and night – of high school in 1976. No real plot,

unless you count drinking, driving and partying, but all the right characters – the nerds, the potheads, the jocks – even the creepy older guy who still hangs out with the kids.

Fat Girl 2001

Director Catherine Breillat **Cast** Anaïs Reboux, Roxane Mesquida 86m

Breillat, never one to dodge controversy, pushes the teen movie to its darkest edge. What starts out as a standard story of sibling rivalry between a pudgy thirteen-year-old and her prettier older sister soon enters some pretty murky waters, touching on underage sex and murderous fantasy before spiralling into shocking brutality. A more unsettling view of sisterly love you will not find.

Ghost World 2001

Director Terry Zwigoff **Cast** Thora Birch, Steve Buscemi, Scarlett Johansson 112m

Former cutesy child star **Birch** gained twenty pounds to play Enid, the best friend of Rebecca (**Johansson**). High-school chums, they aim to remain so for life, spurning college and moving in together, until Becky reconsiders college and falls for Josh (**Brad Renfro**), while Enid becomes attached to middle-aged record collector Seymour (**Buscemi**). The movie's colourful hues emphasize the story's comic-book origins (it's from the series by **Daniel Clowes**), but Enid and Rebecca are two of the most original comic characters and they transfer beautifully to the silver screen.

Heathers 1989

Director Michael Lehmann **Cast** Winona Ryder, Christian Slater 103m

From the opening shot of **Ryder**'s head as a human peg in a game of croquet, you know you're in for a surreal ride. High-school student Veronica (Ryder) is forced to become a lowly member of the elite Heathers' clique. But new arrival J.D. (**Slater**) leads her into a plot to teach the Heathers a murderous lesson. **Daniel Waters**' sharp script ridicules all teen drama: one teacher lectures the students on committing suicide the correct way as "there's only one chance to get it right."

Lilya 4-ever 2002

Director Lukas Moodysson **Cast** Oksana Akinshina, Artyom Bogucharsky 109m

Sixteen-year-old Lilya's heartless mother has swapped Soviet village life for a new beginning in America, but left her daughter behind to fend for herself. As Lilya's life spirals out of control she turns to prostitution and meets Andrei (**Pavel Ponomaryov**), who promises her a better life in Sweden. What follows is a brutal tale of trafficking and pimping, made all the more disturbing by its documentary style.

The Outsiders 1983

Director Francis Ford Coppola **Cast** Rob Lowe, Patrick Swayze, Matt Dillon, Emilio Estevez, Diane Lane 91m

This was probably the first and last taste that actors like **Swayze** had of Method acting. To create a suitably hostile atmosphere between those playing the "socs" and those playing the "greasers" in 1960s Oklahoma, **Coppola** gave the socs leather-bound scripts and put them up in swanky hotels, while the greasers made do with paperback scripts and cheap digs. It worked. Famous faces abound, notably **Tom Cruise** and Nicolas Coppola, aka Francis's nephew, **Nicolas Cage**.

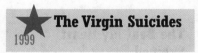 **The Virgin Suicides** 1999

Director Sofia Coppola **Cast** Kirsten Dunst, Kathleen Turner, James Woods 97m

Set in the mid-1970s, saturated in nostalgic Kodachrome colour, **Coppola**'s accomplished debut – based on Jeffrey Eugenides' novel – about five slightly strange teenage sisters, who arouse dangerous passions in their small Midwestern town, is a ravishing, hypnotic movie. **Dunst**, as the sexually awakened Lux, gives a career-best performance.

THRILLERS

Ian Fleming said his books were aimed "somewhere between the solar plexus and, well, the upper thigh". The only defining characteristic of a thriller is that it should offer (or attempt to offer) thrills.

The Beat My Heart Skipped 2005

Director Jacques Audiard **Cast** Roman Duris, Niels Arestrup, Emmanuelle Devos 107m

The French *policier* (police thriller) gets updated while keeping all the themes and gritty "realism" of the greatest French thrillers of the 1960s and 70s. **Duris** is Jean-Paul Belmondo for the new millennium, brutal and tender as the thug torn between a life of crime and his love of classical piano, in a slickly executed remake of the 1978 American indie movie *Fingers* (starring Harvey Keitel and well worth digging out).

The Bird with the Crystal Plumage 1969

Director Dario Argento **Cast** Tony Musante, Suzy Kendall, Enrico Maria Salerno 96m

Argento's directorial debut isn't as assured, nor as bloody, as his later works, but it was a seminal film in the Italian *giallo* (pulp thriller/horror) genre. The story's been done before, and since – there's a woman-killing maniac on the loose, and a witness who has to find the murderer to save himself – and the script falters at the end, but the low-budget élan, with stunning cinematography from a young **Vittorio Storaro** and a creepy soundtrack from **Ennio Morricone** is undeniable.

Blow Out 1981

Director Brian De Palma **Cast** John Travolta, Nancy Allen, John Lithgow 108m

Quentin Tarantino cites this as his favourite **Travolta** movie. You can see why: Travolta, still trying to escape from teen films, stars as a sound recordist who picks up a noise which is the clue to an assassination. Plus, there's some serious homage going on. **De Palma**, at his flashiest and darkest, pays tribute to *Blow Up*, *Psycho* (so no change there then) and Coppola's *The Conversation*, which, at times here, he almost copies scene for scene.

The Butcher 1970

Director Claude Chabrol **Cast** Stéphane Audran, Jean Yanne, Antonio Passalia 94m

In the tiny French town of Tremolat a series of murders takes place. Unlike most thrillers, characters and audience both know who the likely killer is – town butcher Popaul (**Yanne**). The suspense lies in how his friend Hélène (**Audran**) will handle the revelation, how it will affect their relationship and whether she will be his next victim. The movie focuses on them, but although the victims are killed offscreen, there's an indelible sense of foreboding, aided by the stunning back-drop of misty hillsides and caves.

Cutter's Way 1981

Director Ivan Passer **Cast** Jeff Bridges, John Heard, Lisa Eichhorn 105m

This post-Vietnam *noir* was largely ignored on its release as *Cutter and Bone*. Repackaged with a new title and released onto the arthouse circuit, it grew as a sleeper. The masterful **Bridges** is superb as always, while **Heard** gives possibly his best performance as the crazed, tortured Vietnam vet Cutter – and **Eichhorn** does brilliantly with the flimsy material she's given as his wife. Dark and sad, imbued with the anxiety of Reagan's America.

Day of the Jackal 1973

Director Fred Zinnemann **Cast** Edward Fox, Alan Badel, Tony Britton 142m

There's a rather unpleasant wit about **Zinnemann**'s movie (as when the police stenographer complains he can't under-stand a confession because the witness is screaming too much under torture) and a laudable refusal not to "explain" **Fox**'s

assassin. So we're spared the flashbacks to his relationship with his mum. A subtle movie given the subject: the most violent image is a burst watermelon.

★ Diva 1981

Director Jean-Jacques Beineix **Cast** Wilhelmenia Wiggins Fernandez, Frédéric Andréi 123m

Beineix's debut inspired a thousand reviewers to call it stylish. That's what hap-pens if you insert an opera singer into a Hitchcockian thriller. **Andréi** is a postman who tapes **Fernandez**'s diva (who won't record her performances) but gets his tape mixed up with one which is vital evi-dence in a crime. All kinds of shenanigans ensue, beautifully shot by Beineix, who has struggled to match this mix of high culture and low thrills. The chase in the Paris Metro is worth watching for in itself.

★ Don't Look Now 1973

Director Nicolas Roeg **Cast** Julie Christie, Donald Sutherland, Hilary Mason 110m

In **Roeg**'s finest movie the menace, ten-sion and mystery largely emanate from the Venetian setting. John Baxter (**Suther-land**) and his wife Laura (**Christie**) are in Venice to overcome their grief at their daughter's death, but Laura is warned that her husband will die if he does not leave, and the city is racked by a series of murders. In Roeg's skilled hands the viewer gets a shocking denouement (watch out for the recurring motifs) and something deeper, an emotionally rich movie about love and loss.

God Told Me To 1976

Director Larry Cohen **Cast** Tony Lo Bianco, Sandy Dennis, Sylvia Sidney **95m**

Both the *X-Files* and the movie *Unbreakable* were inspired by this horror, sci-fi, religious detective thriller. When a sniper murders fourteen people, Detective Nicholas (**Lo Bianco**) is on the case. But when a father murders his family and a policeman (**Andy Kaufman**) kills his colleagues, Nicholas suspects a more sinister, otherworldly reason behind the seemingly motiveless killings. Too many plot strands fail to make this a classic, but it's definitely one of **Cohen**'s better efforts.

The Killing of a Chinese Bookie 1976

Director John Cassavetes **Cast** Ben Gazzara, Timothy Carey **109m**

John Cassavetes' sombre pace and unique use of colour set this movie apart from your average thriller. Cassavetes regular **Gazzara** is Cosmo, the owner of the Crazy Horse West topless club who has a passion for gambling. After losing money to the Mob, his repayment is to kill another mobster. The director chooses to set aside the usual clichés, focusing on Cosmo and his loyalties to his club and extended family of dancers, intertwined with gambling, murder and double-crossing thrills.

Klute 1971

Director Alan J. Pakula **Cast** Jane Fonda, Donald Sutherland **114m**

There's an intensity to this movie which isn't just due to **Pakula**'s accomplished direction. Take one famous scene, where **Fonda** unzips her dress: **Sutherland** later told an interviewer, "I guess we'd made love an hour before we shot that." Fonda won an Oscar for her performance as Bree Daniels, the prostitute being stalked by one of her clients. But Sutherland as the detective who initially doubts her but feels obliged to protect her matches her all the way.

★ Man Hunt 1941

Director Fritz Lang **Cast** Walter Pidgeon, Joan Bennett **105m**

Lang based this movie about a big-game hunter trying to kill Hitler on the **Geoffrey Household** novel *Rogue Male*. It's hard not to see a certain wish fulfilment in the choice of subject: Lang had fled Nazi Germany, leaving behind a wife who had divorced him partly because of the authorities' disapproval. He adds an anti-fascist message to the movie which, though typical for Hollywood films of the time, wasn't in the book. An effective air of menace throughout and some neat, unobtrusive symbolism.

Marathon Man 1976

Director John Schlesinger **Cast** Dustin Hoffman, Laurence Olivier 126m

This is the movie where **Olivier** advised **Hoffman** to try acting. Less famously, Hoffman told Britain's grandest thesp to try improvising. Olivier wasn't very good at it, partly because he just didn't do that kind of thing but also because he was in excruciating pain. All of which almost overshadows what you see onscreen, a taut thriller in which Hoffman's history graduate is pitted against Olivier's Nazi dentist. Preview audiences were so sickened by the torture scene that it was subsequently cut back.

Ms. 45 1981

Director Abel Ferrara **Cast** Zoë Tamerlis, Albert Sinkys, Darlene Stuto 80m

Ferrara has directed a lot of movies which most of the world has never heard of. A pity really because this film, about a mute woman who gets raped twice and seeks revenge – a kind of feminist *Death Wish* – is well made. The poetry of the streets can be a bit overrated, but garbage has rarely looked quite as good as it does here, clogging up the streets of New York. And **Tamerlis** makes a pleasant change from Charles Bronson as the avenger.

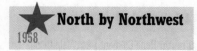 ## North by Northwest
1958

Director Alfred Hitchcock **Cast** Cary Grant, Eva Marie Saint, James Mason 136m

Grant is perfectly cast as Roger O. Thornton, the suave advertising executive who's a victim of mistaken identity and forced to go on the run, luckily (or maybe not) picking up the lovely **Eva Marie Saint** on the way. **Mason** is the epitome of evil urbanity in a movie which packs in a surprising number of laughs. The brilliant set pieces include the famous crop-spraying sequence, while an extra layer of tension is provided by **Bernard Herrmann**'s edgy score.

Play Misty for Me 1971

Director Clint Eastwood **Cast** Clint Eastwood, Jessica Walter 102m

One of only two Clint films scripted by a woman (**Jo Heims**), this isn't Hitchcock but it's more than half decent. **Walter** is superb as the psychotic lover, Evelyn. Her expletive-filled bursts of outrage still seem shocking. **Eastwood** benefits from appearing to be powerless as this madwoman takes over his life. The movie is not without flaws (the romantic interlude is like an outtake from *Love Story*), but mostly this is genuinely chilling.

Plein soleil 1960

Director René Clément **Cast** Alain Delon, Maurice Ronet, Marie Laforêt 119m

In the best adaptation of **Patricia Highsmith**'s *The Talented Mr Ripley*, **Delon** excels as the frighteningly cunning Ripley, paid by Mr Greenleaf to bring his wayward son home, only to murder him and steal his identity. **Clément**'s direction is masterly, shooting Ripley's insidious actions against the backdrop of a postcard-perfect Rome. The movie is a favourite of Martin Scorsese, sponsor of its recent re-release.

Alain Delon as the cold-eyed, multi-talented Monsieur Ripley in *Plein Soleil*.

Shoot the Piano Player 1960

Director François Truffaut **Cast** Charles Aznavour, Marie Dubois 80m

Charles Aznavour may be most famous outside France as the singer who sounds as if his throat muscles are in spasm, but he is subtle and charming here as the piano player sinking into his brother's murky underworld. **Truffaut**'s second feature is an entertaining combo of thriller, gangster movie and comedy and a witty nod to the budget thrillers he liked.

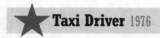

Taxi Driver 1976

Director Martin Scorsese **Cast** Robert De Niro, Jodie Foster, Harvey Keitel 113m

Much imitated, never bettered – **De Niro** is still terrifying as the maladjusted

Vietnam vet Travis Bickle, longing for the day when the rain will "wash all the scum off the streets". **Foster** still unnerves with her sassy child prostitute shtick, and 1970s New York has never seemed seedier, or sadder. Unsettling and poignant – and giving more of an insight into scriptwriter **Paul Schrader**'s psyche than anyone would ask for.

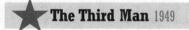

The Third Man 1949

Director Carol Reed **Cast** Joseph Cotten, Trevor Howard, Orson Welles 104m

Graham Greene's work translates well to the big screen, but this movie far surpasses the story on which it is based. The music helps – according to rumour just a tune **Reed** heard being played on a zither in a café. Then there's the war-torn Vienna locations, atmospherically filmed by **Robert Krasker**. But finally it's **Welles**' insouciant performance as the heartless but charming racketeer Harry Lime that can't help but endear him to us, reinforcing the moral ambiguity and betrayed friendships that are such essential parts of Greeneland.

23 1998

Director Hans-Christian Schmid **Cast** August Diehl, Fabian Busch, Dieter Landuris 100m

It's the late 1980s and Karl Koch (**Diehl**) has a new computer. At first he uses it to post on bulletin boards about esoteric literature, but gradually he and his friend David realize they can crack into government files. It all turns criminal when another friend, Pepe, gets the KGB involved. Based on a true story from the early days of computer hacking, this is a dark and stylish look at a young man getting in over his head, and also at the Cold War paranoia of 1980s Europe.

The Unfaithful Wife 1968

Director Claude Chabrol **Cast** Stéphane Audran, Michel Bouquet, Maurice Ronet 98m

Cool, cruel domestic thriller from **Chabrol**, who, when it comes to revealing the rotten core at the heart of bourgeois French respectability, has never been bettered. Starring Chabrol's wife of the time, **Audran**, as the woman in question, the movie also works as a poignant tale of *amour fou*, with a dash of cynical humour thrown in for good measure.

The Usual Suspects 1995

Director Bryan Singer **Cast** Stephen Baldwin, Gabriel Byrne, Kevin Spacey, Benicio Del Toro, Kevin Pollak 108m

With no budget, no track record and no real stars (**Byrne** was then fading, **Spacey** almost unknown), **Singer** and writer **Christopher McQuarrie** created a pleasing, teasing tale of a cop investigating an explosion. The title, for all its obvious echoes of *Casablanca*, came from a magazine article and the film was a poster before it became a script.

> He was dead just long enough for the murder rap to blow over. And then he had lunch.
> **Dave Kujan, The Usual Suspects**

The Wages of Fear 1953

Director Henri-Georges Clouzot **Cast** Yves Montand, Charles Vanel 144m

Four men stranded in Latin America embark on a suicidal mission to drive a couple of truckloads of nitroglycerin hundreds of miles over roads where a sudden jolt might mean certain death. The premise is beautifully simple and **Clouzot** doesn't ease up. But then this is the same director who made the great *Les diaboliques*.

TORTURE PORN

A new mainstream breed of extreme gore, which some very sick puppies find so nasty... it's nice.

Antichrist 2009

Director Lars von Trier **Cast** Willem Dafoe, Charlotte Gainsbourg 109m

Viewers ran retching for the exit from "the most shocking film in the history of the Cannes Film Festival", yet there's more going on than gore. Starting with a slow motion penetration shot, ending with a woman clubbing her husband's penis to pulp before snipping off her clitoris in graphic close-up, the story sees two grieving parents go off to the woods – and go mad (watch out for the talking fox). Sublimely shot, it's at once a profound study in psycho-sexual manipulation and a horror movie so cracking it makes even acorns seem scary.

Captivity 2007

Director Roland Joffé **Cast** Elisha Cuthbert, Daniel Gillies, Pruitt Taylor Vince 96m

Roland Joffé has come a long way since 1984's *The Killing Fields* – arguably in the wrong direction judging from this sadistic lip-smacker. Young model/actress, Jennifer Tree (*24*'s **Elisha Cuthbert**), and her little dog, are held captive in an exact dungeon replica of her apartment. "What is real?" Jennifer asks. "What you can touch" growls her hooded captor. What you can put in a blender would be more accurate. Eyeball smoothies, acid showers, live burial, dental torture: at least there's never a dull moment.

Grindhouse 2007

Directors Robert Rodriguez, Quentin Tarantino **Cast** Rose McGowan, Kurt Russell, Zoe Bell 191m

Tarantino's high concept tribute to "grindhouse": low budget, low taste exploitation flicks supposedly named after the old "bump and grind" burlesque theatres they screened in, though the name aptly also adds a flavour of cheaply churned out mince. Sleaze, slashers, martial arts and general nastiness were order of the day in such places, making this lovingly made, double-bill pastiche look like *Bambi* by comparison. Deliberately noisy-looking film effects and a cool soundtrack add to the ambience.

Hostel 2005

Director Eli Roth **Cast** Jay Hernandez, Derek Richardson, Eythor Gudjonsson **94m**

It was *New York Magazine* who slammed this as the first example of "torture porn" or "gorno" i.e. using glossy, gratuitous violence to titillate viewers. Three clueless young American dudes backpack to Slovakia to find a mythical hostel full of Euro hotties, only to get bloody comeuppance in a culturally underdeveloped nation in thrall to the immoral demands of global capitalism.

Martyrs 2008

Director Pascal Laugier **Cast** Morjana Alaoui, Mylène Jampanoï **99m**

A girl with a background of sexual abuse escapes her orphanage to wreak bloody vengeance on her tormenters. Proof that anything the Yanks can do, Europe can do nastier: this was hit by an 18+ certificate in France – the first instance for such a genre film. Unrelentingly unpleasant, particularly in its brutal treatment of women, **Laugier** said one of his main challenges as director was how to keep his actresses crying all the time.

Holidays from hell: Jay Hernandez wishing he'd stayed home as he experiences the less than cosy facilities at the backpackers' joint in *Hostel*.

TRAINS

The locomotive has inspired movies as great as *Strangers on a Train* and as dire, daft and downright incomprehensible as *Thomas and the Magic Railroad*.

Closely Observed Trains 1966

Director Jirí Menzel **Cast** Václav Neckár, Josef Somr 92m

The Czech Woody Allen, as **Menzel** is known, does a pretty decent job adapting **Bohumil Hrabal**'s funny, slight, yet classic Czech novel for the screen, helped by **Neckár**'s endearing portrayal of bewildered railway trainee Milos coping with (i.e. avoiding) the realities of life on the railways under the Nazis. Not as hilarious as it could be, this is still full of white lies, awkward moments and gentle innocence.

Un flic 1972

Director Jean-Pierre Melville **Cast** Alain Delon, Catherine Deneuve 98m

Melville's final film has been largely and unfairly overlooked. Parisian police commissioner Coleman (**Delon**) does what he can to get through each day, finding solace in his affair with Cathy (**Deneuve**), who also happens to be the girlfriend of the boss (**Richard Crenna**) of a criminal gang. As pursuit of the gang intensifies, so does the rivalry between the two men.

Beginning with a remarkable bank robbery on a deserted beach front, the high point is a twenty-minute sequence in which a helicopter is used to rob a moving train.

The Railway Children 1970

Director Lionel Jeffries **Cast** Dinah Sheridan, Bernard Cribbins, Jenny Agutter 108m

When Mr Waterbury is mysteriously taken away by two strangers, his family are forced to move to a small cottage in Yorkshire, where the three children (**Agutter**, **Sally Thomsett** and **Gary F. Warren**) become enthralled by the nearby railway. Based on the children's novel by **E. Nesbit**, **Jeffries**' directorial debut always stays on the right side of cute in its depiction of an idyllic Edwardian childhood, chock full of adventures and benign grown-ups. It's also powerfully moving.

Sin nombre 2009

Director Cary Joji Fukunaga **Cast** Paulina Gaitan, Edgar Flores 96m

A fascinating fusion of road movie, gangster epic, tragic love story and Western, this vibrant debut reflects its director's

Battle Royale (2000, 113m)

" My first year at NYU grad film, a group of newish schoolfriends invited me to a bootleg viewing party of a film I'd never heard of, *Battle Royale*. Projected in standard-def majesty, on a canted and stained wall in a cosy but cramped apartment in Park Slope, the first two things that came to mind when I heard the title of the main event: a European Big Mac sans cheese, involuntarily due to *Pulp Fiction*, and man, there better be beer. Regarding the cheese, this wasn't an inappropriate way to imagine the film, which includes every kind of topping possible on a burger of violence and social commentary that leaves the viewer completely titillated, utterly mesmerized and slightly disgusted by the secret sauce of blood and guts by the film's end. The film was so audacious in theme (an entire class of naughty high-school students sent to an island and forced to slaughter one another) that I was floored to learn it was the penultimate film of a 72-year-old Japanese auteur filmmaker named Kinji Fukasaku (who'd made his mark decades before with such epics as *Battles Without Honour and Humanity*) and not a videogame-weaned just-out-of-film school director with a taste for spectacle. I went on to watch more of his films, but what remains most clear from that night was what makes a cult film great: the film experience transcended the screen; it wasn't just the film but the social event itself. That night *Battle Royale* became a part of that fixed cinematic experience, collectively shared with a now dear group of friends. "

Cary Joji Fukunaga

One of the best-reviewed features of 2009, Cary Joji Fukunaga's Sin nombre *won directing and cinematography awards at the Sundance Film Festival.*

firsthand experiences with Central Americans seeking the tainted promise of new lives in the US. A tale of a Honduran teenager, a vicious gang member and his would-be apprentices, the bulk of the film takes place in the Tapachula yards and atop the US-bound freight trains on which the immigrants travel.

The Train 1964

Director John Frankenheimer **Cast** Burt Lancaster, Paul Scofield **140m**

If you get your kicks from train crashes, this is for you. The engine crashing into a derailed engine is real – so real that two cameras were smashed filming it. Based on a real-life plot involving Nazi attempts to stuff a load of looted art onto a train, the French resistance's dilemma is how to stop the train without destroying the cargo. The script's not bad either – "With luck, no one will be hurt" says one hero, to which his colleague replies: "No one's ever hurt, just dead."

TRUE STORIES

While many documentary makers (step up Michael Moore) use the genre to grind axes and air grievances, others prefer to focus on human interest, telling tales of derring-do, obsession and – frequently – just plain old weirdness.

Capturing the Friedmans
2003

Director Andrew Jarecki 108m

An "ordinary" Jewish family is torn apart when the father and a son are accused of molesting children that Mr Friedman teaches. This won the Grand Jury prize at Sundance in 2003 for its handling of a nigh-impossible subject. The movie is full of questions, shades of guilt and a spectacular lack of communication among the family. It uses family videos and interviews to challenge the viewer's assumptions as the story unfolds.

The Cove 2009

Director Louie Psihoyos 90m

Flipper was one of the most beloved TV characters, but the fascination with dolphins that he caused created a tragic epidemic that has threatened their exis-

tence and become a multi-billion dollar industry. The largest supplier of dolphins in the world is located in the picturesque town of Taijii, Japan. But the town has a horrifying secret that it doesn't want the the world to know. Part environmental documentary, part horror film, part thriller, *The Cove* shows the true power of film in the hands of people who aren't afraid to risk everything for a vital cause.

Deep Water 2007

Directors Louise Osmond and Jerry Rothwell 93m

Donald Crowhurst was an amateur yachtsman who entered the first solo, non-stop, round-the-world boat race. Almost immediately out of his depth, Crowhurst decided to exaggerate his progress and the press latched on to his story. However, his vessel was in bad shape and facing ridicule and bankruptcy Crowhurst became increasingly desperate. A poignant and powerful meditation on ambition, *Deep Water* uses Crowhurst's original 16mm films and tape recordings to reconstruct his journey.

⭐ **Grizzly Man** 2005

Director Werner Herzog Cast Timothy Treadwell 103m

Herzog's fascination with men driven by obsession and living in defiance of nature is at the forefront of this documentary about **Timothy Treadwell**, a self-styled conservationist who spent his summers living amongst Alaskan Grizzlies until one turned on him and his girlfriend, mauling them to death. Much of the footage comes from Treadwell's own archive. Shot over a five-year period it contains some breathtaking pictures of the bears in their habitats, although as Herzog makes clear Treadwell's assertion that the bears are friends is completely foolhardy.

Lost in La Mancha 2002

Directors Keith Fulton, Louis Pepe 93m

After working for ten years to plan and gather finance for his epic, *The Man Who Killed Don Quixote*, Terry Gilliam was forced to watch the whole thing fall apart when his budget was cut, actors were suddenly unavailable, a freak rainstorm washed him out and unexpected military air manoeuvres started overhead. A compelling disaster movie, but also a fascinating look at preparing for a film – the meetings, the rescheduling, and the nonstop swearing.

Man on Wire 2008

Director James Marsh Cast Philippe Petit 94m

On 7 August 1974, 24-year-old French high-wire artist **Philippe Petit** strung a cable between the towers of the World Trade Center and performed a series of

Man and nature: Timothy Treadwell, with camera, alongside a grizzly bear in Werner Herzog's documentary *Grizzly Man*, much of which is drawn from Treadwell's own recordings.

high-wire stunts as he walked across. The authorities were furious, but in staging "the artistic crime of the century" Petit struck a blow for freedom of expression and became a cult celebrity figure. Riveting and beautifully shot, **Marsh**'s recounting of the chain of events that led to the act features both astonishing archive footage and sensitively staged reconstructions. At the heart of the film is the impish and irrepressible Petit himself.

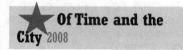

Of Time and the City 2008

Director Terence Davies 75m

This idiosyncratic and hugely personal paean to **Davies**' home town of Liverpool brilliantly blends a poetic verbal account of the director's early life with contemporary and archive footage of the city. It also weaves together the themes that define the director's early works (sexuality, Catholicism, death, loss and the power of cinema), and expresses anger and sadness at the post-1945 slum clearance and subsequent indignities the city's working classes have endured.

Polissons et Galipettes 2002

Compiled Michel Reilhac 67m

Polissons et Galipettes is a revealing – in all senses of the word – compilation of silent-era pornography comprised of stag films originally intended for screening in brothels. Originally shot after hours on the sets of legitimate projects (possibly by well-known industry figures), it's an antique but undeniably hard-core affair (one sequence features a female dog) that may well shock contemporary viewers. Sensual, absurd and surreal, it offers a singular and decidedly eyebrow-raising viewing experience.

Touching the Void 2003

Director Kevin Macdonald **Cast** Joe Simpson, Simon Yates 106m

Based on **Joe Simpson**'s international bestseller, this is an extraordinary true story of endurance. The tale of **Simon Yates**' decision to cut the rope joining him to injured co-climber Joe Simpson on a fateful expedition in Peru, the film resuscitated the documentary in the UK with its nerve-shredding synthesis of dramatic reconstruction and candid interviews.

Zoo 2007

Director Robinson Devor **Cast** Coyote, Jenny Edwards 76m

Inspired by the events that led up to a much-publicized incident in which a secret small town community gathered to indulge in sexual activity with stallions, the controversial *Zoo* explores zoophilia and inter-species intercourse. A subject seldom addressed onscreen and one that is apt to inspire revulsion, this is difficult and uncomfortable viewing made slightly more palatable by the director's artistic approach and thoughtful tone. Not for the faint of heart.

TURKEYS

Some turkeys may well be best served cold: rewarding later revaluation. But there's nothing like watching Warren Beatty and Dustin Hoffman being out-acted by a blind camel (see *Ishtar*, below) to make us glad we're not movie stars.

The Adventures of Baron Munchausen 1988

Director Terry Gilliam **Cast** John Neville, Eric Idle, Sarah Polley 126m

Ostensibly about the legendary baron's impossible adventures, the real conundrum is just how did **Gilliam** manage to spend the $46 million he extracted from Columbia. If you hadn't put up the money, then you might think it's been well spent on stunts such as the one where the baron and a pal climb down from the moon on the same two lengths of rope. Yes, more *could* have been spent on the script and yet more on the editing, but even in its present form it's worth persevering with – for the spectacle and the playful, inventive humour.

Battlefield Earth 2000

Director Roger Christian **Cast** John Travolta, Forest Whitaker 118m

Pulp Fiction had barely restored his star-power before **Travolta** attempted career hari-kiri by realizing his $80 million vanity project: an adaptation of Scientology founder **L. Ron Hubbard**'s sci-fi novel with beyond-appalling special effects. Tis the year 3000. Earth's last surviving "man animals" are enslaved to a superior race of Psychlos, led by Travolta: think the Predator who ate all the pies, accessorized by a droopy Fu Manchu nose clamp, four-foot stilts, rubber lizard-costume gloves and an Amy Winehouse back comb. But sillier.

Catwoman 2004

Director Pitof **Cast** Halle Berry, Benjamin Bratt, Sharon Stone 104m

The 28 writers involved in this DC Comics spin-off came to bitter arbitration over who should get final screen credit – presumably over the fact none of them wanted it. Aside from **Halle Berry** looking smoking in black latex, there's little to recommend a non-super yarn that sees a mild-mannered cosmetics girl transformed into a foxy vigilante by a magic cat sent by an Ancient Egyptian goddess.

Gigli 2003

Director Martin Brest **Cast** Ben Affleck, Jennifer Lopez, Christopher Walken 121m

Affleck, a frequently dodgy prospect (remember *Pearl Harbor*), is Gigli, a lowly Mob thug ordered to kidnap the DA's brother. When Ricki (**Lopez**) is sent to make sure he doesn't mess up, a series of "hilarious" mishaps begin. For a supposed rom-com it lacks both rom (Ricky is a lesbian) and com, but it probably didn't deserve to be shelved by cinemas quite as hastily as it was. Lopez proves that she's not a bad actress, just not a very good one, but she does get the best line: "It's turkey time."

Hell's Angels 1930

Director Howard Hughes **Cast** Ben Lyon, James Hall, Jean Harlow 135m

Aerial action sequences way ahead of their time and the discovery of **Harlow** make this slight story about a pair of brothers who enlist in the RAF during World War I worth a viewing. But it's also a story of filmic excess on a whopping scale. **Hughes** spent a cool $3.8 million, shooting 249 feet of film for every foot used in the final cut and insisting that every print was hand-tinted. Three pilots died during filming. Hughes insisted on doing some stunts and even crashed his own plane.

Ishtar 1987

Director Elaine May **Cast** Dustin Hoffman, Warren Beatty, Isabelle Adjani 107m

A comedy so lame it should have been shot as a mercy to us all. You know it's going to be dire when **Hoffman** and **Beatty** are singers. The duo are on their way to play the Ishtar Hilton and as the plot gets more and more complicated – involving the CIA and a group of rebels – a flock of vultures and a blind camel emerge as the best things in the movie. **May** edited this disaster for months, but only released it when the studio threatened legal action.

One from the Heart 1982

Director Francis Ford Coppola **Cast** Teri Garr, Frederic Forrest, Nastassja Kinski 107m

So much was written about this movie, it's no wonder it buckled under the weight of expectation. **Coppola** spent much of the budget on state-of-the-art electronics so he could play back his scenes immediately after they were shot. This involved Coppola spending hours huddled in a video van, rather than directing. And it shows. The film, about an unhappy couple finding new love in Las Vegas with interesting strangers, sacrificed substance to the demands of technical style. As one industry insider put it: "He took an $8 million project and used the latest advances in video to bring it in for $23 million."

Showgirls 1995

Director Paul Verhoeven **Cast** Elizabeth Berkley, Kyle MacLachlan, Gina Gershon 128m

Basic Instinct writer **Joe Eszterhas** and director **Paul Verhoeven** here reteam for another "erotic drama", which proves the line between good trash and bad can be thinner than a lap-dancer's G-string. True, the story of a Las Vegas newcomer called Nomi (**Berkley**), clawing up the slippery pole from stripper to err, topless showgirl, scarcely sounds intellectual stuff. However, film academics have since reappraised *Showgirls* as a post-modern satire on the capitalist US's degraded porno-culture.

> If you keep jumping to conclusions, you are going to jump to your own conclusion.
>
> **Zack, Showgirls**

Swept Away 2002

Director Guy Ritchie **Cast** Madonna, Adrianno Giannini 89m

Guy Ritchie should've heeded the cautionary tale that **Madonna**'s first ex-husband, Sean Penn, learnt on *Shanghai Express*: never work with the Missus. In a role that speaks volumes about their marriage, the then Mrs Ritchie stars as a spoilt, arrogant rich bitch, who humiliates her husband's boat boy – only to find herself shipwrecked with him. Whilst Madonna's performance is so wooden she could have made a raft out of it, the worst offender is Ritchie's uncharacteristically emasculated pace.

Waterworld 1995

Director Kevin Reynolds **Cast** Kevin Costner, Jeanne Tripplehorn 134m

"Beyond the horizon lies the secret to a new beginning…" ran the tagline. Bet they couldn't wait to see the end though. If it hadn't cost $200 million and been dogged by so many disasters, such as the set sinking in a storm, *Waterworld* might have been an entertaining, futuristic film with impressive action and some nice one-liners. **Costner**'s monosyllabic performance aside, the acting is fine. **Dennis Hopper**, in particular, has a whale of a time as the chief smoker – only in California could the tobacco industry be so despised they base an entire evil cult around it.

The Wiz 1978

Director Sidney Lumet **Cast** Diana Ross, Michael Jackson, Nipsey Russell 134m

Some said, at 34, **Diana Ross** was way too old to play Dorothy in this urbanized, all African-American retelling of *The Wizard of Oz*. They were right. Add in the unmagical screenplay adaptation of **William F. Brown**'s Broadway libretto, plus handing what should have been a fluffy camp extravaganza to gritty director **Sidney Lumet**, and it's no wonder that the then most expensive film musical ever made became an equally monster flop. **Michael Jackson**'s Scarecrow is the best thing here, which says it all.

UNDER-GROUND

Given mainstream cinema's enslavement to storytelling, you could easily forget that film is primarily a visual medium. Some filmmakers have hung on to the idea, creating non-narrative and abstract imagery that is arresting, challenging or pretentious according to your point of view.

Dog Star Man 1961–64

Director Stan Brakhage **Cast** Stan Brakhage, Jane Brakhage **80m**

It's staggering to consider the dedication that went into the production of **Brakhage**'s intoxicating masterpiece, let alone the artistic vision that inspired it. The five-part opus employs natural, cosmological, sexual and biological symbols to build up an increasingly complicated picture of humanity's place in the universe. The multi-layered superimpositions are fascinating, if disconcerting. But it's the materials that were manually appended to the celluloid that make this so enduringly unique.

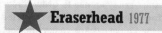 Eraserhead 1977

Director David Lynch **Cast** Jack Nance, Charlotte Stewart, Laurel Near **89m**

Lynch's first major movie portrays the bizarre relationship of Henry (**Nance**, whose hair remained in a frizzy state for the whole five-year shoot) and Mary X (**Stewart**) on discovering they are the parents of a helpless, mewling, phallic-necked baby creature. Essentially about the horror of procreation, it's full of subliminally sexual, nightmarish images of tiny bleeding chickens, exploding womb sacs and Henry's slowly plummeting severed head.

Flaming Creatures 1963

Director Jack Smith **Cast** Sheila Bick, Joel Markman, Marian Zazeela, Mario Montez **43m**

Smith achieved underground fame with this Baudelairean epic, made the same year as Warhol's *Blow Job*. Like Warhol, he had his own coterie, such as Dolores Flores (**Montez**), a transvestite who appears as a fandango dancer. The "earthquake orgy" scene, where a group of Creatures grapple a scantily clad Delicious Dolores (**Bick**) – has been hailed as high art by those seduced by **Smith**'s delirious vision, and as obscenity by the authorities, the New York police seizing the film reels at the premiere.

Man With a Movie Camera 1929

Director Dziga Vertov **Cast** Mikhail Kaufman 68m

Watching this montage masterclass, it quickly becomes apparent that the coming of sound was arguably a loss to film as an art form. Shot in Moscow, Kiev and Odessa, this is a revealing snapshot of a nation in the midst of overwhelming change. Boasting how he's eschewed such counter-revolutionary devices as narrative, character and intertitle, Vertov employs all manner of editorial effects to create "a truly international, absolute language of cinema".

Meshes of the Afternoon 1943

Director Maya Deren **Cast** Maya Deren, Alexander Hammid 14m

Cinema's greatest challenge is to convey thought and few filmmakers have come closer than Kiev-born **Deren** and husband **Alexander Hammid** in this puzzling, menacing journey through a dream. Multiple lookalikes, repeated events and recurring images of keys and knives create an atmosphere of uncertainty, as Deren seems to stalk her

slumbering self. And, amidst this, shots of her feet alighting on different surfaces suggest the sleeping mind's ability to wander with irresistible logic.

Sans soleil 1983

Director Chris Marker **Cast** Jean Négroni, Hélène Chatelain, Davos Hanich 100m

This investigation into the inadequacy of the filmed image is **Marker**'s masterpiece. Scenes shot in Japan, Guinea-Bissau, Iceland and France are restlessly juxtaposed with views of the San Francisco locations of Hitchcock's *Vertigo* to suggest that while photographic representations can enlighten, amuse or provoke, they can never reproduce the intimacy of memory. Exposing the way in which cultural pre-conditioning and censorship corrupt truth, this is an audiovisual barrage of dazzling ingenuity.

Scorpio Rising 1964

Director Kenneth Anger **Cast** Bruce Byron, Ernie Allo 28m

Many of **Anger**'s films were influenced by magician, poet and Satanist **Aleister Crowley**. This "hymn to Thanatos" (Greek for death) is a magical take on *The Wild One*, replete with pop soundtrack, Nazi memorabilia, a homoerotic biker gang and spliced-in scenes from a found black-and-white biblical movie. The provocative and unsettling result is tinged throughout with devilish, sardonic humour.

Allures (1961, 8m)

❝ I chose *Allures* by Jordan Belson (1961). Some very painful omissions – Jonas Mekas's *Walden*, Juraj Herz's *The Cremator*, Paradjanov's *Shadows of Our Forgotten Ancestors*, the Quays Brothers' *Street of Crocodiles*, Herzog's ridiculous and awe-inspiring *La soufrière* and also *How Much Wood Would a Woodchuck Chuck*? Also Tony and Beverly Conrad's *Straight and Narrow* which could never be pirated/downloaded because the flicker frames only work in the cinema. It also has a great and unusually jazzy John Cale/Terry Riley soundtrack from their *Church of Anthrax*.

How such intense cosmological rapture could be channelled into an obscure, eight-minute abstract film is beyond me. It's also beyond me how Jordan Belson's work remains almost invisible to this day. His work has often been overshadowed, but never eclipsed. I waited five years to see *Allures* after having read about it, and my anticipation was duly rewarded. It's a film that singularly soars above the efforts of other abstract filmmakers by transcending any forbidding academic rigour or astrological hocus-pocus. It's a report from another realm, lying in suspension and hidden way beyond the alternative mainstream radar. Celestial synonyms become redundant when attempting to convey the euphoria evoked in the viewer. Belson is that rarest of artists – a conduit, a transmitter of something beyond himself. At once psychedelic and divine, *Allures* embodies our furthermost and innermost wonders. ❞

Peter Strickland

Made with inheritance money outside of mainstream studio financing, Peter Strickland's award-winning Katalin Varga *was hailed as one of the genuine discoveries of 2009. A powerful road movie in which a woman confronts the demons of her past, the film makes astonishing use of its Transylvanian locations.*

Wavelength 1967

Director Michael Snow **Cast** Hollis Frampton, Amy Taubin **45m**

Constantly tinkering with texture, colour, shape, lighting and depth, **Snow** imperceptibly tracks and zooms for 45 mesmerizing minutes, during which time a pitch remorselessly ascends the sine wave. People trespass into the frame. Life goes on through the four large windows at the far end of an 80ft Manhattan loft. What matters in this structuralist landmark is the camera's ability to represent and redefine space and challenge the viewer's perception of reality and illusion.

URBAN NIGHTMARE

Who needs exotic locales when the mean streets where we live throw up ideas for heaps of movies. C'mon now, we've all been trapped inside statues, haven't we?

After Hours 1985

Director Martin Scorsese **Cast** Griffin Dunne, Rosanna Arquette 97m

Worth the price of admission just for **Dunne**'s outstanding turn as a young professional bloke whose night on the town ends with him trapped inside a papier-mâché statue. The most chilling scene, oddly, is the sequence where Dunne is forced to smooch to the tune of "Is That All There Is?", a Peggy Lee classic which here feels as chillingly nihilistic as a Joy Division album.

Blue Velvet 1986

Director David Lynch **Cast** Isabella Rossellini, Kyle MacLachlan, Dennis Hopper 120m

Never comfortable viewing, the tone is set with the opening shot of impossibly blue skies and white fences contrasted with wet, dark beetles. **MacLachlan** plays Jeffrey Beaumont, who finds a human ear and becomes embroiled in a horrific small-town mystery involving the beautiful Dorothy (**Rossellini**) and a psychotic mobster (a very scary **Hopper**). Underneath all of **Lynch**'s trickery, this is a very personal movie with many scenes linking back to the director's childhood.

The Collector 1965

Director William Wyler **Cast** Terence Stamp, Samantha Eggar 120m

Freddie Clegg (**Stamp**) is a mousy butterfly collector who decides to expand his collection to include a human. Art student Miranda (**Eggar**) is the object of his obsession, whom he captures and then keeps in the cellar of his house, hoping she will reciprocate his feelings. A nasty, fascinating, psychological thriller, this was shot in sequence so the actors' relationship could develop in parallel to the one unfolding onscreen.

Dark City 1998

Director Alex Proyas **Cast** Rufus Sewell, William Hurt, Kiefer Sutherland 100m

Wanted by the police for the murder of six prostitutes and pursued by trench-coated alien Strangers intent on manipulating his memory to fathom his soul, John Murdoch (**Sewell**) has a lot on his mind. This is comic-book sci-fi for those who prefer *film noir*. But while the sepia-toned dystopia is designed to sap the spirit, **Alex Proyas** forces us to venerate the mystery of life by questioning whether existence is an objective physical reality rooted in time or space or a figment of our imagination – or, worse still, someone else's.

Delicatessen 1991

Directors Marc Caro & Jean-Pierre Jeunet **Cast** Dominique Pinon, Marie-Laure Dougnac, Jean-Claude Dreyfus 99m

Jean-Pierre Jeunet claims that this surrealist tale of post-apocalyptic cannibalism was inspired by the Jerry Lewis movie, *The Delicate Delinquent*, a stint living above a butcher's shop and a nightmare American vacation with food so bad "it tasted like real humans". Whatever the truth, this black comedy inhabits a Heath Robinsonesque cyberpunk world, where suicide bids are farcical, sex is resolutely unerotic and vegetarian guerillas resort to desperate measures to thwart a grizzly solution to a meat shortage.

Do the Right Thing 1989

Director Spike Lee **Cast** Danny Aiello, Ossie Davis, Ruby Dee, John Turturro 120m

Sal (**Aiello**) is a pizzeria owner with a mostly black clientele. One hot night, a comment that Sal only has Italians and no black people on his walls sparks events that escalate out of control. A black man is killed and Sal's pride and joy is burnt down. Basing his film on a real-life New York incident, **Lee** originally wanted De Niro as Sal, but the lack of star presence is a definite plus. Displays all of Lee's mastery at telling a grim social tale using music, humour and vibrant colour.

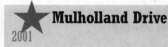 ## Mulholland Drive 2001

Director David Lynch **Cast** Laura Harring, Naomi Watts, Ann Miller 146m

Planned as a TV series but deemed too expensive, **Lynch** rehired the cast, added an ending and released it as a movie. A beautiful woman (**Harring**) emerges from a car wreck with amnesia, and ends up at the apartment of Betty (**Watts**). Then we discover Betty may be a struggling actress named Diane, who is the lover of Camilla (who looks like the woman with no memory). What's going on? Reality and dreams blur against the backdrop of a haunting **Angelo Badalementi** score

VAMPIRES

They may be a permanent pain in the neck but we just can't get enough of these blood-sucking creatures – as long as they're on celluloid obviously.

Billy the Kid vs Dracula
1966

Director William Beaudine **Cast** John Carradine, Chuck Courtney **73m**

The Western /Horror genre didn't have a lot of puff, but what's not to like about a Z-movie that was shot in eight days by the prolific "One-Shot" **Beaudine** (who has anything between three hundred and five hundred films to his name), features wobbly bats on visible wires, and stars a skeletal **Carradine** (who had played the evil count in a couple of Universal Studios' 1940s *Dracula* movies) gurning like a loon?

Bram Stoker's Dracula 1992

Director Francis Ford Coppola **Cast** Gary Oldman, Winona Ryder, Anthony Hopkins **127m**

The famous bloodsucker got a romantic makeover in this luscious adaptation. **Oldman**'s Prince Vlad becomes a creature of the night when he renounces God following the death of his wife, and centuries later believes she is reincarnated in the body of Mina (**Ryder**), the fiancée of Jonathan Harker (**Keanu Reeves**).

Superbly realized – most notably in a scene in which Dracula's shadow seems to move independently of its owner, reaching out to an unsuspecting Jonathan.

Captain Kronos: Vampire Hunter 1973

Director Brian Clemens **Cast** Horst Janson, John Carson, Caroline Munro **91m**

Kronos (**Janson**), a sword-wielding vampire hunter, and his hunchbacked sidekick Grost, find themselves in a small town where the young women have had the youth drained from them. Kronos suspects a vampire at work. This blend of action and horror, with a splash of swashbuckling sword-play on the side, was directed by *Avengers* writer **Clemens**, who'd been given a free rein to instil new blood, so to speak, into the vampire genre. The film flopped but is now regarded as one of Hammer's finest.

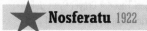 Nosferatu 1922

Director F.W. Murnau **Cast** Max Schreck, Alexander Granach **88m**

Murnau changed the vampire's name hoping the Stoker estate wouldn't recognize the tale; Mrs Stoker sued and got the movie removed from cinemas. The casting of **Schreck** (making his debut) in the title role was a stroke of genius. There are few creepier screen characters (Schreck stayed in make-up all the time on set, unsettling his co-stars), and with Murnau's clever use of black-and-white photography (using the negative to create white trees against a black sky etc), no horror movie has remained so long in our collective memory.

Shadow of the Vampire
2000

Director E. Elias Merhige **Cast** John Malkovich, Willem Dafoe, Cary Elwes 93m

A horror movie within a horror movie, this is the fictional tale about the making of 1922's *Nosferatu*. In this version Max Schreck (**Dafoe**) is a real-life vampire (he did look uncannily like one) paid, not with silver, but with the neck of the leading lady. The story is fuelled by unexplained events during the 1922 shoot, with crew members disappearing and even dying. Scenes from the original movie are blended in and Dafoe is luminous.

Vampyr 1932

Director Carl Theodor Dreyer **Cast** Julian West, Maurice Schutz, Rena Mandel 75m

With a part-sound part-silent soundtrack, largely non-professional cast, and intentionally blurred, dreamy visuals, **Dreyer**'s strange tale of a French village tormented by blood-sucking demons was given short shrift by audiences upon release, leading the director to have a nervous breakdown. Reappraised today, it stands as a classic of the avant-garde, with a hallucinatory quality that transcends surrealism to become genuinely spooky.

Vampyros Lesbos 1970

Director Jesús Franco **Cast** Ewa Strömberg, Soledad Miranda, Andrés Monales 89m

The prolific **Franco** is best known for his soft porn-infused schlock horror, or "horrotica" – an earlier attempt to make a straighter vampire movie, starring Christopher Lee and Klaus Kinski, failed dismally. This one is Euro-pop exploitation at its wobbly peak, giving us a good dose of sultry lesbian vampires, plus a wildly trippy soundtrack from psychedelic composers **Manfred Hübler** and **Siegfried Schwab**.

Zoltan, Hound of Dracula
1976

Director Albert Band **Cast** Michael Pataki, José Ferrer, Reggie Nalder 83m

Vampiric dog and master (an innkeeper called Neidt) are woken from their graves by Russian soldiers and set out for the US in search of Count Dracula's last descendant (**Pataki**), who just happens to have gone camping in the woods with his family. Man's best friend predictably behaves like man's worst fiend, turning all the other campers' pet pooches into the hounds from hell. Definitive so bad it's good fare.

VAMPS

The vampire: a strangely alluring predator who sucks on the blood of innocents. The vamp: well, much the same. Always female, always deadly, and usually without the fangs.

Basic Instinct 1992

Director Paul Verhoeven **Cast** Sharon Stone, Michael Douglas 127m

The coolly beautiful and undeniably smart **Stone** gives iconic vamp: talking dirty, sucking on cigarettes with a sybaritic hiss, staring the fellas out and hiding an ice pick under her bed – all the while, of course, eschewing undies. In a very 1990s hoohah, gay rights groups protested in their droves about the portrayal of bisexuals as unstable and murderous – Camille Paglia, meanwhile, insisted it was her favourite movie.

Body Heat 1981

Director Lawrence Kasdan **Cast** Kathleen Turner, William Hurt 113m

This is *Double Indemnity* (1944) with more sex: Matty Walker (**Turner**) has a torrid affair with listless lawyer Ned Racine (a moustachioed **Hurt**) and decides her husband has to die. A woman is only rarely allowed to be this sexually confident and manipulative onscreen and Turner relishes her moment, making us believe that Hurt is so besotted he will do anything she says. His only protest is: "You shouldn't wear that body."

Appearances can be deceptive: despite the submissive stance, Kathleen Turner as Matty is the one in the driver's seat in *Body Heat*.

The Bride Wore Black 1968

Director Françcois Truffaut **Cast** Jeanne Moreau, Michel Bouquet 107m

Though Tarantino hotly denies he was influenced by it, there's more than an echo of this movie in *Kill Bill* – a vengeful bride, widowed on her wedding day, sets out to seduce and murder each one of the five men she holds responsible. **Moreau** is perfect as the woman for whom our sympathy slowly and systematically diminishes – her cold-eyed, impassive beauty hinting at a motivation slightly darker than a righteous desire for revenge.

> **❝** Kiss me, you fool! **❞**
>
> **Theda Bara, the first vamp, in A Fool There Was**

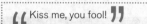
A Fool There Was 1915

Director Frank Powell **Cast** Theda Bara, Edward José 67m

Theda Bara – an anagram of Arab Death – defined the vamp. Lounging around in scanty, Oriental-style clothes, staring sullenly into the camera with huge smoky eyes, Bara (so her studio claimed) was the daughter of an Arabian concubine, born in the shadow of the Sphinx. The real Theodosia Goodman may have been a nice Jewish girl from Cincinnati, but in this classic silent melodrama – as "The Vampire" – with post-coital hooded eyes and dominatrix glare, she set the bar high for generations of man-eaters to come.

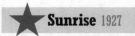
★ Sunrise 1927

Director F.W. Murnau **Cast** Margaret Livingston, George O'Brien, Janet Gaynor 94m

Livingston is often forgotten in all the (deserved) fuss about the visual beauty and delicate psychological nuance of this silent masterpiece. This is a shame, as she tackles with relish her role as "The Woman from the City", a vamp in the classic 1920s mould, all urban and modern, with dark make-up and flapper clothes – who persuades a simple farmer to murder his beloved wife.

VILLAINS

Every movie has a baddie, sure, but these deliciously
dastardly types are in an evil class of their own.

Chitty Chitty Bang Bang
1968

Director Ken Hughes **Cast** Dick Van Dyke,
Sally Ann Howes, Lionel Jeffries 144m

There are many fine aspects to this children's classic, co-written by **Roald Dahl**
from a novel by **Ian Fleming**. **Howes**
sings beautifully and **Jeffries** is superb
as **Van Dyke**'s dad, even though he was
seven months younger. But the real star
is former dancer **Robert Helpman**.
His spider-legged, greasy-haired, longnosed Child Catcher is still responsible
for many an infant nightmare.

The Devil Wears Prada 2006

Director David Frankel **Cast** Meryl Streep,
Anne Hathaway, Emily Blunt 109m

Absolutely fabulous chick flick about the
trials of a supposedly plump, frumpy wannabe news reporter (thin and gorgeous
Hathaway) who takes a job as PA to the
editor of a leading US fashion magazine.
Streep got an Oscar nomination for her
boss from hell, nonchalantly demanding
impossible feats from her assistant. Here
the Devil doesn't just get the best tunes –
she's got the best frocks too.

M 1931

Director Fritz Lang **Cast** Peter Lorre, Ellen
Widmann, Inge Landgut 117m

There's never been a cinematic child
killer to top **Lorre**'s Hans Beckert. A
man living in fear of himself, acting out
of a sick, self-loathing compulsion over
which he has no control, his sympathetic
portrayal of a serial killer rapist in 1930s
Berlin makes **Lang**'s first sound film as
shocking now as it was then. Lorre's first
lead role meant he was forever typecast
in Hollywood as a sinister foreigner.

Misery 1990

Director Rob Reiner **Cast** Kathy Bates, James
Caan 107m

Anjelica Huston and Bette Midler were
both offered the role, but it was **Bates** who
bagged an Oscar for prudish monster
Annie Wilkes. Based on **Stephen King**'s
bestseller it sees a writer (**Caan**) rescued
from a car wreck by a psychotic romantic
fiction addict (Bates). So when he tells her
he's killing off her favourite character, Misery, she's less than pleased – keeping him
under house arrest until he either reverses
Misery's death, or faces his own.

Mr India 1987

Director Shekhar Kapur **Cast** Anil Kapoor, Sridevi, Amrish Puri 179m

That this Bollywood spectacular was one of the best loved hits of the 1980s is largely due to its iconic baddie, played by India's legendary cinema villain, **Amrish Puri**. When crime lord Mogambo (Puri) attempts to evict an orphanage, its benefactor (**Kapoor**) fights back, taking an invisibility drug that transforms him into justice-seeking superhero, Mr India.

A Nightmare on Elm Street 1984

Director Wes Craven **Cast** Robert Englund, John Saxon, Heather Langenkamp 91m

When parents lynch a child-killing school janitor, burning him alive in his own boiler room, they little expect he'll be back to attack their offspring inside their nightmares. Brilliantly merging dream states with reality, it's the intelligence of **Craven**'s slasher that makes this – not just Freddie's iconic razor blade fingers nor the fact it marked a young **Johnny Depp**'s first film role.

Sin City 2005

Directors Frank Miller, Robert Rodriguez, Quentin Tarantino **Cast** Mickey Rourke, Clive Owen, Rosario Dawson 124m

As the title hints, *Sin City* is a world populated by lowlifes. But the big surprise in a stellar ensemble cast that includes **Bruce Willis**, **Jessica Alba** and **Benicio Del Toro** is **Elijah Wood** as a fanged cannibal killer called Kevin. Adapted from **Frank Miller**'s tangled *noir* comic books, it's a beautifully rendered black-and-white world lashed with colour at key moments of violent melodrama.

Villain 1971

Director Michael Tuchner **Cast** Richard Burton, Ian McShane, Nigel Davenport 98m

"Meet Vic Dakin. Then wish you hadn't" went the tagline for this British gangster flick. A sentiment shared by **Burton** after this box office flop inflicted serious GBH to his star status. Modelled on Ronnie Kray, Dakin (Burton) is a mum-loving, sadistic, homosexual crime lord with a bent for rough trade (**McShane**), whose empire is under threat. Teaming British TV comedy writers **Dick Clement** and **Ian La Frenais** with Italian movie tough guy **Al Lettieri** on the screenplay was the bad idea it sounds.

The Witches of Eastwick 1987

Director George Miller **Cast** Jack Nicholson, Cher, Susan Sarandon, Michelle Pfeiffer 118m

Nicholson was perfectly cast as boozy, womanizing, devil-in-disguise Daryl van Horne in this daft comedy-drama based on **John Updike**'s novel. **Cher**, **Sarandon** and **Pfeiffer** are the three amateur witches who conjure him up but don't quite get the dream man they were hoping for, as chaos ensues in their quiet town.

WAR

War – what is it good for? Inspiring great films, for one thing. In the movies war can be hell (*Gallipoli*), glory (*Patton*), hell and glory with the glory of the cause just tipping the balance (*Saving Private Ryan*), absurd (*Oh! What a Lovely War*), a sham (*Breaker Morant*) or simply an inconvenience for a girl trying to get a date (*Pearl Harbor*).

All Quiet on the Western Front 1930

Director Lewis Milestone **Cast** Lew Ayres, Louis Wolheim 138m

This, still the greatest anti-war movie ever made, was a big-budget venture for the time ($1.25m). A group of schoolboys are persuaded to enlist by their teacher but gradually death picks each one off. Initially filmed as a silent movie, making some of the acting look a little OTT, the performances of the lead actors, particularly **Ayres**, carry the film through slow, observational moments. After **Milestone** sent a request for authentic German uniforms for the shoot, he ended up casting real-life German soldiers as so many were living in Los Angeles at the time.

 **Apocalypse Now** 1979

Director Francis Ford Coppola **Cast** Martin Sheen, Marlon Brando 153m

Like many **Brando** movies, the behind-the-scenes story of **Coppola**'s movie is as entertaining as the film itself – there's even a documentary, *Hearts of Darkness* (1991), about it. **Sheen**'s heart attack, **Brando**'s weight, **Dennis Hopper**'s drugs and a Philippine typhoon were just some of the trials facing the crew. Yet Coppola managed to produce a visually and emotionally stunning adaptation of Joseph Conrad's novel, the smell of the napalm almost radiating from the screen. For more of the same, the *Redux* version released in 2001 adds around fifty minutes of cut footage, which either enhances or slows down the film, depending on your viewpoint.

Ashes and Diamonds 1958

Director Andrzej Wajda **Cast** Zbigniew Cybulski, Ewa Krzyzanowska 104m

If **Zbigniew Cybulski** is doomed to be remembered as the Polish James Dean, this movie is to blame. **Wajda**'s troubling film – the last part of a trilogy on Poland's

Come and See (1985, 142m)

" With *Come and See*, the Soviet war movie directed by Elem Klimov, the apocalypse has never felt more physically and psychically real. Russia has suffered the ravages of war like no other nation and so this film is appropriately fearless in delving into the complete horror of war, the complete damage on every human level. Its brutal poetic power adds to its ability to capture the appalling truth behind the rapture and spectacle of mass carnage. It takes it to hallucinatory heights that make it all the more disturbing and experientially real. In making the film, the rumours of the use of hypnotism, live bullets and drugs somehow seem well founded. The utter madness of war consumes its central character – in a vivid, haunting, and uncanny performance, the boy slowly becomes petrified and literally mute from what he witnesses, making this the bravest and greatest film about war ever. "

John Hillcoat

Australian Hillcoat hit the spotlight with the dark Aussie revenge drama The Proposition, *the second of two films scripted by cult musician Nick Cave he has directed. In 2009 he topped that with the post-apocalypse* The Road, *starring Viggo Mortensen, adapted from the Cormac McCarthy novel.*

history – dwells on the struggle of Polish patriots who realize that, with the Nazis defeated, they have found not peace, but a new enemy. Cybulski's hero, asked to gun down a Communist, gets distracted by a blonde bartender. He finally does the job, as fireworks fly, bringing the movie to an iconic, ironic close.

Battle of Algiers 1965

Director Gillo Pontecorvo **Cast** Yacef Saadi, Jean Martin, Brahim Haggiag 135m

An unusual war movie, which made **Pontecorvo**'s reputation. Shot in a black-and-white semi-documentary style, it leaves moral judgements aside to focus on a thrilling reconstruction of the

Algerian civil war, balancing the French army's use of torture with the terrorists' habit of setting off bombs in shops.

Das Boot 1981

Director Wolfgang Petersen **Cast** Jürgen Prochnow, Herbert Grönemeyer, Klaus Wennemann 149m

Jonathan Mostow's *U-571* was praised for its gripping sequences of a hunted war submarine, silently diving to dangerous levels to escape depth charges. But *Das Boot* had done all this and more twenty years earlier. **Petersen**'s classic is the archetypal sub movie, setting the style for subsequent sweaty, claustrophobic underwater war movies like *The Hunt for*

Red October. The director shows that tension and suspense are more important to a good thriller than action and explosions, turning the constraints to his advantage with meticulous camerawork and an intense, cynical script that highlights the sailors' contempt for the Nazis. A 1997 re-release includes an hour of extra footage.

The Cranes Are Flying 1957

Director Mikhail Kalatozov **Cast** Tatyana Samoilova, Alexei Batalov, Vasily Merkuryev 97m

Taking advantage of the thaw that followed Stalin's death in 1953, **Kalatozov** dares to replace the idealized socialist androids (which usually represented the masses in Soviet cinema) with individuals who fall in love, go off to war, get seduced and die. It isn't giving too much away, given the time and the fact that this is an anti-war movie, to say that the love story between **Batalov** and **Samoilova**'s characters is tragic. The scene where the dying soldier sees not his past, but the future which might have been is especially haunting.

Cross of Iron 1977

Director Sam Peckinpah **Cast** James Coburn, Maximilian Schell, James Mason 133m

Sam Peckinpah's only war movie, but then the body count in his Westerns was so high he hardly needed the excuse of war to commence bloodletting. **Coburn** is the German sergeant, sick of war on the eastern front and of the duplicity of officers like **Schell**, who can't see past his own need to win the Iron Cross. Slammed by critics, praised by Orson Welles as

the "greatest war film I ever saw", this is a bittersweet drama whose funereal photography perfectly brings home the claustrophobia and monotony of war.

The Deer Hunter 1978

Director Michael Cimino **Cast** Robert De Niro, John Savage, Christopher Walken 182m

An epic stunner about the effects of the Vietnam War on the lives of people in a small town in Pennsylvania, especially three young steelworkers who enlist in the US army and find themselves caught up in a brutality they had never bargained on. The movie is long, and slow in places, but this is a deliberate ploy to make sure the audience is totally involved in the lives of those onscreen, and so shattered as events during and after the war change the men's lives forever. The Russian roulette scene with **De Niro** and **Walken** will have your heart in your mouth.

The Execution of Private Slovik 1974

Director Lamont Johnson **Cast** Martin Sheen, Mariclare Costello 120m

This superior, eloquent anti-war TV movie, based on a non-fiction bestseller that shocked the US, powerfully recounts the true story of Eddie Slovik, the only US soldier to be executed – in 1945 – for desertion since the Civil War. Director **Johnson** won the prestigious Director's Guild of America award and **Sheen**'s heart-rending performance as the ex-reform-school boy who didn't want to kill anyone, court-martialled as a military embarrassment, remains electrifying. His final scenes with **Ned Beatty** as the chaplain are unforgettable.

Flesh & Blood 1985

Director Paul Verhoeven **Cast** Rutger Hauer, Jennifer Jason Leigh 127m

Paul Verhoeven's first American movie sees **Hauer** as a sixteenth-century mercenary who kidnaps the betrothed princess of a nobleman's son. Despite being kidnapped and raped by Hauer, she (**Leigh**) falls in love with her captor… or does she? Hauer and his men await battle, holed up in a castle, with the princess's feelings consistently ambiguous. The skills of cinematographer **Jan de Bont** (of future *Speed* fame) shine through, giving the film an electrifying pace.

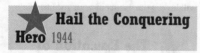

★ Hail the Conquering Hero 1944

Director Preston Sturges **Cast** Eddie Bracken, Ella Raines, William Demarest 101m

As a soldier enlisting for World War II, you want two things: to come back alive, and as a hero. Woodrow (**Bracken**), a small-town lad with such aspirations is invalided out. Too ashamed to go home, he hides out working in a shipyard while his family send letters to him. When some marines hear his story they drag him home where he is mistaken for a hero. **Sturges** regular **Demarest** lights up this fine movie, the only anti-war satire made during World War II by a major studio.

The Hurt Locker 2008

Director Kathryn Bigelow **Cast** Jeremy Renner, Anthony Mackie, Brian Geraghty 131m

The Academy made Bigelow the first female best director in Oscars history for this tense movie focused on an army bomb disposal team stationed in Iraq. Covering their relationships with each other, the locals and private militia, it's a tough, clear-sighted look at male bonding, touching on what compels men to go to war.

Johnny Got His Gun 1971

Director Dalton Trumbo **Cast** Timothy Bottoms, Kathy Fields, Jason Robards 111m

The only film directed by formerly jailed and blacklisted Hollywood screenwriter **Trumbo**, adapting his anti-war novel, is a very grim fable. Mutilated in World War I, Joe is left limbless, deaf, mute and blind. He relives his life in dream and fantasy, and struggles to communicate his wish to be displayed in a freak show. Unlike *Catch-22* and *M*A*S*H* (both 1970), this has no mordant humour to make its message more audience-friendly (although **Donald Sutherland** playing Christ is eye-catching).

King of Hearts 1966

Director Philippe de Broca **Cast** Alan Bates, Genevieve Bujold 110m

A child of the sixties, this comedy combines topical anti-militarism, sentimental glorification of mental illness and such a high body count that it's easy to see why it became a cult movie at the dark end of the swinging decade. **Bates** is the soldier who discovers a small town marked out for blanket bombing and is begged, by the townsfolk (all of whom are former lunatics), to become their king. Anarchic, whimsical, with British soldiers in kilts and circus animals wandering the streets, this is like no other anti-war comedy, ever.

The Life and Death of Colonel Blimp 1943

Directors Michael Powell, Emeric Pressburger **Cast** Roger Livesey, Deborah Kerr 163m

The 1940s caricature of the bluff old warhorse (as satirized in **David Low**'s Colonel Blimp cartoon strip) is fleshed out with a rich, touching life story that shows Blimp's evolution from a dashing young officer. **Livesey**'s portrayal of the decent, cheery Clive Wynne-Candy, lucky in friendship but unlucky in love, is subtle and full of human contradictions. When Churchill railed against the movie, **Anton Walbrook** (who plays Candy's German officer friend) told him, "No people in the world other than the English would have had the courage, in the midst of war, to tell the people such unvarnished truth."

Night of San Lorenzo 1981

Directors Paolo Taviani, Vittorio Taviani **Cast** Omero Antonutti, Margarita Lozane 105m

The extended flashback of a woman who was six when Tuscany was liberated by the Allies, this draws on the Taviani brothers' own memories of the summer of 1944. Unforgettable, romantic, brutal and shocking (especially in the scene where a young Fascist boy is shot dead by the partisans in front of his father), this captures the intensity and fatal unpredictability of war beautifully.

Oh! What a Lovely War 1969

Director Richard Attenborough **Cast** Malcolm McFee, Wendy Alnutt, Colin Farrell 144m

A vicious, surreal satire on World War I, with musical numbers, many based on soldiers' marching songs, linking some of the more terrible events, including a friendly-fire massacre of Irish soldiers and the extraordinary ineptitude of the generals. Some of the sequences sag under their own weight, and in places the original stage show is followed so closely it doesn't quite work on celluloid. But the movie remains innovative and absorbing and the cast reads like a who's who of British theatre and film.

Paths of Glory 1957

Director Stanley Kubrick **Cast** Kirk Douglas, George Macready, Ralph Meeker 86m

The movie that made **Kubrick**, though it was neither a box office nor critical smash. Based on a true story, it highlights the gap between those fighting the war and those leading the charge from the back. **Douglas** is suitably indignant as the lieutenant leading a suicidal charge, whose men are then court-martialled for failing in an impossible task. It was banned in France for its unflattering portrayal of the French World War I army, but Churchill liked it.

Ran 1985

Director Akira Kurosawa
Cast Tatsuya Nakadai, Mieko
Harada 160m

Akira Kurosawa's re-imagining of *King Lear* shifts the story to medieval Japan, where an elderly warlord divides his kingdom between three sons. The result is civil war, brought to life by Kurosawa in moving, majestic battle scenes that influenced Spielberg's opening sequence in *Saving Private Ryan*. "Ran" means chaos in Japanese, and the movie conveys the confusion of war with camerawork that somehow turns bloody clashes into operatic tragedy.

George Chakiris, one of *633 Squadron*'s human stars, dragged away by the Nazis.

Rome, Open City 1946

Director Roberto Rossellini **Cast** Aldo Fabrizi, Anna Magnani 101m

Fellini wrote the script in a week in his kitchen – the only room in his house in Rome which had heat. **Rossellini** shot on silent film stock, dubbing in the sound and dialogue later. This simple story about a resistance leader (**Marcello Pagliero**) on the run made a star of **Magnani** and so impressed Ingrid Bergman when she saw it in a cinema in LA, she fell in love with (and later married) the director. Italian audiences hated its squalid realism, coming round only when it was acclaimed as a masterpiece in France and the US.

633 Squadron 1964

Director Walter E. Grauman **Cast** Cliff Robertson, George Chakiris, Marie Perschy 102m

For men with an emotional age of nine, this movie wrote the book on duty, sacrifice and the importance of a hummable theme tune. The ill-fated squadron's mission is to destroy a Nazi munitions factory, even if it means the squadron is itself destroyed. Heroic stuff, with **Robertson** impassively impressive and some beautiful shots of Mosquito aircraft – the movie's real stars.

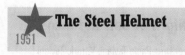 **The Steel Helmet**
1951

Director Samuel Fuller **Cast** Gene Evans, Robert Hutton, Richard Loo 84m

Samuel Fuller's famous opening image, of a steel helmet that looks like a piece of debris but turns out to have a man under it, opens this cracking movie set in the Korean War, as a patrol wanders through the fog in pursuit of a reason for actually being there. Fuller, often portrayed as an idiot savant, here directs a telling movie about war that doesn't draw any easy moral lessons.

Talvisota 1989

Director Pekka Parikka **Cast** Taneli Mäkelä, Vesa Vierikko **195m**

War is a cold hell in this grim movie (the most expensive ever made in Finland) about a group of Finns conscripted into the trenches to be bombarded by Soviet artillery and aircraft. Death is indiscriminate, messy and omnipresent in **Parikka**'s film. Watch it and you'll also find out, if you don't already know, why the Molotov cocktail is named after Molotov.

The War Game 1965

Director Peter Watkins **Cast** Michael Aspel, Dick Graham **48m**

Commissioned by the BBC as an hour-long documentary, the powers that be deemed **Watkins**' work too horrifying for a mass audience. Shelved, it was eventually released in the cinema, winning the 1966 Oscar for best documentary. This is the nightmarish vision of an English city in the throes of a nuclear catastrophe. Part interviews, part acting, it's stunningly realistic.

War Hunt 1962

Director Denis Sanders **Cast** John Saxon, Robert Redford **83m**

Low budget, occasionally pretentious, Korean War movie which marks **Redford**'s movie debut, as a soldier newly assigned to a command dominated by a psychotic **Saxon**. With a moody score by jazz composer **Bud Shank**, this is an unusual war movie, carried by Saxon as a man who would collapse in civilian life, conflict providing a professional alibi for his disturbed personality.

Where Eagles Dare 1968

Director Brian G. Hutton **Cast** Richard Burton, Clint Eastwood, Mary Ure **155m**

"Major, you've got me just as confused as I'll ever be", **Eastwood** tells **Burton** at one point. After a few turns in this far-fetched, fun adaptation of the **Alistair Maclean** novel, you'll probably be as confused as Clint. Not that it matters, the parachute jumps, bomb rigging and motorbike rides keep the momentum going as our heroes try to rescue an American general, imprisoned in one of the world's most impenetrable fortresses.

Zulu 1964

Director Cy Endfield **Cast** Stanley Baker, Jack Hawkins, Michael Caine **135m**

Zulu introduced two new stars to the world: **Caine** and **Mangosuthu Buthelezi** (the future leader of the Zulu nation, seen here playing his great-grandad Warrior Chief Cetewayo). The Zulu actors hadn't seen a movie before, so the crew showed them Roy Rogers films. Like the rest of the world, the Zulus couldn't understand why the cowboy kept stopping to burst into song.

WEEPIES

Great filmmaking is about inspiring strong emotions in the audience, be it excitement, terror, joy, disgust. But the ultimate accolade for any movie must be that it moved its viewers to tears.

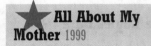 All About My Mother 1999

Director Pedro Almodóvar **Cast** Cecilia Roth, Penélope Cruz, Antonia San Juan 101m

Following the sudden death of her adored teenage son, Manuela (a wonderfully staunch **Roth**) heads for Barcelona in search of the father the boy never knew. **Almodóvar**'s finest film maintains his trademark campery, but with an added element of pathos that is genuinely moving.

The Dresser 1983

Director Peter Yates **Cast** Albert Finney, Tom Courtenay 118m

Backstage drama about an overbearing egomaniac actor (**Finney**) always referred to as "Sir" and his devoted, put-upon dresser Norman (**Courtenay**). As Sir's troupe brings Shakespeare to the provinces, he's drinking too much and unable to remember whether he's playing Lear or Othello. Without Norman cajoling and massaging his ego, the show definitely would not go on. The story of a relationship that's coming to the end of a long road, with moving performances from both leads.

The Elephant Man 1980

Director David Lynch **Cast** John Hurt, Anthony Hopkins 124m

Based on the true story of the rehabilitation of John Merrick, horribly disfigured with Proteus Syndrome, who was rescued from being a sideshow freak by an eminent doctor. **Freddie Francis**'s black-and-white cinematography is stunning, capturing every detail of an authentic-looking Victorian London. Despite being encased in a rubber mask **Hurt** gives a moving performance as a man discovering his inner self and coming to realize that he may just have swapped one freak show for another. The desperately poignant ending will melt the hardest heart.

 The Hairdresser's Husband 1990

Director Patrice Leconte **Cast** Jean Rochefort, Anna Galiena 80m

A young boy develops a crush on his hairdresser and years later marries an almost identical replica of his childhood fantasy, living an eccentric, happy life full of Arabic music and erotic hair-cutting, while

Alain Resnais, fear jerker

Iconic French director of *nouvelle vague* classics *Hiroshima, mon amour* and *Last Year in Marienbad*, **Alain Resnais** is master of the intellectual weepie. He was swept to fame in the late 1950s, a time of change and reassessment of the status quo in Europe, and his films often feature characters carrying enormous burdens, like Emmanuelle Riva in *Hiroshima*, who was punished for falling in love with a German soldier during the war, or yearning for something they have either lost or never really possessed, like Yves Montand in *The War Is Over*, wasting his life longing for a Communist revolution that will never come. Regret, loss, time, memory, passion — these are Resnais's themes, and any tears they provoke are probably shed behind dark glasses and a screen of smoke from your Gauloise. This is sadness with strong social awareness, and often with a provocative slant, but there is an unashamedly emotional core to all his films. His latest film, *Les herbes folles*, is a delightful slice of humanism, proving that, at 87, there are films in him yet.

wife Mathilde wishes never to grow old. **Leconte**'s gentle, absorbing and offbeat love story is one of the most evocative and saddest romances on film. Sensual, funny and beautifully made, it's a story about dreams coming true and whether they can stay fulfilled for ever.

Hiroshima, mon amour
1959

Director Alain Resnais **Cast** Emmanuelle Riva, Eiji Okada 91m

Haunting tale about a French actress who has a brief affair with a Japanese architect when she visits Hiroshima to make an anti-war movie. He insists that, despite visiting the right museums and trying to understand the bomb's effect, she knows nothing of the true horrors, although she tells him of her appalling treatment by her family after she fell in love with a young German soldier. The movie is overwhelmingly moving as it sets one person's tragedy against a vaster tragedy, and the flashbacks set up a brilliant contrast between wartime France and post-war Japan. With lines like: "They make movies to sell soap, why not a movie to sell peace?", it's a classic of intellectual cinema that packs a huge emotional punch.

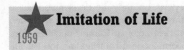

★ Imitation of Life
1959

Director Douglas Sirk **Cast** Lana Turner, Juanita Moore, John Gavin, Robert Alda 125m

Ambitious mum (**Turner**) provides for her daughter financially while neglecting her emotionally and ignoring the needs of her own heart at the same time. The eternally perky **Sandra Dee** plays the teenager whose coming-of-age sub-plot even involves her mother's long-lost boyfriend. Alongside this is the story of

Turner's self-sacrificing housekeeper, Annie (**Moore**) and her rebellious daughter, Sarah Jane. **Susan Kohner** is brilliant as the fair-skinned Sarah Jane, rejected by local boys because she is black, who runs away in order to "pass" for white in the big city. The scene where Annie goes to find her daughter but doesn't give her away to her new friends despite urging her to be proud of her heritage, perfectly captures the perversity of some Americans' attitudes to race.

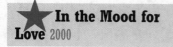

In the Mood for Love 2000

Director Kar Wai Wong **Cast** Maggie Cheung, Tony Leung **97m**

A beautiful and thoughtful story about married love and fidelity. When newspaper editor Chow (**Leung**) moves into a new apartment with his wife, he strikes up a friendship with another new inhabitant, Li-Zhen (**Cheung**). When they discover their respective spouses are having an affair, Chow and Li-Zhen's friendship deepens, but they are determined not to betray their own marriage vows. Leung won best actor at Cannes and the other performances are outstanding, too. If unfulfilled love is your thing, this is your movie.

Jezebel 1938

Director William Wyler **Cast** Bette Davis, Henry Fonda, George Brent **106m**

Rushed out to beat *Gone With the Wind* to the screen, *Jezebel* is a masterpiece of emotional storytelling. **Davis** is a true Southern belle, selfish and flirtatious, who flouts convention and loses her fiancé, Pres (**Fonda**), by wearing the wrong dress to an important ball. When he returns years later she is prepared to beg to get him back but finds he has married a Yankee. As a yellow fever epidemic sweeps the state she is forced to learn about compassion and self-sacrifice, culminating in one of the great doomed-but-defiant movie endings. Davis won her second Oscar and steals every scene. Incidentally, the famous red dress was actually green, as it was deemed to photograph better in black and white.

Mildred Pierce 1945

Director Michael Curtiz **Cast** Joan Crawford, Jack Carson **113m**

An ambitious lower-class mother has an evil, selfish daughter who competes with her for the same man. Was this the story of Mildred Pierce or the story of **Joan Crawford**? Answer: both. It's a superbly made melodrama in which Crawford dominates, deserving her best actress Oscar. **Curtiz** didn't want to cast her, calling her "Phony Joanie" and once, enraged by her habit of glamming up for the cameras, wiping her lipstick from her mouth with his fist. A *film noir* weepie, this gave its star a new career.

My Life Without Me 2002

Director Isabel Coixet **Cast** Sarah Polley, Mark Ruffalo, Debbie Harry **106m**

Low-key tearjerker in which a young, working-class mother (indie sweetheart **Polley**, who went on to direct Julie Christie in *Away from Her*) sets out to check off a crucial to-do list in the two months she has left to live – including embarking upon an affair with the enigmatic **Ruffalo** and setting her husband up with a new partner. **Harry** proves she's still got it in a delicious turn as Ann's irritable mother.

Paris, Texas 1984

Director Wim Wenders **Cast** Harry Dean Stanton, Nastassja Kinski 148m

Sam Shepard's rich but understated screenplay is the perfect tool for **Wenders** to explore this story of a man returning to his family after four years of memory loss. The slow revealing of dysfunctional relationships, **Stanton** getting to know his son, the desert as a metaphor for the emptiness that can overwhelm a person, all of these can make a grown man weep, especially when you add in **Ry Cooder**'s haunting soundtrack.

★ Penny Serenade 1941

Director George Stevens **Cast** Cary Grant, Irene Dunne 119m

It's puzzling that this three-hankie weepie isn't better known. A domestic drama in which a marriage is beset by the most terrible tragedies, it feels incredibly modern – and as a study of grief has yet to be bettered. **Grant** and **Dunne** were genuinely fond of each other, and the warmth and wit that characterizes their screwball comedies (*The Awful Truth* and *My Favourite Wife*) renders them utterly convincing as spouses racked by pain. Grant, in particular, has some devastatingly sad scenes, proving himself to be perhaps the greatest actor of his generation.

A Time to Love and a Time to Die 1958

Director Douglas Sirk **Cast** John Gavin, Liselotte Pulver 133m

Unusual World War II drama told from the German point of view, about a young soldier finding brief happiness during a break from fighting on the Russian front. **Sirk**, who had fled the Nazis, made this intense, sweeping melodrama as a statement of his pacifism and an indictment of the barbarism of sending young men to war. The novel by **Erich Maria Remarque** was burned by Hitler's government. Added poignancy is created by the fact that Sirk's own son died during the same campaign.

Waterloo Bridge 1940

Director Mervyn LeRoy **Cast** Vivien Leigh, Robert Taylor 108m

Leigh, who followed *Gone With the Wind* with this rather more downbeat affair, claimed this movie was her personal favourite – as did **Taylor**. She plays a struggling ex-ballerina, who, brokenhearted by the death of her true love in World War I, resorts to prostitution to survive. Once it transpires that he is alive, keeping her dirty secret becomes too much for her to bear… As with all the best melodramas, it touches on profound issues, including female shame and self-loathing, with a finale that is genuinely devastating.

WESTERNS

The definitive American movie genre has fallen on hard times. But it still allows moviemakers with imagination and wit to explore a rich variety of plots and themes.

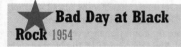 Bad Day at Black Rock 1954

Director John Sturges **Cast** Spencer Tracy, Robert Ryan, Anne Francis, Walter Brennan, Lee Marvin, Ernest Borgnine 81m

Sturges's definitive American anti-Western was the first major Hollywood film to spotlight the unjust treatment of Japanese-Americans in World War II. **Tracy**'s one-armed avenging angel arrives in Bad Rock hoping to deliver a medal. His mission unearths the town's nasty secrets and, Sturges implies, the rottenness of the whole Western mythos. But the director shrewdly includes enough twists on standard Western motifs – especially the final showdown – to make this work on both levels.

Dead Man 1995

Director Jim Jarmusch **Cast** Johnny Depp, Gary Farmer 121m

There are revisionist Westerns where the horse opera plot staples get a little twist. And then there is *Dead Man*. Deep contrast black-and-white photography, an appearance from **Iggy Pop** and a twanging Neil Young score are just a few of the ingredients that tell you this will be an unconventional and slow ride off the beaten track. And that's before you even factor in **Robert Mitchum** as an especially psychotic local powerbroker, and a native American character called "Nobody" with a line in pithy non-sequitur philosophizing. All in all the Western gets thoroughly Jarmusched. No bad thing either.

Flaming Star 1960

Director Don Siegel **Cast** Elvis Presley, Dolores Del Rio, Steve Forrest, Barbara Eden 101m

The Cherokee roots in **Elvis**'s family tree may have helped him excel as the half-breed, doomed by racism on the Texas frontier, as war breaks out between whites and Kiowa. **Siegel**'s violent, pessimistic, liberal Western captures the escalation of violence and hate brilliantly in a movie that, while harking back to historic chaos, hints at struggles to come as the US wrestled with civil rights.

Heller in Pink Tights 1960

Director George Cukor **Cast** Sophia Loren, Anthony Quinn, Margaret O'Brien 100m

Arguably the best showbiz Western, overlooked because neither **Cukor** nor **Loren** had much form in the genre, *Heller in Pink Tights* celebrates the tatty splendour of the theatrical companies that toured the West. There's a neat visual gag involving Loren when her head briefly looks as if emerging from a painted woman's vagina. Cukor's neglected gem focuses on how the West was fun.

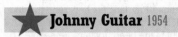 **Johnny Guitar** 1954

Director Nicholas Ray **Cast** Joan Crawford, Sterling Hayden, Mercedes McCambridge 110m

Shane (1953, 118m)

" I have been going to the movies for so long now they're almost as natural a part of my life as day or night or the weather. I think I measure my time here by them. Past, present and maybe the future. To quote *Eureka*: "The world is ever-changing, Mr Farnsworth, like the Universe", and I have always wanted to be part of the realization of those changes. Especially in my work. I have never believed there is a right way and a wrong way, but more that there is a right way for the time and then another way. That is the wonder of imagination.

Movies have been my life and so many have formed me and my thoughts, it is impossible to pick out any single one that has been a Damascene-like revelation. As with everything in life, it has also got so much to do with timing. But looking back and thinking hard, the movie that caught me unawares and which, as time went by, turned out to have, for me, so many strange coincidences and memories both personal and professional (which it is impossible to tell, all these years later, to anyone but myself) is *Shane*. A Western made around the early fifties. For me it triggered a whole new attitude in my expectations regarding film. I was completely sucked into it in spite of – or because of – it being totally different from how I thought it was going to be. The performances – Alan Ladd, Jean Arthur, Van Heflin and Jack Palance – were all wonderful and the direction, photography and editing for such a simple, sparely written screenplay seemed to present everything and every emotion in a totally cinematic way. The image told the story.

When I later read the book on which the film was based I was again very impressed by the skill with which the film had been adapted from the page to the screen… A good book had become a great, classic movie. "

Nicolas Roeg

Nicolas Roeg is one of Britain's most adventurous, versatile and acclaimed directors for his visually arresting and visionary works. His credits include the legendarily psychedelic Performance *(with Mick Jagger), the austere sci-fi fantasy* The Man Who Fell to Earth *(starring David Bowie) and the metaphysical horror fable* Don't Look Now.

Feminist, Freudian, anti-McCarthyist, **Ray**'s nuanced, neurotic Western is all these and more. **Crawford**, cast partly because Ray fancied her, runs a saloon which serves whisky downstairs and a bullet in the head upstairs. Persecuted by a mob (led by the righteous **McCambridge** who gets her kicks from watching houses burn down), Crawford calls on **Hayden**'s guitar-strumming gunslinger for protection, even though she's tougher and more macho than he is. Full of haunting images, fuelled by the jealousy on set, this hallucinatory Western contains so much symbolism critics are still decoding it.

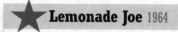 ## Lemonade Joe 1964

Director Oldrich Lipsky **Cast** Karel Fiala, Milos Kopecky, Olga Schoberova 99m

Delicious Czech Western tribute/parody, with musical numbers that betray a puzzling knowledge of **Gene Autry**'s work, and in which one punch knocks down five men in a bar. The place names – Stetson City, Trigger Whisky Saloon – are surpassed only by the song titles, especially ''When the Smoke Thickens in the Bar Do You See My Moist Lips?'' Joe is the hero who rides off with heroine Winifred Goodman, though good and evil are touchingly reconciled in a finale in which a new blend of whisky and lemonade – whiskyoka – is perfected.

Little Big Man 1970

Director Arthur Penn **Cast** Dustin Hoffman, Faye Dunaway, Chief Dan George 147m

Penn's epic, intelligent picaresque Western isn't afraid to draw the obvious parallel – between the US Army's massacre of native Americans and the slaughter of Vietnamese civilians at My Lai – as it sets about reappraising the West through the recollections of the 121-year-old Little Big Man (**Hoffman**). The film moseys off into massacres and speeches after an hour, and some of the caricatures (especially **Richard Mulligan**'s Custer) start to irritate but Penn's deconstruction of the Western has enough brio to keep you watching.

Lone Star 1996

Director John Sayles **Cast** Chris Cooper, Elizabeth Peña, Kris Kristofferson, Matthew McConaughey, Frances McDormand 135m

The best, most neglected Western of the 1990s? **Sayles**' modern Western uses the investigation of a skeleton with a badge as the hook for a fine study of character, community and small town desperation, in which the past haunts the present and where the best most can hope for, as one sergeant puts it, is that one prejudice is overcome by another deeper prejudice.

 ## McCabe & Mrs Miller 1971

Director Robert Altman **Cast** Warren Beatty, Julie Christie 121m

Altman takes some Western stereotypes – the loner who shakes up a town and the whore with a heart of gold – and subverts them brilliantly in a rich, satisfying Western that brings the best out of **Beatty** (as cocky gambler McCabe who ultimately dies from a mixture of stupidity, bullet wounds and exposure) and **Christie** (as the whorehouse madam). In Altman's Western, life is cheap, the landscape is cruel and big business will kill to establish a monopoly. *Nashville* isn't Altman's masterpiece, this is.

Man of the West 1958

Director Anthony Mann **Cast** Gary Cooper, Julie London, Lee J. Cobb 100m

Coop's darkest role, in **Mann**'s bleakest Western, was lauded by Jean-Luc Godard but too strong for many of the star's traditional fans. The tortured hero, Link (Cooper) is a reformed criminal robbed by his old evil boss, Dock (**Cobb**). So bitter is the relationship between the protagonists that Dock rapes Billie (**Julie London**) mainly, Mann suggests, to spite Link. However, she doesn't pay the usual penalty of raped women in a Western – death – and shares scenes of tender erotic power with Link in a noirish classic that shuns the usual clichés.

Monte Walsh 1970

Director William A. Fraker **Cast** Lee Marvin, Jack Palance, Mitch Ryan, Jeanne Moreau 108m

The perpetual dusk in **Fraker**'s sublime elegiac Western reflects the fact that redundant middle-aged cowboys Walsh (**Marvin**) and Rollins (**Palance**) are in the twilight of their lives. In a well-observed, meandering tale, Walsh

hesitates fatally when he should marry **Moreau**'s tart with a heart and then sets out to avenge Rollins' slaying with a gunfight in the abattoir. In its own way, Fraker's melancholy horse opera captures the dying agony of the Old West as evocatively as *The Wild Bunch*; it just doesn't make so much noise about it.

Pat Garrett and Billy the Kid 1973

Director Sam Peckinpah **Cast** James Coburn, Kris Kristofferson, Bob Dylan, Jason Robards, Slim Pickens 121m

Just the kind of melancholic, woozy masterpiece you would expect from a maverick, paranoid genius whose idea of a hearty breakfast was a bottle of whisky. This is probably **Peckinpah**'s darkest, most touching film. The duel between Garrett (**Coburn**) and Billy (**Kristofferson**) ends with the execution of Billy, a bad boy Christ, a denouement which reads like Peckinpah's obituary for his own career.

Pursued 1947

Director Raoul Walsh **Cast** Robert Mitchum, Teresa Wright, Dean Jagger 101m

Mitchum's laconic brooding helps suspend disbelief in **Walsh**'s noirish Western as his character, already haunted by memories of the seemingly pointless slaughter of his family, is the target of various attempted murders. At one point, his lovely bride (**Wright**) tries to bring forward the "till death do us part'' bit of the wedding vows. Although the mystery is resolved with a cliché, this seriously underrated movie may be the first psychological Western.

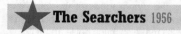 The Searchers 1956

Director John Ford **Cast** John Wayne, Jeffrey Hunter, Vera Miles, Ward Bond, Natalie Wood 119m

Influencing everyone from Martin Scorsese to Buddy Holly and George Lucas, **Ford**'s evocative masterpiece is a moving reconsideration of the certainties that typified his earlier work. **Wayne**'s Ethan Edwards, a wanderer looking for his niece who's been abducted by the Comanches, comes eventually to recognize his own obsolescence. Ford has the confidence to leave many of the tensions within the movie – especially those surrounding Wayne's obsessive, racist quest – unresolved and *The Searchers* is all the better for it.

Sekal Has to Die 1998

Director Vladimir Michálek **Cast** Olaf Lubeszenko, Boguslaw Linda, Jiri Bartoska 109m

A stranger with a secret steps off the train and is forced to confront a local bad guy. It's a classic Western setup but this is World War II Moravia. **Michálek** uses the simplicity of the genre to explore Czech history: his villagers try to destroy evil only to replace it with something just as bad. Richly shot, nicely told, but not quirky or trendy enough to become famous, this pseudo-Western is as unpretentious as its director who, asked to

ponder his movie, often simply replies: ''I dunno''.

Shane 1953

Director George Stevens **Cast** Alan Ladd, Jean Arthur, Van Heflin, Brandon De Wilde 118m

Does Shane die after all? The revisionist theory suggests that Shane rides off bleeding while one of the evil Rykers is not definitively dead. Which makes Joey's cries of ''Come back Shane!'' more urgent than the boy realizes. **Jack Shaefer**'s seminal novel is gorgeously filmed by **Stevens** with **Ladd** divine as an avenging angel in buckskin, reluctantly cleaning up the valley so that Joey's mum (**Arthur**) who he loves – and may love him – can live happily ever after with husband (**Ben Johnson**) and son. The story brilliantly captures a particular moment in the closing of the American frontier yet feels as timeless as a myth.

The Shooting 1966

Director Monte Hellman **Cast** Jack Nicholson, Will Hutchins, Warren Oates, Millie Perkins 81m

Hellman's ambiguous, existentialist Western has an eerie power that still perplexes. **Oates**'s brother goes missing, **Hutchins** fires at nothing, **Perkins** wants her horse shot because it's lame (even though it isn't) and **Nicholson**, as a sociopathic gunman, seems to be impersonating Jack Palance's gunfighter in *Shane*. Meanings and camera angles multiply in a quirky Western which, for once, has a woman – Perkins' anonymous heroine – at its heart.

The Tall T 1957

Director Budd Boetticher **Cast** Randolph
Scott, Richard Boone 77m

As **Randolph Scott** is in danger of being
known chiefly as the man who may or
may not have slept with Cary Grant, it
seems appropriate to pay tribute to this
fine B-Western which earned Scott overdue recognition. Sadly for those hoping
to avoid gay subtexts when discussing
Scott, **Boetticher** would later insist that
Boone's villain was physically attracted to
Scott's hero. The story, scripted by **Burt
Kennedy** from an Elmore Leonard novel,
is an old standby. Scott has to undermine
the solidarity of the outlaw band which
holds him and **Maureen O'Sullivan**
prisoner. But in these capable hands,
it becomes an understated fable about
American progress.

The Three Burials of Melquiades Estrada 2005

Director Tommy Lee Jones **Cast** Tommy Lee
Jones, Barry Pepper, Julio Cedillo, Dwight
Yoakam 120m

Jones sets out to fulfil a promise to his
recently deceased friend to bury him in
his home town in Mexico and decides
the best way to do that is kidnap the killer
and take him along. Jones's long, bleak
contemporary Western makes a plea for
racial tolerance while paying homage
to Peckinpah, Godard and kabuki theatre. But the performances – especially
Jones's – and the details (such as the use
of anti-freeze to embalm the corpse) are
more compelling than the message in
an absorbing tale of three unsatisfactory
burials.

El Topo 1971

Director Alejandro Jodorowsky **Cast**
Alejandro Jodorowsky, Brontis Jodorowsky,
Mara Lorenzio 124m

For some, this is the definitive acid
Western. For others, this is just a way
of saying that the dialogue only sounds
profound when you're high. El Topo (The
Mole) seems like an avenging angel out
of the Sergio Leone catalogue until he
abandons his son to prove his love to a
woman (who leaves him for a woman she
loves) and wakes up, bald and twenty
years older, in a cave full of dwarfs. As
odd as that sounds, this mystical surreal
Western feels even stranger when you
watch it.

Ulzana's Raid 1972

Director Robert Aldrich **Cast** Burt Lancaster,
Richard Jaeckel, Bruce Davison 103m

Aldrich's brutal Vietnam Western is a
dark, violent account of a deadly cat and
mouse game between cavalry and Indians in which even the landscape is harsh.
Lancaster is the scout who sympathizes
with the Apaches but tracks down Ulzana
and his renegades for the US Army. You
can argue the Vietnam allegory both
ways but for some, Aldrich's gritty Western is as much about America's racial
divide.

Acid Westerns

The acid Western was a short lived mutation of the horse opera which discarded the genre's traditional virtue – simple plots that were as reliable as one of John Wayne's trusty steeds – to focus on obscure symbolism, fuzzy camerawork, mood and the implication of existential significance.

El Topo is the most famous acid example – and arguably the most incomprehensible. To some, Monte Hellman's The Shooting and Ride in the Whirlwind (1967) were the first acid Westerns, released the same year as the Summer of Love. But they were far more coherently plotted than many later efforts in this vein. The success of Easy Rider gave the acid Western a decisive boost and, in 1971, that film's star Peter Fonda directed what is probably the best acid Western, The Hired Hand, an existential tale of a doomed drifter which was, unlike many others of its ilk, strongly scripted by Alan Sharp. The Hired Hand has its flaws but it doesn't induce migraines in quite the way that George Englund's Zachariah (1971) does. James Frawley's Kid Blue (1973) in which Dennis Hopper tries to be a good citizen – you can imagine how it turns out – almost sounded the last post for the acid Western. Hollywood discovered other drugs, none of which have yet inspired their own Western microgenre.

Warlock 1959

Director Edward Dmytryk **Cast** Richard Widmark, Henry Fonda, Anthony Quinn, Dorothy Malone 122m

If you're looking for subtexts, this Western's got 'em all. **Quinn**'s lame gambler/ gunfighter is obviously in love with **Fonda**'s marshal in **Dmytryk**'s clever inversion of My Darling Clementine – this time, the former baddie (**Widmark**) triumphs and Fonda's mercenary lawman has to leave town – in a sour Western that touches on Greek myth and Hollywood politics. Fonda's gleeful rogue marshal inspired Leone to cast him in Once Upon a Time in the West.

The Wind 1928

Director Victor Sjöström **Cast** Lillian Gish, Lars Hanson 95m

The first "adult" Western. **Gish** is magnificent as a woman, driven mad by loneliness on a dusty plain in Texas, who murders her would-be seducer and then watches as the wind (created using the propellers of eight aircraft in the Mojave Desert) whips away the sand from the shallow grave in which she's buried her victim. Even MGM had trouble figuring out how to tack a happy ending onto this one, the studio insisting on a more upbeat finish than the original, which saw Gish wandering the desert, certain to die. With temperatures reaching 120°F it was a painful shoot, particularly for Gish, who gave herself third-degree burns simply by touching an overheated door handle.

X-RATED

In the history of the cinema, X has marked the spot where a horror film became too horrific, a space movie alien too grisly or sin a tad too obvious (or prolonged). All these films have been deemed suitable for adults only.

Baise-moi 2000

Directors Virginie Despentes & Coralie Trin Thi **Cast** Karen Lancaume, Raffaëla Anderson **77m**

Written and directed by an ex-prostitute and a porn star, this was yanked from French screens after just three days and it took appeals from Jean-Luc Godard and Catherine Breillat to have it reclassified with a rare X certificate and a warning it was "likely to incite minors to violence". The British censors settled for excising a seven-second shot of a semi-erect penis from a violation sequence. This is clearly a howl of anguish intended to champion female sexuality in a misogynist world. But the hard-core content and relentless nihilism turned many against it.

Behind the Green Door 1972

Directors Jim Mitchell, Art Mitchell **Cast** Marilyn Chambers **72m**

This slice of porno chic is well made and arty (although some of the "artistic" scenes seem amusing now). **Chambers** was famous in the US as the "99.44 percent pure" girl advertising Ivory Snow soap powder. Her purity percentage declines here as she is pleasured by nuns, a boxer and three trapeze artists.

Cannibal Holocaust 1980

Director Ruggero Deodato **Cast** Robert Kerman, Francesca Ciardi, Perry Pirkanen **98m**

"Dear Ruggero", Sergio Leone wrote after seeing this infamous shocker about a documentary crew going missing in the Amazon rainforest, "what a movie! The second part is a masterpiece of cinematographic realism, but everything seems so real that I think you will get in trouble with all the world." And indeed **Deodato** was arrested ten days after the Milan premiere and charged with murder and obscenity. He proved he hadn't made a snuff movie by producing his cast alive and well, but the picture was still outlawed for animal cruelty. Reputedly the most banned film in history, forbidden in over fifty countries.

Child's Play 3 1991

Director Jack Bender **Cast** Justin Whalin, Perrey Reeves, Jeremy Sylvers **90m**

This would have been just another schlocky sequel had a rumour not started that Robert Thompson and Jon Venables, the ten-year-old killers of Liverpool toddler James Bulger, had been inspired to commit their crime by an evil doll named Chucky's black comic rampage at a military academy. The tabloid tirade was led by *The Sun*, whose front page the day after the trial in November 1993 screamed: "For the sake of ALL our kids...BURN YOUR VIDEO NASTY." The film, which was certificated 15 on its cinema release, remains available on DVD in the UK.

The Curse of Frankenstein
1957

Director Terence Fisher **Cast** Peter Cushing, Christopher Lee 82m

Horror in the 1950s was dominated by Commies disguised as aliens and ludicrous monsters until Hammer came up with this little gem, which took the genre back to its roots and became, for many years, the most profitable movie made in a British studio. One reason it made so much money is that they obviously didn't spend a mint on the baron's castle. The film launched **Cushing** and **Lee**, partly because of the relish with which they and **Fisher** set about the story's bloodletting.

Deep Throat 1972

Director Gerard Damiano **Cast** Linda Lovelace, Harry Reems 61m

Not the only slice of arty porn but overshadowing pretenders such as the same year's *Behind the Green Door*, this is a film which reminds you the phrase "adult movie" describes the genre, not how grown-up you have to be to watch it. **Lovelace** has since claimed that between 1971 and 1974 she was forced to commit various sex acts at gunpoint by her husband/manager Chuck Traynor (who, after Lovelace divorced him, married Marilyn Chambers, the second most famous US porn star). This movie was shot in six days, but the only scenes where **Damiano** seems genuinely interested in the film are where Lovelace gives Coke a whole new image.

Emmanuelle 1974

Director Just Jaeckin **Cast** Sylvie Kristel, Alain Cuny, Marika Green 94m

The wonderfully named Jay Cocks, *Time* magazine's movie reviewer when this came out, sneered: "*Emmanuelle* would have to go up against something like *The Greatest Story Ever Told* before it could be called titillating." **Kristel** is the innocent, yet sex-mad, title character, married to the older and sexually wiser Mario (**Cuny**), who, for reasons convincing only for the screenwriter, decides she wants to become a sexual animal.

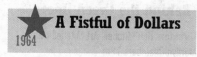 ## A Fistful of Dollars
1964

Director Sergio Leone **Cast** Clint Eastwood, Gian Maria Volonté, Marianne Koch 100m

The debut of The Man With No Name (but who is known to the coffin maker as Joe)

was a brutal affair, mixing the traditional Western and Sicilian morality plays. **Leone** had, as **Eastwood** put it, "an interesting way with violence". Dissed by critics ("They simply made this out of 1001 Westerns they have seen and admired", complained one), this rejig of Kurosawa's *Yojimbo* still works, even after its sequels and imitators.

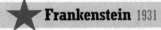

Frankenstein 1931

Director James Whale **Cast** Colin Clive, Boris Karloff, Mae Clarke **70m**

Robert Florey, best known for his musicals, was initially to direct this adaptation of **Mary Shelley**'s seminal horror, until casting disagreements with producer **Carl Laemmle** led to his dismissal. He wanted Bela Lugosi to play Dr Frankenstein, but Laemmle wanted him as the Monster. Lugosi turned the role down, due to the lack of dialogue and his make-up design being rejected. John Carradine also turned the role down, considering it beneath his skills. Sticking closely to Shelley's story, **Whale** took the reigns, creating one of the best horror movies ever, with **Karloff** giving a *tour de force* performance.

Greetings 1968

Director Brian De Palma **Cast** Jonathan Warden, Gerrit Graham, Robert De Niro **88m**

Brian De Palma made his name with two black comedies: *Greetings* and the sequel *Hi Mom!* This one begins with President Johnson on TV; in front of the set is a book entitled *Six Seconds in Dallas*.

Graham plays what is now an archetypal movie misfit: an assassination nut who draws the paths of the bullets on his girlfriend's sleeping body. This, the first movie to receive an X rating, premiered six months after Bobby Kennedy was shot.

I Drink Your Blood 1970

Director David E. Durston **Cast** Bhaskar Roy Chowdhury, Jadine Wong, Rhonda Fultz **90m**

If this film teaches us anything, it's to never feed pies stuffed with rabid dog meat to psychopathic hippies. Self-appointed moral guardian Mary Whitehouse tried to warn the British public when she included a clip in the "video nasty" compilation she showed to the 1983 Conservative Party conference. The British Board of Film Censors was sufficiently convinced to withhold a certificate, but the MPAA in the US proved more courageous in giving this Manson-inspired mayhem the first X certificate for violence alone. An instant cult hit, it influenced, among others, George A. Romero's *The Crazies* (1973) and Josh Becker's *Stryker's War* (1985).

The Killing of Sister George 1968

Director Robert Aldrich **Cast** Beryl Reid, Susannah York, Coral Browne **140m**

A lesbian soap actress (**Reid**) worries that her character, Sister George, is to be killed off. Meanwhile, her younger lover (**York**) has caught the eye of a TV exec (**Browne**). Back in 1969, it wasn't the plot that upset anybody, not even the scene where a drunken Reid takes her frustration out on nuns in a taxi – it was the lesbian love scene that grabbed the headlines. This was proclaimed a first, although women snogging each other onscreen could be traced back to the 1930 Marlene Dietrich movie, *Morocco*. The film holds up better than the fuss might suggest, although it's a bit too long.

Lolita 1962

Director Stanley Kubrick **Cast** James Mason, Shelley Winters, Sue Lyon, Peter Sellers 153m

Vladimir Nabokov told **Mason** many years later that he rather liked this movie (**Kubrick**, he said, had added several things he'd have been pleased to have thought of), but wished it could be remade with a younger girl. It was a view some of the more left-field critics took when the film was released even though, as Mason points out, in the book Lolita ages from twelve to eighteen.

Sue Lyon as Lolita, looking not a bit too old for Humbert Humbert (James Mason), even if she was older than Nabokov had envisioned.

Midnight Cowboy
1969

Director John Schlesinger **Cast** Dustin Hoffman, Jon Voight 113m

This is a touching movie (originally supposed to star Elvis as a gigolo) about a country boy who wants to become a (straight) male prostitute in New York, his descent into seediness and poverty, and his street-hustling pal's eventual death. Maybe it's the strong lead performances, or the way **Schlesinger** keeps it ticking along, or **Nilsson**'s "Everybody Talkin'", but this movie is far more enjoyable than it has any right to be from the synopsis.

Saturday Night Fever 1977

Director John Badham **Cast** John Travolta, Karen Lynn Gorney, Barry Miller 119m

"You can tell by the way I use my walk, I'm a woman's man, no time for talk." That one line, from the brothers Glibb, tells you all you need to know about the movie that made **Travolta**, though *Airplane!*'s 1980 parody of the white-suited dance scene may now be better known than the original. The movie was X-rated because when the authorities finally understood Travolta's dialogue they realized quite how much of it consisted of "fuck".

YAKUZA

Organized crime in Japan has proved just as fruitful a subject for Japanese cinema as the Mafia has for Hollywood. The best yakuza films question the glamour and honour involved in the gangster lifestyle, often with a generous helping of violence.

Drunken Angel 1948

Director Akira Kurosawa **Cast** Toshirô Mifune, Takashi Shimura 108m

In one of **Kurosawa**'s first fully fledged features, **Shimura** plays an alcoholic doctor in post-war Japan who treats a young, small-time hood (**Mifune**) after a gunfight with a rival syndicate. Seeing in the youngster a cause to which he can contribute, an uneasy friendship develops between the pair until the criminal lifestyle once again rears its head. Kurosawa's first film to be made without government interference, *Drunken Angel* was also the first of his many projects with Mifune.

Kids Return 1996

Director Takeshi Kitano **Cast** Kenichi Kaneko, Masanobu Ando 104m

After *Violent Cop* and *Sonatine*, this signalled a slight departure for **Kitano** with its gentler, more contemplative tone. A look at the relationship between two school friends, *Kids Return* charts their inevitable slide into adulthood and the difficult choices they face. As one discovers a talent for boxing, the other finds himself drifting towards a local yakuza gang.

Minbo 1992

Director Juzo Itami **Cast** Masahiro Murata, Yasuo Daichi 126m

A biting satire set in an upmarket hotel that deals with how to deal with yakuza extortion techniques, *Minbo* proved a massive hit in Japan and was regarded as an effective tool in dealing with shakedowns and bribery. Rejecting the favoured portrayal of yakuza as noble samurai-type figures, veteran director **Itami** shows them in a much less flattering light. As a result, he found himself the victim of a gangland knife attack.

Pale Flower 1963

Director Masahiro Shinoda **Cast** Mariko Kaga, Ryo Ikebe 96m

Extremely progressive for its time, Pale Flower follows the life of Muraki (**Ryo Ikebe**), a yakuza mobster who is released from prison after an honour killing only to find that his clan and its rivals have established a truce. At a loss, he begins a destructive relationship with a mysterious woman who's addicted to gambling. Muraki's thirst for killing slowly begins to resurface. Frequently compared to the protagonist of Albert Camus' *L'Etranger*, Muraki uses killing to analyse his existential angst.

Sympathy for the Underdog 1971

Director Kinji Fukasaku **Cast** Koji Tsuruta, Noburu Ando 93m

Famed for his unrelenting view of yakuza life depicted in the *Yakuza Papers* series, with this film **Fukasaku** further enhanced his reputation. The story of a veteran gangster who leaves prison after a ten-year stretch to find the moral code under which he operated long gone, the film looks at the sacrifices and compromises he must make in order to re-establish himself. Taut and economical, it also offers an illuminating look at a changing Japan.

Tokyo Drifter 1966

Director Seijun Suzuki **Cast** Tetsuya Watari, Chieko Matsubara 89m

One of the finest films to emerge from Japan (and made by one of its most original and maverick directors), *Tokyo Drifter* takes a standard Japanese mafia narrative (a former gangster attempts to go straight but soon finds his past life catching up with him) and transforms it into something far more idiosyncratic. Imbued with a dark sense of humour and an eye for the absurd, the film's highly choreographed bursts of violence and stunning framing and cinematography were an obvious influence on Takeshi Kitano.

★ Sonatine 1993

Director Takeshi Kitano **Cast** Takeshi Kitano, Aya Kokumai, Tetsu Watanabe 94m

Although this was only TV comedian **Kitano**'s third movie, few directors have managed to add such a novel slant to the gangster/yakuza film. Murakawa (Kitano) is weary of his life as a yakuza, tired of the constant fear, and wants out, but is asked to settle a dispute between warring factions first. It becomes clear this is a setup and he heads back into the yakuza world, seeking revenge. The violent set pieces are beautifully filmed, all the more chilling for not being overdone.

The Yakuza 1974

Director Sydney Pollack **Cast** Robert Mitchum, Ken Takakura 112m

This underrated film would probably be a lot better known if, as was intended, Martin Scorsese had directed. Instead **Pollack** got the job, directing the first movie to be made from a Paul Schrader script (though Paul's brother Ed and Robert Towne also helped). **Mitchum** is divinely world-weary as the private eye who does a buddy in Japan a favour and, inevitably, gets into trouble. It's far from clichéd – the Japanese setting never feels false and yakuza culture is nicely delineated. The samurai duel in the paper house alone makes this worthwhile.

ZOMBIES

Load up your shotgun and lock up your entrails: prepare to encounter the horror genre that never dies…

Carnival of Souls 1962

Director Herk Harvey **Cast** Candace Hilligoss, Frances Feist, Sidney Berger 81m

A stranger, subtler movie than most about the undead. Mary (**Hilligoss**) appears to be the only survivor of a car crash, but why is she intermittently invisible and why does a ghostly white-faced man keep appearing? An intriguing, eerie (if at times OTT) movie which anticipates directors like David Lynch.

I Walked With a Zombie 1943

Director Jacques Tourneur **Cast** Frances Dee, Tom Conway 69m

Before this, producer **Val Lewton**'s biggest contribution to cinema was persuading Victor Fleming not to shoot a dinner scene in *Gone With the Wind* with two grapefruits in line with Vivien Leigh's breasts. But this movie helped rescue the genre from a clichéd world where monsters roared, heroines screamed and heroes rescued. Loosely based on *Jane Eyre*, the plot centres on whether a plantation manager's wife is mad or, as is feared, a zombie.

The Return of the Living Dead 1985

Director Dan O'Bannon **Cast** James Karen, Clu Gulager, Don Calfa 87m

O'Bannon's comedy splatterfest takes the Romero canon and runs screaming with it. A couple of warehouse workers unwittingly release the "real" zombies that *Night of the Living Dead* was based on, then have to defend themselves alongside a gang of teenage punks against the brain-eating horde. With a host of memorable one-liners (zombie calls for backup: "Send more paramedics!"), the film also has a stonking soundtrack featuring the likes of The Cramps and Roky Erickson.

Shaun of the Dead 2004

Director Edgar Wright **Cast** Simon Pegg, Nick Frost, Penelope Wilton, Bill Nighy 95m

In the world's first "rom-zom-com", Shaun (**Pegg**) spends his nights in the pub and his days in a dead-end job, only snapping out of his coma-like existence when the capital is flooded with zombies. He and his useless pal (**Frost**) decide it's up to them to rescue his mum (**Wilton**), stepdad (**Nighy**), ex (**Kate Ashfield**) and her irri-

Wherefore art thou, Romero?

Since 1968's low-budget black-and-white bloodbath *Night of the Living Dead*, Romero has been on a one-man movie crusade on behalf of zombies. Blending the feel of silent horror with a keen questioning of social stereotypes (witness the genre's first decent female heroine and a black hero), Romero pushed the envelope further a decade on with 1978's *Dawn of the Dead*. "When there's no more room in hell, the dead will walk the earth" ran the poster line. And when the going gets tough, the tough go shopping – the survivors holing up on the top floor of a mall, while the ghouls shuffle about below to piped Muzak; they even get Walkmans in 1985's *Day of the Dead*. Zack Snyder's flashy teen *Dawn of the Dead* remake seemingly brought Romero himself back, with the asylum-seeking zombies of *Land of the Dead* (2005). The septuagenarian filmmaker then convincingly upgraded the genre for the MySpace age in 2007 with the video blog-style *Diary of the Dead*.

tating friends. A low-budget treat, **Wright** and **Pegg**'s post-*Spaced* reunion is a very British homage to the zombie master, a satisfying union of guts and relationships.

28 Days Later 2002

Director Danny Boyle **Cast** Cillian Murphy, Naomie Harris 113m

The opening sequence where **Murphy** wanders around a spookily deserted central London is legendary, but what makes **Danny Boyle** and **Alex Garland**'s second collaboration after *The Beach* truly significant is that its global "Rage" plague turns everyone into really, really *speedy* zombies. Except, according to the exasperated Boyle, "It's NOT a zombie movie. They're infected, not zombies." Tell them that when they're munching your face off.

White Zombie 1932

Director Victor Halperin **Cast** Bela Lugosi, Madge Bellamy 73m

Released a year after *Dracula*, **Lugosi** was paid a not-so-princely $500 for his part, **Bellamy** receiving ten times that for her role as the heroine turned into a zombie on Haiti. Just as *Dracula*'s success launched a cycle of spin-offs, zombies would regularly return to the screen, increasingly looking as if they were written, shot and directed by people in a trance.

Zombie Flesheaters 1979

Director Lucio Fulci **Cast** Tisa Farrow, Ian McCulloch, Richard Johnson 91m

A journalist and a young woman seeking her father head to an island to find it overrun by zombies. Make-up artist **Gianetto De Rossi**'s creations make the movie stand out, audiences in 1979 unaccustomed to such unsettling scenes. Sick bags were even handed out, picture houses convinced audiences wouldn't be able to stomach the blood and guts.

INDEX

M

U V

W

PICTURE CREDITS

The publishers have made every effort to correctly identify the rights holders and/or production companies in respect of the film stills featured in this book. If despite these efforts any attribution is incorrect, the publishers will correct this error on subsequent reprinting.

Inside Covers Moviestore Collection: ©Polygram Filmed Entertainment Gramercy Pictures, Working Title Films (front); © 1994 Jet Tone Production Ltd., Rolling Thunder Colour Section: BFI: xvi) © 2003 Sahamongkolfilm International Limited, Magnolia Pictures,Baa-Ram-Ewe/Sahamongkolfilm Co. Kobal Collection: x, xi) American International Pictures xiv a) © El Deseo S.A./Renn Productions /France 2 Cinema. 1999, El Deseo S.A., Sony Pictures, Renn Productions/France 2 Cinéma/Vía Digital (participation) xvii b) Metro-Goldwyn-Mayer xviii) Nikkatsu xxi a) © Warner Bros Inc, Goodtimes Enterprises xxiii b a) Miramax Films, Fox Filmes do Brasil/Globo Filmes/O2 Filmes/Petrobrás xxiii b) © 1972 Werner Herzog Filmproduktion, New Yorker Films, Werner Herzog Filmproduktion/Hessischer Rundfunk xvi) © Warner Bros Inc, David Foster Productions Moviestore Collection: ix a) Sony Pictures Classics Bridgit Folman Film Gang/Les Films d'Ici/Razor Film Produktion GmbHArte France/Noga Communication - Channel 8 ix b) © 2006 Warner Bros. Entertainment Inc, Thousand Words/Section Eight/Detour Filmproduction 3 Arts Entertainment xii a) © 2004 DreamWorks LLC, Apatow Productions/Herzog-Cowen Entertainment xii b) Park Circus, The Cannon Group/Cineplex-Odeon Films/HandMade Films xiii a) © Paramount Vantage, Ghoulardi Film Company/Miramax Films xiii b) © Miramax Film Corp and Paramount Vantage, Scott Rudin Productions/Mike Zoss Productions xiv b) © New Line Cinema xv a) The Blade Runner Partnership, Warner Bros, The Ladd Company/Shaw Brothers xv b) Cinema 5, British Lion Film Corporation xvii a) © 1995 Universal City Studios, Inc. and Syalis Droits Audio-visuels, Légende Entreprises/De Fina-Cappa xix b) © Captivity LLC, Foresight Unlimited/Russian American Movie Company xx) © 2007 Universal Studios, Big Talk Productions/Ingenious Film Partners/Studio Canal/Working Title Films xxi b) Lionsgate Entertainment, Lee Daniels Entertainment/Smokewood Entertainment Group xxii a) Paramount Pictures, Dino de Laurentiis Cinematografica/Marianne Productions xxii b) © Metro-Goldwyn-Mayer Inc., Polaris/Stanley Kubrick Productions Ronald Grant Picture Collection xix a) © Alexandre Films EuropaCorp Text: BFI: 18 © The Hearst Corporation and Subafilms Ltd, United Artists, Apple Films/King Features Production/TVC London 25 Speciality Films, Janus Film/Les Films de l'Astrophore/SACI 26 Columbia Pictures Corporation 53 Sterling Investment Corporation 105 Columbia Pictures Corporation 123 Historia/Les Films Aleph/Ministère de la Culture de la Republique Française, New Yorker Films Kobal Collection 189 X-Filme Creative Pool/Wega Film/Les Films du Losange/Lucky Red, Canal+ Sony Pictures Classics Moviestore Collection 39 © Michael Powell (Theatre) Ltd, Astor Pictures Corporation 42 Miramax Films, The Australian Film Commission/CiBy 2000/Jan Chapman Productions/New South Wales Film & Television Office 62 Lucasfilm, Paramount Pictures 65 Sony Pictures Classics, BBC Films/Free Range Films/Renaissance Films 72 Universal Pictures International, Focus Features/ Blueprint Pictures/Film4 /Focus Features/Scion Films 79 © Venice Surf Club LLC, Twentieth Century Fox Film Corporation, Fox Searchlight Pictures/Michael London Productions/Working Title Films /Antidote Films /Sound for Film 87 © Renn Productions - France 2 Cinéma - D.A. Films - Nef Filmproduktions GmbH / Degeto pour ARD/WMG - RCS Films & TV, AMLF, Miramax Films 96 Warner Bros Pictures, First Artists/Sweetwall 108 © Loew's Incorporated, MGM 115 © Twentieth Century-Fox Film Corporation, Kent Productions 135 © Channel Four Television Corporation, Polygram Filmed Entertainment, Miramax, Figment Films/The Noel Gay Motion Pic-